Social Problems in America

Social Problems

ELIZABETH BRIANT LEE

and ALFRED McCLUNG LEE

BROOKLYN COLLEGE OF THE CITY OF NEW YORK

n America

A SOURCE BOOK ⟶

REVISED EDITION

Henry Holt and Company · New York

For A. M. L., 3rd and B. H. L.

Preface to the Revised Edition

Science owes its development to problems—the recurrent and the persistent problems with which existing authorities, specialists, theories, and techniques fail to cope. The pinching shoe, the awkward situation, the observation that does not fit existing knowledge, the arrogance of vested authority, the threat of social disaster, the death of a mother from cancer, the alcoholism of a father, the slaughter of loved ones in war, and hundreds of other personalized evidences of minor and major problems drive millions to follow a range of different courses. But such problems so influence the lives of a few thousands directly or indirectly that they become scientists. They turn eventually to systematic study, to systematic searches for "answers."

The intricately interrelated fabric of scientific knowledge—physical, biological, and social—is the weaving together of the experiences gained in millions of such searches for answers to general and specific, direct and derived problems. The general attitude (method) of scientists, regardless of field, stresses observation and the accumulation of sense experiences rather than speculation, and it has gradually resulted in the refinement of more and more precise tools for measurement and techniques for generalization.

Sociology similarly owes its appearance and development, as does all social science, to social problems sufficiently pressing and burdensome to impel their repeated systematic investigation and to prompt experiments with techniques for studying and coping with them. Poverty, strife, authoritarianism, class and caste discriminations, ethnic differences, propaganda, crime, alcoholism and drug addiction, housing, disease, prostitution, physical handicaps, and the others present problems for the study of physical and biological scientists, but they also have highly significant aspects which can only be understood and perhaps miti-

gated in terms of a social frame of reference. They are thus and in this sense social problems. They are a product in part at least of social and societal processes and situations, and they depend for their persistence, recurrence, or temporary prevalence in part at least upon such social factors.

Some distinguish with great care between "social" problems and "sociological" problems. If this distinction does not carry with it a rejection of the study of social problems, it may have merit. A sociological problem is a problem for scientific study which is sufficiently restricted in scope, precise in statement, and related to existing theory to permit of rigorous and fruitful study. At the present stage of the science's development, useful sociological problems are projects frequently based directly upon social-problem situations or in some manner closely related to factors underlying social problems.

Social problems, some insist, are the business of "applied" sociology, and sociological problems are the proper sphere of interest for "pure" or "scientific" sociology. This dichotomy serves chiefly to sever those with a tendency toward speculation from contact with significant factual materials and to excuse social technicians for being ignorant of the great available resources of sociological knowledge. Only through seeing and understanding actual instances of white-collar criminality, unemployment, despair, poverty, panic, and riot can the sociologist bring his theories into some degree of correspondence with social realities. Only by studying the accumulated generalizations of other investigators can the specific instance of crime, poverty, or panic come into some more adequate perspective.

In the foregoing no distinction is made between the social problems studied by the sociologist and those studied by other social scientists. The distinction is in part one of emphasis and in part one of traditional allocation. Human disintegration in an urban or rural slum has its economic, political, geographic, architectural, engineering, and social aspects. On the other hand, sociology, social psychology, anthropology, and education have devoted more attention to racial and ethnic relations than have economics, political science, and geography.

As nearly as possible, the list of social problems taken up in this volume contains those most frequently studied in college courses in social problems, social pathology, social disorganization, and social deviation. An approximation of average usage was sought on this point by examining a great many course outlines. Naturally, with the interpenetration of the various areas of human endeavor, the selected readings might have been grouped in a great many different ways. There might have been, for example, a chapter on social problems in the religious sphere, but it seemed more useful to insert such materials in a number of other chapters. To illustrate, excerpts from Ralph G. Martin and Bishop G. Bromley Oxnam on planned parenthood appear in the chapter on "Birth Through Childhood"; religious influence on courtship and marriage enters at a number of points into the chapters on "Youth" and "Adults"; the controversy over the separation of church and state is discussed in the "Education" chapter. These and many other readings or parts of readings in other chapters might have been gathered together into a sizable and challenging chapter on church-related social problems, but it seemed more functional to the editors to distribute these materials in the manner followed. To learn how problems intertwine with one another, the reader is urged to study the index at the end of the volume.

For convenience, social problems are arranged in this book in eight groups of chapters. Part I presents readings which, it is hoped, will help develop the student's general perspective on social problems. Part II deals with problems arising out of the relationship of man to land, problems of physical resources, technological change, means of transportation, migrations, and rural and urban living conditions. Part III highlights social problems associated with phases of the individual's life-history, from birth through family situations of a problem nature to age and death. In Part IV

problems arising out of contacts with institutions other than the family are touched upon—the educational, economic, political, communicational, and recreational institutions. Part V is devoted to such individual and group deviations as physical injuries, illnesses, and handicaps, mental diseases and deficiencies, juvenile and adult delinquency and crime, and leadership. Parts VI and VII contain readings on problems of social division and social crisis. The divisions of class, status, caste, race, and ethnic background, and the efforts to break through or otherwise adjust to the problems of such divisions are treated. Whole volumes and libraries have been written on man's many social crises, but some effort is made to bring depressions, catastrophes, riots, and wars into the general perspective of the present volume. In Part VIII, the final section, documents are brought together to typify both extremist and sound adjustment processes and techniques for coping with social problems.

The readings presented in the eight Parts are not meant to be of a uniform character. They include summaries and excerpts from objective scientific studies, and these are the largest part of the materials in this collection. As the chapter introductions and review questions indicate, the scientific materials provide the backbone of the volume. In some cases where the nature of a social problem has been clearly outlined by a student of public affairs not classifiable as a sociologist or even a social scientist, the document has nevertheless been used. In addition, for the purposes of contrast and of highlighting the character of problems, other excerpts set forth inflammatory proposals by spokesmen for pressure groups and vivid news reports of problem situations.

Space considerations and the purposes of a college readings text precluded a "debate-manual" approach to individual social problems. In general, throughout the book, statements containing special pleading represent a wide range of viewpoints, but where factual studies could replace speculation they were given preference. For example, a debate manual might give the pros and cons of racial segregation, but factual studies have brought about a high degree of unanimity among sociologists on many significant aspects of this social problem. The economic and other social costs of racial segregation, as estimated by social scientists, are therefore summarized. The excerpts from the United States Supreme Court decisions of May 17, 1954, in Chapter 10 give the weight of enlightened national judicial ruling to condemnations of the mistreatment of minorities.

So that students might pursue contrary as well as scientific statements further, a selection of references to such materials is included in the bibliography at the end of each chapter.

As nearly as possible throughout the book the needs and interests of the college student of social problems are borne in mind. It is hoped that he finds the materials conducive to the development of a scientific approach to the age-long and also the temporary problems that plague mankind. In coping with what Robert Burns so aptly called "man's inhumanity to man"—the largest factor in social problems—only a rigorously thorough and uncompromising knowledge of the facts can furnish an adequate starting point. Once the facts are known, what *can* be done becomes fairly evident.

Malverne, Long Island   E. B. L.
February 1, 1955   A. M. L.

Acknowledgments

Since the first edition of this book appeared, the Society for the Study of Social Problems was formed in 1951. It is now an affiliate of the American Sociological Society and the International Sociological Association, and it works closely with the Society for the Psychological Study of Social Issues (SPSSI). This new society, known as SSSP, has given new momentum and weight to the study of this field through its semi-annual meetings and its quarterly journal, *Social Problems*. We are indebted to those with whom we shared the experience of bringing this new organization into existence, and we believe this new edition of our book reflects in many ways this development.

In its first edition, this source book benefited from broad correspondence with teachers of classes in social problems, social pathology, and social disorganization in colleges and universities throughout the country. In this revised edition, an even larger number of teaching sociologists offered suggestions arising out of their reactions to the first edition. The very number of these cooperators unfortunately makes acknowledgment of each of them by name impossible. They gave us the benefit of their experiences with students in all major types of American colleges. Our work on this and the previous edition was immeasurably enriched by their aid, and we deeply appreciate it.

Our associates at Wayne University and more recently at Connecticut College for Women, New York University, and Brooklyn College of the City of New York have also most helpfully shared with us their experiments and experiences in this area.

The editors of this book naturally take full responsibility for its form and content as it now stands, but we are deeply grateful to the many who made suggestions and criticisms and especially to those who permitted their materials to be reprinted. Our obligations for permission are acknowledged in connection with the papers and excerpts reproduced in the text.

To all these we are indebted. We hope that they find in the following many of their favorite excerpts and many others which will be helpful to their students.

This work was lightened in many ways through the generous cooperation of the staffs of the Wayne County Library Branch at Northville, Michigan, the Wayne University Library, the University of Michigan Library, the Brooklyn College Library, and the Malverne Public Library.

We are appreciative of the interest and patience shown throughout this effort by our sons, Alfred and Briant, to whom we have dedicated this volume. We trust that they and their generation will face society's problems with a conviction that policies based upon clear-eyed social science can help to mitigate some of the worst of them.

E. B. L.
A. M. L.

Contents

PART I

Frames of Reference

─CHAPTER 1 ─→

The Nature of Social Problems

A GROUP of whites and Negroes stand watching a mechanical cotton picker bring economic, social, and psychic chaos to their lives. A lonely girl permits herself to be picked up by a man. The member of a religious or racial minority turns away in dejection from an employment office, denied again a job because of creed or skin color. A public-health report sums up in cold statistics the story of emaciated and scarred bodies ravaged by tuberculosis and syphilis in an overcrowded urban slum or a disintegrating rural area. A juvenile delinquent, raised in an "exclusive" neighborhood, has his thieving or hoodlumism "covered up" by his parents on a promise "not to do it again." A flood rips through homes, factories, and eroding farm land in one of the country's great river valleys. The sun turns a sickly green at noon during a Kansas dust storm, and the people try to wash the earth out of their mouths and keep it from their lungs. And the finest examples of young manhood leave their homes to "save the world for Democracy."

All of these are evidences of social problems. Let us comment briefly on the problems behind each of these evidences.

Technological change forces the rebuilding of the lives of individuals, families, and whole sections of the country with ramifications throughout the United States and the whole world. The mechanical cotton picker is more revolutionary socially than the Emancipation Proclamation. Loneliness and inadequate sex knowledge among our youth help to swell the ranks of the seriously maladjusted and the perverse. Despite the identification of "Nordic-supremacy" myth-making with Nazism, members of American racial and religious minorities still shrink under the cutting lash of discrimination in employment, housing, citizenship, and other social rights, duties, and privileges. Tuberculosis, syphilis, and other diseases—physical and mental—are social as well as physical, biological, and economic phenomena and problems. When well-to-do families "front" for

their delinquent children without handling child personality problems intelligently, they alter delinquency statistics to an extent not possible in less privileged circles, but they do not diminish the role of antisocial behavior in the life of their children and in the affairs of the community. Mankind no longer needs to await in fear and trembling or in casual disregard for disaster to strike. For most disasters, men can plan. Programs of reforestation, anti-erosion techniques, water-control dams, and special organizational preparedness for emergencies place floods and dust storms at least partly within the scope of social planning and treatment. And, finally, the study of war by social scientists has stripped it of much of its romance and its alleged necessity and has pointed to alternative ways—far more constructive ways—to settle international disputes.

All these are social problems which lie behind the evidences mentioned in the first paragraph. On all these and others, social scientists have contributed something for wise social planning both in objective descriptions and analyses and in general perspective. But what do these social problems have in common? What is a social problem?

This Part presents to the student major efforts to define the nature of social problems and to relate social problems to personal disorganization and social maladjustment and change. The four selections in this chapter are concerned with the nature of social problems as such; Chapters 2 and 3 deal respectively with theories of social and personal disorganization and with theories of cultural and societal maladjustment and change.

Frank, in the digest of his influential essay, defines a social problem as "any difficulty or misbehavior of a fairly large number of persons which we [presumably any sizable number of us] wish to remove or correct." He illustrates the complexities of a social problem in terms of housing and concludes that most of our social problems stem from our inability to rid ourselves quickly enough

3

of outworn customs and to take on habits of a more socialized sort.

The three other selections, those by Case and by Fuller and Myers, develop further the conception introduced by Frank. Case elaborates social problem theory in social psychological terms. He indicates that social problems "turn out to be, in a very essential aspect, social *processes,*" that they are, in other words, aspects of "the one all-embracing social process which we call social evolution." This brings us into relationship with the frame of reference—societal change—discussed in Chapter 3.

Fuller and Myers relate social problems to the ideas people have of right and wrong, to social values; they also outline typical stages through which a social problem goes in its "natural history." In their classification, Fuller and Myers discern three types of social problems: the physical, ameliorative, and moral. A physical problem is one "practically all people regard as a threat to their welfare, but value-judgments cannot be said to cause the condition itself." In the case of an ameliorative problem, people agree on the existence of a problem situation but not on the proposals for its amelioration. On the contrary, in the case of a moral problem, there is no unanimity of opinion even as to its problem nature. The Fuller-Myers outline of the phases through which a problem proceeds in its "natural history" includes the phases of awareness, policy determination, and reform. From a commentary on this outline, a footnote at the end of the Fuller-Myers piece offers Bossard's alternative twelve-phase outline. This differs in detail rather than in principle. Try to think of social problems that do not go through such a "natural history."

The four selections serve to indicate (1) necessary elements in a definition of the term "social problem," and to point to (2) a given social problem's interrelationships in contemporary society, (3) the persistence of many problems in human history, (4) the relationship of problem types to culture and to value-judgments, and (5) the phases through which many problems may proceed.

The Character of Social Problems
Lawrence K. Frank

Lawrence K. Frank (1890–   ), formerly director, Caroline Zachry Institute of Human Development, New York. Principal works: *Society as the Patient* (1948), *Projective Methods* (1948), and *Nature and Human Nature* (1951).

A social problem . . . appears to be any difficulty or misbehavior of a fairly large number of persons which we wish to remove or correct, and the solution of a social problem is evidently the discovery of a method for this removal or correction. . . .

Examining social problems and their generating conditions more closely, it appears that each social problem is specifically related to particular social conditions or social factors, namely, one or more social institutions. . . .

Let us take the housing problem for an illustration. There develops a shortage of houses of such a magnitude that many people are distressed. Manifestly, the usual and accustomed operations of house construction have been reduced or interrupted. Now, in the discussion which ensues, we meet these proposals: that the income tax on the interest from real estate mortgages be reduced; that the property tax on newly constructed houses be remitted for a period of years; that insurance companies and savings banks be required to invest a fixed portion of their assets in real estate mortgages; that labor unions in the building trades be supervised by the state; that the producers of building materials be regulated by a state commission; that people be persuaded to move to other cities or towns; that landlords be prohibited from increasing rents above a fixed percentage of existing rents, and so on. It would require many pages to list the various and sundry proposals recently made for solving the housing problem.

From "Social Problems," *American Journal of Sociology, 30* (1924–25): 462–473, pp. 463–469, 473 quoted. Also available in full in Lawrence K. Frank, *Society as the Patient,* New Brunswick: Rutgers University Press, 1948.

It would be taken as a sign of eccentricity or feeblemindedness, perhaps, to question the relevance of these proposals to the housing problem, so let us invoke that familiar figure of the man from Mars who views mundane affairs with an innocent eye. To this visitor, we may imagine the student of social problems, or the man in the street, patiently explaining that we had a serious housing problem. And our visitor would reply with numerous questions, we may assume, about the state of the building art: had we met with some new difficulty in constructing houses which our architects and builders could not overcome? The answer would have to be no, for there was no lack of skill there, nor in the ability of our building trades employees to erect houses. And the producers of building materials were possessed of tools and techniques for manufacturing building materials.

It is evident that our visitor would be somewhat perplexed to understand what was the nature of this housing problem, for surely there was no lack of ability and skill to build houses. When, then, was this housing problem and how were we trying to solve it? Again he would be told, with an exaggerated patience, that there was a shortage of houses for the population and that the legislators and economists, sociologists, social workers, and many other professional and lay-persons, were engaged in finding a way to overcome this shortage, as partially described above. The bewildered gentleman would knit his brows, cough apologetically, and say:

Please be patient with one who is anxious to understand and to sympathize with your difficulties, for I cannot see how, if you are concerned with a housing shortage, you talk about income taxes, mortgages, and all these other seemingly unrelated subjects. If you need houses, why, in the name of intelligence, don't you build them or address yourself to finding ways of building them instead of talking about money, capital, and so on? Your architects and builders know how to construct dwellings, your building-material factories know how to produce materials and the land awaits. Then, wherefore and why?

We should have to delegate an economist, a lawyer, a political scientist, a sociologist, and a historian to explain about the system of private property, the price system, popular government, congestion of population, transportation, and so on. And when they had severally and jointly expounded the complexities of the situation, pointing out that we cannot just build houses, but must rely upon individual initiative and private enterprise to enter the field of building construction, that we must use the "price system" to obtain the needed land which is someone's private property, to buy the necessary materials and to hire the skilled labor, that we must borrow capital on mortgages to finance these expenditures, paying a bonus to induce someone to lend that capital and also pay interest on the loan, together with amortization quotas, and then we must contrive to rent these dwellings in accordance with a multiplicity of rules and regulations about leases and so on—after all these sundry explanations, showing that to get houses built we must not infringe anyone's rights of private property or freedom to make a profit, and that what we want is to find a way of getting houses without interfering with anyone's customary activities, our visitor would suddenly exclaim: "Yes, I begin to see; have you any other such difficult problems, for this is exceedingly interesting."

Then we should go on to explain about the problem of infant mortality, how anyone of adult age may beget children with the sanction and approval of the state, provided they undergo a ceremony called marriage. When they do beget children, despite their physical infirmities and the lack of an adequate income or any technique for taking care of their infants, large numbers of their babies die in the first year of life, but no one can say or do anything to prevent this mortality, because it is against the law and the constitution to interfere with an individual adult woman, especially in the care of her child. We have a difficult problem, therefore, of reducing these appalling losses of life, without restricting the liberty of individual mothers to beget more children than they should have, and to kill off their offspring through ignorance or the poverty which every person is by law entitled to enjoy, without let or hindrance (unless mitigated by charity). Of course, the application of modern medicine and hygiene can cut infant mortality to a very low rate, but about all we can do is to distribute enlightening pamphlets and establish infant-welfare stations, where, if they wish to do so, mothers can bring their infants for inspection and advice.

After telling about infant mortality, we would go into the intricacies of the problem of crime and delinquency, of drug addicts, the labor problem, the traffic problem (which would surely make our visitor puzzled to see how valiantly we are striving to find ways of increasing the number of vehicles and pedestrians on our streets), and all the sundry other social problems. If this visitor possessed the usual Martian keenness and penetration, he would probably interrupt our recital to say:

If it is not indelicate of me to remark, every social problem you describe seems to have the same characteristics as every other social problem, namely, the crux of the problem is to find some way of avoiding the undesirable consequences of your established laws, institutions, and social practices, without changing those established laws, etc. In other words, you appear to be seeking a way to cultivate the flower without the fruit, which in a world of cause and effect is somewhat difficult, to say the least. And from what your historians tell me, every generation has its own peculiar social problems, or as I would prefer to say, its difficulties in keeping "business as usual" (one of your most expressive phrases) despite the exigencies of social life. I am reminded also of an account of the Melanesians written by one of your anthropologists, the late Dr. Rivers, who tells about a tribe or group in which canoe-building used to flourish as a fine art, that died out several generations ago. As nearly as he could discover, there developed such an intricate set of rituals, ceremonies, taboo-raising practices, and the like, around the making of canoes, that it became a dangerous trade, so to speak; for, to omit any step in the propitiation of deities, the collaboration of the priests, the appropriate, ceremonial application of tools, and so on, exposed the wilful or neglectful one to the wrath of the whole community. So the building of canoes, which were really needed for their island economy, became gradually more infrequent and then died out entirely. It would appear that there is somewhat of a kinship between the life of these primitive peoples and of your highly civilized nations, although your institutions are much more rational, as your social theories clearly indicate. I am sorry I can offer no help in solving your problem and I assure you I have been greatly edified by your patient explanations.

Whereupon, our visitor would withdraw to his home planet to write a monograph upon the social customs of the earth dwellers, which would probably appeal to his associates as the report of a field trip among some primitive peoples does to us.[1] His visit and comments while here serve,

however, to call attention to the peculiar character of social problems, for their solution apparently does not involve the discovery of a new technique or tool, nor the removal of obstacles in the way of applying known techniques and tools, at least as they are discussed; for what the discussion and the proposals made for their solution indicate is that a social problem is an enterprise in finding ways of getting something done or prevented, while not interfering with the rights, interests, and activities of all those who are involved in the failure to do, or the persistence in doing, what is the subject of the problem. . . .

This suggests that the rise of a social problem is an augury of something better, or at least more effective, in the way of doing things, and that the bigger and more complicated the problem, the greater the change it portends. From such a point of view, we should look upon our social problems, with all the confusion and even suffering they involve, as incidents of transitions in our social life, wherein we are painfully giving up our old habits and learning new ways of doing things. And if we really want to do something in the circumstances, it would appear to be the part of wisdom to try to help along the transition and get over the agony of change. But since only the young can learn new habits, the old are caught in a situation of acute distress and apprehension.[2] Such an attitude bespeaks a seemingly transcendent faith in human nature, but, in fact, it is merely what all our history reveals. Men will, barring a catastrophe, go on living and reproducing their kind, and, to do so, they must have houses, healthy infants, and all the other accompaniments, necessities, and luxuries of life. So, if the practices of our fathers are not sufficiently accommodating to the exigencies of the life we lead, we will come to terms with one another upon the basis of new practices. The sooner we do this the better, seemingly, for neither young nor old are happy while the transition is dragging along. And these new practices, which appear outlandish, scandalous, subversive, and so on, to our fathers, will in turn be outlawed, scandalized, and subverted by our

---

[1] He might also be struck by the similarity of our social behavior to the actions of certain young monkeys when trapped by a hunter with a bottle: The hunter puts a sweetmeat in a bottle attached firmly to a tree; when the monkey finds the bottle he reaches his hand into it, grasps the bait, and then cannot withdraw his doubled hand, so he remains until the hunter comes around and bags him.

Of course, no visitor would dare to offend us by remarking on this similarity.

[2] Cf. F. J. Teggart, *Processes of History,* New Haven: Yale University Press, 1918, Chap. 4, for an interesting discussion of how these large changes in social life arise and how they are received. Also see Thorstein Veblen, *Theory of Business Enterprise,* New York: Charles Scribner's Sons, 1904.

children, world without end.[3] For neither our fathers, nor we, nor our children, can arrest the evolution of social life which is seemingly accelerated by the progress of science, or the discovery of new techniques for doing more effectively what we have severally tried to do, with less success. . . .

[3] Changes in social relations and practices, it may be noted, come about by a process very similar to "spoiling the baby": at first an aggrieved group plead for mitigation of their disabilities or the reduction in others' privileges from which they suffer. This plea is ignored; then follows a demand, which is sternly refused; then comes agitation, which is repressed in part; yet the clamor goes on, until finally we give in, as we do to an insistent baby. *Cf.* the suffrage campaign, which was won because its proponents made a nuisance of themselves.

In other words, if we could invent a technique for more quickly sloughing off the habits of individual activity or of person-to-person relations, which we learned in the days of agricultural, handicraft life, and would readily learn the habits of *group* activity which the machine process demands, and which we are so hesitant about adopting (as witness the law), then we should perhaps develop a *social* life. Moreover, the social problems which plague us would disappear, because the conflict of habits and customs which generate them would be abolished. But such disclosures and discoveries would conform to the foregoing intimation that social change is produced by scientific advance, for they would imply the development of that for which we eagerly wait—a social science.

A Definition of Social Problems
Clarence Marsh Case

Clarence Marsh Case (1874–1946), professor of sociology, University of Southern California. Author of *The Banner of the White Horse* (1917), *Non-violent Coercion* (1923), *Outlines of Introductory Sociology* (1924), *Social Process and Human Progress* (1931), and *Studies in Social Values* (1944).

According to the etymology of the word, a "problem" of any kind is anything "thrown forward"; that is to say it is anything thrust upon the attention. This definition applies perfectly to what are commonly called "social problems." The phrase itself is one of those much used popular expressions which turn out to be incapable of exact definition when we pause to ask ourselves what we really mean by our phraseology. "Social problems" has long figured as just such a vague but useful expression. Popular as it is, it seems difficult to state, in exact terms, just what a social problem is. Yet while it can hardly be defined so exactly as "social processes," it is possible to state the idea in general terms.

A social problem, as the term is herein understood, means any social situation which attracts the attention of a considerable number of competent observers within a society, and appeals to them as calling for readjustment or remedy by social, *i.e.,* collective, action of some kind or other. The phrase "considerable number" is confessedly vague, but is chosen deliberately to indicate any number, from a vast majority to a small minority if capable and energetic.

The essential feature of this definition is its socio-*psychological* character. That is to say, a "social problem" is not a purely objective situation, which can be recognized by a *stranger,* no matter how proficient in the social sciences, who is not in membership with the social group concerned. In other words, the most learned of sociologists is not competent to go among the lowest of Australian tribesmen and point out to them that they have such and such social problems—for example, improper child feeding, sexual immorality, or poor housing. One guilty of such impertinence would arouse astonishment and ridicule, if not resentment, and might very properly be informed that no such problems existed in that group. This would be strictly accurate, in so far as no considerable number of Australian tribesmen had come to be conscious of any unfavorable conditions of the character mentioned, and requiring remedial action. Consequently, for them no "problems" exist, and the concern of our sta-

From *Outlines of Introductory Sociology: A Textbook of Readings in Social Science,* New York: Copyright by Harcourt, Brace and Co., Inc., in 1924, pp. 627–630.

tistical and philanthropic social scientist counts for nothing against this indifference on the part of the group involved.

This is true because, as shown above, a social "problem" is partly a state of the social mind and hence not purely a matter of unfavorable objective conditions in the physical or social environment. An expert statistician or social worker may be perfectly competent to point out the existence and nature, and even the causes and remedies in some cases, of *adverse social conditions* in any society on earth, but neither he nor any outsider can single out the *social problems* of a social group except by studying the *collective mind* of that group. Social statistics can detect and analyze *adverse social conditions*, but only social psychology and sociology are competent to formulate the *social problems* of the group, because these sciences alone are able to ascertain what the particular life conditions are that have thrust themselves upon the attention of a considerable number of competent observers within the group, being thus "thrown forward" in the collective consciousness as conditions demanding remedial social action. Without this act of *attention*, which takes note and seeks to manipulate and control (See "Introduction" to *Source Book for Social Origins* by W. I. Thomas), there is no social *problem* existent. Hence a group may live under many unfavorable conditions yet have few social problems, or even none at all.

From this it follows that the number and character of "social problems" varies from time to time just as it varies from place to place. The social problems of the United States are quite different from those of native Australia, China, or Greenland, but they are also very different from those of the United States itself a hundred years ago, and doubtless not at all what they will be a hundred years hereafter. At the same time certain adverse social conditions may be identical in all these places and at all these times, for example dearth of natural resources, existence of a polluted water-supply, the presence of dangerous bacteria, unfair distribution of wealth, or ignorance of child care. These are objective natural and social phenomena, actually existent and constantly open to observation and tabulation, but they may or may not at any time or place exist for the group mind, particularly for the *public opinion* there existent on social welfare. When they do they become the objective element in that state of the group mind which consists in the recognition of a certain social problem. The corollary of this is that no complete and final list of specific social problems can be drawn up by the present writer or by any one else.

It is nevertheless possible, and also desirable, to *classify* social problems in a broad general way. . . . The basis of classification used by the present writer may be said to be that of the *source* from which the social problems emerge, or, in the language of our definition, the quarter *from which* the problem in each instance is "thrust forward" upon public attention. From this point of view social problems fall into four groups, . . . namely:—*First,* those which are presented by some unfavorable aspect of the physical environment; *Second,* those arising from defects in the nature of population itself, or unfavorable tendencies in its rate of growth, or its geographical distribution, or disturbing differences in its racial types; *Third,* those growing out of faulty and disrupting social arrangements, *i.e.,* poor social organization, between the members of the group; and, *Fourth,* those springing from the growth and conflict of divergent ideals or social values cherished by different classes or sub-groups within the society. . . .

As herein regarded, social problems turn out to be, in a very essential aspect, social *processes.* More exactly, the recognition and solution of adverse social conditions through the formulation of a series of so-called "social problems" constitutes in itself a definite social process, comprised . . . under the one great all-embracing social process which we call social evolution. Consequently the era of social problems, or of any particular problem, arises in different societies at different stages of social evolution.

Social Problems in Relation to Values

Richard C. Fuller and Richard R. Myers

Richard Corbin Fuller (1907–1944), associate professor of sociology, University of Michigan. Author of "Social Problems," Part 1 of R. E. Park, ed., *Outline of the Principles of Sociology* (1939). Richard R. Myers (1912–   ), professor of sociology and anthropology, Oberlin College.

A common sociological orientation for the analysis of all social problems may . . . be found in the conflict of values which characterizes every social problem. These conflicts are mirrored in the failure of people to agree that a given condition is a social problem, or assuming such agreement, failure to reach an accord as to what should be done about it. It is exactly this disagreement in value-judgments that is the root cause of all social problems, both in the original definition of the condition as a problem and in subsequent efforts to solve it. May we suggest, tentatively, a threefold classification of social problems on the principle of different levels of relationship to the value-scheme? [1]

At the first level, we have what we may call the *physical* problem. The physical problem represents a condition which practically all people regard as a threat to their welfare, but value-judgments cannot be said to cause the condition itself. This is perhaps best demonstrated by such catastrophic problems as earthquakes, hurricanes, floods, droughts, locust plagues, and so forth. That these are "serious" problems from the standpoint of the people which they affect, we can have no doubt. However, we may raise the question whether or not they are "social" problems, since they do not usually occur because of conflicts in the value-scheme of the culture. We find no public forums debating the question of what to do about preventing earthquakes and hurricanes. There is no controversy over how to stop volcanic eruptions and cloudbursts. The causation is thought of as nonhuman, resting in natural forces outside the control of man. Perhaps we may call such causation noncultural or precultural.

Here, we must distinguish between the condition itself and the effects of the condition. While the earthquake itself may involve no value-judgments, its consequences inevitably will call for moral judgments and decisions of policy. People will not agree on how much should be spent in reconstruction, how it should be spent, or how the funds should be raised. There may be serious questions as to whether people in other unaffected areas of the same society should come to the aid of the stricken area. However, the earthquake itself is not a social problem in the same sense as illegitimacy and unemployment. The latter have cultural elements in their causation. . . .

At the second level, we have the *ameliorative* problem. Problems of this type represent conditions which people generally agree are undesirable in any instance, but they are unable to agree on programs for the amelioration of the condition. The essence of the ameliorative problem is one of solution and the administration of reform rather than original agreement that the condition constitutes a social problem which must be eradicated. Crime and delinquency fall in this category. Though there are individuals who offend the dominant community mores by robbing, murdering, raping, and petty thieving, there are no interest groups who openly in forum and legislature seek to perpetuate the interests which these individuals represent. All "right-thinking" people, regardless of race, nationality, religion, or economic status, look upon the ameliorative problem as intolerable. Among other problems which we may place in this class are most physical diseases, mental deficiency and insanity, and industrial and automobile accidents.

In contrast to the physical problem at the first level, the ameliorative problem is truly "social" in the sense that it is a man-made condition. By this we mean that value-judgments not only help to

---

[1] The elements of this classification were stated by Richard C. Fuller in the article, "The Problem of Teaching Social Problems," *American Journal of Sociology, 44* (1937–38): 415–425, on pp. 419–420.

From "Some Aspects of a Theory of Social Problems," *American Sociological Review*, 6 (1941): 24–32, pp. 27–32 quoted.

create the condition, but to prevent its solution. In the case of crime, certain moral judgments of our culture are to a large extent responsible for the criminal act in the first place. To the degree that our mores of conspicuous consumption enter into the motivation of crimes for pecuniary gain, there is a cultural responsibility for such criminal acts. Or again, traditional prison policies based on our belief in severity of punishment may become part of the causal pattern of further criminal behavior in the prisoner after his liberation. These same cherished notions of retribution in punishment of criminals operate to dissuade legislatures from adequately financing probation and parole systems, juvenile delinquency clinics, and the schools for problem children.

At this level, also, we have those physical and mental diseases where traditional beliefs obstruct the application of medical and psychiatric knowledge to the prevention and treatment of individual deficiencies. Certainly illness, disease, and industrial accidents among the low income groups reflect the failure of our culture both in preventing high incidences of risk to these people and in adequately insuring them against the costs of such risks. Specifically, the uneven distribution of wealth and income throughout our various social classes serves both to expose wage-earners and their families to malnutrition, disease, and accident, and to deprive them of the means to meet the economic costs of such disasters. . . .

It is true that all our ameliorative problems have their technical, medical, or engineering aspects similar to those involved in the physical problem. Venereal disease, tuberculosis, insanity, and automobile accidents all necessitate investigation by scientific specialists. The point is, of course, that in the case of such problems, even when the specialists have isolated the causes and are agreed upon programs of control, laymen still are hopelessly divided over questions of policy.

At the third level we have what we will call the *moral* problem. The moral problem represents a condition on which there is no unanimity of opinion throughout the society that the condition is undesirable in every instance. There is no general agreement that the condition is a problem and thus many people do not feel that anything should be done about it. With the moral problem, we have a basic and primary confusion in social values which goes much deeper than the questions of solution which trouble us in the ameliorative

problem.[2] Of course, the ameliorative problem reflects confusion in the value-scheme and thus contains real elements of moral conflict, but such conflict centers more around techniques and means of reform than around fundamental agreement on objectives and ultimate values. Hence, though all "right-thinking" people regard such conditions as crime, insanity, and disease as bad, there are interest groups openly defending and perpetuating the conditions classified as moral problems. Witness the problems of child labor and low wage and hour standards. We have only to read the record of newspaper and Congressional debate on the recently enacted Fair Labor Standards Act to learn that many individuals and groups not only objected to the specific solution attempted in the legislation, but also refused to admit that the conditions themselves were problems over which we should be concerned. In one of the first cases heard under the child labor legislation, one Michigan judge defended the labor of a newsboy on the ground that when he was a boy such work was regarded as excellent character development and training in individual qualities of initiative and self-discipline. Certainly employers in the beet sugar fields of the middle-western states who rely heavily on the labor of children do not define the condition, insofar as it pertains to them, in terms of a social problem. In those families where the labor of children is considered necessary to the maintenance of the family budget, parents and children alike have a stake in the continuance of the condition so abhorred by others. Religious groups have even frowned on governmental control of child labor as an unjustifiable invasion of the home and a threat to the prerogatives of the church. As to long hours and low wages, the opposition of some dominant groups in the southern states to the enactment of the federal legislation indicated no "problem-conscious" attitude on their part. Classical economists and employers have been known to look upon unemployment and low wage and hours standards as the inevitable, if not the necessary, mechanics of competition in the labor market. . . .

Other problems which have less of the economic in their make-up than those mentioned above, but which also occupy the same position in relation to

[2] The term "moral problem" is used by Stuart A. Queen and Jennette R. Gruener in their *Social Pathology*, rev. ed., New York: Thomas Y. Crowell Co., 1940, pp. 38–42. The moral problem, as they define it, pertains to questions of fundamental right and wrong.

the value-scheme, are divorce, race prejudice, and war. . . .

The utility of this classification is in its relativity. The purpose is not to pigeonhole the different problems with finality at any one level, but rather to give us a working basis for observing the position of each problem relative to other problems, and to the value-scheme as a whole. Note that problems will move from one category to another with changes in the state of scientific knowledge and with shifts in the value-scheme. . . . Some day child labor may be looked upon as criminal in the same sense that robbery and murder are now regarded as criminal. Conceivably, war may sometime be defined as wrong as venereal disease.

Nor is there any finality about the problems tentatively classified as ameliorative. Many crimes, such as political corruption, gambling, liquor offenses, and traffic violations are condoned, tolerated, and even participated in by respected and otherwise responsible members of the community.

White-collar crimes are conspicuous in this category. Crimes of this sort reflect the same fundamental confusion of values as the problems which we discussed as moral. Before such offenses can be said to be merely problems of police detection and judicial enforcement, the citizens of the community must get together and agree that something should be done.

It may well be that there are very few contemporary problems which can be said to be purely ameliorative in nature, since most of them reflect no underlying clarity of definition and moral evaluation. If such be the case, it is a revealing commentary on the absence of any firm tissue of cultural integration in the value-scheme. Cultural integration itself is a matter of degree. There is always more or less, but never complete integration. A complete homogeneity of social values would mean we would have no social problems at all unless we include only the purely physical problems discussed at the first level.

The Natural History of a Social Problem
Richard C. Fuller and Richard R. Myers *

Social problems do not arise full-blown, commanding community attention and evoking adequate policies and machinery for their solution. On the contrary, we believe that social problems exhibit a temporal course of development in which different phases or stages may be distinguished. Each stage anticipates its successor in time and each succeeding stage contains new elements which mark it off from its predecessor. A social problem thus conceived as always being in a dynamic state of "becoming" passes through the natural history stages of awareness, policy determination, and reform. . . .

Awareness. The genesis of every social problem lies in the awakening of people in a given locality to a realization that certain cherished values are threatened by conditions which have become acute. Definitions of alarm emerge only as these group values are thought to be involved. Without awareness or "problem consciousness" in certain groups of people, be they scientists, administrators, or like-minded neighbors, no identifiable problem

can be said to exist. Before a social problem can be identified, there must be awareness on the part of people who express their concern in some communicable or observable form.[1] The outstanding characteristic of this initial phase of awareness inheres in the constantly recurrent statements of people involved in a challenging situation that "something ought to be done." As yet, these people have not crystallized their definition sufficiently to suggest or debate exact measures for amelioration or eradication of the undesirable condition. Instead, there is unsynchronized random behavior, with protest expressed in general terms. . . .

Policy Determination. Very soon after the emergence of awareness comes debate over policies involved in alternative solutions. Ends and means are discussed and the conflict of social interests becomes intense. People who propose solutions soon find that these solutions are not acceptable to others. Even when they can get others to

[1] As yet, we have not perfected research techniques which can penetrate covert mental states very satisfactorily.

* See the identifying note on page 9.

From "The Natural History of a Social Problem," *American Sociological Review*, 6 (1941): 320–328, pp. 321–322, 324, 326–328 quoted.

agree on solutions, they find agreement as to means a further difficulty. The stage of policy determination differs significantly from the stage of awareness in that interest groups are now concerned primarily with "what ought to be done" and people are proposing that "this and that should be done." [2] Specific programs occupy the focus of attention. The multi-sided protests have become organized and channelized.

Policy determination on the residence-trailer problem in Detroit indicated discussion on at least three interrelated levels: first, discussion by neighbors and other interested but unorganized groups; second, discussion by organized interest or pressure groups such as taxpayers, trailer manufacturers, real estate organizations, parent-teacher associations, women's clubs, and men's clubs; third, discussion among specialists and administrators in government or quasi governmental units —the police, health officials, Common Council, social workers, and school boards. The interinfluence and cross-fertilization of debate among and between these three levels of participating discussants represent the dynamics of policy determination. . . .

Reform. The final stage in the natural history of a social problem is that of reform. Here we find administrative units engaged in putting formulated policy into action. General policies have been debated and defined by the general public, by special interest groups, and by experts. It is now the task of administrative experts specially trained in their jobs to administer reform. This is the stage of action, both public and private. The emphasis is no longer on the idea that "something ought to be done" or that "this or that should be done" but on the fact that "this and that are being done." Public action is represented in the machinery of government bodies, legislative, executive, and judicial; and in the delegated authority of administrative tribunals, special supervisory officers and boards. This is the institutionalized phase of the social problem in the sense that we have established policies carried out by publicly authorized policy-enforcing agencies. Reform may also be private in character, as witnessed by the activities of private clubs and organizations, private chari-

[2] Newspaper comment on the residence-trailer problem subsequent to 1935 reveals this transition in emphasis from simple alarm to concrete proposals. [They are referring to a case-study of the residence-trailer problem in Detroit given in the omitted sections of the article.—*Eds.*]

ties and other benevolent associations, and church groups.

Decisions of policy remain necessary at the reform stage, but such decisions usually involve quite technical matters pertaining to means and fall within the special bailiwick of the experts concerned with such questions. Of course, such policy questions may be taken out of the hands of the administrators whenever the general public exercises its powers of censorship, veto, or referendum. The already established public agencies may prove sufficient for the administration of reform in connection with a new community problem or it may be necessary to establish new agencies of administration. . . .

[The] stages in the natural history are not mutually exclusive and . . . they tend to overlap. For conceptual purposes, however, the three general phases may be set off from each other; in practical reality, the state of development of a problem at any one time usually contains elements of all three stages. . . .

What of the traditional, older, more pervasive problems which have occupied the attention of teacher and student in social problems texts for the past fifty years or more? What of crime, poverty, insanity, war, family disorganization, prostitution, illegitimacy, and race prejudice? Obviously, we cannot go back into antiquity to record the first awareness of social groups defining such conditions as problems. We cannot trace the earliest conflicts over policy and the first attempts at solution. Anthropological, historical, and contemporary data may be used to demonstrate to the student the universal aspects of these problems in space and time. Such materials, however, are inadequate in that they do not bring the student face to face with the dynamics of the problem. If the student is to understand why these old established problems persist and defy solution, he must examine the values of our social organization which bring the undesirable conditions into existence and which obstruct efforts to remove them. His laboratory for the study of these realities is the local community where the cross-sectional conflicts at the core of the problem can be observed most intimately.

The important fact which the textbooks overlook is that the old traditional problems are given relative emphases in the local community. At the awareness stage, a problem such as crime may be receiving very little attention in community *A*, whereas in the neighboring community *B* it is the all-absorbing focus of interest. Similarly, there may be no discussion of policies relative to race discrimination in *B*, whereas the people of *A* are intensely occupied with such discussion. The administration of relief for unemployment may be in an advanced stage in *B*, whereas little if anything is being done in *A*. Thus, even these problems which are persistently national in scope do not blanket the country with the same stage of development. Such conditions are only latent, dormant, or potential problems in the local area, and before they rise to local consciousness, debate, and control, a local issue is essential to set the natural history going. Although the conflicts of social values which make up the problem, once it has evolved, are much the same in all communities, the natural history technique provides a specific focus on these conflicts as they function in the concrete reality of a local situation. . . .

In the search for temporal sequences in the "becoming" of a social problem, the student does not take problem conditions for granted, as objective "evils" caused by "evils." He seeks to explain social problems as emergents of the cultural organization of the community, as complements of the approved values of the society, not as pathological and abnormal departures from what is assumed to be proper and normal. As such, the natural history technique is a sociological orientation rather than a social welfare orientation. If social problems theory is to come of age, it must cease being a poor relation of sociological theory and become sociological theory in its own right.*

---

* In a comment on Fuller and Myer's paper, *American Sociological Review*, 6 (1941): 328–329 (p. 329 quoted), James H. S. Bossard offers a more detailed "outline of the natural history of social problems which I have presented to my classes in recent years. It follows: (1) recognition of the problem; (2) discussion of its seriousness; (3) attempts at reform, usually intuitively arrived at, often ill-advised, promoted by the 'Well, let's do *something* folks'; (4) suggestions that more careful study is needed—'What we need is a survey'; (5) here follows some change in personnel of people interested; (6) emphasis upon broad basic factors; (7) dealing with individual cases; (8) another change of personnel; (9) program inductively arrived at; (10) refinements of technique of study and treatment; (11) refinements of concepts; (12) another change in personnel."— *Eds.*

CROSS REFERENCES TO STANDARD TEXTS

This list of texts on social problems, social disorganization, social pathology, and social deviation is naturally not a complete one. It includes the more generally used books in print at the time of compilation. At the end of succeeding chapters, the complete bibliographical reference is not given. Merely the author's last name and a shortened title are used with the appropriate page or chapter numbers.

Harry Elmer Barnes, *Society in Transition*, 2d ed., New York: Prentice-Hall, 1952. Pp. 13–14.

Jessie Bernard, *American Community Behavior: An Analysis of Problems Confronting American Communities Today*, New York: Dryden Press, 1949. Pp. v–vii, Chap. 1.

Herbert A. Bloch, *Disorganization: Personal and Social*, New York: Alfred A. Knopf, 1952. Pp. 3–7.

Lawrence Guy Brown, *Social Pathology: Personal and Social Disorganization*, New York: Appleton-Century-Crofts, 1942. Pp. 367–369.

John F. Cuber and Robert A. Harper, *Problems of American Society: Values in Conflict*, rev. ed., New York: Henry Holt and Co., 1951. Chaps. 1–3.

Mabel A. Elliott and Francis E. Merrill, *Social Disorganization*, 3d ed., New York: Harper & Bros., 1950. Pp. ix–xii.

Robert E. L. Faris, *Social Disorganization*, New York: Ronald Press Co., 1948. Chaps. 1 and 2.

John Lewis Gillin, *Social Pathology*, 3d ed., New York: Appleton-Century-Crofts, 1946. Chap. 1.

———, Clarence G. Dittmer, Roy J. Colbert, and Norman M. Kastler, *Social Problems*, 4th ed., New York: Appleton-Century-Crofts, 1952. Chap. 1.

Abbott P. Herman, *An Approach to Social Problems*, Boston: Ginn and Co., 1949. Chaps. 1 and 2.

Paul H. Landis, *Social Policies in the Making: A Dynamic View of Social Problems*, rev. ed., Boston: D. C. Heath and Co., 1952. Pp. 14–15.

Edwin M. Lemert, *Social Pathology: A Systematic Approach to the Theory of Sociopathic Behavior*, New York: McGraw-Hill Book Co., 1951. Pp. 3–7.

Francis E. Merrill, with H. Warren Dunham, Arnold M. Rose, and Paul W. Tappan, *Social Problems*, New York: Alfred A. Knopf, 1950. Pp. vii–ix, 3–13.

Clement S. Mihanovich, *Current Social Problems*, Milwaukee: Bruce Publishing Co., 1950. Pp. vii–x, 1–6, 441.

Martin H. Neumeyer, *Social Problems and the Changing Society*, New York: D. Van Nostrand Co., 1953. Chap. 1.

John Eric Nordskog, Edward C. McDonagh, and Melvin J. Vincent, eds., *Analyzing Social Problems*, New York: Dryden Press, 1950. Chap. 1.

Howard W. Odum, *American Social Problems*, rev. ed., New York: Henry Holt and Co., 1945. Pp. ix–xxv, 463–478.

Harold A. Phelps and David Henderson, *Contemporary Social Problems,* 4th ed., New York: Prentice-Hall, 1952. Chap. 1.

James M. Reinhardt, Paul Meadows, and John M.

Gillette, *Social Problems and Social Policy,* New York: American Book Co., 1952. Chap. 1.

W. Wallace Weaver, *Social Problems,* New York: Dryden Press, 1951. Chap. 1.

OTHER BIBLIOGRAPHY

Richard C. Fuller, "The Problem of Teaching Social Problems," *American Journal of Sociology, 44* (1938–39): 415–435.

———, "Sociological Theory and Social Problems," *Social Forces, 15* (1936–37): 496–502.

Norman D. Humphrey, "The Character of Social Problems," Chap. 1 in A. M. Lee, ed., *Principles of Sociology,* 2d ed., rev., New York: Barnes & Noble, 1951, pp. 3–13.

Edwin M. Lemert, "Is There a Natural History of Social Problems?" *American Sociological Review, 16* (1951): 217–223.

Max Lerner, "What Makes a Social Problem," Chap. 2 in Louis Wirth, ed., *Contemporary Social Problems,* Chicago: University of Chicago Press, 1939, pp. 13–21.

George A. Lundberg, "Societal Pathology and Sociometry," *Sociometry, 1* (1941): 78–97.

———, "What Are Sociological Problems?" *American Sociological Review, 6* (1941): 357–369.

Robert S. Lynd and Helen Merrell Lynd, *Middletown in Transition,* New York: Harcourt, Brace and Co., 1937. Chap. 13.

Elton Mayo, *The Human Problems of an Industrial Civilization,* New York: Macmillan Co., 1933.

Francis E. Merrill, "The Study of Social Problems," *American Sociological Review, 13* (1948): 251–259. Discussion by Albert K. Cohen, Ernest R. Mowrer, and Stuart A. Queen, *ibid.,* pp. 259–262.

Robert E. Park and E. W. Burgess, "Classification of Social Problems," pp. 45–47 in their *Introduction to the Science of Sociology,* 2d ed., Chicago: University of Chicago Press, 1924.

Social Problems, publ. quarterly by the Society for the Study of Social Problems, 1953—.

Willard Waller, "Social Problems and the Mores," *American Sociological Review, 1* (1936): 922–933.

Logan Wilson and William L. Kolb, eds., *Sociological Analysis,* New York: Harcourt, Brace and Co., 1949. Chap. 22.

REVIEW QUESTIONS

1. To what conditions or factors are social problems chiefly related?

2. What are some of the ramifications of the housing problem?

3. To what extent can one compare the solution of the American housing problem with the extinction of the Melanesian canoe-building art?

4. Is the rise of a social problem an augury of something more effective in the way of doing things? Or is a social problem in some other manner transitional?

5. Can you differentiate between habits of individual activity and habits of group activity? How significant are such habits in connection with social problems?

6. What does the etymology of *problem* contribute to a discussion of social problems?

7. In what ways would a sociologist be handicapped in pointing out to Australian tribesmen what their social problems are?

8. In what sense is a social problem a "state of the social mind"?

9. How can social problems be classified according to source?

10. In what senses does a conflict of values characterize every social problem?

11. Differentiate between a physical, an ameliorative, and a moral problem. Is there a movement from one category to another?

12. What stages do Fuller and Myers assign to the natural history of a social problem?

━CHAPTER 2━➤

Social Disorganization

SOCIOLOGY provides three major types of perspective on social problems. As the preceding chapter suggests, these perspectives emphasize personal, group, and societal factors. They are usually termed respectively personal disorganization, social disorganization, and societal maladjustment and change. These are not antagonistic frames of reference. They differ chiefly in the point from which social problems are viewed.

In this chapter, the closely related personal and group perspectives are set forth by leading social theorists. The next chapter deals with societal perspectives on social problems.

"All social problems," observe Ernest W. Burgess and the late Robert E. Park, "turn out finally to be problems of group life, although each group and each type of group has its own distinctive problems." * To an extent, groups are under compulsions from the over-all societal patterns of culture (customs, roles, institutions), and societal maladjustments have their reflection in group disorganization. On the other hand, as Park and Burgess add, "Every social group tends to create, from the individuals that compose it, its own type of character, and the characters thus formed become component parts of the social structure in which they are incorporated. All the problems of social life are thus problems of the individual; and all problems of the individual are at the same time problems of the group." † Considerations of personal and social disorganization are thus inextricably intertwined and are so treated in this chapter. They can only be separated—in an artificial and inaccurate manner—by the individual whose own pressing problems loom so large that his private tree obscures the group clump of trees as well as the societal forest.

Social disorganization is widely thought to occur "when there is a change in the equilibrium of forces, a breakdown of the social structure, so that former patterns no longer apply and the accepted forms of social control no longer function effectively." And the "same dynamic forces that produce social disorganization also bring about the disorganization of the individual. Caught in the maelstrom of social disorganization, many individuals lose their vital group contacts, their sense of personal security, and their interest even in life itself. . . . Individual disorganization and social disorganization thus operate in a vicious circle." *

William I. Thomas, Charles Horton Cooley, Sigmund Freud, and Émile Durkheim, among the older writers, have had notable influence with their theories of personal and social disorganization. Thomas and Znaniecki, in their monumental treatise on *The Polish Peasant in Europe and America,* made a number of contributions to sociology. Among these was a distinguished discussion of personal and social disorganization, substantially illustrated. "The Concept of Social Disorganization" is a summary of part of their conclusions.

Cooley added much to the sociology of the self, the person, group structure, and group relations, and the selections in this chapter show some of the applications of his theories to disorganization problems. He points first to problems arising from contrasts between societal and group standards of right and wrong and between various types of group standards in our society. His insights into delinquency as a group phenomenon, into social reaction to "higher righteousness," and into the rewards and penalties of innovation are quite pertinent. Cooley regards the contrast between formalism and disorganization as an apparent rather than an actual clash because—while different—both are problem-fraught conditions. Formalism is "mechanism supreme," and disorganization is "mechanism going to pieces." In the latter part

---

* *Introduction to the Science of Sociology,* 2d ed., Chicago: University of Chicago Press, 1924, pp. 47–48.
† *Ibid.,* p. 55.

* Mabel A. Elliott and Francis E. Merrill, *Social Disorganization,* 3d ed., New York: Harper & Bros., 1950, pp. 20, 39, 40.

of the Cooley material, he points briefly to ways in which society can be so organized as to atrophy and repress "the larger impulses of human nature . . . to such a degree that they break out, from time to time, in gross and degrading forms of expression."

Cooley thus takes a position resembling that of Freud. Freud contends that it "is impossible to ignore the extent to which civilization is built up on renunciation of instinctual gratifications, the degree to which the existence of civilization presupposes the non-gratification (suppression, repression or something else?) of powerful instinctual urgencies. This 'cultural privation' dominates the whole field of social relations between human beings; we know already that it is the cause of the antagonism against which all civilization has to fight." *

It is common for the uninformed to regard the delinquent child, the dope addict, or the prostitute as a separable individual problem. But Cooley describes, as have others, some of the intricate interrelations that tie together the organized and disorganized, the normal and the abnormal in society.

Durkheim's conception of *anomie,* closely related to the foregoing, has been influential among American sociologists. Talcott Parsons defines this conception as the "state of disorganization where the hold of norms over individual conduct has broken down. Its extreme limit is the state of 'pure individualism' [Correlative with 'disorganization of personality.'] which is for Durkheim as it was for Hobbes the war of all against all. Coordinate with and opposite to [As a polar hypothesis.] the state of *anomie* is that of 'perfect integration' which implies two things—that the body of normative elements governing conduct in a commu-

nity forms a consistent system and that its control over the individual is actually effective—that it gets itself obeyed." *

The selection by Robert K. Merton contains a careful consideration of Durkheim's *anomie* in relation to social structure. He emphasizes particularly "how some *social structures exert a definite pressure upon certain persons in the society to engage in nonconformist rather than conformist conduct.*"

Mowrer, Horney, and Queen contribute further to a perspective on personal disorganization. Mowrer outlines how personal disorganization can range from a person with reduced efficiency to the institutionalized case and the suicide. Horney deals with human maladjustments in "a competitive, individualistic culture." Some of her statements echo, from a different viewpoint, observations in Cooley's "The Conflict of Group Standards." Queen shows how measures of social disorganization in terms of social participation may be achieved.

Objections to conceptions of personal and social disorganization are usually on grounds that criteria stated for disorganization are moralistic and idealistic or class-centered rather than objective. The criteria are frequently said to be vague and seldom subject to measurement or other fairly precise estimation. These common objections might well be borne in mind by the student as he reads the first six selections in this chapter. The seventh selection, by Mills, sums up very briefly some of these objections. In reading this, it should be noted that the Mills analysis is as strong as it is partly because he has not attempted sympathetically to understand the more scientific contributions to disorganization theory.

* Sigmund Freud, *Civilization and Its Discontents,* transl. by Joan Riviere, New York: Jonathan Cape & Harrison Smith, 1930, pp. 63–64. By permission of The Hogarth Press, Ltd., London, copyright owners.

* Talcott Parsons, *The Structure of Social Action,* New York: Copyrighted 1937 by McGraw-Hill Book Co., Inc., p. 377. Reprinted by permission. Two footnotes inserted in brackets, and one omitted.

The Concept of Social Disorganization
William I. Thomas and Florian Znaniecki

William Isaac Thomas (1863–1947), sociologist. Wrote, in addition to *The Polish Peasant,* the following principal works: *Sex and Society* (1907); *The Unadjusted Girl* (1923); with D. S. Thomas, *The Child in America* (1928); and *Primitive Behavior* (1936). Florian Znaniecki (1882–   ), professor of sociology, University of Illinois; professor of sociology at the University of Poznan, Poland, 1919–1939. Principal works in English: *The Method of Sociology* (1934), *Social Actions* (1936), *The Social Role of the Man of Knowledge* (1940), and *Cultural Sciences* (1952).

The concept of social disorganization . . . refers primarily to institutions and only secondarily to men. Just as group-organization embodied in socially systematized schemes of behavior imposed as rules upon individuals never exactly coincides with individual life-organization consisting in personally systematized schemes of behavior, so social disorganization never exactly corresponds to individual disorganization. Even if we imagined a group lacking all internal differentiation, *i.e.,* a group in which every member would accept all the socially sanctioned and none but the socially sanctioned rules of behavior as schemes of his own conduct, still every member would systematize these schemes differently in his personal evolution, would make a different life-organization out of them, because neither his temperament nor his life-history would be exactly the same as those of other members. As a matter of fact, such a uniform group is a pure fiction; even in the least differentiated groups we find socially sanctioned rules of behavior which explicitly apply only to certain classes of individuals and are not supposed to be used by others in organizing their conduct, and we find individuals who in organizing their conduct use some personal schemes of their own invention besides the traditionally sanctioned social rules. Moreover, the progress of social differentiation is accompanied by a growth of special institutions, consisting essentially in a systematic organization of a certain number of socially selected schemes for the permanent achievement of certain results. This institutional organization and the life-organization of any of the individuals through whose activity the institution is socially realized partly overlap, but one individual cannot fully realize in his life the whole systematic organization of the institution since the latter always implies the collaboration of many, and on the other hand each individual has many interests which have to be organized outside of this particular institution. . . .

We can define [social disorganization] briefly as a *decrease of the influence of existing social rules of behavior upon individual members of the group.* This decrease may present innumerable degrees, ranging from a single break of some particular rule by one individual up to a general decay of all the institutions of the group. Now, social disorganization in this sense has no unequivocal connection whatever with individual disorganization, which consists in a decrease of the individual's ability to organize his whole life for the efficient, progressive and continuous realization of his fundamental interests. An individual who breaks some or even most of the social rules prevailing in his group may indeed do this because he is losing the minimum capacity of life-organization required by social conformism; but he may also reject the schemes of behavior imposed by his milieu because they hinder him in reaching a more efficient and more comprehensive life-organization. On the other hand also, the social organization of a group may be very permanent and strong in the sense that no opposition is manifested to the existing rules and institutions; and yet, this lack of opposition may be simply the result of the narrowness of the interests of the group-members and may be accompanied by a very rudimentary, mechanical and inefficient life-organization of each member individually. Of course, a strong group organization may be also the product of a conscious moral effort of its members and thus correspond to a very high degree of life-organization of each of them individually. It is therefore impossible to conclude from social as to individual organization or disorganization, or vice versa. In other words, social organization is not coextensive with individual morality, nor does social disorganization correspond to individual demoralization.

Social disorganization is not an exceptional phenomenon limited to certain periods or certain societies; some of it is found always and everywhere, since always and everywhere there are individual cases of breaking social rules, cases which exercise some disorganizing influence on group institutions and, if not counteracted, are apt to multiply and to lead to a complete decay of the latter. But during periods of social stability this continuous incipient disorganization is continuously neutralized by such activities of the group as reinforce with the help of social sanctions the power of existing rules. The stability of group institutions is thus simply a dynamic equilibrium of processes of disorganization and *reorganization*. Social reconstruction is possible only because, and in so far as, during the period of social disorganization a part at least of the members of the group have not become individually disorganized, but, on the contrary, have been working toward a new and more efficient personal life-organization and have expressed a part at least of the constructive tendencies implied in their individual activities in an effort to produce new social institutions. . . .

The Conflict of Group Standards
Charles Horton Cooley

Charles Horton Cooley (1864–1929), professor of sociology, University of Michigan. Principal works: *Human Nature and the Social Order* (1902, 1922), *Social Organization* (1909), *Social Process* (1918), *Life and the Student* (1927), and *Sociological Theory and Social Research* (1930).

In many cases of what we judge to be bad conduct the man belongs to a group whose standards are not the same as those of our own group by which we judge him. If his own group is with him his conscience and self-respect will not suffer, nor will he, so far as this group is concerned, undergo any blame or moral isolation. Practically all historical judgments are subject to this principle. I may believe that slave holding was wrong; but it would be very naïve of me to suppose that slaveholders suffered from a bad conscience, or found this practice any bar to their success. On the contrary, as it is conventional morality that makes for conventional success, it would be the abolitionist who would suffer in a slaveholding society. It is simply a question of the *mores,* which, as [William Graham] Sumner so clearly showed, may make anything right or anything wrong, so far as a particular group is concerned.

The conflict of group standards within a larger society is also a common example. The political grafter, the unscrupulous man of business, the burglar, or the bad boy, seldom stands alone in his delinquency, but is usually associated with a group whose degenerate standards more or less uphold him, and in which he may be so completely immersed as not to feel the more general standards at all. If so, we cannot expect his conscience will trouble or his group restrain him. That must be done by the larger society, inflicting blame or punishment, and especially, if possible, breaking up the degenerate group. In many, perhaps most, of such cases the mind of the individual is divided; he is conscious of the degenerate standards and also of those of the larger group; they contend for his allegiance. . . .

What may one expect when he breaks convention and strives to do better than the group that surrounds him? Evidently his situation will in many respects be like that of the wrong-doer; in fact he will usually be a wrong-doer in the eyes of those about him, who have no means of distinguishing a higher transgression from a lower.

In general this higher righteousness will contribute to an intrinsic success, measured by character, self-respect, and influence, but may be expected to involve some sacrifice of conventional objects like wealth and position. These generally

From *Social Process*, New York: Charles Scribner's Sons, 1918, pp. 105–107, 153–154, 156–157, 192–193. Reprinted by permission.

imply conformity to the group that has the power to grant them.

The rewards of the first sort, if only a man has the resolution to put his idea through, are beyond estimate—a worthy kind of pride, a high sense of the reality and significance of his life, the respect and appreciation of congenial spirits, the conviction that he is serving man and God. The bold and constant innovators—whatever their external fortunes may be—are surely as happy a set of men as there is, and we need waste no pity upon them because they are now and then burned at the stake.

* * * *

The organization of society may not only fail to give human nature the moral support it needs, but may be of such a kind as actively to promote degeneration. On its worse side the whole system of commercialism, characteristic of our time, is of this sort. That is, its spirit is largely mechanical, unhuman, seeking to use mankind as an agent of material production, with very little regard, in the case of the weak classes, for breadth of life, self-expression, outlook, hope, or any kind of higher life. Men, women, children, find themselves required to work at tasks, usually uninteresting and often exhausting, amidst dreary surroundings, and under such relations to the work as a whole that their imagination and loyalty are little, if at all, aroused. Such a life either atrophies the larger impulses of human nature or represses them to such a degree that they break out, from time to time, in gross and degrading forms of expression.

* * * *

It is the nature of the human mind, working through social organization, to forms norms or standards in every department of life, and to stigmatize whatever falls below these. Such norms are applied with peculiar emphasis to human personality itself, and to the various kinds of behavior in which it is expressed, because these are the matters in which we are most interested. Whether our judgments will prove to be permanently right or only a kind of moral fashion, it is impossible to be sure. It seems to be understood, however, that the word degeneration is used only with reference to standards which are believed to be of a relatively permanent or well-grounded kind, so that it is hard to imagine that the implied judgment could be wholly reversed. A man would hardly be called degenerate for dressing in the fashion of ten years ago, however absurd he might appear; but feeble-mindedness, disloyalty, cruelty, irresponsibility, or gross dissipation might be so called, since it would seem that these must always be detrimental to the common life. . . .

Degeneration . . . is part of the general organic process of life. Every wrong has a history, both in the innate tendencies of individuals and in the circumstances under which they have developed. We no longer feel that we understand crime and vice when we know who are practising them, and how, but we must trace them back to bad homes and neighborhoods, want of wholesome play, inadequate education, and lack of training for useful work. And we need to know also, if we can, what kind of a hereditary outfit each person brought into the world with him, and how it has reacted to his surroundings.

Moreover, the various kinds of wrong hang together in an organic whole; they are due largely to the same causes and each tends to reinforce all the others. Where poverty and apathy have become established, we may expect to find drunkenness and other sensual vices, idiocy, insanity, pauperism, and delinquency. . . .

In the same way all real reform must be general, an advance all along the line. Each particular evil is interwoven with others and with the general process of life in such a way that if you treat it as a thing by itself your work will be superficial and usually ineffective. The method of reform that naturally follows from the organic view is one of team-work, under which each reformer devotes himself to a special line of effort, but always in cooperation with others working in different lines, and always with an eye to the unity of the process in which all are engaged.

Social Structure and Anomie
Robert K Merton

Robert K. Merton (1910–   ), professor of sociology, Columbia University. Principal works: *Mass Persuasion* (1946), *Social Theory and Social Structure* (1949); editor, with Paul F. Lazarsfeld, *Studies in the Scope and Method of "The American Soldier"* (1950); and *The Focussed Interview* (revised, 1954).

Of the types of societies which result from independent variation of cultural goals and institutionalized means, we shall primarily be concerned with the first—a society in which there is an exceptionally strong emphasis upon specific goals without a corresponding emphasis upon institutional procedures. This statement, if it is not to be misunderstood, must be elaborated. No society lacks norms governing conduct. But societies do differ in the degree to which the folkways, mores, and institutional controls are effectively integrated with the goals which stand high in the hierarchy of cultural values. The culture may be such as to lead individuals to center their emotional convictions about the complex of culturally acclaimed ends, with far less emotional support for prescribed methods of reaching out for these ends. With such differential emphases upon goals and institutional procedures, the latter may be so vitiated by the stress on goals as to have the behavior of many individuals limited only by considerations of technical expediency. In this context, the sole significant question becomes, which of the available procedures is most efficient in netting the culturally approved value? The technically most effective procedure, whether culturally legitimate or not, typically becomes preferred to institutionally prescribed conduct. As this process of attenuation continues, the society becomes unstable and there develops what Durkheim called "anomie" (or normlessness).

The workings of this process eventuating in anomie can be easily glimpsed in a series of familiar and instructive, though perhaps trivial, episodes. Thus, in competitive athletics, when the aim of victory is shorn of its institutional trappings and success becomes construed as "winning the game" rather than "winning under the rules of the game," a premium is implicitly set upon the use of illegitimate but technically efficient means. The star of the opposing football team is surreptitiously slugged; the wrestler incapacitates his opponent through ingenious but illicit techniques; university alumni covertly subsidize "students" whose talents are confined to the athletic field. The emphasis on the goal has so attenuated the satisfactions deriving from sheer participation in the competitive activity that only a successful outcome provides gratification. Through the same process, tension generated by the desire to win in a poker game is relieved by successfully dealing oneself four aces or, when the cult of success has truly flowered, in a game of solitaire by sagaciously shuffling the cards. The faint twinge of uneasiness in the last instance and the surreptitious nature of public delicts indicate clearly that the institutional rules of the game are *known* to those who evade them. But cultural (or idiosyncratic) exaggeration of the success goal leads men to withdraw emotional support from the rules.

This process is of course not restricted to the realm of competitive sport, which has simply provided us with microcosmic images of the social macrocosm. The process by which exaltation of the end generates a literal *demoralization*—that is, a de-institutionalization—of the means occurs in many groups where the two components of the social structure are not highly integrated.

From "Social Structure and Anomie: Revisions and Extensions," Chap. XII in Ruth N. Anshen, ed., *The Family: Its Function and Destiny,* New York: Harper & Bros., 1949, 226–258, pp. 230–232 quoted. Footnotes omitted.

Types of Personal Disorganization
Ernest R Mowrer

Ernest Russell Mowrer (1895–   ), professor of sociology, Northwestern University. Principal works: *Family Disorganization* (1927, 1939), *Domestic Discord* (1928), *The Family* (1932), and *Disorganization: Personal and Social* (1942).

It is a truism that the course of all cultural forms is the individual and that the person is a reflection of the culture of the group. Innovations in culture are made largely by trial and error on the part of the individual and accepted by the group unwittingly. These innovations as they accumulate disturb the social equilibrium, but in the process they also lead to the disorganization of some persons. This personal disorganization finds expression in the individual either overtly or covertly. In so far as personal disorganization is primarily a covert process, it is accompanied with little or no serious breakdown in the social organization. When, however, personal disorganization is primarily overt in character, particularly if this overt divergence in response does not meet with strong social disapproval, it creates a disturbance of the social equilibrium out of which social disorganization develops. As the social structure breaks down, the first consequence is the further increase in personal disorganization until new social forms begin to replace the old and this social reorganization is reflected in the increased stability of the personal organization of the group out of which the social disorganization developed. That group of individuals whose life organizations reflected the old social order, however, become increasingly disorganized until they are eliminated, largely by death, though a few may experience a rapid conversion from the old to the new.

As social organization achieves a new equilibrium through the liquidation of those groups whose life organizations reflected the old social organization in favor of those groups whose life organizations the new social order has developed,

ossification begins and initiates a new cycle of personal disorganization. Thus, while the cycles of personal and social disorganization are not synchronized, the cycle of personal disorganization being always somewhat in the lead of social disorganization, there is always some degree of both social and personal disorganization present. Both cycles represent relative rather than absolute increases and decreases, and are based upon the tendency to seek social approval, and hence to rebel covertly rather than overtly.

Upon first analysis, it would seem that the forms of personal disorganization fall into two groups: (1) those forms which develop slowly out of failure on the part of the individual to reproduce in his life organization those attitudes and values which are in harmony with the social organization, and (2) those forms which develop relatively rapidly, due to sudden changes in the social milieu produced by migration and mobility. Upon further analysis, however, this differentiation turns out not to be a fundamental one, since the process of personal disorganization which develops so rapidly with migration and mobility is the source of the migration and mobility and not the consequence, though it is aggravated by changes in physical position which may introduce the person into new social worlds.

Personal disorganization ranges from the person whose efficiency is mildly reduced to those persons who eliminate themselves from society or become such liabilities that they have to be cared for either privately or publicly. Thus, in its extreme form, personal disorganization finds expression in suicide or in psychopathic behavior.

From "A Study of Personal Disorganization," *American Sociological Review, 4* (1939): 475–487, pp. 475–476 quoted.

Culture and Neurosis

Karen Horney

Karen Horney (1885–1952), psychiatrist, dean of American Institute for Psychoanalysis, New York, 1941–1952. Principal works: *The Neurotic Personality of Our Time* (1936), *New Ways in Psychoanalysis* (1939), *Self-Analysis* (1942), *Our Inner Conflicts* (1945), and *Neurosis and Human Conflict* (1950).

We live in a competitive, individualistic culture. Whether the enormous economic and technical achievements of our culture were and are possible only on the basis of the competitive principle is a question for the economist or sociologist to decide. The psychologist, however, can evaluate the personal price we have paid for it.

It must be kept in mind that competition not only is a driving force in economic activities, but that it also pervades our personal life in every respect. The character of all our human relationships is moulded by a more or less outspoken competition. It is effective in the family between siblings, at school, in social relations (keeping up with the Joneses), and in love life.

In love, it may show itself in two ways: the genuine erotic wish is often overshadowed or replaced by the merely competitive goal of being the most popular, having the most dates, love letters, lovers, being seen with the most desirable man or woman. Again, it may pervade the love relationship itself. Marriage partners, for example, may be living in an endless struggle for supremacy, with or without being aware of the nature or even of the existence of this combat.

The influence on human relations of this competitiveness lies in the fact that it creates easily aroused envy towards the stronger ones, contempt for the weaker, distrust towards everyone. In consequence of all these potentially hostile tensions, the satisfaction and reassurance which one can get out of human relations are limited and the individual becomes more or less emotionally isolated. It seems that here, too, mutually reinforcing interactions take place, so far as insecurity and dissatisfaction in human relations in turn compel people to seek gratification and security in ambitious strivings, and vice versa.

Another cultural factor relevant to the structure of our neurosis lies in our attitude towards failure and success. We are inclined to attribute success to good personal qualities and capacities, such as competence, courage, enterprise. In religious terms this attitude was expressed by saying that success was due to God's grace. While these qualities may be effective—and in certain periods, such as the pioneer days, may have represented the only conditions necessary—this ideology omits two essential facts: (1) that the possibility for success is strictly limited; even external conditions and personal qualities being equal, only a comparative few can possibly attain success; and (2) that other factors than those mentioned may play the decisive role, such as, for example, unscrupulousness or fortuitous circumstances. Inasmuch as these factors are overlooked in the general evaluation of success, failures, besides putting the person concerned in a factually disadvantageous position, are bound to reflect on his self-esteem.

The confusion involved in this situation is enhanced by a sort of double moral. Although, in fact, success meets with adoration almost without regard to the means employed in securing it, we are at the same time taught to regard modesty and an undemanding, unselfish attitude as social or religious virtues, and are rewarded for them by praise and affection. The particular difficulties which confront the individual in our culture may be summarized as follows: for the competitive struggle he needs a certain amount of available aggressiveness; at the same time, he is required to be modest, unselfish, even self-sacrificing. While the competitive life situation with the hostile tensions involved in it creates an enhanced need of security, the chances of attaining a feeling of safety in human relations—love, friendship, social contacts—are at the same time diminished. The estimation of one's personal value is all too dependent on the degree of success attained, while at the same time the possibilities for success are limited and the success itself is dependent, to a great extent, on fortuitous circumstances or on personal qualities of an asocial character.

From "Culture and Neurosis," *American Sociological Review, 1* (1936): 221–230, pp. 227–229 quoted.

Social Participation in Relation to Social Disorganization

Stuart Alfred Queen

Stuart Alfred Queen (1890–   ), professor of sociology and head of the department of sociology and anthropology, Washington University, St. Louis. Principal works: *Social Work in the Light of History* (1922); with A. G. Warner and E. B. Harper, *American Charities and Social Work* (1930); with W. B. Bodenhafer and E. B. Harper, *Social Organization and Disorganization* (1935); with L. F. Thomas, *The City* (1939); with J. B. Gruener, *Social Pathology* (1940); and with J. B. Adams, *The Family in Various Cultures* (1952).

It is frequently assumed by leaders in our democratic society that effective organizations of the purposive sort depend on general participation by their members. Thus campus leaders urge their fellow students to take more part in "activities." Politicians urge members of the party to attend rallies, ring door bells, and watch the polls. Trade union officers are concerned about members paying dues, obeying rules, presenting a united front during a strike, rewarding their friends and punishing their enemies. Scout masters emphasize the daily good deed, winning merit badges and taking part in "camporees." Clergymen stress attendance at religious services, marrying within the faith, assisting coreligionaries, supporting denominational institutions, etc. No matter how self-sufficient leaders may feel in making programs and decisions, giving instruction and advice, they commonly give explicit recognition to the assumption that active participation by members is essential to achievement of group ends, if not to group survival itself.

Some work done by sociologists and others indicates that this assumption is not without foundation. The publications of Kurt Lewin, Grace Coyle, Saul Alinsky, Leroy Bowman, and others provide some of the evidence concerning group success and individual participation.

The study and practice of "community organization" indicate that maintenance of a neighborhood or a community as a social group is closely related to the active participation of nigh-dwellers and fellow citizens. I refer here to studies of the U. S. Department of Agriculture (Division of Population and Rural Welfare), colleges of agriculture, Community Councils and Chests, Inc., the Cincinnati Social Unit experiment of 30 years ago, and many others which these will suggest. The research of sociologists and the practice of social workers indicate that the preservation of these locality groups is definitely bound up with the active participation of their constituents.

Some specific studies bearing on this problem are those of Mangus and Cook in Ohio, Lindstrom in Illinois, Anderson in New York, and Wakeley in Iowa. In fact, the very definitions of neighborhood and community imply, if they do not specify, the sharing of locality, tradition, interest, and activity.

A second assumption of leaders in democratic society and students of group life is that persons who are active in one group are usually active in others as well. It is almost a commonplace observation that if you want something done for an organization or a community you should give the job to someone who is already busy. Leaders and workers in churches, community chests, farm bureaus, student government, political parties, and scientific societies are generally found to be men and women who are active in several groups.

Supporting evidence is found in Ray Wakeley's article in *Sociometry*.[1] It appears in the point systems adopted at various colleges and universities to guard against the concentration of student officeholding in a few hands. It is found in the advice offered by the *Social Work Year Book* to the effect that "Effective boards . . . should, through rotation or other means, enlist the service of active

[1] Ray E. Wakeley, "Selecting Leaders for Agricultural Program," *Sociometry*, X (Nov. 1947), 384, 395.

From "Social Participation in Relation to Social Disorganization," *American Sociological Review, 14* (1949): 251–257, pp. 251–253, 254, 256–257 quoted.

and outstanding community leadership." [2] All this implies that there is a wide range of differences in social participation and that persons whose degree of participation is high are especially important for the survival and success of many groups and institutions.

A third proposition for which we have some evidence is that situations in which social participation languishes are also those in which "indices of social disorganization" are high. We refer here to indices of poverty, delinquency, disease, broken homes, mental disorder, suicide, etc. For example, a study made in Kansas City some years ago involved comparison of two districts very much alike as to ethnic composition, economic status and schooling, but very different as to incidence of cases in juvenile court, clinics, and relief agencies. A concomitant variable was membership in organized groups such as clubs, trade unions, and churches. To be sure, there was also another significant variable, namely, residential mobility; so that it is difficult to separate the influence of mobility from that of participation in groups.

We have additional, though still incomplete evidence in the negative relationship between the distribution of the so-called pathologies and of formal schooling. The latter we have found to be positively correlated with social participation scores to be discussed later. Ecological studies in various cities show clearly that poverty, vice, crime, and disease abound in areas where the average amount of schooling is low, and where by inference general social participation is low.

All these data taken together with others of similar character seem to lend strong support to the hypothesis that social participation is negatively related to social pathology and social disorganization, at least so far as spacial distribution is concerned.

The question now arises: Is there any relation between social participation and personal difficulties in the experience of individuals? Faris and Dunham have in various places presented evidence that social exclusion or isolation contributes to certain types of mental disorder, especially schizophrenia. Some more limited studies by students at Washington University have shown that very low social participation for a long period before hospitalization is characteristic of certain mental patients. It also appears that the relation between

mental disorders and social participation operates in reverse or in a circle, for such breakdown serves to exclude the victim from many types of social and cultural activity.

The relation of social participation to poverty seems fairly clear, although the evidence is less precise than we would like. Large numbers of persons combine in their individual experience low income, restricted participation in organized groups, little neighboring, little schooling, little reading, little use of museum, theatre, concerts and other cultural facilities. Supporting data may be found in the second edition of our *Social Pathology*, in Warner's study of *Yankee City*, Davis and Gardner's *Deep South*, Mangus and Cottam's *Farm Population and Rural Life Activities*, and many others.

With reference to crime the evidence is not so clear. There is no reason to suppose that the amount of social participation among "professional" criminals, "white-collar" criminals or juvenile offenders is lower than that of their law-abiding fellows. Indeed, in a comparison of 100 inmates of the Indiana School for Boys with 100 non-delinquents, matched as to age, color, and nativity of parents, Atwood and Shideler found that the social participation scores of the delinquents were even higher than those of the non-delinquents.[3] But it appears that such habitual offenders as vagrants, alcoholics, drug addicts, and petty thieves are relatively isolated persons. Moreover, there is evidence that prejudice against ex-convicts and "jail birds" helps to exclude them still further from participation in many groups.

We might go on to consider hypotheses and the limited data available concerning other personal difficulties and social participation—divorce, illegitimacy, unemployment, prejudice against transients and members of ethnic minorities, etc. But enough has been said to make it plain that here are some important *problems*, some likely *hypotheses*, and some initial evidence. What we need next are dependable *measures* of social participation. . . .

Because of the limitations of scales so far developed, we at Washington University set to work several years ago to devise something which we hoped might be more adequate. Several different schedules were tried out before we finally settled on the one now in use. This one is divided into

[2] Russell H. Kurtz, ed., *Social Work Year Book, 1947*, New York: Russell Sage Foundation, 1947, p. 553.

[3] B. S. Atwood and E. H. Shideler, "Social Participation and Juvenile Delinquency," *Sociology and Social Research*, XVIII (May–June, 1934), 436–441.

four parts: A. Participation in Organized Groups, B. Cultural Participation, C. Neighborhood Participation, D. (Other) Informal Social Participation. . . .*

It was mentioned earlier that the scores in the four sections of our schedule surprised us by the lack of positive correlation. We rather expected that people who are active in organized groups might have little time for neighboring, but we anticipated that the "joiners" would have high scores in cultural participation. At all events when we computed the intercorrelation of scores in the four sections we obtained only negative coefficients.

COEFFICIENTS OF CORRELATION

Sections of Schedule	Pearsonian r
A & B	—.29
A & C	—.18
A & D	—.30
B & C	—.16
B & D	—.39
C & D	—.35

Just in passing, it may be of interest to note the relation between some other factors and the combined social participation scores. Length of residence in a district and amount of schooling were directly and positively related to social participation. Almost the reverse was true of age. There was not a large difference between men and women or between married and single persons.

---

* [Omitted here are details of the procedures and findings of a study made in St. Louis.—Eds.]

As to race, there was less difference than we had anticipated. Whites were higher on cultural participation, Negroes on neighboring. On the Chapin scores white men were highest and white women lowest, Negroes being intermediate. Both races and both sexes were very much alike in informal activities.

There remain many unanswered questions about the scheme we have proposed for measuring social participation. It neglects what might be called "intensity" of social relationships. It does not differentiate between relationships of acceptance and those of hostility, activities which are constructive and those which are disrupting to group life.

But we should not conclude this discussion without pointing out again the possible uses of some social participation scale in studying social disorganization. With such a scale we have a new approach to understanding the difference between conforming and aberrant members of a group. We may test the hypotheses set forth at the beginning of this paper concerning social participation of individual members and the survival or success of a group. We may use this device to measure the success of a program for the social rehabilitation of ex-convicts, convalescent diabetics, unmarried mothers, displaced persons and many other marginal persons. We may use it to compare total populations in depression, war, industrial unrest and so-called normal times. All in all, it seems that here is a device that should prove very useful in studying many aspects of social disorganization.

An Attack on Disorganization Theorists
C. Wright Mills

C. Wright Mills (1916–   ), associate professor of sociology, Columbia University. Co-editor and co-translator with H. H. Gerth of *From Max Weber: Essays in Sociology* (1946). Author of *White Collar* (1951) and, with H. H. Gerth, of *Character and Social Structure* (1953).

One of the pervasive ways of defining "problems" or of detecting "disorganization" is in terms of *deviation from norms.* The "norms" so used are usually held to be the standards of "society." . . . In the absence of studies of specific norms themselves this mode of problematization shifts the responsibility of "taking a stand" away from

the thinker and gives a "democratic" rationale to his work. . . . It is significant that, given their interest in reforming society, which is usually avowed, these writers typically assume the norms which they use and often tacitly sanction them. . . .

The easy way to meet the question of why

From "The Professional Ideology of Social Pathologists," *American Journal of Sociology, 49* (1943–44): 165–180, pp. 169–171 quoted.

norms are violated is in terms of biological impulses which break through "societal restrictions." A paste-pot eclectic psychology provides a rationale for this facile analysis. . . . Thus, more comprehensive problematization is blocked by a biological theory of social deviation. And the "explanation" of deviations can be put in terms of a requirement for more "socialization." "Socialization" is either undefined, used as a moral epithet, or implies norms which are themselves without definition. The focus on "the facts" takes no cognizance of the normative structures within which they lie.

The texts tend either to be "apolitical" . . . or to aspire to a "democratic" opportunism. . . . When the political sphere is discussed, its pathological phases are usually stated in terms of "the anti-social," or of "corruption," etc. . . . In another form the political is tacitly identified with the proper functioning of the current and unexamined political order; it is especially likely to be identified with a legal process or the administration of laws. . . . If the "norms" were examined, the investigator would perhaps be carried to see total structures of norms and to relate these to distributions of power. Such a structural point of sight is not usually achieved. The level of abstrac-

tion does not rise to permit examination of these normative structures themselves, or of why they come to be transgressed, or of their political implications. Instead, this literature discusses many kinds of apparently unrelated "situations." . . .

Present institutions train several types of persons—such as judges and social workers—to think in terms of "situations."[1] Their activities and mental outlook are set within the existent norms of society; in their professional work they tend to have an occupationally trained incapacity to rise above series of "cases." It is in part through such concepts as "situation" and through such methods as "the case approach" . . . that social pathologists have been intellectually tied to social work with its occupational position and political limitations. And, again, the similarity of origin and the probable lack of any continuous "class experience" of the group of thinkers decrease their chances to see social structures rather than a scatter of situations. The mediums of experience and orientation through which they respectively view society are too similar, too homogeneous, to permit the clash of diverse angles which, through controversy, might lead to the construction of a whole.

[1] See K. Mannheim, *Man and Society in an Age of Reconstruction*, transl. by E. A. Shils, New York: Harcourt, Brace and Co., 1940, p. 305.

CROSS REFERENCES TO STANDARD TEXTS *

Barnes, *Society in Transition*, Chap. 1.
Bernard, *American Community Behavior*, Chap. 24.
Bloch, *Disorganization*, Chaps. 4, 6; Appendices 1, 2.
Brown, *Social Pathology*, Chaps. 22–24.
Cuber and Harper, *Problems of American Society*, Chap. 22.
Elliott and Merrill, *Social Disorganization*, Chaps. 1–3, 15, 22; pp. 665–666, 707–708.
Faris, *Social Disorganization*, Chap. 2.
Gillin, *Social Pathology*, Chaps. 1, 10.
——— and others, *Social Problems*, Chap. 19.
Herman, *Approach to Social Problems*, pp. 17–23.
Landis, *Social Policies in the Making*, Chap. 7.

Lemert, *Social Pathology*, Chap. 1.
Merrill and others, *Social Problems*, Chap. 1.
Mihanovich, *Current Social Problems*, Chap. 1.
Neumeyer, *Social Problems and the Changing Society*, Chap. 1.
Nordskog and others, *Analyzing Social Problems*, Chaps. 1, 5.
Odum, *American Social Problems*, Chap. 6.
Phelps and Henderson, *Contemporary Social Problems*, Chap. 1, p. 317.
Reinhardt and others, *Social Problems and Social Policy*, Chap. 1.
Weaver, *Social Problems*, Chap. 2.

OTHER BIBLIOGRAPHY

Franz Alexander, *Our Age of Unreason*, Philadelphia: J. B. Lippincott Co., 1942.
———, "Psychoanalysis and Social Disorganization," *American Journal of Sociology*, 42 (1936–37): 781–813.
Read Bain, "Our Schizoid Culture," *Sociology and Social Research*, 19 (1934–35): 266–276.
Ruth Benedict, "Continuities and Discontinuities in Cultural Conditioning," *Psychiatry*, 1 (1938): 161–167.
Herbert Blumer, *Critiques of Research in the Social Sciences: I, An Appraisal of Thomas and Znaniecki's The Polish Peasant in Europe and America*, New York: Social Science Research Council, 1939.
———, "Social and Individual Disorganization,"

* For complete bibliographical reference to each text, see page 13.

American Journal of Sociology, 42 (1936–37): 871–877.

George Devereux, "Maladjustment and Social Neurosis," *American Sociological Review*, 4 (1939): 844–851.

John Dollard and N. E. Miller, *Personality and Psychotherapy*, New York: McGraw-Hill Book Co., 1950.

Erich Fromm, "Individual and Social Origins of Neurosis," *American Sociological Review*, 9 (1944): 380–384.

———, *Man for Himself*, New York: Rinehart & Co., 1947.

Elton F. Guthrie, "The Crisis Concept in the Approach to the Problem of Personality," *Social Forces*, 13 (1934–35): 383–390.

Karen Horney, *The Neurotic Personality of Our Time*, New York: W. W. Norton & Co., 1937.

Ralph Kramer, "The Conceptual Status of Social Disorganization," *American Journal of Sociology*, 48 (1942–43): 466–474.

Paul H. Landis, *Social Control: Social Organization and Disorganization in Process*, Philadelphia: J. B. Lippincott Co., 1939.

Rollo May, *Man's Search for Himself*, New York: W. W. Norton & Co., 1953.

Elton Mayo, "Psychiatry and Sociology in Relation to Social Disorganization," *American Journal of Sociology*, 43 (1937–38): 825–831.

Ernest R. Mowrer, "Methodological Problems in Social Disorganization," *American Sociological Review*, 6 (1941): 839–849; Raymond F. Sletto, "Comment," *ibid.*, pp. 849–851; Floyd N. House, "Comment," *ibid.*, pp. 851–852.

Edwin H. Sutherland, "Social Pathology," *American Journal of Sociology*, 50 (1944–45): 429–435.

S. Kirson Weinberg, *Society and Personality Disorders*, New York: Prentice-Hall, 1952.

Louis Wirth, "Ideological Aspects of Social Disorganization," *American Sociological Review*, 5 (1940): 472–482.

James W. Woodard, "The Relation of Personality Structure to the Structure of Culture," *American Sociological Review*, 3 (1938): 637–651.

REVIEW QUESTIONS

1. In what senses does the concept of social disorganization refer "primarily to institutions and only secondarily to men"?

2. How meaningful is it to say that social disorganization is "a *decrease of the influence of existing social rules of behavior upon individual members of the group*"? Since various social groups have differing and even conflicting rules, to what rules should one refer as criteria for social organization or disorganization?

3. How is *anomie* related to social disorganization?

4. How do conflicting group standards manage to persist within a society?

5. What interests and social rewards help to maintain such differences?

6. How does individualism differ from personal evidences of disorganization or disintegration?

7. In what view is disorganization "a lack of communication and social consciousness"?

8. Can you think of instances in which the organization of our own society has promoted the degeneration of certain groups? List.

9. Are your instances such that they can be related to Freud's conception of "cultural privation"?

10. Cooley maintains that tendencies toward disorganization relate themselves to one another both in a person and in society. Does it then follow, as he says, that the "method of reform . . . is one of team-work" both personally and socially?

11. Thomas and Znaniecki say that when "an individual rejects any social tradition of his group all other traditions usually lose their hold upon him." How tenable does this conclusion seem to you?

12. Mowrer takes the position that personal disorganization is a necessary step in social adjustment. Can you illustrate this from instances about which you have read or heard?

13. What does Mowrer probably mean when he speaks of "the liquidation of those groups whose life organizations reflected the old social organization"? How are they liquidated?

14. In your own life history, has competition had any such influence on your activities as Horney contends?

15. Would you say that there is any basis for the contention that "success meets with adoration almost without regard to the means employed in securing it"?

16. What relation does social participation have to social and personal organization and disorganization?

17. Doesn't Mills fail to see the similarity between what he calls a "democratic" opportunism and the objective description of social phenomena?

18. What bearing does Cooley's "The Conflict of Group Standards" have upon Mills's criticisms of the norms employed by theorists of social disorganization?

━CHAPTER 3━▶

Societal Change

POPULAR NOTIONS of a societal frame of reference concerning social problems have given rise to such catch phrases as "the dead hand of the past," "social Darwinism," and "the class struggle." Especially during periods of rapid societal change, generations of adolescents stir restlessly against restraints of "dead-hand" customs and institutions inherited from the past. Politicians, with eyes on "lofty" objectives and the "welfare of the state," have turned the unemotional scientific phrases of the kindly Charles Darwin (1809–82)—"survival of the fittest" and "struggle for existence"—into emotion-charged stereotypes with which to justify sacrifices of mass or minority rights and even lives. This gave a name-calling sense to the terms, "social Darwinism" and "social Darwinians." With his perspective warped by personal feelings of acute insecurity and frustration, Marx and his friend Engels developed another oversimplified perspective on societal maladjustment and change. With their fiery *Communist Manifesto*, they made "the class struggle" and "dialectical materialism" catch phrases of popular thought and conflict.

The perspectives on societal maladjustment and change developed by sociologists are not stated in terms of popular catch phrases; they direct attention towards opportunities for human welfare and development through more precise knowledge of social processes. Increasingly as sociologists have developed techniques and criteria for greater sensitivity and objectivity in observation, they have produced more and more helpful insights into the nature of societal processes of growth, change, decay, adjustment, and maladjustment. In this chapter, selections from some of their more general statements in the area of growth and change are presented, together with some pertinent analyses by nonsociologists for purposes of amplification and contrast. In subsequent chapters are many detailed illustrations and applications of these theoretical materials.

What is popularly called the "dead hand of society's past" has concerned sociologists as well

as adolescents and agitators. Cooley, in the first selection, points to the dilemma of deciding what is "dead mechanism" in society, and what still fulfills useful functions, regardless of age. Keller then poses another related problem: he notes how civilization protects man from "the action of natural selection," the claw against claw of the struggle for existence in its harshest forms. But this, he says, is a progressive sort of thing in which the "scaffolding created by his civilization" becomes more and more complex and more and more necessary. When a catastrophe cracks that scaffolding, man "is again an animal among other animals." Keller also outlines the role of competition between tribes and nations in the struggle for existence and in the definition of cultural patterns which survive. A theory concerning the evolution of society and culture, he observes, "is not a logical curiosity." It is a theory summarizing human experience. It should be tested, therefore, by facts of observation and not by tricks of argument.

The problem of cultural maladjustment has concerned many other sociologists and continues to do so. In his studies in the area, Ogburn coined the term "cultural lag," and this is a rough equivalent to "cultural maladjustment." He says that cultural lag is the problem situation brought about by unequal rates of adaptation by culture to changed life-conditions in society.

Queen approaches cultural change and lag with different emphases than Ogburn. Queen prefers the terms "cultural inconsistency" and "institutional malfunctioning" to "cultural lag." He takes this position because certain inconsistencies, such as "the doctrine of the brotherhood of man coupled with the support of war . . . may actually serve to tide over a crisis." He is aware that criteria for institutional malfunctioning may be difficult to devise, but he believes that they might be derived from such concepts as waste and efficiency.

Marx and Engels viewed approximately the same kinds of materials as those faced gravely by

Ogburn, but they bring forth conclusions with significantly dissimilar characteristics. Marx and Engels were impressed by the manner in which the growing bourgeoisie destroyed the romantic illusions of feudalism, replaced them with "egotistical calculation" (termed by others "individualism" or "free enterprise") and the "callous 'cash payment'" ("the profit motive"), and forced man "at last . . . to face with sober senses, his real conditions of life, and his relations with his kind." In turn the bourgeoisie are also to fall. This is because "the bourgeoisie forged the weapons that bring death to itself; it has also called into existence the men who are to wield those weapons—the modern working-class—the proletarians."

The last two selections, by Frank and Brown, turn more directly to the question of what can be done to mitigate social problems of societal deriva-

tion. Frank advocates a change in viewpoint from one stressing "individual wickedness, incompetence, perversity, or pathology" to one in which such individual behavior is related to the fact "that our culture is sick, mentally disordered, and in need of treatment." Objectionable persons are symptoms of societal disorganization or maladjustment. Brown regards Frank's insistence upon treating "society as the patient" as only a partial answer because it overlooks, he contends, "the unique experience of the social variant." From these selections, one gets an impression of the need for both societal and personal attacks upon social problems, for careful and scrupulously objective studies as bases for planning reform programs, and for a willingness to engage in enlightened experimentation.

The Weight of Society's Dead Mechanism
Charles Horton Cooley*

An institution is simply a definite and establish phase of the public mind, not different in its ultimate nature from public opinion, though often seeming, on account of its permanence and the visible customs and symbols in which it is clothed, to have a somewhat distinct and independent existence. Thus the political state and the church, with their venerable associations, their vast and ancient power, their literature, buildings and offices, hardly appear even to a democratic people as the mere products of human invention which, of course, they are. . . .

Too much mechanism in society gives us something for which there are many names, slightly different in meaning, as institutionalism, formalism, traditionalism, conventionalism, ritualism, bureaucracy and the like. It is by no means easy, however, to determine whether mechanism is in excess or not. It becomes an evil, no doubt, when it interferes with growth and adaptation, when it suppresses individuality and stupefies or misdirects the energies of human nature. But just when this is the case is likely not to be clear until the occasion is long past and we can see the matter in the perspective of history.

Thus, in religion, it is well that men should adhere to the creeds and ritual worked out in the past for spiritual edification, so long as these do, on the whole, fulfil their function; and it is hard to fix the time—not the same for different churches, classes or individuals—when they cease to do this. But it is certain that they die, in time, like all tissue, and if not cleared away presently rot. . . .

Underlying all formalism, indeed, is the fact that it is psychically cheap; it substitutes the outer for the inner as more tangible, more capable of being held before the mind without fresh expense of thought and feeling, more easily extended, therefore, and impressed upon the multitude. Thus in our own architecture or literature we have innumerable cheap, unfelt repetitions of forms that were significant and beautiful in their time and place.

The effect of formalism upon personality is to starve its higher life and leave it the prey of apathy, self-complacency, sensuality and the lower nature in general. A formalized religion and a formalized freedom are, notoriously, the congen-

* See the identifying note on page 18.
From *Social Organization: A Study of the Larger Mind,* New York: Charles Scribner's Sons, 1909, pp. 313, 342–345. Reprinted by permission.

ial dwelling place of depravity and oppression. . . .

In America and western Europe at the present day there is a great deal of formalism, but it is, on the whole, of a partial and secondary character, existing rather from the inadequacy of vital force than as a ruling principle. The general state of thought favors adaptation, because we are used to it and have found it on the whole beneficial. . . .

But dead mechanism is too natural a product of human conditions not to exist at all times, and we may easily find it to-day in the church, in politics, in education, industry and philanthropy; wherever there is a lack of vital thought and sentiment to keep the machinery pliant to its work.

What Will the Scaffolding Stand?
Albert Galloway Keller

Albert Galloway Keller (1874–   ), professor of the science of society, Yale University, 1907–1942. Principal works: *Homeric Society* (1902, 1906); *Colonization* (1908); *Societal Evolution* (1915, 1931); with W. G. Sumner and M. R. Davie, *The Science of Society,* 4 vols. (1927); and *Man's Rough Road* (1932).

In truth, since the whole trend of civilization is to interpose barriers to the action of natural selection, societal selection is logically certain to preserve those who would perish under nature. It must always be realized that societal selection operates on a plane of its own, demanding standards of fitness differing from those of natural selection. The only sense that there is in adjudging its results by a comparison with those of natural selection lies in the fact that the biological test is the ultimate and final one. There is a good deal of sense in doing this; in view of our knowledge that man is, at last analysis, an animal in a natural environment, there can be no doubt at all about his ultimate subjection to the laws that control organic nature. His new mode of selection is performable, as it were, only upon a scaffolding created by his civilization—solely in an artificialized environment. If the scaffolding is shaken down, the environment dis-artificialized, by some catastrophe, he is again an animal among other animals. He cannot put more and more dependence upon the scaffolding unless he is constantly strengthening its supports. He can never bid utter defiance to natural law, ignore biological qualities altogether, cut loose once and for all from the earth. It would be dangerous indeed if societal selection were going to become unreservedly counterselective. . . .

In any case we have to live on our scaffolding; even if all societal selection were counterselective, we cannot go back to survival on the basis of mere biological fitness. But we do well to keep an eye on the nature-processes; and those who cry out against counterselection and emphasize the need of biological fitness are performing for us the great service of advertising the presence of limits beyond which it is unsafe to allow variations in the mores to go. . . .

The collapse of any section of the scaffolding of civilization—for instance, as a result of war— shakes the whole structure, even if it does not cast it down; and those who have not been hurled into the pit of brute violence must yet suffer and sacrifice with those who have. . . . If counterselection is no more than tardiness to act, on the part of societal selection, even so it is well to have the dangers of such delay set forth; for if not anticipated, selection must at length be exercised by the brutal, primordial methods of general violence and destruction. . . .

Those who warn of counterselection are inciters to rational action, which, despite the difficulties attending it, we must, as civilized men, try to get the knowledge and skill and fortitude to carry out. . . .

In human society, whatever the case in nature, the sickly mature have often contributed to the strengthening and adjustment of the institutions of society, though by procreation they may have subtracted something from its biological soundness. The question always is the same: What will

From *Societal Evolution: A Study of the Evolutionary Basis of the Science of Society,* rev. ed. (1931), New Haven: Yale University Press, 1947, pp. 260–263, 269–271, 273. By permission.

the scaffolding stand? Is the advantage worth the danger incurred?

* * * *

Survival or non-survival alone is strong proof of fitness or unfitness, but without citation of evidence, in any range of evolution. The more searching question is as to the reasons for triumph or failure in competition, that is, as to what qualities made for fitness or the reverse. It is sometimes objected to evolution in general that it involves circular reasoning: the fittest are those that survive, but they are proved to be the fittest because they survive. This is a shallow quip. Evolution is not a logical curiosity; evolutionists have been too serious and hardworking to have the time to joke that meditators have for their word-juggling. Evolution shows *why* the fittest are fittest, not by verbal contortions calculated to bewilder but by elaborate studies of organisms and their life-conditions. When it is stated that assurance of a general right to life is normal in a society, or that postponement of marriage is characteristic of its more cultured members, to each of these practices is conceded the element of fitness or expediency. It has been proved inexpedient in the fact to confer the right to life only upon some instead of generally and impartially upon all group-members; such discrimination has been tried and given up. The postponement of marriage has fitness because it promotes the standard of living, thereby making for what most people agree is a desirable social result. . . .

War and the military organization, the industrial organization, marriage and the family, medicine and hygiene, and humanitarianism are all societal adjustments not represented in nature. They are what they are because of services discharged to society. Of course they will pinch the individual, from time to time, for there is an inevitable disharmony between the individual and the societal interest.

Societal Change and Cultural Lag
William Fielding Ogburn

William Fielding Ogburn (1886–   ), Sewell L. Avery distinguished service professor of sociology, University of Chicago. Principal sociological works: *Social Change* (1922); *The Social Sciences* (1927); *You and Machines* (1935); *Social Characteristics of Cities* (1937); with M. F. Nimkoff, *Sociology* (1940, 1950); and *The Social Effects of Aviation* (1946).

The thesis is that the various parts of modern culture are not changing at the same rate, some parts are changing much more rapidly than others; and that since there is a correlation and interdependence of parts, a rapid change in one part of our culture requires readjustments through other changes in the various correlated parts of culture. For instance, industry and education are correlated, hence a change in industry makes adjustments necessary through changes in the educational system. Industry and education are two variables, and if the change in industry occurs first and the adjustment through education follows, industry may be referred to as the independent variable and education as the dependent variable. Where one part of culture changes first, through some discovery or invention, and occasions changes in some part of culture dependent upon it, there frequently is a delay in the changes occasioned in the dependent part of culture. The extent of this lag will vary according to the nature of the cultural material, but may exist for a considerable number of years, during which time there may be said to be a maladjustment. It is desirable to reduce the period of maladjustment, to make the cultural adjustments as quickly as possible. . . .

A large part of our environment consists of the material conditions of life and a large part of our social heritage is our material culture. . . . The cultural adjustments to material conditions . . . may be called, for purposes of this particular analysis, the adaptive culture. . . . Some parts of the non-material culture are thoroughly adaptive culture such as certain rules involved in handling technical appliances, and some parts are only in-

From *Social Change: With Respect to Culture and Original Nature,* New York: B. W. Huebsch, 1922, pp. 200–203, 210–212, 280. By permission of The Viking Press, Inc., New York, publishers.

directly or partially so, as for instance, religion. The family makes some adjustments to fit changed material conditions, while some of its functions remain constant. The family, therefore, under the terminology used here is a part of the non-material culture that is only partly adaptive. When the material conditions change, changes are occasioned in the adaptive culture. But these changes in the adaptive culture do not synchronize exactly with the change in the material culture. There is a lag which may last for varying lengths of time, sometimes indeed, for many years. . . .

It is desirable to state more clearly and fully the points involved in the analysis. The first point concerns the degree of adjustment or correlation between the material conditions and the adaptive non-material culture. The degree of this adjustment may be only more or less perfect or satisfactory; but we do adjust ourselves to the material conditions through some form of culture; that is, we live, we get along, through this adjustment. The particular culture which is adjusted to the material conditions may be very complex, and, indeed, quite a number of widely different parts of culture may be adjusted to a fairly homogeneous material condition. Of a particular cultural form, such as the family or government, relationship to a particular material culture is only one of its purposes or functions. Not all functions of family organization, as, for instance, the affectional function, are primarily adaptive to material conditions.

Another point to observe is that the changes in the material culture precede changes in the adaptive culture. This statement is not in the form of a universal dictum. Conceivably, forms of adaptation might be worked out prior to a change in the material situation and the adaptation might be applied practically at the same time as the change in the material conditions. But such a situation presumes a very high degree of planning, prediction and control. The collection of data, it is thought, will show that at the present time there are a very large number of cases where the material conditions change and the changes in the adaptive culture follow later. . . . Furthermore, it is not implied that changes may not occur in non-material culture while the material culture remains the same. Art or education, for instance, may undergo many changes with a constant material culture.

Still another point in the analysis is that the old, unchanged, adaptive culture is not adjusted to the new, changed, material conditions. It may be true that the old adaptive culture is never wholly unadjusted to the new conditions. There may be some degree of adjustment. But the thesis is that the unchanged adaptive culture was more harmoniously related to the old than to the new material conditions and that a new adaptive culture will be better suited to the new material conditions than was the old adaptive culture. Adjustment is therefore a relative term, and perhaps only in a few cases would there be a situation which might be called perfect adjustment or perfect lack of adjustment. . . .

Since lags in social movements causing social maladjustments follow changes in material culture, and since there are many rapid changes in material culture, it follows that there will be an accumulation of these lags and maladjustments. . . . Such a development creates quite a task for those who would direct the course of social progress, the task of eliminating these maladjustments by making the adjustments to material changes more rapid. It is thinkable that the piling up of these cultural lags may reach such a point that they may be changed in a somewhat wholesale fashion. In such a case, the word revolution probably describes what happens. There may be other limiting factors to such a course of development; and our analysis is not sufficiently comprehensive and accurate to make definite prediction. But certain trends at the present time seem unmistakable.

Cultural Inconsistency and Institutional Malfunctioning

Stuart Alfred Queen*

Curiously neither textbook bearing the title *Social Disorganization* † makes effective use of the concepts culture lag and culture conflict. . . . Instead, I adopted the concepts of internal inconsistency and institutional malfunctioning.

Internal inconsistency was restated in terms of mutual incompatibility or contradiction of traits, e.g., in our economic system, the tradition of free competition and the practice of monopolistic control; in our religious complex, the doctrine of the brotherhood of man coupled with the support of war, exclusion of Negroes, and condemnation of radicals. These might perhaps be interpreted as culture lags and conflicts. Yet the very contradictions noted may imply the development of rationalizations which, far from destroying an institution or total culture, may actually serve to tide it over a crisis. Hence, if we continue to employ this concept of internal inconsistency, we must differentiate between discrepancies involved in the appearance of a culture lag or conflict and rationalizations which may constitute an accommodation or a step in reorganization. Another difficulty is that in pointing out contradictions within a culture complex one is tempted to play the role of Sophist or Pharisee, "Thank God, I am not as other men; I see through all this confusion; and I can show you what fools they are who accept it with complacency." Such an attitude can hardly be said to promote scientific objectivity! On the whole, the category of internal inconsistency seems to be of doubtful utility.

Institutional malfunctioning was described in several ways that utilized or might utilize rather precise methods. For example, in studying the economic complex of our culture, use was made of the studies of waste in industry made by the Hoover Committee and others. The criterion of waste was failure to achieve the efficiency (in terms of time, cost, etc.) of the best plant in a given industry. Of course, in some cases this might have been more appropriately related to unorganization than to disorganization. However, by using such a measure at regular intervals of time, one might identify a series of changes properly designated organizing or disorganizing. In studying our governmental complex, some of the criteria employed were the maladjustment of governmental areas (multiplicity, overlapping, expensiveness, lack of homogeneity), miscarriage of justice ("mortality" of criminal cases, conviction of innocent persons, recidivism, etc.), defiance of law by those charged with enforcement and other administration (spoils system, graft, etc.). Unfortunately, there was no well-defined criterion for the rating of governmental areas, or for measuring graft, and other political spoils. However, failure of the system of criminal justice was rather objectively described and partly measured as by the Wickersham Commission, e.g., by ratio of arrests to crimes reported, ratio of convictions to indictments, ratio of recidivists to prisoners released, etc. These illustrations indicate that, while much of the writing on institutional malfunctioning is impressionistic, because criteria are vague and ill-defined, it should be possible to formulate precise criteria and to assemble quantitative data for the objective rating of institutional functioning. When such instruments are devised, their application at regular intervals should yield reliable measures of the direction of change, i.e., toward more or less institutional organization.

The hazards of using such a concept as insti-

† Mabel A. Elliott and Francis E. Merrill, *Social Disorganization*, 3d ed., New York: Harper and Brothers, 1950, and Stuart A. Queen, W. B. Bodenhafer, and E. B. Harper, *Social Organization and Disorganization*, New York: Thomas Y. Crowell Co., 1935.—*Eds.*

* See identifying note on page 23.
From "The Concepts Social Disorganization and Social Participation," *American Sociological Review, 6* (1941): 307–316, pp. 311–312 quoted.

tutional malfunctioning are bound to be great. The temptation to identify positive indexes with "good" and negative indexes with "bad" will be hard to resist. In fact, this will probably be true of all studies within the intellectual framework of social disorganization.

The Bourgeoisie in Societal Change
Karl Marx and Friedrich Engels

Karl Marx (1818–1883), German political philosopher, regarded as the founder of modern socialism. Chief works in English translations: *Poverty of Philosophy* (1847); with F. Engels, *Manifesto of the Communist Party* (1848); and *Capital,* 3 vols. (completed by F. Engels, 1867–1894). Friedrich Engels (1820–1895), German socialist, edited and published Marx's works. Other works by Engels in English translations: *Condition of the Working Class in England in 1844* (1845), *Socialism, Utopian and Scientific* (1878), and *Origin of the Family, Private Property and the State* (1884).

Modern industry has established the world market, for which the discovery of America paved the way. This market has given an immense development to commerce, to navigation, to communication by land. This development has, in its turn, reacted on the extension of industry; and in proportion as industry, commerce, navigation, railways extended, in the same proportion the bourgeoisie developed, increased its capital, and pushed into the background every class handed down from the Middle Ages. . . .

The bourgeoisie, historically, has played a most revolutionary part.

The bourgeoisie, wherever it has got the upper hand, has put an end to all feudal, patriarchal, idyllic relations. It has pitilessly torn asunder the motley feudal ties that bound man to his "natural superiors," and has left no other nexus between man and man than naked self-interest, than callous "cash payment." It has drowned the most heavenly ecstasies of religious fervor, of chivalrous enthusiasm, of Philistine sentimentalism in the icy water of egotistical calculation. It has resolved personal worth into exchange value, and in place of the numberless indefeasible chartered freedoms, has set up that single, unconscionable freedom— Free Trade. In one word, for exploitation, veiled by religious and political illusions, it has substituted naked, shameless, direct, brutal exploitation.

The bourgeoisie has stripped of its halo every occupation hitherto honored and looked up to with reverent awe. It has converted the physician, the lawyer, the priest, the poet, the man of science, into its paid wage laborers.

The bourgeoisie has torn away from the family its sentimental veil, and has reduced the family relation to a mere money relation. . . .

The bourgeoisie cannot exist without constantly revolutionizing the instruments of production, and thereby the relations of production, and with them the whole relations of society. Conservation of the old modes of production in unaltered form was, on the contrary, the first condition of existence for all earlier industrial classes. Constant revolutionizing of production, uninterrupted disturbance of all social conditions, everlasting uncertainty and agitation distinguish the bourgeois epoch from all earlier ones. All fixed, fast frozen relations, with their train of ancient and venerable prejudices and opinions, are swept away, all new formed ones become antiquated before they can ossify. All that is solid melts into air, all that is holy is profaned, and man is at last compelled to face with sober senses, his real conditions of life, and his relations with his kind.

The need of a constantly expanding market for its products chases the bourgeoisie over the whole surface of the globe. It must nestle everywhere, settle everywhere, establish connections everywhere.

The bourgeoisie has through its exploitation of the world market given a cosmopolitan character to production and consumption in every country. To the great chagrin of reactionists, it has drawn from under the feet of industry the national ground on which it stood. . . . In place of the old local and national seclusion and self-sufficiency, we have intercourse in every direction,

From "Manifesto of the Communist Party" (1848), transl. by S. Moore and F. Engels, in K. Marx, *Capital . . . and Other Writings,* ed. by Max Eastman, New York: Modern Library, 1932, pp. 320–355, pp. 322–328, 332, 334 quoted.

universal interdependence of nations. And as in material, so also in intellectual production. The intellectual creations of individual nations become common property. National onesidedness and narrowmindedness become more and more impossible, and from the numerous national and local literatures there arises a world literature. . . .

The bourgeoisie has subjected the country to the rule of the towns. It has created enormous cities, has greatly increased the urban population as compared with the rural, and has thus rescued a considerable part of the population from the idiocy of rural life. Just as it has made the country dependent on the towns, so it has made barbarian and semi-barbarian countries dependent on civilized ones, nations of peasants on nations of bourgeois, the East on the West. . . .

The bourgeoisie, during its rule of scarce one hundred years, has created more massive and more colossal productive forces than have all preceding generations together. Subjection of Nature's forces to man, machinery, application of chemistry to industry and agriculture, steam-navigation, railways, electric telegraphs, clearing of whole continents for cultivation, canalization of rivers, whole populations conjured out of the ground—what earlier century had even a presentiment that such productive forces slumbered in the lap of social labor? . . .

A similar movement is going on before our own eyes. Modern bourgeois society with its relations of production, of exchange and of property, a society that has conjured up such gigantic means of production and of exchange, is like the sorcerer who is no longer able to control the powers of the nether world whom he has called up by his spells. For many a decade past, the history of industry and commerce is but the history of the revolt of modern productive forces against modern conditions of production, against the property relations that are the conditions for the existence of the bourgeoisie and of its rule. It is enough to mention the commercial crises that by their periodical return put on its trial, each time more threateningly, the existence of the entire bourgeois society. In these crises a great part

not only of the existing products, but also of the previously created productive forces, are periodically destroyed. In these crises there breaks out an epidemic that, in all earlier epochs, would have seemed an absurdity—the epidemic of over-production. Society suddenly finds itself put back into a state of momentary barbarism; it appears as if a famine, a universal war of devastation, had cut off the supply of every means of subsistence; industry and commerce seem to be destroyed; and why? . . .

The weapons with which the bourgeoisie felled feudalism to the ground are now turned against the bourgeoisie itself.

But not only has the bourgeoisie forged the weapons that bring death to itself; it has also called into existence the men who are to wield those weapons—the modern working-class—the proletarians. . . .

In the conditions of the proletariat, those of the old society at large are already virtually swamped. The proletarian is without property; his relation to his wife and children has no longer anything in common with the bourgeois family relations; modern industrial labor, modern subjection to capital, the same in England as in France, in America as in Germany, has stripped him of every trace of national character. Law, morality, religion, are to him so many bourgeois prejudices, behind which lurk in ambush just as many bourgeois interests.

All the preceding classes that got the upper hand sought to fortify their already acquired status by subjecting society at large to their conditions of appropriation. The proletarians cannot become masters of the productive forces of society, except by abolishing their own previous mode of appropriation, and thereby also every other previous mode of appropriation. They have nothing of their own to secure and to fortify; their mission is to destroy all previous securities for and insurances of individual property. . . .

What the bourgeoisie therefore produces, above all, are its own gravediggers. Its fall and the victory of the proletariat are equally inevitable.

Society as the Patient
Lawrence K. Frank*

There is a growing realization among thoughtful persons that our culture is sick, mentally disordered, and in need of treatment. . . .

Anyone who reflects upon the present situation in which our Western European culture finds itself cannot fail to see that we have passed from the condition in which deviations from a social norm were to be regarded as *ab*normal. Today we have so many deviations and maladjustments that the term "normal" has lost almost all significance. Indeed, we see efforts being made to erect many of the previously considered abnormalities into cultural patterns for general social adoption.

The disintegration of our traditional culture, with the decay of those ideas, conceptions, and beliefs upon which our social and individual lives were organized, brings us face to face with the problem of treating society, since individual therapy or punishment no longer has any value beyond mere alleviation of our symptoms. . . .

The conception of a sick society in need of treatment has many advantages for diagnosis of our individual and social difficulties and for constructive therapy, although we may find it necessary to prescribe a long period of preparation before the patient will be ready for the remedies indicated. Perhaps the most immediate gain from adopting this conception is the simplification it brings. Instead of thinking in terms of a multiplicity of so-called social problems, each demanding special attention and a different remedy, we can view all of them as different symptoms of the same disease.[1] That would be a real gain even if we cannot entirely agree upon the exact nature of the disease. If, for example, we could regard crime, mental disorders, family disorganization, juvenile delinquency, prostitution and sex offenses, and much that now passes as the result of pathological processes (e.g., gastric ulcer)[2] as evidence, not of individual wickedness, incompetence, perversity, or pathology, but as human reactions to cultural disintegration, a forward step would be taken. At present we cherish a belief in a normal, intact society against which we see these criminals, these psychopaths, these warring husbands and wives, these recalcitrant adolescents, these shameless prostitutes and vicious sex offenders, as so many rebels who threaten society and so must be punished, disciplined, or otherwise individually treated. This assumption of individual depravity or perversity gives us a comfortable feeling that all is well socially, but that certain individuals are outrageously violating the laws and customs that all decent people uphold.

It is, indeed, interesting to see how this conception of a social norm, with individuals as violators and frustrators of normality, runs through so much of our thinking. In political life we cherish a fond belief in the essential soundness and efficacy of representative government. The cumulative evidence of social injustice, of corruption in office, of legislative "deals" and intrigues—the whole slimy trail of graft and misfeasance is treated as the vicious practices of dishonest politicians. We save our belief in democracy and in our representative political organization by imputing all their faults and shortcomings to individual malefactors. The remedy for political chicane is then viewed as investigation and prosecution: "Turn the rascals out."

In our economic affairs we follow a similar practice. Rugged individualism, free enterprise, the money and credit economy, the price system with its supposed free play of economic forces and the law of supply and demand—all these are considered as naturally sound, effective economic practices based upon the very nature of society;

---

[1] *Cf.* the writer's earlier paper, "Social Problems," *American Journal of Sociology*, 30 (1924–25): 462–473.

[2] *Cf.* H. Flanders Dunbar, *Emotions and Bodily Changes*, New York: Columbia University Press, 1935.

* See the identifying note on page 4.

From "Society as the Patient," *American Journal of Sociology*, 42 (1936–37): 335–344. Also available in full in Lawrence K. Frank, *Society as the Patient*, New Brunswick: Rutgers University Press, 1948. Reprinted by permission.

if perverse and selfish individuals did not interfere with these natural forces, frustrate competition, and break these laws, we should have no economic troubles. When our industry and banking and commerce are crippled or paralyzed, we begin to look for the guilty persons who have interfered with normality. Some blame the stifling of competition, others the excess of competition, while others aim their accusations against this or that individual or organized group of individuals whose conduct is deemed to be uneconomic and therefore responsible for our troubles. The confusion over the nature and the perpetrators of these economic misdeeds provides occasion for vivacious, sometimes vituperative, argument, but we generally agree that the trouble comes from individual misdeeds that must be curbed by more laws, more regulation, and more severe punishment.

Likewise, in family life, difficulties are similarly treated in terms of individual wickedness and guilt, to be corrected by severe moral instruction and legal adjudication on a semi-criminal basis, as in divorce. Similarly, the admitted inadequacy of the courts, both civil and criminal, is blamed upon individuals, corrupt judges, unprincipled shysters, and unethical practitioners, whose disloyalty to their high duty has stained the bright garments of Justice and prevented honest administration of the laws.

In every department and aspect of our social life we find the same pattern of thought about our society: that our social ills come from individual misconduct that must be corrected and punished so that these supposed underlying social forces and social laws can operate without hindrance, thereby solving our social problems. Nor is this point of view confined merely to the man in the street and the unscrupulous manipulator who has learned to utilize these social myths for his own purposes. Our social scientists, with few exceptions, are strong believers in these supposed social forces and laws and underlying natural processes that, if left unhindered, would operate smoothly. Much of our social research is a persistent search for these underlying social, political, and economic systems, the discovery of which will, it is expected, bring social progress, just as physical science revealed the underlying physical-chemical processes that gave us our modern industry and technology. Indeed, these conceptions of normality and inherent order in society have dominated both lay and professional thinking for many generations.[3] . . .

When we regard Western European culture that has emerged from an almost incredible background of conflict and confusion and mixture of peoples, and see that for centuries it has not been unified either in ideas and beliefs or in socially approved practices, we can begin to understand the etiology of the sickness of our society. Our culture has no unanimity of individual or social aims, no generally accepted sanctions, and no common patterns of ideas or conduct. All our basic ideas, conceptions, and beliefs have been in process of revision for the last three hundred years or more, beginning with the displacement of the older notions of the universe and man's place therein and going on now to the supersedure of the traditional animistic, voluntaristic conceptions of human nature and conduct and man's relation to his society. The American scene, moreover, has been successively invaded by representatives of widely different nationalities, who have accelerated the decay of the early American tradition that our changing industry has made inevitable. . . .

If we bear in mind this culture disintegration, then our so-called social problems and the seeming perversity of individuals become intelligible. They are to be viewed as arising from the frantic efforts of individuals, lacking any sure direction and sanctions or guiding conception of life, to find some way of protecting themselves or of merely existing on any terms they can manage in a society being remade by technology. Having no strong loyalties and no consistent values or realizable ideals to cherish, the individual's conduct is naturally conflicting, confused, neurotic, and antisocial, if that term has any meaning in the absence of an established community purpose and ideal. The more skilful contrive to profit from the social confusion and their own lack of scruples, while others evade or break laws, become mentally disordered or diseased, or otherwise violate the older codes of conduct, damaging themselves and those whose lives they touch. No one is happy, it is apparent; the successful are driven as relentlessly as the failures by their sense of guilt, their compulsions, and their frustrations.

We see, then, that continued faith in the myths

---

[3] *Cf.* the writer's paper, "The Principle of Disorder and Incongruity in Economic Affairs," *Political Science Quarterly, 47* (1932): 515–525; also the writer's paper, "The Emancipation of Economics," *American Economic Review, 14* (1924): 17–38.

regarding an underlying social system comes from a need to cling to something that offers some sense and meaning in the social confusion and keeps alive the hope that things may be better. Cynicism is, of course, the refuge of the majority of successful men, especially professional men, who shrug their shoulders, acknowledge the decay of their professional scruples, but go on "getting theirs." There is, apparently, no profession or occupation that has not succumbed to the current practice of racketeering, which means that the traditional ethics and sense of responsibility are breaking down, leaving each one to pursue his own personal ends. It is neither fair nor useful to upbraid the individual who cannot singly maintain the old standards, even if they were workable, or withstand the competitive pressure to adopt the unscrupulous practices of the others. Campaigns for social reforms are unavailing since there are no new patterns or sanctions to which we can give allegiance, and we cannot return to the old since they offer no meaningful answers to our present perplexities. The only common faith we share at present is this social mythology which we cling to with increasing difficulty as the absurdity of such beliefs and the futility of our efforts to restore normality become more evident.

Where, then, does the cultural view help beyond providing another apt theory of social confusion which is useful as a point of vantage from which the intellectual can contemplate the vulgar scene? It transfers the focus of attention from the seemingly recalcitrant or perverse individual to the cultural patterns and sanctions. This revision of our thinking will modify the doctrine of individual responsibility and guilt that is not only an active factor in the growing criminality and insanity, but also a complete block to any understanding of the problem or any attempt at modification. If we accept the conception of society as the patient, absolve the individual from guilt, and regard these various social problems as symptoms of progressive cultural change, we can at least relieve some of our anxiety since we then have a

definite and possibly manageable problem.[4] . . .

Instead of clinging to the traditional conceptions of individual autonomy and moral responsibility that were dependent upon a coherent culture for their effective operation, we must begin to think in terms of individuals caught in social confusion wherein individual conduct and ethics are no longer socially tolerable. The individual, instead of seeking his own personal salvation and security, must recognize his almost complete dependence upon the group life and see his only hope in and through cultural reorganization. The tradition of individual striving that was ushered in by the Renaissance has been the very process of this cultural disintegration, for the individual, in striving to be an individual, has broken down the inherited culture of common, shared beliefs and activities. Now that this necessary cultural disintegration has been accomplished, almost to the point of unbearable confusion, we must face the task of constructing a new culture, with new goals, new beliefs, new patterns and sanctions, but predicated upon the enduring human values that must be continually restated and given renewed expression. . . .

Just as the emergence of the doctrine of individual responsibility brought an enormous gain to the individual and to society, so the doctrine of cultural determination will bring another great step forward in human life. It will give us both the courage and the faith to undertake the remaking of our culture, and it will provide the criteria for the new patterns and sanctions for the human needs of individuals who vary in capacities and skills but are basically alike in their physiological, psychological, and social requirements, and especially in their need of a common faith.[5]

---

[4] Cf. Otto Rank, "Psychology and Social Change," *News Letter of American Association of Psychiatric Social Workers*, 4: 3 (January 1935).

[5] Cf. the writer's paper, "Social Planning and Individual Ideas," *International Journal of Ethics*, 45 (1934–35): 81–89.

Comment on Frank's "Society as the Patient"

L. Guy Brown

Lawrence Guy Brown (1895–   ), professor of sociology and chairman of the department, University of Rhode Island. Principal works: *Immigration* (1933), *Social Psychology* (1934), and *Social Pathology* (1942).

Doubtless most sociologists would readily agree with Mr. Lawrence K. Frank that society is sick. However, when society is sick, human nature is equally sick. Consequently the "social physician" will not gain anything by dismissing the individual as the patient and turning to society with his therapeutic measures. Long ago Cooley pointed out the fact that the individual and society do not exist as separate entities. They are inextricably interrelated. Society is a reality only as the objective aspect of human nature. The point of departure is not the individual or society, but the interactive relationship between the two.

It is not possible to change society without changing human nature. This was demonstrated in the Eighteenth Amendment *dèbâcle*. The human nature of the traditional culture remained and was not, therefore, the subjective counterpart of the newly legislated culture. The result was social disorganization and personal demoralization. The "social physician" had cured society but had ignored human nature in the curative process. Had attitudes, ideas, interests, desires, and other aspects of human nature been changed at the same time, the result would have been quite different.

Even in this point of view individual therapy will always have its place. Each individual has his own unique experience, and occasionally one becomes a social variant in a cultural milieu that is not considered a sick society. A black sheep appears in a so-called "good" home where all others are well adjusted. The "social physician" notes that the culture in the home is not sick. If he is a modern social psychologist, he knows that the organic basis of the human nature of the black sheep was undefined at birth; therefore heredity is not the explanation. He is aware that the heredity per se and the environment per se do not hold the explanation of the adjustment of this individual. He knows that the explanation lies in the unique experience of the social variant, which is different from the experiences of all other members of the household. The approach is through the individual who needs a new definition of the situation and a new conception of his role in the group.

In a culture that is not regarded as "sick," one finds mental ill health, the problem child, the psychopathic personality, and the delinquent. In such an instance one does not think of "society as the patient" or talk about individual perversity or congenitally predetermined behavior, but studies the unique experience of the individual for an explanation. If there is an interest in treatment, the student of this situation seeks to redefine the individual to himself and to give him a new definition of his social heritage and a new conception of his role in relation to his cultural milieu.

In most cases the "social physician" must start with the interactive relationship between human nature and society if he wishes to achieve a better society. Social organization cannot transcend the quality of human nature. There will be an occasional need for individual treatment, but a well society will be an actuality only when the whole situation is considered, with human nature and the social order regarded as aspects of the totality.

This point of view does not assume individual depravity or perversity apart from social disorganization. It does not regard society as normal with individuals in rebellion against it. There is no place here for the "time-honored beliefs in human volition and responsibility." This point of view emphasizes the idea that when culture is "sick" and in need of treatment, human nature is also "sick" and in need of treatment. One aspect of the totality cannot be sick apart from the other and one cannot be cured (changed) apart from the other. The social scientist who tries to isolate

From "Society as the Patient" (communication), *American Journal of Sociology*, 42 (1936–37): 717–718. Comments on Lawrence K. Frank, "Society as the Patient," *ibid.*, pp., 335–344.

"society as the patient" and deals with it will find himself confronted with as many difficulties as those who have tried to salvage individuals while ignoring the social order.

CROSS REFERENCES TO STANDARD TEXTS *

Barnes, *Society in Transition,* Chap. 1.
Bernard, *American Community Behavior,* Chaps. 3–6.
Bloch, *Disorganization,* Chaps. 1–3.
Brown, *Social Pathology,* Chap. 3.
Cuber and Harper, *Problems of American Society,* Chaps. 1–2.
Elliott and Merrill, *Social Disorganization,* Chaps. 1, 22.
Faris, *Social Disorganization,* Chap. 2.
Gillin, *Social Pathology,* Chap. 1, pp. 21–22, 201–203.
——— and others, *Social Problems,* Chap. 2.
Herman, *Approach to Social Problems,* Chap. 2.
Landis, *Social Policies in the Making,* Chaps. 1, 5.
Lemert, *Social Pathology,* Chaps. 2–4.
Merrill and others, *Social Problems,* Chap. 1, pp. 279–282, 286–290.

Mihanovich, *Current Social Problems,* Chap. 1, p. 441.
Neumeyer, *Social Problems and the Changing Society,* Chap. 2.
Nordskog and others, *Analyzing Social Problems,* pp. 658–663.
Odum, *American Social Problems,* pp. 63–104, 493–497.
Phelps and Henderson, *Contemporary Social Problems,* Chap. 1.
Reinhardt and others, *Social Problems and Social Policy,* Chap. 1, esp. pp. 26–28.
Weaver, *Social Problems,* pp. 9–16.

* For complete bibliographical reference to each text, see page 13.

OTHER BIBLIOGRAPHY

Robert Cooley Angell, *The Integration of American Society,* New York: McGraw-Hill Book Co., 1941.
Read Bain, "The Concept of Complexity in Sociology," *Social Forces,* 8 (1929–30): 222–231 and 369–378.
H. G. Barnett, *Innovation,* New York: McGraw-Hill Book Co., 1953.
Carl Becker, "Progress," *Encyclopaedia of the Social Sciences,* 12 (1934): 495–499.
Trigant Burrow, "Our Mass Neurosis," *Psychological Bulletin,* 23 (1926): 305–312.
John Bagnell Bury, *The Idea of Progress: An Inquiry Into Its Origin and Growth,* New York: Macmillan Co., 1932.
Alexander Goldenweiser, "Evolution, Social," *Encyclopaedia of the Social Sciences,* 5 (1931): 656–662.
G. W. Hartmann, "Gestalt View of the Process of Institutional Transformation," *Psychological Review,* 53 (1946): 282–289.
Margaret T. Hodgen, *Change and History,* New York: Wenner-Gren Foundation for Anthropological Research, 1952.
Sidney Hook, "Determinism," *Encylopaedia of the Social Sciences,* 5 (1931): 110–114.
Frank H. Knight, "Social Causation," *American Journal of Sociology,* 49 (1943–44): 46–55. Critique of MacIver's *Social Causation.*
Alfred McClung Lee, "Levels of Culture as Levels of Social Generalization," *American Sociological Review,* 10 (1945): 485–495.
———, "Social Determinants of Public Opinions," *International Journal of Opinion and Attitude Research,* 1 (1947): 12–29.
Ralph Linton, "Culture, Society and the Individual,"

Journal of Abnormal and Social Psychology, 33 (1938): 425–436.
Robert Morrison MacIver, "Maladjustment," *Encyclopaedia of the Social Sciences,* 10 (1933): 60–63.
———, *Social Causation,* Boston: Ginn and Co., 1942. See also his "Social Causation: A Rejoinder," *American Journal of Sociology,* 49 (1943–44): 56–58.
———, *Society: A Textbook of Sociology,* New York: Farrar & Rinehart, 1937. Esp. Chap. 28, "Social Evolution and Social Progress."
Karl Mannheim, *Diagnosis of Our Time,* New York: Oxford University Press, 1944.
———, *Man and Society in an Age of Reconstruction,* New York: Harcourt, Brace and Co., 1940.
John H. Mueller, "Present Status of the Cultural Lag Hypothesis," *American Sociological Review,* 3 (1938): 320–327.
Herbert J. Muller, *The Uses of the Past,* New York: Oxford University Press, 1952.
William Fielding Ogburn, ed., *Technology and International Relations,* Chicago: University of Chicago Press, 1949.
Arthur Franklin Raper, "Role of Agricultural Technology in Southern Social Change," *Social Forces,* 25 (1946–47): 21–30.
Joseph Schneider, "Culture Lag: What Is It?" *American Sociological Review,* 10 (1945): 786–791.
Newell L. Sims, *The Problem of Social Change,* New York: Thomas Y. Crowell Co., 1939.
Pitirim A. Sorokin, *Society, Culture, and Personality,* New York: Harper & Bros., 1947.
A. J. Todd, *Theories of Social Progress,* New York: Macmillan Co., 1918.
Wilson D. Wallis and Malcolm M. Willey, "Culture

and Social Change," Chap. 2 in their *Readings in Sociology,* New York: F. S. Crofts & Co., 1930, pp. 49–169.

Louis Wirth, ed., "Social Process," *Publication of the American Sociological Society,* 26: 3 (August 1932).

Kimball Young, *Source Book for Sociology,* New York: American Book Co., 1935, Chaps. 3, 28.

REVIEW QUESTIONS

1. Cooley states that an "institution is simply a definite and established phase of the public mind, not differing in its ultimate nature from public opinion." Discuss some of the implications of this statement.

2. In what senses can it be said that formalism is psychically cheap? What are its influences upon personality?

3. Analyze Keller's comparison of civilization to a scaffolding. How tenable do you think the comparison is?

4. Does evolution show *"why* the fittest are fittest"?

5. Keller says that humanitarianism is a societal adjustment "not represented in nature." What are the implications of that statement?

6. Is Ogburn's "cultural lag" a scientific conception or merely a term for moral condemnation?

7. How does Ogburn think that cultural lag may lead to revolution?

8. Would "slowing up the changes which occur too rapidly and speeding up the changes which lag" in society be possible? What would such efforts be likely to cost us?

9. How does Queen define "internal inconsistency" and "institutional malfunctioning"?

10. In what ways does the analysis by Marx and Engels differ from those by (*a*) Cooley, (*b*) Keller, (*c*) Ogburn, (*d*) Queen, and (*e*) Frank?

11. Some writers have pictured the bourgeoisie as the bulwark of respectable morality. Why do Marx and Engels claim that the "bourgeoisie has stripped of its halo every occupation hitherto honored and looked up to with reverent awe" and "torn away from the family its sentimental veil"?

12. To what would Frank attribute crime, mental disorders, family disorganization, juvenile delinquency, prostitution and sex offenses, and "much that now passes as the result of pathological processes (*e.g.,* gastric ulcer)"? Why?

13. Analyze our "conception of a social norm, with individuals as violators and frustrators of normality," which Frank discusses. How widespread is this conception? What is its significance?

14. To what extent does the Marx and Engels analysis depend upon what Frank calls "continued faith in the myths regarding an underlying social system"?

15. Does Frank take his conception of "society as the patient" too far for the purposes of objective analysis? If so, in what ways?

16. How accurate is Frank's contention that "the individual, in striving to be an individual, has broken down the inherited culture of common, shared beliefs and activities"?

17. To what extent does Brown go to another extreme and make a catch-all conception out of "human nature"?

PART II

Man and Land

━CHAPTER 4━➤

Changing Land and Energy Resources

THE ARTIFICIALITIES of civilization make us forget our basic dependence upon physical resources —land, water, minerals, and climate. Many social problems derive directly from the waste or misuse of natural resources ("land") through lack of planning and through overexploitation. Sumner and Keller's man-land ratio furnishes, therefore, a useful starting point for the selections in the three chapters of Part II. As they formulate it, "Population tends to increase up to the limit of the supporting power of environment (land), on a given stage of the arts, and for a given standard of living." This chapter deals with the "land" side of this ratio; Chapter 5 takes up the man side, problems of population increase, decrease, and movement; Chapter 6 describes and analyzes rural and urban aspects of man-land problems.

Most basic of our physical resources is the land on which our food is grown. The National Resources Planning Board outlines briefly the problems associated with keeping our supply of agricultural land in the United States adequate for our expanding needs. As the demands of population and of the population's standard of living become greater, our production and importation of food must either keep pace or become a limiting factor. Plant-food and growing-space are, after all, essential ingredients in food production. Chapter 22 contains selections which relate erosion and deforestation to floods and dust storms.

The contribution of physical environment to man's well-being can be increased by technological devices, and Ogburn outlines the impact of such devices upon our lives and the problems they mitigate and create. He mentions especially the "hundreds of social effects, as distinct from uses, that flow more or less inevitably" from inventions. He illustrates this and discusses especially such effects as technological unemployment and the revolution in farming, the vast acceleration of transportation and communication and the inevitability of large-scale planning in American society.

Dewhurst and his associates take up an aspect of the physical-resources situation which illustrates vividly how difficult it now is to get a perspective on whether or not the irresponsible overexploitation of natural resources has shortened man's probable stay on this planet. The Twentieth Century Fund investigators headed by Dewhurst trace and project the effects of discoveries and inventions on the availability of mechanical energy for use in workshops, transportation, communication, and the vast range of other human activities including those in our homes. Whether or not the utilization of solar and atomic energy will offset the depletion of such mineral resources as petroleum and coal is difficult to say at this time. Dewhurst and his coworkers are deeply concerned with the social consequences of the rapidly increasing reservoir of energy, and they ponder the suggestion of Sir Henry Clay, that "The so-called capitalist system, so far from failing, has been almost too successful in the interests of its own survival."

Whitney gives an analysis of some sociological consequences of atomic power, a steadying discussion to counterbalance unwarranted speculations and unbridled imaginings.

These five selections cannot explore more than some of the most salient problems connected with man's use of physical resources in the United States. Other related problems appear throughout the chapters of this Part and the rest of the book.

The Man-Land Ratio

William Graham Sumner and Albert Galloway Keller*

William Graham Sumner (1840–1910), professor, Yale University, 1872–1910. Principal works: *Folkways* (1907) and, with A. G. Keller and M. R. Davie, *The Science of Society,* 4 vols. (1927).

Adjustment between men and land involves a struggle between men. Numbers are always surging up against the limit of subsistence, and the mouths do not close upon the food without a preliminary contest which decides who is to have it. This is the familiar struggle for existence, or competition of life, with the powerful urge of self-preservation behind it, and its type is a reflection of the man-land ratio. If there are few men to much land, the struggle is lighter; if the reverse, it is searching and destructive. . . .

The ratio between numbers and land is something that plants and animals cannot alter. If their increase is such as to press heavily upon their food-supply, the only possible immediate outcome, apart from migration, is such elimination of numbers as will leave the survivors provided for. Over a long period, structural adjustments might take place which would enable more individuals to live upon the same area; but even so the immediate mortality would be little if at all decreased. Animal and plant life tends to increase up to the limit of the supporting power of the environment; it cannot advance beyond that dead-line. The case of man is different; he is an animal with superior capacities for speedy adjustment which enable him to operate upon the numbers-land ratio. By the invention of various methods of getting more food out of the land, he virtually increases that term

of the ratio, a feat which allows of a rise in human numbers. We call these adjustments of his the arts of life, or, briefly, the arts. When they deal directly with the extraction from nature of the prime necessities of life, chiefly food, they include the instruments and processes of hunting, herding, and tillage, all of which are, directly or indirectly, ways of exploiting land. And men can also operate upon the other term of the ratio, for they can practice limitation of their own numbers. This is generally put into operation, not so much to avoid the worst as to maintain a standard of living that is traditional, or to attain to a higher one. Thus the arts are seen to be operating upon the land-side of the basic ratio, and the standard of living upon the man-side.

The foregoing considerations may be gathered up, prior to analysis, into a law of population. Numbers vary directly with the arts and inversely with the standard of living. To align this law of human population with the one which covers the case of plants and animals, all that is necessary is the proviso that the modifying arts and standard of living shall remain constant—thus: Population tends to increase up to the limit of the supporting power of the environment (land), on a given stage of the arts, and for a given standard of living. This is, it will be noted, simply a more explicit rendering of the bare man-land ratio.

* See the identifying note on page 30.
From *The Science of Society,* New Haven: Yale University Press, 1927, Vol. 1, pp. 4, 45–46.

Our Changing Land Needs and Resources

National Resources Planning Board

The magnitude of a post-war program of improvements on agricultural land must be governed by the size of the agricultural plant needed

in the future to provide the Nation with adequate supplies of food and fiber and to satisfy export demands for these products. Predictions as to the

From *National Resources Development: Report for 1943,* Part I: "Post-war Plan and Program," Washington: Government Printing Office, 1943, pp. 37–38.

acreage of crop and pasture land needed for these purposes within the next two decades can be made only within broad limits. That acreage depends on the rate of population growth, on foreign demand, and on the effectiveness with which the agricultural plant is used.

Predictions of population in the United States in 1960 range from 137,000,000 to 154,000,000 depending on what hypothesis is used with reference to birth rates, death rates, and immigration.* Using medium estimates of birth and death rates and estimates of net immigration ranging from nothing to 100,000 annually, it would appear that the population in 1960 might reach 147,000,000 to 149,000,000, or 14,000,000 to 16,000,000 more than at present. To provide food at present diet levels for such an additional population would require 35,000,000 to 40,000,000 more than the 311,000,000 acres we had been devoting to domestic food production during the immediate pre-war years, assuming production per acre equal to the average for the years 1936–40.

Present diets of a large proportion of the population are inadequate to provide proper nutrition, but the additional population foods needed are largely those, such as green vegetables, whose production per acre is relatively high. These foods would take the place of some of the cereals now consumed, whose production per acre is relatively low. In fact, the Bureau of Home Economics' standard of an "adequate diet at moderate cost," could be supplied to our entire population from practically the same crop area per capita—about 2.39 acres—as we were devoting to this purpose during the immediate pre-war period. It does not appear necessary, therefore, to make additions to our crop acreage beyond those needed to provide for population increases, or increases in exports of foods, except perhaps to provide for excess consumption among high-income groups.[1] . . .

In addition, some source of production must be found for the acreage which is now devoted to crops but which cannot remain permanently in that use because of destructive erosion and eventually must be retired to grass or forest. The Soil Conservation Service has estimated that there are 76,000,000 acres of such cropland. Its rate of retirement will be slow, but as much as 40,000,000

acres may be retired by 1960.

The question which naturally follows is "What are the sources of the necessary additional agricultural production?" Part of it probably will come from increased production per acre resulting from continuation of the replacement of workstock by tractors and trucks on farms, from improved technology, and from shifts in crop acreage to more productive land. Increased production equivalent to present production on 25,000,000 acres might come from these sources by 1960. Another fairly easily available source of additional crop production is the idle cropland and the plowable pasture in farms. The Census of Agriculture listed 57,000,000 acres of idle or fallow cropland in 1939. In 1938, the Soil Conservation Service estimated that there were 53,000,000 acres of plowable pasture in farms, 22,000,000 of which could be cultivated without special practices to prevent serious erosion. There also were in farms 42,000,000 acres of land which might be used for crops after clearing, 8,000,000 acres of potential cropland in need of drainage and 6,000,000 acres in need of irrigation. Outside of farms there appear to be about 16,000,000 acres of irrigable land, 41,000,000 acres of land which could be used for crops after drainage, and approximately 170,000,000 acres of cut-over land physically capable of producing crops after clearing, without irrigation or drainage.

There appear, then, to be ample sources of additional crop production to meet our domestic needs for food and fiber and at least to maintain our agricultural exports. A substantial public program of soil conservation will be needed, however, to preserve the productivity of the present crop areas that are physically and economically suited to continued cultivation. To the extent that farmers themselves are not able to bring the needed additions to crop areas into production by cultivating idle cropland or plowable pasture or by clearing forest land, public programs of reclamation through irrigation and drainage works and perhaps some land clearing, will be necessary.

During the past 300 years the soil has been destroyed or severely impoverished by erosion on 282,000,000 acres of land in the United States and has been damaged to some degree on 775,000,000 more acres. Damage has been especially severe during the last 50 years, and promises to grow progressively worse unless adequate measures are taken to arrest it. According to Soil Conservation Service estimates, there are 178,000,000 acres of the present crop acreage that can be continued in cultivation only through special cultural practices

---

* World War II upset all such estimates. U. S. population in 1954 was well over 163,000,000.—Eds.

[1] An addition of 5 per cent to the per capita food-crop acreage for this purpose has been included in some calculations. In 1960, such a reserve acreage would amount to about 17,000,000 acres.

which require inputs of labor and materials outside of the normal farm operating outlays. Such practices on the more erodible croplands and on the intensively used pasture lands in farms include construction of contour furrows, terraces, field diversions, and drainageways for water conservation and disposal; stock-water development and fencing to effect better distribution of stock on pasture land and thus reduce overgrazing; planting of eroding slopes; construction of gully-control works and improvement of streambanks to control bank cutting. . . .

While soil losses are being mitigated appreciably by farmers' own efforts, much of the soil conservation work is of such a nature that it cannot be carried out by individual farmers. It requires Government participation and is suitable for Government improvement projects. The costs may be divided between Government and the individual farmers on the basis of benefits derived.

The Social Impact of Technological Changes
William Fielding Ogburn*

Inventions point the way we are going. We adopt them for the immediate use we make of them. But, once adopted, there are hundreds of social effects, as distinct from uses, that flow more or less inevitably. We have seen this vividly in the controversy over the use of atomic energy. One invention, in a more or less stationary world, might not have a great effect on our future. But there are 50,000 patents a year. And they are increasing in number. A half million patents a decade produces a terrific impact on society, starting a turbulent torrent of change.

These changes will make the future quite unlike the past. The 1940's are vastly different from the 1890's, or even the 1920's. The 35 years that are ahead for the average reader of these lines will be even more different. Patents to the number of two million may be expected during this period. History does not repeat itself in an age of change. Hence we should look forward rather than backward. Imagine yourself driving 80 miles an hour across rough country in a veil of mist. You would need to look forward with all the concentration possible. Would you spend your time and energy looking backward? Yet this is what humanity is doing as it is carried along by a rapidly moving civilization. The universities, colleges, and schools are abundantly supplied with teachers of history, but not one has a professorship for the study of the future. It is, of course, easier to remember the past than it is to read the future. Yet we can see the future unrolling in the technology of the present, just as the modern age is the product of yesterday's advances.

The Impact of the Machine. Technology probably seems rather remote from your everyday life. But what you do over the week-end is likely to be determined for you by technology. This would certainly be true if you took a trip by automobile. If you are thinking of changing your work, your choice will be affected by technological developments.

For technology is a very broad term which is used to include inventions of machines and gadgets, tools, and scientific discoveries. Your life is different from that of your grandparents because of it. If you live in a city, your world is a recent creation of factories and railroads, and could not exist without them. If you live in the country, your life differs from that of the city dweller because of mechanical inventions or scientific discoveries.

Whatever happens to technology affects you. When inventors produced "canned music," that is, discovered how film could be made to carry sound, 10,000 musicians lost their jobs in moving picture theaters almost overnight. Your enjoyment of movies was increased because of this invention. You may yet have talking books. The blind already have them, available free from the Library of Congress and most city libraries.

---

* See the identifying note on page 31.
From "Machines and Tomorrow's World," rev. ed., Public Affairs Pamphlet No. 25, 1946, pp. 1–15, 18–31. The pamphlet is based on *Technological Trends and National Policy*, a report of the subcommittee on technology to the National Resources Committee. Professor Ogburn was chairman of the subcommittee. Reprinted by permission.

Medals, Heroes, and Machines

The great role of technology in history is clouded by the devotion with which we worship heroes. General Ulysses S. Grant whipped Robert E. Lee and won the War between the States. We made him President of the United States and he toured Europe as a world hero. But in reality it was the factory machines in the North that prevailed over the hoe and the cotton gin of the South. The mechanical resources of the North were destined to win, whether Grant had ever lived or not. We do not give banquets and victory parades to tools, though. Being hero-worshipers we like our history to be in terms of the exploits of great men. The heroes do not object. The President residing in the White House in times of prosperity claims credit, even though the good times be due to rainfall in the Middle West.

Nor was the Civil War really caused by the fire-eating South Carolinians, or the will and wisdom of Abraham Lincoln. The responsibility may be laid in part at the door of the cotton gin. Before this invention, the seeds were disentangled by hand from the boll of white cotton fibres in which they were enmeshed. The work was so slow and tedious that cotton could not be supplied fast enough to the factories that were clothing the world. With the new speed of the cotton gin, the lands of the deep South became white with cotton, but not without the help of black slaves who were now brought over in larger and larger numbers. Cotton became King. A conflict between the two different economic systems of the North and the South was inevitable. It may be that if the gin had not been invented, cotton would have been much scarcer, slaves fewer, free trade less ardently desired by the South, and more manufacturing would have been done below the Mason and Dixon line. Hence there might have been a lessening of the forces of conflict in the United States in the 19th century.

Automobiles and Radicals. The inventor of the automobile has had more influence on society than the combined exploits of Napoleon, Genghis Khan, and Julius Caesar.

The influence of the automobile on society has been so rapid and so tremendous that it is justifiably called revolutionary. Motor vehicle transportation struck the railroads like a tornado, leaving a path of bankruptcies in its wake. It did not physically tear up the tracks, but it caused the abandonment of hundreds of short local lines, though, for a time at least, it gave increased business to the trunk lines.

The real estate business was also profoundly affected. Areas where the business section impinged on the residence section sunk to the level of blighted areas. Lands adjacent to highways rose in value. Local transportation became abundant for the first time. This achievement, joined to the long distance transportation of the railroads, gave rise to a new population unit called the metropolitan area. The railroads and telegraph created the city of the 19th century. The automobile and the telephone are unmaking it and creating the metropolitan area.

Revolution on the Farm. Today, truck, tractor, and automobile, utilizing the gasoline engine, are revolutionizing the farm. Large-scale production is commercializing agriculture and destroying self-subsistence farming. The gas engine is, of course, not the only influence. Scientific discoveries and inventions affecting marketing and division of labor also contributed to the revolution in agriculture.

The impact of the automobile on county government has been destructive. Built on an area suitable to the days of the horse and buggy, the county is a unit of local government. With the automobile the state capital is no further away than was the county seat. At the same time wealth has become diversified and concentrated. Hence a small, outlying county has difficulty in providing the necessary schools, libraries, hospitals and social services needed by its inhabitants. Five counties in a state might be better than a hundred.

The changes brought by the automobile are really countless. Warfare has been changed by the armored tank. Florida and California have taken on new aspects because of this new type of travel. The character of Sunday is altered. Manners and morals are not the same. The school bus, taking boys and girls to the consolidated school, makes high schools possible for country youth. The automobile camp has been created, and the summer hotel business transformed.

So numerous and far-reaching are these changes that the automobile may be called Radical Number One. The radicalism of the automobile has been, in its way, as basic as that of Lenin, the most famous radical in the past quarter century. Destroying the aristocracy and redistributing wealth, the revolution under Lenin's leadership altered the course of a government and social classes, yet the influence of the automobile has been spread over a far greater range.

The Invention as a Troublemaker. A banker once defined an invention as something which makes securities insecure. Thus, a cheap prefabricated house, paid for at $35 down and $35 a month, that could be set up from a truck in two weeks, would influence the existing mortgage market on present urban homes. A manufacturer once built a new factory and equipped it with $100,-000 worth of new machinery, which he scrapped without using. A new invention had made it out-of-date, and he re-equipped it with the new machines. Thus do inventions create business hazards, and frequently downfalls.

Inventions make trouble not only for business men, but also for statesmen. These difficulties we call social problems. For instance, machines that roll steel cold are taking jobs away from thousands of steel workers who have spent years in developing their skills. Walking the streets, they look for work that cannot be found. Among miners the new drilling and loading machinery is creating similar havoc. This is called "the problem of technological unemployment"; rather impersonal language for one of the most tragic of human misfortunes.

Today we have the problem of social security for the aged. Formerly, when the population was largely rural, old persons were cared for by their relatives. But the modern city has changed all of this. Machinery demands young, strong workers. Transportation inventions scatter the children to distant parts of the country. Urban housing is crowded. The competitive spending, induced by advertising, makes it difficult to save up for old age. Consequently one out of three persons over 65 years of age is dependent on the public for support.

Finding a social problem today that is not affected by a recent change in technology is a difficult task. Choosing at random, crime is largely to be found in cities, created by factory and railroad. The new automobile has become a most common object of theft and a favorite instrument for the criminal in making a get-away. An increase in divorce has followed inventions which have taken the household industries out of the home and placed them in the factory. Indeed, it will be hard for the reader to point out a single present-day social question that is not due in part to a technological change. He may find a few, but not many.

How a Machine Behaves in Society. As an ac-

tor in society, the machine's influence is often indirect rather than direct. To illustrate: An elevator furnishes quick up-and-down transportation, thus saving much time and energy. This is a direct effect. But its operation in reducing the birth rate is indirect. It occurs in the following way: The elevator encourages the construction of tall apartment buildings. These tall buildings are not built for children, as is fully appreciated by any child who has tried to take a bicycle up an elevator. In fact, rearing a child in an apartment house is very difficult. It can be done, but not easily. As a result many apartment dwellers do not have children. The lowered birth rate is, then, an indirect effect of the elevator. It first affects the heights of residence buildings, then, in a roundabout manner, family life and child welfare.

The machine does not always play the lone wolf. It acts in concert with a pack of other inventions. Thus the elevator is not the only invention that produces smaller families. Dozens of urban inventions contribute to the same end. In all probability the power of the elevator in limiting the birth rate is quite small. But if there were no elevators, other things being equal, the birth rate might not be quite as low as it is. The birth rate in the suburbs of Chicago, with individual dwellings, is higher than in the city proper, where there are many tall apartment houses. Such is the case in general with indirect influences. Social developments are complex. The suburbs are only in part built up by the automobile. The steam railroad and the electric line are also important factors, as are the telephone, the radio, and the moving picture. For, without these conveniences, many families would not be so eager to move out into the outskirts of the city. Without them the suburbs would not be so numerous nor so large.

When it is said that the invention of gunpowder destroyed feudalism, it is not meant that a whole social system fell because of this one invention. The gun, by penetrating armor and castle walls more easily than arrows, helped to break up the feudal retainer system centering around the lord and his castle. But other inventions, such as the improvement of the tools, and the better roads and boats that led to the city and to the beginnings of nationalism, were also important.

What of the Future?

If inventions are so useful in unraveling the forces of past history, might they not be of use in penetrating the veil that shrouds the future?

There is no doubt that inventions can throw a flood of light on the world of tomorrow. This is possible not only because technology is a big factor in social change, but also because no invention ever explodes its revolutionary bomb without warning. The warning is the patent or the early demonstration, which precedes its wide use by a quarter of a century, more or less. Thus the phonograph was conceived in 1863, demonstrated in 1877, became successful in 1888, but was not popularized until the 1890's. Even when an invention of importance develops more quickly, as in the case of atomic energy, its widespread adoption may be measured in decades.

The time element is of importance in foreseeing the social effects of a new invention, but so also is our ability to tell which inventions will succeed. Picking a winning invention is a little like betting on a horse at the races. Many inventions do not win. About a decade ago it was announced that sugar could be made from sawdust, but there is no news today that this is actually being done. Industrial power harnessed from the sun's rays has been reported several times, with great prospects for Southwestern United States or Northern Africa. Nothing has come of it. The death rate of inventions is very high. Inventions are like the thousands of eggs fish lay. Only a few survive.

The readers of this pamphlet will live, on the average, about 35 years. These years will be different, radically so in many respects, from those of the past. What will they hold for you? An exact prediction cannot be given, but a knowledge of technological trends will help. Far from being just a dry subject taught to young engineers in the classroom, technology is a key to the future.

Modern Technology Is Huge. To learn the lesson of technological trends we must lift up our eyes and view the whole field. Our aid must be field glasses and not the microscope. The panorama thus seen would show a great variety of fields of invention and discovery. There would be the field of mechanical power, the great modern force; then there are inventions using electricity and transporting power. Chemistry, which makes new things without power, is another class of discoveries. Others are in dealing with metals, in communication and transportation, and in engineering. And so on. But such a procedure would be too technical. We are all interested in what these new scientific discoveries are doing to us, to our homes, to our religion, to our government, to our schools, to our communities, and to our businesses. It is trends in the social effects of technology rather than trends in technology that should interest us as members of a changing society.

Industry. What are the trends in invention and science that are affecting our businesses? Will they expand and grow? Or are we to expect hard times?

There is one invention that has an influence on all our businesses. It is not much discussed; rather it is one of those hidden forces, inconspicuous, not imposing, yet having profound influences. Methods of birth control are slowing up the growth of our population. As a market today the population is not expanding as it has done all through American history. In fact in about 25 years it will cease expanding altogether and begin to decline—unless something is done about it. However, there are other ways to obtain more sales than by increasing the number of purchasers. If the buying power of each individual is increased 10 per cent, the total buying power is the same as if the population had increased 10 per cent. Hence, business can have an expanding market with a decreasing population if the income of the nation can be increased rapidly enough. This depends, in the last analysis, on invention.

Thus the slowing up of population growth makes the attainment of success in business a little more difficult. But other factors may counteract this tendency. The chief ones are the many new inventions and discoveries. Thus, new discoveries are notable in industrial chemistry. There are other great expanding areas of business activity, electricity for instance. Inventions increase the chances of profits. New lands no longer offer opportunities for the ambitious, but there are plenty of new inventions to exploit. Some of these possibilities will be explored in the pages that follow.

Increased efficiency is another outstanding characteristic of modern technology. Tools are much better. The X-ray spots air pockets in cast iron and steel and makes the resulting machinery more reliable. The new cutting tools are incredibly hard, capable of sawing the toughest metals. Coatings for iron prevent oxygen from destroying the metal by rusting. Other alloys protect steel from various destructive agents. Stainless steel can be used with all sorts of chemical substances. This is but one of the 5,000 alloys now in use, almost as many as the stars that can be seen by the human eye. The steel industry can now supply 500 different products in as many as 100,000 different grades, shapes, and sizes. The actual temperature of the heat of molten steel can now be read, making possible the better tailoring of steel.

By lessening waste this increased efficiency throughout the technological world enables us to have more, better, and cheaper products. Again there are forces working in the opposite direction, such as the diminishing supply of metals. But the trend is toward better goods at cheaper prices. This means a higher standard of living.

Machines and Jobs. Taking jobs away from men is a most unfortunate result of this increased efficiency of machines. Note, for instance, the electric eye, one of the greatest inventions of the 20th century. It sees better than the human eye, being able to detect counterfeit money. It does not get tired, being able to assort different objects 24 hours a day, 7 days a week. Counting, opening doors for warehouses, regulating traffic, turning on electric signs at twilight, detecting defective objects on the assembly line, acting as night watchman and reporting burglars, are only a few of the almost innumerable feats the electric eye can perform. No wonder, then, that inventions replace human beings. New machinery that rolls cold steel is displacing tens of thousands of steel workers. We prohibit immigration from Europe in order to protect the jobs of Americans from foreign competition, but at the same time we permit an immigration, via the patent office, of a force of iron men who are threatening many more jobs. But all is not loss. New inventions may create as well as destroy jobs. Television will demand new entertainers, perhaps more than can be readily supplied. New uses of cellulose call for more chemists. Perhaps some of the new inventions create as many or more jobs than others take away.

The impact of invention on industry is manifested in another trend, the relocating of manufacturing establishments. Light industries are moving outward from the city into cheap lands. Before the automobile, plants were located near a railroad. Now they may be found much further away. The location of new businesses, or the moving of old plants, may also be affected by air conditioning. As air conditioning of winter temperatures became perfected, civilization moved northward. Now, with a control of summer temperatures, may not the course of progress be reversed and move southward? It would mean cheaper lands and labor, and a more hospitable winter climate.

Further, the growing size of modern corpora-

tions has been made possible by the transportation and communication inventions. Improved short-haul transportation has aided the development of the chain store with its many small units. Continued growth of the facilities of communication will, then, make for further coordination, but it will not necessarily increase the size of plants or their concentration at one point.

Agriculture. Farming is more than an industry. It is a way of life, duly celebrated by poets and moralists as the cradle of the virtues. All this aspect of rural life is being radically changed by power inventions.

The application of steam to the handicrafts in the 19th century brought on the industrial revolution. But steam was not useful in agriculture, for the boiler was too big for the moving machinery needed. Besides, farmers had the aid of horses, mules, and oxen. But today the gasoline engine is bringing mechanical power to the farms. The industrial revolution has at last come to agriculture. Wheat has already been mechanized and corn is being gathered more and more by harvesting machines. The tractor and mechanical cotton picker are on their way in the cotton fields. As a result, agriculture is being commercialized and subsistence farming is being reduced. Subsistence farming may increase for a time as a refuge for the unemployed, but this is more of a depression phenomenon than a long-time development. The new machinery is suited to large-scale farms. Hence a rural proletariat has developed. The members of this class differ from the city variety in that they wander from region to region, following the crops as they ripen. The farmer's business is being run more like the city man's business.

An efficiency movement may also be found in agriculture. The force is science rather than mechanization. Insects are better controlled. Superior breeding of animals and plants produces remarkable results. Fertilizers are improving. These are only illustrations of a truly brilliant story of achievement.

Technology on the Farm. Growing efficiency and the application of technology on the farms, as in manufacturing, bring unemployment. There is, however, this difference. When the machine was brought to industry, it was followed by a rapid expansion which opened up opportunities for the displaced handicraft workers. But such a reabsorption of the unemployed in agriculture is unlikely. For the market for farm products will expand little because the growth of population is slowing up and the amount of food an individual can consume is limited. Today one farmer feeds 18 persons. With more machinery and science he may soon feed twice as many. But the population will not grow to that extent. Indeed, in the not far-distant future the number of consumers of the farmer's commodities will decrease rather than increase. There is, however, a possibility that farmers will grow more industrial products. The chemical industries, in particular, require increasing amount of such farm products as alcohols, paper, paints, and resins.

with so high a degree of exactness. This is said to make flying over the mountain peaks safe in storms. Ability to land and take off from the tops of office buildings would extend the use of airplanes for city taxi service and for commuting. Such an accomplishment would perhaps mean most, however, to owners of private planes. A helicopter has been made to ascend perpendicularly, and an autogiro has landed mail on the roof of a post office. Compared with the advance of commercial transportation by air, however, progress in this direction has been slow.

HOW MANY PEOPLE ONE FARMER'S WORK FEEDS

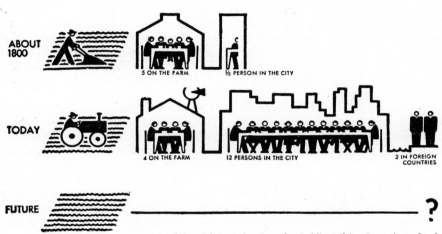

ABOUT 1800
5 ON THE FARM   ½ PERSON IN THE CITY

TODAY
4 ON THE FARM   12 PERSONS IN THE CITY   2 IN FOREIGN COUNTRIES

FUTURE   ?

(Pictorial Statistics, Inc., for Public Affairs Committee, Inc.)

The coming of mechanical power, science, and modern transportation to the farms makes agriculture more like city industries.

Transportation. Recently an airplane covered in one day all the routes that George Washington had traveled during his whole life. Speed is the dominant note in all forms of transportation. In air transportation there are also attempts to gain greater altitudes, planes being conditioned for air pressure. Conquest of altitude flying is significant chiefly for commercial flights of considerable distance. The fog hazard would be eliminated except for landing. Fog has been one of the biggest difficulties in air transportation, and no less than 26 different inventions for mastering it have been reported. These range from infrared lights, through the dispelling of fogs by chemicals, to blind flying by use of the radio beam. Safety devices for flying are being improved. Witness the new altimeter which gives distance above land

Speed and More Speed. Speed also is the keynote in automobile transportation. Experiments with tires, light metals, streamlining, and brakes are in this direction. Rapid automobile changes have quickly outmoded present highways. Scientifically laid out roads with gentler curves and wider paved surfaces are necessary to accommodate the new speeds. The need for wider city streets and roads near the city will soon be critical, if the ratio of cars to population increases very much more. The experiments with steel highways have not yet proved their practicability from either the economic or safety standpoints. While better highway construction reduces the number of accidents, safety is also increased by better visibility, especially in night driving. Adequate lighting, long a technical problem, has greatly reduced accidents and will continue to be developed as night driving near the cities increases.

A home on wheels was inevitable. How much

people will enjoy living in such a home is a question. It seems doubtful if a large proportion of the population will want to live that way, although as a vacation aid the trailer will probably have a great future. Many new uses of the trailer are springing up. Adapted very well to marketing, in rural districts, the trailer so used is a modern counterpart of the old-time peddler. Social services are being brought to out-of-the-way places. Already religion, dentistry, education, public libraries, and political campaigning have been thus carried to the consumers.

New Ideas in Transportation. In the attempt to speed up the railroads, diesel engines, electrification, streamlining, lighter metal, and other new devices are being used. Markers along the railway now advise the engineers what speed to use. As in the case of automobiles and highways, the locomotives and trains are changing more rapidly than the roadbeds. Though short, light trains are still needed for local traffic, the mechanical stoker has lengthened the through trains.

Loading and unloading needs to be made simpler for freight trains. Containers which are the size or truck bodies and that fit into freight cars can be transferred by crane quickly from truck to railroad car. This is a form of packaging which is becoming an important factor in marketing. Refrigeration is increasingly adapted to the vehicles of transportation. Milk has been carried, in a container without ice, from Wisconsin to Florida with a rise of only four degrees in temperature. New methods of cooling, such as the quick freezing of vegetables, fruits, and cream, make it increasingly important to have good methods of refrigeration linked with transportation.

Water transportation is changing less rapidly. The steam turbine and oil have increased the speed and reduced the labor of shipping. Not much use has been made of the radical invention, the rotor ship, which uses wind to turn a rotating cylinder. Nor have science and streamlining, with auxiliary engine, led to any rapid increase in the use of the sailing vessel. Supplementing the submarine, though with a shorter cruising radius, the gasoline-engine-driven speedboat, carrying a torpedo, is an effective war vessel.

In street transportation, the noise of street cars has given way to the odor of the bus. Subways rather than elevated lines are the traffic solution for the big cities.

Transportation creates regions. The discovery of America is due to the ship and compass. Famines are wiped out where there is transportation. Civilian populations cannot escape the destruction of war any more than the front-line soldiers, because of transportation. If there is ever a union of all the peoples of the world, it will rest upon transportation.

Communication. The battle of New Orleans was fought two weeks after the War of 1812 was over because Andrew Jackson had not heard the news. A century and a quarter later, the announcement that Czechoslovakia would be dismembered was heard within a few seconds by millions of radio listeners in scores of countries across the seven seas. So dramatic is the story of the radio, it is well known to every one. Yet the ability of four Russians on a cake of ice at the North Pole to talk with their families back home is no more wonderful than the achievements of the ancient Babylonians in preserving their communications in brick tablets. We have forgotten how wonderful is the alphabet and what it has done for mankind.

The most striking development in this field is the extension of vision. Progress is being made in television from year to year. Many of the major technical problems have been solved. But in a major invention of this type it is not uncommon to have 25 or 30 inventors contributing to it over a considerable period of time. Thirty-three inventors, working for many years, were required to make a successful harvesting machine for wheat. Television is an invention, so to speak, that has to be born an adult. . . .

Another trend of significance is facsimile transmission. For some years rare documents, signatures, and pictures have been sent by wire. The method has been perfected and used by wireless, and years ago a newspaper was distributed in San Francisco a few hours after being set up in New York. Now reasonably priced facsimile machines, over which may be received bulletins and even newspapers, can be plugged in at home in much the same way as radio. Isolated villages and farms, lacking quick newspaper distribution, might find such a service extremely convenient.

Photography has been with us a long time but now-a-days it is becoming surprisingly useful in many new ways. Important is its union with printing. It is being adapted to the typewriter, making cheaper pamphlets and books available for distributing scientific and scholarly productions for which there is little popular demand. Possibly it may replace the typesetter.

Books are also recorded on photographic film. With an illumination projector, film can be read as easily as the pages of a book. Such projectors that sit on a table about the distance of a book from the eyes are now available for the price of a typewriter. This method of communication is of great use to scholars who want copies of rare manuscripts in distant libraries. Libraries, private and public, will soon contain shelves for film as well as for books. Being small, these strips of film are important where storage space is limited. The bulky records of the U. S. Bureau of the Census are being filmed. It has been estimated that if one page of print can be filmed on one square millimeter of film, to be enlarged through a projector to legibility, then all the books of the Library of Congress would require no more space than that needed now to card-catalogue them.

Moving pictures, advertisements, illustrations, recordings of paintings, and still photographs of scenes and events are being reproduced today by color photography and printing. Sound communication also reflects new technological trends. Accurate transmission of sound over great distances has not been in existence more than about a dozen years. Business transactions, the location of industries, the operation of government, and the prevention of crime will be vitally affected by further use of the long-distance telephone. Recordings of sound on discs are now so remarkably good that listeners over the radio must be told that the music is a recording. The recording of books in sound is a subject of research, and the talking book is already an actuality. Recorded sound and the loud-speaker system make it possible for lectures to be given to large audiences when the speakers are unable to be present, suggesting new possibilities in classroom instruction, with possible technological unemployment of teachers.

All these communication inventions make privacy difficult, invade the home successfully, and offer dangerous possibilities for propaganda. But they also remove the disadvantages of isolation for the farmers, and open up new ways of spreading information about science and the arts.

The Community. Technology determines where we live. Primitive man, depending chiefly on his hands to gather roots, nuts, and fruits, and on clubs to kill game, was a wanderer in small bands. When technology brought him his knowledge of planting seeds, he settled down in villages. When science added the plow and taught him the domestication of animals, he then lived in towns in larger numbers. The boat, railroad, and factory brought the great cities.

Once more man's place of living is being changed by invention. The city was once a walled town. Later cities without walls had political boundary lines, and the people, under the necessity of walking to work, were packed into a narrow range of territory. Places of work needed to be close to a waterway or railroad, and a very congested city resulted. Today people can live anywhere, because transportation is everywhere. But practically speaking, they live more and more in metropolitan areas, a hundred miles, more or less, in diameter, around a metropolis as a center. Trends in transportation, including the paved highways, the gasoline engine, and electric power lines connected with a central generating station have brought about this new population unit. Various other inventions also contribute to this grouping of families in villages, hamlets, farms, and in cities and along the paved highway, all in a metropolitan area. The telephone, motion picture, and radio make it more pleasant to live in the suburbs.

While spreading out the city, these same inventions are also changing country life. Bringing the news of the world to the remotest doorstep, they break down the isolation of the small community. The radio for the first time brings the symphony and opera to people familiar only with hymns and ballads. City ways and city manners as well as news of the world are scattered throughout the country.

With a lessening of local differences, communities are being linked together into regions. Large markets for large businesses are created, the areas of government are extended, and the whole country becomes a community.

The Home. The home is like the rock of ages. We feel it is always there, unaffected by the winds of fashion or the surging tides of social changes. But the truth is that technological trends have revolutionized the home, at least in its material aspects, and these changes are not without their reverberations on its spiritual values.

Steam, together with the machines it drives, transformed the home. Once the household was the center of economic activity, almost the only place of production. Everything that was consumed with the exception of such things as gunpowder, salt, and tin pans was produced at home. Human muscles, aided by those of the horse, was the power used in their production.

But it was soon learned that steam, as well as muscle, could supply energy. However, the steam boiler, being larger than a teakettle, proved too big to be housed in a dwelling. Hence a big house, called a factory, was built around it. To the factory went the household occupations, one by one, and with them men, women and children. They now spend much of their time in

washtub, iceboxes, clocks, fans, dishwashers, irons, percolators, toasters, razors, curling irons; and perhaps soon television apparatus, facsimile transmission, electric eyes, burglar alarms, and insect killers.

Construction of dwellings is also joining the trend toward large-scale production. Factory-built houses are now sold through the mail-order cata-

Workers had to work in the neighborhood of the old steam engine

Electricity can be conducted to the worker

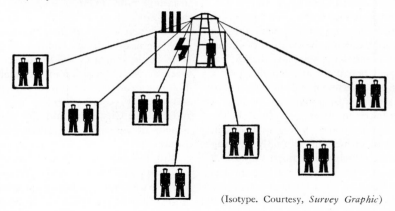

(Isotype. Courtesy, *Survey Graphic*)

factories, stores, schools, theaters, parks, and on the streets, instead of at home. There is now real doubt whether woman's place is in the home. All this has happened within a hundred years.

Effects of Electricity. A new source of energy, running into the home on a wire and available at the touch of a button, has appeared. Will electricity bring back the industries into the home? Hardly, because of the economy of mass production. Still, the manufacture of ice has been transferred from the factory to the home, and possibly others may follow its lead.

The inventions doing most for the home are those using electricity. There are hundreds of them, radio, telephone, vacuum cleaner, electric

logue. The new machines for excavating and foundation work are only for larger buildings or larger numbers of smaller buildings. Modern construction is even better suited to the construction of communities of housing than for the single house. For the house does not exist alone. It is tied in with the community by electric light wires, gas pipe, pavement, sewers, water mains, telephone lines, and sometimes by steam pipes.

Climate in the home is being produced artificially, cool air in summer, hot air in winter, constant moisture content, light at nighttime, artificial sunlight by day. Aiding in this achievement are insulation, and automatic controls. These operate well with oil and gas as fuel and with coal when the furnace is fed by a mechanical stoker. The stoker may discourage tall apartment houses as the elevator encouraged them.

Considerable advance has been made in construction materials. The effect of these new materials, such as steel, concrete blocks, glass bricks, nonbreakable glass sheets, resins and alloys, is to make the home more attractive and more comfortable. Especially do the new inventions encourage recreations and the use of the home as a private club.

Schools. The automobile is shifting rural education from the little, one-room, red school house to the new modern consolidated schools. The school bus is one of the forces pulling the homes of country folk nearer to the few roads that are hard surfaced. The automobile has similarly opened the doors of the high schools to farm youth. Transportation changes also have effects upon the distribution of college attendance. They make it possible for students to go longer distances to the better equipped universities where the specialties desired are most highly developed.

The school is geared to society. Hence the inventions affecting outside institutions affect the school. The many occupations which have sprung up as a result of the machine are forcing the schools to change their courses of study and give greater attention to vocational training. Secondary education has become varied, leading to such specialization as is found in technical high schools.

School buildings are being affected by the architectural and construction trends described in preceding paragraphs. The school today is more than a collection of classrooms. It has a gymnasium, an assembly hall, locker rooms, workshops, music rooms, an art gallery, library, and laboratories, all utilizing new inventions in their respective fields.

The new communication inventions have not been adopted by the schools with the speed that industry has taken them up. For instance, only recently is the motion picture being used in the school; its career has been in the theater. The fact that movies are a source of income for the theater, but an item of expense for the school is the probable explanation. If schools were organized on a chain system basis, they could acquire expensive talking movies more readily. Projectors are becoming cheaper and more educational film is being produced. In time school instruction may be adjusted to make use of this valuable aid. Nor has the radio been adopted by the school as it has by the home.

An aid to visual education is found in the photographic inventions other than motion picture. The sudden emergence of picture magazines and picture newspapers suggests the possible wide use of illustration in the school. These are a product of printing inventions as well as of photography. Already the use of color is influencing the presentation of materials in the schools.

The Church. Religion is everlasting, and truth is abiding. Hence they should be unaffected by technological influence. They are. But if scientific discovery is bracketed as technology, then the forms of religion, though not its fundamental truth, have been considerably influenced by discoveries in biology, anthropology, geology, astronomy—in fact, in all the sciences. The result is "modernism" in religion, and a turning away from the forms of earlier creeds that are out of harmony with scientific discoveries.

The church has made extensive use of the radio in broadcasting Sunday services, which should have the effect, along with the automobile, of decreasing the number of very small churches. It is not known to what extent the movies and the use of the automobile for outings have lessened church attendance. The automobile may have increased attendance and favored the larger churches. The church and religion appear to be less closely related to technology than do other social institutions.

Government. As in the case of the church, there are few, if any, machines invented for government alone. However, trends in material culture do produce trends in government. The growth of nationalism and the totalitarian states has been aided by new inventions in the chemical industries. This has come about as follows. Chemistry makes new substances, often substitutes for items imported from other countries, out of natural resources existing within the country's boundaries. Thus, since the fixation of nitrogen from air has been made possible and other chemical methods have been discovered for obtaining nitrogen, nitrates from Chile are no longer imported. High tariffs favor the chemical industries, making a country more self-sufficient, and hence less dependent upon trade. But chemistry's contribution is probably not a major factor in nationalism.

Technology and War. Warfare, an activity of the state, is profoundly affected by new inventions. Most notable is the development of the atom bomb and germ warfare. The civilian populations have been thrown into war as never before. Hardly a householder in the world is safe from the danger that his home will be bombed and destroyed. His little children are taught to wear gas masks. The atom bomb has had an effect upon recent diplomacy. Because of its threat to civilians, the countries that have developed this new instrument of death the furthest hold a strong position in diplomatic relations. War becomes more deadly as science grows. Science benefits humanity, but it also furnishes the race with the weapons of destruction. Inventions other than explosives thrust the civilian population into war. For industry must be put on a war basis and all the social institutions, even to schools and churches, must be synchronized with the war machine. At one time, a few soldiers were sent away to war and the daily life of the people proceeded much as in peacetime; but not so today. The unity of modern society, a result of the new communication and transportation inventions, has rendered this impossible.

Indeed these inventions tie the whole country close together in peacetime. In the 18th century a village was knit closely together, but a country was a loose collection of rural villages. But now an entire country has become closely knit as was the village of old. Such a situation is reflected in increased strength of the national government. Henry Ford has done as much as anyone to centralize government.

Putting the Government into Daily Life. It is interesting to note the trends in government due to the radio. The chief executive has used it very effectively to strengthen his position. Just as the radio in entertainment magnified the personality of the stars, so it operates in government to augment the prestige of the big shots. The art of political oratory has undergone tremendous changes. There is less waste motion, and responsibility in a national election rests more on a few prominent leaders. In disseminating information and education, the U. S. Department of Agriculture in particular has made wide use of the radio. Since the dividing line between propaganda and the dissemination of information is hazy, the radio can be used for governmental propaganda as well as for political campaigns.

Modern technology is putting government into our daily life. It is no longer something remote in a distant city. We meet it at breakfast and at many times during the day.

This, then, is the way technological trends look from the point of view of the different social, political, and economic institutions. Their influ-

ence is startling and profound. Can we reckon life without them?

Luck, Fate, and Planning

The future is not wholly unknown. Everything is not a matter of chance. We shall all in this country be speaking English 35 years from now, and not Japanese or German. The veil of mist is not completely impenetrable. Hence it is important that we should make plans to meet such future changes as we can foresee. Businesses engage in some planning almost daily. They must buy stocks of goods, acquire raw materials, or construct buildings of a certain size in a particular locality. Planning is something of a gamble, but refusal to plan makes loss certain. Such clearly was the case with the railroads in not planning to meet the new competition from the automobile. They might have reorganized their capital structure. Consolidation of lines would have helped. Some loss of traffic could have been prevented by introducing modern equipment earlier.

Governments plan also. The fathers who wrote our Constitution did a remarkable piece of planning. So did Jefferson when he acquired Louisiana. In fact, planning is part of American tradition. Yet it has not been as thorough going as is desired. We did not plan the cutting of our forests very wisely. We thought we did not need to.

America has been lucky. Any country with half the coal supply of the world within its borders is just lucky. Fate has been on our side, giving us a rich and empty continent to exploit at the exact moment that steam and steel, electricity and chemistry burst forth in all their brilliance. But they ushered in a headlong pace just at the time the continent became filled up. Destiny is still with us, but her course is not so simple to follow.

What is needed is a group of thinkers who will make it their business to devote their whole time to a study of future trends, and whose work will be given adequate recognition. The study of future trends should be furthered by new scientific journals devoted to this field, or adequate space should be given in the existing scientific publications for studies forecasting technological and social trends. In the modern world such a division of labor and specialization is altogether reasonable. Indeed, it is more. It is essential for an adequate attack upon the problems created by social change. Ten years of organized effort devoted to such inquiries would result in contributions of the utmost value to the formation of governmental policies and plans.

Planning Is Inevitable. How the governments will act on the basis of such contributions is another question. Successful planning requires other things besides knowledge—particularly unity of purpose and the will to act. Plans of action often involve policies which are based on values and choices. Governments are very often at the cross-roads of important decisions.

Effect of the Cotton Picker. The United States now faces the second half of the 20th century. What may be expected in technological developments? How far-reaching, for example, will be the effects of the mechanical cotton picker? The good and the bad effects of such a machine are not clearly and distinctly set apart. The cotton picker would cut down sharply the greatest single source of employment for woman and child labor in America. They could not compete with a successful mechanical cotton picker. Their backs and their hands would be spared the labor. But how else, it may be asked, are these people to make a living? Would a larger percentage of them be driven into domestic service? Or might the mechanical picker result in employment of fewer members of a family, but these at better wages, thus releasing women and children for other tasks which might contribute to higher educational and living standards? Does this mean that the surplus labor of the South will flood northern and western cities? What will happen to our Negroes, to farm tenancy, to the political system of the southern states? Will the government plan and act in time, once the spread of this invention is certain?

In some quarters, strange to say, the idea of planning is still unpopular. For plans not only have to be made, but also must be executed. It is not enough merely to see into the future. No one, I suppose, would object to that. The difficulty comes in carrying out plans for the future. That is all right for the individual, but it is different for a government. There the execution of a plan means a strong government. It must be strong enough to command the necessary cooperation of its citizens and institutions. The highly centralized states, such as the Soviet Union with its five-year plan, are in a better position to order and act with dispatch. But in democracies such as England and the United States, plans are just as necessary—as the war has shown. Planning is not as easy for democracies, but who shall say that plans cannot be carried out by a democratic process? Dictators are not necessary. Indeed, if democracies do not plan, they will suffer from the competition of authoritarian states.

This is not to imply that the United States has neglected planning altogether. We had a War Production Board, and have forty-seven state planning boards. Four hundred counties have planning bodies, and there are over a thousand cities with planning commissions.

The first step in planning is looking ahead, trying to figure out what is likely to happen. Only after such knowledge is available do we ask what can be done about it. Planning without knowing trends is like building a house without a knowledge of materials. Scientific discovery and mechanical invention are the keys to the future.

The Rising Tide of Energy
J. Frederic Dewhurst and Associates

J. Frederic Dewhurst (1895–   ), executive director, Twentieth Century Fund. Principal works: with J. H. S. Bossard, *University Education for Business* (1931), and with P. W. Stewart, *Does Distribution Cost Too Much?* (1939).

It is hard to realize today how recently we left the horse and buggy age and entered the power age. A decade or so before the Civil War, human beings did more than two and a half times as much work as they obtained from coal and water power, while horses, mules and oxen furnished three and a half times the amount of "work energy" obtained from minerals and from human beings together. By the end of the nineteenth century the work energy output from minerals had greatly increased—from one billion horsepower-hours in 1850 to more than 30 billion in 1900—

From *America's Needs and Resources,* New York: Twentieth Century Fund, 1947, pp. 680–683, 685–687.

but we were still getting more work out of animals and men than out of coal, oil and water power.[1] The electric trolley was beginning to displace the horse car in the larger cities, and a few playboys were fooling around with horseless carriages. But horses and mules still held their monopoly of the short-haul business in both city and country and did most of the heavy work on the farms.

By 1910 we were getting more than half of the power used in production and transportation from minerals, and the heyday of the horse came in the World War I decade. Nearly 24 million horses and mules were at work in 1910—compared with

ESTIMATED "WORK ENERGY" OUTPUT FROM MINERALS, ANIMALS, AND HUMAN WORKERS, 1850–1960

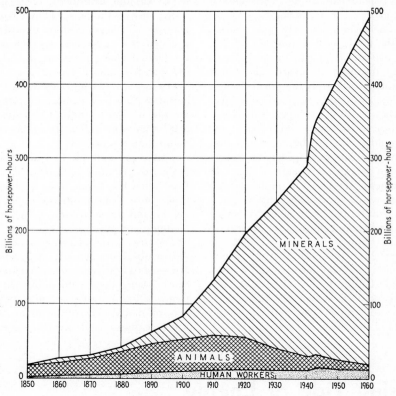

(Source: Appendix 32, Table B, in *America's Needs and Resources*)

---

[1] . . . "Work energy output," as the term is used here, refers to the work performed by animals and human beings plus that obtained from minerals (including water power), in producing the goods and services which make up the national income, or net output of the economy. The "work energy" obtained from minerals and water power refers to that portion of the total supply of mineral energy (estimated as one third since 1900 and as a somewhat larger proportion for earlier decades) used in performing work comparable to the physical work of animals and human workers. It excludes that portion of mineral energy used in chemical and other processing and in providing heat and light.

37 million human workers—and the animals did about a third of the total amount of work done. After that, technological unemployment set in with a vengeance. The automobile in the cities, and soon the tractor on the farms, began to displace work animals, while minerals rapidly became the dominant source of power. By 1940, fully 90 per cent of our energy output came from minerals, and only 10 per cent from human and animal workers combined—a complete reversal of the situation that existed before the Civil War. The trend toward mineral power is still going on, and before another decade has passed it seems

highly probable that animals and human beings together will account for only a negligible proportion of our total work energy supply.[2] [See figure on page 60.]

From 1850 to 1940, national income increased more than 16 times, while total man-hours worked increased less than four times. Output of mineral energy, on the other hand, was 260 times as large in 1940 as in 1850. Total work energy output—comprising that obtained from minerals, animals and human beings—closely paralleled the growth of national income. In other words, we have apparently been getting out of our economic system, without major variations from decade to decade, about as much in terms of finished goods and services as we have been putting into it in terms of total energy expended. We produced our 1850 national income with an "expenditure" of 17.6 billion horsepower-hours of work—a ratio of about 2.8 horsepower-hours per dollar of net output. In 1940, with a total work energy output of 289 billion horsepower-hours, the ratio was about the same.* But mineral energy (including water power), which was of negligible importance in producing the 1850 national income, had almost displaced manpower and animal power by 1940.

Technological Unemployment?

It would appear that "technological unemployment" on a terrifying scale must have been characteristic of our industrial progress during the past century. In 1850, about 7.4 million persons worked more than 70 hours a week to produce a national income of $6.2 billion (in terms of 1944 purchas-

ing power). At the peak of the war effort, in 1944, our national income of $161 billion was produced by 63 million persons working 47 hours a week. With eight and a half times the number of workers, we produced nearly 27 times the net amount of goods and services—but we used 343 times as much mineral energy to do the job. Output per man-hour increased nearly five times—from less than 23 cents in 1850 to nearly $1.05 in 1944. [See figure on p. 64.] With both working hours and productivity remaining at the 1850 level, we would have required in 1944 a working force of 190 million—three times the number actually employed—to have produced the amount of goods we actually turned out in that year. With the shorter work-week of 1944, an additional 100 million workers would have been required! †

This obviously reduces to an absurdity the whole idea of technological unemployment as a *persistent and cumulative phenomenon* in a dynamic economy. Resistance to the introduction of laborsaving machinery is understandable, for it often results in personal tragedy to the individuals who are displaced. Over the long run, however, it is only through technological disemployment that material progress is possible. If all the men operating canal boats in 1830, and livery stables in 1900, and other dying industries, had stayed in the business, and their sons had followed them, railroad travel would still be a luxury that few people could afford and the private automobile a plaything of the idle rich. If the capital, labor and entrepreneurial talent released by technological progress had failed to enter and create new industries we would have been unable to raise our standard of living by producing more of existing goods and a fabulous variety of new, better and cheaper products.

What has happened, in reality, has been not only a vast increase in the amount and variety of goods available to the population and a marked advance in labor productivity, but also a steady expansion in the number and proportion of the population in gainful occupations and a progressive shortening of the work-week. With some costly and painful interruptions, we have "had our cake" in the form of expanding full employment, and "eaten it" in the form of increased leisure and an ever-higher standard of living.

This lessening of human toil and advancement

---

[2] Although many a worker in commerce and industry, and especially in agriculture and construction, still has to "work like a horse" in the traditional meaning of the term, power-driven machinery is now doing most of our work for us—from digging ditches to adding columns of figures. Most occupations in the United States today require more horse sense than horsepower—and take their toll in nervous exhaustion, rather than muscular fatigue. What human work is equivalent to in terms of horsepower-hours is impossible to estimate, and the use of the time-honored ration of 10 man-hours to one horsepower-hour undoubtedly overstates the physical contribution of human labor to total work energy output—and probably involves a greater exaggeration today than in 1850. As the physical work done by human beings constitutes a very small proportion of the total energy used, however, no great error in the total, or in the relative importance of animal and mineral energy, results from converting human effort into horsepower-hours at the traditional ratio.

* See J. Frederic Dewhurst and Associates, *America's Needs and Resources,* New York: Twentieth Century Fund, 1947, Appendix 32, Table B.—*Eds.*

† And what about problems of fatigue and morale associated with increasing mechanization and more and more huge industrial units?—*Eds.*

"WORK ENERGY" OUTPUT—A DIAGRAMMATIC INTERPRETATION

MAN + ANIMAL + MACHINE = GOODS PER HOUR

Although the above chart seems to show man diminishing in stature, the real clue is found in the right-hand column. It shows that by the normal development of machines to substitute for his own and animal power, man will, if he continues to develop and use the machine, produce an abundance of things that make up a good and rising living standard. (*Life, 22,* No. 18, May 5, 1947; based upon J. Frederic Dewhurst and Associates, *America's Needs and Resources.* Courtesy *Life;* copyright Time, Inc.)

of human welfare has been made possible by harnessing tremendous amounts of mineral energy to multiply human effort—with all that this implies in terms of the application of scientific discoveries, engineering and managerial skills and large-scale capital investment. What these accomplishments have meant in terms of labor productivity is suggested in [the "Work Energy" figure]. In 1850,

when an American workman had to work an hour, on the average, to produce 23 cents worth of goods, he had the help of only half a horsepower of energy from animals and minerals. By 1900 his hourly output was twice as large, and his effort was supplemented by nearly twice as much nonhuman power. Output per man-hour had risen to nearly a dollar by 1940, but the nonhuman energy used was now nearly 2.7 horsepower-hours for each hour of human effort. By 1960, if these trends continue, we will be producing six times as much per man-hour as in 1850 —with each hour of human effort supplemented by nearly eight times as much nonhuman energy.

Until the end of the nineteenth century, animals were more important than minerals in supplementing human effort, but their contribution is no longer significant. With the rapid development of electric power and the internal-combustion engine since 1900, minerals have become our dominant source of work energy. In 1940 we used seven times as much mineral energy per man-hour as in 1900 and 70 times as much as in 1850. By 1960, with minerals doing nearly 99 per cent of our nonhuman work for us, we will be using over 100 times as much mineral energy per man-hour as in 1850.

Significance of Mineral Energy

This phenomenol increase in the use of inanimate energy, which more than anything else accounts for the high standard of living and the economic primacy of the United States in the modern world, is not hard to explain. Whether delivered as electricity to the home, farm or factory, produced under the hood of an automobile, or generated in the hold of the *Queen Mary,* mineral energy provides a greater concentration of power in more convenient, compact, mobile and controllable form than would be conceivable with the most ingenious and efficient application of unlimited amounts of human and animal energy.

The pyramids are said to have been built by untold human sweat and sacrifice over years and decades, but a few battalions of Seabees—with their power-driven equipment, and not without sweat, to be sure—could do the job in weeks or months. The famous "Borax 20 Mule Team," with a maximum speed of perhaps 8 miles an hour, was probably the largest aggregation of animal power ever brought under the control of a single driver. But the frailest woman drives around today with three times as much lethal horsepower, and a potential 90 miles an hour, under the hood. In a single day, the Consolidated Edison system in New York delivers enough electricity to do the work of 3 million draft horses or ten times as many hard-working men. The energy output of the Consolidated system in 1946 amounted to nearly 12 billion horsepower-hours— two thirds as much as the total work output from

minerals, animals and human beings combined for the entire nation in 1850. And electric energy is delivered cleanly, instantaneously, and in just the amount needed to drill a tooth or beat an egg—or to operate an electric crane or a subway train in the rush hour. . . . [It] is now delivered at a cost of one to four cents per horsepower-hour (depending upon the amount used), compared with 50 cents for a horse and $10 for human energy. . . . On the whole, animal energy probably costs from 30 to 100 times as much as mineral energy, and human energy from 300 to 1,000 times as much.

The great advantages and economies of this cheapest form of energy, and the lavish expansion in its use in doing the heavy work of the world, account for the fabulous industrial progress of the past century. This rapid upward trend in productivity and material well-being has been so long a part of our daily lives that it has come to be taken for granted as something natural and inevitable— like the growth of population.[3] This assumption that we will in the future, as in the past, obtain more and more goods with less and less human effort overlooks the fact that the period since the beginning of the Industrial Revolution has been short and unique, as human history goes. It may be, as Sir Henry Clay suggests, that "The so-called capitalist system, so far from failing, has been almost too successful in the interests of its own survival: it has encouraged the great mass of our population to believe that the increase of wealth is easy and inevitable, and depends no longer on incentives and appropriate organisation but on scientific research, adequate education, and public direction."[4] . . .

There are good reasons to believe that the technological progress of the past will continue in the future, perhaps at an accelerated rate; but it would be a mistake to assume that further progress is inevitable. Whether we increase output per man-hour during the next decade by 18 per cent or by some other percentage—or not at all—will not be determined by "projecting past trends." It will be

[3] Witness the fact that all future "projections" of gross national product and national income, including the estimates in this survey, "assume" a steady future increase in labor productivity. The only quarrel among the prognosticators is whether the increase per decade will be 10, 15, 20 or some other per cent.

[4] Address delivered at the Twenty-Fifth Anniversary Celebration of the founding of the Industrial Research Department of the Wharton School of Finance and Commerce, University of Pennsylvania, January 10, 1947.

ESTIMATED NET DOLLAR OUTPUT, AND ANIMAL AND MINERAL ENERGY USED, PER MAN-HOURS, 1850–1960

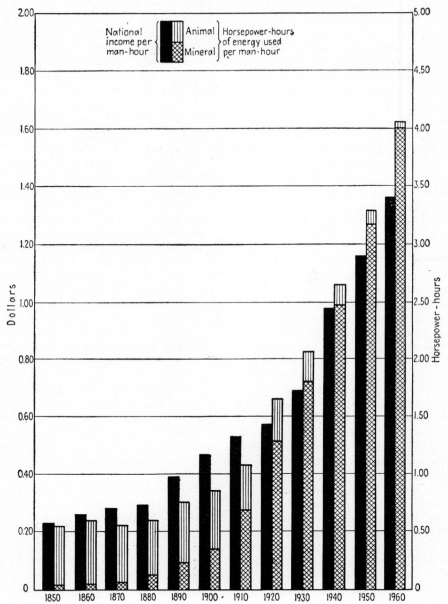

Net dollar output, or national income, per man-hour converted to 1944 prices. (Sources: Table 3 and Appendix 32, Table B, in *America's Needs and Resources*)

determined, as it has been in the past, by a multitude of actions and decisions on the part of individuals: inventors, industrial managers, entrepreneurs, investors, workers and consumers. It is this collective decision, conditioned by their hopes and fears, expressed in the halls of government as well as in the market place, that will determine whether we will continue to multiply the fruits of the Power Age. . . .

A skilled, vigorous population—an individualistic, aggressive people with an extroverted approach toward themselves and their environment—may well have been more crucial to our technical development than the objective factors of climate and resources. . . . This is not to say that "rugged individualism" is a better way of life than any other, even under ideal circumstances, or that further industrialization is *the* true measure of human welfare and progress. But it would be folly to overlook the human element. . . . If it *is* true that our basic individual attitudes and values are changing, it will surely affect the course of our economic development. Continued increases in productivity, inventiveness and daring in the exploitation of new ideas cannot confidently be anticipated without reckoning on the all-important subjective factors. In the last analysis, it is people who make "progress."

Some Sociological Consequences of Atomic Power
Vincent Heath Whitney

Vincent Heath Whitney (1913–   ), professor and chairman, department of sociology, Brown University. Principal work: with Walter Isard, *Atomic Power: An Economic and Social Analysis* (1952).

Fundamentally, the sociological study of atomic power is only a special case of the sociological study of innovation. The history of any one novel idea has, of course, no determinative value so far as any other new configuration of ideas goes. There are nevertheless some general principles of innovation, based on an analysis of innovation as a mental process and on consideration of the experience of prior inventions among diverse social groups.[1] The application of certain of these principles to atomic power can serve two purposes. First, it can replace the aura of mystery and glamour which in the last few years has too frequently substituted for a more rigorous frame of analysis. Second, it can prevent the kind of unwarranted speculations about the far-reaching changes in social organization which are likely to be logical derivations of any consideration of nuclear development based principally on unbridled imagination and wishful thinking.

Atomic power is ordinarily conceived of in terms of the physical components in its production. It is not only correct but necessary to understand the requirements in terms of raw materials, generating and auxiliary facilities, and so on, in coping with problems of nuclear development and in attempting to assess future consequences. It is also necessary to see that, like all other innovations, atomic power represents a novel configuration of ideas. If we assume that technical problems are adequately solved, the use of atomic power in a specific industry or area, or by a given group of people, becomes a function of the two variables of demand and resistance, which are also mental phenomena.

Viewed at this level, it is clear that any innovation may produce one of three results when it is introduced, either by local invention or by diffusion, into the context of an existing social order. It may be generally viewed as harmonious with established culture patterns and value systems, and encouraged, provided it is feasible and functions as an acceptable means to a positively valued goal. It may be interpreted as incompatible, and be actively discouraged where a conflict of ideas occurs. It may be viewed with indifference and fail to become established, through the passive resistance implied in lack of demand.

It is true, as many have pointed out, that both the technical knowledge and the fissionable material necessary to operate a nuclear generating station are theoretically transportable anywhere. The same is not true of value systems and of cultures. The complex structure of beliefs and institutional

[1] Among others, see H. G. Barnett, *Innovation: The Basis of Cultural Change*, New York: McGraw-Hill Book Co., 1953; S. C. Gilfillan, *The Sociology of Invention*, Chicago: Follett Publishing Co., 1935; and Hornell Hart, *The Technique of Social Progress*, New York: Henry Holt and Co., 1931.

From *The Annals*, 290 (November 1953): 67–75, pp. 67–69, 74–75 quoted.

practices of one people may be favorable to change in general and to technological innovation in particular. The social, cultural, and psychological milieu may thus be suitable for the introduction of atomic power. It is certain, however, that opposite and unfavorable conditions will exist among other peoples and in other areas, and that there is nothing inherent in atomic power which will in itself alter these arrangements.

Like any novelty, atomic power can be developed only in the context of some social organization. This means that established procedures exist which have the sanction and force of the customary—and therefore right—way to meet a specific situation. Every culture is composed of interdependent parts. Thus, the introduction of something new always involves some degree of strain and loss. This is why an innovation must be positively wanted by enough people, or by persons with the necessary authority or prestige, if it is to be accepted.

Even the absolute desirability of an innovation is not likely to be the overriding consideration in determining its use or rejection. Rather, it is the desirability of atomic power, or of any other innovation, *relative* to the losses involved in its acceptance. This helps to explain why the assumed benefits of a new energy source are not always apparent to another people. Some consequent degree of industrialization or urbanization may be viewed not as productive of a rise in material standards of living, but simply as a threat to a customary and positively valued way of life. In short, the initial premise, widely held in the United States and other industrialized nations, that atomic power will be "good" is by no means universally accepted.

In westernized countries, the long process of the industrial revolution has led both to a general acceptance of the usualness of change and to a specific willingness to promote and to utilize technological developments. In countries like the United States, people encounter a steady stream of competing ideas and values; therefore, paradoxically, the unfamiliar is not necessarily the strange. Moreover, the strong emphasis upon getting ahead individually and raising living standards nationally favors acceptance of innovations similar to those which have played a part in these processes in the past. Clearly, in these countries atomic power provides the identification with previous experience which is essential if assimilation of a novelty into the social organization is to occur.

As an innovation, atomic power is quite unlike the new style of dress, or birth control, or the ideology of brotherhood, which, in the last analysis, individuals either adopt or do not adopt as parts of their unique life organization. The development of atomic power has necessarily been largely a government monopoly everywhere, and for some time can be expected to involve at most a limited number of private enterprisers. The latter will need both government blessing and some form of subsidy, whether outright or disguised in such forms as continuing government research laboratories or prices for plutonium high enough to make the private sale of nuclear-based power competitive. The vast majority of individuals will simply continue to buy electricity for household and industrial uses, whether it is generated in conventional or in atomic stations. In this sense they can hardly be said to have to face the question of acceptance or rejection of atomic power at all. Certainly, their lives will not be immediately affected whether atomic power is introduced or not.

There is, however, a marked and very real difference between the consequences of atomic power use for the relations of individuals in the already industrialized countries and in those which are economically underdeveloped. In the former regions, atomic power can be a useful adjunct to continuing industrial growth, but there is no evidence that it will alter the nature of the daily routine for the majority of persons. Its most noticeable effect here may be simply to increase the concentration of industrialization already apparent,[2] and, in doing so, to intensify urban-industrial life orientations for the people of such areas. . . .

There is space for only a brief further word about the industrialized nations. What has already been said suggests that their social organization is generally receptive to the use of atomic power. Social change is a usual condition. Technological innovation is expected and welcomed as a means of attaining higher standards of living. The demographic situation is favorable, since the degree of control exercised over both births and deaths makes it possible to maintain a ratio of numbers to available resources which will permit further increases in productivity to be applied to production

---

[2] For the reasoning behind this statement, see Walter Isard and Vincent Whitney, *Atomic Power: An Economic and Social Analysis* (New York: Blakiston Co., 1952), Part II.

and consumption needs rather than to the support of a mushrooming population. Economic arrangements too are more favorable than in the underdeveloped countries, though there is national variation in the availability and cost of capital, the investment in competing power sources, the size of market, the need for additional power or energy resources, the mobility of the labor force, and so on.

There is no evidence that in these countries atomic power will effect the revolutionary changes in social organization which have frequently been predicted in popular and semipopular literature. It is not likely to create a new type of family or of economic system or of class structure. Rather, it will fit readily into established economy and society, and at most promote social changes already in process. In partially industrialized countries like Argentina, it can speed such changes considerably if it is actually utilized. . . .

It is technically possible to build atomic power plants in the most remote areas of the world. The possible should not, however, be confused with the probable, and, except for portable units for such specialized jobs as breaking down icebergs, I see no logical reason for such an undertaking. Only in a few industries, like the electroprocess group, is cheap power of sufficient importance in inducing plant location ever to outweigh other single locational factors such as transportation, markets, labor force, raw materials, and agglomeration economies. An atomic power station in Spitsbergen, or even in Aroostook County, Maine's northern potato empire, would have no function without a market. For a plant of optimum size, a major industrial agglomeration would be required; but other locational factors militate against such a possibility. Hence, atomic power is not likely to develop new population aggregations at remote points.

It is at least conceivable that military considerations might lead to uneconomic industrial concentrations, supported by subsidy, in distant areas like that around Arco, Idaho. It is more likely that, as in the United States in World War II, the concentration of industry in present locations will be strengthened because of their established locational advantages, the investment already made in these areas, and so on.[7] In this country the industrial areas of the Northeast and along the Great Lakes rim are best suited as locations for atomic plants, since they constitute principal areas of demand for power.

It seems probable that atomic power will serve to increase still further the concentration of industry, and therefore of population, in these established areas. It could also spur the industrial growth of such a region as southern California if it became competitive in cost with other power sources. Ecologically, this means a continuing expansion of the major metropolitan districts, presumably with a further dispersion of subcommunities within the metropolitan areas. It does not suggest any more uniform distribution of population in the major industrialized countries, or that such present population centers as New York or London or Moscow or Tokyo will become "ghost towns."

These remarks are necessarily extremely abbreviated. They can only suggest that existing demographic and ecological patterns are likely to be highly consequential for atomic power utilization everywhere. At the same time, they imply that any probable peacetime use of nuclear energy is unlikely to modify radically these same demographic and ecological arrangements.

[7] Atomic power is unlikely to lead to the relocation of basic American industries. This is true even when the use of atomic power to allow new industrial processes is considered. For the evidence, see Walter Isard and Vincent Whitney, "Atomic Power and the Location of Industry," *Harvard Business Review*, Vol. 28, No. 2 (March 1950), pp. 45–54.

CROSS REFERENCES TO STANDARD TEXTS *

Barnes, *Society in Transition*, pp. 8–13.
Bernard, *American Community Behavior*, Chap. 2, pp. 475–477, 485–489.
Bloch, *Disorganization*, Chap. 3.
Brown, *Social Pathology*, Chap. 29.
Cuber and Harper, *Problems of American Society*, Chap. 2.

Elliott and Merrill, *Social Disorganization*, Chap. 1.
Faris, *Social Disorganization*, pp. 267, 465–469.
Gillin, *Social Pathology*, Chap. 1.
——— and others, *Social Problems*, Chap. 2.
Herman, *Approach to Social Problems*, Chaps. 3–4, pp. 228–238.
Landis, *Social Policies in the Making*, Chaps. 1, 21.
Lemert, *Social Pathology*, pp. 81–85.
Merrill and others, *Social Problems*, pp. 5–11.
Mihanovich, *Current Social Problems*, pp. 11–13.

* For complete bibliographical reference to each text, see page 13.

Neumeyer, *Social Problems and the Changing Society*, Chap. 2, pp. 64–68.

Nordskog and others, *Analyzing Social Problems*, pp. 27–30.

Odum, *American Social Problems*, Chaps. 2–4.

Phelps and Henderson, *Contemporary Social Problems*, Chap. 1.

Reinhardt and others, *Social Problems and Social Policy*, Chaps. 3–4.

Weaver, *Social Problems*, pp. 38–41.

OTHER BIBLIOGRAPHY

H. G. Barnett, *Innovation: The Basis of Cultural Change*, New York: McGraw-Hill Book Co., 1953.

Roger Burlingame, *Backgrounds of Power: The Human Story of Mass Production*, New York: Charles Scribner's Sons, 1949.

Stuart Chase, *Men and Machines*, New York: Macmillan Co., 1937.

———, *Rich Land, Poor Land*, New York: Whittlesey House, McGraw-Hill Book Co., 1936.

Robert A. Dahl, ed., "The Impact of Atomic Energy," *The Annals*, 290 (November 1953).

R. E. Dickinson, "Social Basis of Physical Planning," *Sociological Research*, 34 (1942): 51–67, 165–182.

Harold M. Dorr, ed., "Social Implications of Modern Science," *The Annals*, 249 (January 1947).

R. J. Forbes, *Man the Maker: A History of Technology and Engineering*, New York: Henry Schuman, 1950.

S. C. Gilfillan, *The Sociology of Invention*, Chicago: Follette Publishing Co., 1935.

Louis M. Hacker, "Food Supply," *Encyclopaedia of the Social Sciences*, 6 (1931): 332–338.

Walter Isard and Vincent Whitney, *Atomic Power: An Economic and Social Analysis*, New York: Blakiston Co., 1952.

Russell Lord, *Behold Our Land*, Boston: Houghton Mifflin Co., 1938.

Howard A. Meyerhoff, "Some Social Implications of Natural Resources," *The Annals*, 249 (January 1947): 20–31.

Lewis Mumford, *Technics and Civilization*, New York: Harcourt, Brace and Co., 1934.

National Resources Board, *Report*, Part II, "Land"; Part III, "Water"; Part IV, "Minerals," Washington: Government Printing Office, 1934.

National Resources Committee, *Our Energy Resources*, Washington: Government Printing Office, 1939.

———, *Regional Factors in National Planning and Development*, Washington: Government Printing Office, 1936.

———, *Technological Trends and National Policy*, Washington: Government Printing Office, 1938.

John Nolen, "Regional Planning," *Encyclopaedia of the Social Sciences*, 13 (1934): 205–208.

Howard W. Odum and Harry Estill Moore, *American Regionalism*, New York: Henry Holt and Co., 1938.

William Fielding Ogburn, *The Social Effects of Aviation*, Boston: Houghton Mifflin Co., 1946.

President's Research Committee on Social Trends, *Recent Social Trends in the United States*, 1 vol. ed., New York: McGraw-Hill Book Co., 1933. Esp. Chaps. 2 and 3.

Margaret G. Reid, *Food for People*, New York: John Wiley and Son, 1943.

S. McKee Rosen and Laura Rosen, *Technology and Society*, New York: Macmillan Co., 1941.

Rupert B. Vance, "Frontier: Geographical and Social Aspects," *Encyclopaedia of the Social Sciences*, 6 (1931): 503–506.

REVIEW QUESTIONS

1. In what senses does adjustment between man and land involve a struggle between men?
2. State and interpret the man-land ratio.
3. Interpret the National Resources Planning Board selection in terms of Sumner and Keller's man-land ratio.
4. What percentage of our agricultural land must be "retired" per year? What does this mean in the long run to American society?
5. Is Ogburn exaggerating for effect when he says that there is no "professorship for the study of the future"?
6. To what extent was the cotton gin responsible for the Civil War?
7. How influential has the automobile been in bringing about social change? In rural areas? In cities?
8. What interests do bankers have in prefabricated houses?
9. Try to name a social problem that is not affected by a recent change in technology.
10. What have been some of the social consequences of the elevator?
11. Does technology create as many new jobs as it eliminates?
12. What technological changes created the migratory agricultural workers?
13. What influences have communication inventions had upon the privacy of the home?
14. In what ways does technology now determine where we shall live?
15. Why does Ogburn contend that social planning is inevitable?

16. What does he say that social planning can accomplish in this country?

17. What is the chief difference between the types of energy used before and after 1900?

18. Dewhurst and associates say that "technological unemployment as a *persistent and cumulative phenomenon* [is] an absurdity . . . in a dynamic economy." What evidence do they give to support this contention? What, then, is the nature of technological unemployment as a social problem?

19. How rapidly do Dewhurst and associates believe that the "lessening of human toil and advancement of human welfare" can proceed?

20. Why does Sir Henry Clay suggest that "The so-called capitalist system, so far from failing, has been almost too successful"?

21. To what factors do Dewhurst and associates point in asserting that human progress is not inevitable in the energy production field? What do they probably mean by "progress"?

22. What are some of the weaknesses of "projecting past trends"?

23. According to Whitney, what are three possible results from the introduction of any innovation?

24. From what we know now, how revolutionary is atomic energy as a source of power likely to become? List problems likely to come with it.

Shifting Populations

THE UNCERTAINTIES of population statistics have provided ample opportunities for warring propagandists to find apparent support for their contradictory positions and for sincere and objective students to become aware of the inconclusiveness of data on a great many significant points. With a great sweep through recent social history, *Life* in the brief selection on the population theory of Thomas Malthus (1766–1834) points to some of these complexities in the light of certain subsequent developments.

Population problems center about the closely related factors of man-land ratios, the migrations, reproduction, and the limiting influences—disease, accidents, war, and the others. Chapter 4 introduced the man-land ratio, and the workings of this complex of relationships should be borne in mind. Following the first one the selections in this chapter deal chiefly with the highly dynamic problems of migration. Certain problems associated with reproduction are reserved for treatment in the chapter on "Birth Through Childhood," and later chapters discuss various limiting influ-

ences upon population.

Humphrey outlines the evolution of United States immigration and immigration policy since their beginnings. With this as background, he then discusses the problems—imagined and actual —connected with American immigration and emigration. Among the imagined problems is the claim that immigration increases unemployment. Actual problems include the international ill will created by current efforts to exclude worthy potential immigrants and to maintain differential treatment for certain national and racial groups under quota and exclusion rules.

The Senior selection describes in some detail the background of Puerto Rican migration, an illustration of the problems of our newest sizeable migrant group.

In the Caplow reading attention is focused on one aspect of internal migration—the transients. Caplow outlines salient characteristics of the history, life, and times of the hobo or "homeless migratory worker" and the tramp or "homeless migratory nonworker."

Cycle of Population Growth and Decay
From "Life"

The last century and a half has witnessed the greatest increase in population in the history of the world. Today's 2 billion people are the descendants of only 900,000,000 who were living in the year 1800. Had Europe's population multiplied since the beginning of the Christian era as it has in the last 100 years, there would now be one person to each square yard of European land.

The specter of overpopulation has always haunted demographers. Most famous of these students was England's Thomas Malthus, whose

first pamphlet on the subject appeared in 1798. According to Malthus, mankind tends to increase in geometric progression, but its food supply rises in arithmetic progression. Starting with the unit 1, population growth would normally be at the rate of 1, 2, 4, 8, 16, 32, 64; food supply, at the rate of 1, 2, 3, 4, 5, 6, 7. Unchecked, a people might multiply within 150 years to 64 times its original size, but the supply of food would increase only seven times. Believing that the sole checks to population growth are starvation, war,

From "All Countries Are Following the Same Cycle of Population Growth and Decay," *Life,* (September 3, 1945), p. 47. Reprinted by permission.

vice and disease, Malthus concluded that man is probably doomed to perpetual misery through overpopulation.

Malthus was too gloomy. In the century following his pamphlet, Europe not only tripled its population but greatly raised its standard of living. The tremendous population spurt during the 19th Century resulted not from a higher birth rate but almost wholly from a lower death rate. This was brought about by modern medicine and by better food and housing, results of the industrial revolution. . . .

At the start of the period [in such a country as Sweden about 1750], the birth and death rates are in equilibrium at a high level. Population is about stationary. With the coming of the industrial revolution and modern medicine, the death rate begins to drop while the birth rate stays up. This divergence results in a doubling of the population despite a steady drain of emigration. But by 1900 the birth rate is falling sharply and by 1930 the two rates are again in equilibrium at a low level.

There are many reasons for this drop. One is birth control. Another is the rising standard of living, for the well-to-do have fewer children. Another is urbanization. Children are likely to be an economic liability in a city instead of an asset as they are on farms.

What occurred in Sweden has occurred in virtually all the countries of Western Europe. It is happening in the U. S. today. It will happen before long in the U.S.S.R. . . . Presumably when the countries of Asia become industrialized, they, too, will have a further increase in population, followed by a leveling off. It seems to be almost a law that people multiply under the impetus of industrialization and science, then assume stationary or declining populations when the change is complete.

Immigrants and Immigration Laws
Hubert H. Humphrey, Jr.

Hubert H. Humphrey, Jr. (1911–   ), United States Senator from Minnesota since 1948.

Immigration laws crystallize and express a society's basic human values, for they deal with our relationship to people other than our immediate neighbors. In a sense, they may be said to codify our prejudices or our freedom from prejudice. They reveal how our actual practices correspond with our professed ideals. A nation's immigration policy is thus an index of its strength, wisdom, and morality. Our immigration laws recall the biblical admonition to "Love ye therefore the stranger: for ye were strangers in the land of Egypt." (Deuteronomy 11:19). It is well to remember that at one time we or our ancestors were all immigrants to this country.

From the beginning of our history those who founded the United States recognized a national need not merely to tolerate immigration but to encourage it; not alone to admit those who were wealthy or skilled, but in the words of George Washington, to give haven to "the oppressed and persecuted of all Nations and Religions."

Indeed, one of the reasons announced in the Declaration of Independence for the American Revolution against England was the British effort to impede free immigration into the colonies. In the first years of our Republic we deliberately sought to stimulate immigration. We needed help to build our industries and to assist in the development and expansion of our frontiers. The wisdom of this policy is now manifest everywhere in our land. Refreshed by a constant stream of new settlers with new ideas and new imagination, and with fresh yearning for freedom, we have erected a vast industrial network and created a democratic community. James Madison's predictions at the Constitutional Convention of 1787 have been confirmed: "that part of America which has encouraged them [the foreigners] has advanced more rapidly in population, agriculture, and the 'arts.'"

Abandoning Our Traditional Welcome. Not until 1882 did we depart from our original policy of unimpeded immigration. Then, under the in-

From "The Stranger at Our Gate—America's Immigration Policy," Public Affairs Pamphlet No. 202, 1954, pp. 1–3, 5–22, 26, 28. Reprinted by permission.

fluence of ideas similar to those expressed earlier by the Nativist and Know-Nothing movement, we permitted for the first time bars against the entry of an immigrant class because of its race. Between 1882 and 1924 we did a complete about-face in our immigration policies.

At first Chinese alone were excluded. But the categories of excludables were swiftly expanded. In 1917, after three different Presidents had vetoed a similar measure, Congress enacted a literacy test for admission aimed at shutting off entry of the so-called "new" immigrants from southern and eastern Europe. The 1917 law also established the notorious "Barred Zone" provision, sealing off immigration from most of the Orient. When, in turn, these devices were found insufficiently restrictive, they were supplemented by the rigid quota plans of 1921 and 1924 which represented the final hardening of a national anti-immigration mood into a national policy. The basic principles of the 1924 law without the Oriental exclusion provisions were re-enacted in the McCarran-Walter Immigration Act of 1952.

Since the 1880's, arguments for a more humane and generous immigration law have largely gone unheard. Despite the contributions to our national economy and our national culture made by our immigrant populations, despite their energy, their creativeness, and their industry, despite the crying need for charity and generosity in the face of the growth of oppressive European totalitarianisms, it has nevertheless become increasingly difficult to persuade Congress of the need for an immigration law premised on reasoned hospitality.

Five Myths of Immigration

In the first place, immigration laws are not easy to understand. Few citizens or Congressmen have time to digest the mass of scientific and historical material required for an appreciation of the problems in this field. The McCarran-Walter Act runs to 302 pages, and is virtually unreadable by anyone except an expert.

In addition, certain persistent myths have become widely accepted as facts. They almost always turn up in discussions in this area and they account for some of our undemocratic immigration policies. These myths are:

1. Rigid laws are needed to prevent the country from being flooded with immigrants.
2. Immigration threatens American living standards.
3. Certain races or nationalities are undesirable.

4. Immigrants do not make good citizens.
5. There isn't room for many more people here.

Not one of the five assumptions can be supported by statistics, science, or history. Let's look at them:

Myth No. 1: Rigid laws are needed to prevent the country from being flooded with immigrants. If that is so, why haven't millions, eligible under immigration laws, migrated from Canada and South America which are exempt from quota limitations? The fact is that most people cling to familiar soil or well-known pavements. They will suffer poverty or endure dictatorship rather than turn from friends and relatives to start afresh in a strange country where a strange language is spoken. We do not know how many people from southeastern Europe would come to our shores if allowed to do so. But it is interesting to remember that even when immigration from Europe was unlimited—which no one proposes today—the highest average annual immigration, in ratio to the total United States population, was only 1.28 per cent of our population for the decade 1840–1850. This peak figure certainly does not represent a tidal wave.

Myth No. 2: Immigration threatens American living standards. Organized labor, which is sensitive to any attack on living standards, has tossed this myth into the ashcan. Leaders of both the American Federation of Labor and the Congress of Industrial Organizations opposed the McCarran-Walter Act and argued for a liberalized immigration policy. Labor has learned that immigration normally creates more jobs and increases the national wealth. Millions of native Americans earn good livings from industries founded or developed by immigrants. The type for this pamphlet (and for practically every newspaper, magazine, and book published in the United States) was set at low cost on the linotype machine invented by Otto Mergenthaler, an immigrant from Germany. Other immigrants gave us the typewriter, the telephone, the electric elevator, the blast furnace, the oil refining process, and many other sources of wealth.

Recent immigrants have brought old world skills and technical processes with them. Judah Lifszyc, a Polish scientist, had a secret process for producing clear dextrose syrup. He opened a factory in Wenatchee, Washington, cooperatively owned by some 700 farmers, which is producing 30 tons of syrup daily from surplus wheat and potatoes that used to be dumped. Refugees from

Amsterdam created high-paid jobs for Americans when they moved the center of the world's diamond industry to New York City.

Immigrants are consumers as well as workers and producers. The more consumers, the more capital investment and the more employment. During the great period of immigration, from 1870 to 1930, the population increased about three times, but the number of jobs—despite widespread adoption of labor-saving machinery and techniques—increased about four times.

Myth No. 3: Certain races or nationalities are undesirable. Like the old belief that the world is flat, this myth has been hard to dispel. As recently as a generation ago a few scientists still clung to the idea that certain people were inherently or biologically inferior, but today not a single competent authority accepts the theory of superior and inferior peoples. Dr. Margaret Mead, the distinguished anthropologist, says "all human beings from all groups of people have the same potentialities." The concept of inferior peoples, she adds, "is artificial, and cuts off good ancestors for our great-great-grandchildren." Dr. Ralph L. Beals, former president of the American Anthropological Association, comments: "All scientific evidence indicates that all peoples are inherently capable of acquiring or adapting to our civilization. Upon this point of view the American Anthropological Association has unanimously endorsed an official statement by its executive board."

There will be marked individual differences, of course, in any national group. There will be idiots and geniuses, scoundrels and statesmen, weaklings and Samsons. But the average person, whether he be an Eskimo or an Ecuadorean or a resident of Easton, Pennsylvania, is the same fellow the whole world over. He has the same innate ability to compose a great symphony, invent a better mousetrap, or develop a spineless artichoke. And there's the same risk that he may abuse his dog, yell at telephone operators, or pilfer the poorbox.

Myth No. 4: Immigrants do not make good citizens. The Scots were once rated as poor timber for citizenship and for decades it was widely believed that the Irish could never become good Americans. History has shown otherwise. The slurs against recent immigrants have no more validity.

Again and again it has been demonstrated that the foreign-born commit proportionately fewer crimes than the native Americans. E. H. Sutherland, an authority on criminology, found in 1933 that 536 native whites per 100,000 were committed to prisons of all types as against only 402 foreign-born whites. The sons and daughters of immigrants contribute more to delinquency than the foreign-born.

Home ownership is a good index of adjustment to a new environment. The 1940 census showed that proportionately more foreign-born people own homes than native whites.

Recent immigrants have made rich contributions not only to industry and science but also to music, literature, drama, and art. Over the years the foreign-born have changed our eating habits. What would our diet be without occasional opportunities to sample ravioli, chile con carne, blintzes, shish kebab, sukiyaki, and crepes suzette?

Myth No. 5: There isn't room for many more people here. There is plenty of room and plenty of need for them. Representative Harrison Gray Otis of Massachusetts was wide of the mark when he declared: "When this country was new it might have been good policy to admit all. But it is so no longer."

Mr. Otis was speaking in 1797.

In 1950 the United States had 51 persons per square mile. Compare this with 480 in Great Britain and 807 in Belgium. How large a population could be comfortably supported cannot be forecast exactly, but the experience of the past fifty years shows that the limit is not yet in sight.

Some experts predict that at the present small rate of immigration the population will reach a peak of about 190,000,000 in 1975.

Our Permanent Immigration Laws

Our permanent immigration laws were codified in June, 1952, when the Congress enacted, over President Truman's veto, the McCarran-Walter Immigration and Nationality Act (Public Law 414). This new act is the first comprehensive revision of our immigration statutes ever attempted.

The law has some good features. It was sensible to make an orderly codification of the many haphazard and piecemeal laws on immigration and naturalization. It was wise to remove the longstanding prohibition against citizenship for Japanese and other Asian aliens. It was encouraging to permit the entry, for the first time since 1917, of Asians who were formerly ineligible for permanent residence, although only a handful were allowed to come.

While the new law takes these steps forward, in the opinion of many authorities it takes other steps backward. It has been argued that it reaffirms and even strengthens the racist provisions of the old laws, that it rates northern and western Europeans as superior people, and that it classifies southern and eastern Europeans, Asians, and Africans as inferior.

Few of our federal laws are based on racial prejudice. Critics of the new law assert that none results in more serious racial discrimination than our new 1952 immigration act. They point to the fact that the peoples whom they claim have been classified as inferior have been outspoken in their resentment.

Northern and western European countries have been scarcely less bitter. Visitors and seamen from England, France, Norway, Denmark, Sweden, and other western European states complained that the new law requires that they undergo complicated loyalty checks as if they were potential criminals. The world's leading scientists have, in some cases, been reluctant to arrange international conventions in the United States lest their delegates suffer needless insult.

Reports from abroad indicate that the McCarran-Walter Act is intensifying the ill-will toward the United States that stemmed from previous immigration laws. The hundreds of millions of dollars we are spending to cultivate allies will be at least partly offset if our immigration law implies that most of the world's people are not good enough to live in the United States. You can't call a man inferior and then expect him to be on your side.

Why should the United States care whether other nations like or dislike us? That was the attitude of some of our Congressmen when the 1924 immigration law was drafted. A clause excluding Japanese was debated. The Japanese embassy warned that the proposed law would weaken the democratic forces in Japan and give the militarists the anti-American ammunition they were looking for. Secretary of State Hughes agreed and urged Congress not to "affront a friendly nation." But the insult was voted. The Japanese militarists strengthened their grip. Seventeen years later they considered themselves strong enough to attack Pearl Harbor.

This doesn't mean that the 1924 immigration law was the direct cause of the Pearl Harbor raid.

But our international rudeness may have been one factor contributing to the build-up of the Japanese war parties. To a far greater extent than most Americans think, other nations judge us by our immigration laws.

The National Origins Quota System

The major target of our restrictive immigration policy was southern and eastern European immigration. Bias against immigration from this area grew rapidly as the influx of northern and western Europeans slackened. For some years Americans who regarded Italians, Greeks, Poles, Hungarians, Russians, and their neighboring peoples as inferior looked for a way to make discrimination against this group effective. They found it in the National Origins Quota System, first written into the 1924 immigration act.

The National Origins Quota System lies at the heart of the McCarran-Walter Act. The quota for any given nationality is determined by finding out what proportion that nationality contributed, by birth or descent, to the total American population of 1920—a most difficult statistical problem—and then applying this percentage to the total quota of 154,000. The result of this system is that about five-sixths of the over-all quota goes to northern and western countries of Europe, while one-sixth goes to the southern and eastern European countries. For example, Great Britain is entitled to send 65,361 persons a year; Germany, 25,814; and Greece only 308.

The quota system is in some measure supplemented by the issuance of immigration visas outside the quota system, but these are granted mainly to immigrants who are the children or spouses of citizens or to persons born in Canada or Latin America.

Most of the quotas of the favored countries are wasted because their citizens don't wish to emigrate. From 1930 to 1944 the northern and western nations used on the average only 17 per cent of their quotas. The total authorized quota ceiling for the 28-year period from 1925 to 1952 is 4,362,354. Of this, a total of only 1,923,509 was used. In other words, 56 per cent of the quota has been wasted.

In the southern and eastern countries qualified applicants for visas must wait years—and sometimes more than a lifetime—to be considered. Displaced persons admitted to the United States in the post-war years were charged against one-half of their countries' quotas for future years. By this plan, the quota for Greece has been reduced 50 per cent until the year 2013; for Yugoslavia until 2114; for Estonia until 2146, and for Latvia until 2274.

The National Origins Quota System would appear to be a futile attempt to turn the clock back a hundred years and restore the immigration pattern of the mid-19th century. The purpose—to discriminate against southern and eastern Europeans—was publicly acknowledged when the system was devised in 1924, and many feel that it was reaffirmed in 1952 by the Senate Judiciary Committee, which wrote the McCarran-Walter Act. A slight relaxation of the National Origins Quota System had been proposed in order that unused quota numbers might be redistributed to countries that wanted them. The change was rejected because—"To distribute the unused quotas on the basis of the registered demand would shift more quota numbers to the countries of southern and eastern Europe."

Individual Congressmen were even more candid in the debate. One member said that although he was not a follower of Hitler's theory of racial origins, "there is something to it."

"I believe," he continued, "that possibly statistics would show that the western European races have made the best citizens in America and are more easily made into Americans."

The Congress of 1924 at least used the most recent census figures on the national origins of the population. Knowing that the percentage of southern and eastern Europeans had increased since 1920, the framers of the McCarran-Walter Act refused to accept 1950 census figures for the national quotas. The 1920 census is still used as the base, and only the white population is included in the calculations. By the 1952 act, the annual quota of any country is fixed at one-sixth of 1 per cent of the number of inhabitants in continental United States in 1920 of that national origin.

Quotas based on one-sixth of 1 per cent of the 1920 white population are much smaller than they would be if they were based on the same percentage of the 1950 population. A nation that has increased its population 43 per cent in thirty years is thus restricting its immigration out of all proportion to its capacity to absorb new people. Instead of being a law to regulate immigration in the wisest and most humane manner, the McCarran-Walter Act thus becomes primarily a stop sign.

Discrimination Against Asiatics. Sponsors of the new law have argued that the law does not discriminate. They point out that small quotas have been assigned to Asian countries for the first time and that Japanese may now become United States citizens. But what offends Asian peoples and those Americans who find prejudices repugnant is the broad use of a relatively new device for discrimination. The McCarran-Walter Act endorses the fiction that there is a huge geographical area inhabited by inferior peoples. This area, called the Asia-Pacific triangle, is defined as including every country that is wholly situated north of the 25th parallel of south latitude and between 60 degrees east and 165 degrees west longitude. Immigration of persons born in countries wholly situated in this area is sharply restricted. Except for slightly higher quotas for China and Japan, not more than 100 persons a year may ever enter from any of the countries in this zone. The 25th parallel bisects Australia; the 60th meridian is on the eastern edge of Iran and 165 degrees west longitude is just west of the Aleutian Islands.

The McCarran-Walter Act not only discriminates against every person born within this vast triangle, which includes the populations of Afghanistan, Burma, China, Indonesia, Japan, Korea, India, and the Pacific Islands, but also discriminates against those born elsewhere if half of their ancestry can be traced to the triangle. The law says that any prospective immigrant "born outside the Asia-Pacific triangle who is attributable by as much as one-half of his ancestry" to peoples within the triangle shall be chargeable to the annual quota of 100 for the Asia-Pacific triangle or, in certain cases, to the token quotas of 100 for Asian countries.

Thus the English-born son of an English father and an Indian mother cannot use the liberal English quota. He would have to wait at least a decade or so under India's quota of 100.

The code of racial prejudice twists like a cowpath. To keep out Italians, Greeks, Turks, and Slavs, the McCarran-Walter Act relies on place of birth, not the ancestry of the applicant. To keep out Asians, the law ignores place of birth and relies on ancestry. For both groups, however, the law consistently ignores individual worth.

The Immigration and Naturalization Act of 1952 brings racial prejudice to our front door by penalizing, for the first time in the history of our immigration laws, the predominantly Negro population of the British West Indies. Immigrants from these colonies formerly were permitted to enter without restriction under the liberal quota of the mother country, and at the most about 2,500 did so each year. The new law sets a limit of 100 for each colony or dependent area that may be charged to the quota of the governing country. This limitation has been denounced by the colonial legislatures, by newspapers, and by West Indian leaders. They have pointed out that there are no quotas for the neighboring states of Cuba, Haiti, and the Dominican Republic.

There would appear to be no explanation that squares with American traditions. During debates on this measure in the House, one of the authors of the bill announced that the reason for this provision is that the St. Thomas Labor Conference in the Virgin Islands and the Virgin Islands Civic Association had written the House Immigration Sub-Committee urging the new limitation as a means of "protecting" those islands from large migrations from Jamaica. This hardly appears to be a sufficient justification for so grievous a discrimination against colored immigrants. In the minds of most people this provision looks like an expression of anti-Negro prejudice.

Barring the Gate

In practical effect our immigration code keeps many deserving people out of the United States even when the quotas for their countries are still unused. One way in which this has long been done is by giving authority to consular officials abroad to bar visa applicants if for one reason or another those applicants are believed to lack the qualifications established in the immigration laws. The discretion of subordinate officials on these matters is virtually absolute since there is now no way to prosecute an administrative appeal or to secure judicial review of an adverse decision regardless of its accuracy.

Thus, persons of adequate means may be excluded if they "in the opinion of the consular officer or the attorney general are likely at any time to become a public charge." An unfavorable determination of a consular official may be right or wrong, but under this provision a wrong opinion would bar the immigrant just as surely and just as completely as a correct one. An American citizen can challenge the decision of a customs official who tries to prevent him from importing a sack of beans but he cannot appeal the ruling of a consul who prevents him from bringing in his

mother or any other person whose admission he wishes to facilitate.

Also barred is any applicant who the consular officer or Attorney General "has reason to believe" might "incidentally" engage in activities "prejudicial" to the United States. This loose language could conceivably be used to keep out almost anybody. A member of the British parliament, resolutely anti-Communist but also critical of United States actions in the United Nations, could be denied a visa because a consular official feared that he might express his differences with American policy on the lecture platform.

Our present immigration law excludes persons convicted of two or more nonpolitical crimes with sentences totaling five years. This provision gives foreign courts the power to screen our immigrants. It even means accepting the verdicts of totalitarian courts that operate under laws alien to our concepts. Thus, the Belgian war bride of an American airman has not been allowed to enter the United States because, as a slave laborer for the Nazis, she was convicted of falsifying documents to get food ration tickets.

While the victims of Fascist courts are excluded, the ex-Fascists themselves get two advantages under the new act and, although once barred along with Communists, they now are eligible for admission. First, the present law provides that former members of totalitarian parties may qualify if they terminated their membership five years earlier and have since opposed the party's ideology. This test is relatively easy to meet since the Nazi-Fascist parties which we fought in World War II technically went out of existence more than five years ago, and since the State Department has ruled that a former member need not prove affirmatively that he opposed such a totalitarian program for the last five years but merely prove that he did not advocate it. Secondly, the present law includes a definition of "totalitarian" which restricts the term to those who have advocated a dictatorial rule "in the United States," a phrase which has been interpreted by the State and Justice Departments as inapplicable to the Nazi and Fascist parties.

The 1952 Immigration Act further removed foreign professors from the non-quota status which traditionally they had enjoyed. It subjected their entry to the red tape and delay of obtaining a regular quota visa or of securing a preference quota visa as one whose presence is "needed urgently" in the United States. This change reflects a fear of ideas and a lack of confidence in the ability of our universities to select only well-qualified persons for their teaching staffs.

A Medieval Punishment. A case can be made for deporting a person who used fraud to enter the United States. But many competent critics feel that the McCarran-Walter Act unnecessarily goes to the extreme length of deporting immigrants for minor reasons, even when no law of the United States has been violated.

The new law makes it easier to deport an alien who is suspected of having become a public charge within five years of entry. Under the old law, the government had to prove the alien was in fact a public charge. But the McCarran-Walter Act permits deportation if in the "opinion" of the Attorney General (and, realistically, an immigration inspector) the alien is such a charge.

Similarly immigration officers are given authority to decide whether an alien committed to a mental hospital is suffering from a condition that developed in the United States or in the country from which he came. Experienced psychiatrists often find it hard to tell when mental diseases began. But the alien is nonetheless required to prove conclusively that his mental sickness began after a certain date.

Deportation is also made an extra penalty for violation of the alien registration law, which carries stiff penalties of its own. An alien can be deported if he neglects to notify the Attorney General of a change of address within ten days and if the Attorney General does not think the oversight excusable.

Membership—at any time after entry—in an organization required to register under the McCarran Internal Security Act is made a ground for deportation. The publication of lists of subversive groups is a relatively new device. Many good Americans and many good immigrants innocently joined, ten, fifteen, or twenty years ago, "front" organizations that have since been declared subversive. There is no penalty whatever for comparable membership by native citizens but aliens may be deported even though they may have long since rejected the organization and the principles it represents. The failure of this section of the law to recognize repudiation of totalitarian beliefs denies us the association and support of many persons who are today more firmly welded to democratic beliefs.

This feature of the new law introduces for the first time in American history a system of retroactive punishment for aliens.

The United States Constitution prohibits *ex post facto* laws. But this has been held applicable only to criminal cases and the Supreme Court has ruled that deportation is not technically criminal punishment, although in many respects it is admittedly harsher and severer. Deportation punishes not only the alien but also his wife and children who in fact may be citizens. This situation has long been recognized in our immigration code which has always included some provision for relief in hardship cases. The possibility that injury may be worked on innocent parties, however, is intensified under the 1952 Act which sharply restricts the grounds for suspension of deportation and establishes almost impossible conditions for the adjustment of the status of an alien no matter how worthy his claim.

Moreover, the McCarran-Walter Act does much to deprive resident aliens from ever attaining a feeling of security. The new law prescribes deportation *at any time* if it is discovered that the immigrant should have been excluded originally because of his race, nationality, politics, or anything else. There is no statute of limitations as long as he is unnaturalized. An alien who has been a model resident for twenty-five or thirty years is no safer than the person who arrived last month. Indeed, the long-time resident's position is worse. There may have been nothing fraudulent in his case, but how can he find witnesses so many years later to help establish his innocence? And if witnesses are found, how can they be positive in their recollection? That is why every crime save murder has a statute of limitations.

Much is rightly said about the immigrant's responsibility to his new country. More should be said about America's responsibility as a host to newcomers. Pulling up roots from foreign soil and moving a family to the United States is an enterprise that demands courage, vision, and money. The average immigrant family plans, sacrifices, and saves for months and years to fulfill its dream. When the family reaches American soil, there is no overnight indoctrination in United States laws and customs. Our language, our cities, our people, and our concepts cannot be assimilated in a couple of years.

What the immigrant needs is time to get settled and to learn about the United States. He should have friendly help during this period.

Second-Class Citizenship

Chief Justice Marshall wrote that a naturalized citizen becomes "a member of the society, possessing all the rights of a native citizen and standing, in the view of the Constitution, on the footing of a native. The Constitution does not authorize Congress to enlarge or abridge those rights."

An immigrant who obtained his citizenship through fraud should, of course, be deprived of it. But if citizenship was fairly won, there should be no strings attached.

Although native Americans may live abroad until they die without losing their citizenship, the new law terminates the citizenship of any naturalized American who is absent anywhere abroad for five years or more. This provision was aimed particularly at Jews who left the United States to help develop Palestine. The drafters of the bill which ultimately became the Nationality Act of 1940 had not thought of including this provision until after receiving testimony from an official of the State Department. The enactment of this section of the law seems largely attributable to his observation that "it will be desirable to put in a provision to cover each person who goes to a third country. The principal cases we have, I may say, are these scientists that are principally Russian and German Jews who have been naturalized in this country and later went to Palestine. We have other cases but I mean that there are more of that particular body than in any other category." Thus, Ezra Pound, who broadcast for Mussolini during the war, is still an American citizen—but a naturalized citizen who spent more than five years in Israel or Germany would lose his citizenship.

Second-class citizenship is humiliating to the naturalized immigrant, unbecoming to our democratic tradition, and hurtful to the nation. The person who knows he is getting an unfair deal cannot serve his country as well as the citizen who is treated fairly.

Any American citizen who helped the Russians in their campaign to alienate our friends would be denounced in Congress for subversion and hustled off to jail. Yet there are many who feel that the McCarran-Walter Act has gratuitously placed a powerful propaganda weapon in the hands of the Russians, and the Russians are making the most of it. Philip M. Hauser, professor of sociology at the University of Chicago and former acting director of the Census Bureau, reported after a long stay in the Orient:

Public Law 414 (the McCarran-Walter Act) is well known to the peoples of the world and it is not favorably known. It does untold damage to the United States in creating attitudes of distrust and hostility. . . . It is absurd to think that we can retain our position as the world leader in the fight for freedom and democracy with the peoples whom we explicitly and openly brand in our legislation as undesirable and inferior. . . . We have unwittingly placed into the hands of the ruthless, adroit and unscrupulous propagandists of the U.S.S.R. a major weapon with which to attack us. . . . The U.S.S.R. is skillfully and continuously making the most of our ethnic and racist doctrines as promulgated in Public Law 414.

Professor Hauser's opinion is supported by the first-hand observations of many other experts. Our new immigration law has created resentment and hatred not only in Asia but also in Africa, in the Caribbean, in Latin America and, of course, in Italy and Greece.

The mistrust of non-Americans that is manifested in the new law is one reason why international scientific congresses are keeping clear of our shores. The International Congress of Psychology will be held in Canada, not the United States, in 1954, to avoid any embarrassment to delegates who might be refused visas. The International Congress of Genetics decided that Italy and Canada would be more hospitable than the United States for its next two meetings. The International Astronomical Union and other important scientific groups have likewise turned down invitations to America. Leading American scientists are gravely concerned about their foreign colleagues' boycott.

Congress has been alert to catch even the slightest flaws in the Voice of America program. Many citizens of other nations do not hear the Voice of America broadcasts because the McCarran-Walter Act speaks so loudly.

How About the Reds?

Some good Americans, admitting that the McCarran-Walter Act is marked with racial bias and other defects, say that a tough law is essential to keep out Communist agents.

No American could object if the provisions of the Act had a reasonable relationship to our national security. But the McCarran-Walter Act gives no more protection against Communist immigration than a more equitable and less discriminatory law would give.

The National Origins Quota System certainly is no safeguard against Communists. Neither is the Asia-Pacific triangle. And France, the western nation with the heaviest proportion of Communists, enjoys a fairly liberal immigration quota under the McCarran-Walter Act.

Moreover, those who pushed hardest for the adoption of the present act seemingly show little concern with the influx of illegal migrants from Mexico and Canada. Communists could easily, if they so wished, bypass our consular officers by sneaking across the line from Canada and Mexico, as hundreds of thousands of persons do every year. No real effort has been made to stop them.

Gladwin Hill, the New York *Times* correspondent, reported in January, 1953, that an estimated 1,500,000 Mexican "wetbacks" entered the United States in 1952 without the formality of tipping their hats to an immigration officer. This illegal immigration was about ten times greater than the 154,000 persons allowed from Europe and Asia by the McCarran-Walter Act.

Why hasn't Congress cracked down on the vast, illegal migration from Mexico? Because, Mr. Hill says, farm owners want cheap Mexican labor.

No good American opposes statutes designed to protect us from invasion by agents of a foreign power or by those bent upon espionage or subversion. The McCarran-Walter Act, however, cannot be justified or explained in these terms. Its most restrictive and unfair provisions bear no relation whatever to considerations of internal security. Many devoted Americans believe that attempts by the sponsors and authors of the McCarran-Walter Act to masquerade the discriminatory provisions of the laws as a protection against Communist infiltration into the country represents an effort to exploit anti-Communist feelings for purposes totally unrelated to our security. . . .

The imperative need for thoroughgoing amendment of the McCarran-Walter Act has been acknowledged by thinking Americans of every political background, by both Republican and Democratic national administrations. It represents a challenge to be met by the common action of all the American people, no matter what their party affiliation. . . .

Conclusion

No doubt . . . [a variety of] immigration proposals will be introduced during the next few years to achieve many of these same reforms. Bills have been introduced to minimize the discriminatory features of the national origins system by pooling immigration quotas and assigning them on the basis of need and national interest [and to make other changes]. No matter which of these measures ultimately becomes law, one thing appears certain: a basic rethinking of our present inflexible and restrictive immigration policies is necessary to bring our immigration practices into accord with our democratic aspirations. Ill-conceived and bigoted immigration laws have been a blemish on our record of democratic achievement. The immigration laws of any society both reflect and shape its fundamental character. Freedom of movement, both in emigration and immigration, have long been acknowledged as among the most fundamental of human freedoms; it is the hallmark of totalitarianism that it seeks rigidly to limit the free movement of people. It seeks to deny to its own subjects the freedom to live elsewhere. It seeks to deny to others access to its soil or contact with its peoples. Conversely, the very essence of democracy is that people remain free to choose where and in which country they wish to live and build their future. It is essential that so fundamental and significant an area of American life and law as immigration be revised so that bigotry may give way to knowledge, and expediency to the justice of humanitarianism.

Puerto Rican Migrants

Clarence Senior

Clarence Senior (1903–   ), Chief, Migration Division, Department of Labor, Commonwealth of Puerto Rico; lecturer, Columbia University. Principal works: *Puerto Rican Migration* (1947), *The Puerto Rican Migrant in St. Croix* (1947), with C. W. Mills and R. K. Goldsen, *The Puerto Rican Journey* (1950), and *Strangers and Neighbors: The Story of Our Puerto Rican Citizens* (1952).

All but a handful of Puerto Ricans who move their homes from the island go to the continental United States.[1] There is little reason to assume that any significant numbers of them will go to the so-called countries of immigration in Latin America. Nationalistic restrictions on foreigners in the labor force, visa and customs difficulties, transportation costs, and other obstacles limit the possibilities, although there are Puerto Rican groups in the Dominican Republic, Cuba, Venezuela, Mexico, Brazil, and several other Latin American countries.[2] Probably a factor at least as important as American citizenship is the widespread acceptance of the ideas and aspirations flowing from the continental United States since the third quarter of the nineteenth century. Even before this country took over from Spain, there were Puerto Rican communities on the continent.

These factors have meant that the main migratory current has been directed toward the continental United States. There are only two significant exceptions aside from the Latin American countries already mentioned. Hawaiian sugar growers recruited canefield workers on the island in the 1890's and thus laid the basis for a "colony" in those Pacific islands which numbers about 10,000 today. A minor current has flowed to the United States Virgin Islands in recent years, primarily to replace a dwindling labor force on the

sugar-growing island of St. Croix. Interestingly enough, the Puerto Ricans are in demand largely because of the long-continued out-migration of those inhabitants of St. Croix who are in the productive age categories.[3]

By 1930 the census reported Puerto Rican-born persons in all forty-eight states. The largest numbers found by the 1940 census were in New York 63,281; California 1,892; New Jersey 780; Pennsylvania 607; Maryland 294; District of Columbia 289; Florida 272; Illinois 259; Texas 254; and Michigan 208. They were predominantly (96.3 per cent) city dwellers, and the overwhelming majority were living in New York City. Only six other cities contained more than 200 each: San Francisco, Philadelphia, Washington, Chicago, Baltimore, and Los Angeles, in that order.

Recent Migration

Only since World War II has net out-migration helped significantly to reduce population pressures. About 4,000 persons per year were lost through migration between 1908, when dependable figures first became available, and 1945. The annual net outflow since has been as follows: 1945, 13,573; 1946, 39,911; 1947, 24,551; 1948, 32,775; 1949, 25,698; 1950, 34,703; 1951, 52,900.

A combination of factors produced the sharp upturn:

1. The disposition to migrate was founded on the heavy unemployment on the island, with all it implies in terms of low wages, lack of opportunities for advancement, and so forth. This provided the "push" which is found in all migrations.

---

[1] The only direct information on the outflow to other areas indicates that only 1.7 per cent of those leaving went to other countries. "Encuesta Sobre las Personas que Salieron de Puerto Rico en Noviembre de 1946" (San Juan: Negociado del Presupuesto, 1947), p. 11.

[2] The question is examined in Kingsley Davis, "Future Migration into Latin America," in *Postwar Problems of Migration*, New York: Milbank Memorial Fund, 1947; and Clarence Senior, *Puerto Rican Emigration*, Río Piedras: Social Science Research Center, 1947, 166 pp.

[3] Clarence Senior, *The Puerto Rican Migrant in St. Croix*, Río Piedras: Social Science Research Center, 1947, 42 pp.

From "Migration and Puerto Rico's Population Problem," *The Annals*, 285 (January 1953): 130–136, pp. 130–133, 135–136 quoted. Reprinted by permission.

2. The "pull" was provided largely by plentiful job opportunities on the continent at a time when unskilled and semiskilled labor was in demand. The favorable labor market attracted those whose aspiration levels had been raised by schools, radio, newspapers and magazines, and the example of relatives, friends, and neighbors who had previously migrated and had advanced themselves economically.

3. The cost to the migrant influences the strength of the "pull." Boats, which took 4½ to 5 days and which cost around $150, were largely replaced after the war by planes which made the trip in 8 to 10 hours. This resulted in the "first airborne migration in history." Much of the ensuing publicity has, in fact, arisen from the dramatic features of the movement rather than the numbers involved, which have never been large. Competition between the non-scheduled companies forced reduction of the fare to as little as $35, but safety standards were also driven down. Several wrecks costing many lives led the insular government to add its own inspection requirements to those of the federal government. Now two regularly scheduled companies furnish passage for $64 on 6½- to 8-hour flights.

Two streams of migration flow from the island; they differ significantly in origin, destination, and length of stay. One flows up in the spring and back in the fall; the other is "permanent." The first consists of farm workers; the second of city people.

The Farm Workers

The Puerto Rican sugar cane season lasts from late fall to late spring, and thus workers are available when needed here. Most of them come under a work agreement formulated and enforced by Puerto Rico's labor authorities, and return at the end of the continental farm season. They are placed in areas of agricultural labor shortages in co-operation with the federal Farm Placement Service. Through the work agreement, the Puerto Rican Department of Labor strives to protect the workers from the abuses still so widely characteristic of labor relations in agriculture, which lags at least a century behind industry in this field.[4]

The work agreement provides that the local prevailing rate of wages shall be paid, and that the worker shall be guaranteed 160 hours of work

[4] See *Migratory Labor in American Agriculture,* Report of the President's Commission on Migratory Labor, Washington: Government Printing Office, 1951, 188 pp.

or wages per month and acceptable housing, rent free. It requires the employer to bring the migrant under workmen's compensation, since most states do not require such insurance for farm labor. It also requires the posting of a performance bond and the opening of the employer's books to the agents of the insular Department of Labor. The Migration Division of the Department, with offices in New York and Chicago, has a staff to investigate complaints, secure enforcement, and help both employer and worker to solve their problems. The chairman of the Senate Subcommittee on Agricultural Labor has praised the program as unique in the field and as tending to improve labor standards.[5]

The numbers involved in the farm-workers stream are increasing. Those protected by the work agreement numbered 3,000 in 1947 and had risen to 12,500 in 1952. Several thousand others established satisfactory relations with their employers during their first season or two, and now come each summer on their own. One obstacle to the program is the private labor contractor who wants to help some employers to secure workers without paying prevailing wages or assuming the responsibilities required by the agreement. Last season eight such agents were jailed for illegal recruiting on the island.

Continued high levels of employment on the continent will result in a chronic farm labor shortage for which the Puerto Rican supplies a highly satisfactory answer. Most of the season migrants work on sugar cane during the winter. Swinging a machete is heavy, grueling work in the tropical sun. Most of the "stoop labor" tasks on farms in the continental United States are less exacting. The Puerto Rican worker is widely accepted as making an outstanding contribution throughout the Middle Atlantic and New England states, where he is best known.

The Urban Migration

The other stream flows from the cities of the island to the cities of the mainland. It is the migration for settlement in a new environment; it accounted for a net outflow from the island of

[5] *Migratory Labor,* Hearings before the Subcommittee on Labor and Labor-Management Relations, Part I, Washington: Government Printing Office, 1952, pp. 793–811; P. A. Pagán de Colón, "Farm Labor Program in Puerto Rico," *Employment Security Review* (March 1952) pp. 23–26; "How to Hire Agricultural Workers from Puerto Rico," New York: Department of Labor of Puerto Rico, 1952, 15 pp.

249,918 persons in the decade 1942–51. These migrants enter urban service, trade, and industrial occupations. They settle in the industrial centers. About 80 per cent now live in New York City. The 1950 census showed 246,300 first- and second-generation Puerto Ricans there. The Welfare and Health Council of New York City estimated that on April 1, 1952 the figure was 321,-000. Contrary to the general impression, the Puerto Ricans are not all concentrated in one or two areas, but are found in 351 of the 352 health areas into which the city is divided.[6]

Outside of New York the migrants are found in relatively small clusters in Bridgeport, Newark, Passaic, Trenton, Camden, Philadelphia, Pittsburgh, Buffalo, Youngstown, Cleveland, Lorain, Gary, Chicago, Aurora, Joliet, Savanna, and Milwaukee, and "points west" as far as Utah, Arizona, and California. The tendency is toward dispersion, and the government's policy is to encourage and facilitate such movement.

Characteristics of the Settlers

What kind of person migrates? How does he compare with the rest of the population? A good deal of light can be shed on these questions. The answers will help us to evaluate migration as a long-range means of alleviating population pressure. The migrant is much more likely than the "average" Puerto Rican to come from an urban area; he is above his compatriots in literacy, in skill, and in occupational standing. He is slightly older than the average and is more likely to be in the labor force. He was, while on the island, employed more regularly than his peers, and he received a slightly higher than average income.[7]

The whole life pattern of the migrant displays urban characteristics as opposed to those of the Puerto Rican peasant. Ninety-one per cent of all persons in the sample had lived in the island's urban centers before coming to New York, com-

---

[6] *Population of Puerto Rican Birth or Parentage, New York City: 1950*, New York: Welfare and Health Council, 1952, 57 pp.

[7] This picture is drawn from the results of two studies which agree closely on major features. One interviewed a sample of all persons migrating in November 1946 ("Encuesta," etc., *op. cit.*); the other analyzed the characteristics of 5,000 persons in 1,113 households in the two core areas of Puerto Rican settlement in New York City in 1948. (C. W. Mills, Clarence Senior, and Rose Goldsen, *The Puerto Rican Journey: New York's Newest Migrants*, New York: Harper & Bros., 1950, 238 pp.) This study was more detailed than the one made in 1946, so data from it will be cited below.

pared with the 28 per cent of the total population classified as urban in the 1940 census. The two largest cities, San Juan and Ponce, accounted for the majority of the migrants. Overwhelmingly (79 per cent), they had been born in the urban centers and were not recent migrants from farm or village.

Occupational history reflected the urban origin: only 5 per cent had ever engaged in farming, although 39 per cent of Puerto Rico's workers were so occupied in 1940. Even more important is the contrast between the migrants and the 1940 labor force on the basis of skill: skilled workers, migrants 18 per cent, island 5 per cent; semiskilled workers, migrants 41 per cent, island 20 per cent; unskilled workers, migrants 21 per cent, island 50 per cent. Thus it can be seen that skilled workers are represented among the migrants over three times as frequently as in the general population, the semiskilled twice, but the unskilled less than half.

Fifty-four per cent of the migrants were in the labor force, compared with 52 per cent of the urban adult population and 35 per cent of the total population. Only 4 per cent of those in the labor force were unemployed when they left the island, in sharp contrast to the 10 to 20 per cent annual average in recent years. Most of the migrants had quit jobs to make the change, and 71 per cent of those had worked steadily for the full year prior to their departure. The income of those who came just before the war averaged about 25 per cent above that of the island's industrial workers, but the gap narrowed during the war.

The schooling of the migrant is superior to that of the average islander; only 8 per cent of the migrants were illiterate, contrasted with 32 per cent on the island. The migrant is thus seen to be the end product of a selective process which has chosen those who, on the average, are superior to the average Puerto Rican in significant respects. . . .

Government Policy

Labor shortages on the continent after World War II, coupled with expanded and cheaper transportation facilities from Puerto Rico, made the island a happy hunting ground for private, fee-charging, recruiting agencies. These agencies accepted fees from Puerto Ricans with little or no regard for the interests of the workers or the continental communities in which they were placed. Many abuses resulted. Men and women were recruited for areas where they were not needed. Not only was there no work for them when they reached these areas, but the absence of such work and lack of funds created community problems of caring for stranded people. The picture was further complicated when the fee-charging agencies tied in with travel agencies whose interest was solely in selling tickets.

These abuses and the exorbitant charges of the recruiting agencies resulted in a 1947 law regulating labor contractors and abolishing fee-charging agencies in Puerto Rico. All contracts for workers recruited on the island must be approved by the insular Secretary of Labor. One basic policy decision was that no Puerto Rican worker could be recruited for the continent unless a labor shortage was certified by the responsible local, state, and federal labor officials.

These considerations, along with those steps already described which were taken for the protection of agricultural workers, apply to those recruited on the island. However, the majority of the migrants come on their own in search of "greener pastures." The official policy is that generally the government neither encourages nor discourages such migration. It early recognized, however, that the voluntary migration of substantial groups often gives rise to personal problems for the migrant and friction in his new community. It therefore maintains a Migration Division in the Department of Labor.

The Division co-operates with the 1,800 state and local offices affiliated with the United States Employment Service, to help Puerto Ricans move to labor shortage areas. It helps to interpret the economic and cultural background of the migrant to the local community and endeavors to speed the adjustment process by explaining to the migrant the new attitudes and habits required in his new situation. It maintains a staff of placement specialists, social workers, labor inspectors, community organizers, educators, and bilingual speakers to serve employers and workers and civic, labor, and social welfare organizations. It issues literature in both English and Spanish, produces and distributes educational films, organizes radio programs and conferences, and strives to build and maintain an atmosphere of good will and understanding between the migrant and the community.

Forecasts of widespread and serious continental labor shortages at the outbreak of the Korean war led the government to call the attention of employers and manpower officials to the presence of a substantial reservoir of unemployed and underemployed on the island. An Employment Development Section was created in the Economic Development Administration to canvass prospective employers outside of New York City, and a fund of $100,000 to underwrite transportation expenses advanced by the employer was voted. The failure of widespread shortages to develop hampered the program, and it was ended.

The Migrant in His New Home

The situation the migrant faces either in New York City or outside is not essentially different from that faced by most of the 40,000,000 immigrants who have helped to build the United States. It is complicated at present by war-born shortages of housing, schools, and recreation and other community facilities. It is made somewhat easier by a more widespread realization today of the realities of culture contact and conflict and by the existence of a number of organizations seeking better understanding between ethnic groups.[12] The co-operation of such groups has been of inestimable value in helping to smooth the adjustment process and in aiding the migrants to enjoy the rights and responsibilities of full citizenship.

---

[12] Examples of such civic action are cited in Clarence Senior, *Strangers and Neighbors: The Story of Our Puerto Rican Citizens,* New York: Anti-Defamation League, 1952, 54 pp.

Transiency as a Cultural Pattern

Theodore Caplow

Theodore Caplow (1920–   ), assistant professor of sociology, University of Minnesota.

The existence of transiency has been a prominent feature of American life for half a century. Despite fluctuations in the composition, function, and status of the hobo group, it has continually increased in size, and is today of surprising magnitude. Between ten and twenty thousand illegal train riders are apprehended daily on American railroads.[1] Between two and three thousand were killed every year between 1920 and 1938, and a somewhat greater number injured.[2] Estimates of the total population vary from 300,000 to 3,000,000. The rapid turnover of personnel is constantly returning hobos to settled life and recruiting others, so that the number of former transients doubtless runs into the millions. . . .

Vagrancy or transiency exists to some extent within all highly developed civilizations, and all vagrant classes show certain common characteristics in their relation to society. These may be briefly summarized. 1. Vagrancy as a mass phenomenon always arises in a period of rapid change and social disintegration, but may persist after the implementing conditions have disappeared. 2. A certain degree of cohesion always exists within the vagrant class, ranging from a vague *esprit de corps,* to the development of complete dialects, hierarchies, and parasitic economic systems.[3] 3. The efforts of the authorities to suppress the class as a whole, while keeping some or all of the individuals from starvation, sets up an ambivalence between repression and relief.

It must be emphasized, however, that beyond the general functional similarities, transiency in the United States is a unique and indigenous de-velopment with no close analogue.[4] The key to the understanding of its history lies in the distinction between the hobo, a homeless migratory worker, and the tramp, a homeless migratory non-worker. The hobo was often regarded as a hardy successor to the pioneers, while the tramp was seen as a social menace.[5] While this distinction was attacked as early as 1904,[6] it persisted both in fact and in theory, until the end of the twenties when the position and composition of the transient group was altered with unprecedented rapidity by the onset of the Great Depression. The number of transients [then] increased markedly at once. . . .

This period saw the advent and disappearance of the child tramp.[7] Primarily, the child tramp was the product of economic conditions, but in many respects he seems to have been involved in a mass movement. A survey by the Children's Bureau in the spring of 1932 estimated the number of transient boys at over 200,000. Other estimates vary from 100,000 to half a million or more. A considerable number of girls were involved. . . . In September 1935, less than 3 per cent of youth were found among transients[8] and that proportion is probably a maximum for the five years following. The vigorous efforts of government and social agencies along with a change in the underlying attitudes leading to youth transiency were the major factors involved.

Youth transiency was only one of the aberra-

---

[1] Association of American Railroads. The writer was informed by a railroad executive compiling these statistics that they were arbitrarily cut by 75 per cent to avoid duplication.

[2] *Fifty-first Annual Report on the Statistics of Railways in the United States,* Interstate Commerce Commission, Washington, D. C., 1938.

[3] For an interesting example, see Ronald Fuller, *The Beggar's Brotherhood,* London: George Allen and Unwin, 1936.

[4] Nigel Harvey, "Concerning Casuals: Life on the Roads," *Spectator,* 160 (1938): 742.

[5] Nels Anderson, *The Hobo,* Chicago: University of Chicago Press, 1923. Interviews with hobo celebrities illustrate the strength of the prevailing attitude.

[6] Jack London, *The Tramp,* Chicago, 1904. [Re-issued as Chap. 2 of his *War of the Classes,* New York: Macmillan Co., 1905.—Eds.]

[7] Thomas Minehan, *Boy and Girl Tramps of America,* New York: Farrar and Rinehart, 1934.

[8] *A Survey of the Transient and Homeless Population in 12 Cities,* Div. of Social Research, Works Progress Administration, Washington, D. C., 1937.

From "Transiency as a Cultural Pattern," *American Sociological Review,* 5 (1940): 731–739.

tions which appeared in Hobohemia during 1929–1933. For one thing, the total number was exceedingly large. In January, 1933, the Committee on Care of Transient and Homeless estimated that the number of homeless persons in the United States was approximately 1,500,000. It must be remembered that January, a mid-winter month, would represent a very low total relative to other months.

Almost as striking as the number of children was the rather high proportion of unattached women. Both prostitutes and female hobos were on the road in considerable numbers at this time. In addition, between 10 and 25 per cent of the child tramps were girls. By June, 1934, however, the women transients numbered only a little over 1 per cent. By the end of 1934, the crisis had passed although there was still an enormous hobo population and the new hobos were more various as to background. "The transients are now coming from all walks and conditions of life. Homes of college professors, farmers, electricians, musicians, technicians, southern cotton pickers, northern mill workers, and congested urban dwellers were all represented." [9] . . .

From 1936 onward, the hobo population remained in comparative equilibrium. Its composition and function are markedly different, however, from those existing in previous periods. Recent investigations agree to a surprising extent with each other, and with the following observations made in the latter part of 1939 as to the personnel of the transient class.[10] The majority of transients are between the ages of 20 and 35. I encountered only one individual under 18. The child tramp as a type has disappeared. Nor is the old man much more typical. A large proportion of homeless men in the higher age groups are not really transients. They tend to remain in one city, or within a fairly circumscribed neighborhood, either as retired tramps or as displaced individuals who have been driven by necessity to the mission and the flophouse. Probably not more than 1 per cent of the transients are women. Women very often "thumb" rides, but they do not in that case identify themselves with the hobo class, nor do they have any important points of contact with the hobos. The woman rider on a freight train is generally under the protection of a man. A very high proportion of the transients are native-born whites. An overwhelming majority declared themselves willing and able to work. They are generally unmarried and more or less unskilled.

In terms of function, this population is exceedingly diverse. They fall into two main categories: the travelers, and the hobos. The travelers are individuals en route to a real destination as transients. These include college students, migrant laborers, criminals, soldiers on leave, salesmen, workers going home for a visit, and many others with purposes of their own who cannot afford the legitimate charges of long-distance transportation. They travel by train, occasionally paying for their food and shelter but more often relying on the usual hobo methods at least for lodging. In the West especially, there survives the tradition that the proper way for a poor man to travel is by freight. A ninety-two-year-old prospector criticized a group of hitchhikers in the American River valley, "Mixing with everybody, getting into trouble, if you were worth your salt you'd hop a train." The decline of hitchhiking continues to increase the number of those who are forced on to the trains.

The larger proportion is comprised of men "on the road." Almost every hobo will give a definite destination, Chicago, St. Louis, Los Angeles, New Orleans, or another of the important railroad termini. However, being "on the road" is a definite condition fully recognized in most parts of the country. The members of this class are typically mature but young. They leave home because of unemployment, the desire to travel, family disorganization, petty crime, trouble with a woman, ill health. By far the most frequent reasons given are economic pressure and wanderlust. The high proportion of the latter factor is striking. For the less favored classes of the American population, a few months on the road may constitute a sort of Grand Tour obtainable in no other way. It is very unusual to encounter a hobo who has been continuously on the road for more than three years. The average period spent as a hobo seems to be about a year and a half. Many state their intention of returning home; some have returned and settled down only to leave again. The transient, staying in a strange community for a few days or hours, almost invariably meets residents who "know what it's like. I've been on the bum myself." Mer-

[9] Ellery F. Reed, *Federal Transient Program: An Evaluation Survey*, New York, 1934.

[10] John N. Webb, *The Transient Unemployed*, Div. of Soc. Res., WPA, Washington, D. C., 1935; Freda P. Segner, *Migrant Minnesota: An Analysis of Minnesota Transient Cases*, a Works Progress Administration Project, St. Paul, November 1936; *Unattached Non-resident Men*, Chicago Relief Administration, Chicago, 1939. . . .

chants, garage attendants, farmers, even an occasional social worker or policeman include themselves in this category, and it is often from them that informal assistance to the hobo will come most readily. The increasing number of settled and respected persons tends toward a progressively greater acceptance of the hobo population, which they regard almost automatically as a normal and recognized class. . . .

Today the absence of formal organization [among the migrants] is striking. The mores of the hobo class are technics transmitted with amazing rapidity because of their utility in confronting the dangers and hardships of the life. The common language consists of technical terms only, in contrast to the vocabularies formerly reported which embodied common attitudes and emphasized strong group sentiment.

The fairly intricate hierarchies formerly described have quite disappeared. There is no distinction of status as between the tramp, the hobo, and the bum. Indeed, the first of these words is obsolete, and the second used rarely and then as interchangeable with the third. The word "bum" in this connection has no derogatory connotation. . . .

The hobo has in no sense ceased to identify himself with society at large. The formal relation the hobo must maintain toward the institutions and individuals who maintain him is that of an unfortunate; but more and more he conceives this condition not as personal failure but as economic maladjustment which he shares with large numbers of the stable population. Furthermore, he considers his homeless condition to be a temporary circumstance, which in most cases it is. . . .

As a matter of fact, the hobo does not always take even his position as an unfortunate very seriously. The relative advantages of life on the road and in a community are discussed more often than any other single topic. While few will advocate it as a permanent condition, many find it a satisfying experience. For the recidivistic transient, there is the traditional romanticization, "There's something about a train whistle that gets in your blood." It is comfort rather than the more spiritual values which the ideal of home life represents to the transient. Food, clothes, shelter, a clean bed, baths, women. The consensus is "no woman will look at a guy on the bum." The simpler comforts and "three squares" become tremendous values to the hobo to whom the securing of minimal subsistence and shelter is a matter of continuous cal-culation. For those who return to the road at intervals, there is a sort of balance between security and new experience, and the desire for one grows in proportion as the other is satisfied.

With the attraction of mobility growing greater in our culture and the mobility of labor becoming less, this attitude becomes more and more general. It is perhaps greater among rural and semi-rural populations where social mobility in a given environment is more limited. A similar situation has long existed in Sweden. If this state of affairs continue, it may, reinforced by a degree of economic disorganization, lead to transiency as an expected phase of the life-pattern among certain strata.

Although the hobo is not a psychological outlaw, his experiences are not particularly socializing. Seeing the seamy side of institutional culture, he is apt to prize the symbols of the social organization very lightly. While the range of political opinion among hobos seems to be a fair sampling of the general population, the hobo is conscious of himself as a member of an underprivileged group. If he does not develop an emotional set against the existing order, he is at least likely to be skeptical and resentful of the totems or taboos of community life.

Engaged in a struggle for subsistence, his attitude toward the police, the missions, the social agencies, the Salvation Army, and the various charities and churches that aid him is one of thoroughgoing unemotional antagonism. Toward the railway police, it is one of open warfare. Most of these attitudes are reciprocated to some degree. The transients constitute a real burden upon the resources of the community, and are assumed to be a danger to property and morals. . . .

Although officials view the transients as a semi-criminal element and pursue a more or less systematic policy of repression, the attitude of the local resident may be quite different. As a matter of fact, communities in which the police policy is most drastic may be receptive to transients because they have not been "overworked." Many experienced hobos boast of avoiding the jails and shelters, and relying for food and lodging on the less formal methods of "bumming" bakeries, groceries, and back doors, of panhandling, and a variety of technics euphemistically called "living off the country." These range from petty theft to odd jobs. Lodging may be found in boxcars on sidings, in haystacks, barns, under bridges, in city parks, cheap flophouses, office buildings, and most important, in established jungles. With notable exceptions, the assumption that the hobo is responsible for much damage to property seems unwarranted. Stealing vegetables from a field or groceries from a parked truck is a universal practice, but major theft seems to be unusual.

The traditional classification of the vagrant as a criminal may be a rationalization for the natural animosity of a relatively stable society toward the stranger. The tendency for "the road" to become a definite and recognized American pattern may break down this outgroup identification, and eventually affect the institutional procedures. Should this occur, a modification of the antisocial behavior of transients could be expected since the present patterns are for the most part so clearly functional. There is no reason to suppose that the motivation which induces hundreds of thousands to adopt the life of the road will disappear in the near future. In the face of powerful deterrents, the transient pattern becomes more and more an acceptable and recognized mode of behavior.

CROSS REFERENCES TO STANDARD TEXTS *

Barnes, *Society in Transition*, Chaps. 2–4.
Bernard, *American Community Behavior*, Chap. 2.
Bloch, *Disorganization*, Chap. 19.
Brown, *Social Pathology*, pp. 499–500.
Cuber and Harper, *Problems of American Society*, Chap. 14.
Elliott and Merrill, *Social Disorganization*, Chap. 28.
Faris, *Social Disorganization*, pp. 454–465.
Gillin, *Social Pathology*, Chap. 19.
———— and others, *Social Problems*, Chaps. 7, 8.
Herman, *Approach to Social Problems*, pp. 203–228.
Landis, *Social Policies in the Making*, Chaps. 3, 22–24.
Lemert, *Social Pathology*, pp. 84–85.
Merrill and others, *Social Problems*, Chaps. 11, 14–15.

Mihanovich, *Current Social Problems*, Chap. 2.
Neumeyer, *Social Problems and the Changing Society*, Chap. 5.
Nordskog and others, *Analyzing Social Problems*, Chap. 2.
Odum, *American Social Problems*, Chap. 8.
Phelps and Henderson, *Contemporary Social Problems*, Chap. 10.
Reinhardt and others, *Social Problems and Social Policy*, Chaps. 8–9.
Weaver, *Social Problems*, Chaps. 4, 22.

* For complete bibliographical reference to each text, see page 13.

OTHER BIBLIOGRAPHY

Nels Anderson, *Men on the Move*, Chicago: University of Chicago Press, 1940.
M. K. Bennett, "Population and Food Supply: The Current Scare," *The Scientific Monthly, 68:* 1 (January 1949): 17–26.
A. M. Carr-Saunders, *World Population*, New York: Oxford University Press, 1936.
Henry Hill Collins, Jr., *America's Own Refugees: Our 4,000,000 Homeless Migrants*, Princeton: Princeton University Press, 1941.
Robert C. Cook, *Human Fertility: The Modern Dilemma*, New York: William Sloane Associates, 1951.
Maurice Rea Davie, *Refugees in America*, New York: Harper & Bros., 1947.
Imre Ferenczi, "Freedom from Want and International Population Policy," *American Sociological Review*, 8 (1943): 537–542.
Lyonel C. Florant, "Negro Internal Migration," *American Sociological Review*, 7 (1942): 782–791.
D. V. Glass, ed., *Introduction to Malthus*, New York: John Wiley & Sons, 1953.
Everett Cherrington Hughes and Helen MacGill Hughes, *Where Peoples Meet*, Glencoe, Illinois: The Free Press, 1952.
R. R. Kuczynski, "Population: History and Statistics," *Encyclopaedia of the Social Sciences*, 12 (1934): 240–248, 253–254.

Paul H. Landis, *Population Problems: A Cultural Interpretation*, New York: American Book Co., 1943.
Frank Lorimer and others, *Foundations of American Population Policy*, New York: Harper & Bros., 1940.
Carey McWilliams, *Factories in the Field*, Boston: Little, Brown and Co., 1939.
Adena M. Rich, "Current Immigration Problems," *Social Service Review*, 21 (1947): 85–106.
Victor Roterus, "Effects of Population Growth and Non-Growth on the Well-Being of Cities," *American Sociological Review*, 11 (1946): 90–97.
Henry S. Shryock, Jr., and Hope Tisdale Eldridge, "Internal Migration in Peace and War," *American Sociological Review*, 12 (1947): 27–29.
T. Lynn Smith, *Population Analysis*, New York: McGraw-Hill Book Co., 1948.
Edwin H. Sutherland and Harvey J. Locke, *Twenty Thousand Homeless Men*, Philadelphia: J. B. Lippincott Co., 1936.
Dorothy Swaine Thomas, *Migration Differentials*, New York: Social Science Research Council, 1938.
William I. Thomas and Florian Znaniecki, *The Polish Peasant in Europe and America*, 2d ed., New York: Alfred A. Knopf, 1927, 2 vols.
Warren S. Thompson, *Plenty of People*, New York: Ronald Press Co., 1948.

Jacques Vernant, *The Refugee in the Post-War World,* New Haven: Yale University Press, 1953.

Caroline F. Ware, "Emigration," *Encyclopaedia of the Social Sciences,* 5 (1931): 488–493, and "Im-

migration," *ibid.,* 7 (1932): 587–595.

Pascal Kidder Whelpton, "A History of Population Growth in the United States," *The Scientific Monthly,* 67 (1948): 277–288.

REVIEW QUESTIONS

1. To what does *Life* attribute the great increase in population since 1800?
2. Why does *Life* regard Thomas Malthus as too gloomy?
3. What kinds of social conditions have stimulated public opinion in favor of immigration? against immigration?
4. What is the distinction between the old and the new European immigration?
5. What is happening to our aliens?
6. How do we limit immigration? How do our laws attempt to define the "quality" of the newcomers?
7. What are the "quota" laws? How do they utilize the national origins plan?
8. What are the exempt and the preferred classes among immigrants?
9. What are some of the proposals for further restriction of immigration?
10. Does immigration increase unemployment? What was the immigration situation during the depression of the 1930's?
11. How did our immigration quota law function during World War II?
12. Are immigrants disproportionately responsible for crime?
13. What kinds of organizations have raised the cry of "America for the Americans"?
14. What kinds of organizations are now working for fair play for refugees and other immigrants?
15. What are some of the current proposals for relaxing the quota laws?
16. What did the establishment of quotas for certain oriental peoples accomplish? Would the extension of such arrangements to other Asiatics make similar contributions?
17. How can a degree of flexibility be introduced into the immigration laws?
18. Distinguish between the several kinds of Puerto Rican migrant to this country. Are their numbers increasing?
19. What is the work agreement that Senior refers to? What is a recruiting agency?
20. How extensive is our transiency pattern in the United States?
21. Differentiate between the hobo and the tramp. How firmly is this distinction adhered to among transients?
22. Caplow claims that vagrancy or transiency "exists to some extent within all highly developed civilizations." To what extent does he believe that it is similar throughout the world?
23. How broadly does Caplow think that transiency has been accepted as a cultural pattern in the United States?
24. From the materials presented in this chapter, what now strike you to be some of the outstanding population problems? Why?

City and Country Dwellers

As URBAN and industrial America evolved, it brought into being the production assembly line. This complex arrangement co-ordinates mechanical contrivances and men in order to offer to the world a steady stream of automobiles, electric refrigerators, radios, airplanes, and atomic bombs. For periods each day, millions of men and women learn to subordinate their personalities—even to erase them—to a rhythmical and thoughtless routine in return for earnings.

And the assembly-line spirit, as it evolves, has its counterpart in the spirit of depersonalization, anonymity, and mass action which developed in urban and rural slums and in colorless nonslum residential areas. It permeates the crowded commutation back and forth between home and factory, the union meetings and union organizational structure, the machine-made recreation of bars, movies, radio, television, and even the home, which is partly decentralized into maternity wards, restaurants, sleeping quarters, dance halls, and funeral "homes," to mention but a few of the offshoots. Hence, Allport, viewing one such depersonalized individual, asks, "Throughout the day Sam is on the go, implicated in this task and that—but does he, in a psychological sense, *participate* in what he is doing? Although constantly *task-involved,* is he ever really *ego-involved?*" In the answer to these questions lies at least a partial insight into many pressing contemporary rural and urban social problems.

Our perspective on problem situations in other sections of rural and urban America tends to be warped by our own backyard and location within it. To illustrate, slums are costly to us all both financially and socially whether we live in them or not, as Rumney and Shuman suggest in their compilation of statistics, but those who do not live or work or visit in slums seldom realize this.

The problems occasioned by city and country conditions of living together range through many fields, and only a few of the ones more directly related to the man-land relationship are outlined in this chapter. Rose presents a careful sociological study of the living arrangements of unattached persons. As he says, "the inadequacy of housing for unattached persons . . . is not being given the degree of public or expert attention that would seem to be merited by its seriousness." The Supreme Court of the United States ruled on May 3, 1948, that restrictive covenants are unenforceable, but private agreements and neighborhood pressures still help to preserve racial ghettos. *Fortune* raises the question of whether or not street traffic will strangle our cities and outlines briefly some of the prices we pay for street traffic congestion. Whetten shows how the suburban movement has not only attracted people from the cities but has also depopulated rural areas and placed great strains on suburban institutions. Hill, as a result of his study of population changes in the wealthy farm state of Wisconsin, asks if farm *people* are expendable—if they are to be permitted to exhaust themselves by selective migration.

Problems created by urban-rural differentials and migrations appear in other chapters, especially in the discussions of educational (10), economic (11), and delinquency and crime (17) problems.

Is the Urbanite Ego-involved in His Tasks?
Gordon W. Allport

Gordon W. Allport (1897–   ), professor of psychology, Harvard University; editor, *Journal of Abnormal and Social Psychology;* president, American Psychological Association, 1939. Principal works: with P. E. Vernon, *Studies in Expressive Movement* (1933); with Hadley Cantril, *Psychology of Radio* (1935); with H. S. Odbert, *Trait-Names* (1936); *Personality* (1937); with Leo Postman, *Psychology of Rumor* (1947); *The Individual and His Religion* (1950); *The Nature of Personality* (1951); and *The Nature of Prejudice* (1954).

Take, for example, Citizen Sam who moves and has his being in the great activity wheel of New York City. Let us say that he spends his hours of unconsciousness somewhere in the badlands of the Bronx. He wakens to grab the morning's milk left at the door by an agent of a vast Dairy and Distributing system whose corporate manœuvers, so vital to his health, never consciously concern him. After paying hasty respects to his landlady, he dashes into the transportation system whose mechanical and civic mysteries he does not comprehend. At the factory he becomes a cog for the day in a set of systems far beyond his ken. To him (as to everybody else) the company he works for is an abstraction; he plays an unwitting part in the "creation of surpluses" (whatever they are), and though he doesn't know it his furious activity at his machine is regulated by the "law of supply and demand," and by "the availability of raw materials" and by "prevailing interest rates." Unknown to himself he is headed next week for the "surplus labor market." A union official collects his dues; just why he doesn't know. At noontime that corporate monstrosity, Horn and Hardart,

swallows him up, much as he swallows one of its automatic pies. After more activity in the afternoon, he seeks out a standardized day-dream produced in Hollywood, to rest his tense, but *not* efficient mind. At the end of his day he sinks into a tavern, and unknowingly victimized by the advertising cycle, orders in rapid succession Four Roses, Three Feathers, Golden Wedding and Seagram's which "men who plan beyond tomorrow" like to drink.

Sam has been active all day, immensely active, playing a part in dozens of impersonal cycles of behavior. He has brushed scores of "corporate personalities," but has entered into intimate relations with no single human being. The people he has met are idler-gears like himself meshed into systems of transmission, far too distracted to examine any one of the cycles in which they are engaged. Throughout the day Sam is on the go, implicated in this task and that,—but does he, in a psychological sense, *participate* in what he is doing? Although constantly *task-involved,* is he ever really *ego-involved?*

From "The Psychology of Participation," *Psychological Review, 53* (1945): 117–132, pp. 121–122 quoted.

The Cost of Slums

Jay Rumney and Sara Shuman

Jay Rumney (1905–   ), professor of sociology, Newark Colleges, Rutgers University. Principal works: *Herbert Spencer's Sociology* (1933); *The Science of Society* (1935, rev. ed. with Joseph Maier, 1953); *English Sociology in the Twentieth Century* (1945); and with Sara Shuman, *Social Effects of Public Housing* (1944); *The Cost of Slums in Newark* (1946). Sara Shuman (1919–   ), research assistant, Newark Housing Authority.

The Financial Cost of Slums

The following table gives a general idea of the extent to which slums and blighted areas in various cities contribute to the cost of their maintenance. These ratios are not comparable because the studies on which they are based were made by very different methods. Therefore, it would be incorrect to conclude from the table that the blighted area in Hartford contributed twice as much to its support as did the Atlantic City slum.

In some cases the revenue refers to the potential income from taxes levied on the property in the area, in other cases it is computed from the actual income from taxes, allowance being made for delinquencies. Some of the investigations include revenue from sources other than property taxes. On the expenditure side there are as many variations in the methods of determining the cost of services in the slum areas. Although, for these reasons, the figures for the various cities cannot be compared, they show that in slums costs consistently exceed revenues. . . .

The Social Cost of Slums

There have been numerous investigations, in the past 15 years, showing the high incidence of illness, fires and anti-social behavior in slums as compared with the city average, or good residential areas in the city. A number of these studies are summarized below. . . .

Detroit, Michigan, 1938.[1] In comparison with a normal residential area, the slum area had—

3 times as many deaths from pneumonia
10½ times as many deaths from tuberculosis
6 times as many infant deaths
15 times as many crimes

Birmingham, Alabama, 1940.[2] The four districts with the worst housing had the highest proportion of problem families. More than two-thirds of the housing was reportedly sub-standard

[1] City of Detroit Housing Commission, *Fifth Annual Report,* 1938.

[2] Housing Authority of the Birmingham District, *Social and Economic Survey of the Birmingham District,* 1940.

RATIO OF EXPENDITURES TO REVENUE IN SLUMS IN 13 AMERICAN CITIES

		Expenditures	Revenue	Ratio
Cleveland, Ohio	1932	$1,356,978	$ 225,035	6.0
Atlantic City, N. J.	1933	153,372	17,071	9.0
Chicago, Ill.	1933	3,200,000	586,061	5.5
Elizabeth, N. J.	1933	220,739	47,317	4.7
Hartford, Conn.	1933	465,697	104,244	4.5
Indianapolis, Ind.	1933	92,775	11,312	8.2
Boston, Mass.	1934	310,624	44,800	6.9
Birmingham, Ala.	1935	2,132,923	317,086	6.7
Camden, N. J.	1935	201,534	44,723	4.5
Atlanta, Ga.	1935	74,380	7,539	9.9
Toledo, Ohio	1935	18,040	4,229	4.3
Los Angeles, Cal.	1942	4,610,244	2,070,000	2.2
Newark, N. J.	1942	552,219	167,462	3.3

From *The Cost of Slums in Newark,* Newark: Housing Authority of the City of Newark, New Jersey, 1946, pp. 28–29, 32–34.

and more than 45 per cent of the families were involved in economic, social or health difficulties in 1940. Because of the extent of the problems in these areas they also received the largest amount of economic assistance, social adjustment and health service.

An earlier study, 1936,[3] gave the following results:

	Blighted Areas	City
Fire per square mile	131.0	54.0
Infant deaths per 1,000 births	76.8	63.8
All deaths per 1,000 population	14.3	10.5
Reportable diseases per 1,000 population	31.6	19.1

Washington, D. C., 1940.[4]

	Substandard Tracts	City
Tuberculosis deaths per 100,000 population	177.0	89.1
Pneumonia deaths per 100,000 population	101.0	80.3
Infant mortality per 1,000 births	62.0	46.8

Denver, Colorado, 1941.[5] Infant mortality rates in some of the worst housing districts was more than five times those of the best sections of the city. Juvenile delinquency in 1932–36 in these districts was 64.8 per 1,000 of the school population as compared with 29.5 for the city as a whole. . . .

Philadelphia, Pennsylvania, 1943.[6]

	Public Housing	City
Juvenile delinquency per 1,000	1.84	2.84
Adult offenses per 1,000	.66	33.18
Tuberculosis death rate, per 1,000	.33	5.98
Pneumonia death rate per 1,000	.33	5.86

[3] Jefferson County Board of Health, *Final Statistical Report of Surveys of the Blighted Areas*, 1936.
sults:

[4] U. S. Senate, subcommittee of the Committee on the District of Columbia, *A Resolution Authorizing an Investigation of the Program of the National Capital Housing Authority, Hearings* on S. Res. 184, Part 1, 1944.

[5] University of Denver Reports, *Housing in Denver*, Bureau of Business and Social Research and the School of Commerce, Accounts and Finance, 1941.

[6] Philadelphia Housing Authority, *Homes for War Workers and Families of Low Income*, 1943.

Fires were reduced from 28 before the project was built, to 1 in the same area.

Los Angeles, California, 1944.[7]

	Blighted Areas	Good Areas
Incidence per 10,000 persons (nurse home visits)		
Tuberculosis	705	91
Communicable diseases	69	14
Venereal diseases	13	1
Health Service	356	54
Fire alarms	256	142
Police arrests	350	100
Juvenile delinquency cases	68	10

Pittsburgh, Pennsylvania, 1944.[8]

	Public Housing	Low Economic Area
Per cent of illegitimate births	6.9	13.1
Deaths per 1,000 population	11.8	22.0
Infant mortality per 1,000 births	41.6	71.0
Infectious diseases per 1,000 pop. under 15 yrs	56.6	43.8
Juvenile delinquency per 10,000 pop. 10–17	383.0	570.0

. . . The United States.[9] Slums and blighted districts comprise about 20% of the metropolitan residential areas and contain 33% of the population, yet they contribute—

45% of the major crimes
50% of the arrests
55% of the juvenile delinquency
60% of the tuberculosis victims
50% of the disease
35% of the fires
45% of the city service costs
          and only
  6% of the tax revenues (real estate).

[7] Planning Commission of the City of Los Angeles, *Comparison of Blighted and Good Areas in Los Angeles*, 1945.

[8] Bureau of Social Research, Federation of Social Agencies of Pittsburgh and Allegheny County, *Juvenile Delinquency in Public Housing*, 1944, and *Vital Statistics of Public Housing Residents*, 1945.

[9] W. E. Reynolds, *Post-War Urban Redevelopment*, Federal Works Agency, Washington, 1939.

Living Arrangements of Unattached Persons
Arnold M. Rose

Arnold M. Rose (1918–   ), professor of sociology, University of Minnesota. Principal works: with Gunnar Myrdal and Richard Sterner, *An American Dilemma*, 2 vols. (1944); *The Negro in America* (1944); with Caroline Rose, *America Divided* (1948); and editor, *Race Prejudice and Discrimination* (1951).

Social problems receive differing degrees of attention from those who are affected by them and from the general public. This seriousness of the problem—measured either by the number of persons affected or by the degree of the need—is not necessarily an index of the amount of interest in the problem. This paper will describe a social problem—the inadequacy of housing for unattached persons—and suggest its degree of seriousness. This problem is not being given the degree of public or expert attention that would seem to be merited by its seriousness, although the closely-related problem of housing for families is being given a large amount of public and expert attention. A companion article [1] will describe the variations in interest in the problem for the unattached and attempt to get at some of the reasons for the variations and the general lack of interest. By means of these two articles, we hope to demonstrate the lack of correlation between the existence of a social problem and the amount of interest in it.

In 1940 there were at least 12,285,000 unattached persons in the United States.[2] They constituted about 9.3 per cent of the total population, or about 14.2 per cent of the population 20 years of age and over. It is probable that there were many more unattached persons during the depths of the depression in the 1930's (when it was esti-

mated that there were 1½ million homeless, mostly unattached),[3] and in the midst of the war boom of the 1940's (when it was estimated that 30 to 50 per cent of those who migrated to boom cities were at least temporarily unattached).[4] For the purposes of this paper, an unattached person will be regarded as one who does not have parents, collateral families, spouse, or children living with him and who has not joined an institution which incidentally provides living arrangements. Although this definition is occasionally unsatisfactory in deciding whether certain marginal persons are unattached or not, it is the one used because it is desired to examine the living arrangements of those persons in urban American society who do not live either as a member of a family or in an institutional home.

The existence of large numbers of unattached persons is a modern phenomenon, a consequence of the Industrial Revolution that came to England in the late 18th century and to the United States in the middle of the 19th century. The requirements of industry and the attractions of cities, as well as the relative inability of rural areas to support all the persons born in them, brought unprecedented numbers of single, young people from farms to cities, and from small cities to large cities.[5] Most of them ultimately got married, but for a while they were unattached, and some never got married at all (almost 10 per cent of the popula-

---

[1] Arnold M. Rose, "Interest in the Living Arrangements of the Urban Unattached," [*American Journal of Sociology*, 53 (1947–48): 483–493.]

[2] This figure includes lodgers in private households, one-person families, members of quasi households (such as lodging houses and hotels), servants and hired hands living in private households. The figure is a minimum estimate because it does not include related persons living with families (no matter how remote the relationship), those who had no place of residence at all, transients who were unknown to their neighbors and thus were missed by the Census.

[3] John N. Webb, *The Transient Unemployed*, Washington: Works Progress Administration, 1935, pp. 1–3, 12, 88–93.

[4] Howard B. Myers, "Defense Migration and Labor Supply," *Journal of the American Statistical Association*, 37 (March, 1942), 75.

[5] John H. Clapham, *An Economic History of Modern Britain*, Cambridge, England: University Press, 1926, esp. chapters 2 and 14. Adna F. Weber, *The Growth of Cities in the Nineteenth Century*, New York: Columbia University, 1899, esp. chapters III–VI.

From "Living Arrangements of Unattached Persons," *American Sociological Review*, 12 (1947): 429–435.

tion never gets married).[6] A special type of these migrants were those who emigrated from Europe: beginning with the new immigration from southern and eastern Europe about 1880, the proportion of unattached immigrants rapidly rose until immigration was all but cut off by the first World War and the restrictive laws of 1921 and 1924.[7] The Industrial Revolution also brought the business cycle and increased seasonal and casual employment.[8] Since these had the social effect of reducing the marriage rate and breaking up families, they irregularly increased the number of unattached.[9] There are other miscellaneous types of unattached whose numbers were relatively stable: the "homeless men," the temporarily unattached (including some travelling salesmen), and some prostitutes.

Although large numbers of unattached persons have been in American cities for almost a hundred years, few suitable living arrangements for the bulk of them have developed. The "Y's," the Eleanor Clubs, the Arlington Farms, and other organized residences built to meet their housing needs serve only a small proportion of the unattached. Most of the unattached live in what might be termed the cast-offs among residences: they live in rooming houses or lodging houses that have been converted from family residences; they live in spare rooms rented out in family homes. The problem can be conceived of as one of cultural lag. It would seem that society still considers the condition of being unattached as either a temporary or an unusual condition. This would help to explain the fact that few residence structures, with the exception of hotels that are usually too expensive for permanent residence, have been built to meet the special needs of the unattached, either by private

capital or by the federal government. It has been shown, by the example of the Mills' Hotels in New York City, as well as by other lodging houses built about the same time in other cities, that even the cheap lodging house can be made adequate for the residents and profitable for the owners. But although the Mills' Hotels are over 40 years old, practically no other private capital has entered the field of building houses for the unattached poor, and not much more for those unattached who earn fairly good wages and salaries. There are some exceptions, of course, but apparently even most of these date back to pre-World War I days, and many have a philanthropic motive behind them. The federal government has, during the last fifteen years, concerned itself with clearing slums and providing adequate housing for the underprivileged, especially in cities. But, until the need for labor in war industries practically forced the government to start building dormitories in 1942, it paid no attention to the housing needs of the unattached in cities.[10] This was true even when the well-motivated slum-clearance projects drove lodgers out of family households and razed rooming houses. City planners and students of housing have tended to ignore the unattached in their studies and plans for the past 25 years.[11] All these facts suggest that there is a blind spot in the thinking of the experts as well as of the general public when it comes to the housing of the unattached.

The income of the average unattached person is half to two-thirds as large as that of the average whole family,[12] and if the indigent unattached were eliminated from consideration, and age of income earners held constant, this discrepancy would be even less. Further, since families always have more than one member, and usually not all the members are income-earning, the average fam-

[6] U. S. Bureau of the Census, *Sixteenth Census of the United States: 1940. Population*, Vol. IV, Part I, Washington: Government Printing Office, 1943, p. 17.

[7] Marcus L. Hansen, *The Immigrant in American History*, Cambridge: Harvard University Press, 1940, p. 150. Caroline F. Ware, "Immigration," *Encyclopaedia of the Social Sciences*, VII, New York: The Macmillan Co., 1932, pp. 587–594.

[8] Karl Pribram, "Unemployment," *Encyclopaedia of the Social Sciences*, XV, New York: The Macmillan Co., 1935, pp. 147–162 (esp. pp. 147–148, 152).

[9] Samuel A. Stouffer and Paul F. Lazarsfeld, *Research Memorandum on the Family in the Depression*, New York: Social Science Research Council, 1937, pp. 139–186. Robert C. Angell, *The Family Encounters the Depression*, New York: Charles Scribner's Sons, 1936. Ruth S. Cavan and Katherine H. Ranck, *The Family and the Depression*, Chicago: University of Chicago Press, 1938.

[10] The federal government through C.C.C. camps and F.S.A. labor camps, did provide some very inexpensive barracks for certain types of unattached persons in rural areas during the 1930's. Also the government entered the housing field briefly during the first World War to build some temporary barracks for unattached war workers.

[11] Unpublished manuscript by the author, "Interest in the Living Arrangements of the Urban Unattached." [See footnote 1.]

[12] National Resources Committee, *Consumer Incomes in the United States, Their Distribution in 1935–36*, Washington: Government Printing Office, 1938, pp. 4, 18. U. S. Bureau of the Census, *Sixteenth Census of the United States: 1940. Population and Housing, Families, Income and Rent*, Washington: Government Printing Office, 1943, p. 9.

ily member has only a little over one-third the income available to him of the average unattached person ($411 compared to $1151 in 1935–36).[13] Considering these facts, the income of the average unattached person could not be said to be so relatively low that he could not afford adequate housing.

At any given income level, the average unattached person spends a greater proportion of his income for housing than does the average family.[14] The average urban tenant family paid a monthly rent of $25.22 in 1940, while the average urban tenant person living by himself paid $19.47.[15] Considering what the unattached person got for his money, and the smaller number of his needs that could be satisfied by his housing (for example, he can seldom have food preparation, laundering, social amusement, minor recreation, carried on in his one room that families can have in their homes or apartments), the rent for unattached persons could be said to be relatively high. Available studies[16] of rooming houses—taken as the currently single most important form of living arrangement for self-supporting unattached persons—show that the furniture in furnished rooms is often cheap and insufficient, the sanitary facilities are frequently outmoded and insufficient, the presence of vermin is frequent, the rooms are often not kept clean, there are seldom any common rooms or other facilities for the entertainment of guests. These facts make the relatively high rents for furnished rooms seem even higher. The greater turnover of population in furnished rooms also does not justify high rents, since vacancies are of shorter duration in furnished rooms than they are in unfurnished apartments for families, so that the vacancy rates per year are about the same.[17]

Alternative explanations do not seem to stand up therefore, and we are obliged to seek the conditioning factors of inadequate living arrangements for the unattached in lack of public and expert interest or knowledge.

The actual living arrangements for the unattached can best be considered under the three historical types of unattached persons who made most use of them, the immigrants, the hoboes and other indigents, and the native-born, self-supporting migrants to cities. Unattached immigrants lived mainly as roomers and boarders in the homes of families of their own nationality. Other living arrangements developed logically out of this: The boarding boss system was one in which a single man or a couple took in boarders as a business. The cooperative non-family group was one in which a number of unattached persons got together to rent a house or apartment, buy furniture and hire a housekeeper (or sometimes do their housekeeping themselves). The labor camp had a boarding boss system where the "boss" was an employee of the company rather than an independent entrepreneur. Mainly for immigrant women, there were charitable or semi-charitable boarding homes sponsored by religious, ethnic, or philanthropic groups. Immigrants also lived in regular lodging, boarding and rooming houses. There were grave inadequacies in all these types of living arrangements, the most important of which were extreme overcrowding, poor sanitary facilities and lack of cleanliness, invasion of the privacy of families, and lack of opportunity for recreation and social contact. After the laws restricting immigration were passed in the early 1920's, the number of foreign-born in the United States began to decline, and the proportion of unattached declined still more rapidly, so that their living arrangements are no longer a major problem. A similar problem exists today, however, for Negroes who have migrated from the rural South to the urban North.

The chief type of residence for unattached "homeless men" and the unemployed is the common lodging house. Although some of these call themselves "hotels" they are very cheap, and are the poorest form of living arrangements for the unattached. Most of them can be classified under one of three types: the room-type lodging house (where several beds are put in a single room,

---

[13] National Resources Committee, op. cit., pp. 4, 18.

[14] Ibid., p. 30.

[15] U. S. Bureau of the Census, Sixteenth Census, Population and Housing, op. cit., p. 9.

[16] See, for example: (1) Community Service Society, "Life in One Room," mimeographed report by the Committee on Housing, Community Service Society, New York, 1940. (2) Information Bureau on Women's Work, Toledo, Rooms, Inquire Within, Toledo, Ohio, 1927. (3) James Ford, Slums and Housing, Cambridge: Harvard University Press, 1936. (4) Edith Abbott, The Tenements of Chicago: 1908–1935, Chicago: University of Chicago Press, 1936. Many other sources, most of them written before World War I, are available on the characteristics of rooming houses.

[17] Chicago Plan Commission and Work Projects Administration, Residential Chicago, Vol. I of the Chicago Land Use Survey, Chicago Plan Commission, 1942, pp. 232–234.

Although these data were not published until 1942, they were collected in 1938—before the war housing shortage.

which is otherwise like a room in a rooming house), the cell-type lodging house (where each lodger has his own small cell, very scantily furnished and not separated at their tops from similar cubicles), the "flophouse" (which is usually simply a bare room where lodgers sleep on boards, sometimes covered with thin mattresses and sometimes with piles of rags or newspapers). In addition to the common commercial lodging house, there are the model lodging houses built by philanthropists (the Mills' Hotels, for example), the missions sponsored by religious groups, and municipal lodging houses built by cities for men and women who are completely without funds. These indigent persons devise all sorts of other living quarters for themselves: they sleep in taverns, in all-night movies and restaurants, in police stations, on park benches, in doorways and hallways, in vacant lots and abandoned buildings. During the depression of the 1930's, they even built whole villages, commonly called "Shantytowns," for themselves in public grounds. Among the unemployed during the depression, families were better off than unattached persons, since they were less often evicted and more often supported in their homes by relief payments.

Single young people who came from rural areas to cities to earn their living and make their fortunes in expanding commerce and industry at first lived in boarding houses. These were usually quite adequate to satisfy the social and recreational needs of a home for the unattached as well as their physical needs (for a place to sleep, eat and do laundering). But these did not have enough flexibility with respect to time for eating and coming home at night, and did not have enough privacy, to be popular. When the restaurant and the rooming house came into existence, the boarding house declined, until by the year 1900 they were very few in number in large cities.

Living in rooming houses, or as a roomer in a family home, is now the most popular form of living arrangement for unattached persons. Most of the available evidence indicates that rents in rooming houses are high for the services rendered, and that furniture and other facilities tend to be inadequate. The unattached person who comes from a given social level or who has a given income sinks a step or two in the quality of furniture he uses when he lives in a rooming house rather than in a family home. The roomer in a family home, on the other hand, has as wide a variety of quality in his living quarters as families

do, since families of all income levels—except at the very top—take in roomers.

The organized boarding home and the residence club also exhibit a wide variety as far as their quality is concerned, but they are non-profit making and sometimes even partially supported by philanthropic groups so that their rents are not high in comparison to what the renter receives. They have also become more popular in recent decades, since their restrictions have been reduced and since some of them have eliminated the practice of charging for meals whether they are taken or not. Such homes are not numerous, relative to other forms of living arrangements, and the number of rooms in them has not kept pace with the increasing demand. It requires a fairly large accumulation of capital to build and maintain an organized boarding home or residence club.

Insofar as private capital has gone into providing housing for the unattached, it has gone into the building of hotels. Hotels are not for the unattached alone, of course, but cater in large measure to transients and moderately well-to-do families. Hotels provide a fairly satisfactory living arrangement for high salaried unattached persons, but they are too expensive as a permanent residence for the bulk of the unattached. A development of the last several decades, which combines some of the desirable features of both the hotel and the family home, is the apartment hotel. It is used by unattached persons as well as by families. The apartment hotel also tends to be expensive and sometimes requires a high initial outlay of money for furniture and other household essentials.

The rooming house and the lodging house, which together provide housing for a very large proportion of unattached persons, are usually converted structures.[18] That is, they were originally constructed to serve functions other than those which they are now serving. Few, if any, buildings are built with the intention of making rooming houses out of them. Thus, rooming houses tend to be old buildings, and not always suited for their purpose. Their sanitary facilities are old fashioned and perhaps worn out. The rooms are not spaced properly for individual living. There may be no fire exit, and if there is one it is likely to be through someone's private room, which is usually

---

[18] The rank-order correlation, for the community areas of Chicago, between the proportion of units in converted structures and the proportion of roomers in the population is +.69.

kept locked. In various other ways, the rooming house in a converted structure is an undesirable place to live.

The most rapidly growing cities, region of country held constant, are the ones which have the largest proportions of unattached. Rapidly growing cities have many advantages, but their housing facilities probably tend to be insufficient in number. The areas within a city in which the unattached can find furnished rooms tend to be the poorest ones. They are areas from which upper and middle class families have moved, and which industry and commerce are invading. Or they are along noisy arteries of transportation. The areas of Chicago in which the unattached are concentrated have been found by correlation,[19] to be areas of economic blight, of commercial and industrial invasion, of old structures in poor condition, of dwelling units lacking such facilities as inside bathrooms and central heat, of overcrowded residences owned by absentee landlords. These areas also have well-defined social characteristics: relatively few children in the population, a high sex ratio, proximity to red light districts, high venereal disease rate, high schizophrenia rate. Thus, the areas are characterized by a high degree of social disorganization to which the unattached contribute after they have been there a while. They have two main advantages for the residents: (1) They tend to be near most of the places of work. (2) They tend to be near the centers of amusement,[20] and have characteristic service institutions which especially cater to the needs of the unattached.

World War II increased the disadvantages of unattached living. The pressure on living quarters for the unattached increased so markedly that they were living in all the odd corners that unemployed men found for themselves during the depression of the previous decade.[21] The federal government belatedly went into the field of building housing for the unattached 15 months after it began on war housing for families.[22] But the dormitories were insufficient in number,[23] and generally not nearly as adequate as the war housing built for families. Private owners of furnished rooms raised rents markedly for the unattached, despite O.P.A.* price ceilings because the O.P.A. could not adequately police the large number of furnished rooms and because the new rooms or "improved" rooms put on the market were not subject to O.P.A. control for their initial pricing. The O.P.A. even hurt the unattached as far as hotel rooms were concerned, because hotels found it more profitable to charge daily rates rather than weekly rates and so forced their guests to move every 5 days. This situation continues after the war, but, of course, there is an acute shortage of housing for families also.

The over-all picture, then, is one of inadequate living arrangements for the great bulk of the unattached population in American cities. There has been little interest, either on the part of private capital or on the part of the general public (as manifested through government) in remedying the situation. It is not mainly a matter of charity, since most of the unattached have relatively more money than do family heads to spend upon their living quarters. It is largely a matter of getting either government action or of getting private capital together to finance large projects. The new projects can be modeled after the existing residence clubs, if the aim is to provide adequate living arrangements to meet the needs and desires of the unattached. The various occupational groups will need somewhat different facilities.

The very poor among the unattached need hous-

[19] Coefficients of rank-order correlation, for the community areas of Chicago, have been worked out between each of the indicated characteristics and the proportion of roomers in the population. The data have been taken from a variety of sources: (1) Chicago Plan Commission and Work Projects Administration, *Residential Chicago*, Vol. I of the *Chicago Land Use Survey*, Chicago, 1942; (2) Arthur J. Todd *et al.*, *The Chicago Recreation Survey, 1937*, Chicago: The Chicago Recreation Commission, 1937; (3) U. S. Bureau of the Census, *Sixteenth Census of the United States: 1940, Population and Housing: Chicago, Ill.*, Washington: Government Printing Office, 1942; (4) Chicago Department of Health, *Health Data Book*, Chicago: Dept. of Health, 1939, pp. 85–86; (5) R. E. L. Faris and H. W. Dunham, *Mental Disorders in Urban Areas*, Chicago: University of Chicago Press, 1938, Appendix B.

[20] The rooming house areas in Chicago (1937) have a disproportionately large number of liquor establishments, billiard halls, cabarets, penny arcades, movie theatres. They have a low number of bowling alleys and dance halls.

[21] Lyonel C. Florant, "The Impact of the War on the Norfolk Negro Community," (Unpublished manuscript, Richmond: Population Study, Virginia State Planning Board, May 26, 1942). Mary Skinner and Alice S. Nutt, "Adolescents Away from Home," *Annals of the American Academy of Political and Social Science*, 236 (November, 1944), 51–59.

[22] The Defense Housing Act of October 14, 1940, as amended January 21, 1942.

[23] Unpublished statistics made available through the courtesy of Miss Corienne K. Robinson, National Housing Agency, Federal Public Housing Authority (Letter, August 28, 1942).

* Office of Price Administration, a Federal agency during World War II period.—*Eds*.

ing badly also. It is questionable whether private enterprise would find it profitable to build for this group, although the Mills' Hotels and other philanthropy-sponsored lodging houses built around the turn of the century made regular profits. Today, because of increased building costs and higher land values, housing for hoboes and the unemployed would probably have to be a matter for philanthropic or government support. New building would not be necessary if remodeling went along with conversion of older buildings. It might be that some social service functions should be given along with board and lodging for indigents,

in order to increase their capacity for self-support.

Some of the unattached persons themselves will continue to prefer to live in rooming houses, lodging houses, or one of the other forms of living arrangements now predominant. There are aspects of privacy, anonymity, cheapness, about some of these places which they prefer, and certainly no one should try to force them to live elsewhere. But the United States can do what Great Britain had accomplished by the 1920's—give these places a continual and thorough inspection, and require them to meet certain minimum standards of cleanliness and completeness.

The United States Supreme Court Declares Restrictive Covenants Unenforceable

The historical context in which the Fourteenth Amendment became a part of the Constitution should not be forgotten. Whatever else the framers sought to achieve, it is clear that the matter of primary concern was the establishment of equality in the enjoyment of basic civil and political rights and the preservation of those rights from discriminatory action on the part of the States based on considerations of race or color. . . .

White sellers, one of whom is a petitioner here, have been enjoined from selling the properties to any Negro or colored person. Under such circumstances, to suggest that the Negro petitioners have

been accorded the same rights as white citizens to purchase, hold, and convey real property is to reject the plain meaning of language. . . .

The power of the federal courts to enforce the terms of private agreements is at all times exercised subject to the restrictions and limitations of the public policy of the United States as manifested in the Constitution, treaties, federal statutes, and applicable legal precedents. Where the enforcement of private agreements would be violative of that policy, it is the obligation of courts to refrain from such exertions of judicial power.

From Chief Justice Vinson's 6–0 opinions of the Court in the cases of Shelley v. Kraemer and McGhee v. Sipes et al. and of Hurd v. Hodge et al. and Urciolo et al. v. Hodge et al., all decided May 3, 1948 (respectively cases numbered 72, 87, 290, and 291, October term, 1947).

Will Traffic Strangle Our Cities?
From "Fortune"

Those who suffer from traffic congestion in New York City face a maddening truth: although their pain can be relieved, it will probably go on indefinitely. In the world's largest traffic sore, their suffering seemed to approach unbearable proportions this year. Week after week, the postwar

surge of vehicles grew more and more gaseous, torpid, and impenetrable. Less than a year after gas rationing was lifted, over 390,000 cars, trucks, taxis, and busses were writhing their way through the stone grid of Manhattan Island every working day. For the fume-drenched people in those ve-

From "The Traffic Outrage," Fortune, 34: 4 (October 1946): 122–129, 254, 257, 260, 263, 264, p. 123 quoted. See also "A Day in New York's Traffic Jungle," ibid., pp. 266–267.

hicles it would be meager consolation to know that the city's traffic was now almost exactly what it had been at the all-time peak in 1941. After three years of rationed driving on relatively open streets, the congestion seemed worse than it had ever been before.

Today, everyone who drives into New York City knows what to expect. Morning and afternoon, cars from New Jersey, Westchester, and Long Island choke up some $325 million worth of six-lane parkways and expressways that have been hailed as the world's finest. A single flat tire or road repair job, by cutting three lanes to two, can mean a half-hour's delay for hundreds of cars. Any weekday morning a driver is doing well if he can cross the George Washington Bridge and crawl down the six miles of the west-side elevated highway to midtown Manhattan in twenty-five minutes. Once off the highway, he will begin his worming way across town at three miles an hour or so, pushed by busses, shouldered by taxis, blocked by trucks. After 9:30 A.M. he may well find every midtown garage and parking lot jammed solid, so he will circle for perhaps twenty or thirty minutes looking for a stretch of free curb space. He may gamble on parking on an "express street." If caught, it will cost him a $15 ticket for a first offense and up to $50 for a fourth. But the police are scarce and many drivers now accept infrequent fines as a reasonable charge for the parking they cannot buy. A few will pay for curb space with Christmas gifts to the cop on their street. By 10:00 A.M., cars have clotted solidly along Manhattan's midtown and downtown streets and a third hard core has formed across the river in downtown Brooklyn. By late afternoon, after the congestion has reached its peak, the tortuous disentangling of homeward cars begins to choke the main traffic arteries again.

Within these daily churning tides of vehicles, the city's *real* traffic sufferer—the non-driver—fights his painful way. In busses, trucks, streetcars, taxis and on foot, he strains to move along city streets that have been narrowed from four lanes to two by private cars parked bumper to bumper. His pain will be much worse if some heedless double parker has squeezed the passage to a single lane. A few blocks' progress in bus or cab is such a time-wasting labor of sudden starts and infuriating halts that he will usually prefer the faster and less laborious struggle on foot through sidewalk swarms. . . .

The struggle against too much traffic is very much the same in every other big U. S. city today. The statistics elsewhere are smaller, and no other city suffers from the natural traffic bottlenecks peculiar to the shape of Manhattan Island. But in Chicago and Philadelphia and San Francisco, in Boston and Baltimore and a score of other cities, traffic congestion has become a postwar agony for millions. What it is now costing the U. S. in lost time, labor, and trade is anybody's guess. Estimates run as high as $25 million a day. For the New York City region, the loss is certainly far above the unchallenged guess of $1 million a day, which New York's Regional Plan Association ventured in 1927. . . . The toll in human and mechanical efficiency is incalculable. Such losses, however, are only a fraction of the total traffic bill.

The toll is so serious that it is pertinent to ask whether traffic congestion might not one day choke all cities to death. The answer lies in a paradox: the traffic that chokes is precisely what makes cities thrive. Traffic makes business good, and good business makes more traffic. And no one yet knows how much traffic a big city can stand before the costs of congestion cut too deeply into the profits that heavy traffic creates. Presumably when that point is recognized and reached, those who have profited will provide their own remedies to reduce traffic congestion to the viscosity of healthy, heavy circulation. Such remedies might include a total parking ban throughout Manhattan's congested areas, night deliveries by big trucks, and construction of off-street loading berths in buildings that are now taking over the public streets and sidewalks as private terminals.

But there is little chance that these or other traffic remedies will soon be applied in New York City. For in the worlds largest city there are, monstrously enlarged, all the basic barriers to traffic relief—political, legal, psychological, and financial. Because of these, the city's traffic victims are helpless. Those who could help them have stubbornly refused to apply even the simple medicines that could ease their suffering. These self-centered groups, blind to the costs of traffic congestion, see only the costs of the relief—and will not pay them. Congested traffic, in short, still seems too profitable to too many people.

Suburbanization
Nathan L. Whetten

Nathan L. Whetten (1900–   ), professor of sociology and dean of the Graduate School, University of Connecticut. Principal works: *Studies of Suburbanization in Connecticut* (1936–1939); with C. C. Zimmerman, *Rural Families on Relief* (1938); and *Rural Mexico* (1948).

One of the most important internal population shifts in history has been taking place gradually over a period of years in the United States. I refer to the clustering of people in and around the periphery of our larger cities. According to the United States Census of 1950, considerably more than half of our total population (56 per cent) is now living in what are defined as the 168 standard metropolitan areas. These include the major cities together with the outlying districts which are deemed to be closely integrated with and dependent upon them. The total number of inhabitants living in these metropolitan areas now reaches 84 millions as compared with only 66 millions in the rest of the entire nation.[1]

Not only are the majority of our people concentrated in the metropolitan areas, but the population of these areas is increasing at a much more rapid rate than the rest of the country. During the past ten years, for example, the population of the metropolitan areas increased 21 per cent as compared with an increase of only 5.7 per cent in the rest of the country outside of the metropolitan areas. Stated in another way it may be said that 80 per cent of the population growth in the U.S.A. during the past ten years occurred in the metropolitan areas. This is particularly interesting when we realize that the metropolitan areas are the ones with the lower birth rates and that the greatest natural increases in population are found in the more isolated rural districts. This can only mean a tremendous shifting of peoples in toward the metropolitan centers.

There are many factors which have contributed towards metropolitan growth in the United States. Improvements in farm technology have enabled a smaller number of persons on farms to raise the

agricultural products required to feed a rapidly increasing total population. The output per farm worker has doubled since 1910,[2] while tremendous improvements have been made in the yields of crops and herds. For example, the average cow in 1790 produced 1,000 pounds of milk per year; today the average cow produces 5,000 pounds, and there are records of animals producing as much as 50,000 pounds. There was a 30 per cent increase in the yield of corn per acre between 1920 and 1945. The farm tractor has been rapidly replacing the horse as a source of power on the farm, and this is freeing land for the growing of food that formerly had to be used for the growing of feed for farm animals. Thus, the number of horses in the United States declined from 21½ millions in 1915 to only 2 millions in 1950.[3]

All of this has tended to free an increasingly large proportion of the inhabitants to engage in non-farm work. In 1820, 72 per cent of the working population of the United States was engaged in agricultural pursuits and only 28 per cent in non-agricultural pursuits. By 1940, these percentages had shifted to 82 per cent engaged in non-agricultural pursuits and only 18 per cent in agriculture. In 1940 there were only about as many agricultural workers in this country as there were in 1885 when the total population was less than 75 millions.[4] In the meantime, accelerated industrialization, the expansion of international commerce, the rapid growth of the service industries and improved transportation and communication facilities have encouraged the congregation of peoples into large urban aggregates. Thus, 30.7 per cent of the total urban population now live in the 25 largest cities.

[1] Calculations from "Population of Standard Metropolitan Areas: April 1, 1950," U. S. Bureau of the Census, 1950 Census of Population, Preliminary Counts, Series PC-3, No. 3.

[2] *Agricultural Outlook Charts.* BAE, USDA, Washington, D. C., October, 1950, p. 5.

[3] Data from BAE, USDA.

[4] Carl C. Taylor and others, *Rural Life in the United States* (New York: Alfred A. Knopf, 1949), p. 246.

From "Suburbanization as a Field for Sociological Research," *Rural Sociology, 16*: 4 (December 1951), 319–330.

But while numerous recognizable forces have been violently hurling population elements in the direction of the larger cities, many of these elements have failed to stick permanently in the cities but have bounced back a short distance into what might be referred to as the suburban areas. In fact, it is really in the suburban areas where the most rapid increases in population are now taking place. Of the 84 million people living in the metropolitan areas in 1950, 35 million, or 42 per cent, live in the areas outside of the central cities. In these areas, the increase during the last ten years was 35 per cent as compared with an increase of only 13 per cent for the central cities. Fully half of the population increase for the entire nation since 1940 has occurred in the metropolitan areas *outside* of the larger cities.[5]

Since we know that employment opportunities for the vast majority of the local inhabitants do not exist in the suburban areas, we must conclude that the common pattern for the gainfully employed is to use the suburb quite largely as a place to sleep and in which to keep their families while they commute to their jobs in the larger cities. Thus, *The New York Times* recently estimated that about half of all the passengers now carried by American railroads are commuters, and that on a typical working day about half-a-million people move by train into lower Manhattan and the business section of Brooklyn from Long Island, Connecticut, Westchester and New Jersey.[6] This is in addition to the thousands who pour into New York by auto and bus each day from suburban areas in all directions.

There is considerable evidence, moreover, to the effect that the process of suburbanization is not confined to the fringes of the larger cities, but that it is taking place even around the smaller ones. After a careful analysis of the 1940 census data Donald J. Bogue, of Scripps Foundation for Population Research, recently concluded that cities of all sizes are experiencing suburbanization. He states that from 1930–40, "the diffusive movement into suburban areas was characteristically a rural one. Upstart hinterland cities of all sizes lying outside the range of direct competition with the metropolis began to grow faster than the central and satellite cities. In doing so they tended to accumulate rural populations about themselves. Even small cities were diffusing into rural territory and

fostering their own tiny suburbs. Almost every area which grew at a pace in excess of the national rate of growth in the 1930–40 decade was accomplishing decentralization in one of its forms."[7]

The suburban movement is undoubtedly a two-way process. Not only is the population from the city moving out to the nearby rural areas but the adjacent farm areas confronted by the expansion of cities are themselves caught up in the suburban movement. This may begin when a daughter from the farm family finds employment in a city office building, or a son gets a job in a department store. Part of the farm is later sold off as building lots; the agricultural enterprise becomes a part-time farm and the farm family gradually takes on a semi-urban orientation. The rural non-farm population has increased from 39 per cent of the total rural population in 1920 to 56.9 per cent in 1950 (preliminary census data).

In view of all of these developments one might well be wondering whether or not the really typical American of the future will be found living in *Suburbia* rather than in Mainstreet, in Plainville, or in Middletown. Certainly such a prospect does not seem very far fetched in the Northeast.

Reasons for Migration to the Suburban Areas

The reasons for migrating to the suburbs are as diverse as the backgrounds of the suburbanites themselves. It should be said at the outset that not all clusters of population within a metropolitan area, but outside the central city, are suburbs. In those instances where the central city has merely overflowed its boundaries and spilled into the immediately adjourning territory, the built-up section is too closely identified with the parent city to be classified as a suburb. We would also rule out from consideration so-called industrial suburbs or satellite cities where industry has moved out some distance away from the central city and resulted in a second smaller industrialized city. In other words, what we have in mind here is the residential suburb situated at some distance from the city and necessitating daily commuting on the part of large numbers of the urban employed population.

Speaking of this group, then, one may ask why they should prefer to live at considerable distance from their work and undergo all of the inconveniences of several hours' daily travel than to live

---

[5] U. S. Bureau of the Census, *op. cit.*

[6] *New York Times,* Sunday, February 11, 1951.

[7] Donald J. Bogue, *Metropolitan Decentralization: A Study of Differential Growth,* Scripps Foundation Studies in Population Distribution—No. 2, August, 1950, p. 16.

in the city. In this connection the following facetious definition of a commuter may be of interest:

"A commuter is a man whose life is divided into two principal parts: coming and going. He is a goat in antelope's clothing. He feeds on timetables, asterisks, and footnotes. He thrives on duplicated scenery. His life is one long series of two-hundred-yard dashes." [8]

Generally speaking, suburbanization may be viewed as both a flight from the city and as an attraction towards the romantic ideal of country living. In the former case, it is a sort of escapism and may reflect deep insecurities of urban life.[9] While people find themselves dependent on the city for earning a livelihood, they flee from it as a dangerous place in which to live and especially in which to rear a family. The first aspect of this is perhaps associated with the problem of health. People have long regarded the city as a less healthful place to live in than the country. This belief may be illustrated, and will perhaps be reinforced, by an article appearing recently in *Life Magazine* under the title of "Science." The opening sentence reads: "Every time a New Yorker takes a breath he inhales 69,000 particles of grit and dust. His lungs are nearly black. Almost everywhere in the United States the city dweller lives in a sea of coal, grime, sulphuric acid, ammonia and other aerial garbage that—whether or not fog may be involved—is generally called 'smog.' " [10] The magazine contains a full page of colored photographs purporting to show a comparison between the lungs of a farmer and those of a New Yorker. The farmer's lungs appear to be a beautiful pink color while those of the New Yorker are dark and dingy. The caption for the farmer's lungs reads: "Farmer's lungs are still clean and pink after 39 years of life, most of it spent in rural parts of the U. S. where he breathed no lung-clogging smoke or smog." The caption for the New Yorker's lungs reads: "New Yorker's lungs after 40 years are blackened by carbon. Carbon itself is harmless to body but in city smoke it may be accompanied by harmful chemicals." The writer does not wish to pass judgment on the validity of these "scientific" observations but merely to call attention to the fact that they fit in very nicely with the traditional conception of the harmful effects of city life.

Closely related to the problem of health is that of congestion as a reason for people leaving the cities. Couples with growing children are especially apprehensive about the lack of lawns, play grounds and space between dwellings as well as about congestion within the dwellings. The problem of what the youngsters can do during their spare time when not in school, or otherwise closely supervised, looms large to parents. The impersonal relations characteristic of the city are also a repelling force especially to families with young children. The next-door neighbors may be completely unknown; they may have widely differing social backgrounds and standards; and this may cause a deep feeling of insecurity among parents and children alike.

In the immediate future, fear of the atom or the hydrogen bomb may accentuate the flight from the larger cities. It has been remarked that what would be the most attractive bombing run in the world extends from Boston to Washington, D. C. Over this stretch, the bombing crews would never be out of sight of choice bombing targets. Thoughts of what bombs might do to city water systems, power lines and transportation systems, with consequent interruptions to food supply, will probably stimulate still more people to search even more diligently for a secluded spot in some inconspicuous outlying area. A glance at the ads in the New York papers these days will show that real estate dealers are already fully aware of the sales value of the bomb in disposing of rural properties.

In addition to the forces of expulsion there are also forces of attraction at work. These become especially effective because the majority of our urban population either have rural backgrounds themselves or they are only a generation or two removed from the land. Those who were born in rural areas may reflect on their childhood and, perhaps forgetting the more unpleasant aspects, develop nostalgia for the open space, the green sod under foot, the clear skies overhead and the abundance of fresh air and sunshine. Even those who were born in cities may have developed a yearning for life in the country from the reminiscences of their parents, from summers spent on the farm with their grandparents, or perhaps from the glowing accounts of rural living as depicted in literature. The idealized small community setting with its *gemeinschaft* relations has a romantic appeal to persons enmeshed in the complexities of an urbanized *gesellschaft* type of life.

[8] H. I. Phillips, "The 7:58 Loses a Passenger," *Collier's*, April 11, 1925, p. 11.

[9] Solon T. Kimball, *The New Social Frontier: The Fringe*, Michigan AES, Special Bulletin 360 (East Lansing: June, 1949), p. 16.

[10] *Life*, February 12, 1951, pp. 60–61.

The prospect of home ownership looms large as an attraction to many suburbanites. Many seem to feel that until they can move into a home which they can claim as their own, even though heavily mortgaged, they are merely living a temporary existence. They feel blocked from home ownership in the city and turn towards the outlying districts. In this connection it is interesting to take note of the construction of hundreds of what might be called "suburban developments" with their neatly arranged rows of compact little houses all of the same variety, each placed on a neat little plot, sometimes even equipped with antenna for the installation of television and often containing a picture window through which the young family might obtain a nice view across the street into the neighboring picture window. Usually these houses all sell for about the same price; and payments are arranged like rent on a monthly basis so that complete home ownership automatically becomes effective after 15, 20, or 25 years. It would be interesting to learn to what extent these little homes become permanent habitations for large numbers of families or to what extent they prove to be only temporary. Another interesting problem in this connection is whether or not the smallness of the house in these compact suburban developments tends to limit the size of the family of the occupants. In other words, does the family tend to confine its size to the available room, and if so, can it be said that contractors and construction companies exert unintended influence on the birth rate in this type of development?

The suburban movement also includes what might be called a "back to the land movement." This encompasses a large population of urban workers who, for various reasons, prefer to live in what might be referred to as the "deep country" out beyond any of the closely built-up developments or compact villages. These are rather venturesome souls who have a deeper love for mother nature and for the land than for close neighbors or for some of the modern conveniences and services available in compact communities. These open-country dwellers are usually faced with the necessity of providing their own water systems, septic tanks and cesspools, garbage disposals, and many other items. An automobile is as indispensable as a cook stove and many families would feel unduly isolated without two cars, especially when the husband drives one to work. These families quickly learn that it is expensive to bring plumbers, electricians and carpenters from the city, and the husband or wife soon learns to putter around the house fixing leaky water taps and even wielding a respectable paint brush. All of this provides variety which breaks the monotony of specialized urban employment.

These back-to-the-land movements gather momentum during depression years when urban families begin searching for ways of cutting down rent and supplementing the family income by means of part-time farming. Families with medium or low incomes feel that by raising a few chickens, planting a vegetable garden, and growing their own fuel they can reduce living expenses. The movement is by no means confined to periods of economic depression, however, but is associated generally with the improvement of rapid transportation systems and the expansion of metropolitan communities. As early as 1929 it was estimated that 70 per cent of the farms in southern New England were operated on a part-time basis.[11] There are many other tracts of land of considerable size that are merely used as residence areas for families entirely dependent on city incomes. A few of the occupants of these holdings may be persons trying to retain their Wall Street salaries while paying a farmer's taxes; but, most of them are probably middle and upper class families who are not so much concerned about the economics of the arrangement as about the alleged satisfactions of privacy and real country living. The deep-country home has an especially strong appeal to people having sufficient income to equip it with all of the modern conveniences and gadgets now available to urban residents.

In addition to these various groups entering the suburbs from the cities, mention should also be made of those persons who move directly in toward the suburban areas from the smaller and more remote towns, villages and rural areas. We do not know how large this group is. Among them one would probably find local school teachers, persons employed in the local service industries, vegetable gardeners, and many others. Some of these undoubtedly are motivated by the desire to avail themselves of the "cultural," educational and shopping facilities found only in a large metropolis. They, like many others, are frankly seeking certain advantages offered by a highly urbanized society yet trying to avoid the disadvantages.

---

[11] John D. Black, *The Rural Economy of New England* (Cambridge, Mass.: Harvard University Press, 1950), p. 562.

Thus, they move in toward the big city, but they do not move all the way in.

Problems for Research

There are many aspects of suburbanization which we do not now thoroughly understand and which, in view of the growing importance of the movement, need to be explored. Among these we shall mention a few with the understanding that the list is by no means exhaustive.

1. There is need for further identification and classification of suburban populations into meaningful groupings or community types.[12] These probably would include aristocratic suburbs inhabited by wealthy families with their clipped hedges, country clubs and servants, and their severe restrictions against "undesirables"; compact suburban developments; quaint and picturesque country villages; and the more expansive rural areas containing part-time farms and non-farm dwellings interspersed among the farms.

2. There is need for more information regarding the extent and selectivity of the migration. We have tried to indicate that while the movement to the suburban areas includes people with a wide range of social and economic characteristics, nevertheless there does appear to be a concentration of persons in certain categories. The most common among these seem to be family units consisting predominantly of young adults and young children who are struggling to become home-owners, who yearn for life in a small community setting or who seek to obtain for themselves the traditional alleged values of rural life while retaining their urban employment. These characteristics have been observed in studies carried on in Connecticut, New York, and Michigan, but the studies have been somewhat limited in scope and need to be extended into other areas. Since the suburban movement, as was suggested earlier, involves migration both from the city outward and from the rural areas inward, information about the social and economic differences of the people participating in the various streams would be valuable.

3. There appears to be need for information concerning the impact of suburban living on personality. Do such factors as dual community allegiance, hours of daily commuting, the absence of the husband or father from the family, and the predominance of women during the daylight hours, in any way influence the personalities of the children or of the other members of the family?

4. Data are needed concerning the acquiring of social status in relation to the suburban movement. Are young families who want to "get ahead" impelled to move from the city merely in order to "keep up with the Joneses" even though *Suburbia* offers no particular advantages to them in personal well-being? Is there a pattern of mobility from suburb to suburb which is pursued or is expected as one advances in the social hierarchy?

5. There is need for intensive studies of social conflict in local areas affected by the suburban movement. Ofter the suburbanites enter as newcomers to older established communities and when they arrive in large numbers, greatly disturb the *status quo*. They tend to carry into the older communities new ideas with reference to the expansion and modernization of schools, water systems, playgrounds, and community centers. Although many move to the suburb looking for a *gemeinschaft* type of society, they want to find it in a *gesellschaft* setting. They may admire the homey atmosphere of a rural community, but they often deplore the inconveniences of rural life and the unbusinesslike dealings of local merchants, servicemen, and officials. They sometimes meet "head on" with farmers and older residents interested in preserving the heritage of the past and who view with alarm any proposals which might have the effect of increasing local taxes. Thus, social cleavages quickly develop between the newcomers and the older residents. Sometimes the influx of newcomers so profoundly affects the structure of the local community that there is obvious need for re-examination, and possibly reorganization, of the local governmental structure.

6. The relations of the suburban areas to the parent city need to be thoroughly studied. The urban administrator is likely to hold the point of view that the suburbs are "strangling" the city. He would probably argue that a city such as New York, which serves as motherland for hundreds of surrounding towns and villages, must provide costly services such as traffic and parking facilities, police protection, water supply and waste disposal for nearly twice the city's regular population yet can tax only those inhabitants living within its political boundaries.[13] On the other

---

[12] Further study should also be made of the adequacy of the delineation and classification of standard metropolitan areas used by the United States Census in 1950.

[13] W. Laas, "Suburbs are Strangling the City," *New York Times*, June 18, 1950.

hand, it can be shown that in some instances the revenue-producing advantages rest with the cities and towns where the industrial and commercial establishments are located rather than with the suburban communities where the workers live. This is often the case when the suburbanites are drawn primarily from the lower income groups rather than from the upper.[14] Some would argue for the reorganization of governmental units obliterating political boundaries in the metropolitan areas and displacing these by a sort of city state organization which would definitely tie the central city and its contributory areas closely together

into one governmental unit so that coordinated planning and administration could prevail. This proposal would probably not be very enthusiastically received by the suburbanites, especially those searching for the small community situation. But, undoubtedly, there is need for further study of the political structure and its implications.

7. We should be interested in learning to what extent the suburbanites are actually experiencing the realization of their aspirations in the suburban area. It might well be asked whether or not, for certain groups, suburban living turns out to be a delusion; and to what extent it is a "way out" for those who find themselves caught up in the web of urban occupations yet who feel insecure and thwarted by the prospect of continued residence in the city.

In conclusion, it should be pointed out that conscientious pursuit of the answers to some of these questions would lead one beyond the generally recognized boundaries of sociology and deep into such neighboring disciplines as psychology, political science and land economics. The very nature and complexity of the problems would call for inter-disciplinary cooperation. That such cooperation would be both stimulating and feasible, however, seems obvious where important and meaningful projects are involved.

[14] A forceful example of this is found in the towns of East Hartford and Manchester, Connecticut. In East Hartford is located the famous Pratt and Whitney Aircraft Corporation. At the present time about one-half of the total town revenue of East Hartford comes from the taxes of this concern. Many of the Pratt and Whitney workers, however have moved to comparatively low-cost housing developments in the neighboring town of Manchester. It is claimed that the tax revenue from some of these housing developments in Manchester is insufficient to pay for the additional burden placed on the town as a result of the required expansion of school facilities, fire and police protection, water supply and other public services. Manchester is thus faced with rising taxes to meet these needs. On the other hand, East Hartford has been able to lower the tax rate because of the revenue from Pratt and Whitney.

Are Farm People Expendable?
George W. Hill

George W. Hill (1900–   ), chairman, department of sociology and anthropology, University Central de Venezuela, Caracas, Venezuela. Principal works: *Man-Land Adjustment* (1938) and *Man in the "Cut Over"* (1942).

Through the ceaseless experiments of scientists in our agricultural laboratories and the effective distribution of their findings through such media as the state-wide extension service, Wisconsin's farmers are learning that their natural or physical resources are exhaustible.

What about people in agriculture? The human resource. Here we are still in an exploitative era. The soil, humus, rainfall, and the flora, all of these we have learned to our sorrow are not expendable. People are! At least so we continue to promote our agricultural policy.

Is this a harsh statement? Let's try to get at the facts.

To start with we have to remind ourselves of the obvious, which we so often completely overlook. Wisconsin has grown up. It's come of age. No longer is there a steady influx of young, ambitious immigrants of child-bearing age. No longer is there the need of buying the neighboring farm or two or three near-by farms to find a place for the sons who wish to follow farming. No longer is the population pyramid that of a rapidly growing vigorous society. On the contrary, the age pyramid

From "Recent Population Changes in Rural Wisconsin," *Rural Sociology, 12* (1947): 169–172, pp. 169–171 quoted.

is becoming inverted; it is losing its wide base made up of the young ages and the concentration by ages is shifting toward the top of the pyramid.

Unfortunately, separate statistics for the farm population are not available for census years earlier than 1920. But even in the short span between the census of 1920 and the one in 1940, remarkable differences are present to show the aging of our farm population. In 1920, 36.1 per cent of the farm population was under fifteen years of age, and 20.0 per cent was over forty-five years. In 1930, these percentages were 33.8 and 23.2, and in 1940, they were 28.3 and 28.4. In other words the proportions of the aged and the very young in our farm population have been reversed.

The foregoing contrasts would be even greater were census data available to permit calculations for a span of two or three generations. . . .

Farmers are becoming citified. They, too, ride in automobiles, use tractors, have running water; a large number have indoor toilets, electricity, etc. But just as their city brethren, they likewise have learned the art of family limitation. . . .

Wisconsin's farm families best able economically and socially to have and to rear children are the ones who are contributing less and less to the maintenance of our farm population. Certainly we can't say they have any "surplus" to throw off to the cities. In fact, many of them . . . already find themselves approaching a deficit status. Added to the lowering fertility is an ever-increasing tempo of cityward migration. With more than half of our counties losing between 45 and 60 per cent of their 20 to 24 year-old girls in the past decade, it's time that we began to think of human conservation. Without these girls there won't be many farmer marriages, and whatever bachelors may be worth otherwise, they won't long assure us an agricultural population.

CROSS REFERENCES TO STANDARD TEXTS *

Barnes, *Society in Transition*, Chaps. 9–12.
Bernard, *American Community Behavior*, pp. 22–34, 141–147, 274–279, 324–328.
Bloch, *Disorganization*, pp. 44–49, 167–169.
Brown, *Social Pathology*, Chaps. 22–24.
Cuber and Harper, *Problems of American Society*, Chaps. 18–19.
Elliott and Merrill, *Social Disorganization*, Chaps. 22–23.
Faris, *Social Disorganization*, pp. 127–136, 459–469.
Gillin, *Social Pathology*, Chaps. 19, 22–23.
——— and others, *Social Problems*, Chaps. 11–12.

Herman, *Approach to Social Problems*, pp. 78–94, 132–145, 195–196, 473–476.
Landis, *Social Policies in the Making*, Chap. 2.
Lemert, *Social Pathology*, p. 30.
Merrill and others, *Social Problems*, Chap. 2.
Mihanovich, *Current Social Problems*, Chap. 2.
Neumeyer, *Social Problems and the Changing Society*, Chaps. 3–4.
Nordskog and others, *Analyzing Social Problems*, pp. 267–272, 631–636.
Odum, *American Social Problems*, Chap. 5.
Phelps and Henderson, *Contemporary Social Problems*, Chap. 10, also pp. 181–182, 394–398.
Reinhardt and others, *Social Problems and Social Policy*, Chaps. 6–7.
Weaver, *Social Problems*, Chap. 24.

* For complete bibliographical reference to each text, see page 13.

OTHER BIBLIOGRAPHY

Donald J. Bogue, *Metropolitan Decentralization: A Study of Differential Growth*, Oxford, Ohio: Scripps Foundation for Research in Population Problems, 1950.
———, *The Structure of the Metropolitan Community: A Study of Dominance and Subdominance*, Ann Arbor: University of Michigan, 1949.
Ralph Borsodi, *Flight from the City*, New York: Harper & Bros., 1941.
Thomas R. Carskadon, "Houses for Tomorrow," 3d ed., Public Affairs Pamphlet No. 96, 1947.
Miles L. Colean, *Renewing Our Cities*, New York: Twentieth Century Fund, 1953.
Edward H. Faulkner, *Plowman's Folly*, Norman: University of Oklahoma Press, 1943.

———, *A Second Look*, Norman: University of Oklahoma Press, 1947.
Walter Firey, "Ecological Considerations in Planning for Rurban Fringes," *American Sociological Review*, 11 (1946): 411–421. Amos H. Hawley, "Discussion," *ibid.*, pp. 421–423.
———, *Land Use in Central Boston*, Cambridge: Harvard University Press, 1947.
Noel P. Gist and L. A. Halbert, *Urban Society*, 3d ed., New York: Thomas Y. Crowell Co., 1949.
C. Horace Hamilton, "The Social Effects of Recent Trends in the Mechanization of Agriculture," *Rural Sociology*, 4 (1939): 3–19.
Ernest Theodore Hiller, *Houseboat and River-Bottoms People*, Urbana: University of Illinois Press, 1939.

A. B. Hollingshead, "Human Ecology," Part 2 in A. M. Lee, ed., *Principles of Sociology*, 2d ed. rev., New York: Barnes & Noble, 1951, pp. 65–118.

———, "Re-examination of Ecological Theory," *Sociology and Social Research*, 31 (1946–47): 194–204.

Solon T. Kimball, *The New Social Frontier: The Fringe*, East Lansing: Michigan Agricultural Experiment Station Special Bulletin 360, June 1949.

J. H. Kolb and Edmund deS. Brunner, *A Study of Rural Society*, 3d ed., Boston: Houghton Mifflin Co., 1946.

David E. Lilienthal, *TVA—Democracy on the March*, New York: Harper & Bros., 1944.

Charles P. Loomis and J. Allan Beegle, *Rural Social Systems*, New York: Prentice-Hall, 1950.

Carey McWilliams, "Small Farm and Big Farm," Public Affairs Pamphlet No. 100, 1945.

Robert K. Merton, Patricia Salter West, Marie Jahoda, and Hanan C. Selvin, eds., "Social Policy and Social Research in Housing," *Journal of Social Issues*, 7 (1951): 1 and 2.

A. G. Mezerik, *The Revolt of the South and the West*, New York: Duell, Sloan and Pearce, 1946.

Arthur E. Morgan, *The Small Community*, New York: Harper & Bros., 1942.

Lewis Mumford, *The Culture of Cities*, New York: Harcourt, Brace and Co., 1938.

Howard W. Odum, *Southern Regions of the United States*, Chapel Hill: University of North Carolina Press, 1936.

Richard W. Poston, *Small Town Renaissance*, New York: Harper & Bros., 1950.

Arthur Raper, *Tenants of the Almighty*, New York: Macmillan Co., 1943.

Svend Riemer, *The Modern City*, New York: Prentice-Hall, 1950.

Edgar A. Schuler and others, *Outside Readings in Sociology*, New York: Thomas Y. Crowell Co., 1952. Chap. 8.

T. Lynn Smith, *The Sociology of Rural Life*, rev. ed., New York: Harper & Bros., 1946.

Nathan Straus, *The Seven Myths of Housing*, New York: Alfred A. Knopf, 1944.

Carl C. Taylor, "The Contributions of Sociology to Agriculture," *1940 Yearbook of Agriculture*, Washington: Government Printing Office, 1941, pp. 1042–1055.

Rupert B. Vance, Gordon W. Blackwell, and Howard G. McClain, *New Farm Homes for Old*, University: University of Alabama Press, 1946.

Robert C. Weaver, *The Negro Ghetto*, New York: Harcourt, Brace and Co., 1948.

Vincent Heath Whitney, "Rural-Urban People," *American Journal of Sociology*, 54 (1948–49): 48–54.

Louis Wirth, "Urbanism as a Way of Life," *American Journal of Sociology*, 44 (1938–39): 1–24.

Carle C. Zimmerman, *The Changing Community*, New York: Harper & Bros., 1938.

REVIEW QUESTIONS

1. To what extent did "Citizen Sam's" activities involve his ego? Of what significance is ego-involvement?

2. In view of the high costs of slums summarized by Rumney and Shuman, what are some of the reasons why slums persist?

3. How extensive is the classification, "unattached persons," in the United States? What kinds of people does it include?

4. Give some of the reasons why you think the problem of housing the unattached person has been neglected. Would you agree with Rose as to the pressing nature of the problem?

5. What was a race-restrictive covenant? For what purposes was it used?

6. Why does *Fortune* assert that although traffic congestion can be relieved, "it will probably go on indefinitely"?

7. Who suffers from traffic congestion? Who benefits from traffic congestion?

8. How does the "explosion" of our cities strain suburban institutions?

9. What forces of expulsion and attraction have brought about the development of Suburbia?

10. Why does Hill think that we are still in an exploitative era so far as the human resources of agriculture are concerned?

11. Why does Hill take a pessimistic view of present tendencies in Wisconsin migration?

PART III

Problem Periods in Family Life

CHAPTER 7

Birth Through Childhood

IN OUR changing society the processes of societal adjustment to changed life conditions occasion maladjustments in customary life experiences. These problem periods occur at critical or transitional ages from conception to the grave. Fortunately modern science is rapidly helping us to cope with some of the more serious of these new problems as well as with others of longer duration.

From time to time controversy has raged over who should have children and how many they should have. In such discussions, misinformation is common with regard to the relative roles of heredity and environment in the formation of the personality. Kornhauser, through his Poll of Experts, summarizes leading testimony on significant aspects of the heredity-environment controversy. Martin outlines the struggle of the Planned Parenthood Federation of America for "better babies." He sums up briefly the present American position on birth control medically and legally and outlines Roman Catholic belief on this point. Oxnam gives the substance of a resolution on planned parenthood signed by 3200 Protestant and Jewish clergymen. Upham, as a former president of the American Medical Association, furnishes the attitude being taken by leading physicians toward child-spacing.

Unfortunately those who have babies do not always want them, and some who do not have babies suffer from not having them. Seeley tells, in a 1946 article, of the "black market" in babies that resulted in New York City from these only partially satisfied needs, but the conditions she describes still persist and are to be found in other cities and, on a smaller scale, in villages and towns. Davis sets forth salient problem aspects of children whose parents have failed to "make a go of it," an increasingly common affliction of American married life.

In homes which have wanted children, Gruenberg mentions an area in which advice is gradually helping people cope with personal and social problems which are common now. He discusses in detail how sex education from an early age in the home and through supplementary aid in the schools can help to launch better adjusted children into society.

Does Heredity Make You What You Are?
Arthur Kornhauser

Arthur Kornhauser (1896–   ), professor of psychology, Wayne University. Principal works: with F. A. Kingsbury, *Psychological Tests in Business* (1924); *How to Study* (1924, 1937); *Psychology for Business Students: Syllabus* (1940); *Detroit as the People See It* (1952); and with Robert Dubin and Arthur M. Ross, eds., *Industrial Conflict* (1954).

"He has his mother's eyes, and her nasty temper, too.". . ."That Jones family is full of brains; they're all smart as a whip.". . ."Naturally, Larry took to drink; look at the old soak his father was."

Are opinions like these valid? Do we *inherit* our strengths and weaknesses, or pick them up as we go?

There is a pleasant illusion to the effect that our good qualities are of our own making, while our bad traits are due to heredity. When it comes to

American Magazine Poll of Experts conducted by Arthur Kornhauser, "Does Heredity Make You What You Are?" *American Magazine* (May 1946). Reprinted by permission.

our children, however, we look eagerly for signs that they have inherited our virtues.

What are the facts? To find out, we took some questions along these lines to a number of the best-qualified experts. They are leading scientists in the field of human heredity—psychologists, biologists, anthropologists, who have made special studies of these problems. They are on the staffs of outstanding universities and research institutes throughout the United States.

We would have liked these authorities to answer such general questions as: How important is heredity in shaping our lives? Or: Does heredity have greater or less influence than environment? But there are no answers to such questions, save in vague generalities.

Heredity and environment are both indispensable. In general, neither can be labeled more important than the other. The part heredity plays is vastly different, depending on which human characteristics are considered and on whether the environment gives people the opportunity to develop their inherited capacities. So the vital questions we put to the experts inquired about *particular* characteristics of people living under normal American conditions.

We focused on 10 important human traits, such as intelligence, temper, energy, etc. Regarding each, the question was how important a person's *heredity* is in causing him to be better or worse than other people in that trait.

Among the 10 characteristics put before the experts, the one in which *heredity* was judged most clearly to play a leading role is *intellectual ability;* that is, how bright or how dull a person is. Here are the experts' answers on that trait:

1. Differences between individuals are determined *almost completely by heredity;* affected little or not at all by normal differences in environment   11%
2. *In large measure by heredity,* but also affected considerably by normal differences in environment   80%
3. *Somewhat by heredity,* but in larger measure by differences in environment   8%
4. *To no significant extent by heredity;* almost completely by environment   0%
5. No judgment possible on basis of existing evidence   1%

More than 9 out of 10 believe that inherited capacity is the major factor in our intelligence.

The experts' conclusions regarding *musical talent* are nearly the same; 4 out of 5 state that superior or poor musical ability depends in large measure on heredity.

A majority of the experts also place 2 other characteristics among those where heredity is most important in accounting for differences between people. These are: first, *dexterity and freedom from clumsiness;* and, second, amount of *energy and vigor.*

At the other extreme, *environment* was judged most clearly predominant in causing people to have *race feelings and prejudice.* More than 9 out of 10 experts declare that feelings against other races are not at all due to a person's heredity.

We also asked the experts about 2 other traits often charged against heredity—*criminal tendencies* and *alcoholism.* The answers definitely deny that the traits of the criminal and the drunkard can be blamed principally on their heredity. Environmental influences are thought more largely responsible by an overwhelming majority of the authorities.

The other 3 characteristics we asked about are: good or bad *disposition* (cheerful, gloomy, etc.), *quick temper,* and degree of *general nervousness.* These traits occupy a middle ground between the two sets already mentioned. Heredity and environment are judged nearly equal in influence for these, but with a slight majority of experts saying environment predominates.

On all these points there are disagreements among the experts, due to the scarcity of clear-cut facts. The final answers are not known. As many as 1 in 5 of the authorities flatly declare that no judgment can be given at present about certain of the characteristics. When leading scientists remain that uncertain, the rest of us have to warn ourselves not to be too sure of our own ideas on the subject.

In sharp contrast, the scientists are definite and in agreement about a physical trait, like eye color. On this, 99 per cent of the answers say "determined almost completely by heredity." Even for the mental qualities judged *most* influenced by heredity this reply is given by only 1 expert in 10. Most of the authorities do not think that any of our mental traits are determined *completely* by our heredity. The right environment can almost always lead to better development of our characteristics.

We put several other disputed points about heredity to the experts. For one thing, many people believe that whenever they see a child who is like his parent in being selfish or dishonest, ex remely ambitious, or lacking ambition, he must have *inherited* these qualities. The authorities unanimously reject this conclusion. They emphasize the fact that children *learn* these traits to a large extent from the example their parents set and the training they give. Though heredity may well play some part, we are never justified in assuming that simply because the same behavior occurs in parent and child, it *must* have come about through inheritance.

Another belief we checked on is the idea that some of the things a parent has learned can be passed on by heredity to his or her children. For example, if a mother, as a girl, developed a special fear of cats, will her children inherit this tendency? Will the fact that a father became a skilled mathematician make his son inherit better mathematical ability than if the father had never studied mathematics? The answer is again practically unanimous that such beliefs are false. Parents cannot change or improve what their children *inherit*. But, naturally, the parents' own development can profoundly affect what they give their children through the *environment* they provide.

The experts also threw into the discard the idea that the thoughts and fears of an expectant mother may be transmitted to her unborn child. They emphasize that there is no way in which this could possibly occur. Certainly not, that is, if it refers to the specific contents of the mother's mind.

A few of them do point out, however, that the mother's emotions, worry, or nervousness may affect the *physical* condition of the unborn infant, and in this way may indirectly make the child more nervous, tense, or emotional than it would otherwise have been. These effects would not be hereditary; they are results of the *environment* inside the mother's body. But the more important fact, on which the experts agree, is that there is no truth to the old idea that particular mental experiences of the mother have specific effects on the child.

One vital theme runs through the experts' replies regarding heredity. It is this: The effects of heredity and environment depend on each other.

No matter what good qualities our heredity gives us, they amount to nothing unless the environment lets them come out. No matter what bad qualities we inherit, the right treatment will make them less bad than they otherwise would be.

Imagine an environment in which children grew up without ever hearing any music. Even remarkable inherited musical talent would get nowhere; it would have no chance to develop. But, given normal circumstances, some of the children become gifted performers, while others cannot learn to carry a tune. Whenever some children are deprived of opportunities to develop any of their abilities, it tends in the same way to waste native talents and superior intellects.

The case is similar for traits like cheerfulness, temper, or energy. For example, insufficient food, or family emotional strains, can go far to ruin what could have been highly favorable characteristics.

Body build or inherited physical defects likewise have altogether different effects on personality, depending on how they are received in particular surroundings. If the person who is unusually short, or ugly, or has dark-colored skin, is treated as an outcast or inferior, then the physical condition results in emotional troubles. With a different social environment, the same individuals might become happy, well-adjusted persons.

In a word, heredity is not something we must submit to in resignation. Rather, the challenge is to find or create environments which will make the most of our hereditary possibilities. It is conceivable that the future may bring drugs, injections, surgery, and new educational methods that will overcome or correct all sorts of inherited mental quirks and defects.

But even now, without looking into the dim future, it is the conviction of most of the experts that our mental characteristics depend in considerable degree on our surroundings. As we improve the conditions under which people grow up, we shall do a much better job of letting each person go as far as his own heredity makes possible.

Birth Control: Where Do We Stand Today?

Ralph G. Martin

Ralph G. Martin (1920–   ), journalist. Author: *Boy from Missouri* (1946); *The Best Is None Too Good* (1948).

Thirty years ago birth control was only a whispered word at a drugstore counter; today it rocks the world.

And what is it?

The simplest definition: population control by contraceptives.

And why does it rock the world?

Because it affects the life and death of millions of people, because it's become one of the great throbbing issues of our time, argued in laws, hot words and papal pronouncements.

Pageant doesn't plan to argue. But it recognizes an urgent need to tear the top off the subject.

You can start on the second floor of an old building on Main Street in Mineola, New York, one of Planned Parenthood Federation's 594 clinics. Why start there? Because Planned Parenthood has become a synonym for birth control, because this Federation is the one big group internationally geared to the problem. They'll send advice and literature to anyone anywhere in the world, but their main concentration is here.

And this Mineola clinic is typical. Everything meticulously clean, a faintly antiseptic smell coming from the doctor's office, and pictures of babies everywhere.

"Some people are surprised to see all these baby pictures," said Registered Nurse Pearl Z. Britting. "They've picked up the idea somewhere that all we want to do is stop women from having babies. And that's just not true. We believe in babies, the more the merrier—as long as women are healthy and can afford them."

She opened a pamphlet and pointed. "That's our charter," she said:

1. To make medical advice on birth control available to married women who want it.

2. To provide a consultant and referral service to physicians for childless couples who desire advice on infertility.

Or you can put it this way: they'll help women to have children and they'll help women to prevent having them (for reasons of health and economics).

Nurse Britting emphasized other things: that the clinic only gave contraceptive information to married women; that their typical patient was a woman well enough to have a sex life, but for whom pregnancy would be dangerous; that fees were based on ability to pay and started from minus-nothing ("we reimburse those who can't afford to pay for transportation"). And they've had 10,000 patients since the Mineola clinic opened in 1935.

The stress was on privacy. Nurse Britting told of another clinic that didn't do so well because it used a cottage near the heart of a small town. "And just about clinic time, all the neighbors would sit out on their porches to see who was coming to the clinic."

They use women doctors only, because patients prefer them. For those women in the middle age group of greatest danger, they also give cancer detection exams, the Papanicolaou smear test. Of the first 1,000 checked, Dr. Evelyn V. Berg sent 525 to their own doctors and clinics for further examination.

Point Two in the clinic charter gears itself to the fact that one out of every 10 couples in this country seemingly can't have children. For them, the clinic gives repeated physical exams of the pelvic area, temperature charts to find the optimum fertility time, and if that doesn't work, the women are turned over to more elaborate fertility clinics [Parenthood Federation operates 28 of the 152 such clinics in this country—*Eds.*]. Treatment success runs to 20 per cent.

What's the next stop? Well, in any discussion of birth control, you'll always hear somebody mention, "Catholic opposition." So you check into it, and it's true. Catholic opposition to birth control is complete and unyielding. And nobody questions the fact that Catholics form the strongest force against it. And why?

From "Birth Control: Where Do We Stand Today? Legally, Medically, Religiously, Politically," *Pageant* (July 1952).

"Do you believe in the teaching and practice of Birth Control?"

THE PUBLIC'S ATTITUDE

■ = YES VOTE

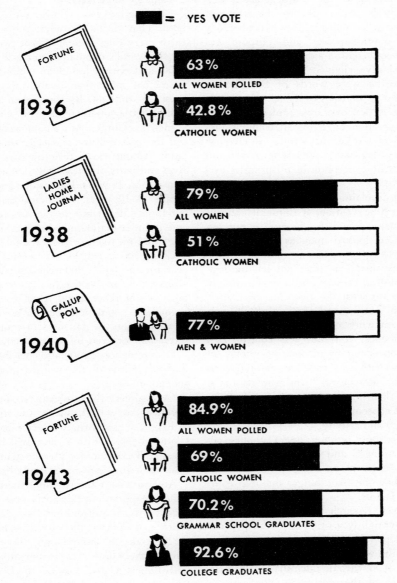

FORTUNE

1936

63% ALL WOMEN POLLED

42.8% CATHOLIC WOMEN

LADIES HOME JOURNAL

1938

79% ALL WOMEN

51% CATHOLIC WOMEN

GALLUP POLL

1940

77% MEN & WOMEN

FORTUNE

1943

84.9% ALL WOMEN POLLED

69% CATHOLIC WOMEN

70.2% GRAMMAR SCHOOL GRADUATES

92.6% COLLEGE GRADUATES

(The Wexton Co. for Public Affairs Committee, Inc. Reprinted by permission from Herbert Yahraes, "Planning Your Family," Public Affairs Pamphlet No. 136, 1948, p. 9.)

To Catholics everywhere, birth control is mainly a moral issue.

Pope Pius XI, in his encyclical "On Christian Marriage," said, "Since the conjugal act is destined primarily by nature for the begetting of children, those who in exercising it deliberately frustrate its natural power and purpose, sin against nature and commit a deed which is shameful and intrinsically vicious."

Equally specific were words of St. Thomas Aquinas. "Next to murder, by which an actually existent being is destroyed, we rank this sin by which the generation of a human being is prevented." And St. Augustine wrote, "Intercourse even with one's legitimate wife is unlawful and wicked where the conception of offspring is prevented."

Their point is plain. Birth control, by which they mean birth prevention, is immoral—always has been and always will be, because it opposes the Natural Law looked upon as binding upon all men. . . .

Catholics say this: God does not tell mothers how many children they are to have. He simply forbids tampering with the functions of nature. There is such a thing as spacing of children within the framework of God's law. It is done through continence, restraint, self control. . . .

Contraception is put by orthodox Catholics in the same class with sins called unnatural, such as homosexual intercourse. "And the reason is that it is like them a perversion, an abuse of the sexual act and consequently a positive destruction of sexual energy and activity."

That's the current position: the Catholics say it's morally wrong * and Planned Parenthood Federation urges it as an economic and social need. Meanwhile the issue bulges out into complicated other factors.

The more you research the subject, the more you realize how tightly it's tied up with the problems of world population. Everybody agrees that huge parts of the world's people are overcrowded and underfed. It's a chronic dilemma that can rip apart the peace of the world. So what's to be done?

Food and health experts suggest improved farming methods, new chemical fertilizers, mass inoculations, a Point Four program of public health. Others recommend migration of surplus

---

* See the following selection for a statement by an eminent clergyman, representative of a widely held Protestant and Jewish viewpoint.

populations to the underdeveloped countries of the world, and still others claim the quickest weapon is birth control.

Here are some facts:

Every second beat of your pulse a new baby is born. That means 25 million more people on this earth every year. It took almost two million years for the world's population to reach 900 million by 1800, and within less than a hundred years that figure has more than doubled (current total almost 2½ billion). By the end of this century it will be half again as large.

Here's a sample: Asia's population *increase* during the past century equals Europe's *total* population. Countries all over the world like Puerto Rico and parts of Africa will double their population within 25 years. India alone added 50 million people in 10 years. If medical science suddenly cut India's death rate to the low American level, and if India maintained her present birth rate— she could fill five earths in a single century.

China has averaged one serious famine every year for the past 2,000 years. An American Red Cross report in 1929 gave these reasons for stopping famine relief there: relief resulted always in immediate population increase which meant increased misery in the form of more hunger and starvation for even more people than before.

Demographers (population scientists) point out that two-thirds of the world's people just don't get enough to eat.

"And unless the problems of underdeveloped countries are solved, one of two things is likely to happen," said Britain's UN representative, Sir Gladwyn Jebb. "Either there will be an outburst of anarchy, or some attempt will be made to solve their problems on Stalinist lines."

And so what's the solution? Is it more important to export new fertilizers and farming techniques or birth control kits?

Some, at least, say the latter:

"Next to the atom bomb, the most ominous force in the world today is uncontrolled fertility," said Robert Cook, *Journal of Heredity* editor. "The scramble for bare subsistence by hordes of hungry people is tearing the fertile earth from the hillsides, plunging millions of human beings into utter misery. The peoples of all nations are rushing into a desperate genetic crisis."

India decided it couldn't wait to find out what was best. It asked the United Nations World Health Organization for help—birth control help —and got it: *a string of beads.*

That string of beads may some day turn out to be one of the most important strings in the world, because it's a method of birth control; it ties in with the rhythm of fertility and sterility occurring in the monthly cycle of a woman's menstrual periods.

"We designed those beads in different colors," said Dr. Abraham Stone, director of the Margaret Sanger Research Bureau, closely affiliated with Planned Parenthood on a research basis. "Pink for the menstrual period, red for the fertile period and green for the safe period. The woman can even wear it as a necklace, but each day she moves a bead, and the color tells her if she can have intercourse without too much danger of conception."

Promoting the project, now part of India's national planning, Dr. Stone set up five pilot clinics early this year, outlined a mass educational program of films and posters, along with a slogan, "India must produce more and reproduce less."

Nobody can safely guess at the success of this project, but Dr. Stone hopes for 60 per cent. . . .

In another book, *The Sterile Period in Family Life,* published under the imprimatur of the late Cardinal Hayes, authors V. J. Coucke and Dr. J. J. Walsh say, "As regards the end of marriage, we must assiduously keep in mind that the end of this institution was not that children should or even could be born in every family, but that through this institution the conservation of the species should be sufficiently provided for."

Pope Pius XI in his encyclical of 1931 discussed the idea of the Rhythm Method. This the Church neither approves nor disapproves, but merely tolerates, and only if three factors are present:

1. There is a sufficiently serious reason for a couple to use this method, sufficiently serious to justify side-stepping the first purpose of marriage. 2. Both husband and wife are truly willing to follow the method—neither one can force the other to adopt this system. 3. The use of this method must not cause moral sins against chastity.

Rhythm control is only one of many birth control methods. For men, *coitus interruptus* (withdrawal before climax) probably predates the calendar. Fallopius introduced the sheath in 1564, Casanova developed it in the 18th century and British Dr. Condom soon afterwards crusaded for it. For women, the last count showed 636 brands of contraceptive products, the most effec-

tive of which is the individually fitted diaphragm used with jelly. Altogether contraceptives today are a 250-million-dollar industry.

The National Research Council in the United States has allotted $100,000 to its Committee on Human Reproduction for a great many projects, one of which is the search for a simple contraceptive. The general scientific feeling right now is that existent contraceptives are too complicated for primitive peoples.

You find this much when you talk to doctors about birth control—they're not much concerned with its social-economic-moral-legal right or wrong, but with how all this affects their individual patients.

Again, the viewpoints vary.

"Mathematical calculations based on menstrual dates are scarcely reliable or opportune in moments of sexual excitement. It places too much of a strain on human nature," said Dr. George Kosmak in the American Medical Association *Journal.* He based his statement on the fact that woman's sexual desire is at a peak when the rhythm method demands abstinence.

And Dr. Abraham Stone added a postscript, "At this stage we do not consider the thermometer a contraceptive device."

Still, rhythm control can work. But it takes strict control and its success isn't as predictable.

When contraception becomes a matter of life and death for their patients, few doctors disagree. The A. M. A. put it simply: "In all cases the legal justification is the medical need of the patient."

With the exception of two states, there just isn't any legal problem. Judicial interpretation has so loosened local laws that you can now set up birth control clinics, disseminate information, sell and distribute contraceptives anywhere in 46 states.

That isn't true in Massachusetts and Connecticut. The Massachusetts State Supreme Court ruled that doctors cannot prescribe contraceptives to protect the health or even the lives of their patients. They did rule that druggists could sell some devices—but only for the purpose of preventing venereal disease. As for birth control clinics, state police shut them all down in a series of raids in 1938.

Connecticut prohibits the *use* of any device to control conception. This law applies to doctors and nurses. And when a doctor asked the Connecticut Supreme Court if the law would be construed to interfere with his prescription of contraceptives for patients to whom pregnancy meant almost certain death—they voted 3 to 2 that it would. So Connecticut doctors can legally perform abortions on patients for whom, they are convinced, childbirth would mean certain death —but these same doctors are not permitted under the law to prescribe contraceptives to prevent contraception.

What does it all add up to?

It all adds up to one of our most complicated controversial problems. You find "authorities" on every side contradicting one another. But nothing much anyone says is going to change minds. The only value in discussion is to make it clear that neither side is merely perverse or ignorant. This at least contributes to the cause of tolerance and may lift the level of controversy from the depths to which it usually sinks.

To the vast millions of Americans, the problem is pointed and personal. Should we have a child every 12 months? Should we practice continence or use contraceptives? What's morally right and what's morally wrong? How many children can we afford? Whom should we listen to most of all? The priest? The state? The doctors?

The American mood seems to be changing. Once not so long ago, birth control was totally taboo; today colleges openly discuss contraceptives in their marriage courses, restrictive laws are loosening, and many organizations have come out in its favor.

Yours is the final word. But this much is for sure—birth control is no longer something that can be hush-hushed out of existence.

Planning Our Children

G. Bromley Oxnam

G. Bromley Oxnam (1891–   ), bishop, Washington Area, Methodist Church; former president, Federal Council of the Churches of Christ in America. Principal works: *Social Principles of Jesus* (1923); *Youth and the New America* (1928); *The Ethical Ideals of Jesus in a Changing World* (1941); and *Labor and Tomorrow's World* (1945).

Thirty-two hundred Protestant and Jewish clergymen have signed a resolution urging the inclusion of planned parenthood services in hospitals and other agencies throughout the nation because they believe that such service makes fundamental contribution to the preservation of the American family. It was but yesterday that some persons, in the name of religion, condemned the use of anesthesia at childbirth, arguing suffering was the just lot of women because of the sin of Eve. Similarly, there are those who now illogically condone planned parenthood if continence or the "rhythm theory" are practiced, but condemn it if scientific means are used. They miss the religious reason which rests on the respect for personality. Planning for our children so that the mother's health may be preserved and healthy children born should be our real interest. When we make available to mothers sound scientific information which is used for the high moral objective of bringing to our families healthy, happy children, we are wisely using scientific means for moral ends. Religious leaders are awake to the dangers to family life which planned parenthood can help to correct. Communities which fail to provide proper marriage counseling, sex education and child-spacing service are recreant to their trust. Fundamentally, the family rests upon the acceptance and the practice of the law of love as it is revealed in the prophets and Jesus.

From "The Fight for Better Babies," *Look* (April 1, 1947). Reprinted by permission, Federal Council of the Churches of Christ in America. See also the publication, *"Moral Aspects of Birth Control"* (1938).

Medical Attitude toward Child Spacing

J. H. J. Upham

J. H. J. Upham (1871–   ), dean, College of Medicine, Ohio State University, 1927–1941; president, American Medical Association, 1937–1938.

Childbirth ranks among the major causes of death in the United States. The latest available figures on this killer show that 78,000 babies are born dead each year, 72,000 die in the first month and 7,000 mothers die in childbirth. There can be no doubt that a very substantial part of this waste of human life is the result of ignorance on the all-important subject of parenthood—ignorance on the part of parents who have been woefully unprepared for marital responsibility; ignorance on the part of physicians who have been inadequately trained in the field of human reproduction. Parents and prospective parents by the millions are completely uninformed on the importance of child spacing to the health of the mother and all her children. Physicians—as is shown by an unusually comprehensive survey just completed by Dr. Alan Guttmacher of Johns Hopkins—have a better understanding of the need for child spacing than they have training in conception control. While 96 per cent approve of it for some reason, only 25 per cent had any kind of training in their medical schools. However, it is an indication of progress that 73 per cent of those who were graduated after 1934 had some training in this field. The extension of planned parenthood services to the millions now denied it through the medium of adequately trained medical personnel will be one big step toward the reduction of infant mortality and the improvement of maternal health.

Black Market in Babies

Evelyn Seeley

Evelyn Seeley, free-lance writer; instructor in journalism, New York University.

There are two black markets in babies in New York:

First and foremost is run by the ruthless operators who cash in on the unmarried mother's desperation and the adoptive parents' longing for whatever the traffic will bear.

The other is more sentimental than commercial.

The price of the money-making "baby brokers" ranges from $500 to $10,000. Right now $1000 is a typical low figure here—$500 down and $500 when you get the child. Fees of $2500 and $5000 are not extraordinary and several $10,000 fees have been reported.

These people often work in doctor-lawyer teams, sometimes drawing in nurses or ex-social workers, and there are believed to be several nationwide chains. They work mostly through private or proprietary hospitals, having been pretty thoroughly ostracized in the public institutions. They work fast, sometimes forcing their way into hospitals with adoption papers all prepared. Their patients register as "Mrs." and the babies are placed in nurseries outside the city. . . .

Among the other groups of intermediaries are many good persons, well-meaning, kindly, who have come into the adoption field for emotional rather than financial reasons. Among them also are bitter people whom experience and observation have made scornful, with good reason, of rigid and moralistic social agency procedure. Many of them refuse to accept money from adoptive parents, or will take just enough to cover the expenses of the mother. You find an occasional doctor or social worker who has not only risked her professional standing but spent her own income in this work.

Some of these placements will be thoughtful, careful and good. The danger is in the general lack of training, of standards, of responsibility to authority.

Doctors, for instance, who pride themselves on the precision and skill with which they deliver a child, will proceed to give that child away without recourse to professional knowledge.

Such a doctor will get great emotional satisfaction from relieving the panicky unmarried mother-patient and giving her child to the frustrated patient who has tried vainly to become a mother.

This practice has stopped, it is believed, in public hospitals because of a two-year campaign of ostracism of doctors who indulge in it. It still thrives, however, in private institutions.

The commercial placement is, of course, the greater menace. With money involved, the mother may be trapped into an unwilling surrender. The child may be placed with the highest bidder. A wealthy home may not mean the child's happiness, and social workers meet many problems adolescents adopted into such homes.

Tragic stories emerge from unskilled placement of mental defectives or children who develop handicaps which the average home cannot handle.

The agencies now admit publicly that the "baby brokers" have the upper hand in this vital area.

The agencies admit that they are alarmed by this rapidly growing black market and their diffi-culties in solving this problem. Recently the United Hospital Fund, the Welfare Council of New York, and the New York Academy of Medicine formed the New York City Committee on Adoptions to investigate the black market and try to find out what happens and why. They will try to figure out the bottlenecks in the City's adoption practices carried on through five placement agencies—the State Charities Assn., Child Adoption Committee, the Spence-Chapin Child Adoption Service, the New York Foundling Home, the Catholic Home Bureau and the Free Synagogue Child Adoption Committee. They will try to get back from the "baby brokers" a job that should be theirs. . . .

If . . . [the Committee] gives a candid report, it will have to admit these facts:

Three to five babies are being born every day in New York who need adoptive homes, but only one or two of them will be placed through an authorized agency—the black market *will take care* of the rest.

Ten times as many parents as babies wait anxiously on agency lists, and some of them give up and turn to the black market. Other would-be parents never come near the agencies at all. . . .

It is estimated that 500 to 1000 unmarried mothers bear children in New York each year. Known to the City Dept. of Welfare are 500 to 600 children awaiting placement, and many others known to the courts have not yet been referred for placement. Adoptions in New York [in 1945] ran to 1395, but nobody knows nor can one find out how many children were secretly placed here and never legally adopted. Less than one-third of these babies were placed through the agencies.

Children of Divorced Parents
Kingsley Davis

Kingsley Davis (1908–   ), professor of Sociology, Columbia University. Principal publications: editor, *World Population in Transition* (Vol. 237, *The Annals,* January 1945); with Ana Casis, *Urbanization in Latin America* (1946); editor with Harry C. Bredemeier and Marion J. Levy, Jr., *Modern American Society* (1948); and *Human Society* (1949).

In the United States, as in other Western nations, the child of divorced parents constitutes a relatively new, acute, and unsolved social prob-lem. This is due primarily to the peculiar social structure that Western peoples have developed. It is not due, as many people believe, to the rising

From "Children of Divorced Parents: A Sociological and Statistical Analysis," *Law and Contemporary Problems, 10* (1944): 700–720, pp. 719–720 quoted. Reprinted by permission from *Law and Contemporary Problems,* published by the Duke University School of Law, Durham, North Carolina. Copyright 1944 by the Duke University Press.

divorce rate. The divorce rate has risen steadily and is likely to rise still more, yet such a trend merely increases the incidence of, but does not create, the problem. There are societies in which the divorce rate is higher than in the United States, but where the problem of the divorced child hardly exists. In primitive or archaic kinship societies the allocation of the child to the mother's or the father's family is usually automatic, and the child has substitute parents and many kinsmen living with or near him; consequently, the adjustment after divorce is quite easy. Our society, on the other hand, has a small family system with little emphasis on extended kinship, with equalitarian rights of the parents in the child, and with intense emotional involvement in both the marital and the parental relationship. As a consequence the child's future must be decided in each divorce case by the discretion of the court, with few principles other than the vague "welfare of the child" to guide it. The parents often use the child as an instrument of mutual conflict. They also compete for his custody, though not for his support. The public exaggerates the disadvantages of the child's situation, and seeks to prove by this means that divorce itself is an evil. In our culture, therefore, the child of divorce is a social problem in the sense that the societal machinery for dealing with him does not operate automatically or satisfactorily. Though he is really better off than the child whose parent has died, he is more of a problem because his condition is felt to be somebody's fault, with all that this implies.

With the possible exception of the last two decades, the number of children affected by divorce each year in the United States has not risen as fast as the divorce rate. According to our estimates the number in 1940 was 176,000—only 0.4 per cent of the total number of children in the population. In the same year the number of children whose parents had *ever* been divorced was, by our estimate, 1,533,000, which was 3.6 per cent of the total child population. Such figures are merely approximate, but may be sufficiently accurate to aid social agencies having to deal with the problem. It should be remembered, however, that these estimates relate only to legal divorces. The number of children affected by permanent desertion and separation, independently of the law, is entirely unknown, but the chances are that it is substantially larger than the number affected by divorce—yet the social problem is essentially the same, and perhaps worse.

For the future there seems every reason to believe that the divorce rate will climb steeply after the war, until approximately one-third of all marriages are being dissolved. Because of the recent rise in the birth rate the number of children affected will climb almost proportionately. The peak year (1945 or 1946) may see as many as 300,000 children involved in divorce cases.

The statistics, tentative at best, indicate the numerical extent of the problem. The sociological and anthropological analysis tries to show the causes of it. Neither approach, unfortunately, can give a certain answer to the two great questions of the future: In what ways will the social structure change so as to make the child of divorced parents less of a social problem? and when will the secular increase in the divorce rate reach a turning point? About the only certainty is that both changes are bound to eventuate sometime. It is doubtful if either can be accomplished deliberately by legal means, although the law will likely play a part. Since a high divorce rate does not necessarily threaten societal stability if ways are available for safeguarding the children, it may be that America will eventually have a divorce rate that will seem astounding by present standards. If so, it is safe to assume that the present chaos concerning the children will not then prevail. Some social mechanism will have been evolved for taking care of them. The remedy, therefore, does not necessarily lie in reducing the number of divorces. Divorce is here to stay. Instead, some means of neutralizing the effects of divorce on the child may be found by the creation of new institutional relationships that will replace the kinship bonds of primitive and archaic societies.

How Sex Education Can Help

Benjamin C. Gruenberg

Benjamin C. Gruenberg (1875–   ), educator. Selected works: *Parents and Sex Education* (1923); *The Story of Evolution* (1929); *Science and the Public Mind* (1935); with N. E. Bingham, *Biology and Man* (1944); *About the Kinsey Report* (1948); and *Our Children Today* (1952).

Why do so many young people get into sex difficulties that bring them to the attention of the police or of magistrates? The most frequent answers are bad homes and "undesirable companions." It is easy to blame the home because in all the groups that populate this country the family is accepted as the center of all that is best in life. It is in the nursery or at the mother's knee that the child normally acquires basic attitudes toward others, essential values, and convictions as to right and wrong. This is in keeping with the traditions of all nations and all religious groups. Yet a large proportion of the homes have *not* been meeting the child's need for suitable guidance regarding sex.

Nearly every new feature in the changing life of the past century has been blamed for the unsatisfactory conditions.

Some blamed the growth of cities. There is crowding. Young people move about freely, unknown among strangers and far from the family's sight.

Some blamed immigration, the coming of people whose ways were different from those of the earlier arrivals.

Some blamed the decline of religious influence in the home or the exclusion of religious teaching from the public schools.

Others have blamed alcohol or the saloon; burlesque shows, and pool rooms; or dance halls and commercialized entertainment generally.

Still others blamed "yellow" journals for exploiting crime and vice. They said the papers were "putting ideas into young people's heads." And there was "obscene" literature and art. In due course the "cheap movies" came along.

Profound social change has accompanied what we sometimes call the industrial revolution or the growth of democracy. It has brought greater freedom for the individual to go off and start his own business instead of clinging to his father's trade, greater opportunities in education, for girls as well as for boys, and greater freedom of young people to choose their mates as well as their companions—freedom from the older ways of living. And it has included far-reaching changes in the family as the basic institution of society.

Many people have been displeased by the changes in behavior that followed the increased freedoms. But to others the changes indicate not so much a breakdown of positive morality as of hypocrisy and concealment. And some have seriously questioned whether a social order is really healthy if it keeps up appearances through fears and coercions; or whether children are better off living with frustrated and mutually hateful parents than they would be if the parents were divorced. . . .

In all except some comparatively small communities, children have been receiving their home training and guidance from homes with differing traditions and practices. Accordingly, boys and girls in ever larger numbers have been reaching their teens utterly at sea as to the meaning of marriage and family living and as to the place of sex in adult life.

Home vs. School. A great deal of what these children were learning in their homes, moreover, conflicted with what they learned in the schools. The autocratic father, for example, did not jibe with the school's teachings about "equality" and free speech for everybody. The inferior position of women in immigrant homes could not be reconciled with the relative independence and authority of the teacher. The self-conscious silences and evasions of home did not go with the smut and ribaldry of the outside world. What children learned in their homes conflicted with

From "How Can We Teach About Sex?" Public Affairs Pamphlet No. 122, 1946, pp. 2–8, 13–15, 29. Reprinted by permission.

what their playmates and schoolmates—and then their fellow workers—had learned from their different kinds of homes.

And the churches, for the most part, were not very helpful. They were rather aloof from young people's most disturbing needs. They were also without a unifying philosophy, so that they often added to the perplexity of the rising generation. It is these confused and bewildered children who became, through the years, the confused and troubled parents of succeeding generations of "problem" children or "wild" adolescents—and unhappy adults.

How Far Parents Fail. In discussing why so many parents (three-fourths of them, in a study of 2,000 Catholic adolescent boys) fail to give their children the "early sex information to which they are entitled," a recent investigator concludes that "the parents simply do not know how to broach the subject. They feel unfit to give this information because no one has ever taught them how to tell the facts; through the years they have been straightening out their own twisted attitudes on the subject gathered at a similar back-fence source of information." [1]

The same writer quotes Dr. Felix M. Kirsch of the Catholic University of America to the effect that 98 per cent of Catholic parents "never received the proper information themselves and hence cannot impart it" to their children; and also that "the terminology" with which the parents are familiar "is either vulgar or even obscene, and they naturally feel embarrassed about using such language in the presence of their children."

Since education and moral guidance are so closely organized among the Catholics, it would seem fair to assume that conditions in the country generally have been no better than those described by Drs. Fleege and Kirsch. For example, from personal interviews with 291 boys in a midwestern city (80 per cent of them from twelve to fifteen years old), it was learned that "only 13 per cent of the boys rate their parents' efforts in sex education as fair or adequate." The combined results of six earlier studies covering over 2,000 persons showed that "approximately 50 per cent of the families made *no* attempt to give instruction in this field."

Fleege's own studies of the "sources from which 2,000 Catholic boys obtained their infor-

mation on sex" led him to conclude that "unwholesome sources outnumbered wholesome sources nearly three to one." And speaking specifically of the problems of adolescents, Dr. Fleege says, "The best way of making certain that our present adolescents will not find themselves in a similar plight when they become parents would be to instruct them now both as to the facts and the proper vocabulary."

Noble Experiments. When people began to worry about what was happening to youth, some parents were wise enough to know that their failure was largely due to ignorance. They therefore determined to inform their children and so reverse the traditional policy of silence. But even with this sincere desire to help their children, most parents were still burdened with a medieval attitude toward sex. For them, sex was still vile. Their desire to help children consequently included a desire to destroy all interest in sex. Teachers as well as parents worked on the theory that children's questions should be answered fully and honestly to *destroy* "morbid" curiosity, although in other matters teaching was supposed to encourage curiosity.

Parents and teachers discovered, moreover, that even when they knew the "facts" and even when they knew the right words, they were quite unable to *tell* their children anything important. They could not *speak* about sex and reproduction, about what they considered right attitudes toward one's own sexuality and toward the opposite sex, about promiscuity and prostitution, about standards and ideals of sex behavior. The old-fashioned taboos on which they had been raised blocked every honest effort to help their boys and girls. For these parents, like their own children, had been getting "sex education" of a silent but potent sort from very infancy. The young child learns from the hemmings and hawings of parents and from the nudgings or sly winks of others. From smirks and snickers as well as from awkward silences he learns of hidden and shameful meanings, at home and outside.

The well-meant, but often futile, efforts of many parents demonstrate the fallacy of starting "sex education" at adolescence—when boys and girls are on the verge of manhood and womanhood. For by that time many of them are already conditioned to secrecy and evasion—or to reckless defiance of convention—and to that extent estranged from their parents.

If we are to break the vicious circle, education

---

[1] Urban H. Fleege, *Self-Revelation of the Adolescent Boy,* Bruce Publishing Company, 1945, pp. 274–5.

in regard to sex must begin in infancy; and for that we have to catch the parents while they are still young and ready to learn. Progress is being made in that direction. . . .

Why Schools Have Held Back. The principals and superintendents who have recognized the need and the school's responsibility have been held back chiefly by two kinds of fear: The "public" might object. And untoward "incidents" in the schools might cause trouble. The bogeys that are most frequently mentioned are the parents and "the church."

We know a good deal about what parents think about these matters. We have the results of opinion polls, numerous resolutions and manifestoes of parent groups, responses to inquiries by schoolmen, and letters to editors. Articulate parents have left no doubt that they are looking for help from the schools. They want the schools to play a more positive role. Perhaps the best indication of what parents think is to be seen where parents cooperate most closely with teachers in the interests of their children. Here "sex education" is decidedly more advanced than in other schools. In many public and private schools teachers are aware of the parents' problems and of the role of parents in the home. There are study or discussion groups for parents in which ideas are clarified. Teachers are ready to help the parents in terms of the home's needs; and they are as much concerned with the attitudes the children cultivate as they are with the information absorbed.* . . .

The Church Not an Obstacle. When school leaders speak of the church, particularly of the Catholic Church, as the major obstacle to the introduction of scientific and sound social hygiene education into the schools, we must assume that they do so in good faith. And yet there is no official doctrine in this respect on which all the bishops and archbishops of the Catholic Church agree. Since the first World War, considerable Catholic literature advocating suitable sex education has appeared both in this country and abroad. In 1930, Felix M. Kirsch wrote, "In no case may we allow youth to stumble upon the significance of sex. . . . If the knowledge [regarding sex] is not furnished from pure sources, it will come in a vile way." And the Catholic

leaders advocate essentially the same basic principles regarding sex education as have been formulated by non-Catholic psychologists and educators.

Certainly no responsible religious leaders say: "Leave this education to the gutter or to nature." They do not even say: "Leave it to the parents," for they know better. They say that this is an educational responsibility. Of 368 Catholic pastors who replied to the question, "In view of present-day dangers to chastity, do you think it necessary that our youth be instructed in sex matters?" three hundred and forty-nine answered "Yes"—90 per cent. And some of the best organized work in the field of social hygiene education—or human relations education, or sex education—is being done in scattered parochial schools and academies throughout the country and in the schools of some of the large Catholic parishes.

It would be unfair to say that the fears of school authorities are never warranted. We can say only that outside opposition is of diminishing importance. But most objections to sex education as a responsibility of the school boil down to one that is seldom mentioned. And that is the fact that so many teachers are incapable of carrying out the task. But even if qualified teachers should show up they would find the set-up in most schools hostile to the informal, casual, and personal guidance which children and young people need.

The obstacles and difficulties within the school come largely from a traditional—and obsolete—conception of "education." Certainly the school has to transmit information and doctrine; it has to build up ideas, as in mathematics or history. But professional educators have been coming to realize that they have the responsibility of developing sound attitudes and ideals in addition to transmitting information and ideas. They are more and more aware of the role that the emotions play in the educational processes and also of the importance of the emotions and attitudes as major concerns of education. As for sex education in particular, they are rapidly learning from what has been done in personal and family counseling as well as from the effective work done in many kinds of schools in all parts of the country. . . .

The soundest kind of education regarding sex normally comes about in the home where the parents are themselves mature and adjusted regarding sex, and where such questions as children ask are answered simply and casually. But for

---

* See Benjamin C. Gruenberg, "How Can We Teach About Sex?" Public Affairs Pamphlet No. 122, 1946, pp. 20–25.—Eds.

reasons already considered, such homes are not the prevailing kind.

Community leaders and community spokesmen must look to the school as the first line of attack. Whatever society intends for its future, it must first put into its schools. It has become necessary for schools to supplement the home in many ways, including help with scientific knowledge about sex. The school needs also to supplement the home in overcoming attitudes that may be embarrassing to children in their daily relationships and in their future development. Such help may require individual counsel or special school plans rather than new lessons or "teaching" strange facts.

The schools are called upon to reach far beyond their walls and particularly into the homes. All who are not satisfied with the practical results of the prevailing modes of casual "sex education" must help the schools and parents work out more suitable approaches.

CROSS REFERENCES TO STANDARD TEXTS *

Barnes, *Society in Transition*, Chap. 3, pp. 319–321.

Bernard, *American Community Behavior*, pp. 211–215, 253–255, 514–517.

Bloch, *Disorganization*, Chap. 5.

Brown, *Social Pathology*, Chap. 7.

Cuber and Harper, *Problems of American Society*, pp. 278–280.

Elliott and Merrill, *Social Disorganization*, pp. 145–154, 261–262, 464–469.

Faris, *Social Disorganization*, pp. 268–278.

Gillin, *Social Pathology*, Chaps. 14–15.

—— and others, *Social Problems*, Chap. 13.

* For complete bibliographical reference to each text, see page 13.

Herman, *Approach to Social Problems*, pp. 204–209.

Landis, *Social Policies in the Making*, Chaps. 4–6, 14.

Lemert, *Social Pathology*, pp. 73–79.

Merrill and others, *Social Problems*, Chaps. 11–13.

Mihanovich, *Current Social Problems*, Chaps. 8, 10.

Neumeyer, *Social Problems and the Changing Society*, Chap. 7.

Nordskog and others, *Analyzing Social Problems*, Chap. 6.

Odum, *American Social Problems*, Chap. 13.

Phelps and Henderson, *Contemporary Social Problems*, Chap. 6.

Reinhardt and others, *Social Problems and Social Policy*, Chap. 11.

Weaver, *Social Problems*, Chaps. 20–21.

OTHER BIBLIOGRAPHY

Grace Abbott, *The Child and the State*, Chicago: University of Chicago Press, 1938, 2 vols.

Edith M. H. Bayler and Elio Monachesi, *The Rehabilitation of Children: The Theory and Practice of Child Placement*, New York: Harper & Bros., 1939.

Gordon W. Blackwell and Raymond F. Gould, *Future Citizens All*, Chicago: American Public Welfare Association, 1952.

James H. S. Bossard, *Parent and Child*, Philadelphia: University of Pennsylvania Press, 1953.

——, *The Sociology of Child Development*, rev. ed., New York: Harper & Bros., 1954.

Elvira H. Brigg, "The Tragedy of Birth Certificates," *Survey Midmonthly*, 79 (1943): 200.

Dorothy Burlingham and Anna Freud, *Infants Without Families*, New York: International University Press, 1944.

"Children of Divorced Parents," a symposium, *Law and Contemporary Problems*, 10 (1944): 697–866.

Kingsley Davis, "The Forms of Illegitimacy," *Social Forces*, 18 (1939–40): 77–89.

J. Louise Desport, *Children of Divorce*, Garden City: Doubleday and Co., 1953.

Robert L. Dickinson and Woodbridge E. Morris, *Techniques of Conception Control*, Baltimore: Williams & Wilkins Co., 1941.

Everett W. DuVall, "Child-Parent Social Distance," *Sociology and Social Research*, 21 (1937): 458–463.

Martha C. Ericson, "Child-Rearing and Social Status," *American Journal of Sociology*, 52 (1946): 190–192.

Erik H. Erikson, *Childhood and Society*, New York: W. W. Norton & Co., 1950.

Federal Council of the Churches of Christ in America, "Moral Aspects of Birth Control," New York, 1938.

Arnold Gesell and Frances L. Ilg, *The Child From Five to Ten*, New York: Harper & Bros., 1948.

——, *Infant and Child in the Culture of Today*, New York: Harper & Bros., 1943.

Max Sylvius Handman, "Abortion," *Encyclopaedia of the Social Sciences*, 1 (1930): 372–374.

Norman E. Himes, *Medical History of Contraception*, Baltimore: Williams & Wilkins Co., 1936.

John J. Honigmann, *Culture and Personality*, New York: Harper & Bros., 1954. Esp. Chaps. 10–11.

James L. Hymes, Jr., "How to Tell Your Child about Sex," 10th ed., Public Affairs Pamphlet No. 149, 1954.

H. S. Jennings, "Eugenics," *Encyclopaedia of the Social Sciences*, 15 (1935): 617–621.

Clyde Kluckhohn, Henry G. Murray, and David M. Schneider, eds., *Personality in Nature, Society and Culture,* rev. ed., New York: Alfred A. Knopf, 1953.

Margaret Kornitzer, *Child Adoption in the Modern World,* New York: Philosophical Library, 1952.

Alfred McClung Lee, "Child and Family," Chap. 31 in Lee, ed., *Principles of Sociology,* 2d ed., rev., New York: Barnes & Noble, 1951, pp. 299–307.

David M. Levy, *Maternal Overprotection,* New York: Columbia University Press, 1943.

Maud Morlock, "Babies on the Market," *Survey Midmonthly, 81* (1945): 67–69.

Theodore M. Newcomb, *Personality and Social Change,* New York: Dryden Press, 1943.

Fritz Redl and David Wineman, *Controls from Within,* Glencoe, Illinois: Free Press, 1952.

John Winchell Riley and Matilda White, "The Use of Various Methods of Contraception," *American Sociological Review,* 5 (1940): 890–903. See also *ibid.,* 6 (1941): 33–40 for a related article.

Margaret Sanger: An Autobiography, New York: W. W. Norton & Co., 1938.

William Carlson Smith, *The Stepchild,* Chicago: University of Chicago Press, 1953.

William I. Thomas and Dorothy Swaine Thomas, *The Child in America,* New York: Alfred A. Knopf, 1928.

U. S. Department of Labor, Children's Bureau, *White House Conference on Children in a Democracy, 1940,* Washington: Government Printing Office, 1940.

White House Conference on Child Health and Protection, *The Young Child in the Home: A Survey of Three Thousand American Families,* New York: D. Appleton-Century Co., 1936.

Leontine Young, *Out of Wedlock,* New York: McGraw-Hill Book Co., 1954.

Henry L. Zucker, "Working Parents and Latchkey Children," *The Annals,* 236 (November 1944): 43–50.

REVIEW QUESTIONS

1. After reading Kornhauser's summary of expert opinion, to what general extent can you attribute to heredity virtues and weaknesses in character?

2. What is the relationship between birth control and world population?

3. To what extent does public opinion support a program of disseminating birth-spacing information in the United States?

4. What is the chief argument against birth control?

5. What are the two chief types of black market in babies discovered by Seeley? Which type represents the greater problem?

6. Which are in greater supply in New York City, would-be foster parents or children available for adoption? What factors enter into this contrast?

7. How considerable a problem, according to Davis,

does the child of divorced parents represent at the present time in the United States?

8. To which does Davis believe a child can adjust most satisfactorily: parents separated by divorce or by death?

9. When does Gruenberg believe that sex education should begin? How should it be carried on? With what social problems can one thus cope?

10. What contradictions appear between home and school in the teaching of sex roles?

11. Why do parents still have difficulty carrying out their obligations in the field of sex education?

12. Why have the schools held back in sex education?

13. Why does Gruenberg say that the churches are not opposed to school sex education programs as such?

Youth

To AN EXTENT extraordinary in human societies, adolescents in western civilization undergo a period of marked storm, stress, and conflict with their elders. Davis analyzes the sociology of the parent-youth conflict in this transitional period, and he deals especially with the problems associated with the disillusionment of youth. Green points to the confusing differences in adjustment a modern middle-class boy feels impelled to make to parents, siblings, and playmates. In part he echoes the findings of Freud concerning the unpreparedness of middle-class youth for the aggressions a competitive world turns upon them. Komarovsky summarizes similar findings for middle-class girls. She shows how competitive pressures on these girls motivate some to adjust in terms of the current "feminine" role and others, the "modern" role.

Men and women work out their heterosexual adjustments in our society in terms of courtship and eventually—to follow the societally prescribed pattern—of marriage and a family. As Kinsey and his associates * have concluded from their extensive study of human sexual behavior, "A list

---

* Alfred C. Kinsey, Wardell B. Pomeroy, and Clyde E. Martin, *Sexual Behavior in the Human Male*, Philadelphia: W. B. Saunders Co., 1948, p. 578.

of the social problems which most often arise out of human sexual activity would give first places to venereal disease, bastardy, rape, and the contribution by adults to the delinquency of minor children. On the other hand, personal conflicts most often develop over masturbation, oral contacts, and the homosexual." They claim study and aid is needed in these areas, "not because they are rare, but because they are widespread." They have found that "no legislation or social taboos have been able to eliminate them from the history of the human animal." The selections by Deutsch, Folsom, and Graham outline these and related problems arising out of the inconsistencies of our moral code and practice, the tyrannous relics in our customs of outworn imperatives, and the walls of anonymity and loneliness that separate people in our large cities and other urbanized areas. Deutsch digests and interprets salient features in the findings of Kinsey and his associates with regard to the sex habits of American men. Folsom discusses the problems that face us in translating our factual knowledge about human sexuality into ethics, legislation, social policy, and religious guidance. Graham tells how a "social contact bureau" or "friendship service" bridges gaps between "lonely hearts" in a large city.

Parent-Youth Conflict
Kingsley Davis*

Why does contemporary western civilization manifest an extraordinary amount of parent-adolescent conflict?[1] In other cultures, the outstanding fact is generally not the rebelliousness of youth, but its docility. There is practically no custom, no matter how tedious or painful, to

---

[1] In the absence of statistical evidence, exaggeration of the conflict is easily possible, and two able students have

warned against it. E. B. Reuter, "The Sociology of Adolescence," and Jessie R. Runner, "Social Distance in Adoles-

* See the identifying note on page 120.
From "The Sociology of Parent-Youth Conflict," *American Sociological Review*, 5 (1940): 523–535, pp. 523–529 quoted. Reprinted by permission.

which youth in primitive tribes or archaic civilizations will not willingly submit.[2] What, then, are the peculiar features of our society which give us one of the extremest examples of endemic filial friction in human history?

Our answer to this question makes use of constants and variables, the constants being the universal factors in the parent-youth relation, the variables being the factors which differ from one society to another. Though one's attention, in explaining the parent-youth relations of a given milieu, is focused on the variables, one cannot comprehend the action of the variables without also understanding the constants, for the latter constitute the structural and functional basis of the family as a part of society.

The Rate of Social Change. The first important variable is the rate of social change. Extremely rapid change in modern civilization, in contrast to most societies, tends to increase parent-youth conflict, for within a fast-changing social order the time-interval between generations, ordinarily but a mere moment in the life of a social system, become historically significant, thereby creating a hiatus between one generation and the next. Inevitably, under such a condition, youth is reared in a milieu different from that of the parents; hence the parents become old-fashioned, youth rebellious, and clashes occur which, in the closely confined circle of the immediate family, generate sharp emotion.

That rapidity of change is a significant variable can be demonstrated by three lines of evidence: a comparison of stable and nonstable societies;[3]

cent Relationships," both in *American Journal of Sociology,* 43 (1937–38): 415–416, 437. Yet sufficient non-qualitative evidence lies at hand in the form of personal experience, the outpour of literature on adolescent problems, and the historical and anthropological accounts of contrasting societies to justify the conclusion that in comparison with other cultures ours exhibits an exceptional amount of such conflict. If this paper seems to stress conflict, it is simply because we are concerned with this problem rather than with parent-youth harmony.

[2] *Cf.* Nathan Miller, *The Child in Primitive Society,* New York: Brentano's, 1928; Miriam Van Waters, "The Adolescent Girl Among Primitive Peoples," *Journal of Religious Psychology,* 6 (1913): 375–421 and 7 (1914): 75–120; Margaret Mead, *Coming of Age in Samoa,* New York: William Morrow and Co., 1928, and "Adolescence in Primitive and Modern Society," pp. 169–188 in V. F. Calverton and S. Schmalhausen, eds., *The New Generation,* New York: Macaulay Company, 1930; A. M. Bacon, *Japanese Girls and Women,* New York: Houghton, Mifflin Co., 1891 and 1902.

[3] Partially done by Mead and Van Waters in the works cited above.

a consideration of immigrant families; and an analysis of revolutionary epochs. If, for example, the conflict is sharper in the immigrant household, this can be due to one thing only, that the immigrant family generally undergoes the most rapid social change of any type of family in a given society. Similarly, a revolution (an abrupt form of societal alteration), by concentrating great change in a short span, catapults the younger generation into power—a generation which has absorbed and pushed the new ideas, acquired the habit of force, and which, accordingly, dominates those hangovers from the old regime, its parents.[4]

The Birth-Cycle, Decelerating Socialization, and Parent-Child Differences. Note, however, that rapid social change would have no power to produce conflict were it not for two universal factors: first, the family's duration; and second, the decelerating rate of socialization in the development of personality. "A family" is not a static entity but a process in time, a process ordinarily so brief compared with historical time that it is unimportant, but which, when history is "full" (i.e., marked by rapid social change), strongly influences the mutual adjustment of the generations. This "span" is basically the birth-cycle—the length of time between the birth of one person and his procreation of another. It is biological and inescapable. It would, however, have no effect in producing parent-youth conflict, even with social change, if it were not for the additional fact, intimately related and equally universal, that the sequential development of personality involves a constantly decelerating rate of socialization. This deceleration is due both to organic factors (age—which ties it to the birth-cycle) and to social factors (the cumulative character of social experience). Its effect is to make the birth-cycle interval, which is the period of youth, the time of major socialization, subsequent periods of socialization being subsidiary.

Given these constant features, rapid social change creates conflict because *to* the intrinsic (universal, inescapable) differences between parents and children it adds an extrinsic (variable) difference derived from the acquisition, at the same stage of life, of differential cultural content by each successive generation. Not only are parent and

[4] Soviet Russia and Nazi Germany are examples. See Sigmund Neumann, "The Conflict of Generations in Contemporary Europe from Versailles to Munich," *Vital Speeches of the Day,* 5 (1939): 623–628. Parents in these countries are to be obeyed only so long as they profess the "correct" (i.e., youthful, revolutionary) ideas.

child, at any given moment, in different stages of development, but the content which the parent acquired at the stage where the child now is, was a different content from that which the child is now acquiring. Since the parent is supposed to socialize the child, he tends to apply the erstwhile but now inappropriate content. . . . He makes this mistake, and cannot remedy it, because, due to the logic of personality growth, his basic orientation was formed by the experiences of his own childhood. He cannot "modernize" his point of view, because *he* is the product of those experiences. He can change in superficial ways, such as learning a new tune, but he cannot change (or *want* to change) the initial modes of thinking upon which his subsequent social experience has been built. To change the basic conceptions by which he has learned to judge the rightness and reality of all specific situations would be to render subsequent experience meaningless, to make an empty caricature of what had been his life. . . .

Although, in the birth-cycle gap between parent and offspring, astronomical time constitutes the basic point of disparity, the actual sequences, and hence the actual differences significant for us, are physiological, psycho-social, and sociological—each with an acceleration of its own within, but to some degree independent of, sidereal time, and each containing a divergence between parent and child which must be taken into account in explaining parent-youth conflict. . . .

Psychosocial Differences: Adult Realism *versus* **Youthful Idealism.** The decelerating rate of socialization (an outgrowth both of the human being's organic development, from infant plasticity to senile rigidity, and of his cumulative cultural and social development), when taken with rapid social change and other conditions of our society, tends to produce certain differences of orientation between parent and youth. Though lack of space makes it impossible to discuss all these ramifications, we shall attempt to delineate at least one sector of difference in terms of the conflict between adult realism (or pragmatism) and youthful idealism.

Though both youth and age claim to see the truth, the old are more conservatively realistic than the young, because on the one hand they take Utopian ideals less seriously and on the other hand take what may be called operating ideals, if not more seriously, at least more for granted. Thus, middle-aged people notoriously forget the poetic ideals of a new social order which they cherished when young. In their place, they put simply the working ideals current in the society. There is, in short, a persistent tendency for the ideology of a person as he grows older to gravitate more and more toward the status quo ideology, unless other facts (such as a social crisis or hypnotic suggestion) intervene.[5] With advancing age, he becomes less and less bothered by inconsistencies in ideals. He tends to judge ideals according to whether they are widespread and hence effective in thinking about practical life, not according to whether they are logically consistent. Furthermore, he gradually ceases to bother about the *untruth* of his ideals, in the sense of their failure to correspond to reality. He assumes through long habit that, though they do not correspond perfectly, the discrepancy is not significant. The reality of an ideal is defined for him in terms of how many people accept it rather than how completely it is mirrored in actual behavior.[6] Thus, we call him, as he approaches middle age, a realist.

The young, however, are idealists, partly because they take working ideals literally and partly because they acquire ideals not fully operative in the social organization. Those in authority over children are obligated as a requirement of their status to inculcate ideals as a part of the official culture given the new generation.[7] The children are receptive because they have little social experience—experience being systematically kept from them (by such means as censorship, for example, a large part of which is to "protect" children). Consequently, young people possess little ballast for their acquired ideals, which therefore soar to the sky, whereas the middle-aged, by contrast, have plenty of ballast.

This relatively unchecked idealism in youth is eventually complicated by the fact that young people possess keen reasoning ability. The mind, simply as a logical machine, works as well at sixteen as at thirty-six.[8] Such logical capacity, combined

---

[5] See footnote on p. 128 for necessary qualifications.

[6] When discussing a youthful ideal, however, the older person is quick to take a dialectical advantage by pointing out not only that this ideal affronts the aspirations of the multitude, but that it also fails to correspond to human behavior either now or (by the lessons of history) probably in the future.

[7] See amusing but accurate article, "Fathers Are Liars," *Scribner's Magazine* (March, 1934).

[8] Evidence from mental growth data which point to a leveling off of the growth curve at about age 16. For charts and brief explanations, together with references, see F. K. Shuttleworth, *The Adolescent Period*, Washington: Society

with high ideals and an initial lack of experience, means that youth soon discovers with increasing age that the ideals it has been taught as true and consistent are not so in fact. Mental conflict thereupon ensues, for the young person has not learned that ideals may be useful without being true and consistent. As a solution, youth is likely to take action designed to remove inconsistencies or force actual conduct into line with ideals, such action assuming one of several typical adolescent forms—from religious withdrawal to the militant support of some Utopian scheme—but in any case consisting essentially in serious allegiance to one or more of the ideal moral systems present in the culture.[9]

A different, usually later reaction to disillusionment is the cynical or sophomoric attitude; for, if the ideals one has imbibed cannot be reconciled and do not fit reality, then why not dismiss them as worthless? Cynicism has the advantage of giving justification for behavior that young organisms crave anyway. It might be mistaken for genuine realism if it were not for two things. The first is the emotional strain behind the "don't care" attitude. The cynic, in his judgment that the world is bad because of inconsistency and untruth of ideals, clearly implies that he still values the ideals. The true realist sees the inconsistency and untruth, but without emotion; he uses either ideals or reality whenever it suits his purpose. The second is the early disappearance of the cynical attitude. Increased experience usually teaches the adolescent that overt cynicism is unpopular and unworkable, that to deny and deride all beliefs which fail to cohere or to correspond to facts, and to act in opposition to them, is to alienate oneself from any group,[10] because these beliefs, however unreal,

are precisely what makes group unity possible. Soon, therefore, the youthful cynic finds himself bound up with some group having a system of working ideals, and becomes merely another conformist, cynical only about the beliefs of other groups.[11]

While the germ of this contrast between youthful idealism and adult realism may spring from the universal logic of personality development, it receives in our culture a peculiar exaggeration. Social change, complexity, and specialization (by compartmentalizing different aspects of life) segregate ideals from fact and throw together incompatible ideologies while at the same time providing the intellectual tools for discerning logical inconsistencies and empirical errors. Our highly elaborated burden of culture, correlated with a variegated system of achieved vertical mobility, necessitates long years of formal education which separate youth from adulthood, theory from practice, school from life. Insofar, then, as youth's reformist zeal or cynical negativism produces conflict with parents, the peculiar conditions of our culture are responsible.

---

for Research in Child Development, 3: 16 (1938), figs. 16, 230, 232, 276, 285, 308.

Maturity of judgment is of course another matter. We are speaking only of logical capacity. Judgment is based on experience as well as capacity; hence, adolescents are apt to lack it.

[9] An illustration of youthful reformism was afforded by the Laval University students who decided to "do something about" prostitution in the city of Quebec. They broke into eight houses in succession one night, "whacked naked inmates upon the buttocks, upset beds and otherwise proved their collegiate virtue. . . ." They ended by "shoving the few remaining girls out of doors into the cold autumn night." *Time*, October 19, 1936.

[10] This holds only for expressed cynicism, but so close is the relation of thought to action that the possibility of an entirely covert cynic seems remote.

---

[11] This tentative analysis holds only insofar as the logic of personality development in a complex culture is the sole factor. Because of other factors, concrete situations may be quite different. When, for example, a person is specifically trained in certain rigid, otherworldly, or impractical ideals, he may grow increasingly fanatical with the years rather than realistic, while his offspring, because of association with less fanatical persons, may be more pragmatic than he. The variation in group norms within a society produces persons who, whatever their orientation inside the group, remain more idealistic than the average outsider, while their children may, with outside contacts, become more pragmatic. Even within a group, however, a person's situation may be such as to drive him beyond the everyday realities of that group, while his children remain undisturbed. Such situations largely explain the personal crises that may alter one's orientation. The analysis, overly brief and mainly illustrative, therefore represents a certain degree of abstraction. The reader should realize, moreover, that the terms "realistic" and "idealistic" are chosen merely for convenience in trying to convey the idea, not for any evaluative judgments which they may happen to connote. The terms are not used in any technical epistemological sense, but simply in the way made plain by the context. Above all, it is not implied that ideals are "unreal." The ways in which they are "real" and "unreal" to observer and actor are complex indeed. See T. Parsons, *The Structure of Social Action*, New York: McGraw-Hill Book Co., 1937, p. 396, and V. Pareto, *The Mind and Society*, New York: Harcourt, Brace and Co., 1935, vol. 3, pp. 1300–1304.

The Competitive Demands upon the Middle-class Boy

Arnold W. Green

Arnold W. Green (1914–   ), professor of sociology, Pennsylvania State University. Author of *Sociology* (1952).

The modern middle-class child, . . . particularly the boy, who has found surcease from anxiety and guilt by blind obedience and "love" for his parents, is not allowed to stabilize his relationships with others on that basis. His play-group, which may be denied him until he has reached school age, makes him feel a certain shame and inadequacy in attempting to approach its members with familiar techniques.[1] He also early discovers that he is involved in competition with others, as an individual with his contemporaries, and as a representative of his family unit with other families. . . .

Before the child has developed a real self-awareness he becomes part of a process of invidious comparison with other families: he uttered his first word two months earlier than the Jones' boy; he weighed so many pounds at the end of his first year. At Sunday School he received the Bible for perfect attendance; at public school his grades in arithmetic were higher than two-thirds of the other members of the class. He may take piano lessons in view of the day when Mrs. Smythe's pupils will be on public exhibition before the parents of the neighborhood. Everything he accomplishes or fails to accomplish becomes an inevitable part of the family's attempt to maintain or improve its standing in the community.

But effective competition demands a certain degree of independence, firmness of purpose, perhaps aggressiveness. Even for the "normal" middle-class child the transition from submission to some degree of independent behavior is made difficult.[2] And for the child whose personality has been absorbed, an especially exacerbated conflict arises. He is expected to "do things," to accomplish, perhaps to lead in some endeavor, like other children, but his earliest social conditioning was dependence, submission, inferiority; his accomplishments, if any, are on a god-scale—in phantasy. He is desperately attempting to stabilize all later relationships on the basis of his earliest conditioning. Any pressure to compete only exaggerates his anxiety, guilt, and feelings of inadequacy. Life in the modern middle-class home insures that he shall feel that pressure.

[1] The play-group has immeasurable sociological significance for it is secondary in importance only to the family of orientation in the socialization process. Unfortunately, the only good empirical studies of the play-group available are of institutionalized children or slum children whose gang behavior is regarded as a social problem.

[2] See Ruth Benedict, "Continuities and Discontinuities in Cultural Conditioning," *Psychiatry, 1* (1938): 161–167. . . .

From "The Middle Class Male Child and Neurosis," *American Sociological Review, 11* (1946): 31–41, pp. 40–41 quoted. Reprinted by permission. Compare with Karen Horney, "Culture and Neurosis," pp. 30–31.

Contradictions in Middle-class Female Roles

Mirra Komarovsky

Mirra Komarovsky (1906–   ), chairman of the department of sociology, Barnard College, Columbia University. Principal works: with G. A. Lundberg and M. A. McInerny, *Leisure: A Suburban Study* (1934); *The Unemployed Man and His Family* (1940); and *Women in the Modern World* (1953).

Members of an undergraduate course on the family were asked for two successive years to submit autobiographical documents focused on [incompatible sex roles imposed by our society upon the college woman]; 73 were collected. In addition, 80 interviews, lasting about an hour each, were conducted with every member of a course in social psychology of the same [women's] institution—making a total of 153 documents ranging from a minimum of five to a maximum of thirty typewritten pages.

The generalization emerging from these documents is the existence of serious contradictions between two roles present in the social environment of the college woman. The goals set by each role are mutually exclusive, and the fundamental personality traits each evokes are at points diametrically opposed, so that what are assets for one become liabilities for the other, and the full realization of one role threatens defeat in the other.

One of these roles may be termed the "feminine" role. While there are a number of permissive variants of the feminine role for women of college age (the "good sport," the "glamour girl," the "young lady," the domestic "home girl," etc.), they have a common core of attributes defining the proper attitudes to men, family, work, love, etc., and a set of personality traits often described with reference to the male sex role as "not as dominant, or aggressive as men" or "more emotional, sympathetic."

The other and more recent role is, in a sense, no *sex* role at all, because it partly obliterates the differentiation in sex. It demands of the woman much the same virtues, patterns of behavior, and attitude that it does of the men of a corresponding age. We shall refer to this as the "modern" role.

Both roles are present in the social environment of these women throughout their lives, though, as the precise content of each sex role varies with age, so does the nature of their clashes change from one stage to another. In the period under discussion the conflict between the two roles apparently centers about academic work, social life, vocational plans, excellence in specific fields of endeavor, and a number of personality traits.

One manifestation of the problem is in the inconsistency of the goals set for the girl by her family.

Forty, or 26 per cent, of the respondents expressed some grievance against their families for failure to confront them with clear-cut and consistent goals. The majority, 74 per cent, denied having had such experiences. . . .

Sixty-one, or 40 per cent, of the students indicated that they have occasionally "played dumb" on dates, that is, concealed some academic honor, pretended ignorance of some subject, or allowed the man the last word in an intellectual discussion. Among these were women who "threw games" and in general played down certain skills in obedience to the unwritten law that men must possess these skills to a superior degree. At the same time, in other areas of life, social pressures were being exerted upon these women to "play to win," to compete to the utmost of their abilities for intellectual distinction and academic honors. . . .

Another aspect of the problem is the conflict between the psychogenetic personality of the girl and the cultural role foisted upon her by the milieu.[1] At times it is the girl with "masculine" interests and personality traits who chafes under the pressure to conform to the "feminine" pattern. At other times it is the family and the college who

---

[1] Margaret Mead, *Sex and Temperament in Three Primitive Societies,* New York: Morrow & Co., 1935.

From "Cultural Contradictions and Sex Roles," *American Journal of Sociology,* 52 (1946–47): 184–189, pp. 184–185, 187–188 quoted. Reprinted by permission.

thrust upon the reluctant girl the "modern" role.

While, historically, the "modern" role is the most recent one, ontogenetically it is the one emphasized earlier in the education of the college girl, if these 153 documents are representative. Society confronts the girl with powerful challenges and strong pressures to excel in certain competitive lines of endeavor and to develop certain techniques of adaptations very similar to those expected of her brothers. But, then, quite suddenly as it appears to these girls, the very success in meeting these challenges begins to cause anxiety. It is precisely those most successful in the earlier role who are now penalized.

The Sex Habits of American Men
Albert Deutsch

Albert Deutsch (1905–   ), journalist and free-lance writer. Principal works: *The Mentally Ill in America* (1937, rev. ed. 1949); *History of Public Welfare in New York State* (1940); editor and co-author, *Sex Habits of American Men: A Symposium on the Kinsey Report* (1948); *The Shame of the States* (1948); and *Our Rejected Children* (1950).

The public and professional reception accorded the now celebrated "Kinsey Report"[1] is unprecedented in the history of American science. Within ten weeks after its publication in January, 1948, it reached second place on the list of non-fiction best sellers. The name of the senior author, Professor Alfred C. Kinsey, became a byword in the American household. Within two months of publication, a Gallup poll indicated that one out of every five Americans had already read or heard about the book—an extraordinary proportion. . . .

Sexual Behavior in the Human Male is the first of a series of at least nine volumes planned for publication as the Kinsey project proceeds during the next twenty years. It is, as the authors state in their very first words, "a progress report from a case history study on human sex behavior." Successive volumes are planned, at roughly two-year intervals on sexual behavior in the human female, sex factors in marital adjustment, legal aspects of sex behavior, the heterosexual-homosexual balance in humans, institutional sex problems, prostitution, sex education, and other special problems.

It is important to remember that this first volume represents a "progress report," and that its findings are presented as tentative, not final although ". . . the authors consider these findings of sufficient general validity to warrant their publication at this time." They have gone to great pains in discussing the limitations, shortcomings and defects in their initial publication. . . .

The Kinsey report is based on the case histories of the 5,300 white males interviewed during the first nine years of the survey. It also contains much collateral data stemming from the rest of the 12,000 histories taken up to that time. Approximately 1,000 case histories of Negro males were excluded from the first volume because the sampling was not considered adequate as yet. On the basis of preliminary findings, however, Dr. Kinsey tells us that no significant difference has been discovered between the sex habits of white and Negro males, the latter generally revealing very much the same patterns found in whites of corresponding economic, social and educational status. . . .

[The] Kinsey group divided the American population into twelve main biologic and socio-economic groups—sex, race-cultural group, marital status, age, age of adolescence, educational level, occupational class of subject, occupational class of parent, rural-urban background, religious group, religious adherence (degree of active connection with a particular group), and geographic origin. Each of these twelve main categories was in turn broken down into sub-groups for tabulating purposes.

The population is divided into three main educational groups—those who have never gone beyond grade school, those who have gone to high

[1] Alfred C. Kinsey, Wardell B. Pomeroy, and Clyde E. Martin, *Sexual Behavior in the Human Male*, Philadelphia: W. B. Saunders Company, 1948.

From the chapter by Albert Deutsch, "Kinsey, the Man and His Project," in *Sex Habits of American Men: A Symposium on the Kinsey Report,* edited by Albert Deutsch, and published by Prentice-Hall, Inc., New York. Copyright 1948 by Prentice-Hall, Inc.

school, and those who are college-trained. Another Kinsey classification divided people into nine socio-economic groups ranging from the underworld (those depending mainly on illicit activities for a livelihood) through unskilled, semi-skilled, and skilled laborers, lower and upper white collar workers, professionals, business executives and the leisure class (social registerites).

The sexual behavior of these groups is measured and compared in the Kinsey study by the incidence and frequency of "sexual outlets." These outlets refer to sexual orgams resulting from six main types of sexual activity—self-stimulation (masturbation), nocturnal emissions, heterosexual petting, heterosexual intercourse (pre-marital, marital, extra-marital, with prostitutes), homosexual activity and animal contacts.

The findings published in the first Kinsey report, tentative though they are, nevertheless deal a shattering blow to widely prevalent and deeply rooted concepts of sex and marriage. Its startling revelations, presented in coldly objective statistical order, reduce to myth many of the traditional ideas that had been taught to civilized men as facts for centuries. . . .

The Kinsey report explodes many popular notions as to when sex activity begins and reaches its peak in humans, although psychoanalysts and others familiar with Freudian theory are not surprised by the findings. The Kinsey data confirm the observations of Sigmund Freud that sex attitudes and habits start in infancy and that sex life, in fact, begins virtually at birth. Kinsey reports that a complete orgasm (except for ejaculation) has been observed in a five-months-old male, and in a girl infant of only four months. Since the orgasm is the key factor of statistical measurement in the Kinsey project, I have asked Kinsey for a definition of the term as he uses it. Here it is: *Orgasm is the sudden release of the erotic tension built up by the sensory or psychic stimulation.* . . .

Pre-adolescents, the Kinsey survey reveals, have a capacity for frequency of sexual orgasm far greater than most adults. One pre-adolescent child was observed to experience 26 orgasms within 24 hours when sexually aroused. In the pre-adolescent age, the child responds sexually, in a physical sense, to a great variety of stimulating situations of indefinite character—taking a shower, receiving punishment, feeling shame or anger, seeing an accident, friction with clothing, riding horseback, getting an examination mark in school, fast car riding, fear of a house intruder or "being scared"

otherwise, receiving grade cards at school, seeing a movie, listening to music or an adventure story, entering an empty house, sex-play with other children, etc.

There is a far greater amount of sex activity in that period of life known as adolescence—when the child rather suddenly acquires physical stature and adult conformation along with growth of pubic hair, change of voice and ability to ejaculate. Adolescence is usually associated with the teenage period, but Kinsey notes that some boys arrive at this stage at four or five years of age, while there are occasional cases of college seniors who have not yet passed adolescence.

Contrary to the traditional idea that the male's "prime of life," sexually, is reached in the thirties or forties, the Kinsey survey reveals that the height of sexual capacity and activity in human males is usually reached in the late teens. (Kinsey uses sexual activity in a comprehensive sense, including—besides intercourse—masturbation, nocturnal emissions, homosexual experiences, etc.)

Over twelve per cent of all thirteen-year-old American boys have already had sexual intercourse. At 14, one out of every four has had such experience. Over 86 per cent of American males have pre-marital intercourse by the time they are 28; only a small percentage remain virgins till marriage.

A remarkable conclusion by the Kinsey group, on the basis of their survey, is that the sex pattern of the average American male is firmly established by the time he has reached 16 years of age and that with rare exceptions, no circumstance, however catastrophic, materially alters that pattern in his later life. Those who are most sexually active in their adolescent years, for example, are likely to remain most sexually active through marriage and middle age.

So firmly established are these sex habits, and so closely are they related to the social and educational group for which the growing boy is destined, that Professor Kinsey feels he is able to predict with a high degree of certainty whether a sixteen-year-old boy is destined to go to college or not just by reviewing his sex history!

This set of facts has tremendous significance for the future of marriage, parenthood, law enforcement and education.

The revelation that a human male actually arrives at the height of his sexual needs in his late teens demands the immediate attention of experts already grappling with the problem of delayed marriage imposed by our modern way of life.

The problem of the sexually active male adolescent is complicated, the Kinsey group points out, by the fact that the average adolescent girl gets along satisfactorily with one-fifth the activity of her male counterpart. The frequency of sexual outlet of the female in her twenties and early thirties, they add, is still below that of the average adolescent male.

The significance of these observations is readily apparent. . . .

[Caution] should be heeded in evaluating other figures in the Kinsey report that have received wide publicity, such as these:

Eighty-six per cent of American males have pre-marital intercourse by age thirty.

One out of every six American farm boys has sexual contacts with animals.

Thirty-seven per cent of American males engage, in some time of their lives, in homosexual activity climaxed by orgasm.

Ninety-five per cent of American males engage in forms of sexual activity, at some time of their lives, that are punishable as crimes under the law.

Nearly 70 per cent have, at some time, intercourse with prostitutes.

Only a very small proportion of males imprisoned as sex offenders are involved in behavior materially different from that of most males in the general population, the Kinsey group states.

The task of conducting a "clean-up campaign" against *all* sex offenders—as is periodically demanded by the public following a particularly shocking "sex crime" case—is rendered extremely difficult in light of the statement that fully 95 out of every 100 Americans are involved in one or more illicit sexual activities!

There are, of course, sex attitudes and practices that are dangerous to person and to public weal. . . . But implicit in the Kinsey report is the need for careful revaluation of our present legal codes relating to sex. . . .

Two further implications of the Kinsey findings —both of them tentative and both reassuring to those concerned with modern sex morality—merit passing mention in this summary:

1. The younger generation is not going to the dogs, morally.

2. The recent world war has not resulted in looser sexual behavior among those who fought in uniform.

The Kinsey group, on the basis of their tentative statistics, crack down hard on the ubiquitous Jeremiahs who go about bewailing the evil ways of the younger generation. Modern youth, they report, is no wilder than that of father's, or even grandfather's, day. They remind us that our present-day fathers were themselves the "flaming youth" of that jazz age in the "roaring twenties" that followed World War I. It is true that the evidence indicates that boys of the lower social level are reaching adolescence a year or so sooner than boys of the same level a generation or two ago. This they are inclined to attribute to the fact that the better sanitation, medical care and nutritional standards which have improved the general health of lower-income groups during the past thirty years and, along with it, the capacity for sexual activity. There is also more masturbation and petting among lower level boys than there used to be probably as a result of infiltration of upper level ideas.

But with respect to pre-marital intercourse with prostitutes or other women (which, it is claimed, has been increasing), the Kinsey group declare:

. . . the records for the older and the younger generation are, by the admission of the older generation when it contributes its own histories, so nearly identical that no significant differences can be found. . . .

The violent social and political changes witnessed during the past generation have no significant effect on the nation's sex patterns, Kinsey states on the basis of his findings. We have gone through two world wars of unprecedented scale, periods of economic prosperity and depression, jazz and jitterbug ages, political upheavals, changes in educational and religious attitudes, revolutionary developments in our means of transportation and communication. Yet, in war and peace, sex patterns have remained essentially as they were down the centuries.

As for wartime effects on the sexual behavior of men, Dr. Kinsey flatly contradicts the widespread opinion that America has experienced a "moral breakdown.". . .

Those who had experience with prostitutes while in uniform were generally the kind who would have the same experience in civilian life, and those who avoided prostitutes did so for the same reason they would have at home, according to Kinsey . . . "The high officer who complained that too many mothers thought that the army had invented sex had considerable justification for his complaint," says Kinsey.

Very few adults ever depart from the sex patterns established in their teens, Kinsey emphasizes again and again. Many individuals do acquire certain details of sex activity in later life, and some think they have acquired entirely new sex attitudes. Upper level persons like to think they have become more liberal, sexually emancipated, free of their former inhibitions, rational instead of traditional in their behavior, ready to experiment with anything. Nonetheless, it is rare that such "emancipated" persons actually engage in sex behavior which is foreign to the pattern laid down in their youth.

There is the upper level male who boasts of his many wild experiences with girls in the tropics, of his conquests of women in many ports, after returning from army service. But when such men contributed their objective records to Kinsey's scientific study, it usually turned out that they never brought themselves to having actual intercourse with any of the girls.

The Kinsey report will continue to arouse a great deal of heated controversy in the months and years to come. Its findings are at odds with many prejudices, taboos and false concepts that have been venerated as the truth for centuries. No subject has such an explosive effect on human emotions and human temperaments as sex. Yet, for our own sake and for that of our children, it would behoove us to heed . . . plea[s] for tolerant, courageous analysis made by . . . scientists of unquestioned wisdom and integrity.

Kinsey's Challenge to Ethics and Religion
Joseph K. Folsom

Joseph K. Folsom (1893–), professor of sociology, Vassar College. Principal works: *Culture and Social Progress* (1928); *Social Psychology* (1931); *The Family* (1934); *Youth, Family and Education* (1941); and *The Family and Democratic Society* (1943).

"Maybe its true, but it's not good policy to *broadcast* detailed truth without some consideration of how people are going to use it." Such is a common reaction to Kinsey. It is not peculiar to traditionalists nor to those lacking reverence for modern science. For example, Margaret Mead, in an eloquent Appendix on "The Ethics of Insight Giving" says: "When one writes in a way that is easily accessible to all interested citizens, I believe one should put oneself in those readers' place, and not force them either to accept or to reject [or to choose which to do?] interpretations the implications of which they would not have chosen to hear had they been fully aware of them." The sudden removal of a previously guaranteed reticence has left many young people singularly defenseless in just those areas where their desire to conform was protected by a lack of knowledge of the extent of non-conformity."[1] The most important aspect of the Kinsey studies is their challenge to reexamine the relation of science to ethics and religion and this connected issue of intellectual paternalism versus complete intellectual democracy.

The medieval harmony of science, ethics, and religion, documented by St. Thomas Aquinas, became more and more disturbed by the rapid development of science. In 1790 Kant seemed to solve the problem in a novel and revolutionary way, by making a complete separation of science and ethics. However the ethics which actually operate in our society have never yet been reduced to any single principle, but are based on several different types of thinking. Wayne Leys has done a great service to social science by making explicit these ethical thoughtways.[2] He compares Kant's ethic of pursuing an ideal of social relations with the casuist ethic of following precedents, the Bentham utilitarian ethic of estimating the pleasant and painful consequences to all affected, the Hegelian ethic of loyalty to the larger whole, or destiny toward which history moves, and the Deweyan pragmatic ethic of solving the essential problem. The last seems like a kind of negative, objectivist, practical utilitarianism: doing what will most reduce complaints and conflicts.

The alarm over the Kinsey reports seems to be

---

[1] Margaret Mead, *Male and Female*, New York: William Morrow and Co., 1949, p. 450.

[2] Wayne Leys, *Ethics for Policy Decisions*, New York: Prentice-Hall, Inc., 1953.

From "Kinsey's Challenge to Ethics and Religion," *Social Problems, 1* (1954): 164–168.

based on a fear that our fellow citizens are largely guided by an extremely realistic form of casuistry which says, "When in Rome do as the Romans *do* —read their laws—but also notice which laws are enforced." It is well known, of course, that many a person will thus appeal to custom when what the Romans do fits in with his felt needs, but when it does not, he may turn to an idealistic, utilitarian, or even a Hegelian argument. This is one of the commonest types of rationalization.

F. S. C. Northrop vigorously opposes this type of casuistry which would derive ethics from actual practice. Furthermore, Northrop sees a similar error in Hegelian and Marxian thinking. Hegel on the level of nations, and Marx on the level of classes, assume that in some important sense the "ought" can be derived from the "is." Yet Northrop rejects also the Kantian solution of making ethics independent of science. He believes that ethics can and should be derived from science.[3] The Kinsey reports would belong mostly to Northrop's descriptive "social science." Biology, psychology, and studies such as Kardiner's [4] which attempt to apply universal criteria to several cultures would seem to belong mostly to Northrop's "human and natural science," which he regards as a proper basis for ethics. However, while Kinsey's titles "Human Male" and "Human Female" seem to the anthropologist like a bit of ethnocentric conceit, there are many things in the reports which contribute to omni-human natural science in Northrop's sense. Such for example are the data on the tremendous age, sex, and individual differences.

There is a job to be done, and Northrop has suggested what it is. It is to translate our factual knowledge about human sexuality into ethics, legislation, social policy, and religious guidance. The time has now come to do it. Not because Kinsey has told us anything so very surprising, anything that was not known, in rough approximation, before. Rather, because he has told it so statistically to so many people that now there may be enough steam up to do what should have been done a long time ago.

This task should be done gradually through discussion. In this writer's view the discussion should be in no way secret, however benevolent and high-minded; but it should be *led* by men and women of unquestionable honesty, devotion to the general good, and free from any concealed personal motive or bias. Given the present organization of our intellectual life, these discussion leaders should be clearly distinguished from the factual researchers, although both groups require intellectual and moral integrity.

The kind of discussion we need is well represented by *Sex Ethics and the Kinsey Report* by Dr. Seward Hiltner,[5] a clergyman and member of the University of Chicago theological faculty. Hiltner not only understands Kinsey's methods and results with uncommon acumen, but shows theoretical skill after the fashion of a Max Weber. He is interested in *patterns,* not of sex behavior and "outlets," but of sex attitudes and values. He constructs seven types, each logically consistent within itself, and most of them also well represented empirically. The first three are mass types correlated with Kinsey's three socio-educational levels: the "child-of-nature" attitude of the lower level, the "respectability-restraint" attitude of the middle level (especially before 1920), and the "romantic" attitude (romantic toward licit and illicit sex and not merely toward conventional courtship and choice of mate) of the upper level, now filtering down to other levels. Then there are three consistent patterns which Hiltner has observed among thoughtful individuals but which do not appear in the Kinsey data, either because Kinsey did not ask the necessary questions, or because the holders of these attitudes are too few. These are the "no harm" attitude, the "toleration" attitude, and the "personal-interpersonal" attitude. The last named is the one frankly admired by Hiltner. It is implied in the works of Erich Fromm.[6]

The person with this attitude "believes that the ordering of sex by society should be for the realization of personal and interpersonal values, not for the sake of control of such." It is neither legalistic nor libertarian, biologistic nor spiritistic, unreflectively conformist nor yet rebellious for the sake of proving non-conformity. "It does not consider naturalness or unnaturalness as adequate criteria." Hiltner [7] measures all these six types against a seventh type as a standard. This is

---

[3] F. S. C. Northrop, *The Meeting of East and West,* New York: The Macmillan Co., 1946, pp. 245, 256–258.

[4] Abram Kardiner, *et al., The Psychological Frontiers of Society,* New York: Columbia University Press, 1945.

[5] Seward Hiltner, *Sex Ethics and the Kinsey Report,* New York: Association Press, 1953.

[6] Erich Fromm, *Man for Himself,* New York: Rinehart and Co., 1947; *Psychoanalysis and Religion,* New Haven: Yale University Press, 1951.

[7] Seward Hiltner, *Sex Ethics and the Kinsey Report,* New York: Association Press, 1953, p. 177.

the *Christian view* * of sex, which Hiltner derives, in an objective, scholarly manner, from the Bible and Christian history, but also "taking into account the modern knowledge." The Christian view turns out to be essentially the personal-interpersonal attitude with the addition of Christian theological support. It is summarized in five points, here condensed: (1) sex is good if it serves the fulfillment of man as a total being, i.e., God's will for man, (2) the aim of all human interrelationships is to foster love, (3) the aim of sex is toward a progressive integration of the several necessary levels of sexual function, (4) human sex requires both intensity and steadfastness with a proper relationship between them, (5) the good of any sex act always depends in some measure upon the inner meaning to the persons involved, but the sole ultimate standard is the judgment and love of God.[8]

How is this Christian view different from the traditional sex mores? For one thing, it is adequate and inspiring on the positive side, whereas the traditional code emphasizes the negative, and the concrete. Hiltner thinks that Kinsey has distorted the Judaeo-Christian view by reading it through the ideas of his subjects. He asserts that this Judaeo-Christian tradition assigns more positive value to the sex act itself, than is generally realized. He agrees in general with D. S. Bailey, an Anglican clergyman, who reads real flesh and not merely a symbol in the Biblical doctrine on "one flesh." [9] These scholars both seem to feel that although the sex act should be kept within marriage, yet it has a God-sanctioned value which is not dependent upon marriage as an institution nor upon the intention to procreate.

John J. Kane argues that the Catholic attitude toward sex has been seriously misunderstood by many Catholics as well as outsiders. Actually it is warmer, healthier, more positive than it seems. Catholic thought is not responsible for the identification of sex with the obscene or pornographic. But there is a certain caution in verbalizing it. "Since conjugal love is both a legitimate and beautiful kind of love, and since it is expressed in sexual union, the marital sex union should also be considered in that light." [10] If this approach

differs significantly from the approach of the other branches of the Judaeo-Christian tradition, the difference, according to the present writer, involves a general tendency to leave many things publicly unsaid, to assume a benevolent, paternal control over the circulation of symbols and ideas. This may have had value in protecting the sex drive from fears and disgusts as well as guarding it against superfluous stimulation. This may account for a certain kind of healthy-mindedness in the Catholic attitude toward sex. The question is, can any such paternalistic control stand up indefinitely in the open ideological market of modern society, or must it be replaced by other controls?

Hiltner's Christian view, or in purely humanistic terms, his personal-interpersonal attitude, emphasizes "man as a total being." Two serious problems will arise: one has to do with the individual man as a total being, and the other with the total population of men as endowed with the same human needs and intrinsic worth.

In the total of needs, drives, and interests which make up the individual man, there is a class of *defensive* drives such as anger-and-aggression, and fear-and-escape. In a sense these are antagonistic to the rest of the personality; they are necessary evils, weapons held in reserve against emergencies, and they operate through a branch of the nervous system which is antagonistic to the branch concerned with hunger, sexual excitation, and the routine bodily processes. Anger does sometimes become linked with sexual desire, and the result may be sadism. Do we want more of that? Do we want to encourage the very natural linkage of sex with jealousy, a partly defensive emotion, because of the useful weapon this gives against sexual infidelity; or would we minimize jealousy as an evil and try to find adequate substitute weapons? We do wish to link sex more closely with tender love toward the mate, a linkage which seems to be deficient in some persons and cultures. Yet we fear that tenderness toward other love-objects such as children, one's own sex, or the spouse of one's friend, might lead to erotic feeling.

Perhaps no group of drives plays so large a part in the higher development of man as do the *exploratory* drives of curiosity, acquisition, construction, aesthetic creation, and the like. The full story of man as a total being is not understood until we recognize that man strives to make new connections, craves new experiences, strives to enter all fields he can within the limits of time, energy, and empirically adequate safety. Denis de Rougemont seems to recognize that sexual ad-

---

* The Jewish view seems to be incorporated within this.
  [8] *Ibid.*, pp. 179–180.
  [9] D. S. Bailey, *The Mystery of Love and Marriage, A Study in the Theology of Sexual Relations,* New York: Harper & Bros., 1952. See *Genesis* 2:24 and *Ephesians* 5:31.
  [10] John J. Kane, *Marriage and the Family, A Catholic Approach,* New York: Dryden Press, 1952, p. 258.

venture provides some positive values which cannot be dismissed merely by calling them bad names. His answer is that marital fidelity is also a value, a faith chosen for its own sake, and to choose it means to renounce the values both of "spontaneity" and "manifold experience." [11]

Kinsey's outstanding discovery about sex differences is that males are erotically stimulated by a much greater variety of objects and mental images than are females. He thinks this is due to some biological difference. Hiltner is inclined to question this interpretation. That there is such a *biological* difference, however, is suggested by Slater and Woodside. "If the race were so constituted that female orgasm occurred before male, she might very well thereupon terminate coitus before the chance of conception had occurred. A male constitution that provided for ejaculation at the earliest possible moment after intromission would be a selective advantage." [12] More generally, we may theorize, nature is wasteful, and reproduction may be best assured by having an excess of male *excitement* present all the time, at the same time that the female, for short periods, may seem almost insatiable. Clearly ethics cannot be derived simply from natural law any more than it can from existing custom. But, on the other hand, an ethic of human fulfillment would continually seek harmless ways to use rather than waste, to integrate rather than to keep separate, the various and abundant potentialities of man.

The other serious problem is the problem of humanity as a whole population. Does the Christian view of sex hold that persons, when they cannot achieve the ideal, should renounce sex altogether? Must sex be used only during some limited period of one's lifetime, depriving especially men in youth and women in older years, often at the very times they are strongest in biological drive? Strange to say, these absolute deprivations would be much easier to endure were it not for the existence of a rather elastic supply of surplus sexuality in the non-deprived people of the opposite sex. Conversely, the surplus sexuality of these latter would not bother them so much were it not for their knowledge of the absolute deprivations existing among potential partners. One might almost say that sex, like "nature," abhors a vacuum, and that this characteristic is likely to increase the more we rationalize (in Max Weber's sense) and civilize our sexuality.

The problem is not a simple choice between two alternates. At least four distinct values are involved: (1) sexual exclusiveness, (2) permanence of marriage or intimate relationships, (3) male initiative in courtship and economic production, (4) better intersexual balance and wider satisfaction of the biological sex need. Any three of these can be attained better by sacrificing, or honestly subordinating and risking, the fourth. The least discussed possibility, though not necessarily the most hopeful, is the subordination of value three. That is, if boys were to marry soon after sexual maturity, taking wives a few years older, expecting more economic responsibility and courtship initiative from the girls, much of the problem as Kinsey portrays it might be relieved, and there would also be less widowhood.

But perhaps there are weightier considerations than these. If so, they will endure the strain of public exposure and discussion. Sex may be a dangerous thing, but now that we have radioactive dust floating about, any alarm over the insidious consequences of the "Kinsey bomb" should seem to be somewhat amusing.

---

[11] Denis de Rougemont, *Love in the Western World*, New York: Harcourt, Brace and Co., 1940, p. 290.

[12] Eliot Slater and Moya Woodside, *New Patterns in Marriage*, London: Cassell and Co., 1951, p. 175.

The Lonely Hearts
Lee E. Graham

Lee E. Graham (1918–   ), free-lance writer of articles and stories.

In a city of seven million, . . . there are thousands of lonely hearts. They don't lack vitamins, a double Scotch, or a book club subscription. They don't suffer from dishpan hands, pink toothbrush, of five o'clock shadow. Nor are they actual social misfits whom Dale Carnegie, himself, couldn't

---

"None But the Lonely Heart," *The New York Times Magazine* (September 1, 1946), p. 27. Reprinted by permission.

help. All they need is a little aid in finding friends.

To make their hearts less lonely, a streamlined kind of matchmaking, tactfully referred to as a "social contact bureau" or a "friendship service," has been devised. There are over a dozen such places in town—none of which, incidentally, are required to be licensed—each run by a silken-voiced woman with an I-would-like-to-help-you glow in her eyes. And, indeed, for a nominal down payment, she can.

Supposing Mary Smith, private secretary, sees one of their ads in the subway or on a bus, swallows her pride, and decides to investigate. Lighting a cigarette for nonchalance, she telephones at home, and learns that an interview is free. She arrives the next day after work, mutters, "I never thought I'd come to a place like this," is convinced in a few minutes that it was a marvelous idea, has her vital statistics and preferences recorded, pays her membership fee (usually $25), and leaves with the promise that as many introductions as possible will be supplied during the next six months.

The silken-voiced woman then combs her files for compatible males, and soon Mary is phoned or written to by Joe Doakes for a date. If Mary doesn't like Joe after going out with him, she asks for another contact. If Joe happens to make her heart beat a little bit faster, she continues to see him—providing he wants to continue—and the rest is up to her. Even so, she still has the privilege of meeting more men. The average is five to a customer, although one fussy schoolteacher managed thirty-two. The procedure is exactly the same for Joe Doakes.

The results of this organized effort to make the right romance paths cross are summed up in an interview with a woman who has been handling lonely hearts for ten years. Sitting behind three telephones and a wide desk, she said: "I've had over ten thousand clients and am responsible for at least eight hundred marriages. And I'm sure there are more I haven't heard about. Not that we are a matrimonial bureau. Think of this as a nonsectarian clearing house for men and women who want to defeat loneliness."

She stopped to answer a call her secretary had switched in, and then continued:

"The most difficult clients to handle are the short fat men, the too tall girls, and the overanxious women past 45. Naturally, appearance is important, but just being sweet and friendly goes a long way. There is a faster turnover among brunettes than blondes, and girls born in New York are least in demand. The rules of opposites being attracted usually holds good—Southerners will insist upon Yankees, and Germans are often interested in the French.

"But when a client is on the rebound, he invariably wants to meet a girl who looks like the sweetheart who quarreled with him or like the wife who divorced him. And when a date is a flop, I must confess the man is usually the better sport about it. In general, we don't get wolves or coquettes, because the people who come here are serious and want more than a casual relationship."

Still, with all the chances, for boy to meet girl provided by jamming into subways, going to church, sitting on park benches in the spring, joining clubs, and battling for seats in downtown movie palaces, how do the lonely hearts explain their paradoxical plight?

An energetic red-headed nurse replies, "You can't go around talking to men you don't know. And the only ones I meet are married doctors or patients who want to talk about their operations." A middle-aged widower confesses, "I don't know how to approach strange women any more. My wife was my only companion for twenty years."

A lady professor admits, "Men are intimidated by my position. They don't think of me as a woman." An ex-G.I. says, "I'm sick of kids you can pick up in a bar. I want an older clean-cut kind of gal—one who'll understand me." A little Brooklyn stenographer moans, "Where I work there's nothing but lots of other girls. Sure, the boss is a man—but he never looks at me." And a bespectacled young lawyer complains, "I'm too busy during the day to look for women. Anyway, most of them concentrate too much on their appearance. I want one to share my mental life."

These answers are not the glib rationalizations of people who are especially unattractive or overwhelmingly shy. If you met all the participants in a Gallup poll, you wouldn't find a more average group. They're tall, dark, and handsome; short, fair, and plain. Some are divorced, some are widowed, and the rest have never been married, but continue to hope. Their ages vary from 18 to 50, but an occasional octogenarian crops up among them like the one who just left to take his fifth bride. Most have high-school diplomas, quite a few their college sheepskins, and Phi Beta Kappa keys dangle from a couple of vest chains. They go to the movies, try to answer $64 questions, and miss three-inch steaks like anybody else. Eight out of ten are not native New Yorkers; a great many hail from the Middle West, where speaking to a stranger on the street is not rebuked by silence and a cold stare. Their dilemma, as Mrs. [Franklin D.] Roosevelt remarked, is "the third greatest problem in our nation," and their number is legion.

CROSS REFERENCES TO STANDARD TEXTS *

Barnes, *Society in Transition,* Chap. 8.

Bernard, *American Community Behavior,* Chaps. 11, 24.

Bloch, *Disorganization,* Chap. 7.

Brown, *Social Pathology,* Chap. 8.

Cuber and Harper, *Problems of American Society,* Chap. 11.

Elliott and Merrill, *Social Disorganization,* Chap. 4.

Faris, *Social Disorganization,* Chap. 10.

Gillin, *Social Pathology,* Chaps. 11, 14, and 15.

—— and others, *Social problems,* Chap. 13.

Herman, *Approach to Social Problems,* Chap. 12.

* For complete bibliographical reference to each text, see page 13.

Landis, *Social Policies in the Making,* Chaps. 12–15.

Lemert, *Social Pathology,* Chap. 8.

Merrill and others, *Social Problems,* Chaps. 11–13.

Mihanovich, *Current Social Problems,* Chaps. 8–10.

Neumeyer, *Social Problems and the Changing Society,* Chap. 7.

Nordskog and others, *Analyzing Social Problems,* Chap. 6.

Odum, *American Social Problems,* Chap. 11.

Phelps and Henderson, *Contemporary Social Problems,* Chap. 8.

Reinhardt and others, *Social Problems and Social Policy,* Chaps. 10, 11.

Weaver, *Social Problems,* Chaps. 18, 19, and 21.

OTHER BIBLIOGRAPHY

Ray E. Baber, *Marriage and the Family,* 2d ed., New York: McGraw-Hill Book Co., 1953.

Howard Becker and Reuben Hill, eds., *Family, Marriage and Parenthood,* Boston: D. C. Heath and Co., 1948.

Peter Blos, *The Adolescent Personality,* New York: D. Appleton-Century, 1941.

Ernest W. Burgess, Paul Wallin, and Gladys Denny Shultz, *Courtship, Engagement and Marriage,* Philadelphia: J. B. Lippincott Co., 1954.

—— and H. J. Locke, *The Family,* 2d ed., New York: American Book Co., 1953.

Ruth Shonle Cavan, *The American Family,* New York: Thomas Y. Crowell Co., 1953, Chap. 11.

Luella Cole, *Psychology of Adolescence,* 3d ed., New York: Rinehart & Co., 1948.

Helene Deutsch, *Psychology of Women,* New York: Grune & Stratton, 1944, Vol. 1.

James Lee Ellenwood, *Just and Durable Parents,* New York: Charles Scribner's Sons, 1948.

Marynia Farnham, *The Adolescent,* New York: Harper & Bros., 1951.

Ruth Fedder, *A Girl Grows Up,* 2d ed., New York: McGraw-Hill Book Co., 1948.

E. Franklin Frazier, *Negro Youth at the Crossways,* Washington: American Council on Education, 1940.

Fred S. Hall, "Child Marriage: United States," *Encyclopaedia of the Social Sciences,* 3 (1930): 397–398, 429.

Ernest Havemann and Patricia Salter West, *They Went to College: The College Graduate in America Today,* New York: Harcourt, Brace and Co., 1952.

Robert James Havighurst and Hilda Taba, *Adolescent Character and Personality,* New York: John Wiley & Sons, 1949.

August B. Hollingshead, *Elmstown's Youth,* New York: John Wiley & Sons, 1949.

John E. Horrocks, *The Psychology of Adolescence, Behavior and Development,* Boston, Houghton Mifflin Co., 1951.

Elizabeth B. Hurlock, *Adolescent Development,* New York: McGraw-Hill Book Co., 1949.

Charles S. Johnson, *Growing Up in the Black Belt,* Washington: American Council on Education, 1941.

Alfred C. Kinsey, Wardell B. Pomeroy, and Clyde E. Martin, *Sexual Behavior in the Human Male,* Philadelphia: W. B. Saunders Co., 1948.

——, ——, ——, and Paul H. Gebhard, *Sexual Behavior in the Human Female,* Philadelphia: W. B. Saunders Co., 1953.

Raymond G. Kuhlen, *The Psychology of Adolescent Development,* New York: Harper & Bros., 1952.

Paul H. Landis, *Adolescence and Youth,* New York: McGraw-Hill Book Co., 1945.

——, *Your Dating Days,* New York: Whittlesey House, McGraw-Hill Book Co., 1954.

—— and Mary G. Landis, *Building a Successful Marriage,* 2d ed., New York: Prentice-Hall, 1953.

Alfred McClung Lee, "Courtship, Marriage, Divorce," Chap. 32 in Lee, ed., *Principles of Sociology,* 2d ed. rev., New York: Barnes & Noble, 1951, pp. 308–317.

Marguerite Malm, *Adolescence,* New York: McGraw-Hill Book Co., 1952.

Meyer F. Nimkoff, *Marriage and the Family,* rev. ed., Boston: Houghton Mifflin Co., 1947.

Stuart A. Queen and John B. Adams, *The Family in Various Cultures,* Philadelphia: J. B. Lippincott Co., 1952.

William I. Thomas, *The Unadjusted Girl,* Boston: Little, Brown and Co., 1927.

Frederick M. Thrasher, *The Gang*, 2d ed., Chicago: University of Chicago Press, 1936.

Willard Waller, *The Family: A Dynamic Interpretation*, rev. by Reuben Hill, New York: Dryden Press, 1951.

————, *The Old Love and the New*, New York: Boni & Liveright, 1930.

Goodwin Watson, *Youth After Conflict*, New York: Association Press, 1947.

Helen L. Witmer and Ruth Kotinsky, eds., *Personality in the Making: The Fact-Finding Report of the Mid-Century White House Conference on Children and Youth*, New York: Harper & Bros., 1952.

REVIEW QUESTIONS

1. Give some of Davis's reasons why western civilization manifests such an extraordinary amount of parent-adolescent conflict. What do you think of his ideas?
2. Why is it easily possible that parent-adolescent conflict has been exaggerated?
3. What can be learned about parent-youth conflict through comparing stable and changing societies?
4. How does the keen reasoning ability of young people complicate their relatively unchecked idealism?
5. How does life in the modern middle-class home insure that a son in it shall feel competitive pressures?
6. Why do Komarovsky's upper middle-class college girls often define their culturally set personality traits with reference to their definition of the male sex role?
7. Would Komarovsky's female role contradictions apply to other class groups in our society?
8. What basic social problems do male and female role contradictions present?
9. What is the relationship of social class level to sexual activity among American boys and men?
10. To what social problems do you think that the Kinsey study, as reported by Deutsch, point? How are we likely to find solutions for these problems?
11. How does Folsom suggest that we go about utilizing the Kinsey findings? What does he mean by the "personal-interpersonal" attitude?
12. According to Folsom, how does the Christian view differ from traditional sex mores?
13. Of what does a "lonely hearts" service consist? As a problem-solving device, would you say that it is worth any risks involved?
14. What do you think of the comment that a person "on the rebound . . . invariably wants to meet a girl who looks like the sweetheart who quarreled with him or like the wife who divorced him"?

CHAPTER 9 →

Adults

THE PROBLEMS of our confused adolescent period have, as one would expect, their counterparts in problems associated with our changed sex roles in the adult community. Mead introduces this discussion with her essay on "What Women Want." In this selection, she objectively describes and analyzes the American woman's current situation and ways in which to deal with its maladjusted features. Deutsch sheds additional light on the adult phase of male sex roles in his interpretation of the Kinsey report's adult findings.

These selections extend our conception of personality problems and provide a background for marriage maladjustments. The following six essays then relate such problem personalities to breakdowns in parental and marital arrangements. Vincent's findings indicate bias in sampling methods may have given a distorted impression of the problem of unwed motherhood. Elmer outlines the extent and character of the problems of children born out of wedlock and especially of their parents. Green analyzes the remote and nominal relationship of many middle-class fathers to their children, the indefiniteness of the roles and functions of their wives, and some of the consequences thereof. King furnishes a careful discussion of the Negro maternal family and the problems it presents to the Negro community in various parts of the United States. McLean helps to bring the implications of the chapter's selections together by analyzing emotional background factors in marital difficulties. Thorman summarizes statistics on trends in divorce and desertion and attempts to interpret the significance of persistent increases in divorce rates. Burgess and Wallin discuss the character of marriage counseling, the nature of the role of the counselor and his methods, and marriage counseling as an emerging profession. Many regard this activity as a fairly successful type of marriage "repair shop."

The status of modern woman, the vast increase in divorce, our lack of adherence to our proclaimed moral codes, the emotional isolation of many fathers from their families because of working conditions—all these are features of the marital chaos in large sections of our society in these times. Fortunately, as some selections are careful to indicate, ways are being found which are proving effective in mitigating these pressing social problems.

As the American population has accumulated more and more older people, interest in the health and welfare of the aging has steadily increased. Tibbitts points out the many ramifications of retirement as a relatively new phenomenon in our society, the tremendous number of problems accompanying it, and some of our efforts to meet them.

Only the short-lived miss age. But to all men, soon or late, comes death. "As sex dominates the first half of life," Eliot notes, "so death dominates the latter half." He not only suggests psychological and sociological characteristics of death as a social problem but summarizes his findings with regard to ways in which families change as a result of bereavement. With deep understanding, Eliot writes, "The art of death should be part of the art of life, even as the art of love."

What Women Want

Margaret Mead

Margaret Mead (1901–   ), associate curator of ethnology, American Museum of Natural History. Principal works: *Coming of Age in Samoa* (1928); *An Inquiry Into the Question of Cultural Stability in Polynesia* (1928); *Growing Up in New Guinea* (1930); *The Changing Culture of an Indian Tribe* (1932); *And Keep Your Powder Dry* (1942); *Male and Female* (1949); with Frances Macgregor, *Soviet Attitudes Toward Authority* (1951); and *Growth and Culture* (1951)

If we have to make some adjustments so that women will feel that they have as much choice as men, and if, given choice, many of them elect to work outside the home at least part of the time, what will happen to the home? Will it become so difficult to bring up children to be full human beings that outraged voices will sound throughout society and shout women back into the home again?

If we look at history, present and past, and at the position of women all over the world, among savage and civilized peoples, we find that it is possible for society to do almost anything with the relationships between men and women. There are cultures where women are dominating and men responsive, where women manage the finances and men wheedle pocket money out of them and spend their time daydreaming of forgery and alchemy, where women initiate the love affairs and no man would be so foolhardy as to make the first advances, where both men and women enjoy and rear the children; cultures where fathers are indulgent and loving and mothers stern disciplinarians, where girls grow up envying boys and wishing they had been born boys, and cultures where boys grow up envying girls, wishing they had been born girls. Human beings are exceedingly plastic, and the relationship of men and women to each other is a very flexible thing.

If in assaying our own society we find that we have educated women to want to act in terms of their full individuality, and not as members of the sex that bears children, and that this education isn't working very well, what alternatives can we consider? There are scientists—especially from the fields of biology, medicine, and psychiatry—who feel the answer would be to re-emphasize women's biological role: bearing and feeding children. They would recommend educating girls, not to be persons first and women second, but to be women primarily, women who will see the only choice they want to make as a choice among potential fathers of their children. They point to the neurosis from which childless women suffer, and conclude that although human beings are very flexible, they are not so flexible that we can ignore the fact that woman was born to reproduce the race.

These exponents of a biological rather than a social outlook make a plausible argument, supported by many case histories of maladjusted women. American culture may in time return to a respect for the biological realities, but at present that is not our direction. We are not likely to abandon coeducation and bring up children from infancy with different toys and different kinds of exercise in order to limit the horizon of girls and so condition them to their biological role. The whole trend in the U. S. is away from every sort of biological limitation on human activity and achievement. If you are born with the wrong-shaped nose, it can be operated on. If your cheek bones are too high, rouge can be put on to change the effect. If your eyes are too close together, an eyebrow pencil can make the correction. Straight hair can be curled, weak eyes reinforced by glasses, the deaf made to hear by better and better hearing devices. Facial surgery, false limbs, and every sort of skill and device are brought to compensate for physical defect, while the congenitally unsociable take courses in how to make friends. And we are not willing to honor other accidents of birth. Primogeniture was swept away almost at once in America, for why should mere order of birth give one brother privilege over another? Biological facts of ugliness, sickness, physical handi-

From "What Women Want," *Fortune,* 34: 6 (December 1946): 172–175, 218, 220, 223, 224, pp. 175, 218, 220 223, and 224 quoted. Reprinted by permission.

cap, and death are limiting facts—and the American is interested in transcending limitations, not in conforming to them. Death—which is the one biological fact that we have found no way to transcend with technological devices—we ignore as far as possible. The effects of age, especially on women, are staved off with every known device. Congruently with this tendency to ignore and deny any biological limitation, less than 3 per cent of those responding to the *Fortune* Survey question about who had an easier time, men or women, mentioned that women bore children. Women were described as "bringing up children," "looking after children," "having all the care of the children." By ignoring the fact that women bear children, and by feeding the newborn out of bottles, we make it possible for social patterning to transcend biological limitations. There is no evidence that suggests women are naturally better at *caring* for children than men would be. In other words, with the fact of childbearing out of the center of attention, there is even more reason for treating girls first as human beings and then as women.

If a return to a stronger social emphasis on women's biological role is therefore unlikely in the U. S., what are the other possible solutions? There are many who will press for the diffusion of homemaking among a mass of community agencies, nursery schools, day-care centers, laundries, diaper services, play schools, and infirmaries. Women who work outside the home because they must [1] thus will no longer carry the impossible double burden they carry now, and women who work outside the home because they elect that way of life can have their children adequately cared for. There is no doubt that we need many more of such resources to care for the children of working mothers, to get rid of door-key children playing in the streets because there is no one at home, and

---

[1] In a study made in 1945 by the Women's Bureau of some 13,000 women employed in ten war-congested areas, of every 100 women who said they intended to keep on working, eighty-four gave as their reason support for themselves and others, eight gave such special economic reasons as home ownership or to be free from debt or to educate their children, and only eight said they would continue to work primarily because of interest in their jobs. When we place these figures beside the steadily increasing number of employed women in the U. S. (1880: 2,647,-000; 1920: 8,550,000; 1940: 11,000,000; an expected 16,-000,000 by 1950) [1953: 19,000,000—*Eds.*], it will be seen that failure to take into account this great army of women who *must* work seriously distorts any understanding of the position of women in America.

also to remove from the home a lot of useless drudgery that is out of line with our standards of efficiency. But, if we really take out of the home everything that the woman as homemaker is supposed to do in it, it is questionable whether we shall have homes at all. This solution has been tried, in wartime, in almost every large country. Child specialists have studied children who grow up in institutions, and the results are discouraging. Unless all the institutions where the children are taken care of in droves are staffed by a very large number of women *and* men to replace the missing parents, the children don't come out human. They don't know how to fall in love, marry, and have children—to say nothing of their becoming responsible, self-initiating human beings.

To get the kind of human beings on which a society like America depends (individuals with enterprise, self-starters able to form a committee and tackle any problem at the drop of a hat) we need to bring up our children in homes—and in homes where mothers have as high a position as fathers. This war has taught us what kind of personalities are developed in traditional Japanese or Nazi homes where women are reduced to a despised position. We are doubly committed by our general repudiation of biological limitations and by our demand for upstanding individuals who neither bully nor cringe, to having our children reared in homes by parents who can look each other in the eye with mutual respect. Yet the home as it is now constructed violates our feelings about choice, a freedom that is necessary if American women are to feel themselves as dignified as men in their social roles. Are there other solutions?

Bring Men Home. If we can't go back to treating women as special child-bearing creatures but must treat them as persons, and yet can't give up the home for a lot of institutions that aren't able to develop children's personalities, there is at least one other possible solution. We can meet women's demand for choice and for work that brings them out of their isolated houses and flats if at the same time that we make it possible for the married women to get out of the home we also encourage the married man to take more of a share in it. This is not a plea for getting fathers to wash dishes. There is no proof at all that children's personalities are dependent upon anybody's washing dishes. The Samoans eat off leaves, the Eskimos pass a large hunk of meat from hand to hand, the Malays cook rice in green bamboo, crack the bamboo, and throw it away. The only possible connection between housekeeping and bringing up children is that while an adult is doing something with the hands, it is easy to watch and talk with a child. But cleaning the car is equally suitable, or planting the garden, or feeding the goldfish, for that matter. The best fathers and the best mothers probably do some physical things—walk, skate, climb, swim, whittle, build models, shine the silver—with their children. But there is no reason why most of the present drudgery of housekeeping, the sort of drudgery that takes up the hours that might be spent in some different surroundings, shouldn't go out of the home altogether. Then groups of women will work in canning factories, instead of each one canning at home, and those who like laundries will work together in laundries, as the women of Europe once laughed and gossiped as they washed their clothes on the riverbanks. What would remain in the home would be shared living, a family eating, sleeping, and playing together. It is actually the arranging of this shared living that keeps the middle-class woman tied to her house—no matter how many frozen vegetables she is able to buy—and keeps the woman who works sagged and tired from trying to coordinate her home activities and her work hours. Yet women have no special biological fitness for fetching children from school, for telephoning to moving men, for selecting seeds for the summer garden, for buying phonograph records, or for choosing the upholstery for the car. All of these activities are merely human, and many of them are pleasant and offer a welcome counterpoint to a man's office routine. That one of women's great desires is to get American men to take more of a share in the *human* as opposed to the vanishing *production* side of home life showed up in the *Fortune* Survey. There the larger number of women expressed themselves as specifically wanting fathers to take equal part in disciplining the children, and a large number of both sexes felt that such questions as when to have children or how to spend money should be decided not by one sex or the other but by both. When men take a greater part in these activities that we call living, as opposed to making a living, we shall approach again the sort of balance between the sexes that we had in early America, on our American farms, when both worked together at the same tasks, often within earshot of each other.

Woman's Choice. Letting men into the home and giving them a greater share in making choices about the way in which life is to be enjoyed would probably not effect a great revolution in American social life. A large proportion of women would probably elect homemaking—without outside work—as a full-time occupation for generations to come, unless war or new forms of political organization compelled them to do otherwise. Given freedom of choice, given the possibility of a marriage in which bringing up children and holding a job or pursuing a career do not present an impossible combination, most women will find one reason for their discontent removed and continue to give their time to homemaking. That is what their mothers did, and that is the basic picture of home life that they absorbed as small children. But such a pattern of life would include choice. Young people consider whether they will get a car and a smaller house, or a larger house and wait for the car, or whether they will build a shack at the seashore or go somewhere different each summer. They might also come to consider how the work is to be divided. Shall they both work and share the expense of getting the drudgery out of the house, and share also the task of keeping life going at home, or shall the girl elect to spend her full time at home, even if it means some drudgery because they won't be able to afford laundry services and precooked foods?

The position of women in America at present is explosive and potentially harmful. It keeps a great number of employed women working unhappily, troubled and anxious about the home they also have to manage somehow. It makes a great number of educated women feel they are faced with an unbearable choice and leaves them correspondingly unhappy whichever choice they make. It produces many maladjusted children who reflect their mothers' discontent. It makes for a general uneasiness in society. Once the vote was an issue. Yet, when women were given the vote, it was found that the vote—such a terrible issue when they were denied it—became a mild enough routine of life. Only a few women went into politics, only a few became active party workers. But a disturbed area of life, a sense of festering injustice, was removed. The participation of women as citizens was improved, and life went back on a more even keel. A climate of opinion that ceases to regard married women as if they were inherently different from other human beings, that regards marriage as the privilege of all human beings and homemaking as a job for any pair of parents who take it on, would have the same stabilizing effect on women's present confused discontent.

A climate of opinion in itself is important only because it results in change. Once parenthood is regarded as a joint job for both parents and women are no longer regarded as persons to whom a certain amount of drudgery is biologically appropriate, we can make the inventions required to take a good part of the drudgery out of the home. Some of these will be technological: for example, precooked-food service and dish-washeries that launder the dishes the way laundries now do the linen. Some of them will be institutional:

for example, residential emergency centers where children can be cared for when there is illness in the home. Some of them may even be new forms of housing and new neighborhood ways of living in which a group of women share in the care of the children. When we eliminated slavery we opened the way for a million labor-saving inventions in field and factory. Elimination of the semivoluntary slavery to housekeeping that we now impose on married women in the U. S. should open the way for an equally significant set of inventions in that key spot of our civilization, the home, where not "things" but human beings are produced and developed.

Class Differences in Male Sex Roles
Albert Deutsch*

Perhaps the most significant result of the Kinsey survey [1] is the revelation that there is no single "American sex pattern," but rather there are scores of different patterns, based mainly on social differences in the population. Dr. Kinsey and his colleagues have found wider differences in the sex habits of social groups living within the same community than anthropologists have reported between peoples separated by vast geographical distances.

The sex habits of the grade school son of a semi-skilled laborer in an East Side New York tenement and the college-destined son of the business executive living in the swank apartment house around the corner may contrast more widely than those of an African jungle boy and an Eskimo youth. The discovery of these tremendous variations in American sex habits is of incalculable importance, since our moral and legal codes are based largely on the assumption that "normal" Americans share a common pattern of sex behavior.

Human sex patterns, Kinsey observes, are based on three major factors—the biologic, the psycho-

logic, and the social. Of these, the social factor is the most important. The individual's sex habits are formed mainly by his cultural environment— the social group in which he moves . . . or for which he is destined. The Kinsey group discloses a remarkable aspect of the close relationship between sexual patterns and socio-educational levels. One might take, for example, the family studied by the Kinsey group which included a semi-skilled worker and his five sons. Four sons never went beyond high school; their sex habits conformed to the lower-level socio-educational group. The fifth son, whose sex habits were akin to those of the college-level group, later went through college. Kinsey doesn't know, at this point, exactly what is the basis of this extraordinary link between sex habits and educational status; he knows only that the close relationship exists. The boy's sex pattern accords not so much to the socio-educational group into which he is born, but to the one he eventually moves into in later life.

There are sharp differences between the sex attitudes and habits of these socio-educational groups, but remarkable conformity among most individuals belonging to the same group. . . .

Implicit in [Kinsey's] revolutionary report is a plea for greater public and private tolerance of

[1] Alfred C. Kinsey, Wardell B. Pomeroy, and Clyde E. Martin, *Sexual Behavior in the Human Male*, Philadelphia: W. B. Saunders Company, 1948.

* See the identifying note on p. 133.

From the chapter by Albert Deutsch, "Kinsey, the Man and His Project," in *Sex Habits of American Men: A Symposium on the Kinsey Report*, edited by Albert Deutsch, and published by Prentice-Hall, Inc., New York, pp. 26–29, 32–33. Copyright 1948 by Prentice-Hall, Inc. Reprinted by permission.

the vast differences in the sex habits of Americans. A revaluation of our ideas of normal and abnormal sex behavior is indicated. Such terms as unnatural, bestial, frigid, under-sexed and over-sexed, as used in our moral and legal codes, have little validity in the light of the Kinsey findings. The Kinsey study reveals a tremendous range of variety in the frequency and types of sexual behavior of apparently normal Americans. . . .

The average American boy of grade school level, between the ages of 16 and 20, masturbates only half as often as the college-level youth of the same age, but has seven times more sexual intercourse than the latter. Kinsey points out that mothers afraid to send their sons to college for fear of moral corruption there evidently are unaware of the histories of boys who stay at home.

Kissing is a common part of love-making among people in the upper social levels, but is widely abhorred as filthy and unhygienic and even perverse among those in the lower levels. Upper level family circles display a far greater acceptance of nudity than do lower level families. Those in the upper levels tend to be far stricter about non-marital sexual intercourse, but far more tolerant of masturbation and petting. Emphasizing the global peculiarities in sex attitudes, Kinsey observes that a Latin American audience may view complacently an artistic film about nudity that would shock the average American audience, but may hiss down as "obscene" a typical Hollywood movie with kissing scenes. . . .

The laws regarding sexual behavior are written, interpreted and enforced mainly by people in the upper educational and social levels, who mostly conform to the particular pattern of their kind. Most sexual mores are imposed on modern society by those belonging to the 15 per cent of the population which is college-trained. But the Kinsey study shows that a vast gulf lies between this 15 per cent and the 85 per cent who never go to college. The upper level group tends to view sex from a moral standpoint—on the basis of what's right and wrong. The lower level group, on the other hand, regards sexual behavior from the viewpoint of the natural and the unnatural. To most members of this group, sexual intercourse seems natural and therefore right, whether or not it has legal sanction. They view as disgusting perversions many of the love-making habits (such as deep-kissing) considered "civilized" by upper level people.

In general, Kinsey notes, the upper level condemns lower level morality as lacking in the proper ideals and righteousness. The lower level regards upper level sex mores as artificial and insincere. Legends of lower level immorality are matched by legends of upper level perversions.

"One is inclined to accept the particular legends that apply to the group to which one does not belong," Kinsey observes.

The data on extra-marital relations reveal a striking difference between upper and lower level sex patterns. The report indicates that anywhere between 30 and 45 per cent of married American males have intercourse with women other than their wives. Over 60 per cent of married males who never go beyond grade school engage in such extra-marital relations. The Kinsey group reveals another curious fact of social significance: Lower level married males tend to have most extra-marital intercourse in the early years of wedded life, but become increasingly faithful to their wives with the passage of time. In the upper levels, on the other hand, extra-marital intercourse shows a gradual increase during the course of marriage of college-trained men. Dr. Kinsey, with the keen wit that characterizes so many passages in his absorbing book, observes that some may interpret these data to mean that the lower level starts out by trying promiscuity and finally concludes that strict monogamy pays off better; another interpretation would be that the upper level starts out by trying monogamy and finally decides that variety is more desirable. Neither interpretation is quite correct. Kinsey adds: the main factors are to be found in different sexual adjustments in marriage at different levels, and also in the force of the mores underlying most of these class differences.

Unwed Mothers

Clark E. Vincent

Clark E. Vincent (1923–   ), instructor, University of California at Berkeley. Author of "Middle-Class Illegitimacy," in William Petersen, ed., *Five Studies of American Society,* New York: Anchor Books, Inc., forthcoming, 1955.

A preliminary survey of the available data on unwed motherhood reveals that historically a variety of etiological factors have been emphasized. Studies made during the 1920's stressed such causal factors as "immorality" and "mental deficiency." During the 1930's the findings pointed to the factors of a "broken home," "poverty," "little education," and "domestic occupation." Within the past two decades, unwed motherhood has been explained increasingly as an accepted pattern of life in a given sub-culture. However, the most frequent emphasis at the present time appears to be upon psychological processes. The majority of current studies conclude that unwed motherhood is a product of unresolved parent-child conflict and represents an "unrealistic way out of inner difficulties."

Equally evident from such a survey is the fact that in the majority of investigations reported, the samples of unwed mothers were taken from public institutions, welfare agencies or psychiatric clinics. Out of 48 studies surveyed, 39 or 81.3 per cent used samples of unwed mothers taken from psychiatric clinics, social agencies, charity institutions and private therapy cases. Another 10.4 per cent of the studies drew samples from a particular socio-economic or ethnic sub-group, and the remaining 8.3 per cent comprised statistical analyses of available data from a national or international level of incidence.

This method of sampling has prolonged the picture of the unwed mother as being an extremely young, poor, uneducated or psychologically disturbed female. This portrayal has persisted despite the impressions of many professional people working with the unwed mother that this is a phenomenon occuring quite frequently among middle-income, normal and well-educated women. . . . This sampling procedure is in part related to the ease with which such

groups can be studied. It is also related to, and in turn reinforces, a like-causes-like approach which tends to regard unwed motherhood as bad and then emphasizes bad or pathological etiological factors. . . .

The findings reported in the present paper * resulted from a deliberate attempt to sample unwed mothers who do not go to agencies, clinics or institutions. The data were based on a 71 per cent response from 576 doctors who provided information on 137 unwed mothers delivered in private practice in Alameda County, California, during 1952.

The following findings suggest the need for more inclusive samples in studies of unwed motherhood and raise additional questions for future research. Of the 137 unwed mothers delivered in private practice:

83.9 per cent were white;

51.8 per cent were 22 years of age or older;

38.0 per cent had attended or completed college and 34.3, 24.8, and 35.8 per cent respectively of their fathers, mothers and alleged sexual mates had attended or completed college;

60.5 per cent were employed in professional or white collar jobs or were college students, and only 8.8 per cent were employed in semi-skilled or unskilled jobs;

36.5 per cent of 74 who were working, received a salary of 251.00 dollars or more per month;

78.4 per cent of those who came from out of the state to have their baby in California had attended or completed college;

50.0 per cent of those who had attended or completed college were mated sexually with a man seven or more years their senior;

70.0 per cent of those with less than a 12th

* [Detailed analyses and tables omitted.—*Eds.*]

From "The Unwed Mother and Sampling Bias," *American Sociological Review,* 19 (1954): 562–567, pp. 562, 566–567 quoted. Footnotes omitted. Reprinted by permission.

grade education were mated sexually with a man the same age or not more than two years their senior;

90.0 per cent of those who had attended or completed college were mated with an alleged sexual mate who had attended or completed college.

Occupational association appeared to be operative as a situational factor in some of the 89 cases for which occupational data were available for both the unwed mother and the alleged sexual mate.

Unmarried Parents
Manuel Conrad Elmer

Manuel Conrad Elmer (1886–   ), professor of sociology and head of department, University of Pittsburgh. Principal works: *Social Statistics* (1926); *Family Adjustment* (1932); *Social Research* (1939); with Verne Wright, *General Sociology* (1939); *The Sociology of the Family* (1945); and *Cultural Changes in Venezuela* (1953).

There is a tendency in the various states to adopt legislation recognizing the principles of responsibility of both parents for children born out of wedlock. The general non-support and desertion laws place liability for support of the child upon the father. . . . In general only the economic responsibilities are recognized, although there are instances, as is the case in North Dakota, where the child may take the surname of the father. Constructive measures more important than those dealing with the economic support of the child will be developed when we fully comprehend the social significance of the 75,000 to 100,000 illegitimate children being added to our population each year who do not have the opportunity for normal home environment. This problem will continue for some time even though constructive efforts are put forth to reduce the number of illegitimate children. . . .

Helen I. Clarke * indicated that social legislation relating to children of unmarried parents is moving in the direction of (*a*) giving the unmarried mother and her child a status comparable to that of lawful parents and children, (*b*) giving the illegitimate child the right to inherit property through its mother, (*c*) requiring support for the child from the man judged to be its father, (*d*) extending the procedures for legitimatizing the child, (*e*) placing the responsibility for establishing paternity and legitimatizing the child upon a state agency, and (*f*) placing the welfare of the mother and child above the financial interests of the community.

Clarke stated that "a large per cent of unmarried mothers come from low wage earning groups, the unmarried father contributes inadequately to the support of the child; hence, dependency has been increased by illegitimacy.". . .

The subject of the unmarried mother has been very extensively exploited, reasonably in view of the fact that the mother is recognized generally as the most important person in the rearing of children and in the care of the home. Likewise, the maternity of the child is more readily determined than its paternity. . . . An unmarried father ordered by the court to make payment for the support of his child seldom follows the order very carefully. . . .

Society generally looks upon the male parent as the financial provider and the mother as the parent who provides the love, affection, and socially approved forms of behavior. Owing to this overemphasis upon the economic role, the courts as well as society take the attitude that a financial settlement takes care of the father's obligations. This accords with the popular assumption of a good father's being an "adequate provider." The need of the child for a father's care and affection, the need of the father for an object of care and affection, and the contribution of a male parent which the child needs for his growth and development are overlooked. Further, while it is recognized that if a young unmarried mother is given the responsibility for her child she will develop attitudes desirable for the child and of value to her-

* *Social Legislation*, New York: D. Appleton-Century Co., 1940.—*Eds.*

From *The Sociology of the Family*, Boston: Ginn and Co., 1945, pp. 386–391. Reprinted by permission.

self, this same characteristic is not given sufficient weight in the case of the father. The assumption is that the father of the child is merely a temporary mate of the mother for which privilege he paid a fee toward the care of the child. The paternal responsibilities and reactions are assumed to be nonexistent in the case of unmarried fathers.

Recognition of the rights of individuals has been of rather slow growth. Most adults still remember when the policy of forcing a person to marry was generally conceded. Marriage for the purpose of giving a child a name, where the desire or intent of establishing a home is not present, has been found to complicate the difficulties rather than bring about a solution.

When marriage was to a large extent a convenient solution of the economic problem of providing a livelihood for a young woman, and a housekeeper for a young man, the matter of a happy relationship was of secondary importance. This attitude was further emphasized by the many legal handicaps of women as well as by the difficulty of becoming socially adjusted in a society which largely placed the blame upon the woman for a break in family life. Hence, when young people had violated the social and moral code and consequently the birth of a child was imminent, it was natural to feel that the only solution was a forced marriage. In many cases this solution was not only satisfactory but actually desired by both parties. In other cases the union was unfavorable from every aspect, and led only to further social and individual maladjustment. Regarding the unfavorable type of forced marriage Colcord very pointedly stated: "More surprising than all else, perhaps, is the attitude toward marriage, seemingly borrowed from the comic pages, that it is a suitable punishment for those who have offended. To hear marriage being

proffered to a man who has raped a young girl as an alternative to a prison sentence makes one feel as if this world we live in were as topsy-turvy as a madman's dream. It is not a high concept of marriage but a low one which contemplates its use either as quick-sale or as retribution." [1] Eubank concluded, "Forced marriages, loveless and consummated for the sole purpose of legitimizing the child, are almost foredoomed to failure." [2] . . . Our changing demands upon the family, and the refining of our concept of the objective of a family, require more than can be achieved by forced marriages.

The problem of children of unmarried parents in the population has two aspects. First, there is the child itself and the resultant inadequacy of his training and preparation for normal life in the community. Even when such a child has intelligent rearing or is adopted into another family, adjustments and modifications are necessary. The other aspect concerns the attitudes which result in children's being born out of wedlock. This indicates a social situation which is not in conformity with the established order and consequently results in the need for the reorganization of other lives, not directly concerned but closely associated with the persons concerned. Any attempts to rectify this situation are remedial and corrective. The scar of the surgery is never entirely obliterated. The elimination of the situations which give rise to the presence of any considerable number of children of unmarried parents in the population is the only adequate method to be followed.

---

[1] Joanna C. Colcord, "What Has Social Work to Do with the Founding of New Families," *The Family*, 7 (1926): 133–139.

[2] Earle E. Eubank, *A Study of Family Desertion*, Chicago, 1916.

Middle-class Parents
Arnold W. Green*

The father's work takes him far from the place of residence, where most of his associates are only slightly less strangers to him than they are to his

family. He is a white-collar worker. As a salesman, office worker, minor bureaucrat, or professional man, his job-techniques revolve around

* See identifying note on page 131.

From "The Middle-class Male Child and Neurosis," *American Sociological Review*, 11 (1946): 31–41, pp. 35–38 quoted. Reprinted by permission.

manipulating the personalities of others, instead of tools. Since he has internalized the supreme middle-class value, individual success, he tries to use his associates as means to further his career; in fact, he has himself been conditioned to view his associates, education, hobbies, intellectual interests, in terms of their possible value to his career.[1] On the job he views himself not so much as functionally associated with others in a common purpose, as a self-contained unit establishing "contacts" with others. His work relations are not defined in fixed terms of status and role to the extent that they were in the past for he is on the move, or views himself in that way. He has, then, a well-developed tendency to view his relations with others *in terms of what he, as a mobile, displaced person, can get out of them.*

Yet the modern middle-class father cannot use his *child* either in the new sense of manipulating others to his own advantage, nor, be it noted, in the ways available in the past. . . .

In terms of dollars alone, the cost of raising a modern middle-class child represents a serious threat to the personal ambition of the father.[2] At the very time when, in terms of his primary success-goal, he should have time and money available for further study if a professional man, money for clothes, entertaining, household furniture and an automobile for purposes of presenting a "front" in any event; at this time when his career is in its initial and hence its crucial stage, the presence of the child represents a diversion of energy and funds, so long, of course, as the career remains his primary goal. A certain degree of ambivalence directed toward the child is inevitable. Not the depth, but the present height of the middle-class birth-rate is the noteworthy phenomenon, indicating an amazing vitality of the old rural-familistic values which find little support in modern social structure.

With the advancing individuation of modern society, not only has individual success become a supreme value, but also individual, hedonistic enjoyment. The child again presents an interference with most of the recreation available to the mid-dle-class father, for whether commercialized (movies, sports events, plays) or social (golf, bridge, tennis, dinner parties), these are designed not for family-wide participation, but individual- or couple-participation. . . .

And how about the mother? She enters marriage and perhaps bears a child with no definite role and series of functions, as formerly. Her old role within the patriarchal family, with its many functions, its economic and emotional security, its round of community participations, is lost, but no well-defined role has taken its place. She feels inferior to men because comparatively she has been and is more restricted.[3] If she works after marriage she faces sex discrimination on the job and perhaps her husband's criticism if his traditional role of bread-winner is important to him.

Half-seriously she prepared for a career prior to marriage, half-seriously because a career is regarded by most middle-class girls as insurance against the grim possibility they will not be married; through a "good" marriage (the folk phrase "she married well" refers not to personality adjustment but to the bank balance and career prospects of the husband) the middle-class girl attains far more status than is possible through a career of her own. But the period of phantasy dalliance with a career, or an embarkation upon one, leaves her ill-fitted for the drudgery of housecleaning, diapers, and the preparation of meals. The freedom which the urban apartment and modern household devices have brought the middle-class housewife has been commonly misinterpreted as well as exaggerated. While the Victorian housewife had more work to do, that work was part of a well-integrated system of household and community activities. While the modern middle-class housewife has more leisure-time than either her mother or grandmother, she must still work at a number of household jobs for which she has not been trained, which are usually not an essential part of her value-system, and which are isolated from her social activities. One sociologist has expressed this dilemma facetiously: half her working day is spent doing something she does not like, the rest is spent thinking up ways of getting even with her husband. The re-

---

[1] See Arnold W. Green, "Duplicity," *Psychiatry, 6* (1943): 411–424.

[2] Basing their estimates on a family income of $2,500, Dublin and Lotka figure that the parents spend between $9,180 and $10,485 in rearing a child through the age of 18. See Kingsley Davis, "Reproductive Institutions and the Pressure for Population," *Sociological Review, 29* (1937): 1–18.

---

[3] The extent of the actual emancipation of women has been commonly exaggerated. Within all classes in our culture, as in all other cultures, women are trained to regard themselves as inferior to men in some degree. It is usually desired that the first child shall be a boy, by wife as well as husband.

sulting boredom frequently leads to a period of indecision early in the marriage over whether to have children or resume the career. . . .

And so it is inevitable that the child shall be viewed with some degree of ambivalence by both father and mother, for he represents a direct interference with most of the dominant values and compulsions of the modern middle class: career, social and economic success, hedonistic enjoyment. There is some doubt that *under modern middle-class conditions,* children automatically bring husband and wife closer together.[4]. . .

---

[4] See Ernest W. Burgess and Leonard S. Cottrell, Jr., *Predicting Success or Failure in Marriage,* New York: Prentice-Hall, 1939, esp. p. 413. In their sample they found a slight negative correlation between number of children and self-rating of marital adjustment. . . .

Modern "scientific child care" enforces a constant supervision and diffused worrying over the child's health, eating spinach, and ego-development; this is complicated by the fact that much energy is spent forcing early walking, toilet-training, talking, because in an intensely competitive milieu middle-class parents from the day of birth on are constantly comparing their own child's development with that of the neighbors' children. The child must also be constantly guarded from the danger of contacting various electric gadgets and from kicking valuable furniture. The middle-class child's discovery that the living-room furniture is more important to his mother than his impulse to crawl over it, unquestionably finds a place in the background of the etiology of a certain type of neurosis, however absurd it may appear.

The Negro Maternal Family
Charles E. King

Charles E. King (1911–   ), professor of sociology, North Carolina College, Durham.

According to the census of 1930, there were 3,792,902 families without a male head in the United States, including all population groups.[1] The census of 1940 shows an enumeration of 5,353,240 families without a male head in the United States for all population groups.[2] This gives a numerical increase of 1,560,338 families without a male head for 1940 over the number for 1930. In the ten-year period, 1930–1940, the percentage change shows an increase of families without a male head amounting to 41 per cent. Because these families are headed by women the term *maternal* has been applied to them. There are several reasons for the existence of these families. Many are due to desertion by the husband, insanity of the husband, imprisonment or death of the husband. Wives are generally from three to five years younger than their husbands and this gives wives the probability of a longer life than their husbands.

The major interest here is concerned with the Negro maternal family, since this group of the

population has a higher rate of maternal families. . . .

It is the intention here to show that this family pattern is the product of the economic and culture system of the rural South. The Negro maternal family is found primarily in the *rural South among the low income, uneducated* members of the population. It is found to some extent in urban areas,[9] but primarily among groups that have migrated from the rural South and are dwelling in the slum areas of southern and northern urban centers.

The slave plantation of the South is the place of origin of the Negro maternal family.[10] Family life among Negro slaves was loosely organized. The father's function in the slave family was generally biological [11] rather than sociological. That is his function ceased to be important to the

---

[1] *Fifteenth Census, Population,* Table 37, vol. VI, 1930.
[2] *Sixteenth Census, Population and Housing, Families,* Table 1, 1940.

[9] E. Franklin Frazier, *The Negro Family in Chicago,* Chicago: University of Chicago, 1932.
[10] E. Franklin Frazier, "Traditions and Patterns of Negro Family Life in the United States," E. B. Reuter, ed., *Race and Culture Contacts* (New York: McGraw-Hill, 1934), p. 195.
[11] *Ibid.*

From "The Negro Maternal Family: A Product of an Economic and a Culture System," *Social Forces,* 24 (1945–46): 100–104. Reprinted by permission.

family group after conception took place. The rearing, care, and discipline were by the mother, while the food, clothing, shelter, and protection were provided for by the slave owner. Hence the role of the father was unimportant and unnecessary in making a close knit unit in the Negro slave family. Also contributing to the loose organization of the slave family was the slave owner's desire to increase his labor supply by reproduction. Often he would encourage sexual unions between a slave woman and a slave man other than her husband, if this man were apparently more prolific than her husband. Neither husband nor the wife could show resentment to such efforts of the slave owner since he alone had the power to grant permission for a marriage, or for "taking up with" a man or a woman, or he could dissolve any union at his will. The husband was also helpless to object if the slave owner chose to take the woman for his concubine.

In the event of a sale the children always went with the mother. The children developed more of an attachment to the mother than to the father. In fact the father as such was unknown to many children of the slave family.

The economic and culture patterns of the plantation system made the Negro woman the dominant personality in the slave family. Whatever family activities that prevailed were centered around the mother. The children learned traditions, customs, superstitions, religious beliefs from the mother. If the children received any special favors of the master, it was through the effort of the mother.[12] The whole of the slave family life came to be centered around the mother. The slave owners and the Negro slaves became adjusted to this family pattern and accepted it as the only arrangement for the slaves. Without doubt there might have been affectional bonds existing between father and mother that would have made for stable family organization, but the slave owners did not consider the slaves as their equals, and therefore the slaves did not need close, well-organized family life as did the slave owners. The family unity of the slaves was thought of as a necessity no more than that of the animals on the slave plantation. The loose organization of the family life, the varying fatherhood, and the freedom of sex relations for the woman would have been considered as highly immoral among the white slave owner class, but such was not considered immoral for the Negro slaves. The slaves were considered more as amoral with regard to American social standards.

Being excluded from the general social pattern of American society, the slaves had no alternative but to conform to the family organization imposed by the culture of the plantation system. The slaves were so completely adjusted to this family pattern that, after emancipation, many Negro husbands and fathers left the woman in her accustomed position as head of the family, and the Negro maternal family continued to prevail to a great extent in the plantation areas throughout the South.

Emancipation changed the status of the slave to that of hired hand or tenant. The master was no longer bound to provide the economic needs of the Negro as he had prior to emancipation. The provision of family support, the assumption of the responsibilities of the headship of a permanent family organization were difficult adjustments for many emancipated Negro fathers to make after having been for generations reared in a plantation slave society. Thus many would leave the family or be satisfied to leave everything to the woman. Many women, finding that a husband was not an advantage to them, ceased to develop an attitude for permanent attachment to a man through marriage. From this particular group of the Negro population has largely developed the maternal family population that exists at present, as maternal families tend to perpetuate themselves for several generations.[13]

There are distinctly four types of maternal families existing today, namely: the unmarried mother type, the deserted mother type, the divorced mother type, and the widowed type. No arbitrary difference can be made regarding the pattern of living. Among the unmarried, deserted, and divorced, age of the mother and age of the child or children, make the distinction. Generally, the three types just mentioned live on the same pattern. The older children assist the mother with support and discipline of the younger children. In the event the children are very young a neighbor or relative such as the mother's mother will take care of the children. The widowed mother usually assumes full responsibility of discipline and support. The widowed type of maternal family fol-

---

[12] Charles S. Johnson, "Negro Personality Changes in a Southern Community," E. B. Reuter, ed., *Race and Culture Contacts,* p. 213.

[13] E. Franklin Frazier, "Traditions and Patterns of Family Life in the United States," in Reuter, *Race and Culture Contacts,* pp. 196–197.

lows the conventional family since it has been conditioned to normal life during the life of the father. The children, too, are usually mature, or nearly so, and the mother is taken care of by the children.

In the majority, the maternal families are headed by unmarried mothers. This has been substantiated by four studies.[14] In the study of the Georgia area [15] it was discovered that of the 150 families in the area over 40 per cent of them were maternal and over 50 per cent of this group were families headed by unmarried mothers. In other words, 31 of the 61 maternal families were headed by unmarried mothers. These women do not become mothers through any moral weakness but through deliberate choice. Johnson states ". . . there are competent, self-sufficient women who not only desire children but need them as later aids in the struggle for survival when their strength begins to wane, but who want neither the restriction of formal marriage nor the constant association with a husband. They get their children not so much through weakness as through their deliberate selection of a father." [16] Powdermaker says, "The economic consideration may serve to keep a woman from marriage or to make her leave her husband." [17]

Women of the maternal group can find regular employment more constantly than the men. They find employment as domestic servants, cooks, and washerwomen in the nonfarm areas of the South and in larger towns and cities. The farm does not offer sufficient employment for a woman alone to take care of her family; besides, landlords are reluctant to rent to, or share with a woman. Therefore, the maternal families locate in the non-farm villages, towns, and cities except in the case of widows. They usually own their farms and are in position to hire labor or have sons old enough to supervise their farms.

These women are accustomed to supporting themselves and, finding that men are more constantly unemployed or earning inadequate means and seeing many married women of their class having to be the sole support or breadwinner for the family, decide against formal marriage since it promises the additional burden of having to support the husband. Also many men refrain from marrying, or, if married, resort to desertion after finding themselves economically unable to support a family. Therefore, illegitimate births occur not so much from the result of immorality on the part of women as from the desire to become mothers and from the need of children to aid them in old age or when their health fails. This is also true of the deserted women of this class. Their husbands usually desert them shortly after marriage and often the second child is born after they have separated from their husbands. Illegitimacy is rare among widows since they are usually beyond the child-bearing age and are also of a different culture. The family prior to widowhood had become compact and self-conscious and has standards of a higher level. According to Johnson, "Ownership of property tends to restrict illegitimate relations because of the economic complexities introduced and the serious effects upon credit and leadership in the larger community of looseness in domestic relations." [18]

The problem of support in the maternal family of the unmarried and deserted types is most difficult and inadequate for a normal standard of living. In the study of the Georgia area it was found that 66.7 per cent of the maternal families' earnings by the mothers ranges from $1.00 to $3.99 per week.[19] Such low income makes it necessary to place the child to work at a very early age before it has completed the basic years of elementary school. However little a child earns it helps with food, rent, and clothes. The maternal family is fortunate if the grandmother is able to contribute to the support of the children or if the father of the child, or the mother's present lover contributes to food, rent or clothes occasionally. There is very little chance for the members of the maternal family of the unmarried type and the deserted type to improve their situation since their educational training is so low that it makes them incapable of self-improvement. Their educational status makes them incapable of increasing their earning power, and their low earning power makes them unable to pursue educational development. It was found among 61 maternal families of the Georgia area [20] that over fifty per cent

[14] Charles S. Johnson, *Shadow of the Plantation*, p. 66; Hortense Powdermaker, *op. cit.*; Charles E. King, *op. cit.*; E. Franklin Frazier, *The Negro Family in Chicago*.

[15] Charles E. King, *op. cit.*

[16] Charles S. Johnson, *Shadow of the Plantation*, p. 66.

[17] Hortense Powdermaker, *op. cit.*, p. 155.

[18] Charles S. Johnson, "Negro Personality Changes in a Southern Community," Reuter, *Race and Culture Contacts*, pp. 218–219.

[19] Charles E. King, *op. cit.*, Table IV, p. 35.

[20] *Ibid.*, Table V, p. 36.

of the mothers had an educational level ranging from illiteracy to the third grade.

In the community the maternal family has practically the same status as the conventional family. Its social worth is judged on the basis of the character of the mother. There is no ostracism of the family if the mother is considered to be of good character. The mother can easily prove that she is not a lewd woman and that she is respectable if she refrains from letting herself become "common" with men, from allowing married men to pay her attention, and from having quarrels, or fights, occur on her account. As long as she carries on conventional courtship no social stigma will be placed against her.

In school the children of unmarried mothers are accepted without any restrictions by their schoolmates. No objections are made by parents of conventional families when their children select playmates from among children of unmarried mothers. If the child is a very bad child, conventional parents will restrict their child's association in this instance; and the same will be done in case the bad child comes from a conventional family.

No objection is offered when children of unmarried mothers appear in plays and concerts in the community or school. The children of unmarried mothers feel as free to acknowledge their fathers without embarrassment as the children of conventional families do. The child of an unmarried mother has no social opposition to prevent his being successful in participation in the life of the community. Relative to the above discussion, Johnson says,

An incidental value of this lack of a censuring public opinion is the freedom for children thus born from warping social condemnation. The group adjustment to this situation entails a widespread and commonly accepted practice of child adoption, which gives family status to all children. There are, thus, virtually no orphans. Normally, the child of an unmarried daughter in a family is treated as if it belongs to the mother's parents, and the status of the mother is similar to that of an older sister.[21]

If an unmarried mother is active in any community activity, she has equal opportunity for participation with the members of the conventional family.

The maternal family will continue to exist as long as the economic insecurity of men exists; as long as public opinion of the white and black members of the larger society allows the unmarried woman the right of motherhood without loss of social status; as long as the educational level remains too low to raise the social standards to higher levels.

[21] Charles S. Johnson, "Negro Personality Changes in a Southern Community," Reuter, *Race and Culture Contacts*, p. 215.

The Emotional Background of Marital Difficulties

Helen V. McLean

Helen V. McLean (1894–   ), psychiatrist and clinical consultant at the Chicago Institute for Psychoanalysis.

What is apparent to a psychiatrist is that all the developmental and constitutional weakness and flaws of a human personality are put to a severe strain and test in the long pull of a marital relation. Those flaws which most commonly make their appearance in marriage can be briefly stated.

1. The Unconscious Wish to Be Dependent. For a man whose early life has been one of spoiling by an indulgent mother, the responsibilities of marriage will become very much of a burden. For such an individual, marriage with a motherly woman may be successful until her attention is in part diverted from her husband to her children. Then he may turn from her and under the guise of an extramarital sexual interest, seek a woman who will gratify his dependent needs in an irresponsible relation. For a woman who wishes unconsciously to be a child, caring for a home and children will often produce great tension which finds expression in irritability, psychosomatic disorders, or in psychosis.

2. A Destructive Hostile Attitude toward the

From "The Emotional Background of Marital Difficulties," *American Sociological Review*, 6 (1941): 384–388, pp. 386–388 quoted. Reprinted by permission.

Marital Partner. In casual sexual affairs, destructive feelings can often be successfully masked but in any permanent relation, the disguise of love will soon be torn off and the rage which is the real bond between two individuals becomes all too apparent. Any outsider viewing the marriage of a man and woman whose relation is essentially hostile in character, will exclaim, "How can they stand each other; he is terribly cruel to her, and she's a martyr who makes everyone suffer." It is exactly because of the outlet for unconscious destructive feelings combined with punishment for the hostility each inflicts on the other that such a marriage survives in the face of all rational reasons for its dissolution. When, however, the psychic equilibrium of either individual is altered, the desire for freedom from such a hateful relationship will be spontaneously felt. If the need of either one is merely to protest by means of divorce against the destructive and self-destructive feelings which find their satisfaction in the particular marriage, such a protest on the part of the more mature ego-attitudes of the personality will probably be temporary in nature and following divorce, the destructive forces will again gain ascendency so that the next choice of a love object will be another individual both cruel and martyr-like in character.

3. Sexual Guilt May Exist as a Result of Unduly Repressive Measures in Childhood or of Unusually Intense Heterosexual Temptation by a forbidden person (father or brother, mother or sister), or as a result of both these conditions. Since unconscious guilt over sexual feelings exists in an overwhelmingly large majority of the members of civilized society, its existence may account for many marital difficulties. Psychiatric experience reveals that the guilty feelings which were defined in the individual as a child may become clearly evident only after marriage. Frigidity, which is a common psychosomatic disturbance in women of all classes, is found to arise out of feelings of guilt and consequent fear of sexual relations. A lack of complete responsiveness on the part of the woman in marriage is disturbing not only to her but also to her husband, for he considers her incapacity for complete pleasure as an indication of some inadequacy in himself. With this, as with other pathological manifestations, a vicious circle of emotional interreaction between the man and woman is initiated.

In the normal individual, the choice of a marital partner will be determined by both rational conscious interest in, and an unconscious perception of, complementary emotional suitability of the given person. Too often, however, a chance resemblance of the man or woman to some individual who has previously been of emotional significance is the determining factor. There is a total disregard of many character or personality traits which will eventually prove distasteful. Many a man has married a woman because in some physical detail she resembled his mother, sister, or one of the objects of his childish affection; many a woman has found herself married to a weak, helpless man, the opposite in character and temperament of the father who had disregarded and rejected her childish love. Disappointment will be experienced in such a marriage and rage felt against the partner who is unjustly blamed for the disillusionment.

Divorce and Desertion
George Thorman

George Thorman (1912–   ), probation officer, Marion County Juvenile Court, Indianapolis, Indiana.

Divorce is now breaking up marriages three times as rapidly as it did a half-century ago. In 1890 there was one divorce to every sixteen marriages performed that year. By 1910, the figure jumped to one divorce to every eleven marriages, and by 1920 one divorce to every six marriages. In 1940 there was one divorce to every five marriages, and it is estimated that in 1946 there was one divorce to every three marriages. [In 1951, the rate was one divorce for every 4.2 marriages, lower than before World War II.—*Eds.*]

Some people believe that our divorce rate is so

From "Broken Homes," Public Affairs Pamphlet No. 135, 1947, pp. 7–10, 20–22, 6–7. Reprinted by permission.

high because our marriage laws are too lenient. Others say that it indicates a state of moral laxity and a lack of ethical standards. Sociologists, however, point out that these explanations do not go far enough. What is happening is this: Our world is changing rapidly and marriage is in a process of adjusting itself to these changes. We live in a civilization that is becoming more and more complex—one which gives rise to new problems and new situations and new perplexities. These new problems call for new solutions and new adjustments. To make the adjustment to these changed conditions isn't easy. It puts a strain on all of our institutions and is felt in every other human relationship—political, economic, legal, moral, and religious.

Marriage in a Changing World. The rapid increase in divorce is reflecting the difficulty we are having in making marriage suit modern needs and fit in with our changing world. The family, like other institutions, is in a process of change. New pressures are causing strain and tension in the relationships between husbands and wives, and making it more difficult for them to stay happily married.

The industrial revolution, for example, has done away with the economic basis of the home. Most husbands and wives no longer earn their living working together in the home. Instead of living on farms or in small towns, most people have been drawn to the factories and live in congested quarters in the cities. Life has been speeded up. Our way of living has been changed, putting new strains upon our emotional and mental life. The rise of industry has freed women, given them economic independence, and changed their attitude toward marriage.

Studies have shown that people who have similar education, religious affiliations, and family background have a better chance of making their marriage succeed. They have also shown that husbands and wives who share a great many activities, like the same things, and have the same friends, are often more happily married than those who do not have these things in common. Urban centers, however, make it difficult for married couples to share much of their lives. For cities provide a vast range of activities and contacts. Husbands have their business friends and their poker clubs; wives have their bridge clubs and social functions. Each leads his life independently of the other. When common goals and interests no longer hold the marriage together, it may wither and die.

New Attitudes toward Marriage. A marriage is no longer "good" just because it lasts. Women who were once content to endure cruelty or immorality on the part of their husbands now are rebelling. They expect more from marriage than economic security, legalized sex relations, unrestricted procreation, and female domesticity. They refuse to be dominated by their husbands; they demand love and affection. There is a growing conviction that a sound marriage must be built on the sharing of common goals and common interests. All this represents a comparatively new attitude toward marriage, giving rise to new expectations—especially on the part of women. It has resulted in dissatisfaction with many marriages which would have been regarded as successful a half-century ago. That is why our increasing divorce rate does not necessarily mean that there are more unhappy marriages. It may simply mean that more people who are unhappily married seek divorce than before because they find less reason to stay married. Convention is no longer so powerful a factor as it was. New values and new ethical standards have developed. If a marriage is too restrictive, too binding on the individual, revealing a lack of capacity to adapt, the result is often divorce.

The rise in our divorce rate, then, is in part the price we are paying for not being able to adjust readily to certain changes in our modern civilization. It is a part of the price we must pay for a new set of values in marriage. It is a symptom that marriage must take full account of the social and economic emancipation of women, the importance of freedom, and individual happiness. Many marriages which were once held together by the external pressure of economic necessity or of social disapproval will fall apart once these props are removed. A modern marriage must be held together from within, rather than from without. Our rising divorce rate registers that fact. . . .

Desertion: The Poor Man's Divorce

Full statistics are not available, but it is estimated that about 50,000 homes are broken each year by desertion, usually by the husband. In some cases the desertion becomes the basis for a divorce, but often no legal action is taken to break the marriage bonds in any official way. The desertion is simply accepted as the end of the marriage. There is no divorce, largely because divorce proceedings cost money. That is why desertion is sometimes called the "poor man's divorce" or the "poor man's vacation." While some have the money to pay for the legal proceedings of divorce, others use desertion as an easy and cheap escape from an unhappy marriage.

In some cases desertion offers the *only* escape. For example, South Carolina does not grant divorces on any grounds whatsoever. Therefore, any citizen of South Carolina must obtain his divorce elsewhere (and this is a relatively expensive procedure) or take the law into his own hands by deserting his family. In other cases, religious scruples may keep a husband from obtaining a divorce, but he may feel justified in leaving his wife.

Economic Causes. The factors which cause desertion are similar in most respects to those which cause divorce. At one time it was thought that most husbands who deserted their families did so because they wanted to escape financial responsibility for supporting them. Sometimes this is the chief reason for the desertion. In many cases the deserting husband is the father of a large family, and frequently he deserts his wife and children at a time when the going is rough. His wife may be pregnant and he wants to run away from the responsibility of feeding and clothing another child. Or he may be deeply involved in debt and cannot see his way out.

Psychological Factors. But finances are rarely the whole story. The husband who deserts is frequently a person who has difficulty facing a crisis. He cannot stand too much pressure. His first impulse is to get away. His desertion is a symptom of his emotional immaturity. He wants to escape the unpleasant, and make his escape as easily as possible. Sometimes he regrets his impulsive action and returns to his family voluntarily.

Alcoholism and Desertion. Alcoholism also seems to be closely related to desertion. But here again, it must be remembered that while alcoholism may be the direct cause of the disorganization and desertion, it is the result of some more basic personality maladjustment. The alcoholic is usually a person who is overwhelmed by his problems, unable to cope with difficulties, and finds release in his drinking. It is no wonder, then, that the responsibilities of marriage and caring for a family are often too much for him,

and that he chooses desertion to escape from them.

Often the desertion is only another event in a series of family disputes. The family has gradually become disorganized over a long period, and the desertion is the result of this gradual disintegration of the home. The desertion is a symptom of some dissatisfaction with the marriage relationship or some personal maladjustment that leads to conflict between the two partners. Sexual maladjustment, cultural differences, financial disputes, temperamental differences are all important factors in creating the tensions that make the marriage intolerable and in the end break it. . . .

The Price of Broken Homes

[The] price we pay for our broken homes cannot be measured in dollars and cents alone; nor can it be counted only in terms of what it means in the lives of children. For adults, too, have a need for security. The death of a husband or wife is a threat to security both emotionally and financially. Desertion and divorce are also costly in terms of human values. A mother who has been deserted may feel quite bitter about her fate. She may find it difficult to manage her family and care for her children properly. The added responsibility of these new problems may put a severe strain upon her, both physically and emotionally. A husband who has been divorced may feel that "this is the end." He has already gone through a trying period of marriage difficulties. His failure to make the marriage succeed may leave him with mixed feelings: hostility toward his former wife and guilt over his own responsibility for not making the marriage work. Not only has his home become disorganized, but he himself has become personally disorganized. He feels lonely, bitter, and hopeless.

Of course, not all adults pay so heavy a price. And again, it is important to remember that in many cases the divorce, separation, or desertion may be a welcome release from an unhappy situation. But in other cases the price for this freedom has been too high. That is why marriage counselors believe it is important to count the cost before reaching a decision. Divorce or separation may not be the only answer, and both marriage partners have a responsibility to study their problems carefully and make their decisions after they have taken all the factors into consideration. When a marriage is broken, friendships of long standing may be broken. Personal habits, plans, ways of living—all change. The immediate effects are often shattering. For love does not always end with the divorce decree. There is bound to be pain, especially to the person who has had the divorce thrust upon him by another. And divorce brings with it a terrific blow to pride, even

though it may finally be accepted as the only way out. While many persons make a complete recovery from the immediate suffering and injury inflicted by the break, others remain lonely, thwarted, and bitter throughout life unless they receive adequate counseling during their period of readjustment.

Marriage and Family Counseling
Ernest W. Burgess and Paul Wallin

Ernest W. Burgess (1886–   ), professor emeritus of sociology, University of Chicago. Principal works: with R. E. Park, *Introduction to the Science of Sociology* (1921, 1924); with L. S. Cottrell, Jr., *Predicting Success or Failure in Marriage* (1939); with Harvey J. Locke, *The Family* (rev. ed., 1953); and, with Paul Wallin, *Engagement and Marriage* (1953). Paul Wallin (1910–   ), professor of sociology and anthropology, Stanford University. Principal work: with E. W. Burgess, *Engagement and Marriage* (1953).

Where are young people to turn for information and knowledge [about factors making for and against success in marriage]?

At present, they go first to their friends, their parents, their ministers, teachers, or physicians. But many hesitate to bring their problems to those who are closest to them. They feel they will not understand. Or they know in advance what the advice will be. They want someone who is more detached and objective. Often the only other source of help they know about is a newspaper column. One of the earliest of these was self-styled "Advice to the Lovelorn." Today the names of Dorothy Dix, Beatrice Fairfax, Doris Blake, Mary Haworth, Ann Landers, Samuel G. and Esther B. Kling, are familiar to adolescents and youth.

The nature of the questions asked and of the replies received are well known to newspaper readers. Real problems of life are presented by these questions. Over a month's period they offer a picture of the troubles and perplexities faced by young people before and after marriage. But they present only one side; generally the woman's. Nevertheless, the columnists do not hesitate to diagnose and prescribe for the entire range of human problems.

Their advice can generally be anticipated. They usually apply the mores, or what the guardians of public morality believe right, to the problem

of the reader. Blame for the situation is freely visited upon the person held responsible. They seldom neglect the opportunity of saying or implying "let this be a lesson to others."

Few people are aware of the existence of a new service in our cities to deal with these very same problems. They do not know that marriage counseling centers have been established. They have not heard of the marriage counselor who has training, experience, and competence to counsel with persons on their problems before and after marriage. They have no information on the nature, the procedure, and the results of professional marriage counseling. . . .

Marriage counseling services are now increasing. In 1932, there were three centers: Marriage Guidance Clinic in New York established by Abraham Stone, M.D., in 1929; Institute of Family Relations in Los Angeles, founded by Paul Popenoe in 1930; and the Marriage Council of Philadelphia, initiated by Emily H. Mudd in 1932. At present there are counseling services in all large cities. The greatest number of these offering family counseling, approximately 240, are under the auspices of Family Service Societies. Originally the services of these family organizations were available to economically dependent families. Now many of them are open on a fee basis to all people in the community in need of individual, marital, and family counseling.

From *Engagement and Marriage,* Philadelphia: J. B. Lippincott Co., 1953, pp. 724, 729, 747–748, 749–751, 752, 753.

Marriage counseling is increasingly being offered under the auspices of other organizations. Catholic, Jewish, and Protestant churches now provide counseling services in some localities. The Roman Catholic church has organized an extensive program of group counseling through its pre-Cana conferences for unmarried young people and Cana conferences for married couples. Organizations specializing in family life education, like the Association for Family Living in Chicago and the Merrill-Palmer School of Detroit, maintain a department of marriage counseling. In many communities qualified and sometimes unqualified individuals have set up private offices and are giving their full time or part time to marriage counseling.

A recent development has been the growth of marriage counseling in colleges and universities. Generally such counseling service has been on an informal basis in connection with courses on marriage. The instructor announces more or less casually that he is willing to talk with students about their problems.

In a few universities marriage counseling centers or clinics have been established as at Florida State University, Furman University, Ohio State University, Pennsylvania State College [University], Southern Methodist University, Stephens College, the University of Utah and Utah State Agricultural College. . . .

The purpose of marriage counseling is educative and therapeutic, namely, to help persons if possible, to avoid, and if avoidance is impossible, then to solve problems which arise in courtship, engagement, and marriage.

At the present time there is lively discussion and even controversy over the nature of the role of the counselor and his relation to the client. One group likens the marriage counselor to the physician who makes a diagnosis of the condition of the patient and prescribes a remedy. The physician can draw upon the knowledge of the biological sciences and upon medical discoveries. He also utilizes his own previous experience in the cure of ailments. So the marriage counselor in analyzing a problem presented by a client and in prescribing a plan of treatment makes use of the knowledge of the sciences of human behavior—anthropology, biology, psychology, and sociology. He also develops skill in analyzing and treating problems by reason of his experience with many previous cases of a similar sort.

A second group assigns the counselor a more passive role. The counselor is defined as an expert listener who stimulates the client to feel and think through a problem to his own diagnosis and plan of treatment. The counselor from this point of view serves as a catalytic agent, enabling the client to secure (1) catharsis through release of repressed emotional reactions, (2) insight into his problem, (3) reorientation of attitudes, and (4) a decision upon a course of action.

A third group combines something from the diagnostic, the functional, and the client-centered approaches and modifies their procedures in some degree to fit the emotional climate of the client, the type situation, and the background, training, personality, and skill of the counselor.

In counseling of all three types the counselor needs training in the psychodynamics of human relations, both in their psychological and in their sociological aspects.

It is evident that marriage predictive and success schedules are more appropriate where the counselor takes an active rather than a passive role in counseling and where his role is more educative than therapeutic. But in practice often no sharp distinction can be made between education and therapy. A client may have a problem, be a problem, or both have and be a problem.

The majority of people who go for assistance to counseling centers before and after marriage *have* problems. These cover a wide range: cultural differences, financial difficulties, relations with in-laws, and inadequate sex knowledge. The minority *are* problems. For example, a few may be chronically neurotic or have mental conflicts. Marriage counseling needs to make provision for both types of assistance. Perhaps marriage counseling centers should emphasize the educative and preventive functions and continue to refer those with marked personality problems to clinical psychologists and psychiatrists. . . .

Predictive and measurement instruments may be of value to the marriage counselor in the following ways: (1) predictive scores provide him with a numerical index of the probabilities that a couple will succeed or fail in marriage; (2) the engagement success and anticipated contingency schedules indicate areas where the relation of the engaged couple may be aided by counseling, thus improving the chances of marital success; (3) the schedule on personality traits indicates the presence or probability of problems of personal adjustment which may be reduced or forestalled by counseling; (4) the engagement and marital success schedule locates areas of conflict or dissatisfaction which may serve as appropriate starting points for discussion; and (5) the engagement and marriage success schedules may be given the client a second time in order to find out the effect of the counseling experience.

It is important to emphasize that marriage prediction and measurement schedules are aids to counseling and not the central core of marriage counseling. Predictive and success schedules are helpful in diagnosis just as the clinical thermometer is helpful to the physician. But in diagnosis and in treatment the counselor, like the physician, must place his chief reliance upon intensive study of the case, upon the knowledge obtained from his scientific training, upon his past experience, and upon the intelligence, flexibility and "will to do" of the client.

Counseling differs from the practice of medicine in one important respect. The counseling process involves the participation of the person in a more active and dynamic manner than that of the patient in medical diagnosis and therapy. The essence of personality adjustment consists in the meeting and solving of problems. Life for the modern man and woman is continuous adjustment to a changing social environment. Counseling means that the aid of a professionally trained person is enlisted in meeting a problem which the client has failed to solve and which he feels he cannot solve alone. In the interests of the personality development of the client it is important that he does not become dependent upon the counselor by having a solution imposed upon him. To avoid this, the client must actively participate in the diagnosis of the problem and in working out a plan of treatment. The marriage counselor does not or should not make any decision for the couple. He is rather a disinterested third person trained in this field and with a wisdom that comes with familiarity with many similar experiences. He should be, first of all, a good listener to whom both members of the couple can unburden their feelings, attitudes, expectations, resentments, and hostilities. In releasing these repressed feelings the persons experience catharsis and are thus freer to gain insight into their problems as a first step in readjustment.

Up to this point marriage counseling has been presented as an individual matter. It has been discussed as an interpersonal relation between the counselor and the person.

But counseling also takes place in group situations. Here the group is utilized as the dynamic influence in changing attitudes and motivation. Three types of group counseling will be briefly described: (1) group discussion, (2) psychodrama and sociodrama, and (3) participant experimentation.

Group discussion is at present the most usual form of group marriage counseling. Its common characteristic is the presentation and discussion of a problem of concern to young people before or after marriage. Sometimes the group is limited either to engaged or married couples.

Group discussion may be guided in a more or less authoritarian manner by the adult leader; or it may be relatively unguided. In either case the group tends to exercise a decisive influence in the formation of attitudes.

Psychodrama and sociodrama tend to merge in the presentation of marital conflicts. Role taking is a stock device in the dramatic portrayal of the problem. The husband acts out his own role and then may be requested to play the part of his wife. Members of the staff who are in the audience will also be asked to take the husband's or the wife's role. By this procedure the interaction of a husband and wife in a marital conflict becomes objectified. The husband is enabled by playing his wife's role to see the situation as she sees it. When his role is played by his wife and by others, he obtains a more detached perspective by which to view his own conduct.

The psychosociodramatic depiction of marital situations is therapeutic and educative and may be used for purposes of research. Frequently it is employed primarily as education for marriage in college classes. In this case the class is the audience. Problem situations are chosen and students in the class play the roles of the engaged or married couples and of the other characters.

Participant experimentation is a recent form of the group method in premarital and postmarital education. Some of its features are common to group discussion and to the psychosociodrama. But while the intention of most therapeutic and educational methods is to manipulate the participants toward given ends, such as the acceptance of certain norms, participant experimentation acts to encourage the group members to develop their own strategies to meet problems and expected shifts in family role. If the degree of manipulation by the leader is placed upon a continuum, most classroom groups would fall at the pole of extreme manipulation of accepting given ends decided upon by the leader, action groups near the middle and participant experiment groups near the pole of minimum manipulation. The group is experimental in that it provides (1) through unrehearsed role playing in typical family life problem situations the opportunity for the participants to formulate tentative strategies and (2) through discussion the opportunity to study these strategies and thereby to increase knowledge of interpersonal relations. The group provides an atmosphere of spontaneity for creating alternative solutions to problems and for testing and increasing the insight of the participants through self-examination and evaluation. Participant experimentation thus acts as an agent in increasing self-awareness, broadening experience, and facilitating understanding in couples.

Accordingly, the procedure in this form of group counseling is participant in the sense that every one in the group takes part with a common objective. They are all, for example, engaged couples interested in preparation for marriage. Its procedure is experimental since there is no rigid pattern and no predetermined outcome. Problems are selected by the group. They are presented by

informal role taking. Discussion follows the role taking and the attempt is made to arrive at consensus. . . .

The term "marriage counselor" at present is being restricted to persons who have had specialized training in one or more of the sciences of human behavior—biology, psychology, psychiatry, social work, and sociology. . . .

Marriage counseling may now be regarded as an emerging profession. There is increasing public recognition of the importance of its service to society. In addition, it is making progress in realizing the four chief characteristics of a profession, namely:

1. A sound basis for its activity in scholarship or/and research.
2. Adequate training of its personnel at a graduate level of advanced study.
3. High standards of personal and educational qualifications for the practice of the profession.
4. Certification of qualifications by formally established organizations of persons engaged in the activity.

Retirement Problems in American Society
Clark Tibbitts

Clark Tibbitts (1903–   ), chairman, Committee on Aging and Geriatrics, U. S. Department of Health, Education, and Welfare. Editor of: *Living Through the Older Years* (1949); *Planning the Later Years* (with Wilma Donahue, 1950); *Growing in The Older Years* (with W. Donahue, 1951); and *Social Contributions by the Aging* (1952).

Retirement is a relatively new phenomenon in our society and the challenge of a new way of life for most Americans. In rural, preindustrial days there were comparatively few older adults, and most of them were occupied with the responsibilities of making a living until overtaken by final illness or death. Until well into the last quarter of the nineteenth century, the population 65 years of age and older numbered fewer than two million— less than 3.5 per cent of the total. The population 50 years and over accounted for less than 12 per cent of the whole. Well over two-thirds lived in rural areas, and three-quarters of the older men were gainfully employed. The older women were also usefully occupied, for in the days of the self-

sufficient, productive family unit they were busy cooking, sewing, cleaning, teaching and entertaining the young, and caring for the sick.

Partial or complete retirement from these tasks is a development, primarily, of the last fifty to seventy-five years. Fundamentally, it is an outgrowth of the scientific and technological achievements of the time. Control of the environment and discoveries in the causes and treatment of disease have so extended life that the 50-year-old adult may now anticipate, on the average, at least twenty-five additional years. Simultaneously, technological inventions and application of mechanical power have brought about a two- or threefold increase in worker productivity. This has been re-

From "Retirement Problems in American Society," *American Journal of Sociology, 41* (January 1954): 301–308.

flected, in turn, in a 40 per cent reduction in the length of the work week since 1870 and in the separation of a majority of older persons from the work force. Today, only about 42 per cent of males and nearly 10 per cent of females over 65 years of age are gainfully occupied. And among males the dropping-out from the work force is already observable in the age span 45–54.

Corresponding changes appear to have taken place in family life and in occupations of older women. Industrialization, with separation of the principal earner's job from the home; lightening of farm and household work; and partial or complete removal of some household tasks from the home have brought about a marked shift from the consanguinal, economic unit to the conjugal, two-generation family in which there are few, if any, essential roles for the older generation. Urbanization—64 per cent of Americans now live in urban areas—and growing mobility have interfered further with the utilitarian and social functions of older people in the homes of their children.

Widowhood and the increasing excess of older women over men is a special phase of the retirement phenomenon. The growing differential in death rates as between the sexes is increasing the number and proportion of unmarried, older women without residual household duties.

The absolute and relative increases in numbers of retired persons are also, of course, functions of the high birth rates of the latter part of the nineteenth century, which were followed by declines in the present century, and of the large influx of young adults prior to World War I.

What is retirement? There is no single definition; the term is used in at least three different ways. It is, perhaps, generally understood to mean separation or withdrawal from one's principal or career occupation in gainful employment. Recent gerontological research discloses that it is applied with almost equal force to housewives at the end of the child-rearing period—usually between the ages of 45 and 55 years.

Some workers, however, shift to new occupations, and some housewives find paid work after their children have left. Following these adjustments, retirement may then come to mean complete or final separation from the work force.

Many older persons continue or take up other forms of productive activity, such as community service, arts and crafts, gardening, and home maintenance. Retirement may then denote the end of all contributory activity beyond that of mere self-maintenance.

Even these three categories, however, fail to account for all variations. Some workers, particularly the self-employed, do not retire abruptly but taper off by reducing the time or effort devoted to their jobs. Others shift to part-time employment. Women whose careers have been in homemaking also retire gradually, at least as long as their husbands are alive. And an increasing proportion of women have two careers—families and paid employment and, thus, two retirements.

For the purposes of the present discussion, retirement is roughly defined to include (1) persons who report themselves as no longer in the regular work force and (2) unemployed women whose children have matured and left home. Creative activity, community service, and the like are regarded as retirement interests.

The total number of persons aged 65 years and over in 1953 exceeds 13.4 million (8.4 per cent of the total population) and is increasing at the rate of about 325,000 annually. In addition, there are 32 million between 45 and 64 years of age—20 per cent of the total population.

The number of males aged 45 years and over who are not in the labor force is 4.8 million, of whom some 3.6 million are aged 65 and older. The females 45 and over not in the labor force number about 16.7 million, and 6.2 million are 65 or more years of age.

Among the 16.7 million women who have reached 45 years of age and who are not in the labor force, there are probably some 10–12 million who have been, but no longer are, responsible for children.

Marital status also changes rapidly with age. From 15 per cent at age 50–54 years, the proportion of men who are not married increases to 26 per cent at ages 65–69 and to 56 per cent at age 80 and over. The increase among women is much more rapid, from 25 per cent not married at 50–54 years to 51 per cent at 65–69 and to 88 per cent in the top age group.

There are no data to indicate how many older persons are in their usual occupations and how many have shifted to different jobs, how much time older women spend in housework, and how those who are wholly or partially retired are occupying their time. Prevalence of handicapping illness increases with age, but there are relatively few invalids among the retired.

Just when to retire from work is a critical and complex problem. In the 1930's the principal that retirement should occur at some specified point between 60 and 70 years of age was generally adopted. But, for the individual, the question turns on financial condition, energy and health, performance capacity, need to maintain position or status in the family and community, the wish for stimulating activity, the ability to retain or find work, and the desire for time to devote to other interests.

There is a great deal of evidence that most aging and even aged persons wish to continue in gainful employment. Self-employed business and professional workers and farmers like to continue as long as possible. The great majority of salaried workers and wage-earners resist retirement as long as their health continues good, and many keep on even longer. Women who worked while their children were growing up tend to keep on working, and increasing numbers who did not work are seeking jobs in their newly freed time.

For the employer the decisive factors are the supply of qualified workers, their cost and productive capacity, the need to advance younger workers, and the hiring and retiring practices and pensions.

Society's position is also complicated. Fear of the cost of supporting an increasing retired population is responsible for much of the shift in attitude since the 1930's. Some point to the from $10 to $12 billion contribution of older people to the national product and insist that we cannot get along without it. During the war, employment of older workers was essential, there are still acute shortages in some occupations, and federal manpower agencies are anxious to maintain the health, skills, and work habits of older persons in view of the world situation. There is also growing recognition of the current waste of skills and experience and of the individual problems and frustrations brought on by retirement at a fixed age.[1]

On the other side, there is concern that fulfilment of defense orders and rising productivity will create an oversupply of workers and restrict opportunities for young people entering the labor force.

The long-time downward trend in the employment of older men has already been noted. For the trend to be arrested, a number of adjustments will be required: current prejudices will have to be abandoned; research will be necessary on the development of objective criteria for hiring and retirement; the length of the work week may have to be reduced; more opportunities for tapering off and for part-time work may have to be developed, as well as procedures for moving older workers into positions of lesser responsibility, and there must be provision for counseling, rehabilitation, and retraining.

Adjustment to the changes of the later years is, basically, an individual matter. It can be successful, however, only in an environment which provides opportunity. And, since it is society which creates roles, attitudes, and social values, institutions, facilities, and services, the individual or personal problems of retirement have their societal counterparts. Just as society and the community have provided a climate favorable to the development and self-realization of those of other ages, so now they must define the problems of maturity and create a climate in which older adults may continue as socially integrated, contributing, self-sufficient individuals.

Fairly numerous studies of the adjustment of various occupational and population groups of the retired show that the principal problems faced by the individual are maintenance of income to meet the requirements of active and healthful living; discovery of new occupations or social roles; finding opportunity for social contacts, companionship, and affection; maintenance of health; and procurement of suitable living arrangements. Although most studies show that the majority of older persons adjust well, large numbers are bewildered and confused and frustrated in their efforts to retain or find useful roles, social contacts, and security.[2]

Obtaining sufficient income for shelter, food, clothing, increased medical needs and for active living is commonly regarded as the most pressing need of retired persons and their dependents. At the same time people wonder how many can be supported without lowering the general standard of living.

Considerable progress has been made, particularly in the last twenty years, in providing basic money income to the retired. Of the 13.4 million

[1] National Committee on Aging, *Criteria for Retirement* (New York: G. P. Putnam's Sons, 1953).

[2] Ruth S. Cavan; Ernest W. Burgess; Robert J. Havighurst; and Herbert Goldhamer, *Personal Adjustment in Old Age* (Chicago: Science Research Associates, 1949); Robert T. Monroe, M.D., *Diseases in Old Age* (Cambridge: Harvard University Press, 1951).

persons aged 65 and over on July 1, 1953, about 4.1 were employed or were wives of employed persons. Among the remaining 9.3 million, about 3.8 million were receiving old age and survivors insurance. Other public retirement systems—civil service, veteran and armed forces, and the railroads—were making payments to some 1.1 million persons aged 65 or more. Nearly 0.5 million were beneficiaries of private pension plans. These figures overlap considerably, but it may be said that perhaps two-thirds of all the aged are receiving payments under a public plan or earnings from employment.

Despite this progress, the income continues to be a pressing problem. Old age and survivors insurance payments are low—averaging less than $600 per year to primary beneficiaries, on the assumption that there will be other income, as from savings or part-time employment. Actually, only one in eight has a supplemental income of as much as $600, and the majority of beneficiaries appear to be physically unable to work.

The problems of women are particularly acute. As wives of social security beneficiaries they receive an amount equal to one-half that of the primary benefit—when they reach 65. As widows, they receive a three-quarter benefit, at 65, and private pensions rarely make any provision for them. Not more than one-tenth of the women over the age of 65 are gainfully employed.

The 1950 Census established the fact that the median income of family units in which the head was 55–64 years of age was $3,258 but dropped to $1,903 for families in which the head was 65 or more. About 30 per cent of the older families had less than $1,000, and about 32 per cent had $3,000 or more. Older persons living alone or with nonrelatives averaged $646 per year.

Other sources of income include public assistance payments (to 2.6 million in July, 1953); room, board, clothing, and gifts from relatives; community-supported living accommodation and medical services; and produce from gardens. A few are able to live on personal savings, but only 8 per cent report a net worth of as much as $25,000.

As a consequence many older persons are poorly housed, eat badly, neglect health, and withdraw from organizational and community activities. And many become burdens on their children, who, in turn, must support families of their own and save for their own retirement years. Moreover, continually rising prices depress the value of pensions and financial holdings and lead to prolonged uncertainty and worry.

Some students argue that the economy is not endangered by population aging and retirement. For one thing, the over-all ratio of persons who are not gainful workers per 100 gainful workers has declined from 209 in 1870 to 135 in 1952. Aged persons who are not workers or the wives of workers have increased from 2 per cent of all nongainful workers to 10 per cent over the same period. But there has been marked decline in the proportion of children in the population and marked increase in the employment of young and middle-aged women. If present trends continue, the ratio of 135 dependents to 100 workers will not change much during the next generation.[3]

Furthermore, it is pointed out that productivity and the national income will continue to outstrip population changes. Some authorities forecast that the rise in manufacturing production by the year 2000 will be twice as large as the increase in population.[4] Another group predicts that the national income in 1975 will be twice what it is today and that the per capita increase will approximate 65 per cent.[5] Thus, if economic progress can be maintained, our standard of living is not threatened by the growing number of retired persons. Even today the major obstacle to making adequate provision for this new element in American society would seem to be the outlays essential for military defense.

Insurance and pension plans are now regarded as fixtures, and attention is focused on their improvement. Major questions revolve about the integration of present systems; extension of coverage to all retired persons, including those forced by disability to drop out early; increasing benefits and making them responsive to the rising standard of living and the decreasing purchasing power of the dollar; short- and long-time implications of funding versus pay-as-you-go systems; and provision of financial protection against costs of long-term illness.

It is a question whether pension and insurance plans can be arranged so that they encourage rath-

[3] *Pensions in the United States: A Study Prepared for the Joint Committee [of the Congress] on the Economic Report, by the National Planning Association* (Washington, D. C.: Government Printing Office, 1953), pp. 39–49.

[4] *Retirement Policies and the Railroad Retirement System: Report of the Joint Committee [of the Congress] on Railroad Retirement Legislation* (Washington, D. C.: Government Printing Office, 1953), Part I, pp. 408–10.

[5] *Pensions in the United States*, pp. 33–49.

er than discourage the older person who wishes to continue in gainful work. Though designed to protect the older worker, most of the 14,000 private pension systems tend to place him at a disadvantage when he seeks to change jobs, when he wishes to continue beyond a fixed retirement age, or when, unemployed, he applies for work. But in the future it seems certain that there will also be greater opportunity for increased savings during the working years and, correspondingly, less need for burdening the middle generation with the support of their parents.

Economists at the National Conference on Aging raised the question of greater provision of income in kind. While urging the changes suggested above, they recognized that cash incomes cannot be expected to meet all needs of retired persons. They suggested, therefore, that more facilities and services be made available at the expense of the community, as is now the case with public health, education, and recreation.[6]

Even though the number of older persons who remain in paid employment remains at its present level, three-fourths of those beyond middle age will have to look elsewhere for their principal occupations. American society rewards usefulness and self-sufficiency with recognition and social status. Recent research reveals the strength and universality of the need for a purpose in life, and this is usually satisfied by some sort of contributory activity. One of the critical problems of retirement, therefore, is the discovery of status-giving social roles to replace those of the earlier years.

Herein, it may be suggested, lies the new challenge to American society. Throughout history the tasks of making a living and nurturing the new generation precluded leisure, except in limited amounts. But now the situation is different. No other culture has offered the length of life and the amount of free time now enjoyed by the industrialized countries of the Western world. What shall be done with it? An alternative is to encourage retired adults to live out their years in pursuit of time-filling hobbies, at such entertainment as circumstances afford, and in reflective vegetation—as a reward for past contributions. Or they may be regarded as a new and rich source of energy, experience, and wisdom capable of attaining a self-

realization and carrying important community responsibilities.

While there is considerable evidence of constriction of interests in retirement, there are parallel indications that those who are withdrawn from family and social life are not contented. Some try to find opportunities for broader participation in community affairs. The natural tendency of the mature individual is to turn to activities that will preserve and improve the environment for oncoming generations.[7]

At any rate, the first alternative appears to promise boredom, deterioration, dependency, conservatism, depression, and institutionalization. The second promises continued growth, preservation of the vital functions, purposeful living, continued social usefulness, and self-sufficiency.

Most basic capacities hold up—indeed, in some cases, do not reach their peak—until well into the sixth or seventh decade of life. Much present-day decline and loss of function can be postponed. By and large, the second alternative is the best. The question then becomes: In retirement can a way of life be developed in which the individual has purpose, comparative independence from children, and incentive to maintain health and self-sufficiency, society becoming the beneficiary of the product of his energy and maturity?

Household responsibilities, of course, partially occupy the time of a good many mothers well into the later years, and some find opportunity to be useful in the homes of their children. Similarly, some retired men turn to repair and maintenance of the home, gardening, and postponed hobbies. But these are not enough; most people need more formal interests as substitutes for the responsibilities of the earlier years.

Is there opportunity for self-realization through development of appreciation and creativity in the broad area of the fine arts and crafts and for vast enrichment of the culture through the efforts of retired people? In several parts of the country older persons seem to be finding new satisfactions and, indeed, new lives in thoughtfully developed, organized, community-sponsored situations. The creative arts are meaningful when they are undertaken in groups, when one gains recognition from them, and when, as sometimes, they yield supple-

---

[6] Federal Security Agency, *Man and His Years: Account of the First National Conference on Aging 1950* (Raleigh, N. C.: Health Publications Institute, 1951), chap. iii.

[7] Maurice E. Linden, M.D., "Growing Up or Growing Down: The Challenge of the Geriatric Patient," *Danville [Pa.] State Hospital Mental Health Bulletin* (1952), Vol. XXX, No. 3.

mental income. How widespread and significant this may be remains to be seen. It appears that there is much room for exploitation.

Voluntary community services may offer another outlet, but the evidence is conflicting. Many formerly active drop out as their careers terminate; others look to the field for a new occupation. Certainly, a great variety of useful tasks are performed by volunteers associated with both private and public community agencies, and most agencies clamor for more help. A striking example is the American Red Cross, which has more than a million volunteer workers. A new phenomenon is the banding-together of groups of retired businessmen for the purpose of offering consultation services to individuals or small organizations for little or no fee.

Many retired persons do not know of the opportunities in this field. Some who do seem to lack confidence in their capacities, some encounter the same discrimination as in gainful employment, some find that voluntary services are not so conducted as to recognize the values of maturity or yield a sense of accomplishment and recognition, and others lack the health or income to follow their interests. Can more agencies develop conditions of selection, training, work, and rewards broadly meaningful and satisfying to retired persons? Should more of our rising national income be used to place some of these important, voluntary occupations on a salary basis?

Another area worth exploration is that of citizenship. An everyday complaint is that government has become too large and removed from the people. Yet, government has grown in response to needs, and its functions will probably not be reduced. Indeed, today, it is faced with more complex responsibilities than ever before. Is it possible that mature, retired adults may come to be seen as a vast resource of senior citizens available to serve as consultants, members of survey teams, of commissions and advisory groups, as councils of elders, or, merely, as thinking, informed members of the community? If so—and there are beginnings—the potentialities for civic betterment challenge the imagination.

In solving these problems, the choice may lie between continued utilization and, through it, continued social integration of the retired, or the appearance of a huge pressure group of social, financial, and medical dependents.

The fundamental problem is that of shifting from a technological society focused on ever in-

creasing productivity of goods and wealth to one in which the highest values are placed on forms of consumption that yield the greatest degrees of personal satisfaction and social gain.[8]

A major problem of retired persons is to find replacements for earlier sources of social contacts, companionship, and affection. The independence and mobility of children create an affectional loss that many parents find hard to fill. Widowhood, reached by a majority of women by age 65, aggravates the loss. That work provides social contact is powerfully appreciated when retirement comes and the contacts are lost. Removal from the community or death of friends further constricts the social sphere.

Retired individuals, gradually bereft of companionship, characteristically become lonesome, complaining, and self-centered and may make excessive demands on children, physicians, case workers, ministers, and others. Their children, who must devote their energies to their own young, find themselves burdened with salvaging the social life of the older generation. Feelings of guilt and serious family problems result.

Not only do they give a sense of usefulness, but new interests in the creative arts, community service, continuing education, and citizenship activities automatically solve a large part of the problem through providing new friendships which satisfy the need for companionship.

Many private and public community agencies are experimenting with clubs for older adults, recreational programs in parks, playgrounds, and community centers; centers with programs in education, dramatics, crafts, social events, tours of interesting places, friendly visiting, and games, overnight camping; and development of such interests as nature study, photography, and collecting.

Although organized educational and recreational programs have, thus far, appealed to only small numbers of retired persons, these derive much satisfaction from them. Individual problems of family relationships, boredom, psychosomatic illness, and eating habits are being resolved.[9] It appears worthwhile to continue to experiment with varied types of facilities, programs, leadership, and methods of appeal.

[8] George A. Lundberg, *Leisure* (New York: Columbia University Press, 1934).

[9] Susan H. Kubie and Gertrude Landau, *Group Work with the Aged* (New York: International Universities Press, Inc., 1953).

Declining health is generally a predisposing factor in retirement rather than a consequence. There is a marked inflection in the curve of chronic illness during the 45–55-year decade. Nevertheless, there is evidence of premature deterioration when retirement deprives the organism and the mind of activity. Moreover, low retirement incomes and lack of information often impede proper nutrition, medical care, and rehabilitation services. Health improves when retired persons rediscover a purpose in life. Surgery, drug and dietary therapy, physical medicine, and occupational therapy, in a few experimental programs, are restoring older persons and lifting the burden of their care from family and community. Current research offers great promise in bringing the chronic diseases and the aging process itself under control. But facilities to care for the extremely ill and the infirm for whom there is no prospect of improvement must be expanded.

Retirement from family duties and from work creates problems of living arrangements for many older persons. Departure of children generally reduces the amount of space needed. Reduced income sometimes makes it essential to seek less expensive housing. Rural homes must often be vacated in favor of the young family taking over the farm. Illness, declining energy, or loss of spouse may also dictate a change in living arrangements. And, for some, completion of family or career offers opportunity to migrate to a more attractive section of the country.

Many variations in living arrangements are sought, dependent upon personal preferences, income, health, marital status, availability of space with children, and importance of community contacts. Most retired persons seem to prefer to maintain their own homes, even beyond the point at which it has become a physical and financial burden. Some, voluntarily or involuntarily, seek living in groups or institutions. It is quite likely that many live as they do because they know no alternative.

Communities are faced with the problem of making a variety of living arrangements available, in one way or another, to declining families and retired individuals. The solution is not easy. Not enough is known about personal preferences. Housing is an expensive commodity, not easily

turned over if it is of special design. Because of the low incomes and shorter life-expectancy of retired persons, private enterprise has been slow to take an interest. Unfavorable attitudes toward public housing have retarded effort through that medium. The belief that older persons will not share facilities has withheld efforts.

Nevertheless, the awareness and the urgency of needs are forcing some progress. The University of Chicago is conducting research into preferences in type and location of housing. Villages for the retired which provide housekeeping and health services, workshops, and recreational facilities are dispelling the notion that all older people are unwilling to live in more or less segregated neighborhoods or communities. England, New York State, and Chicago are showing the feasibility of reserving units for retired persons in large public projects. Extension of hospital, home management and housekeeping, social case work, food, and visiting services into the home is enabling many infirm and ill to remain where they seem best satisfied. So, too, studies of housing design are yielding suggestions for greater comfort and safety.

Migration to warm climates is creating housing as well as other problems for some states. While it appears that most persons will retire in their own communities, enough will migrate to create special situations in Arizona, California, Florida, and perhaps elsewhere.

Larger numbers of very old, ill and infirm, and socially isolated persons are increasing the demand for institutional and "foster-home" facilities. Traditionally, institutionalization has meant admission of defeat and complete withdrawal from the community, relinquishment of total assets, and a vegetative existence. But there are improvements: institutions are no longer being established in isolated locations; medical, rehabilitation, and food services are being extended; and programs are being developed for purposeful activity and the maintenance of community contacts. These are only pioneering ventures, however, and many problems remain.

Indeed, this sentence applies to the entire field; housing and living arrangements for the retired have become recognized as one of the major phases of the total problem.

Adjustment to Bereavement
Thomas D. Eliot

Thomas Dawes Eliot (1889–   ), emeritus professor of sociology, Northwestern University. Principal works: *The Juvenile Court and the Community* (1914); *Outlines of Social Economy* (1925) and *American Standards and Planes of Living* (1931).

As sex dominates the first half of life so death dominates the latter half. As sex was dodged in vain, so death is dodged in vain. As sex is being faced, so death must be faced.[1] Each, indeed, may have a phase, like the far side of the moon, which we may never see: life before conception, life after organic functional unity ceases. But, hitherto, our sacraments, ceremonials, theologies and taboos have been mere defense mechanisms to help us escape from inescapable realities.

Sex has its sex hygiene, its sex education and its social hygiene. Though far from mastering its arts we are, as a result of research, at least aware of certain avoidable errors and certain useful controls and sublimations. There is a mental hygiene of sex.

But what do we know about the mental hygiene of death? about the sublimation of grief? Some of us think we know death, but what we know is empirical, like what most of us know about sex.

We are "acquainted with grief," but while some of us have won out, it has been "by grace of God and force of habit," not by knowing "the truth which makes us free." Collectively we have not "swallowed up death in victory" and death still has its sting.

Death has been joked about almost as much as sex: there is again a close psychological analogy—the joke is the escape from repression of an intolerable reality-experience which cannot be seriously faced. When the reality is upon us, it ceases to be funny.

Great souls have, to be sure, always pondered the problem of the cessation of self, and have written great words into the human record. They have done so, however, as seers, poets, prophets, philosophers, novelists, biographers, not as scientists. Physicians have made a beginning on the physiological side, psychologists and physicists have shown skeptical or credulous but inconclusive interest in "psychical research." It remains to apply modern techniques of case histories, group studies, and documentary analysis to the attitudes and actual behavior of people toward death. Only upon such a basis, slowly to be accumulated, compared and worked over, can a social psychology of death be built up which can be of social value.

The art of death should be part of the art of life, even as the art of love, but all three are as yet in their infancy, and uncoordinated.

* * * *

It is difficult to isolate the true bereavement features from the socioeconomic features which have been so extensively studied by social workers.[2] For the social psychologist, however, the latter are of interest only as they influence personal attitudes and family interactions. . . .

[Let] us note some ways in which families have been observed to change as a result of bereavement.

(1) The role of a family member exists in relation to the configuration and functioning of the family as a unit. A death tends to disturb this unity. The shifting of the roles of the various members under bereavement represents a reshaping of the configuration.

(2) The consensus of the family in respect to these roles, i.e., in respect to its own pattern, may result; or, family conflict may develop as a sequence to incompatible conceptions of the role of certain members under the new conditions.

(3) Such conflicts or jealousies, or the lack of a common personal or domestic object or symbol of

---

[1] It is interesting to note how certain writers who have faced sex frankly in their earlier works have turned toward problems of death in later works: Hall, Carpenter, Wells, Shaw, Ellis, Freud, Jung occur to the writer.

[2] E.g., Mary E. Richmond and Fred S. Hall, *A Study of Nine Hundred and Eighty-Five Widows . . .* , New York: Russell Sage Foundation, 1913.

From "A Step Toward the Social Psychological of Bereavement," *Journal of Abnormal and Social Psychology,* 27 (1932–33): 380–390, pp. 380–381 quoted, and from "The Bereaved Family," *The Annals,* 160 (March 1932): 184–194, p. 188 quoted. Reprinted by permission.

affectional attachment (conditioning stimuli) may result in decreased family solidarity.

(4) Acceptance of new interpersonal responsibilities may increase family solidarity.

(5) Removal of authority, of habit-stimuli, of home, or of support may lead to revision of family folkways.

(6) Maturity of children who lose their parents may lead to individualism or turning to their own families.

(7) The will, or personality, of the deceased, acting psychologically as a dynamic complex in each member's memory, and reenforced by consensus, may activate the behavior of the entire family.

CROSS REFERENCES TO STANDARD TEXTS *

Barnes, *Society in Transition*, Chap. 8.

Bernard, *American Community Behavior*, Chaps. 11, 24.

Bloch, *Disorganization*, Chaps. 5, 8, 13–16.

Brown, *Social Pathology*, Chaps. 9, 11, 25.

Cuber and Harper, *Problems of American Society*, Chap. 17.

Elliott and Merrill, *Social Disorganization*, Chaps. 15–21.

Faris, *Social Disorganization*, Chap. 10.

Gillin, *Social Pathology*, Chaps. 11–13, 16, 20.

—— and others, *Social Problems*, Chaps. 13, 17.

*For complete bibliographical reference to each text, see page 13.

Herman, *Approach to Social Problems*, pp. 222–228, 414.

Landis, *Social Policies in the Making*, Chaps. 12–17.

Merrill and others, *Social Problems*, Chaps. 11–13.

Mihanovich, *Current Social Problems*, Chaps. 10, 13.

Neumeyer, *Social Problems and the Changing Society*, Chaps. 7, 11.

Nordskog and others, *Analyzing Social Problems*, Chap. 6.

Odum, *American Social Problems*, Chaps. 12, 14, 23.

Phelps and Henderson, *Contemporary Social Problems*, Chaps. 9, 15–17.

Reinhardt and others, *Social Problems and Social Policy*, Chap. 10.

Weaver, *Social Problems*, Chaps. 18–21, 27.

OTHER BIBLIOGRAPHY

Aging, bi-monthly publication, U. S. Department of Health, Education, and Welfare, Committee on Aging and Geriatrics, Washington, D. C.

Robert Cooley Angell, *The Family Encounters the Depression*, New York: Charles Scribner's Sons, 1936.

Ruth Nanda Anshen, ed., *The Family: Its Function and Destiny*, New York: Harper & Bros., 1949.

Ray E. Baber, *Marriage and the Family*, 2d ed., New York: McGraw-Hill Book Co., 1953.

Milton L. Barron, *People Who Intermarry*, Syracuse: Syracuse University Press, 1946.

Floyd A. Bond and others, *Our Needy Aged: A California Study of a National Problem*, New York: Henry Holt and Co., 1954.

James H. S. Bossard, ed., "Toward Family Stability," *The Annals*, 272 (November 1950).

Henry A. Bowman, *Marriage for Moderns*, 3d ed., New York: McGraw-Hill Book Co., 1954.

Ernest W. Burgess, issue ed., "Aging and Retirement," *American Journal of Sociology*, 59:4 (January 1954).

—— and Paul Wallin, *Engagement and Marriage*, Philadelphia: J. B. Lippincott Co., 1953.

Ruth Shonle Cavan, *The American Family*, New York: Thomas Y. Crowell Co., 1953.

John F. Cuber, *Marriage Counseling Practice*, New York: Appleton-Century-Crofts, 1948.

Thomas D. Eliot, "The Adjustive Behavior of Bereaved Families," *Social Forces*, 8 (1929–30): 543–549.

——, "—of the Shadow of Death," *The Annals*, 229 (September 1943): 87–99.

Joseph K. Folsom, *The Family and Democratic Society*, New York: John Wiley & Sons, 1943.

Robert G. Foster, *Marriage and Family Relationships*, New York: Macmillan Co., 1944.

E. Franklin Frazier, *The Negro Family in the United States*, Chicago: University of Chicago Press, 1939.

John C. Gebhart, "Funerals," *Encyclopaedia of the Social Sciences*, 6 (1931): 527–529.

Ernest R. Groves and Gladys Hoagland Groves, *The Contemporary American Family*, Philadelphia: J. B. Lippincott Co., 1947.

Margaret Jarman Hagood, *Mothers of the South*, Chapel Hill: University of North Carolina Press, 1939.

Robert J. Havighurst and Ruth Albrecht, *Older People*, New York: Longmans, Green and Co., 1953.

Jerome Himelhoch and Sylvia Fleis Fava, eds., *Sexual Behavior in American Society: An Appraisal of the First Two Kinsey Reports*, New York: W. W. Norton & Co., 1955.

Norman E. Himes, with the medical collaboration of Abraham Stone, *Practical Birth Control Methods*, New York: Modern Age Books, 1938.

Raymond P. Kaighn, *How to Retire and Like It*, rev. ed., New York: Association Press, 1954.

Alfred C. Kinsey, Wardell B. Pomeroy and Clyde E. Martin, *Sexual Behavior in the Human Male*, Philadelphia: W. B. Saunders Co., 1948.

―――― and Paul H. Gebhard, *Sexual Behavior in the Human Female*, Philadelphia: W. B. Saunders Co., 1953.

Mirra Komarovsky, *Women in the Modern World*, Boston: Little, Brown and Co., 1953.

George Lawton, *Aging Successfully*, New York: Columbia University Press, 1946.

―――― and Maxwell S. Stewart, "When You Grow Older," Public Affairs Pamphlet No. 131, 1947.

Harvey C. Lehman, *Age and Achievement*, Princeton: Princeton University, 1952.

Clarence W. Leib, *Outwitting Your Years*, New York: Prentice-Hall, 1951.

John Levy and Ruth Munroe, *The Happy Family*, New York: Alfred A. Knopf, 1938.

Ferdinand Lundberg and Marynia F. Farnham, *Modern Woman: The Lost Sex*, New York: Harper & Bros., 1947.

Margaret Mead, *Male and Female*, New York: Wm. Morrow and Co., 1949.

Meyer F. Nimkoff, *Marriage and the Family*, Boston: Houghton Mifflin Co., 1947.

Walter B. Pitkin, *The Best Years*, New York: Current Books, 1946.

Amram Scheinfeld, *Women and Men*, New York: Harcourt, Brace and Co., 1944.

Leo W. Simmons, *The Role of the Aged in Primitive Society*, New Haven: Yale University Press, 1945.

M. B. Smith, *The Single Woman of Today: He Problems and Adjustment*, New York: Philosophical Library, 1952.

Edward J. Stieglitz, *The Second Forty Years*, Philadelphia: J. B. Lippincott Co., 1946.

"Symposium on Divorce: A Re-Examination of Basic Concepts," *Law and Contemporary Problems*, 18, 1 (Winter 1953).

Clara Thompson, "The Role of Women in This Culture," *Psychiatry*, 4 (1941): 1–8.

Clark Tibbitts, ed., *Living Through the Older Years*, Ann Arbor: University of Michigan Press, 1949.

――――, ed., "Social Contribution by the Aging," *The Annals*, 279 (January 1952).

Andrew G. Truxel and F. E. Merrill, *Marriage and the Family in American Culture*, New York: Prentice-Hall, 1953.

Willard Waller, *The Family: A Dynamic Interpretation*, rev. by Reuben Hill, New York: Dryden Press, 1951.

――――, *The Old Love and the New*, New York: Boni & Liveright, 1930.

――――, *War and the Family*, New York: Dryden Press, 1940.

Louise M. Young, "Personality Patterns in Unmarried Mothers," *Family*, 26 (1945): 296–303.

Carle C. Zimmerman, *Family and Civilization*, New York: Harper & Bros., 1947.

―――― and Nathan L. Whetten, *Rural Families on Relief*, Washington: Government Printing Office, 1939.

REVIEW QUESTIONS

1. If more women find it possible and want to work outside the home, what will happen to the home?
2. Is it possible that it will become, as Mead suggests, "so difficult to bring up children to be full human beings that outraged voices will sound throughout society and shout women back into the home again"?
3. Why does Mead think that a stronger social emphasis on women's biological role is unlikely in the United States?
4. Are we likely to achieve the sort of balance between the sexes that Mead suggests?
5. To what extent can housekeeping now be regarded as "the semivoluntary slavery . . . we now impose on married women"?
6. List some of the consequences of the fact that most sex-related legislation, as Deutsch points out, is enacted by college-trained legislators.
7. Is there any likelihood of sex mores being standardized throughout American society?
8. How do Vincents' findings correlate with the popular stereotype of an unwed mother?
9. What are the chief problems Elmer sees in connection with unmarried parents?
10. What steps are currently being taken to cope with injustices to the children of unmarried parents?
11. What are the "old rural-familistic values which find little support in modern social structure," to which Green refers?
12. How would you compare the conclusions of Green and Mead with regard to the emerging roles for middle-class men and women?
13. What is happening to the Negro maternal family in various parts of the United States?
14. What kinds of problems does King associate with the Negro maternal family?
15. What weaknesses or flaws in personality does McLean believe most commonly make their appearance in marriage?
16. What bearings do McLean's points have on divorce as a social problem?
17. How fast is the divorce rate growing? What are some of the outstanding factors contributing to this rise? Can you account for the recent drop in the rate?
18. Why is a marriage no longer regarded as "good" just because it lasts?
19. What is the extent of desertion? Why is it called the "poor man's divorce"?

20. What prices does Thorman say we pay for broken homes? Who pays these prices most directly? Who indirectly?

21. What qualifications do Burgess and Locke recommend for the marriage and family counselor?

22. How should marriage and family counseling services be sponsored and organized? Why?

23. Who have traditionally offered marriage and family counseling services? Why should or shouldn't they continue to do so?

24. What forms does marriage counseling take?

25. Do you think that the governmental licensing of marriage counselors would make their services more or less acceptable?

26. How rapidly is our population over sixty-five increasing?

27. What are we doing to provide for the care of the aged?

28. What are the chief types of adjustment families make to bereavement?

PART IV

Major Institutional Problems

—CHAPTER 10—→

Education

As THE educational system of the United States has expanded, especially during the first half of the twentieth century, the struggle over what is taught in texts and classrooms has become progressively more determined and sophisticated. Benedict condemns those "critics and exhorters" of the public-school system who "have argued only that some particular set of facts should be taught in our schools." She urges that we should not be afraid of facts and that we should use our vast educational machinery primarily to transmit our democratic heritage, our democratic ways of thinking and of acting. Konvitz devotes himself to the struggle of church groups to maintain and to destroy the secular—the religiously nonpartisan—character of public education. The United States Supreme Court, in its interpretation of the religious clause in the First Amendment to the Federal Constitution, attacks various devices by which public schools have been used to undermine freedom of conscience and religion. In its epoch-making decision against segregation in the public schools the Court proclaims the failure of the separate but equal doctrine.

Those who labor to maintain democratic institutions must be eternally vigilant. The *Platform* selection points up the plight of our schools with too many children for too few rooms, too few and too poorly paid teachers, and unclarified educational objectives.

Problems associated with education also appear in many other chapters. To illustrate, the Mobilization for Understanding Private Enterprise in Chapter 13—Mass Communications—warns businessmen to interest themselves in what local schools are teaching. Several selections in Chapter 17 on delinquency and crime relate the schoolteacher and education to efforts to cope with such problems. Other significant points in the field of education are discussed in the chapters on leadership, class, race, ethnic differences, and elsewhere.

Transmitting Our Democratic Heritage in the Schools

Ruth Benedict

Ruth Benedict (1887–1948), associate professor of anthropology, Columbia University. Principal works: *Patterns of Culture* (1934); *Zuñi Mythology* (1935); *Race: Science and Politics* (1940); and *The Chrysanthemum and the Sword* (1946).

Controversies about education in recent years have in one way or another turned upon the issue of the role of the schools in transmitting our cultural heritage. There have been those who have blamed the schools for every "un-American" trait they believed to be increasing in our society. Some of these critics place on the schools responsibility for the decreasing religious affiliations in our cities and rural areas; some attack them for the moral relativism they see in our decade. Such criticisms assume that an educational system can, of and by itself, have such far-reaching effects as these; and

From "Transmitting Our Democratic Heritage in the Schools," *American Journal of Sociology*, 48 (1942–1943): 722–727. Reprinted by permission.

this same assumption is just as basic in a very different argument: that education should shoulder the responsibility for ushering in a new social order. In so far as these critics and exhorters have argued only that some particular set of facts should be taught in our schools—American history or the Bible or Thomas Aquinas or the achievements of the TVA—there is no need for further discussion; the school curriculum can easily be improved without claiming that our educational system makes or breaks the social order. But the assumption made by these critics has consequences of its own which go far beyond the changes in curriculum they urge. It is an assumption that can be examined in the light of comparative studies of other cultures, and such an examination can throw light on the whole relation of education to social change.

It is instructive to study a long series of societies, identifying those where culture is relatively stable and those where it is highly unstable. One does not find that those which are stable educate their children in one fashion and those which are unstable in another. There are a great many different ways of rearing children: they may be treated like little adults from birth and divide their day into work and play almost exactly as their parents do; they may be little outlaws who consider the adults fair game, pillaging their fields and evading responsibilities; they may be privileged beings whose every wish is gratified, however inconvenient. But none of these or other ways of rearing children correlates with whether or not the culture is reproduced in the next generation. Stability of culture over generations is not a function of the particular kind of education that is given to children. It is a function rather of social conditions in the whole tribe or nation. Anthropologists have to study rapidly changing cultures over and over again, and usually with sinking hearts. When a Plains Indian tribe is put on a reservation, the differences between older and younger generations are very great, and transmission of culture most inadequate. The livelihood techniques the parents knew can no longer be used, for the buffalo have disappeared from the plains, and horses can no longer be raided from other tribes. The older ways of life no longer work, and with them go the religious rites that guaranteed them and the respect which the young once showed their elders. These drop out, and the tragedy is that it is hard to replace them. Then one generation is not like another: transmission of culture has been interfered

with by all the external and internal condition which are present in an unstable society. Sometimes the anthropologist can study cultural change under more favorable conditions: when incentive to activity are increased; when there is more lei sure because iron tools, for instance, have been in troduced; and when the arts of life therefore flourish and new developments take place.

Under such social conditions—whatever the method of education—transmission of culture i achieved only in part. But a homogeneous society faced by no new circumstances sufficiently drasti to disturb its balance transmits its culture genera tion after generation, no matter how it breaks the rules of education that seem to us essential. Our problems in transmission of culture arise from the rapidity of social changes in our society; and no method of education can prevent this. The choice open to our school systems are only whether they will cling to the teaching of subjects and attitude. which the child can no longer use profitably ir the world in which he will live or whether they will give him equipment he can use. They canno possibly make a stable world of an unstable one Those critics who blame the schools for change they resent in our culture are making the educa tional system a scapegoat for vast changes in the structure of modern society which they do no take into account.

Once we are sufficiently skeptical about the no tion that schools—or parents—have it in thei power to indoctrinate our children so that they will maintain the status quo, we can face the cru cial problem of the relation of education to the social order. All the problems in this relationship whatever the tribe or nation studied, concern the degree to which the method of education fits the requirements of that society. It is not a matter of identifying some good educational policies and some bad ones. The "best" education can be a weakness in a society that does not give the adoles cent scope to put his learning into practice; it can breed sullenness and frustration. The "worst" can be well adapted to all that will ever be required of him as an adult.

Nothing is more striking in some primitive so cieties than the rapid intellectual development of children which flattens out somewhere in early life so that a man of twenty, perhaps, has already all the skills and all the knowledge of a man of fifty. This fact has sometimes been read off as an inherent characteristic of simpler peoples; it is said that their mental powers are capable of only limited development. It would be truer to say that they do not expand if the society requires nothing further of them. If men can supply their needs of livelihood and gain prestige among their fellows without adding to their skills or their knowledge, they early reach a mental plateau. This is not a characteristic of all primitive societies, for in many tribes a man must accumulate "wisdom" and special techniques throughout his life in order to take any desired position in the society. It is this continuing stimulus to mental achievement supplied by the responsibilities society puts upon its members which in any society, our own included, prevents the arrest of intellectual development.

Not only intellectual development but also training of the emotions and will-power are relative to the social order in which they occur. Life in some primitive cultures requires tough and violent people if they are to carry on; they can fill their roles with less cost to themselves and to their fellowmen if they have been reared not to expect universal kindness. Primitive people are generally more permissive to their children than we are, and their methods of child-rearing often seem to us extraordinarily attractive. They are not all of them the better for it. In some tribes where sorcery is a common practice and greatly feared, children are believed to be unaffected by black magic. They live in a charmed circle. At adolescence they become liable to all the machinations of their fellow-tribesmen, and they are unprepared. Sorcery in such tribes is a daily terror the intensity of which is possible just because the children were secure and happy in their childhood. There are other tribes where the maladjustment between education and adult requirements is quite the opposite. Life in the band is co-operatively regulated; all members share the labors and the rewards of labor. But the boy's education is, as they say, "like breaking a colt." He must be humiliated by his elders, and they send him on lying errands to make game of him. He must be chased out of bed to jump into icy water. He is taught that he has only himself to depend on. "Rely on no one. Your hands are your friends. Your feet are your friends. Your eyes are your friends. Rely on these." The education he is given does not fit the cooperative arrangements of band life; and the aggressions, the mean gossip, the bickering of tribal life, are objective measures of the lack of consonance between child-training and the kind of character structure which can operate to advantage in the culture.

In our own culture there are of course many inconsistencies between education and the world for which it offers training. I shall not discuss the curriculum, though it is obvious that in any changing society the curriculum must be reconsidered constantly. The matters which are affected when we try to make our education consonant with our total cultural life go far beyond the curriculum. They include attitudes which our children learn in the course of studying their lessons and the institutional organization of our schools. And we cannot plan without analyzing our own culture. The more clearly we see its general outlines, the more wisely we shall propose.

We are constantly in danger in our schools of underestimating the cultural changes that occur in such a society as ours. Education in our world today must prepare our children to adapt themselves to unforeseeable conditions. It must give them a basis upon which they can make their own decisions in situations not yet on the horizon. The controversies of our decade will die out or be re-embodied in quite different events. The phrasing will change. In the first decade of this century the duty of thrift was one of the absolute values on which all my teachers were agreed. Starting little bank accounts was a learning activity which would bear the fruit of the good life from childhood to old age. The object was to create in school a sentiment for valuing accumulation rather than for present expenditure. My schoolmates and I have lived through the nemesis of this teaching, through periods when one's whole duty was to spend and the hoarder was antisocial. Then, too, we were taught that the world was through with war and that in our day and age ethics and humanitarianism were so developed that the voice of the whole earth was unanimous for peace. We have lived through the first World War and the Long Truce, and today we do not know where the second World War . . . [has taken us]. The absolute values of peace which we were taught in school are something for which people are jailed.

A clearer analysis of our culture would have made it unnecessary for that generation of school children to unlearn painfully these lessons they had been taught. If, instead of trying to educate us to recognize an absolute good in hoarding, our teachers had chosen out of the cultural values of American civilization that pre-eminent one of initiative and independence, if they had been able to teach us that according to our abilities we could get somewhere if we showed initiative and independence and that we would be honored for them by our fellow-men, they could have subordinated saving money to the due place which it holds in an American scheme of things. They could have put their teaching on the ground that some attainable goals are worth saving for. If, instead of pacifism, they had taught us that peace was the dearest possession of any people and the one most worth giving one's greatest efforts to perfect, if they had taught us that war was the greatest calamity but one which, no matter what men's ethical sentiments were, would follow from certain acts, the generation they taught would not have had to unlearn the lesson.

"Transmitting our culture" in a changing society means self-examination and a certain detachment; for, unless our analyses are good, our teachings may go into limbo with the passing of some special set of circumstances. A stable society is not faced with such necessities. It can inculcate saving for generation after generation, or it can inculcate stripping one's self of all possessions. If these are integrated in the whole economic pattern of their culture, they can be taught to each generation in minute detail. Stable societies, too, have teachings either about the glories of war or about the virtue of peacefulness; these are consequences of the state of warfare or lack of warfare in which they live, and generation after generation maintains the status quo. The great challenge of education in our changing world today is that it requires so much more of our educators than a stable society need require.

This challenge is intensified when we try to state what we mean by transmitting our heritage of democracy. Here, too, we must stress those things without which our culture would be unrecognizable. Fortunately, in America there is a certain basic agreement. In contrast to European and South American nations, the United States from the first has had a tradition of liberty and opportunity, and despotic power has been at a minimum. It is true that there are marked divergencies in current definitions of what democratic heritage we want to transmit, divergencies which turn upon whether the speaker is demanding liberty and opportunity for a special group to which he belongs or whether he is demanding these privileges for all Americans on the same terms. What is essential to all of them, however, is that they identify our way of life with adequate scope for personal achievement. All the definitions are drawn from experience in our culture where initiative and independence are traits every man wants for himself.

The transmission of our democratic heritage means primarily, then, preparing children in our schools to act as adults with initiative and independence. Our culture does not go about this with the directness that is characteristic of many tribes which set this same goal. With us, children are dependent, and yet as adults they must be independent. They are commanded as children, and as adults they command. This is in strong contrast to those societies which make no qualitative differences between children and adults. The qualities they value in grown men they boast of also in little boys even if the child flouts his father or even strikes him. "He will be a man," his father says. Such tribes do not have the problem we have in our culture: the unlearning of dependence and docility when the child reaches man's estate. Nevertheless, this discontinuity in the life-cycle is basic in our culture, and we have used it to good advantage. We greatly prolong infancy, and we define it as a period of learning. We give ourselves, therefore, the opportunity to equip our children with all that a long-continued and uninterrupted course of teaching can give them. We do not always take full advantage of our opportunity, of course, but the opportunity is there. The child on the threshold of manhood has spent years sitting at the feet of the older generation, and his teachers have had a remarkable chance to pass on to him all they know and value.

One great danger we face under this system is not that the child will be rebellious or insufficiently docile—but that he will learn his lesson of docility too well. Our schools impose the school schedule, the subject matter, the personnel, the forms of discipline; in all these matters the child takes what is offered. As long as he accepts these arrangements as the condition of his progress toward adulthood, his docility in these matters need not interfere with a later independence. But the training is overwhelmingly in docility rather than in self-reliance and independence, and many adults have obviously been overinfluenced by this training. They find dependency hard to relinquish. Progressive education, with its greater encouragement of the kind of behavior the child will need as an adult in our culture, is clearly on the right track. There are many classroom customs which could be introduced and which could give the child greater experience in responsibility and initiative. All such methods bridge the gap between school and life and lessen the numbers who find it difficult or impossible to make the transition.

The spread of progressive education is at least in part a compensation for increased restrictions on children's opportunities for independence and responsibility in our modern cities. In the earlier days of our democracy, village and even city life provided more chances for genuine autonomy. Boys shouldered their fishing rods and organized their own games and filled their free time according to their own ideas. A bully at the fishing hole was the affair of the older boys who swam there. Their chores, too, were genuine responsibilities. A boy might have to milk the cows and tend store, but his work belonged in the scheme of things. He was doing the things his father also did. Today he listens to the radio or plays in supervised playgrounds or on the street with one eye on the policeman. His father's work is away from home and he cannot contribute to it. The changed conditions in our cities make it harder for the child to get experience in the kind of behavior upon which success in his adult life will depend; and, unless our schools offer such opportunities, the persistence of childhood dependency into adulthood—our so-called "regressions"—will inevitably become a greater social problem.

Just as our system of child-rearing runs the danger of inadequately transmitting our cultural heritage because the child may learn the lesson of dependency too well, so, too, it may fall short because he learns too well the lesson of external sanctions for moral behavior. Our moral tradition is based on internalized sanctions; we do not regulate private life by constant external supervision as is the custom in some European countries and in many native tribes of Africa. Our democracy needs as many individuals as possible with the capacity for self-discipline, individuals who will subordinate immediate and shifting wishes to a chosen goal. But self-discipline is not a lesson which is learned directly by enforced discipline. In many societies the step from one to the other is never made. It is not automatic. In our culture we make the transition the hard way, and all our psychiatric discussions of the punishing superego are documentation of this difficulty. For our transition internalizes not the actual consequences of the comprising act but the outside punisher himself, a punisher who when he is internalized can be overwhelmingly inhibiting. Many societies follow a different course. From earliest childhood they inculcate genuine self-dis-

cipline, and individuals in such societies do not have to make such expensive transitions as are common in our culture. Parents in such tribes are not so afraid as we are of placing responsibility for his acts genuinely in the child's hands. If the baby sells his tanned-skin dress to a white man for a dime, no adult punishes him; they would consider that extraneous to the issue. The dress was his, and he alone is responsible for what he has done with it. But at the next feast he has no fine dress to wear. He learns the consequences of his act; he does not learn the punishing parent. Even very extreme disciplines are left in the child's hands. From our point of view these disciplines seem arbitrary and out of all proportion to the goals sought. They may be rubbing one's self with nettles or letting wads of grass burn into one's skin or drawing blood from sensitive parts of one's body. The point is that even these are readily assumed by the child himself, not imposed by an outside authority. Democratically organized societies have often fared well by giving the child experience in genuine self-discipline. They put upon the child the responsibility for going out to seek a vision and for taking the initiative in obtaining his own instruction in hunting. Data from such societies make it clear that absence of enforced discipline does not necessarily mean license or laziness. This notion, so common in conventional discussions of our educational system, can arise only in a society which has systematically minimized opportunities for preadult self-discipline.

These specific points of strain in our educational system occur just because of the contrast in our culture between the child's world and the adult world, and all our problems are acute at the period of transition itself. Gradually our schools are coming to realize that it is just at this transition period where they have failed the child. Vocational training and job-placement assistance are being provided, but the problem is only partly met, as statistics in unemployment and criminology abundantly show. Primitive democratic societies which, like us, require one set of behavior for the child and another for the adult have remarkable basic likeness in their procedure at the period of transition. They have great graduating ceremonies—the conclusion of puberty rites—and automatically give the graduates as a group their new responsibilities as adults, providing them with the necessary tools and equipment. They do not leave the transition to each adolescent's fumbling attempts, and they do not put obstacles in the way of his access to the means of production. It seems fair to say that it is at this point of transition from childhood dependency to adult independence that our culture most often fails adequately to transmit our democratic heritage and that our educators must work with our social planners if our current wastage is to be lessened.

These examples of what education can do to insure the transmission of our democratic heritage are not based on "the nature of the child" or on an absolute standard of what a mature individual should be or of what a good society is. They depend upon surveying some of the major wastages in our civilization and upon citing ways in which some other cultures have met similar situations. Such knowledge of comparative cultures can often be useful; and it highlights the truth that our democracy, with its special demand for initiative and independence, is a special way of functioning as a human being that has to be learned. All that we know about the learning process we need to apply socially to this task of transmitting our democratic heritage in a changing world.

The Churches and Education
Milton R. Konvitz

Milton R. Konvitz (1908–   ), professor, New York State School of Industrial and Labor Relations, Cornell University; editor, *Industrial and Labor Relations Review*. Chief publications: *The Alien and the Asiatic in American Law* (1946); *The Constitution and Civil Rights* (1947); *Essays in Political Theory* (1948); *Civil Rights in Immigration* (1953).

Religious freedom, as based on the rigorous separation of church and state, has traditionally been regarded as one of the foundation stones of American democracy. Against this background, many view with apprehension increasing efforts on the part of the churches to use state funds and power on behalf of religious education and, by one means or another, to invade the public school system. . . .

In colonial times and in the early days of the Republic the states supported the churches and the church schools. For the last hundred years, however, and until the end of World War I, the sharp separation of church and state was considered an inviolable principle of American democracy. Practically the only aid the church received was tax exemption of its property. And even this measure of support was under violent attack. President Garfield, for example, said: "The divorce between church and state ought to be absolute.". . . Garfield followed the precedent set by President Grant, who . . . [in] no uncertain terms . . . urged "the taxation of all property equally."

Today a President would be committing political suicide were he to make such proposals.

From the middle of the 19th to the middle of the 20th century we have gone a long way in closing up the distance between church and state; and the end is not in sight. The churches are well organized and aggressive; and ambitious politicians have learned it is easier to be on the side of the churches than against them. The churches blame the scientists and the politicians for the unchristian destruction of Hiroshima and Nagasaki; they blame the godless schools for juvenile delinquency and crime. They speak for decency, public order, and morals. They say they are on the side of God and that God is on their side. Who else can make such a claim? And if they make such a claim, who dare oppose them? . . .

While the pressure to secure public funds for parochial schools comes from the Catholic Church, the pressure to bring the Bible and religious instruction into the public schools, and then gradually convert the public schools into parochial schools, comes from the Protestants. While the Catholics have been forthright in affirming their objectives, this cannot always be said of the Protestant groups. . . .

The Bible has been taken into the public schools on the argument that it is a non-sectarian

From "Whittling Away Religious Freedom: The Current Threat to Separation of Church and State," *Commentary, 1: 8* (June 1946): 4–13, pp. 4–5, 8–12 quoted. Reprinted by permission.

book; and many state courts have agreed with this contention. Notwithstanding the objection of the Catholics and Jews that the Bible ordinarily used in the public schools is the Protestant Bible, which is not the Bible of the other faiths, a survey made in 1940 discloses that out of forty-three states for which facts are available, thirty-three have Bible-reading.

There is no such thing as a non-sectarian Bible. The Catholics use the Douay version; the Jews use the Jewish Publication Society's or some other Jewish translation of the Old Testament; the Protestants ordinarily use the King James version. These versions vary sharply in respect to what is included and what is excluded, in the translation of important words, in marginal notes, and in other ways. To the non-believer the differences may seem unimportant, but to the adherents of the various faiths the differences are of great significance. The attack on Bible-reading, therefore, comes not so much from the godless groups, but from religious groups who justifiably identify Bible-reading in the public schools with Protestantism.

In addition to pressure to introduce the Bible into the schools, there is strong pressure today for so-called non-sectarian religious education in these schools. It is argued that separation of church and state should not necessarily mean the exclusion of a state interest in religion and in religious education. It was the multiplicity of sects that led to separation. Today, when the sharp lines that once separated the sects are in the process of decay, the emphasis is on common convictions and responsibilities, not on divisive factors. People now, it is said, are seeking a common faith, in which the emphasis will be on personal and social values, and not on dogmas. The schools had to become secular because of the sectarianism of the churches. The secular schools encouraged religious toleration, guaranteed rights of minorities, freed the schools from church control and the churches from state control. But this, it is argued, was not a permanent solution. The time has come to bring religion back into the schools: a non-dogmatic religion that will unite the pupils. While parochial schools divide children along sectarian lines, non-sectarian religion will make of them one body. This non-sectarian religion is to be independent of ecclesiastical authority and institutions and is to have little to do with theology and ritual.

This proposal has a wide appeal today. Even some rabbis (among them Dr. Bernard Heller) have been won as sponsors. But the inherent danger should be easily apparent. The religion meant is obviously one consisting of only those elements of Protestantism upon which the Protestant churches can agree. When Protestants argue that the trend today is away from sectarianism towards unity, they mean intra-Protestant sectarianism. They cite the movement to unify the Episcopalian and Presbyterian churches. They do not—and cannot—cite a movement to unite the Catholic and Protestant churches, or to unite Judaism with Christianity.

The Federal Council of Churches of Christ in America is named as strong evidence of the unity movement. But the Council represents only Protestant sects. (And not all such sects are affiliated; Unitarians and Universalists have been declared ineligible because their theology is too liberal—they are not "Churches of Christ.") . . .

In any case it should be clear that "non-sectarianism" in this discussion is Protestant non-sectarianism. To bring "non-sectarian" religious education into the public schools means to convert our public schools into Protestant parochial schools. . . .

If the Protestants capture the public schools, non-Protestants will feel the need to withdraw their children and provide their own schools for them. But if the Protestant schools will be supported by the state as public schools, the state will need to support all other parochial and private schools. This is exactly what the Catholic Church has urged and what the Protestants have opposed. The inconsistency in the Protestant position is quite apparent, to an outsider. It would become apparent to the Protestants, too, if they decided to call things by their right names—if they stopped proposing religious education and urged instead Protestant religious education. . . .

[Another makeshift program is the released or dismissed time plan.] The released time plan originated in Gary, Indiana, in 1913, and since then it has spread to about 1,000 communities in ten states. Originally it meant releasing an hour or a half-hour earlier at the end of the day, once a week, pupils who signified a willingness to go for religious instruction to their respective churches or church schools. Those who did not want this instruction stayed in school until three o'clock or the regular dismissal time. But . . . many variations on the theme have developed.

Released time developed among Protestant

groups who envied the Catholic parochial schools and the Jewish after-school classes. Released time was opposed by Catholics on obvious grounds: The plan involved cooperation among the faiths; but Catholics do not wish to seem to approve of the claims of Protestants and Jews that children require instruction in Protestantism and Judaism. . . .

The plan was also opposed by Jews. Their reasons were: Released time violates the principle of separation of church and state. The public schools are for secular education exclusively. Religion is a private matter and should be the concern of the parents and of the religious bodies, but not of the public schools.

The United States Supreme Court Speaks on Church and Education

In 1940 interested members of the Jewish, Roman Catholic, and a few of the Protestant faiths formed a voluntary association called the Champaign Council on Religious Education. They obtained permission from the Board of Education to offer classes in religious instruction to public school pupils in grades four to nine inclusive. Classes were made up of pupils whose parents signed printed cards requesting that their children be permitted to attend; they were held weekly, thirty minutes for the lower grades, forty-five minutes for the higher. The council employed the religious teachers at no expense to the school authorities, but the instuctors were subject to the approval and supervision of the superintendent of schools. The classes were taught in three separate religious groups by Protestant teachers, Catholic priests, and a Jewish rabbi, although for the past several years there have apparently been no classes instructed in the Jewish religion. Classes were conducted in the regular classrooms of the school building. Students who did not choose to take the religious instruction were not released from public school duties; they were required to leave their classrooms and go to some other place in the school building for pursuit of their secular studies. On the other hand, students who were released from secular study for the religious instructions were

required to be present at the religious classes. Reports of their presence or absence were to be made to their secular teachers.*

The foregoing facts, without reference to others that appear in the record, show the use of tax-supported property for religious instruction and the close cooperation between the school authorities and the religious council in promoting religious education. The operation of the state's compulsory education system thus assists and is integrated with the program of religious instruction carried on by separate religious sects. Pupils compelled by law to go to school for secular education are released in part from their legal duty upon the condition that they attend the religious classes. This is beyond all question a utilization of the tax-established and tax-supported public school system to aid religious groups to spread their faith. And it falls squarely under the ban of the First Amendment (made applicable to the States by the Fourteenth) as we interpreted it in *Everson* v. *Board of Education*, 330 U. S. 1. There we said: "Neither a state nor the Federal Government can set up a church. Neither can pass laws which aid one religion, aid all re-

---

* Excerpts from supporting documents are appended to the foregoing from place to place in the original document; these excerpts merely add detail and are therefore deleted from the present version.—*Eds.*

From People of the State of Illinois *ex rel.* Vashti McCollum, Appellant, *vs.* Board of Education of School District No. 71, Champaign County, Illinois *et al.*, 68 S.Ct. 461 (1948). Justice Hugo L. Black delivered the 8 to 1 decision of the Court. Justice Felix Frankfurter delivered a supplementary opinion in which five other justices concurred. The excerpts from Frankfurter's opinion follow the asterisks. The only dissenting Justice was Stanley F. Reed.

ligions, or prefer one religion over another. Neither can force or influence a person to go to or to remain away from church against his will or force him to profess a belief or disbelief in any religion. No person can be punished for entertaining or for professing religious beliefs or disbeliefs, for church attendance or nonattendance. No tax in any amount, large or small, can be levied to support any religious activities or institutions, whatever they may be called, or whatever form they may adopt to teach or practice religion. Neither a state nor the Federal Government can, openly or secretly, participate in the affairs of any religious organizations or groups, and *vice versa*. In the words of Jefferson, the clause against establishment of religion by law was intended to erect 'a wall of separation between Church and State.' " *Id*. at 15–16. The majority in the *Everson* case, and the minority . . . agreed that the First Amendment's language, properly interpreted, had erected a wall of separation between Church and State. . . .

To hold that a state cannot consistently with the First and Fourteenth Amendments utilize its public school system to aid any or all religious faiths or sects in the dissemination of their doctrines and ideals does not, as counsel urge, manifest a governmental hostility to religion or religious teachings. A manifestation of such hostility would be at war with our national tradition as embodied in the First Amendment's guaranty of the free exercise of religion. For the First Amendment rests upon the premise that both religion and government can best work to achieve their lofty aims if each is left free from the other within its respective sphere. Or, as we said in the *Everson* case, the First Amendment has erected a wall between Church and State which must be kept high and impregnable.

Here not only are the state's tax-supported public school buildings used for the dissemination of religious doctrines. The State also affords sectarian groups an invaluable aid in that it helps to provide pupils for their religious classes through use of the state's compulsory public school machinery. This is not separation of Church and State.

* * * *

It is pertinent to remind that the establishment of this principle of separation in the field of education was not due to any decline in the religious beliefs of the people. Horace Mann was a devout Christian, and the deep religious feeling of James Madison is stamped upon the Remonstrance. The secular public school did not imply indifference to the basic role of religion in the life of the people, nor rejection of religious education as a means of fostering it. The claims of religion were not minimized by refusing to make the public schools agencies for their assertion. The nonsectarian or secular public school was the means of reconciling freedom in general with religious freedom. The sharp confinement of the public schools to secular education was a recognition of the need of a democratic society to educate its children, in so far as the State undertook to do so, in an atmosphere free from pressures in a realm in which pressures are most resisted and where conflicts are most easily and most bitterly engendered. Designed to serve as perhaps the most powerful agency for promoting cohesion among a heterogeneous democratic people, the public school must keep scrupulously free from entanglement in the strife of sects. The preservation of the community from divisive conflicts, of Government from irreconcilable pressures by religious groups, of religion from censorship and coercion however subtly exercised, requires strict confinement of the State to instruction other than religious, leaving to the individual's church and home, indoctrination in the faith of his choice. . . .

Separation means separation, not something less. Jefferson's metaphor in describing the relation between Church and State speaks of a "wall of separation," not of a fine line easily overstepped. The public school is at once the symbol of our democracy and the most pervasive means for promoting our common destiny. In no activity of the State is it more vital to keep out divisive forces than in its schools, to avoid confusing, not to say fusing, what the Constitution sought to keep strictly apart. "The great American principle of eternal separation"—Elihu Root's phrase bears repetition—is one of the vital reliances of our Constitutional system for assuring unities among our people stronger than our diversities. It is the Court's duty to enforce this principle in its full integrity.

We renew our conviction that "we have staked the very existence of our country on the faith that complete separation between the state and religion is best for the state and best for religion." *Everson* v. *Board of Education*, 330 U. S. at 59. If nowhere else, in the relation between Church and State, "good fences make good neighbors."

The United States Supreme Court Speaks on Segregation in the Schools

Today, education is perhaps the most important function of state and local governments. Compulsory school attendance laws and the great expenditures for education both demonstrate our recognition of the importance of education to our democratic society. It is required in the performance of our most basic public responsibilities, even service in the armed forces. It is the very foundation of good citizenship.

Today, it is a principal instrument in awakening the child to cultural values, in preparing him for later professional training, and in helping him to adjust normally to his environment.

In these days, it is doubtful that any child may reasonably be expected to succeed in life if he is denied the opportunity of an education. Such an opportunity, where the state has undertaken to provide it, is a right which must be made available to all on equal terms.

We come then to the question presented: Does segregation of children in public schools solely on the basis of race, even though the physical facilities and other "tangible" factors may be equal, deprive the children of the minority group of equal educational opportunities? We believe that it does.

In Sweat v. Painter, supra, in finding that a segregated law school for Negroes could not provide them equal educational opportunities, this court relied in large part on "those qualities which are incapable of objective measurement but which make for greatness in a law school."

In McLaurin v. Oklahoma State Regents, supra, the court, in requiring that a Negro admitted to a white graduate school be treated like all other students, again resorted to intangible considerations: "* * * his ability to study, engage in discussions and exchange views with other students, and, in general, to learn his profession."

Such considerations apply with added force to children in grade and high schools. To separate them from others of similar age and qualifica-

tions solely because of their race generates a feeling of inferiority as to their status in the community that may affect their hearts and minds in a way unlikely ever to be undone.

The effect of this separation on their educational opportunities was well stated by a finding in the Kansas case by a court which nevertheless felt compelled to rule against the Negro plaintiffs:

> Segregation of white and colored children in public schools has a detrimental effect upon the colored children. The impact is greater when it has the sanction of the law; for the policy of separating the races is usually interpreted as denoting the inferiority of the Negro group.
>
> A sense of inferiority affects the motivation of a child to learn. Segregation with the sanction of law, therefore, has a tendency to retard the educational and mental development of Negro children and to deprive them of some of the benefits they would receive in a racially integrated school system.

Whatever may have been the extent of psychological knowledge at the time of Plessy v. Ferguson, this finding is amply supported by modern authority. Any language in Plessy v. Ferguson contrary to this finding is rejected.

We conclude that in the field of public education the doctrine of "separate but equal" has no place. Separate educational facilities are inherently unequal. Therefore, we hold that the plaintiffs and others similarly situated for whom the actions have been brought are, by reason of the segregation complained of, deprived of the equal protection of the laws guaranteed by the Fourteenth Amendment. This disposition makes unnecessary any discussion whether such segregation also violates the Due Process Clause of the Fourteenth Amendment.

Because these are class actions, because of the wide applicability of this decision, and because of the great variety of local conditions, the formulation of decrees in these cases presents problems of considerable complexity. On reargument, the

---

From the unanimous May 17, 1954 Supreme Court ruling in four cases involving state laws in South Carolina, Virginia, Kansas, and Delaware, as delivered by Chief Justice Earl Warren. Footnotes deleted.

consideration of appropriate relief was necessarily subordinated to the primary question—the constitutionality of segregation in public education.

We have now announced that such segregation is a denial of the equal protection of the laws.

The Plight of the Schools
From "Platform"

With the Standing Room Only sign hung out in most of the nation's public schools, our educators are faced with a challenge of titanic proportions. They are being called upon to teach more young people than at any time in the country's history: a record-breaking total of nearly 30 million boys and girls—nearly a fifth of the entire population—is enrolled in the public schools this year. And they are expected to give these youngsters the best education that the taxpayers' $7.5 billion can buy. . . .

Perhaps no nation has ever asked or expected more of its schools than we do today. We have agreed that the public schools must educate all the children of all the people and to a remarkable extent we have succeeded in reaching this goal, for four out of five children between the ages of five and seventeen are now in school. At the same time, we have asked that the schools give all these children, who in a single classroom may range from the dull to the remarkably gifted, the education that will best fit them—as individuals and as citizens—to take their places in our society. In our insistence on these twin ends, we have plunged our public schools into a double crisis. . . .

"Perhaps the most predictable, the most avertable, and the least prevented of all crises is the present one in the elementary schools—except perhaps for the one of the day after tomorrow which is shaping up in the high schools," Fred M. Hechinger, education editor of the *New York Herald Tribune,* and George Kerry Smith of the U. S. Office of Education have written.

A steady increase in school enrollment is the first fact with which the schools must account. The national birth rate started climbing in 1939, just as the nation was recovering from the depression; by 1945, Hechinger and Smith point out, "the first forerunners of the new crop began to show up in the schools." Since then, contrary to expectations, the upward trend has continued, "steady at first and downright spectacular a few years later."

And the end is not even in sight. This fall [1953], for instance, . . . the number of pupils had soared to almost two million more than last fall, the biggest one-year rise on record. Next year, judging from birth records, there will be another increase of more than two million. These mammoth jumps, moreover, are piling up on top of eight successive increases that began in 1945. All told, the elementary schools are trying to teach seven million more pupils than they had eight years ago—an increase of 35 per cent, nationally, in grade school students. And by 1959, according to present estimates, eight million more children will enter the schools.

"All this would not be too serious if we were dealing with a short one-, two-, or even five-year crisis," Hechinger and Smith commented in their article in *The Saturday Review* (Sept. 12, 1953). But we are not. For after the record crop of war babies, the expected slump in the birth rate just did not come, and it's safe to guess that, short of a major economic disaster, nothing will push it down. There are good grounds for believing, along with these experts, that "the days of the small American family seem to be past. Unless there will be a new approach to providing for public education, we shall continue to live in a continuous crisis."

The schools are already pitifully overburdened and overcrowded to the bursting point. Forty per cent of our school buildings are more than 30 years old, 16 per cent of them more than 50 years old. Last August, the late Lee M. Thurston, then U. S. Commissioner of Education, pointed out that "three classrooms out of every five will be overcrowded. One out of every five pupils will

From "U. S. Schools: How Well Do They Teach Our Children?," *Platform* (January 1954), publication of the Club and Educational Bureaus, *Newsweek* magazine.

go to school this coming fall in a schoolhouse which does not meet minimum fire safety conditions."

Pinning the situation down somewhat, the National Education Association pointed out recently that about 632,000 children attend school in double shifts or other improvised arrangements. A study of more than 100,000 city elementary school classes showed these unsavory results: "One third of the elementary school children are in classes of 36 or more. One child in eleven is in a class which has 41 or more pupils." Twenty-five, the N.E.A. recommends, is the proper number of pupils for elementary classes, 30 the absolute maximum. Under present conditions, if the classes surveyed in the report were reduced to 30 pupils each, 12,380 more classes would be needed, the report concluded. Indeed, former Commissioner of Education Earl J. McGrath once estimated that in order to fill the classroom shortage completely, we would need "additional floor space equal to a one-story building 52 feet wide, extending from New York to San Francisco."

American communities have responded to this growing need for schools handsomely, engaging, since 1946, in the largest school-building program on record. In the period from 1946 to 1950, an average of 10,000 new classrooms were built annually. For the last three years, the total is close to 150,000. But even this is not enough, for present building programs must not only keep pace with the shifting, growing school population, but must also make up for an enormous backlog of building which had accumulated during the depression and war years. The U. S. Office of Education estimates that the nation ought to be adding some 73,000 new classrooms this year—53,000 units to accommodate increased enrollments, another 20,000 as the annual replacement for classrooms that no longer are usable.

The supply of teachers has not been able to keep pace with the flood of children pouring into the schools. Already critical, the teacher shortage, from all indications, is bound to get a good deal worse before it gets better.

At the end of 1953, the total number of teachers (including classroom teachers, principals and supervisors) was 1,088,584. This total, while 38,-000 more than the previous year, nowhere approached current needs. During the school year of 1952–53, for example, our children suffered from a shortage of 53,000 teachers. This year, the shortage of elementary schoolteachers is expected to reach 72,000. During the next three years, 45 states are expected to run short of elementary schoolteachers, 20 states will be short of high schoolteachers. In fact the high school situation, not critical now, may make our present crisis in the grade schools seem trifling a few years hence. As Hechinger and Smith have pointed out, "By 1959, the public high schools may have about six million more students than they have today . . . an increase of almost 100 per cent . . . One indication of things to come: the 1953 college class of prospective high school teachers was 36 per cent below that of 1950."

All told, the number of new teachers that must be lured into the schools is overwhelming. Yet young people have not been quick to enter the field, and even experienced teachers already in it have been dropping out. "In the past year," *Newsweek* reported (Oct. 12, 1953), 60,000 teachers left the field, an annual decline which had never appeared in any other line of work."

The numerical shortage, grim as it is, is by no means the whole story. The tighter the shortage gets, the more the schools must relax their standards and allow less strictly qualified teachers to fill the gaps. Yale's President Griswold has complained (*The Atlantic,* Nov. 1952) that "of 600,-000 elementary teachers in our public schools, 300,000 do not hold college degrees and, according to the National Education Association, 100,-000 are so poorly prepared that their continued presence in the classroom is considered 'dangerous to the mental and emotional health of America's youth.' " There are reasons for these conditions, Dr. Griswold added, "but there is no excuse."

A *New York Times* editorial of last August, "Teach—Or Drive a Truck?", pondered over the following incident:

There must be some lesson for us, as the new school year approaches, in the incident reported from Summit, N. J., 1950 population 17,929. A high school teacher there . . . has just notified the board of education that he is quitting his job, which pays $85 a week, and is taking a job driving a brewery truck for $137.50 a week.

The Summit teacher, *The Times* observed, was doing fairly well as teachers' pay goes nationally, earning as he was a yearly $4,420. For teachers' salaries range from a low of $2,400 to a high of $7,200; the national average last year was $3,400.

More money is needed if more teachers are to

be recruited and more money is needed if building is to keep up with the rocketing school population. Yet we are already spending more on schools than ever before. How can school expenditures be raised to meet these overwhelming needs? . . .

We could, it has often been pointed out, spend a good deal more on education if we really tried. As it is, only a minute fraction of the national income is spent on the schools. In 1950, for instance, Dr. Griswold points out, we spent 2.7 per cent of our gross national product on all education, including higher education. In the same year, 1.1 per cent of the gross product was spent on radios, television sets and musical instruments, and 6.9 per cent on new and used cars. "These figures and others showing the amounts we spend each year on pleasures and creature comforts quite apart from our necessities prove to my satisfaction, at least, that we could spend more on education . . . Our excuse that we cannot afford to do so is a lame one."

Vital as these problems are, they deal with what Benjamin Fine, education editor of *The New York Times,* has called "the peripheral aspects of education." In comparison with the fundamental battle raging over the content of public education, they could almost be described as mild.

Much of this controversy has centered around the philosopher John Dewey and the progressive education movement which was modeled, at least theoretically, on principles he propounded. Progressive education is difficult, if not impossible, to define exactly. As Dr. Willard E. Goslin, former superintendent of the Pasadena public schools, has pointed out, it "means whatever the individual wants it to mean who happens to be using it at the moment."

But there is no denying that the movement has been both important and far-reaching. The rebellion, Fred M. Hechinger has written (*The Reporter,* Aug. 5, 1952), "has changed the face of all education. There are still only a few 'progressive schools'. . . in the country, especially among the public schools, but there is hardly a school that has not been influenced by what was a startling 'movement' some half a century ago.". . .

The two problems that face the schools today are closely related, for both arise from the fact that we have come near to achieving the ideal of universal free education. We have solved the problem of who should be taught (although not the problem of how to pay for it), but the questions of what should be taught, and how, are more pressing than ever before.

Is the way the schools *are* going about their business the way they *should be* going about it? What kind of education is best in a society where nearly every child goes to school? Faced with huge numbers and tremendous diversity, what should our schools aim for? Should the emphasis be placed on the traditional disciplines, traditionally organized? Or does this approach ignore realities and lead to certain failure?

Some of the precepts of the new education are not challenged by even its severest critics. The schools of the past, they agree, were in many respects too rigid and unyielding. The use of more effective teaching methods—where they actually are more effective—is certainly all to the good. And it is all to the good that children are now considered to be human beings and are treated with respect—as long as their new freedom doesn't degenerate into license.

Yet fundamentally, the many critics of today's public schools believe, the general performance of the schools—particularly that of the high schools—is highly unsatisfactory and it is mirrored in the caliber of the product they turn out. Not all the critics see the same difficulties or make identical criticisms. But as Canon [Bernard Iddings] Bell has written, "All the disillusioned have come to share a simple common fear. We are producing—at great expense and with the most incongruous self-congratulation—a nation of Henry Aldriches.". . .

When Americans committed themselves to the ideal of free public schooling for all, "they were not thinking in terms of the trivia that fascinate many present-day educationists," [Professor Arthur E.] Bestor contends. "They did not intend, by making education universal, to debase and destroy it. They were not seeking to water down the great tradition of disciplined and liberal study. They were undertaking the heroic task of raising an entire nation to the highest attainable level of intellectual competence."

Is this an impossible goal? If we are prepared to admit that, this side believes, we must be prepared to abandon the very concept on which this nation was founded—the concept that all citizens are rulers and all citizens are capable of being rulers.

Today, Bestor believes, it is of crucial importance that every citizen have "an *education,* not a headful of helpful hints." To understand and judge modern problems, citizens need a thorough grounding in such disciplines as history, economics, political philosophy, geography and, in the atomic age, science. It will do them little good to know how to make simple repairs around the house, it's argued, if, through ignorance and lack of training in thinking through complex issues, they make decisions that result in having the house blown up by an atomic bomb. We will come to regret teaching future citizens how to get along in the water at the expense of the basic disciplines if they grow up to fall prey to some glib demagogue because his arguments make sense to those who have neither the knowledge nor the training in disciplined thinking necessary to counter them. . . .

The schools cannot be divorced from the rest of the society from which they spring, for they are, and will become, what we choose to make of them.

"As a people, we have been unwilling to be clear and coherent about what we want the United States to be, and the consequent confusion has had a tremendous impact on public education," Professor Richard Boyd Ballou wrote in *The New Leader*. "A people tolerant of the level of the average political discussion, or movie or radio program, or of comic books is hardly likely to press for the quality of public education . . . democracy deserves." As Norman Cousins, editor of *The Saturday Review*, has observed, "Our school system is no better and no worse than we ourselves deserve."

In the end, only the public, by action or inaction, can determine the direction public education will take. If, through inertia or indifference, we delegate the task, or allow the school system to become a headless monster, blundering along without direction, this does not alter the fundamental responsibility.

CROSS REFERENCES TO STANDARD TEXTS *

Barnes, *Society in Transition,* pp. 122–123, 336–356, 514, 664–665.
Bernard, *American Community Behavior,* pp. 202–206, 330–333, 378–380, 395–399.
Bloch, *Disorganization,* pp. 216–218.
Brown, *Social Pathology,* Chap. 26.
Cuber and Harper, *Problems of American Society,* Chap. 15.
Elliott and Merrill, *Social Disorganization,* pp. 244–245, 630–632, 649–651, 720–721.
Faris, *Social Disorganization,* pp. 469–473.
Gillin, *Social Pathology,* pp. 360, 490, 501, 599.
——— and others, *Social Problems,* Chap. 14.
Herman, *Approach to Social Problems,* pp. 414–415, 431–434.

Landis, *Social Policies in the Making,* Chap. 26.
Merrill and others, *Social Problems,* Chap. 15.
Mihanovich, *Current Social Problems,* pp. 390–391.
Neumeyer, *Social Problems and the Changing Society,* Chap. 13.
Nordskog and others, *Analyzing Social Problems,* Chap. 9.
Odum, *American Social Problems,* Chap. 21.
Phelps and Henderson, *Contemporary Social Problems,* Chap. 8.
Reinhardt and others, *Social Problems and Social Policy,* Chap. 12.
Weaver, *Social Problems,* pp. 599–601.

OTHER BIBLIOGRAPHY

Alan Barth, *The Loyalty of Free Men,* New York: Viking Press, 1951, Pocket Books, 1952. Esp. Chap. 9.
Arthur E. Bestor, *Educational Wastelands,* Urbana: University of Illinois Press, 1953.
Paul Blanshard, *American Freedom and Catholic Power,* Boston: Beacon Press, 1949. Esp. Chaps. 3, 4.
———, *Communism, Democracy, and Catholic Power,* Boston: Beacon Press, 1951. Esp. Chap. 7.
Joseph L. Blau, ed., *Cornerstones of Religious Freedom in America,* Boston: Beacon Press, 1949. Esp. Chaps. 3, 8, 10.

Theodore Brameld, *Minority Problems in the Public Schools,* New York: Harper & Bros., 1946.
Edmund deS. Brunner, *Community Organization and Adult Education,* Chapel Hill: University of North Carolina Press, 1942.
Ernest W. Burgess, W. Lloyd Warner, Franz Alexander, and Margaret Mead, *Environment and Education,* Chicago: University of Chicago Press, 1942.
R. Freeman Butts, *A Cultural History of Education,* New York: McGraw-Hill Book Co., 1947.
William G. Carr, ed., "International Frontiers in Education," *The Annals,* 235 (September 1944).
Stanley H. Chapman, "Church Schools," *Journal of Educational Sociology,* 18 (1944–45): 340–350.

* For complete bibliographical reference to each text, see page 13.

Kenneth B. Clark, "Desegregation: An Appraisal of The Evidence," *Journal of Social Issues*, 9 (1953): 4: 1–77.

Committee on Religion and Education, *The Relation of Religion to Public Education: The Basic Principles*, Washington: American Council on Education Studies, 1947.

Lloyd and Elaine Cook, *Intergroup Education*, New York: McGraw-Hill Book Co., 1954.

Norma E. Cutts and Nicholas Moseley, *Bright Children: A Guide for Parents*, New York: G. P. Putnam's Sons, 1953.

Edward Darling, *How We Fought for Our Schools: A Documentary Novel*, New York: W. W. Norton & Co., 1954.

Harold J. Dillon, *Work Experience in Secondary Education*, New York: National Child Labor Committee, 1946.

Joseph K. Folsom, *Youth, Family, and Education*, Washington: American Council on Education, 1941.

William Gellerman, *American Legion as Educator*, New York: Teachers College, Columbia University, 1938.

Charles Hunter Hamlin, *Educators Present Arms: The Use of the Schools and Colleges as Agents of War Propaganda, 1914–1918*, Zebulon, N. C.: Record Publishing Co., 1939.

Harvard Committee, *General Education in a Free Society*, Cambridge: Harvard University Press, 1945.

R. F. Havighurst, W. L. Warner, and M. D. Loeb, *Who Shall Be Educated?* New York: Harper & Bros., 1944.

H. Gordon Hullfish, "Keeping Our Schools Free," Public Affairs Pamphlet No. 199, 1953.

Sidney L. Jackson, *America's Struggle for Free Schools*, Washington: American Council on Public Affairs, 1941.

Charles S. Johnson, "Education and the Cultural Process: Introduction to Symposium," *American Journal of Sociology*, 48 (1942–43): 629–632.

Francis P. King, *Financing the College Education of Faculty Children*, New York: Henry Holt and Co., 1954.

Robert H. Knapp and Joseph J. Greenbaum, *The Younger American Scholar: His Collegiate Origins*, Chicago: University of Chicago Press and Wesleyan University Press, 1953.

Vashti Cromwell McCollum, *One Woman's Fight*, Garden City: Doubleday & Co., 1951. The story of

the famous McCollum case, carried to the United States Supreme Court, a successful effort to maintain the separation of church and state in the public schools.

Carey McWilliams, *Witch Hunt*, Boston: Little, Brown & Co., 1951.

Scudder Mekeel, "Education, Child-training, and Culture," *American Journal of Sociology*, 48 (1942–43): 676–681.

Ernest O. Melby and Morton Puner, eds., *Freedom and Public Education*, New York: Frederick A. Praeger, 1953.

"Militarism in Education," National Council Against Conscription, Washington, D. C., 1950.

Neal E. Miller and John Dollard, *Social Learning and Imitation*, New Haven: Yale University Press, 1941.

Conrad H. Moehlman, *School and Church: The American Way*, New York: Harper & Bros., 1944.

Gerald Hamilton Jeffrey Pearson, *Psychoanalysis and the Education of the Child*, New York: W. W. Norton & Co., 1954.

Robert Bruce Raup, *Education and Organized Interests in America*, New York: G. P. Putnam's Sons, 1936.

Florence Greenhoe Robbins, *Educational Sociology: A Study in Child, Youth, School, and Community*, New York: Henry Holt and Co., 1953.

Joseph Slabey Roucek, ed., *Sociological Foundations of Education*, New York: T. Y. Crowell Co., 1942.

Porter Sargent, *Between Two Wars: The Failure of Education, 1920–1940*, Boston: The Author, 1945.

"Segregation and the Schools," Public Affairs Pamphlet No. 209, 1954.

George R. Stewart, *The Year of the Oath*, Garden City: Doubleday & Co., 1951. The controversy over a special "loyalty" oath for faculty members of the University of California.

Ann Tanneyhill, "From School to Job: Guidance for Minority Youth," Public Affairs Pamphlet No. 200, 1953.

V. T. Thayer, *The Attack Upon the American Secular School*, Boston: Beacon Press, 1951.

Robert Ulich, *Crisis and Hope in American Education*, Boston: Beacon Press, 1951.

Thorstein Veblen, *The Higher Learning in America: A Memorandum on the Conduct of Universities by Business Men*, Stanford, California: Academic Reprints, 1954 (originally publ. 1918).

Willard Waller, *The Sociology of Teaching*, New York: John Wiley & Sons, 1932.

REVIEW QUESTIONS

1. How does Benedict say that self-discipline is best learned? How does she know this?
2. Why is it dangerous that a child will learn his lesson of docility too well?
3. From the mid-nineteenth to the mid-twentieth

century, Konvitz says that "we have gone a long way in closing up the distance between church and state." To what does he and to what would you attribute this development?
4. Why does Konvitz believe that there is danger of

our public schools being converted into Protestant parochial schools?

5. What is meant by "released time"? In what sense does "released time" break down the separation of church and state?

6. For how definite a separation between churches and public schools does the Supreme Court call?

7. What practices do the U. S. Supreme Court decisions ban?

8. What is meant by the "separate but equal doctrine?"

9. Do you think there has been a shift back toward the teaching profession on the part of young people?

CHAPTER 11

Earning A Living

FOR GENERATIONS, economic theory oversimplified social problem analysis with the assertion that all social problems are fundamentally economic problems or at least economically based. As the selections in this chapter indicate, economic factors are significant but not enough so to account adequately for many social problems. Within the area of problems traditionally assigned to economists, economists themselves now recognize that joint approaches by cooperating social scientists from several viewpoints are far superior to merely an "economic" analysis. French and his associates tell how "the miracles of technology and the development of mass production industries have been accompanied step by step by painful gropings toward satisfactory human relations in the industrial sphere." Bell discusses recent studies of social relations within the factory and raises the objection that they contain "no view of the larger institutional framework of our economic system within which these relationships arise and have their meaning." Arnold asks whether the "American way" is one of producers competing in a free market for consumer business or of producers combining through mergers, price-fixing agreements, and patent pools to offer the consumer a product at a fixed price. In other words, just what do we mean by "free enterprise" or the "enterprise system"?

Always, there are the poor and disadvantaged.

Altmeyer gives in simplified form a description of the extensive social security system now operative through government, a system broadly expanded in recent years.

In employment, as in so many other parts of American life, minorities still are far from being given their full freedom of opportunity in the United States. The largest underprivileged minority, as we saw in the chapter on adults in family life, consists of about one-half of the population: the women. From the Women's Bureau of the U. S. Department of Labor comes a brief description of the current economic status of women workers, with particular reference to the differential between men's and women's earnings. Flowerman writes on the typically anti-Jewish query, Why don't Jews change their occupations? He believes that the important consideration is whether or not a job is personally satisfying and socially desirable. Haas and Fleming point to sound personnel practices through which Negroes may be assimilated into a plant situation. In the final selection, Fuller draws attention to several aspects of the problem of migratory labor, ones not always apparent from statistical analyses.

As economic problems come to be regarded more and more as social problems, to be attacked by techniques known to the various social sciences, our perspective of them will improve, and our ability to mitigate them will increase.

Conflict and Cooperation in Industry

John R. P. French, Jr., Arthur Kornhauser, and Alfred Marrow

John R. P. French, Jr. (1913–   ), program director, Research Center for Group Dynamics, University of Michigan. Alfred J. Marrow (1905–   ), director of research and president of the Harwood Manufacturing Corp., a textile manufacturing company. For identifying note on Arthur Kornhauser, see page 111.

The miracles of technology and the development of mass production industries have been ac-

companied step by step by painful gropings toward satisfactory human relations in the indus-

From "Conflict and Cooperation in Industry," *Journal of Social Issues*, 2: 1 (February 1946), pp. 2–4. Reprinted by permission.

trial sphere. Slowly and haltingly the men who manage and the men who labor have been feeling their way toward a more satisfactory "government of industry." This pertains both to the formal structure of economic authority and responsibility and also to the informal personal relationships which go so far to determine whether work is a good and self-expressive, or a stultifying, segment of life.

That there have been important advances no one can doubt who stops to recall the appalling conditions which have been described as characteristic of the mines and factories of England a century ago. In this country, too, the history of child labor, 12 and 14 hour days, sweat-shop conditions, lack of safety and health measures, stand in striking contrast to present day conditions.

The changes in all these matters, as well as the enormous increase in wage rates, have not come smoothly and without struggle. The 19th century is thickly dotted with intense and often violent industrial disputes. These conflicts arose from the organized effort of working people to improve their lot, even when it led them to transgress the accepted rules and the "rights" of property. Resistance by employers expressed itself sharply in opposition to the trade unions which groups of workers attempted to form as the principal means by which they could try to enforce their demands upon these employers. The long fight for the right to organize and to bargain collectively has extended on into very recent years. In fact, many labor leaders and employers recognize that this fundamental battle is not yet fully concluded.

Many of the most bitter and violent outbursts between employers and employees have occurred in conflicts over the right of unions to exist and to use their power to force concessions from unwilling managements. In the effort to combat unions and to curtail their power, large corporations have used both the instruments of government in so far as these were available to maintain "law and order" and to "protect the public interest" and also have built up their own special means of self-defense in the form of elaborate spy systems, the hiring of thugs and strike-breakers, and the domination of local communities. Until recent years, the courts, the police and the militia could be depended upon by the corporations to prevent any important or sustained gains in power by unions. The history of industrial conflict in this country contains many instances of fatal clashes between the organized workers and the armed forces of government or the private police and company guards of the corporation.

While this history of bitter conflict is undeniable, it must be seen in proper perspective. At best, the record does not make cheerful reading. But morale differs enormously from company to company. Management's policies and personalities do count. Great corporations have succeeded in carrying on peaceful labor relations over the decades and have steadily improved the wages and conditions of their employees without being clubbed into it. Strikes and lockouts are spectacular and consequently command public attention. For the most part, however, industry proceeds more or less smoothly with its more prosaic tasks of production. The occasional outbursts must not be assigned exaggerated importance. At the same time, they need to be evaluated realistically. They are deeply significant symptoms of unsolved human problems of industry.

The Changes during the 30's and 40's. It is ordinarily recognized that labor made great gains during the period of the New Deal. How enormous and basic these changes have been, however, is rarely appreciated. The problem and the role of organized labor in America have taken on altogether new dimensions. Labor union membership alone is one indication of the startling transformation. Before 1933, unions had for the most part fluctuated in the neighborhood of two million to three million members; they have now increased to fourteen or fifteen million. The great mass production industries were almost unorganized before the 30's. Now such industries as steel, automobile, rubber, textiles, and electrical equipment have some of the largest and strongest unions. The organized labor movement has grown to a point where it exercises a telling influence upon both the economic and political affairs of the nation.

This new position of labor has greatly changed the nature of the struggles between management and working people. Corporations are no longer as able to use the old methods, either governmental or private, for resisting the demands of unions. Great aggregates of power now find themselves opposed to each other, each wielding enough influence to keep from being "pushed around" and each able to prevent the machinery of government from being used in a highly one-sided manner.

Not less significant than organized labor's increase in numbers is the remarkable change which has occurred both in management circles and among the general public (white collar, professional, and other non-wage-earning groups) in the acceptance of unions. Perhaps most astonishing is the readjustment that has been taking place in the thinking of management executives themselves. There can be little question that most of them now recognize that unions are here to stay. Neither they nor the middle class are opposed to the *existence* of labor unions even though large numbers do object to particular actions and policies. The fight for recognition has been won in most industries. Management's resistance to further union advances is now carried on within a framework of organized dealings. It seems highly questionable whether the violent outbreaks of the past will be repeated in this new period. The spirit of desperation on the part of labor groups is disappearing as is the imperious brooking of no opposition to its dictates by powerful management. Antagonisms are now more likely to work themselves out within the broad fields of public relations, psychological appeals to working people, and pressures on government.

Management vs. Worker
Daniel Bell

Daniel Bell (1919–   ), lecturer in sociology, Columbia University and labor editor, *Fortune* Magazine.

Recent studies represent a significant departure from the earlier approach of the industrial engineer, who evaluated the worker's output on the basis of some purely mechanical measure, and sought to find ways to greater efficiency through time and motion studies measuring the worker's physical capacities. Like the earlier studies, however, the new investigations are not focused on "industrial relations" or "labor problems" as these terms are commonly understood, i.e., on large economic issues or on the top-level relations between the trade union and the employers. Primarily, they are studies of actual behavior and actual social relations *within the factory:* the attitude of the worker toward his supervisor and his employers; the relation between the formal structure of authority as defined by the employer's organizational chart and the structure that actually develops; motives for restriction of output; worker resistance to technological change; and so on.

* * * *

Perhaps the most important accomplishment of these studies . . . is that in their course more researchers have talked to more workers and explored more factory situations than in any other investigations in the past fifty years. The mass of material which has already accumulated is tremendous. Yet one is struck by the paucity of conclusions. The reason for this, one feels, is that no one has approached this material armed with basic hypotheses about the nature of our industrial system. Without general hypotheses, the researchers merely "psychologize," asserting that the workers "feel" this, or that management "feels" that. There is no view of the larger institutional framework of our economic system within which these relationships arise and have their meaning.

Over the past twenty years, America has been going through a profound social revolution, and a new class structure is developing whose contours are only now beginning to appear.[1] As a product of the increasing complexity of industry, the broadening role of research, new avenues in public service, and the general job shift away from manufacturing and toward service and commerce, there has emerged a new social stratum: the class of technical and managerial employees. Within the working class, on the other hand, technological advances have tended at once to degrade the skilled worker and to replace the raw muscle-power of the purely manual worker, creating instead a general class of semi-skilled machine tenders.

[1] See my article "The Changing Class Structure of the United States," *New Leader*, June 15, 1946; also Lewis Corey, "The Middle Class," *Antioch Review*, Spring 1945.

From "Adjusting Men to Machines," *Commentary, 3:* 1 (January, 1947): 79–88, pp. 79, 86–88 quoted. Reprinted by permission.

Thus a class of interchangeable factory "hands" is at last becoming a reality, and the "promise" of the factory system, as described by Marx, is only now being fulfilled. At the same time, the industrial working class in the United States is declining in relation to the total work force.

This creates a peculiar problem in social mobility: the chances of striking out for oneself or rising to the top have diminished steadily, and yet there are more status-carrying skilled jobs available than ever before. But this, precisely, is the nub of the problem: these new technical-managerial jobs require a degree of skill that is attainable only by long education; unless one gets on the social escalator early, one may never get on it.

This is the situation that the worker faces today. As a result of the depression and the increasing specialization of work, a wide gulf is being opened between skilled groups with professional status and the mass of semi-skilled machine tenders (machine tenders not only among industrial workers, but among white-collar workers as well, since new business machines threaten the role of the office worker too). The insecurity of the skill-less in a world that increasingly uses skill as the basis of reward is now the chief fact in the life of the masses, and the worker tends more and more to base his attitudes on the assumption that he—and his son—will remain in the working class.

From such an analysis of the institutional situation—an analysis that the factory researchers do not make—certain new questions and propositions emerge. One might look for the development of certain types of militancy among workers—a militancy not necessarily political in its tone or motivation, but one just as likely to be anti-Semitic or anti-Negro or nihilistic. Again, one might look for the beginnings of an elite psychology in the technical-managerial groups, perhaps of a kind that has played such a significant role in statist movements and societies. The concepts of "group solidarity" and "status" that have emerged as such basic factors, could, under this approach, be clarified, and their specific effects on understanding and action more exactly defined. (And, incidentally, such an approach might well prove more illuminating to those concerned with the social future of our democracy, and not merely with increasing the productivity of its industrial machine.)

Behind the refusal to adopt such an approach, one senses a disdain for what is called "armchair sociology"—or for anything that is not strictly empirical research involving a formidable statistical apparatus. Yet while researchers in this field often display a parvenu arrogance toward theory, a great deal of pretentious, senseless, and extravagant writing fills their own work, much of it inspired by the theoretical system they have taken over from Pareto. Under his influence, all action is defined in terms of equilibrium. A Newtonian model is set up in which force and counterforce, action and reaction, are modulated in pendulum fashion to create "laws of behavior." In a stable system with fixed points, this may be useful; but it is doubtful whether such a mechanical analogy is truly enlightening for the analysis of dynamic structures.

Despite their claims to scientific objectivity, these researchers rest on the unstated assumption that mechanical efficiency and high output are the sole tests of achievement—of "good" results. There are under way no studies to see what kinds of jobs can best stimulate the spontaneity and freedom of the worker, and how we can alter our industrial methods to assure such jobs. The present organization of industrial production, inhuman as it may be, is accepted as an inalterable "given." Sociologists tend to work on the behaviorist assumption that the human being is a bundle of conditioned reflexes—equally malleable, psychologically, to any situation. But it is possible that the increasing "rationalization" of living (its organization for greater efficiency), pervading all areas and narrowing all choices, is itself the root cause of the stresses and breakdown in social living that everybody decries.

One of the most striking omissions in all these researches is the failure to relate the problems of work and leisure. If one asks a worker what he thinks of his job, the reply may be: "It's all right." But if one probes below this surface, the question arises of whether work contributes anything to leisure-time occupation, or leisure-time occupation to work. And, probably, little relationship would be found. Yet real job satisfaction comes only when work and leisure shade off into each other. The sense of wholeness that one associates with the old artisan class, and with the creative person of today, arises when no sharp distinction can be drawn between work and leisure. Today, in the increasing fragmentation of life, the world of the factory is one life, the world outside another, and we find a corresponding standardization of the job in one area and standardization of leisure in the other.

Another unstated assumption underlies the persistent tendency to pose the problem of industrial harmony in terms of the difficulties of *communication*. It is assumed that people don't understand each other because of emotional blocks or antiquated verbal habits, or because issues of feelings and status are involved. (This has its counterpart in the theory that permanent peace can be established if nations can be made to "understand" each other.) But industrial relations—like international relations—happen to be much less a problem of setting up a smoothly functioning organization than a problem of accommodating diverse and conflicting *interests*. And these interests are real. The question of how to distribute increased income resulting from higher productivity, for example, cannot be flim-flammed away as a problem of verbal misinterpretation.

One sociologist has asserted that industry can function best when there is a balance of down-the-line and up-the-line pressures—that is, when the authority of management is balanced against the needs and suggestions of workers. But industry is no abstract rational system where only organizational problems prevail. Industry operates within a framework of *cost* factors, and every step it takes—including the employment of research sociologists—is reckoned in these terms. When a firm fires an aging worker because he cannot meet production norms, it is the cost factor that operates. Few of the researches we have discussed, concentrating as they do on greasing the skids as ordered, actually show any understanding of the chain of irresponsibility that constitutes an industry's line of command, with each man along the line responsible for carrying out a policy he has had no voice in shaping, and which he is yet required to "sell" to those below him or lose his job.

The real policy decisions are made by a few, and they are not made with concern for the men at work, but with an eye to the logic of cost, efficiency, and competition. The effect of technological change, for instance, is to downgrade workers, change the age composition of the labor force, pull more women into the factory; but changes are introduced without any consideration of their ultimate and far-reaching effects. The only factors that count are market decisions.

We must consider also the two polar concepts in this research—status motivations and solidarity motivations. They have not been defined, nor their implications fully considered. We are told that money-incentive schemes do not spur a worker so much as prestige considerations: the invidious comparisons between the rank of one job and the next, the trappings of office that one individual is allowed and not the other, etc. Yet we are also told that group solidarity is the factor which makes possible increased output, or controls the rate of work.

The two concepts have been used carelessly. It is likely that in the white collar ranks, in the higher supervisory positions, and among management, the status motivation is predominant, while among workers, the solidarity motif is most useful in explaining actions. But more direct studies are needed to clarify these motivations and define the conditions which produce each.

The gravest charge that can be leveled against these researches is that they uncritically adopt industry's own conception of workers as *means* to be manipulated or adjusted to impersonal ends. The belief in man as an end in himself has been ground under by the machine, and the social science of the factory researchers is not a science of man, but a cow-sociology. Burleigh Gardner has written: "The more satisfied [the worker] is, the greater will be his self-esteem, the more content will he be, and therefore, the more efficient in what he is doing." Surely this is a fitting inscription to go under the Model T symbol of Huxley's *Brave New World*.

One striking fact about a field that has turned up so much material in these past few years is how rarely in its literature one comes upon the name of Thorstein Veblen. Perhaps this is not accidental, for that lonely protestant struck off from the hard flint of his iconoclasm the most brilliant flashes we have had into the caverns of our industrial world. Perhaps these researches are themselves an illustration of Veblen's observation about the development of occupational ruts and the "trained incapacity" they foster.

Which Is the American Way?
Thurman W. Arnold

Thurman Wesley Arnold (1891–　　), lawyer, member of firm of Arnold, Fortas & Porter, Washington, D. C. Chief works: *The Symbols of Government* (1935); *Cases on Trials, Judgments and Appeals* (1936); *The Folklore of Capitalism* (1937); *The Bottlenecks of Business* (1940); and *Democracy and Free Enterprise* (1942).

The great economic tradition of America is that of industrial freedom—the freedom of every man to produce and sell in an uncontrolled market. This may be called the economics of opportunity. It assumes that every man in America material wealth a nation can have—an expanding productive plant. If there is to be freedom of opportunity, invested capital values must not be protected against new enterprise or new techniques under the cloak of corporate franchises, as-

EVOLUTION OF A CARTEL

ORGANIZES TRADE ASSOCIATIONS, SET TRADE REGULATIONS PRICES, ETC.

ENTERS POLITICS

ELIMINATES INDEPENDENT COMPETITORS

PREVENTS NEW ENTERPRISES

NEW INVENTION

BUYS UP PATENTS SO NOBODY CAN USE THEM

PRODUCTION

AND LIMITS PRODUCTION

ENTERS INTO AGREEMENTS WITH MONOPOLIES OF OTHER COUNTRIES

(Graphic Associates for Public Affairs Committee, Inc.)

must be free to take a chance, to gamble on his abilities or on the efficiency of his organization, and to win or to lose. And out of that race to produce and distribute will come the only real sociations, or patent pools, or any other organized device. Established enterprise must constantly meet the challenge of new enterprise. The opportunity to create a new business enterprise is

From Thurman W. Arnold, "Cartels or Free Enterprise?," 5th ed., Public Affairs Pamphlet No. 103, 1948, pp. 4–6. Reprinted by permission.

the impulse that makes the profit system work.

Opposed to this idea is the idea of an economics of security for established organizations. Before the war this idea pretty well dominated mass production and distribution all over the world. As the industrial revolution of the twentieth century knit the world closer together with faster and cheaper transportation and with mass production and distribution of goods, commerce became more closely organized and integrated than it had ever been before. Vast areas of that world of commerce accepted an idea which is the opposite of the philosophy of free enterprise.

turning loose such a flood of goods that it is no longer safe to leave it in independent hands. The individual producer, who was the unit in Adam Smith's economy, could never produce so much goods and sell them at such ruinous prices as to destroy investment and disrupt business. But the modern industrial organization can, if such action is to its interest. Its control of a large proportion of the productive capacity in its field gives it power to produce surpluses which the management of our great industries fears may bankrupt

WHICH IS THE AMERICAN WAY?

ECONOMICS OF A FREE MARKET

PRODUCERS   CONSUMER

ECONOMICS OF SECURITY

PRODUCERS   CONSUMER

(Graphic Associates for Public Affairs Committee, Inc.)

This idea has taken on various forms. It is based on the assumption that a few men in control of established business institutions must hold control of production and distribution in vast areas of the world's economy as benevolent trustees for the common good of all. It assumes that the machinery of modern industry is capable of

competition and create nation-wide unemployment. These great organizations, which are created to restrict competition, are often called—for want of a simpler word—"cartels" or monopolies.

The term "cartel" is ordinarily used to describe a ring of producers or distributors who have acquired control over domestic or foreign markets by agreements to maintain prices or control production and distribution. In the United States the same result is more often accomplished by corporate mergers, consolidations, and holding companies. This is because certain big business groups by merging their interests into large corporations have sought to avoid the Sherman Act, which makes monopoly agreements illegal. Economically, however, it makes no difference whether a group of men control the market under the protection of an agreement or under the cloak of a corporate franchise. Therefore, for the purpose of this pamphlet, no distinction will be made between the two. Both of these types of combination will be referred to as cartels.

Often these cartels have agreements with similar producers abroad to control world production and distribution of their product. But for the sake of convenience we shall use the term "cartel" mostly for domestic combinations.

No one can question that what I have called the economics of security—as reflected in the cartels—is opposed to every American tradition. The economics of opportunity represents our prevailing ideal. But that ideal, with our present concentration of economic power, creates a series of contradictions between economic facts and economic theory. Never in our history has so much been said in praise of free competitive enterprise. Yet never in our history has there been a greater concentration of economic power in a few hands. Our

great sprawling industrial empires are afraid to compete with new enterprise to furnish goods at lower prices. They are even more afraid of the government intervention without which a controlled market soon becomes intolerable. One may compare our present confusion between our economic ideals and our business practice to the endless debates and continuous bewilderment of the old days when we insisted on having liquor and having prohibition at the same time.

For a while it seemed as though the great depression had destroyed our belief in an economy of great mergers. For a few years at least men turned to programs of government planning as a way out of their bewilderment. But government planning was new and terrifying to many businessmen. The more they saw of it, the more frightened they were. Today we are turning back to belief in big corporations controlled by little stockholders as the American way of economic life. We have been reassured by the ability of these business concerns to produce war materials under government direction. And so a great campaign has been started to convince us again to trust in their management to give us full production in time of peace. Tons of literature . . . have been issued to preach this lesson to the American people.

Social Security
Arthur J. Altmeyer

Arthur J. Altmeyer (1891–   ), U. S. Commissioner for Social Security, 1946–1953.

Within the general framework set up by the Social Security Act, each state decides for itself who is covered by unemployment insurance, who may receive benefits and under what conditions, how much the benefits shall be, and for how many weeks of unemployment they may be paid.

The state unemployment insurance laws cover nearly all industrial and commercial jobs except that most states include only concerns that have a given number of workers (most often 8 or more) on their payrolls for a certain number of weeks in the year. In 1953, payrolls covered by these laws

represented nearly three-fourths of all civilian wages and salaries paid in the United States. The excluded jobs are mostly on farms, in domestic service in private homes, in small concerns, and in government. Self-employment is not covered since it is practically impossible to tell when a person who works on his own account is "unemployed."

To receive an unemployment benefit under a state law you must:

1. Have registered for work at a public employment office and filed a claim for benefits.

From Arthur J. Altmeyer, "Your Stake in Social Security," 1st ed., Public Affairs Pamphlet No. 206, 1954, pp. 2–14, 16–19, 26–28. Reprinted by permission.

2. Have had a given amount of employment
and wages in jobs covered by the state law in the
last year or two.

3. Be able to work and be ready to take suitable
work if it is offered to you.

After you file your claim, you must—in all but
two states—serve a waiting period, usually a
week. Then, if you are qualified and have not
found a suitable job in the meantime, your benefit becomes payable for the following week.

Even though you have the necessary wage credits, you can be disqualified from benefits for any
one of several reasons. These are:

1. If you have quit your job voluntarily without
good cause. Some state laws go further and say,
"without good cause attributable to the employer"
or "connected with the work."

2. If you were discharged for misconduct related to your job.

3. If you refuse, without good cause, to apply
for or accept suitable work. Each state law defines
"suitable work" but the federal act specifies that
a worker may not be disqualified for refusing to
take a job in certain circumstances involving labor
standards or labor disputes.

4. If you are unemployed because of a stoppage
of work resulting from a labor dispute. In two
states this disqualification results only in a longer
waiting period and benefits are paid after that if
the strike continues.

In some states, disqualification amounts only to
postponement of benefits for a few weeks; in
others, benefit rights are reduced as well as postponed. A few states cancel all benefit rights of a
disqualified worker and he cannot draw unemployment insurance until he again has earned
enough wage credits to qualify.

Most states originally set the weekly unemployment benefit at about half the full-time weekly
pay, except that there are top and bottom limits.
The top limit ranges among the states from $20 to
$35 a week for a worker without dependents;
eleven states make additional allowances for certain dependents. The benefit may be as low as
$3 a week, but is $5 or more in most states. In
1953, benefits for total unemployment averaged
$23.32 a week in the country as a whole.

The length of time for which you may continue to receive benefits if you continue to be unemployed also differs from state to state. In most
states, the number of weeks depends on the claimant's past employment and wages. In some of
these states, benefit duration may be as short as

5 weeks for some workers; in some others, as long
as 26 weeks. Fifteen states pay benefits up to a
given number of weeks—ranging from 16 to 26—
to any qualified claimant whose unemployment
lasts that long.

In 1953, when employment was at a high level,
a weekly average of nearly 800,000 persons drew
benefits under the state unemployment compensation laws, and payments totaled over $1,000,000,-
000.

Unemployment benefits are financed by contributions by your employer under the state laws.
In two states, employees also contribute. The federal government makes grants to states to cover
the cost of administering the state programs.

Each state deposits its contributions in its account in the Unemployment Trust Fund in the
United States Treasury. All reserves are invested
in obligations of the United States Government at
interest, which is added to each state's account.
States may withdraw money from their accounts
only for benefit payments.

Assets in the state accounts in the Unemployment Trust Fund at the end of 1953 totaled more
than $8,500,000,000. This Fund also carries an
account for the railroad unemployment insurance
system which is supported by employer contributions.

There are two ways in which the Social
Security Act can be important to you when you
are old. (1) You may be insured and entitled to a
federal old-age benefit based upon your past wage
record. (2) Or even if you are not insured, and
your total resources of all kinds—earnings, savings, benefits, aid from friends and relatives, and
so on—come to less than your state welfare agency
finds you need for subsistence, you may receive
old-age assistance.

The Social Security Act set up an old-age insurance program in 1935 for industrial and commercial workers. The program was broadened in
1939 to include benefits for dependents of retired
workers and survivors of insured persons, and
later it was extended to additional groups, including self-employed persons.

In the 1940's, many people who were already
old or were reaching old age could not qualify for
insurance benefits because they had not been able
to work after the program came into effect or had
not had enough employment in the jobs it covered. The result was that the needy old people on
the assistance rolls outnumbered old-age insurance
beneficiaries until February, 1951. At that point,

the insurance program forged ahead, and it has been increasing its lead steadily, both in the number of old people receiving monthly benefits and in the amount paid to them. While the total number of old people in the United States has been increasing, the rolls of the needy aged have been declining in recent years.

By the end of 1953, more than half of our retired population was getting insurance benefits under this or some other federal law.

Nearly all the workers in industry and commerce and the majority of persons working on their own account now have the protection of old-age and survivors insurance. Regularly employed workers in agriculture and in domestic service in private homes are also covered, as are some workers in government jobs and in nonprofit charitable, religious, and educational organizations. Railroad workers have a separate system that is partly coordinated with Social Security.

About 12,000,000 jobs in the United States were still outside this insurance system early in 1954. Some 4,000,000 of these are covered, more or less adequately, by federal, state or local-government retirement programs. The chief groups that now are without protection are farm operators, the less regularly employed workers in agriculture and domestic service, and self-employed professional persons.

As the law now stands, an insured person may receive a monthly retirement benefit when he or she has reached age 65 and is not earning $75 a month in covered employment or more than $900 a year in self-employment. A monthly benefit also is paid to the wife of such a worker when she reaches age 65 or at any age if she is living with him and caring for a child of his under age 18. Benefits similarly are paid to unmarried children under age 18.

To receive retirement benefits for yourself and your family, you must be "fully insured." This is measured in terms of calendar quarters, that is, quarters of the calendar year beginning January 1, April 1, and so on. A person is fully insured when he or she has received $50 or more in covered employment in half the number of quarters that have elapsed between December 31, 1950 and the quarter in which he becomes 65 or dies. He may include in that number quarters before 1950 in which he had such wages. A self-employed person must have had $100 or more in net earnings in each of the same number of quarters; any year in which he has more than $400 is counted as four

quarters. No one is insured unless he has at leas[t] six quarters of coverage.

The amount of a benefit is based on the work[-] er's average monthly earnings until he become[s] 65 (or, if this is to his advantage, the time afte[r] age 65 when he applies for benefits).

There are two formulas for figuring the benefi[t] one for persons who have had less than six qua[r-] ters of coverage since 1950, when the law wa[s] amended, and one for those who have had si[x] quarters or more since that time. The secon[d] which now applies to most claimants, is as fo[l-] lows: 55 per cent of the first $100 of the worker['s] average monthly earnings under the program plu[s] 15 per cent of the remainder up to $200. A clai[m-] ant whose average has been $300 a month, th[e] top amount that can be counted, receives a month[-] ly benefit of $85. The minimum monthly bene[-] fit of a retired worker is $25. The benefit of [a] wife, dependent husband, or child is half th[e] worker's amount. The total for a family cannot b[e] more than 80 per cent of the average wage o[r] $168.75, whichever is less.

In all, more than 4,700,000 old people were ben[-] efiting under old-age and survivors insurance a[t] the end of 1953. This number includes retire[d] workers and their wives or husbands and age[d] survivors of insured workers who had died. Abou[t] 2,600,000 old people, including some of the bene[-] ficiaries counted above, were receiving old-age as[-] sistance because they were in need of suppleme[n-] tal aid.

Old-age and survivors insurance is paid for b[y] contributions of employees, employers, and sel[f-] employed persons. Employees and employers eac[h] now pay 2 per cent of the covered worker's wag[e] or salary, not including anything over $3,600 [a] year. These contribution rates are scheduled to in[-] crease eventually to 3¼ per cent each. A self-em[-] ployed person, for whom there is no employe[r] contribution, pays 1½ times the employee rate o[f] his earnings up to $3,600.

Old-age assistance is the second line of defens[e] against hardship and want in old age. Under th[e] Social Security Act, the federal government make[s] grants to states to cover a certain proportion of th[e] costs of state assistance programs that meet ce[r-] tain general requirements of the federal act. Th[e] state programs differ widely in defining "need["] for assistance, in residence requirements and othe[r] conditions for eligibility, and in levels of assistanc[e] payments.

The amount of assistance an old person receive[s]

supposed to be the difference between the amount he has to live on, including aid from relatives and friends, and the amount he requires for subsistence according to the standards set by the state agency. States, however, usually set a top limit on the amount that can be paid to any individual regardless of what they find he requires. When funds are limited, states may limit the things for which allowance is made (usually food, shelter, clothing, medical care, and so on) or may scale down all payments to some percentage of their standard.

Payments for old-age assistance, including medical care, averaged $51.07 in November, 1953 for the program as a whole, which is in operation in all states, the District of Columbia, Alaska, Hawaii, Puerto Rico, and the Virgin Islands.

When Congress added monthly survivors benefits to the federal insurance system in 1939, it created, at one stroke, a tremendous addition to the security of families, young and old, throughout the United States. The face value of this insurance today is $300,000,000,000, more than the face value of all other life insurance.

The Social Security Act also provides a second line of defense for fatherless children in what is called Aid To Dependent Children. This is provided under approved state programs to needy children who have been deprived of parental support or care by reason of the death, absence from the home, or disability of one or both parents. As in the case of old-age assistance, more than half of the cost of this assistance program, is supported by federal grants.

The children of a deceased insured worker receive survivor benefits until they reach age 18; a widow, regardless of her age, who is caring for children is entitled to benefits and, in some circumstances, a divorced wife who has children of the deceased in her care.

For all these types of benefits, the worker need have been only "currently insured"—that is, he need have had only six quarters of coverage out of the thirteen consecutive quarters ending with that in which he died. Young workers, who have only recently entered the labor market, therefore may build up this insurance quickly, at a time when they have had little or no chance to make other savings and when young children may need support.

Survivor benefits are also paid to the widow of a "fully insured" worker at age 65 if she has not remarried, and, in certain circumstances, to an aged widower or aged parents. In addition, lump sums may be paid on behalf of insured persons to the widow or widower or other person who paid the worker's burial expenses.

Generally speaking, aged survivors receive benefits until they die. Children receive them until age 18 unless they marry before that age, and a widow under age 65 who is caring for children receives her benefit until the youngest child reaches age 18. Like retirement benefits, survivor benefits are suspended for any month in which the beneficiary receives more than $75 in wages for covered work.

The benefit of a widow, widower, former wife or aged parent is three-fourths of the retirement benefit amount which has been described above. If only one child is entitled to benefits, his payment is also three-fourths of that amount; if more than one is entitled, each child receives half that amount and an additional one-fourth is divided equally among all the children.

The Social Security Administration has estimated that at the end of 1953 there were about 2,100,000 children under age 18 whose fathers had died. More than 1,000,000 were receiving benefits under old-age and survivors insurance; about 300,000 were benefiting under the veterans' compensation program, and about 100,000 under the railroad retirement program and retirement programs for federal employees. Some 300,000 needy children whose fathers had died were receiving aid to dependent children under the Social Security Act.

Thus more than three times as many fatherless children had insurance benefits as were receiving assistance under the act by reason of the father's death.

The big gap in social security in the United States is lack of insurance protection against the costs and losses from sickness and disability. Most other modern industrial nations, and many others, provide such protection through insurance to replace part of the wages workers lose when they are sick or permanently disabled. They also make arrangements, usually called health insurance, to meet costs of needed medical care.

A large part of the relief bill of the United States results from sickness and disability. Two of the assistance programs under the Social Security Act—Aid to the Blind, and Aid to the Permanently and Totally Disabled—deal only with the disabled. Much of the assistance given to families under the Aid to Dependent Children program and much of the general relief supplied by states and localities is needed because of the physical incapacity of breadwinners. Many of the old people on the old-age assistance rolls are there because of their disabilities, or those of others on whom they would naturally have depended.

As a matter of fact, the public not only pays for the support of these needy persons but also pays most of their medical care. Public funds also provide institutional care for the sick and disabled. Federal, state, and local governments own and operate three-fourths of all hospital beds in the United States. Government pays for nearly all care of mental and tuberculous patients.

Much of this economic burden of sickness, disability, and premature death could be avoided through prompt and adequate medical care. Likewise, much of the dependency resulting from these causes could be prevented by spreading the cost—through social insurance—over the whole population. When the cost is spread in this way, ordinarily self-supporting families can pay their share.

Permanent disability is like old age in that it reduces or destroys a worker's capacity to earn his living. When chronic disability forces a person to quit work before he reaches age 65, he has at least as much need of insurance protection as he would have at retirement age. He has the extra expenses that illness causes in a home and may have a family that needs support for years to come. Yet when he ceases to earn, any insurance benefits for which he or members of his family may qualify ultimately are likely to be cut down or lost because his average earnings are lowered.

Temporary disability, like unemployment, cuts off the earnings of many workers for shorter periods. Like permanent disability, it may reduce or cancel the protection a worker otherwise would have under existing social insurance programs. These interruptions of earnings and the costs of medical care of the breadwinner and others in the home frequently wipe out a family's savings.

Government insurance to cover medical costs is not "socialized medicine." When medical care is "socialized," the government employs and directs the doctors. Under health insurance, care is provided by private doctors, engaged in private practice, who then are paid out of the insurance fund for the care they give insured persons, just as such doctors now are paid under the Blue Shield plan.

Private voluntary health insurance plans have spread in recent years, but chiefly among people in the middle and higher income brackets and in the large cities. All forms of private insurance to cover costs of medical care, including all nonprofit plans such as Blue Cross and Blue Shield and all commercial insurance, together cover only about one-sixth of the nation's $10,000,000,000 annual medical bill.

Social security in the United States clearly still has big gaps in what it covers. But what about the programs we already have? Are we doing as well as we should and can do in the three fields in which the largest groups of our people have a stake—unemployment insurance, old-age and survivors insurance, and public assistance?

Most of our troubles in unemployment insurance arise from the arrangements for financing it. The Federal Unemployment Tax Act permits employers to deduct from the federal tax not only what they have paid under state unemployment insurance laws but also the amounts which they have been excused from paying by the employer "experience-rating" provisions of those laws. When times are good and state reserves in the Unemployment Trust Fund are large, it is natural that states should want to reduce the tax on employers. The only way the federal act permits them to do so is on the basis of the individual employer's past "experience" with unemployment.

All but six states measure such experience by adding up the unemployment benefits paid to former employees. This is an illogical basis, because the likelihood of a laid-off worker's being obliged to claim benefits is not affected so much by his employer as by conditions in the labor market. A sensible way to measure the employer's "experience" would be the number of workers laid off or the decline in the payroll, not the amount of benefits paid to former employees.

But the present basis of experience rating has proved worse than illogical. It has given employers a reason to resist payment of benefits to their workers, since every claim paid cuts down their chance to get a reduction in their contribution rate. Even though the benefits are paid out of a state fund, a claim for benefits is likely to be regarded as a contest between the employer and his former employee.

When the Social Security Act was passed, we had no experience to tell us what unemployment insurance was likely to cost. The Social Security Board was therefore very conservative in recommending to the states what benefit amounts and duration should be. It was intended that benefits

ould average at least 50 per cent of wages. As
ages and living costs have risen, however, the
ates have failed to make a corresponding in-
rease in the top benefit. Benefits averaged 41 per
nt of wage loss in 1939 but have fallen to 33 per
nt.

Most states have increased the length of time
uring which benefits may be paid, but from 1946
rough 1950 between one and two million bene-
ciaries reached the end of this period every year
ithout finding work. It is easy to imagine what
ould happen in a period of severe and general
nemployment.

There has also been a steady increase in the
mount of wages and length of time a worker
ust have worked to be eligible for benefits. And
arsh conditions have been added that may dis-
ualify a claimant.

Unemployment insurance is intended to com-
nsate for involuntary unemployment. There-
re a worker should be disqualified who has quit
s job voluntarily without good cause, has been
scharged for misconduct, or has refused suitable
ork. Twenty states, however, go beyond this
d require that quitting must have been for good
use *attributable to the employer*. These states
squalify a worker who has left his job because
orking conditions were undermining his health
because he was obliged to move to another lo-
lity or because he was offered a better job that
d not materialize. States also have become in-
easingly strict in denying benefits to workers on
e ground that they have refused "suitable"
ork. Often skilled workers are required to ac-
pt unskilled jobs.

The general federal tax on payrolls was in-
ded to keep down unfair competition between
ployers in states that had unemployment in-
rance laws and those that did not. Actually, the
ect of experience rating has caused an opposite
uation. States are discouraged from trying to
prove their program lest they put the state's
ployers at a competitive disadvantage.

Here [old-age and survivor's insurance] the pic-
re is brighter, though the federal insurance sys-
m still does not cover all workers and still con-
ns injustices.

Benefits do not compensate workers' losses ade-
ately. In February, 1953, nearly 11 per cent of
e aged beneficiaries were receiving supplemen-
y old-age assistance, and nearly 6 per cent of
e beneficiary families with children also received
d to dependent children.

The present benefit formula is relatively unfair
to workers in the middle wage brackets, to workers without dependents, and to long-time contributors. But it is only right that a larger proportion
of the employers' contributions be used to pay
benefits to the groups most in need of protection
—low-wage earners, dependents of insured persons, and workers who were nearing old age
when the system started. Today, when the worker's contribution rate is 2 per cent and the self-
employed person's rate is 3 per cent, contributors
get at least their money's worth in protection and
most of them considerably more. But eventually,
when the contribution rates rise to the maximum
scheduled in the law ($3\frac{1}{4}$ per cent for employees
and $4\frac{7}{8}$ per cent for self-employed persons), this
will not be true for many persons.

If social insurance in the United States covered
all major risks causing wage loss, covered all
workers, and paid adequate benefits, there would
be far less need for public assistance, though some
would remain. As we have established and improved social insurance, we have cut down needs
for assistance. There are relatively fewer people
on relief rolls, and some of those on the rolls get
smaller amounts than they would otherwise have
to have because they have some income from social insurance. More than 5,000,000 people in the
United States, however, still count on public assistance for at least some of their daily bread.

Most of these people are being aided through
the four assistance programs under the Social Security Act—old-age assistance, aid to the blind, aid
to totally and permanently disabled persons over
age 18, and aid to families with children who are
dependent for one of the reasons specified in the
act. Federal funds pay more than half the costs
of these programs. Under the present law, the
federal grant to each state must be proportionate
to the amount the state itself can and wishes to
make available out of its own funds or out of
state and local funds combined.

Some states are much wealthier than others.
They also differ greatly in the amount they set
aside for public aid, in the need for such aid, in
the conditions under which it is given, and in the
levels of payment to needy persons. The differences in the assistance that needy individuals and
families receive are greater, however, than these
circumstances warrant. A person who gets a certain amount of aid in his own state might get
much more or much less or nothing at all in a
neighboring state.

Especially in view of the large contribution of federal funds, it is hardly fair for such wide differences to persist in the aid available to persons in similar circumstances in various parts of the country. It is also unfair that some kinds of needy persons—like the sick and disabled—should get no federal funds. . . .

Most of the public attention directed toward social security has centered on the federal Old-Age and Survivors Insurance System, which is basic to our program in the United States.

Nearly everyone is agreed that this system should be extended to cover all the major groups now excluded, and the President has made recommendations in that direction. There is no reason why we should not bring into the system all the chief groups that now have no substantial protection under retirement and survivors insurance. These include more than 3,000,000 farm operators; some 2,700,000 farm employees; the 100,000 to 200,000 domestic workers now excluded by the provisions requiring "regular" employment in these fields for coverage; and about 500,000 self-employed persons in professional groups now excluded (largely at their own request)—accountants, architects, funeral directors, lawyers, physicians and other medical practitioners, professional engineers and so on. About 190,000 ministers now excluded could be covered under voluntary arrangements such as those used to cover other employees of non-profit organizations.

The federal system also excludes more than 4,000,000 persons who are under retirement plans for public employees. Many of these have little or no provision for surviving dependents of a covered employee who dies. In many cases also, an employee who leaves work covered by the retirement plan may lose all rights to benefits he built up in his past service, getting only a return of his contributions.

Most public employees could have better and sounder protection if these retirement plans were related in some way to old-age and survivors insurance. The arrangements should be such that workers covered by the retirement plans would have the full protection of their own plans in return for higher contributions paid by them or their employers, in addition to the protection of the general system.

There is a temporary provision, giving a wage credit of $160 a month for active service in the armed forces. A permanent plan should be developed for relating the special retirement system for members of the armed forces to the Old-Age and Survivors Insurance System in a similar manner to that suggested for public employees. Likewise, the partial coordination now existing between the Railroad Retirement System and the Old-Age and Survivors Insurance System should be greatly simplified and strengthened.

The top wage on which benefits are based and the formula for computing benefits should be revised. A change is necessary to take account of the general increase in wages and living costs in recent years and of the future injustice that will arise under present provisions for workers in the middle wage brackets, single persons, and persons who have contributed to the system for many years.

The President in his message recognized the need for increasing benefits as well as for increasing the maximum annual earnings upon which benefits and contributions are based. He pointed out that, due to the rise in wage level, the present maximum of $3,600 covers the full earnings of only 40 per cent of regular male workers, whereas the original maximum of $3,000 covered 94 per cent. However, the President recommended an increase to only $4,200, although a maximum of $7,500 would be required to include 94 per cent of such earnings. It is interesting to note that labor organizations have long favored an increase in the maximum and have stated their willingness to pay contributions based on a higher maximum such as $6,000.

In my opinion the wage base should be raised from $3,600 to at least $6,000. The benefit formula should pay at least 60 per cent (instead of 55 per cent) of the first $100 of the worker's average monthly wage or earnings from self-employment plus 30 per cent (instead of 15 per cent) of any amount above $100 up to $400 a month additional, if no increase in the benefit is provided for each year that the worker has been covered.

If the benefit amount is increased by 1 per cent for every year that a worker has been covered, as was true prior to 1950, the basic formula would not need to be so high; but even so it should be at least 55 per cent of the first $100 average monthly earnings and 20 per cent of any amount above that.

These changes would mean that the $100-a-month worker who has contributed for twenty years would have a retirement benefit of $66 a month, rather than the present $55. A $300-a-month worker who has paid in for the same ength of time would get $114 a month rather than $85. Thus we would keep the principle of relatively larger benefits for low-paid workers, since the first beneficiary would have more than half as much as the second though his former earnings were only one-third as much. At the same time, workers in the middle brackets who now are young would get their money's worth.

The present law gives the wife of a beneficiary half as much as her husband receives but not until she reaches age 65. Wives are usually several years younger than their husbands, so that aged couples ordinarily cannot have the wife's benefit for several years after the husband reaches retirement age. In general, women do not work outside their homes as long as men. For these reasons, the qualifying age for benefits to women—wives' and aged widows' benefits and retirement benefits for which women qualify on the basis of their own earnings—should be reduced from 65 years to 60 years.

Benefits should be paid to insured workers who become permanently and totally disabled before age 65 and to their eligible dependents on the same basis as those paid in old-age retirement. As has been pointed out, their wage loss and need for benefits are the same or greater.

Nearly all the persons who apply for retirement benefits have stopped work because they were physically unable to continue or because they could not get a job. If benefits were paid to insured workers who had to quit before retirement age, and if persons who kept on working after that age got a sizable increase in benefit for every additional year they worked, we would have a flexible retirement age. This would be fairer for the individual and would help to conserve and use the skills of old people who could and wanted to stay on the job. . . .

Eventually our first line of defense against hardship and want will be a comprehensive contributory social insurance program that offsets income losses due to unemployment, disability, old age, and death, and helps meet the costs of medical care. How long it will take such a system to develop is not clear, but it will eventually develop. Probably, like other countries, we shall continue to meet particular needs, one by one. Then we shall find we have many gaps and inconsistencies among the provisions. Finally we shall find it simpler and more effective to eliminate these complications by adopting a comprehensive, unified program.

Undoubtedly we shall find it desirable to have workers and employers share the costs of such a system equally so as to focus attention on the social objectives of providing enough protection and eliminate the bad attitudes which develop when the employer pays the entire costs. Government, federal or state, should also share in the cost of insuring against the risks, again to keep attention focused on the social objective.

Division of responsibilities between the federal and state governments must be considered carefully because of the size of our country as well as its governmental system and traditions. Whether or not the federal government itself administers all these kinds of social insurance, it must be responsible for seeing that each of the risks and all persons subject to them are covered and that benefits are adequate.

Conceivably the federal government itself could maintain a single system covering all risks. Employers would make only one payroll report and one remittance of contributions. There would be only one central record system, one network of local offices. Since benefits are related to wage loss, they would be adjusted automatically to wage levels throughout the country.

Alternatively, the federal government might administer social insurance covering the long-term risks—permanent total disability, old age, and death—and the states, the system covering the short-term hazards of unemployment, temporary disability, and medical care.

Supplemented by public assistance to meet immediate need in any part of our country, and strengthened by preventive measures to avert, insofar as is possible, the underlying causes of risks to earning, health, and economic independence, our program would be worthy of the name of social security.

We now spend about 5 per cent of our national income for health and welfare programs, federal, state, and local. This figure includes all the social insurance, public assistance, and other government health and welfare activities such as hospital construction, vocational rehabilitation, child welfare, school lunches, and institutional care. If this seems a high figure, it is encouraging to know that it is a smaller part of our national income than we spent before World War II even though unemployment insurance and old-age and survivors insurance have developed since that time.

If we expanded and strengthened the social insurances and amended public assistance as I have suggested, we should probably spend about 7 or 8 per cent of our national income for health and welfare. This does not mean that total expenditures, counting both public and private costs, would be increased. Health insurance, for example, is a means of spreading existing costs by a prepayment system. The economic losses from unemployment, disability, old age, and death exist now, whether or not we spread the costs through social insurance and public assistance. We cannot make them disappear by ignoring them. We can reduce them by proper preventive measures. Indeed, social insurance, by preventing destitution reduces the social as well as the economic consequences of these hazards, since destitution feed on itself. . . .

In a modern democracy, freedom means equal opportunity. Social Security does not mean that anyone shall be guaranteed the good things of life without effort on his part. It does not mean dead level of uniformity, but a basic protection of which each of us can build effectively his desire standard of well-being. It means genuinely equal opportunity in a free society.

Economic Status of Women Workers
From U. S. Department of Labor, Women's Bureau

During the postwar period there has been a substantial increase in the wage rates of women workers, particularly professional, technical, and clerical workers and operatives in factories and service industries. Yet the median income of women, nearly all of which is derived from wages and salaries, has risen only slightly in the postwar period, from $901 in 1945 to $1,045 in 1951, while that of men (also obtained largely through earnings) rose from $1,800 in 1945 to about $3,000 in 1951, latest year recorded in the Consumer Income Report of the Bureau of the Census.

Women's average income from wages and salaries in 1951 was less than half (44 per cent) of that received by men in 1951. Only ½ of 1 per cent of women wage earners received as much or more than a $5,000 income from their work, whereas 12 per cent of the men workers received wages or salaries of $5,000 or more. At the lower end of the scale, 81 per cent of the women and only 37 per cent of the men received less than $2,500 from wages or salaries.

Part of this wide differential between men's and women's earnings is due to the fact that most men work continuously during the year, while women's employment is more intermittent, particularly that of married women, whose earnings tend to be low, according to the explanatory statement of the Bureau of the Census. But there are other more fundamental reasons why census figures show up such a wide discrepancy between the earned income of men and women workers. One of these is the fact that women workers tend to congregate in occupations traditionally employing women and that these occupations have a relatively low wage scale. In some of the occupations newer to women and with a higher wage scale, women are slower than men to receive advancement to the better-paid positions. Another reason for the discrepancy between men and women's income from salary or wages is the fact that women still are paid less than men, in a multitude of cases, for doing the same or comparable work. While the principle of equal pay for equal work is generally accepted in theory, it is by no means universal in practice.

In Colorado, one of the States in which women's organizations are supporting an equal-pay bill in the State legislature, the Business and Professional Women's Clubs recently completed a State-wide spot survey which revealed that in most instances Colorado women are being paid less than men for doing comparable work. In one community of 15,000 residents, the survey revealed that:

Men employed in manufacturing work in the town received $1.45 an hour; women doing similar job are paid 97½ cents an hour.

In dry-goods stores, women employees receive $2 a month to a man's $300.

Bookkeepers in one garage—if they are men—ea

From "The Status of Women in the United States 1953," Women's Bureau Bulletin 249, U. S. Department of Labor, Washington: Government Printing Office, 1953, pp. 11–12 quoted.

$350; women only $237. In another garage there was no salary discrimination.

One bank pays women $191.37 for doing the same job that pays a man $304.50.

There is no reason to believe that what is true in Colorado would be measurably different in other States where there are no equal-pay laws. Even in the States that have equal-pay laws, the coverage is in most cases limited, and legal loopholes exist which make it difficult to enforce them completely. However, the principle of equal pay is being put more and more into practice not only in compliance with State laws, but by voluntary action on the part of employers. Trade unions frequently include equal-pay clauses in union contracts, since equal pay benefits men as well as women by discouraging employers from hiring women for less money, or, as sometimes happens, from replacing men with women at lower rates.

The Women's Bureau of the U. S. Department of Labor, women's organizations, civic groups, unions, and individual leaders have been active for many years in promoting the equal-pay principle. Last year (1952) the Women's Bureau called a National Conference on Equal Pay, and following the conference a national committee was formed of voluntary organizations and trade unions to stimulate further efforts toward the elimination of wage inequalities between men and women. Known as the National Committee for Equal Pay, it has headquarters at 1817 Eye Street NW., in Washington, D. C.

Should Jews Change Their Occupations?

Samuel H. Flowerman

Samuel H. Flowerman (1912–   ), director of research, Postgraduate Center for Psychotherapy, New York City.

Prophetic voices are again warning American Jews that their economic position spells trouble for them—especially if there is a major depression. Well-meaning neighbors (and some not so well-meaning) urge the need to "normalize" Jewish occupational "maldistribution"—and not infrequently Jews themselves are heard singing the same ominous tune.

Typically, J. F. Brown, a social psychologist, calls upon Jewish leadership to dissuade fellow-Jews from entering those businesses and professions which they have already too conspicuously "overpopulated." Zionists call for a return to manual labor and the soil. Others tell us that Jewry's only hope of survival—elsewhere as well as in America—is to retire from all positions of economic concentration, prominence, or control; to retreat from all points at which they conspicuously come in contact with Gentile customers; to abandon all handling of goods that adds nothing to the value of such goods; and to seek their sustenance exclusively as farmers, mechanics, and factory hands. . . .

The lot of the Jew in America is inextricably woven into the fabric of democracy in America. If our form of political democracy should falter, nothing the Jew can do—now or in the future—can save him. On the other hand, as a citizen in a democracy, the Jew has a great stake in its development. He has—and must exercise—the same duties and obligations, but also the same rights and privileges as any other citizen. For him to waive his rightful opportunities is as injurious to him and as disloyal to the democratic faith and to his country as would be the neglect of his duties and obligations.

What does all this mean, job-wise, for the Jew in America? He must maintain his right to choose the life calling for which he has the ability, opportunities, and desire. This in turn means freedom to choose, to the highest possible degree, untrammeled by parents, tradition, school and college officials, self-imposed or government-supported restrictions. This does not imply a game of blind man's buff; our schools and government must continuously provide the most up-to-date information on occupations and job trends. In the schools the task of preparing for a job must

From "Should Jews Change Their Occupations? A Rational Approach to the 'Maldistribution' Problem," *Commentary, 3* (1947): 320–328, pp. 320, 328 quoted. Reprinted by permission.

The
BASES OF JOB DISCRIMINATION
(COMPLAINTS TO FEPC, FISCAL YEAR 1943–44)

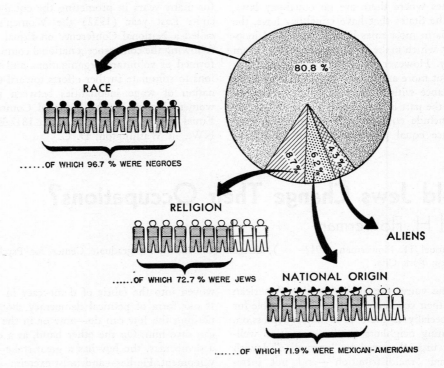

RACE

......OF WHICH 96.7 % WERE NEGROES

80.8 %

8.7 %

6.2 %

4.3 %

RELIGION

......OF WHICH 72.7 % WERE JEWS

ALIENS

NATIONAL ORIGIN

......OF WHICH 71.9 % WERE MEXICAN-AMERICANS

THOSE CHARGED WITH DISCRIMINATION

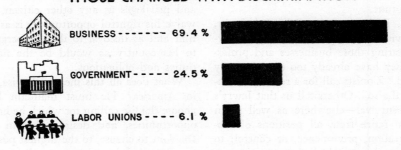

BUSINESS - - - - - - 69.4 %

GOVERNMENT - - - - - 24.5 %

LABOR UNIONS - - - - 6.1 %

SOURCE: First Report, FEPC, based on 4,081 complaints for fiscal year 1943-44.

(From the President's Committee on Civil Rights, *To Secure These Rights,* Washington: Government Printing Office, 1947, p. 54) be considered as integral a part of our formal education as learning to read and write. The widened occupational horizons made possible by such learning materials—which implies some form of curriculum revision—must be vigorously supplemented by adequate counseling facilities for young people and their parents.

Too early specialization of training must be assiduously avoided, chiefly because of the complexity of our occupational structure and the uncertainties of our economic system. Preparation for broad job "families" (related occupations) rather than for highly specific vocations is much to be preferred; this gives a youngster more than one string to his bow.

Finally, a stable economy is far and away the best insurance against the menace of assaults by one group against another's economic position. Full employment; adequate provisions for social security; a stable price structure; adequate housing; a government elected by all of the people and responsive to their wishes—these are the necessities. For it is only under such a system of life that the selection of a career, of a school, the finding and holding of a job, will depend only on an individual's ability, and not on his ancestry. It is to the achievement of this kind of society that we should bend our efforts.

The acid test in selecting any occupation must be: Is the work personally satisfying and socially desirable? And not: Is it good or bad for the Jews? What is good for other Americans is good for the Jews.

Employment of Negroes

Francis J. Haas and G. James Fleming

Francis J. Haas (1889–1953), late bishop, Roman Catholic Diocese of Grand Rapids, Michigan; author of *Shop Collective Bargaining* (1922) and *Man and Society: An Introduction to Sociology* (1930). G. James Fleming (1904–   ), executive editor, *Amsterdam News*.

"Employers need only to approach the matter [of employing Negroes] practically and objectively, using the proved rules of good management practice as a guide," observes the American Management Association in its special research on *The Negro Worker*.[1] Those who have made this kind of approach and who have been both earnest and honest have been able to overcome the worst of their fears, the record shows. They have been able to control those group prejudices which first caused employers to say, "Our workers won't stand for this."

At first, personnel men—accustomed to past traditions which excluded Negroes from certain occupations—were confused, even where they were not bitterly opposed. One investigator observed: "In the absence of any well-defined techniques for overcoming some of the objections to the use of Negro workers, personnel directors frequently found themselves confused when confronted with new and complicated situations. Likewise the selection of competent workers for training and placement often presented a difficult task for interviewers and personnel representatives."[2]

Some personnel directors were afraid of their shadows and, instead of providing their companies with personnel leadership and direction, tried to do no more or go no further than they thought their employers would approve at first presentation. Increasingly, however, personnel men—not all by any means—have come to see that there is economic soundness in nondiscriminatory employment practices because, instead of a part of each personnel dollar being spent in finding ways *not* to employ or utilize some otherwise acceptable workers, under a regime of fair employment all of each personnel dollar is used for the exclusive purpose of employing needed workers.

---

[1] New York, 1942, p. 2.

[2] Julius A. Thomas, "Wartime Changes in the Occupational Status of Negro Workers," *Occupations, the Vocational Guidance Magazine*, April 1945, p. 404.

From "Personnel Practices and Wartime Changes," *The Annals*, 244 (March 1946): 48–56, pp. 54–55 quoted. Reprinted by permission.

UNEMPLOYMENT HITS
MINORITY GROUPS HARDEST

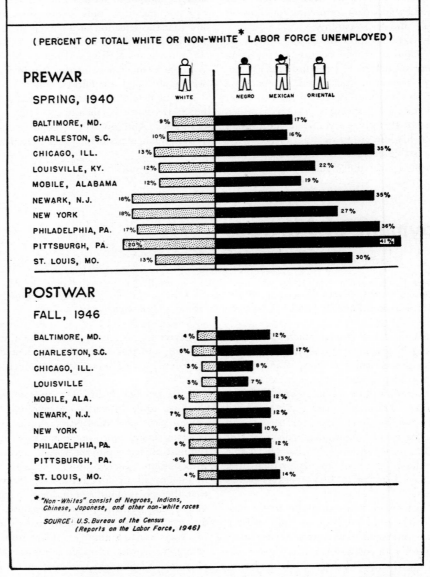

(PERCENT OF TOTAL WHITE OR NON-WHITE* LABOR FORCE UNEMPLOYED)

PREWAR

SPRING, 1940 — WHITE · NEGRO · MEXICAN · ORIENTAL

	WHITE	NON-WHITE
BALTIMORE, MD.	9%	17%
CHARLESTON, S.C.	10%	16%
CHICAGO, ILL.	13%	35%
LOUISVILLE, KY.	12%	22%
MOBILE, ALABAMA	12%	19%
NEWARK, N.J.	16%	35%
NEW YORK	18%	27%
PHILADELPHIA, PA.	17%	36%
PITTSBURGH, PA.	20%	41%
ST. LOUIS, MO.	13%	30%

POSTWAR

FALL, 1946

	WHITE	NON-WHITE
BALTIMORE, MD.	4%	12%
CHARLESTON, S.C.	5%	17%
CHICAGO, ILL.	3%	8%
LOUISVILLE	3%	7%
MOBILE, ALA.	6%	12%
NEWARK, N.J.	7%	12%
NEW YORK	6%	10%
PHILADELPHIA, PA.	6%	12%
PITTSBURGH, PA.	6%	13%
ST. LOUIS, MO.	4%	14%

* "Non-Whites" consist of Negroes, Indians,
Chinese, Japanese, and other non-white races

SOURCE: U.S. Bureau of the Census
(Reports on the Labor Force, 1946)

(From the President's Committee on Civil Rights, *To Secure These Rights,* Washington:
Government Printing Office, 1947, p. 60)

Wartime experience has shown them that there are good and bad, efficient and inefficient workers among all groups, regardless of race, religion, or national origin. They have also discovered that Negroes *can* be trained and have been trained for occupations requiring all levels of skill, and covering every occupation listed in the *Dictionary of Occupational Titles*.[3]

Personnel officials have learned the answers to the arguments raised against employment of Negroes, along these lines:

Anti-Negro Argument 1:

Negroes have no mechanical aptitudes.

Personnel Department Rebuttal:

Thousands of Negroes completed defense courses in mechanical skills; over 100 plants reported (to Thomas) the employment of Negroes in every technical, professional, and supervisory job listed in the *Dictionary of Occupational Titles;* Negroes in the Army Air Forces were flying fighter planes in combat.

Argument 2:

Negroes and whites cannot work together (mix together).

Rebuttal:

Negroes and whites do work together as schoolteachers and policemen in many cities; as contruction workers in others; as welders, carpenters, power drillers on street transportation systems (even Philadelphia Transportation Company and Capitol Transit Company, Washington).

Argument 3:

The Negro is more susceptible to disease, has more disease.

Rebuttal:

All workers in a company, regardless of race, are required to submit to medical examination; those diseased are not employed, thus all workers are equal from point of view of disease. (If no medical examinations are given, the responsible management should provide for same.)

Argument 4:

Why force Negroes on us in the factories?

Rebuttal:

The smart personnel man will always start his nondiscrimination program with employment of a Negro or Negroes in his own department or on the top management level. (Davis suggests a "neat," attractive, well-qualified colored girl in the employment office itself.)[4] Some personnel directors add Negro interviewers or "assistant personnel directors" to their staffs.

Sometimes an employer faced an individual employee who said: "If you employ Negroes I will have to quit this company, though I'll hate to." And the employer had to reply: "We'll be very sorry to lose you after all these years, but this is a free country and there is no way I can stop you from leaving." Usually, after that answer the white worker would return to his job and settle down to learning how to work in the same plant with Negroes.

Migratory Labor
Varden Fuller

Varden Fuller, associate professor of agricultural economics, University of California, was executive secretary of the President's Commission on Migratory Labor, 1951.

People who are concerned with migratory labor —government officials, employers, and interested observers—are inclined to simplify migratory movements and to perceive them as systematic by classifying them into "patterns" or "streams." By identifying these patterns or streams and drawing them on a map, the directions and sizes of the various movements are portrayed. But the notion of migratory patterns, as currently used, contributes about as much to misunderstanding as it does to clarification.

True, the seasonal movement of people from one area to another follows fairly well-defined routes. But this does not mean that the same in-

[3] *Ibid.,* p. 403.

[4] John A. Davis, *How Management Can Integrate Negroes in War Industries,* Albany: New York State War Council, p. 8.

From "No Work Today!," 1st ed., Public Affairs Pamphlet No. 190, 1953, pp. 6–9. Reprinted by permission.

DISCRIMINATION IN EMPLOYMENT MEANS ...

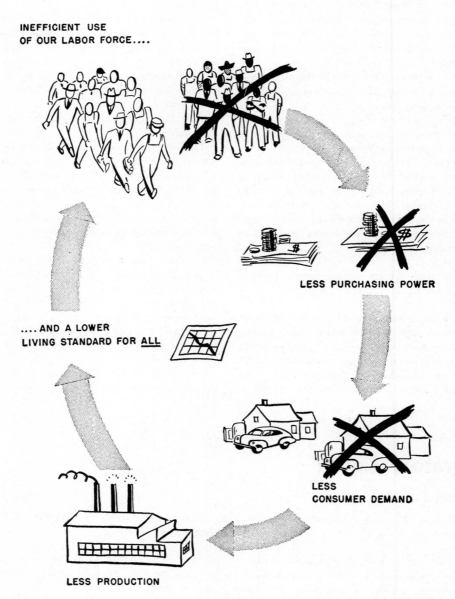

INEFFICIENT USE
OF OUR LABOR FORCE....

LESS PURCHASING POWER

....AND A LOWER
LIVING STANDARD FOR ALL

LESS
CONSUMER DEMAND

LESS PRODUCTION

(From the President's Committee on Civil Rights, *To Secure These Rights,* Washington:
Government Printing Office, 1947, p. 142)

FAIR EMPLOYMENT PRACTICES WOULD
HELP BRING ...

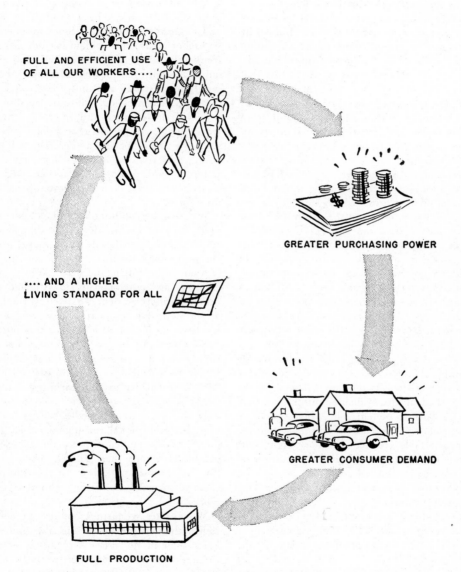

(From the President's Committee on Civil Rights, *To Secure These Rights,* Washington: Government Printing Office, 1947, p. 143)

dividual families move regularly along these routes, that such families have known destinations, that they have assurance of employment on arrival, and that they "follow the sun" systematically from one harvest to the next. If one pays attention to the experiences of individual families, the orderliness, the stability, and the regularity and assurance of employment that are implied by the concept of migratory patterns are all cast in doubt. After surveying work and migration histories of individuals and families, the picture that emerges is one of trial and error, of disappointment or rebuke here or there, of a great deal of frantic movement within the season and from one season to the next, most of it based on rumor or on the chance that things will prove to be better somewhere else. A few have fairly certain work connections, but they are mainly individuals and small groups who work in the minor crops and in the smaller areas which lie outside the paths of the major movements. (Within the major migratory labor areas, the aggregate movement may seem to resemble a pattern, but it is a mistake to assume that the lives of the majority are patterned on anything except harsh uncertainty.

This uncertainty is a double one: (1) There is the hazard of whether there will be a crop on which to work. (2) There is always doubt whether the migrant will get the work he expects even if there is a good crop. In consequence, a hopeful trek of hundreds of miles may end with the crushing discovery that the crop is late or has failed or that other migrants have arrived earlier and have filled up the available housing and that there is no work to be had. The whole system of migratory labor is so chaotic and unsystematic that a comfortable balance of labor supply and demand is rare and unusual. Either surpluses or shortages are more normal.

These hazards and uncertainties help to explain why migratory workers earn so much less than many people think they ought to. Quite frequently, one encounters the belief that migrants in a certain pattern should get at least 200 days of employment a year. This is arrived at by adding up the estimated days of crop activities that lie along the route. Unfortunately, this estimate does not allow for the many disappointments that befall the migrant worker. Actually, according to the surveys that have been made, the male adult migratory worker who gets more than 100 days of farm employment during the year is lucky. And many of these are short days that start late or end early.

Migrants do not work at individual jobs like tending a machine, or occupying a station on an assembly line, or driving a truck. A hundredweight of cotton or a hamper of beans is the same whether picked by a child or by an adult and earns the same wage. Since farm employers and labor contractors seldom exclude women and frequently allow children as well, and since the family usually needs the earnings, the entire family often works as a unit. Moreover, except in the rare instances of child-care facilities being provided, it is easier and safer for children to work along with parents than to be left behind in camp or in a locked automobile. Children as young as seven and eight years of age are often found at work in the fields, and child-labor laws, even where they do exist, have proved difficult to enforce.

When crop conditions are favorable and the work force of the locality is not diluted with excessive labor, the family may make impressive earnings. Such fortunate experiences are the exception rather than the rule. When migrants' earnings are systematically investigated and the disappointing experiences as well as the favorable are brought into the picture, the record is not one to evoke envy—not, at least, by prevailing American standards of income. The most recent national survey of migratory labor earnings, made by the U. S. Department of Agriculture for the year 1949, revealed that average earnings of adult male workers were approximately $600 for the year; only one out of four earned $1,000 or more. Even with such additional earnings as wives and children are able to contribute, the typical family earned no more than $1,000. These are gross earnings and do not allow for the transportation expense incurred in moving about in search of work.

Wage rates to farm labor are higher in the North than in the South and also higher in the West than in the East. Accordingly earnings in Colorado ought to be comparatively favorable. Yet, the National Child Labor Committee found in a Colorado study, that 1949 migrant earnings from all sources averaged $1,424 a family. "About 80 out of each 100 families had, somehow, to support themselves, travel from job location to job location on an annual cash income of less than $2,000," reports the Committee.

CROSS REFERENCES TO STANDARD TEXTS *

Barnes, *Society in Transition*, Chap. 13.
Bernard, *American Community Behavior*, Chaps. 5, 7–9, 13–15, 23.
Bloch, *Disorganization*, pp. 57–58, 282–284, 488–505.
Brown, *Social Pathology*, Chap. 29.
Cuber and Harper, *Problems of American Society*, Chaps. 5, 19.
Elliott and Merrill, *Social Disorganization*, Chaps. 10, 11, 29.
Faris, *Social Disorganization*, Chap. 4.
Gillin, *Social Pathology*, Chaps. 25–28.
―――― and others, *Social Problems*, Chaps. 9, 10, 17.

Herman, *Approach to Social Problems*, pp. 290–291, 340–351, 444–452, 457–461, 467–473.
Landis, *Social Policies in the Making*, Chaps. 18–20.
Merrill and others, *Social Problems*, pp. 37–38, 40–41, 226–227, 313–314.
Mihanovich, *Current Social Problems*, Chaps. 6, 7.
Neumeyer, *Social Problems and the Changing Society*, Chaps. 9–11.
Nordskog and others, *Analyzing Social Problems*, Chap. 4.
Odum, *American Social Problems*, Chap. 20.
Phelps and Anderson, *Contemporary Social Problems*, Chaps. 12–13.
Reinhardt and others, *Social Problems and Social Policy*, Chap. 5.
Weaver, *Social Problems*, Chaps. 25–26.

* For complete bibliographical reference to each text, see page 13.

OTHER BIBLIOGRAPHY

Nels Anderson, *Men on the Move*, Chicago: University of Chicago Press, 1940.
Thurman Wesley Arnold, *The Folklore of Capitalism*, New Haven: Yale University Press, 1937.
E. Wight Bakke, *Citizens Without Work*, New Haven: Yale University Press, 1940.
Reinhard Bendix and S. M. Lipset, eds., *Class, Status and Power: A Reader in Social Stratification*, Glencoe, Illinois: Free Press, 1953.
Morroe Berger, *Equality by Statute*, New York: Columbia University Press, 1952.
A. A. Berle, Jr., and Gardiner C. Means, *The Modern Corporation and Private Property*, New York: Macmillan Co., 1932.
Herbert Blumer, "Sociological Theory in Industrial Relations," *American Sociological Review*, 12 (1947): 271–278.
Robert A. Brady, *Business as a System of Power*, New York: Columbia University Press, 1943.
Nathaniel Cantor, *Employee Counseling*, New York: McGraw-Hill Book Co., 1945.
Paul Hubert Casselman, *The Cooperative Movement and Some of Its Problems*, New York: Philosophical Library, 1952.
Neil W. Chamberlain, *Collective Bargaining*, New York: McGraw-Hill Book Co., 1951.
Russell W. Davenport, with Editors of *Fortune*, *U.S.A. The Permanent Revolution*, New York: Prentice-Hall, 1951.
Jerome Davis, *Capitalism and Its Culture*, New York: Farrar & Rinehart, 1935.
Thomas D. Eliot, *American Standards and Planes of Living*, Boston: Ginn and Co., 1931.
Abraham Epstein, *Insecurity: A Challenge to America*, New York: Random House, 1938.
Herman Feldman, ed., "Labor Relations and the Public," *The Annals*, 248 (November 1946).

John Kenneth Galbraith, *American Capitalism: The Concept of Countervailing Power*, Boston: Houghton Mifflin Co., 1952.
Alvin W. Gouldner, *Wildcat Strike*, Yellow Springs, Ohio: Antioch Press, 1954.
Walton H. Hamilton and Irene Till, "Antitrust in Action," Temporary National Economic Committee Monograph No. 16, Washington: Government Printing Office, 1941.
E. T. Hiller, *The Strike*, Chicago: University of Chicago Press, 1928.
Leo Huberman, *The Labor Spy Racket*, New York: Modern Age Books, 1937.
Alfred W. Jones, *Life, Liberty, and Property*, Philadelphia: J. B. Lippincott Co., 1941.
Arthur Kornhauser, Robert Dubin, and Arthur M. Ross, eds., *Industrial Conflict*, New York: McGraw-Hill Book Co., 1954.
David Lasser, *Private Monopoly: The Enemy at Home*, New York: Harper & Bros., 1945.
David E. Lilienthal, *TVA—Democracy on the March*, New York: Harper & Bros., 1944.
Lewis Meriam, *Relief and Social Security*, Washington: Brookings Institution, 1946.
Robert K. Merton, Ailsa P. Gray, Barbara Hockey, and Hanan C. Selvin, eds., *Reader in Bureaucracy*, Glencoe, Illinois: Free Press, 1952.
C. Wright Mills, *The New Men of Power*, New York: Harcourt, Brace and Co., 1948.
Wilbert E. Moore, *Industrial Relations and the Social Order*, rev. ed., New York: Macmillan Co., 1951.
Lowry Nelson, "Migratory Workers: The Mobile Tenth of American Agriculture," Planning Pamphlet No. 82, Washington, D.C.: National Planning Association, 1953.
Louis Ruchames, *Race, Jobs and Politics: The Story*

of FEPC, New York: Columbia University Press, 1953.

George P. Schultz and John R. Coleman, *Labor Problems: Cases and Readings*, New York: McGraw-Hill Book Co., 1953.

Eugene Staley, ed., *Creating an Industrial Civilization* (Corning Glass Co. Conference), New York: Harper & Bros., 1952.

Mary van Kleeck, "Towards an Industrial Sociology," *American Sociological Review*, 11 (1946): 501–505.

Morris S. Viteles, *Motivation and Morale in Industry*, New York: W. W. Norton & Co., 1953.

Charles R. Walker and Robert H. Guest, *The Man on the Assembly Line*, Cambridge: Harvard University Press, 1952.

W. Lloyd Warner and J. O. Low, *The Social System of the Modern Factory*, New Haven: Yale University Press, 1947.

William F. Whyte, ed., *Industry and Society*, New York: McGraw-Hill Book Co., 1946.

William H. Whyte, Jr., *Is Anybody Listening?*, New York: Simon and Schuster, 1952.

Clair Wilcox, "Competition and Monopoly in American Industry," Temporary National Economic Committee Monograph No. 21, Washington: Government Printing Office, 1940.

REVIEW QUESTIONS

1. How has the human aspect of industry changed during the past fifty years?
2. On what basis does Bell raise the objection that "there is no view of the larger institutional framework of our economic system" apparent in recent studies conducted on social relations within the factory?
3. What does Bell mean by "cow-sociology"?
4. What, according to Arnold, is a "cartel"? Why does he regard it as a dangerous form of organization?
5. In what ways does Arnold say that "free enterprise" is limited in the United States?
6. What are some of Altmeyer's suggestions toward minimizing poverty?
7. In what ways should women be regarded as a minority group? Can you suggest others than those brought out in the Women's Bureau selection?
8. How does Flowerman answer those who talk about the occupational "mal-distribution" of Jews?
9. How do Haas and Fleming reply to the allegations that Negroes "have no mechanical aptitudes"?
10. According to Fuller, what misconceptions arise from indicating migratory movements of laborers as "patterns" or "streams"?

Government and Political Power

To THE STUDENT of social problems, political power is of interest as one of the several expressions of social power—expressions which are largely convertible from one form to another. Since social power is administered—as it must be—by human agencies, there is more or less abuse of the control of that power. There is more or less of a problem situation among the affected groups of people.

The control of social power politically by political leaders and by businessmen has concerned many writers. Blaisdell and Greverus discuss briefly the struggle between business and political power wielders for the control of the federal government, for the use of federal agencies to achieve their goals. Prentis, as a spokesman for the National Association of Manufacturers, worries especially about political enterprisers, a tendency frequently observed among business enterprisers.

In the political field, the political specialist is a key figure. Whether he is a ward leader, a county political chairman, a state boss, or a lobbyist in a legislature or in an administrative establishment, he is a political specialist with technical ability, prestige, and domination which he can sell or use for his own purposes. Clugston tells how the Kansas City *Star* merged the business and political bossdoms of Kansas City, Missouri, with the fall of Pendergast. He also describes some of the purposes that its bossdom has served for the *Star* and affiliated interests.

As in so many other fields, discrimination against minorities because of poverty, among other things, is also regarded as a pressing problem in the political realm in the United States. Waldron describes how a legal aid society attempts to overcome at least a part of the handicap suffered by the poor when they have a legal problem.

Since the beginnings of the United States, all slightly deviant political philosophies have been called "foreign" and attempts made to associate them with foreign sources in order to discredit them. During recent decades the "red" menace, linked chiefly with the U.S.S.R., has occupied untold hours of political and newscasting oratory, thousands of columns of editorial comment, cartoons, and news stories, and World War II was said to have been fought to eliminate the threat of "fascism." Neither the intense anti-red propaganda nor the war has obliterated these movements in the United States. It is therefore useful to present Schlesinger's discussion of communism in a free society and Cleveland's plea that in avoiding the Communist short cut we not take "that other short cut—absolute certainty through authoritarian national government."

The Control of Social Power
Donald C. Blaisdell and Jane Greverus

Donald C. Blaisdell (1899–   ), deputy chief, U. S. Resident Delegation to International Organizations, Geneva. Chief publications: *The Farmer's Stake in World Peace* (1935, 1936, 1937), *Government and Agriculture* (1940), with Jane Greverus, *Economic Power and Political Pressures* (1941), and "Government under Pressure" (1942).

The methods by which control of power is sought are as varied as the groups which seek it. The role of the general public in the contest may to a large extent be ignored, since the public is generally too formless, to inchoate, to apply pressure at given points for a given purpose, and is

From "Economic Power and Political Pressures" (Temporary National Economic Committee Monograph No. 26), Washington: Government Printing Office, 1941, pp. 5–6, 16.

largely the passive instrument which both business and government use to strengthen their own arms. . . .

The expansion of government activity has been along the lines of providing social services favorable to many groups which would otherwise not be furnished at all, and of regulating economic activity in the public interest.

Business, on the other hand, has fought such regulation and the expansion of social services, and even more bitterly has fought the idea of government ownership. The fight occurs largely in the political arena, but it does not end with the election of Congressmen and Senators. Election is but one phase of the process. The selection of candidates, the drafting of platforms, the party caucus, all function largely in advance of the legislative process. Pressures on Congress while legislating and appropriating, manipulation of law enforcement and administration, and use of the judicial process to achieve individual or group ends, take place during or after the legislative process.

Through the press, public opinion, and pressure groups it is possible to influence the political process. While all three of these factors have played a part in the process since our beginnings as a nation, the extent and consciousness of their use has grown inordinately. They are employed by all contestants in the struggle for control, but reflect the viewpoint of business more accurately than that of others. . . .

Among the noteworthy characteristics of the struggle for power between government and business are—

1. The invisibility of most of the action.
2. The continuity of the struggle.
3. Its varying intensity.
4. Its constantly shifting battleground. . . .

In the contest for domination of public policy, four characteristics [of the participants] are [also] of primary importance. They are: length of life, cohesion, visibility, and resources. Length of life, or staying power, is vital because the contest is a continuing one, and an organization which continues to function over a long period of time gathers experience, techniques, and familiarity with the problems which are probably not shared by its opponents.

Cohesion in an organization makes for mutual support, which is invaluable under stress. The more an organization suffers from disunity, or internal dissension, the less is it able to direct its strength toward any particular goal, and the more easily its aims are defeated.

The extent to which the activities of a contestant, whether it is government or a pressure group, are invisible to the general public or to other groups often determines the outcome of a particular maneuver or a whole phase of the battle. A part of the struggle for power is carried on more or less openly, although even then it may be disguised, as propaganda frequently is. Congressional hearings provide another spotlight. The committee meetings in which policies are decided are not open to the public, however, a circumstance which fosters invisibility in political action.

In a conflict between economic and political forces it is inevitable that resources should play an important part. Propaganda is expensive, law suits are expensive, lobbies are expensive. The word "resources" should, of course, include more than money, as there have been occasions when money was of no avail against militant groups who worked with reforming zeal. The record indicates, however, that the side which spends the money usually wins the election.[1]

---

[1] See H. D. Anderson, *Popular Government in California*, Stanford University Press, 1941.

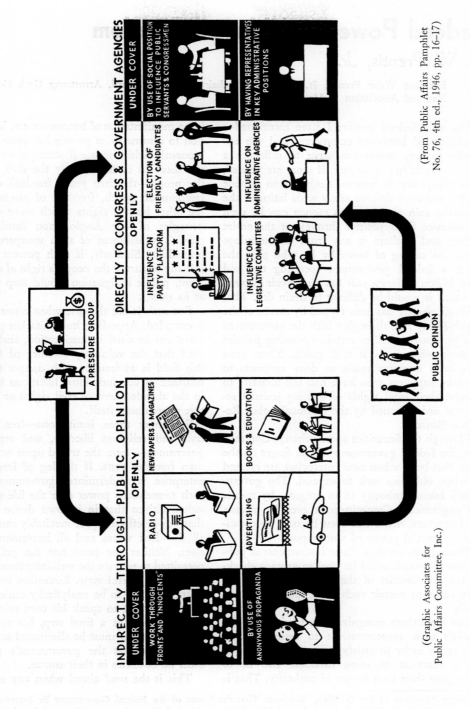

(From Public Affairs Pamphlet No. 76, 4th ed., 1946, pp. 16-17)

(Graphic Associates for Public Affairs Committee, Inc.)

Federal Power and Human Freedom

H. W. Prentis, Jr.

Henning Webb Prentis, Jr. (1884–   ), chairman of the board, Armstrong Cork Co. President, National Association of Manufacturers, 1940.

The only federal powers I have mentioned—regulation of interstate commerce, and the authority to levy taxes—can serve to influence a wide sector of man's activity. If more are needed, there are plenty in reserve. Authority to provide for the common defense offers wide latitude; the power to coin and regulate money can be used to influence fiscal policies throughout the entire nation; and if there is any truth in the adage about the calling of tunes by he who pays the piper, a federal government spending ten and more billion dollars a year has a reservoir of power which it would be difficult to drain dry. That reservoir already has been tapped by means of the Walsh-Healy Act, through which the government as a purchaser specifies certain operating policies of those who supply it with goods. There even have been attempts made to deny contracts to potential suppliers who have had the temerity to exercise their legal rights of seeking judicial review of orders issued by the National Labor Relations Board.

Through the Securities and Exchange Commission, the federal government has its finger on the pulse that beats when new enterprises are created or when old ones seek to expand. The government's latent authority to investigate, by means of Congressional Committees or even by income tax inspectors, needs not even be used to constitute a potential power of vast import.

These, then, are those "new instruments of public power" which could be used to provide shackles for the liberties of the people. How far we have come to permit such power to rest in any hands.

Our forefathers recognized the tendency of the people's own representatives to assume larger powers, in order to satisfy pressure groups or to use a short-cut to some desirable end or to strengthen their own tenure of authority. That is

but a manifestation of human nature. The temptation to assume these powers lies primarily in the economic field, because if attempts were made to use them to curtail directly the civil liberties of the people—the free press, freedom of religion, freedom of speech, freedom of assemblage, and the other human rights which were won by the struggles of our Anglo-Saxon forefathers—the public's punishment of such usurpers would be immediate. Similarly, if such powers were used initially to curtail the people's right of self-government, public indignation would stop the process at its outset.

But such is not the case when economic liberty is curtailed. Appealing humanitarian purposes always can be cited in justification, and yet I contend that the voluntary sacrifice of freedom in this field is as fraught with danger to the continuance of our individual liberty as it would be in the abandonment of civil rights or representative government itself.

For these three institutions—free enterprise, civil and religious liberties, and representative government—form the tripod upon which all human freedom rests. If the leg of free economic enterprise is undermined, government assumes such tremendous power over the life of the individual citizen that in its own desire to exercise that power effectively, it inevitably must suppress all dissident voices and all implements of criticism. Neither the press nor the pulpit can be permitted to restrain the well-intentioned activities of an all-powerful state. Education must not encourage people to be analytically critical. The individual's right to speak his own mind must be curtailed, and as a final step, his access to the ballot box either must be eliminated or made purposeless, so that the government's plans need meet no obstacles in their course.

This is the road ahead when any of our basic

Excerpt "Negative of the Question, 'Resolved: That the Power of the Federal Government Be Increased,' " Appendix C, pp. 30–33, in National Association of Manufacturers, *Limited Government and Personal Freedom*, New York, no date, pp. 31–33 quoted. Mr. Prentis's remarks were part of a radio debate November 22, 1940. Reprinted by permission.

liberties are sacrificed. It is not surprising that we will not sacrifice them deliberately. That is not our danger. From other countries we have learned that individual liberty almost always is extinguished by gradual consent of the people themselves, by their giving up one right after another until there has emerged a totalitarian state ruled by a dictator or a small group with authority equivalent to that of any ancient despotism.

It is no minor and incidental question that we are debating. It reaches to the heart of our heritage of freedom. Throughout human experience, where freedom has been partly won and then lost, it has been lost sometimes by sudden violence, but just as often by gradual surrender.

As a famous Englishman, John Stuart Mill, said a century ago, in words that have been echoed by many another philosopher and statesman in Europe and America:

"A people may prefer a free government, but if, from indolence, or carelessness, or cowardice, or want of public spirit, they are unequal to the exertions necessary for preserving it; if they will not fight for it when it is directly attacked; if they can be deluded by the artifices used to cheat them out of it, if by momentary discouragement, or temporary panic, or a fit of enthusiasm for an individual, they can be induced to lay their liberties at the feet even of a great man, or trust him with powers which enable him to subvert their institutions; in all these cases they are more or less unfit for liberty; and though it may be for their good to have had it even for a short time, they are unlikely long to enjoy it."

The Kansas City Version of Political Control
W. G. Clugston

W. G. Clugston (1889–   ), writer. Principal publications: *Animal Crackers* (play, 1925); *Rascals in Democracy* (1940); *Politics in Kansas* (play, 1944); *Facts You Should Know About Kansas* (1945); and *Eisenhower for President?* (1951).

The late T. J. (Tom) Pendergast is generally looked upon as the man who made Kansas City notorious for corrupt political bossism. It is true that Pendergast built up, under the Democratic label, an organization which enabled him to pose as the ironfisted dictator of all public affairs, until Franklin D. Roosevelt's Department of Justice sent him to the penitentiary for forgetting to pay income taxes on a big insurance graft. All police, city hall, and county officials had to bear the stamp of his approval. All franchise favors were dished out through him; all boodle from public improvements and all rake-offs from protected vice passed through his hands.

But, as Lincoln Steffens pointed out in *The Shame of the Cities,* no corrupt city boss ever held power for long without a behind-the-scenes alliance with the dominant business and financial leaders of the community. In the milieu in which it flourished, the Pendergast machine served well and faithfully the economic overlords who really own and rule Kansas City.

From earliest days, Kansas City aggressively sought to be a favorite trading center and "wildlife" playground of the big cattlemen, smalltown merchants, oil promoters, gamblers, and fundamentalist soul savers of the Southwest. The aggressive commercialists who ran the town wanted to make sure that none of these free-and-easy spenders would be lured to other cities when they left home on "business" trips. They wanted a wide-open town, with every form of vice and entertainment easily available. So these purse-minded businessmen and civic leaders had a two-fold incentive for permitting Pendergast to flourish and build up a powerful political machine. His organization protected them from costly and troublesome political upsets, and it provided them with a handy straw man to belabor when criticism of indecencies became noisy. Whenever reformers complained about existing evils and corruptions, Old Tom's gang was blamed. He was piously denounced as the entrenched agent of the Devil, who had an unbreakable stranglehold on the city.

Ostensibly, the *Star* opposed and fought the Pendergast machine. But the fact remains that

From "Kansas City: Gateway to What?" Chap. 12, pp. 256–276 in Robert S. Allen, ed., *Our Fair City,* New York: Vanguard Press, 1947, pp. 272–275 quoted. Reprinted by permission.

although that machine controlled all the tax agencies of the city, the records show that neither the newspaper nor its millionaire executives ever were soaked very hard by the tax collectors. And some of Tom's key henchmen were intimate cronies of the *Star's* top editors.

After Pendergast finally was convicted and imprisoned by the federal government, the business overlords let out loud huzzahs of self-righteous acclaim and proclaimed a new day. It was they who took over and began runnings things themselves. Under the leadership of the *Star* they organized a Citizens' Nonpartisan Committee as a cover device for their political rule, and Democrats and Republicans, who knew on which side their bread was buttered, climbed on perfumed bandwagons.

Voters were told that the prime objective of the new movement was the wiping out of all the old evils and corruptions. Most of the gambling dens were chased across the state line into Kansas City, Kansas, and other forms of vice were given to understand they would have to operate more discreetly. The old boasting about K. C. being a wide-open town became *verboten*.

Under the *Star's* tutelage a new boast was adopted, to the effect that Kansas City had become one of the most virtuous, law-abiding and God-fearing communities in the country. To provide some basis of fact for this hoopla, the new regime did suppress some of the most outrageous vices, grafts, and rake-offs, and many small homeowners were given long overdue tax adjustments. But behind this facade of sanctimonious respectability the Roberts-Kemper-Nichols * leadership forged on Kansas City the iron chains of a

---

* "The representatives of three Kansas families, all of whom got their start working with or under [William Rockhill] Nelson, joined forces after his death and achieved a domination of the city even more complete than his."—p. 272. Nelson was founder, long-time editor, and publisher of the *Star,* which with its morning edition is the only daily general newspaper in Kansas City.—*Eds.*

crushing and reprehensible business hegemony that is stifling every form of liberal thought and action.

There are few if any other great American centers of population where these tactics have been as successful as in Kansas City. With the most powerful radio station in the area and a complete monopoly of the press in their possession, the masters of the *Star* have been able to suppress virtually every independent movement and cause. Working hand in glove with the Kemper financial interests and cheek by jowl with the Nichols promotional schemes, the *Star* has been able to control and direct every form of civic activity from the Chamber of Commerce to the City Hall. No local movement can hope to succeed without its blessing and approval. Often, it has exercised this power far beyond local confines. In 1936, the *Star* and its bulky Roy Roberts saddled on the Republican Party Alf M. Landon as its candidate for President, and in 1944 they had a big hand in the sordid behind-the-scenes machinations that put Harry S. Truman on the Democratic ticket and thus in the White House.

Millions throughout the Missouri Valley have been led into such muddled, confused thinking by the *Star* that they have often been unable to see where their own best interests lie. The area's attitude toward establishment of a Missouri Valley Authority similar to T.V.A. is an outstanding example of this. Kansas City pays more for electricity than many other cities its size. It has been demonstrated that the people of Missouri and Kansas would save forty million dollars a year if they had a Missouri Valley Authority to serve them. But despite all this, Kansas City has been made the hotbed of opposition to a Missouri Valley Authority, with the *Star* never letting up crusading against it. And newspapers, public officials, and local businessmen throughout Kansas and Western Missouri have, with rare exceptions, been browbeaten, hoodwinked, and worse into echoing the *Star's* jeremiad in defense of the power trusts.

Poor Man's Justice
Webb Waldron

Webb Waldron (1882–1945), magazine editor and writer. Chief works: *The Road to the World* (1922); *We Explore the Great Lakes* (1923); *Shanklin* (1925); *Blue Glamour* (1929); *Fortunate Isle* (1934); *Uncharted* (1936); with Paul Starrett, *Changing the Skyline* (1938); and *Americans* (1941).

A legal aid society is the bargain basement of its profession. Its doors are always open to clients unable to pay for a lawyer. This has been true for two thirds of a century in the case of the New York Society, the oldest in the network of such organizations which now span the continent. Last year the New York Legal Aid Society represented more than 32,000 persons in cases ranging from an 80-cent wage claim to criminal actions for grand larceny and manslaughter. Yet the fee asked of all clients was the same: "Fifty cents—and if you can't afford that, we'll take your case anyway."

In sixty-six years the Society has given legal aid to a million and a quarter persons—all sorts of people with all sorts of woes. A boy from Kansas, starving and friendless, wounded when he attempted suicide and then cast into the Tombs for having concealed weapons. . . . A low-paid worker caught between a landlord threatening eviction and an installment selling firm threatening criminal prosecution if he moves his cheap furniture. . . . A woman seeking her freedom from a man incurably insane. . . . And today, as twenty-five years ago, soldiers and sailors caught in some sort of jam.

They come in a steady stream to the Society's offices. The 50-cent retainer fees hardly pay the telephone bill. Most of the financial support comes from the lawyers of New York—their practical way of serving the law's ideal of an even break for every human being, regardless of his station in life.

The New York Society, not only the oldest but the largest of 134 legal aid societies in the United States, has twenty-two full time salaried attorneys on its staff. Many prominent lawyers annually volunteer to try, free, several criminal cases. Junior attorneys from the city's finest firms work one month a year as voluntary defenders, their salaries paid by their employers. All maintain the highest professional standards and the utmost thoroughness in preparing cases.

Well Worth the Effort. Legal Aid Society lawyers have a sympathetic understanding of the troubles of ordinary people. A navy man is married to a girl who had a child by another man. He wants to adopt the little boy and give him his name. Someone has told him that the Society can help. A staff lawyer helps the anxious couple to put through the adoption. In the process he manages to make the man feel that he is doing a swell thing, and sends him away in a glow of good feeling. "This kind of work gives us special pleasure," says the attorney. "We're helping to build something—a family, a secure future for a child."

Marie, aged twenty, comes to the Society in distress and fright. She has been fired from her job in a war plant because she cannot prove her citizenship. Her father brought her to America when she was a baby, but disappeared when she was in her teens. Since then she has been on her own. Is she a citizen or not? Her livelihood is at stake. A Legal Aid Society attorney tracks down Marie's father, finds that he became a citizen when Marie was thirteen, which automatically made her a citizen, too. So the Society promptly gets her a certificate of derivative citizenship; thankfully Marie goes back to her job.

Investigation shows that in the United States more than half of all claims under $100 are abandoned because the claimant fears a lawyer's fee would eat up the whole sum. Last year the Society collected $58,318.23 for its clients. Broken down into items of a few dollars each for thousands of poor people, this becomes a significant symbol of justice confirmed.

No case is too trivial for the Legal Aid Society. Susie, a domestic, worked five days and should have been paid $5.80. Instead she received only

From *Survey Graphic*, 31 (1942): 590–591. Reprinted by permission.

$5. The Society wrote several letters to the employer and finally got the 80 cents. Naturally Susie was not asked to pay even the 50-cent retainer fee.

Many more Legal Aid Society cases are settled over the phone or by letter than before a judge. The ability and disinterestedness of the attorneys are so well known that defendants often prefer to settle rather than fight them in court.

Tom, a dishwasher, was bilked of $1.25—a day's pay. A phone call to the employer got the money and a few days later Tom sent in his 50-cent fee with a letter of thanks. "We didn't want to take it," says Louis Fabricant, Legal Aid Society attorney-in-chief, "but he didn't give us his return address. Yet realizing that he felt impelled to send it was a rich reward for us all."

Recently the Society received a touching appeal from a thirteen-year-old girl who was being graduated from grammar school. Her parents were on relief—a fact she had managed to conceal from her classmates—and they could not afford to buy her a white dress for graduation. The girl knew that in the city treasury to be held until she became of age was a little money awarded her years before as damages in an accident case. She wrote to the Society, asking what could be done.

At the suggestion of a Legal Aid Society Lawyer with a daughter of his own, the Surrogate's Court gravely decided that the purchase of a white dress, shoes, slip and hair-bow was an eminently justifiable demand on the funds in the treasury of the City of New York. A good deal of trouble to save a girl's pride, perhaps, but the Society felt it was well worth the effort.

No Personal Axe to Grind. In taking care not to accept clients who really can afford a lawyer, a rather flexible dividing line is employed. This line is a weekly income of $25 for a single person, or $40 for a family. Men in uniform, free service always. Registration cards of applicants usually read: Property—none; Wages—$10, $15, $18 a week; Rent—$12, $15, $20 a month. Sometimes the Society is imposed on by people who falsify this information, but the occasions are rare.

Lately the Legal Aid Society has been of immense help to men in the armed forces. Under the terms of the Soldiers' and Sailors' Civil Relief Act of 1940, the man in uniform was endlessly harassed by landlords, merchants and loan companies unless his debts dated from before October 17, 1940. A new amendment to the act—drawn up in part by the Society's lawyers—now gives the service man a moratorium on debts incurred right up to the date of induction. But there still are many technical steps through which soldiers and sailors need guidance.

A Legal Aid Society attorney never promotes a trial when there is no convincing defense. Instead, in criminal cases, he does his best to get a confession; by throwing himself on the mercy of the court the defendant almost always gets a much lighter sentence than if he had been tried and found guilty. "And furthermore," says Edward R. Tighe, head of the Society's criminal branch, "confession is the first step toward rectitude. All sorts of helping hands stretch out to the man who admits his guilt."

There have been numerous cases of convicted innocent men freed through the efforts of the Society. Recently a man, accused of swindling a Johns Hopkins professor, swore that he had been staying in a Detroit rooming house on the day of the crime. The Society attorney got photostatic copies of the rooming house register showing the defendant's signature, yet the jury chose to believe the professor's testimony and found the accused man guilty. The judge and district attorney in the case were so impressed by the Society's defense, however, that each sent a detective to Detroit to investigate further. Both came back with affidavits that the man actually had been seen at the rooming house on the date in question. The verdict was set aside.

Courts treat Legal Aid lawyers with special respect. They know that these men have no personal axe to grind, that their sole interest is in defending the legitimate rights of their clients.

Nationwide Legal Aid. The Society's fight for equal justice runs back to 1876, when a handful of public-spirited German-American citizens banded together to provide free legal advice for immigrant fellow-countrymen who often were cheated or jailed through their ignorance of our language and laws. Soon this group made its facilities available to all poor people. Carl Schurz, Elihu Root, and Theodore Roosevelt were among the early directors of what, in 1896, became the present Society. Its growing success spread the idea nationwide.

The 133 similar legal aid organizations throughout the United States last year handled 295,251 cases and collected $611,844 for their clients. These far-flung units frequently cooperate. A few years ago a man in Utah was killed crossing railroad tracks outside the plant where he worked. The Utah Industrial Commission awarded his widow damages, but the company appealed to the state Supreme Court. The Salt Lake City Legal Aid Society won the case for the widow. The company then appealed to the U. S. Supreme Court. The Salt Lake City group wired a lawyer in the Boston Legal Aid Society who was especially skilled in workmen's compensation cases. He went to Washington, found the papers from Utah waiting for him, worked night and day for three days preparing his case, then presented it before the Supreme Court. The Court sustained the widow's claim.

The New York Society is constantly striving to *prevent* evils by campaigning for new and better laws. The Small Claims Court, first established in New York in 1934 and widely copied since then, was sponsored by the Legal Aid Society. The New York State installment legislation of 1942,

eliminating weasel-worded small-print clauses in selling contracts, was another clearcut victory for the Society, which enlisted the cooperation of the leading installment merchants. The Society has also been behind various laws against loan sharks.

Legal Aid Society lawyers keep urging their clients: "Consult us before you borrow money, sign papers, or take any other legal step. Our advice is free and it may save you trouble later."

The Legal Aid Society is the only law office in New York where business never falls off. The slack summer months of the ordinary barrister's office are unknown, for the Society's twenty-two lawyers are busier than ever handling the flow of about 150 new applicants every day. For these little men with big problems, the Legal Aid Society is turning "Equal Justice for All" from a copybook phrase into reality.

What About Communism?
Arthur M. Schlesinger, Jr.

Arthur M. Schlesinger, Jr. (1917–   ), associate professor of history, Harvard University. Principal works: *The Vital Center* (1949) and, with R. H. Rovere, *The General and the President* (1951).

The existence of a group like the American Communists poses difficult questions to a free society. The American people have been debating these questions for years, in many cases without reaching settled conclusions. Such complex problems cannot be solved here. But, in order to aid the reader in formulating his own answers, a number of considerations are set forth in the following pages, which should be borne in mind in any discussion of the problems of Communism and free society.

The word "Communist" has a specific meaning. It means a member of the Communist party. The word "fellow traveler" also has a specific meaning. It means a man who, without being an actual party member, follows the party line faithfully, especially on questions of foreign policy. In responsible discussion these words should be used in these senses, and no other. But the problem is rendered more difficult by the fact that many conservatives are less interested in identifying genu-

ine Communists than in smearing liberals as Communists, and by the additional fact that many Communists and fellow travelers do their best to conceal their political affiliations. The question then arises: is there any way in which Communists and fellow travelers who pose as ordinary liberals can be fairly reliably detected?

Some people say that all radicals or dissenters are actual or potential Communists or fellow travelers. If a person denounces the capitalist system or race discrimination or the repression of civil liberties, these people argue, he is "practically" a Communist.

Others argue, however, that to use Communism so loosely is to make the word meaningless. Many radicals, they point out, are as profoundly anti-Communist as are conservatives. Socialists, for example, oppose the capitalist system, and political repression; yet they believe in democracy, civil freedom and constitutional processes; and they are deeply hostile to the Communists. In

From "What About Communism?" 5th ed., Public Affairs Pamphlet No. 164, 1954, pp. 23–24, 25–32.

Europe today the Socialists are a fundamental part of the anti-Communist coalition. It is in the countries where the Socialists are strongest—Britain, Norway, Sweden, Denmark, Belgium, Austria—that the Communists are weakest.

How, then, to identify the Communist? The point to remember, this second group argues, is that Communists are not to be defined primarily by their attitude toward capitalism; since many people criticize capitalism who detest Communism. Orthodox Communists are to be defined primarily by their *attitude toward capitalism plus their attitude toward the U.S.S.R.*—by the consistent shifts of their political line in obedience to the policy of the Soviet Union. Fellow travelers are similarly to be defined by their acceptance of the thesis of Soviet infallibility in foreign affairs.

If you find a man who believed strongly in collective security until August 1939, who then became an isolationist until June 1941, who then demanded a second front, and who now opposes the Marshall Plan and the North Atlantic Pact, inveighs against Tito and supports the Progressive Party—if he meets not just one but all of these tests—then it is fairly safe to assume that you have found at least a reliable fellow traveler. . . .

In the recent court trial the leaders of the Communist Party contended that it was a peaceful and constitutional party, dedicated to non-violent change. The government contended that the leaders of the party taught and advocated the methods of violent revolution. The jury decided in favor of the government. The case has been appealed and will not be settled finally until the Supreme Court passes upon the constitutionality of the Smith Act under which the Communist leaders were indicted.

Other commentators have taken a position midway between that of the Communists and of the Department of Justice. They argue that the attitude of the Communist leaders toward violence has been entirely opportunistic. The American Communists have advocated violent revolution, they claim, when the Soviet Union was ordering a policy of revolutionary extremism, and they have stopped advocating violent revolution when the Soviet Union called for a united front policy. While the Communists certainly have no objection in principle to the overthrow of governments by force, this does not necessarily mean that revolution is their specific policy at any given moment. These commentators make one other point:

there is a profound difference from the viewpoint of law between an abstract belief in the inevitability, or even the desirability, of revolution, on the one hand, and concrete conspiratorial preparations for a revolutionary coup on the other. Thus Thomas Jefferson could speak of the usefulness of periodic revolution. Abraham Lincoln wrote, "This country with its institutions belongs to the people who inhabit it. Whenever they shall grow weary of the existing government, they can exercise their constitutional right of amending it, or their revolutionary right to dismember or overthrow it." John Dulles declared in 1949, "I don't believe that we need to have a violent revolution certainly not today. The people still have it in their power peacefully to check this thing, (statism) but if we don't do it and do it soon we will have to fight our way back, as Thomas Jefferson said, through revolution."

Such statements as these, whether uttered by conservatives or by Communists, are quite different from the storing of arms, the secret drills, the clandestine preparations for military action. "The wide difference between advocacy and incitement, between preparation and attempt, between assembling and conspiracy, must be borne in mind," Justice Brandeis has written. In general, American law has sought to stop, not *unpopular thoughts,* but *illegal acts.*

In order to avoid registration as foreign agents under the Voorhis Act, the American Communist Party disaffiliated itself in 1940 from the Comintern. The Communists claim today that they are serving the best interests of the American working class; and that the best way of serving working class interest anywhere is to protect and advance the cause of the Soviet Union. The American Communists are no more bound to the decisions of Moscow, they contend, than American Roman Catholics are to the decisions of Rome.

Others, assert, however, that the Communist leaders in this country have acted effectively as agents of the Soviet Union from the day the first Comintern representative disembarked in New York, and that the relationship of blind obedience to every new phase of Soviet policy was not altered in the slightest by the formal act of disaffiliation from the Comintern in 1940, nor by the dissolution of the Comintern itself in 1943. On this basis, some people argue that the leaders of the party, at least, should be required to register under the Voorhis Act. The case of the Communists and Moscow is distinguished from that of the Catholics and Rome by pointing out that Catholic discipline is much less taut and all-embracing than Communist discipline. A Catholic, as a citizen, must make decisions of living based on conscience and free will. Only under very grave circumstances is he excommunicated. Thus Catholics could write to Cardinal Spellman criticizing his attacks on Mrs. Roosevelt without fear of penalty, whereas Communists who had dissented from the party leadership in such a manner would be expelled.

It is not clear, however, that all ordinary Communists are to be considered as agents of foreign governments. "When we speak of the Communist party as a conspiracy directed by Moscow," ex-Communist Louis Budenz recently said, "we cannot realistically accuse every individual rank-and-file Communist of being consciously in that conspiracy." Many were attracted by Communist cries against social injustice, only to discover that they were involved in defending even greater injustices. "This belated realization," says Budenz, "is the reason why there are thousands of ex-Communists in America today, and why the turnover in Red Membership is so high."

The Communist themselves, and some non-Communist Americans, are bitterly critical of "red-baiting"—that is, attacks on Communists and the identification and exposure of Communist or pro-Communist activity. To attack Communism in any way, it is said, is to weaken the cause of liberalism and to play into the hands of the fascists.

Other Americans, however, inquire with skepticism why the Communists should be granted an immunity from criticism which the Communists would concede to no other group in society. Republican-baiting, Democrat-baiting, Catholic-baiting and so on seem to be fine from the Communist viewpoint; so why should an exception be made for Communist-baiting? The attempt to forestall anti-Communist activity, then, is held to be a strategy of defense rather than the application of any general principle. Moreover, agreement to this strategy, it is pointed out, means agreement to the general proposition that America is doomed to the choice between Communism and fascism, and that therefore to hurt one is to help the other. America is not condemned to so bleak a choice, these people argue; the proper American liberal position is to offer rigorous opposition to both Communism and fascism.

The problem is very different, however, when non-Communist liberals are denounced as Communists by individuals opposed to all non-conformist or unpopular views. A democracy deals with Communism by responsible debate and factual exposure. The method of the witch-hunt, with its reckless denunciations and unsubstantiated accusations, is generally adopted by those less interested in preserving a free society against Communism than in silencing all persons who disagree with them at whatever cost to freedom. These methods, especially when employed from the ambush of congressional immunity, are sometimes almost as dangerous to democracy as the methods of the Communists themselves.

Some people argue that the Communists have forfeited all claim to democratic treatment in this country, and that the interests of national security and of the preservation of freedom require that the Communist Party be outlawed.

Other equally patriotic Americans, including [Ex-]President Truman, [Ex-]Governor Thomas E. Dewey and FBI Director J. Edgar Hoover, have opposed this proposal. They have opposed it in part because such action, short of a situation of genuine national emergency, would be contrary to the American tradition of civil freedom. They have opposed it in part also on practical grounds. When the Communist Party of Canada was outlawed, its leaders, after a due interval, set up a new party, called it the "Labor Progressive Party" and set it to doing business at the same old stand. The opponents of the illegalization of the Communist Party argue that such action has little effect unless accompanied by an arrest of the party's leaders and active members. Otherwise all that is outlawed is a name; and, at the same time, the Communists are provided with an issue tailor made to win them the sympathy of many Americans who see no national emergency justifying so sharp a contraction of political freedom.

Some argue that it is foolish to grant the Communists full freedom of action, when their only object is to use freedom in order to destroy it. Wherever they have achieved power, it is pointed out, they have swiftly crushed out the right of political opposition. Why should we guarantee them the rights which they concede to no one else? Why should we give them the slightest opportunity to gain power in the U. S. and destroy freedoms for the rest of us? Thus many who do not advocate the open illegalization of the Communist Party feel that Communist activity should be weighted down by various legal disabilities, as provided in the McCarran Act, so as to preserve the general freedom of society.

The opponents of such proposals reply that our whole traditional conception of free society is based on a belief in the free competition of ideas. This does not mean, it is argued, just competition among the ideas we happen to like. Such a procedure would give the "we" group—i.e., whatever group happens to have power at a given moment —altogether too much control over the mind of the country. Hence basic to the conception of free society is what might be called the right to hold loathsome ideas. As Justice Oliver Wendell Holmes once said, "We should be eternally vigilant against attempts to check the expression of opinions that we loathe and believe to be fraught with death, unless they so imminently threaten immediate interference with the lawful and pressing purposes of the law that an immediate check is required to save the country."

The question to be faced, this group argues, is: in view of the Korean crisis is the present danger to our country from the Communist Party great enough to outweigh the dangers involved in the departure from our traditional principles of civil freedom? Do its ideas "so imminently threaten immediate interference with the lawful and pressing purposes of the law that an immediate check is required to save the country"?

This test, as established by the Supreme Court, is known as the "clear and present danger" test. This phrase means that free speech can properly be suppressed only when it creates a clear and present danger, not just of changing some one's mind, but of bringing about "substantive evils" which the government may constitutionally seek to prevent. "It is only the present danger of immediate evil or an intent to bring it about," wrote Justice Holmes, "that warrants Congress in setting a limit to the expression of opinion." "If there be time to expose through discussion the falsehoods and fallacies," added Justice Brandeis, "to avert the evil by the processes of education, the remedy to be applied is more speech, not enforced silence. Only an emergency can justify repression."

Does this mean that we are helpless before a conspiracy? Of course not, this group argues. Those who commit acts in violation of law must be swiftly punished. But having an ugly idea is not an act in violation of law. And trying to suppress that idea is really a vote of no-confidence in the strength of one's own democratic ideas. Does

the present emergency, they ask, justify embarking on a national program of repression?

Some people argue that, so long as membership in the Communist Party is legal, Communists should be allowed to work for the government like any other citizens. Even if it might not always be wise to employ Communists, they add, the policy of ferreting them out through investigation does far more harm than the presence of a few Communists would do. Loyalty investigations, they say, turn quickly into witch hunts which drive able men out of government and place a premium on timidity and mediocrity.

But others contend that on the contrary, the right to work for the government is not one of the necessary rights of citizenship. "The petitioner may have a constitutional right to talk politics," observed Justice Holmes in deciding the case of a policeman who had lost his job for political reasons, "but he has no constitutional right to be a policeman." And clearly, the first condition of government employment is loyalty. As Roger Baldwin, former head of the American Civil Liberties Union, has put it, "A superior loyalty to a foreign government disqualifies a citizen for service to ours."

It is conceded that difficult problems arise with the application of this principle. Determinations of disloyalty are hard to make. Most people would agree that the witch-hunt approach to questions of loyalty in the government service can only result in injury to innocent people, confusion and demoralization. Most of these evils could be avoided if loyalty investigations were limited to jobs genuinely related to the national security, and if the individual against whom the charges are made were granted the full and customary protections of Anglo-Saxon justice. In this way the essential goals of civil freedom and national security could both be safeguarded.

Those who would exclude Communists as teachers in institutions of higher learning argue that a university is a community of scholars dedicated to free and disinterested inquiry; that intellectual integrity is incompatible with undeclared or unknown loyalties; and that Communists by definition are thus disqualified from membership in an intellectual community. They argue further that it has always been a prime Communist objective to gain influence over the youth of the country.

Those who oppose the policy of exclusion argue that the benefits which a university might derive from expelling Communists would be less than the disadvantages entailed by setting in motion the whole appalling machinery of investigation, detection and trial. They point out that it is possible for teachers to be Communists without indoctrinating their students with Communism. Where the "clear and present danger" test might justify loyalty checks in government, these persons say, it does not justify them in the colleges. The small number of pro-Communist teachers in the colleges, it is said, have had no kind of impact sufficient to provoke such drastic countermeasures; nor do they present any specific danger to national security.

Some people draw a distinction between colleges and pre-college education. In college the student is relatively mature; he is exposed to several different teachers; he can benefit by the crosscurrents of opinion. In lower schools, however, the student is less mature and often is exposed to only a single teacher. In such circumstances, some people feel, measures should be taken particularly in the public schools, to insure that the immature student not be influenced by anti-Catholic, antisemitic or pro-Communist teachers. Others continue to feel, however, that even in the lower schools the disadvantages of the machinery of detection outweigh the advantages gained in ridding the schools of a few harmful individuals.

Some feel that Communism can only be met in the last resort by police measure directed to the detention of Communist leaders, the break-up of the party and the suppression of their means of propaganda and political action.

Others feel that this approach treats symptoms, not causes. The symptoms must certainly be treated, particularly if they threaten to infect all of society; but this is not enough. The basic appeal of Communism, they feel, comes from the existence of poverty and injustice and from the frustration, drabness and insecurity of life for many people in our society. In the long run, they argue, we can defeat Communism in our midst only by removing the internal sources of its appeal. This means constructing a society of our own in which people will feel free, secure and strong—a society capable, moreover, of protecting itself against the external threat of aggression. Only by giving all those who dwell in our society a vigorous sense of belonging to it—of vital membership in it—can we finally destroy the roots of Communist power.

Loyalty, Security, and the "Tolerant Center"
Harlan Cleveland

Harlan Cleveland (1918–   ), executive editor, *The Reporter*.

I was visited the other day by a young man just home from fighting in Korea, who is looking for a job. He has college behind him, and two years in the Marines besides. His question was simple: "I've been offered a job in Washington," he said. "Should I take it?"

I thought back to the time when I had left school, when coming down to Washington seemed the obvious thing to do. I didn't remember having asked anybody that question in just that way. So I said, "Sure. Why not?" But I wasn't going to get off that easily.

"What about this security thing?" he asked. It took me an hour to reply, and I wrestled with my conscience every step of the way.

First of all, I said, it will take you anywhere from three to six months to get cleared. But that's the least of your worries.

Second, you'll find you never are really cleared. At any moment you may become a "controversial" character. This can happen without your doing or saying anything you regard as controversial, since there is no way to guarantee that informers against you have a responsible regard for the truth. Since you will not be told what the nameless accuser has said, you will find it practically impossible to refute it, or even to find out whom you should refute it to.

If anybody ever does drop anything "derogatory" into your file, there's no way to get it out.

From "Loyalty, Security, and the 'Tolerant Center,'" an address by Harlan Cleveland at the Sixth National Conference on Civil Liberties of National Civil Liberties Clearing House, Washington, D. C., March 19, 1954, as printed in *The Reporter*.

You can try burying it under a mountain of contrary testimony, but that's dangerous too; people have been fired for having a "voluminous security file" even after they had been cleared.

Third, suppose you do get into what is called, in whispers, "security trouble." You can hardly expect your boss to support you, with three Congressional committees ready to accuse him of coddling you if he does. Moreover, you'll find that the system set up to adjudicate your case is not judicial. Scott McLeod has explained it very honestly, this way: "Our Anglo-Saxon judicial system goes back through the centuries, and common law has been developed all through that time. The integrity-security system goes back to April of '47, and we've had very little experience with it. . . . We are not trying to punish him for some act he has committed in the past. . . . We are trying to protect the Government from what may occur in the future. Since you can't prove future behavior—future acts are not susceptible to present proof—there is no proof in this system. It's not a judicial system."

Pursuant to this principle, you can be declared ineligible for Government employment on the basis of (these are Vice-President Nixon's words) files showing that they contain "information indicating subversive activities or associations" or "information indicating untrustworthiness, drunkenness, mental instability or possible exposure to blackmail." Don't ask, "What information?" Don't ask, "In whose opinion does the information indicate these things?" Such questions are taboo.

Fourth, you'll find its even dangerous to resign. Some politician, or a security officer with a yen to get into politics, may claim later that you were fired as a traitor, a pervert, a drunk, or a blabbermouth—he doesn't know which, but it doesn't matter, because the American people don't want any of those kinds of security risks in their Government. If you look for a job outside the Government, your new employer will wonder whether you're a security risk, and it will be up to you to prove you're not. A friend of mine, returning recently from an overseas assignment, told me proudly last week that he had been careful to build up a large file of documentary proof that he had really resigned!

Fifth, if you are unfortunate enough to have to write down your views about policy, you will have to learn to be a master of ambiguity. You will stay away from predictions and judgments about matters on which you can be proved wrong by events. You will also avoid predicting an unpleasant event that *does* come true, lest you be held responsible.

Sixth, if you raise any question about these matters, you'll be told it's a privilege and not a right to work for the Government. But if you leave the Government, you'll find that most private companies and most universities and foundations have some sort of security system too, especially if they have dealings with the Government or are seeking business that is ultimately financed, one way or another, by the Government.

My young friend stopped me. "Does that mean," he asked, "that it's a privilege and not a right to work *anywhere?*" Maybe there's a good answer to that one, but I didn't think of it then and I haven't thought of it yet. Instead I went on.

If, finally, you manage to remain non-controversial with respect to your actions, and to look sufficiently harmless with respect to your future behavior, you may rise to the top of the civil service. But if the precedent set by this Administration is any guide to its successors, you will have to leave the Government just when you have had enough experience to be really useful in a policy making position—because a new Administration will come in and it can't afford to have a "holdover" carry its appropriation request up to Capitol Hill.

You can avoid most of these dangers only in one way: by deciding from the outset that your job is political, and getting in solid with the right Senators and Congressmen. You may thereby help to break down the internal discipline of the Executive Branch, and to eat away the principle of the separation of powers. But there's safety in it for you—if not for the nation.

So ended the lesson to my young Korean veteran. Should I, in all honesty, have said less? And if the balance of joys and sorrows in the Federal service has changed so much in fifteen years, what poison is it that has infected us so?

Is the trouble Communism, or McCarthyism, or what? The front pages are so preoccupied these days with the Senator and his curious associates that we are tempted to lay at his door all the folly and unreason of our time, and to blame him besides for the deep uncertainties that sit in our own souls. He and others less flamboyant are certainly transmission belts for more than their share of confusion. But he is a latecomer. The Communists have been planting fear and suspicion and bitter controversy among us for a couple of decades, and even they didn't start it.

As far as our generation is concerned, the story can be said to begin with those two massive events of the 1930s: the Great Depression, and our collective discovery that we, the last great isolationists, were thoroughly part of the world, and for good. These events seem to have caused the profound uncertainties among us. People came to feel that they were being kicked around by forces beyond their control, that our supposedly sovereign national state was suddenly unable to cope with the big decisions: boom or slump, peace or war. Somehow our history hadn't prepared us for the blind irrationality of events, for the feeling that we had been sucked into some gigantic game of roulette, with our own destiny as the stake.

In Europe a search had already begun for short cuts to some foolproof system that would make the affairs of men comfortably predictable again. Two kinds of short cuts emerged: the Communist kind and the Fascist kind. One rested its doctrine on absolute, universal laws of history; the other sought its absolute in the frame of the national state. Both swept away the sovereignty of the individual, and replaced it with the sovereignty of a governmental apparatus.

In the midst of our confusion, it was the Communists who first set out to gain power at any cost.

Lenin had said: "We must be ready to employ trickery, deceit, lawbreaking, withholding and concealing truth."

Lenin had said: "We can and must write . . . in a language which sows among the masses hate, revulsion, scorn and the like toward those of differing opinions."

Lenin had said: "We must train men and women who will devote to the revolution, not merely their spare evenings, but the whole of their lives."

So the Communists—starting something that was new and different in our free society—adopted a strategy of two-faced lives, of deception and fraud and double-dealing. They set out to dissolve the "stickum" that holds us together, to boil away the glue of mutual trust that lies at the core of our morale as a nation.

Many Americans believed, at first, that the Communists were moving toward the same goals of social progress and human freedom as the rest of us, only they were disagreeably rough in the way they went about it. They were supposed to be the express subway, while we preferred to take a local. The catchword of those days has a familiar ring: "I agree with what they're trying to do, but I disapprove of their methods."

But, especially since the war, we have had a closer look at what was involved in their short cut. People we knew, or thought we knew, turned out to have secret lives, hidden loyalties, a double standard of truth. Some of these held Government positions, and refused to testify about charges that their conduct was treasonable, that the Kremlin was a higher loyalty than their patriotism as Americans. A few were convicted in court of offenses connected one way or another with their secret lives.

As the story came to light, we reacted with healthy violence against the people who had deceived us—and against some bystanders, too, who got involved by accident or naíveté.

Knowing what we now know about the Communist attack, all of us would agree, I'm sure, that a practicing Communist has no business in the Government of the United States. You probably wouldn't hire a Communist in your organization. And yet the investigations designed to expose the Communists in our midst, and the procedures created to keep them out of Government, have us all disturbed.

Why?

Is it because "we agree with what they're trying to do, but we disapprove of their methods?" Many sensible people would say that if certain forms we've learned to respect are followed, if the accused can confront their accusers, if the presumption of innocence is maintained, if witnesses are not bullied, if, in short, American fair play prevails, then everything will be all right.

Certainly these historic principles are important. And certainly, too, if these are the tests, the investigating committees and the Federal loyalty program, whether under President Truman or under President Eisenhower, should get pretty low marks. The kinds of Anglo-Saxon procedures that we are used to, that we are proud of, have been flouted and trampled on in the competitive rush to find and expose the next Alger Hiss.

Many of us are busy proposing better rules of procedure for Congress, and a few hardy souls have even tackled the much more difficult problem of rules for the Executive Branch. I'm sure that better procedures are important, and during the discussion period I should like to put in my two cents' worth on that subject. But first I'd like to

THE WITCH-FINDER GENERAL

(As an introduction to his address, Mr. Cleveland read an excerpt from Extraordinary Popular Delusions and the Madness of Crowds, by Charles Mackay, a book published in 1841.)

Among the ill-weeds which flourished amid the long dissensions of the [English] civil war, Matthew Hopkins, the witch-finder, stands eminent in his sphere. This vulgar fellow resided, in the year 1644, at the town of Manningtree, in Essex, and made himself very conspicuous in discovering the devil's marks upon several unhappy witches. . . . In the course of a very short time, whenever a witch was spoken of in Essex, Matthew Hopkins was sure to be present, aiding the judges with his knowledge of "such cattle," as he called them. As his reputation increased, he assumed the title of "Witch-finder General," and travelled through the counties of Norfolk, Essex, Huntingdon, and Sussex for the sole purpose of finding out witches. In one year he brought sixty poor creatures to the stake. The test he commonly adopted was that of swimming, so highly recommended by King James in his *Demonologie*. The hands and feet of the suspected persons were tied together crosswise, the thumb of the right hand to the toe of the left foot, and *vice versa*. They were then wrapped up in a large sheet or blanket, and laid upon their backs in a pond or river. If they sank, their friends and relatives had the poor consolation of knowing they were innocent; but there was an end of them: if they floated, which, when laid carefully on the water, was generally the case, there was also an end of them; for they were deemed guilty of witchcraft and burned accordingly.

Another test was to make them repeat the Lord's prayer and creed. It was affirmed that no witch could do so correctly. If she missed a word, or even pronounced one incoherently, which in her trepidation . . . was most probable . . . she was accounted guilty. . . .

Hopkins used to travel through his counties like a man of consideration, attended by his two assistants, always putting up at the chief inn of the place, and always at the cost of the authorities. For about three years he carried on this infamous trade, success making him so insolent and rapacious that high and low became his enemies. The Rev. Mr. Gaul, a clergyman of Houghton, in Huntingdonshire, wrote a pamphlet impugning his pretensions, and accusing him of being a common nuisance. . . .

It is consoling to think that this impostor perished in his own snare. Mr. Gaul's exposure and his own rapacity weakened his influence among the magistrates; and the populace, who began to find that not even the most virtuous and innocent were secure from his persecution, looked upon him with undisguised aversion. He was beset by a mob at a village in Suffolk, and accused of being himself a wizard. An old reproach was brought against him, that he had, by means of sorcery, cheated the devil out of a certain memorandum-book, in which he, Satan, had entered the names of all the witches in England. . . . In vain he denied his guilt. The populace longed to put him to his own test. He was speedily stripped, and his thumbs and toes tied together. He was then placed in a blanket, and cast into a pond. Some say that he floated, and that he was taken out, tried, and executed upon no other proof of his guilt. Others assert that he was drowned. This much is positive, that there was an end of him.

---

suggest that no legal or procedural discussion goes to the root of the matter.

What really has us worried is this: We sense that some of the men who make the loudest noises against the Communist short cut really believe, not in the democratic system the Communist are out to destroy, but in that other short cut—absolute certainty through authoritarian national government.

This is, in fact, the only reasonable way to explain why Senator McCarthy, and his friends and imitators in Congress and the Executive Branch, are so willing to help the Communists dissolve the "stickum" of mutual trust that holds us together, and undermine the individual rights that stand in the way of absolute power for anybody.

In a relay race, the first man doesn't need to cross the finish line himself; he need only pass the baton to another man who starts running in the same direction. If McCarthy is willing to run with the baton of deceit and suspicion and mutual distrust, he is either an unwitting dupe or a conscious ally of his alleged adversaries. And, as he is fond of implying, does it matter which?

We are used to thinking of these two short cuts as two extreme and opposite ends of the political spectrum. This way of thinking is now out of date. The Communists, at least, are quite aware that the two extremes can accomplish more if they work together—or, to put it another way, the Communists have a scheme for making fellow travelers out of the most violent anti-Communist.

If this idea sounds fanciful to you, try this exeriment. Try, for a disagreeable moment, to imagine the point of view of a Communist conspirator in America in March, 1954.

He has, to begin with, a continuing assignment to sow confusion, fear, and mutual suspicion. But even though that effort hasn't been going badly from the Communist point of view, it isn't enough by itself to enable a very small and unpopular group of men to neutralize America's giant strength while the Soviet Union rakes in a few more satellites in Europe and Asia. The next step is political action, designed to polarize all major political views into two widely divergent groups, shouting vituperation at each other and paralyzing the action of Government.

He *wants* a ruthless anti-Communist crusade, the more overzealous the better. He *wants* the crusaders to say, "There are only two choices—the Communists or us."

The fact is that the Communists and their Russian bosses are not afraid of other extremists. They are at home on the barricades of pitched battle between extremes. What worries them is the political Center—the masses of people who don't easily get worked up, who prefer the alternation of two moderate parties to a choice between two breathless and immoderate contenders for their absolute loyalty.

The Communists know that their chance for power can come only by eroding the tolerant Center. They know the center can be eroded from the "Right" as well as from the "Left." So they have a double task ahead: first, to strengthen the most extreme forms of McCarthyism, and second, to join and try to assume leadership of those segments of opinion that can't stomach McCarthyism. This is, precisely and to the letter, what they are now working overtime to do in Europe.

There is startling evidence coming out of Europe about how the Communists have infiltrated, financed, and in a measure controlled the revival of Fascist groups in Italy and Nazi groups in Germany. Those of you who read *The Reporter* will see some of this evidence spread on the record in our April 13 issue. But let me mention a couple of facts by way of example.

Item: One neo-Nazi newspaper in West Germany was started with a subsidy from the Communist Central Committee in East Germany.

Item: That ill-starred pair, Cohn and Schine, sought information during their European trip last year from two Germans, one of whom appears to have been a professional double agent and the other the director of a well-known Communist-front organization in Munich.

Item: In Italy, the Communist Party financed a magazine written by and for veterans of Mussolini's last political gasp, the Salò Government; these Fascists in turn formed a party which got nearly 6% of the vote in the Italian elections last year. The magazine, according to its own statement, was set up "to combat the tendency of Communists, Socialists, ex-Facists of the Left and revolutionaries of every kind to fight each other rather than the common enemy." The common enemy was defined as De Gasperi and Christian Democratic and other moderate parties.

If their actions are already so clear in Germany and Italy, we should expect the Communists to try their best to infiltrate similar groups in this country, goading them to be even more reckless in the future than they have been in the past. The evidence here is scanty. But the parallel effort by the Communists to capture the leadership of the anti-McCarthyism movement is already plainly written down in the *Daily Worker*.

Listen to these sentences from the Communist Party's new manifesto, which bears the title "The American Way—to Jobs, Peace, Democracy," and which was printed in the *Daily Worker* with pictures of the Statue of Liberty and the Liberty Bell, crack and all.

Speaking of "the attack on our democratic heritage" and the "grave danger to our democratic liberties," the Communists proclaim: "McCarthyism is on the rampage. It is trying to browbeat into submission every independent point of view, every thinking person. It burns books and destroys art and culture. It aims . . . to wipe out all vestiges of liberty. McCarthyism seeks to turn America into a land of yes-men, a land where patriotism is replaced with jingoism, independent thought with conformity, courage with servility. . . . We call for the defense of the Constitution and its Bill of Rights, for an end to the 'dictatorship of fear.' "

This sounds insanely paradoxical, coming from the enemies of freedom and justice. Their description of McCarthyism is the twin brother of *our* description of life in the Soviet Union and its satellites. But is it more topsy-turvy than a "peace" campaign alongside of military aggression, or the dead-pan reiteration of the term "people's democracies" to describe satellites run by policemen?

The tragedy of this kind of thing is that the atmosphere is already full of such tension and uncertainty that the Communists can stain our principles and soil our words in the minds of millions of people by the simple act of coming out for our principles and using our words. They can even call into question the Fifth Amendment to our Constitution, by the simple act of pleading it.

In this game of playing both ends against the middle, they can thus accomplish two things at once: They pretend there is a basis for agreement with them on broad American principles, and they provide ammunition for the noisiest anti-Communists to use. Can't you see the *Daily Worker*, with the words I have quoted, being waved at a television camera? Can't you hear the sentence starting with those well-known words, "I hold here in my hand . . ."? Can we altogether dismiss the idea that the words were printed *so that they would be waved by that hand?*

This all sounds like a pretty gloomy prospect. Most of us, Republicans and Democrats, think our freedoms are better protected and fewer bystanders are hurt if we remain, if not in the middle of the road, at least somewhere on the road rather than driving up onto one sidewalk or the other. What can we do about it?

Criticism comes easier than craftsmanship, as somebody said more than two thousand years ago. The panel that is going to carry on this discussion is a distinguished group of critics and craftsmen. I would suggest for their consideration only a couple of bromidic but eternal verities.

One, we have to keep our shirts on in the face of vituperation from both political extremes. This doesn't mean running away from a fight, whether that fight is with the Communists at a Berlin conference or with another kind of extremist over a fried-chicken luncheon at the Capitol. It does mean resisting the emotional temptation to join either extreme merely because it is clobbering people or policies we despise.

Two, we have to stick to the principles of our American democracy, which have worked so well for so long. Plato, who was no democrat, nevertheless wrote my favorite definition of democracy. He called it "a charming form of government, full of variety and disorder, and dispensing a sort of equality to equals and unequals alike." It's time we got back, particularly in the Federal Government, to a system of law that dispenses "a sort of equality."

This means a system that depends on the courts rather than on policemen for its judgments. It means a system that rests these judgments on past and present deeds, not on guesses about a person's future intentions. It means that even during election campaigns, we have to remember about the presumption of innocence and due process of law.

It means we have to stop using the idea of "security risks" as a political prostitute, available for the excitement and pleasure of the highest bidder. (In this respect, there's not a whole lot to choose between the numbers racket conducted by the Republican Administration in recent months and the official Democratic attempt to show that the Truman Administration got rid of even more risks.)

With so many handy villains about, to the Left and to the Right, we of the "tolerant Center" sometimes have a hard time remembering, that the preservation of our freedoms depends mostly on how we ourselves act. So saying, we can add the immortal exhortation of Walt ("Pogo") Kelly:

"Resolve then that on this very ground, with small flags waving and tinny blasts on tiny trumpets, we shall meet the enemy, and not only may he be ours, he may be us."

CROSS REFERENCES TO STANDARD TEXTS *

Barnes, *Society in Transition*, Chap. 12.
Bernard, *American Community Behavior*, Chaps. 12, 21, 25, 28.
Brown, *Social Pathology*, Chaps. 23–24, 30–31.
Cuber and Harper, *Problems of American Society*, Chap. 20.
Elliott and Merrill, *Social Disorganization*, Chaps. 25, 33.
Faris, *Social Disorganization*, Chap. 12.
Gillin, *Social Pathology*, Chaps. 24, 32.

——— and others, *Social Problems*, pp. 96–101, 445–446.
Herman, *Approach to Social Problems*, pp. 157–163, 452–455, 478–481.
Lemert, *Social Pathology*, Chap. 7.
Merrill and others, *Social Problems*, Chap. 4.
Mihanovich, *Current Social Problems*, Chap. 15.
Neumeyer, *Social Problems and the Changing Society*, Chaps. 15–16.
Nordskog and others, *Analyzing Social Problems*, Chaps. 10, 12.
Odum, *American Social Problems*, Chaps. 19, 27.
Reinhardt and others, *Social Problems and Social Policy*, Chaps. 2, 20.

* For complete bibliographical reference to each text, see page 13.

OTHER BIBLIOGRAPHY

Jack Anderson and Ronald W. May, *McCarthy: The Man, The Senator, The "Ism,"* Boston: Beacon Press, 1952.

Stephen K. Bailey and Howard D. Samuel, *Congress at Work,* New York: Henry Holt and Co., 1952.

Alan Barth, *The Loyalty of Free Men,* New York: Viking Press, 1951; Pocket Books, 1952.

Roger N. Baldwin, "The Truth Shall Make You Free," *Survey Graphic,* 35 (1946): 498–500.

Morroe Berger, Theodore Abel, and Charles H. Page, *Freedom and Control in Modern Society,* New York: D. Van Nostrand Co., 1954.

Paul Blanshard, *Communism, Democracy, and Catholic Power,* Boston: Beacon Press, 1951.

Emery A. Brownell, *Legal Aid in the United States: A Study of the Availability of Lawyers' Services for Persons Unable to Pay Fees,* Rochester, N. Y.: Lawyers Co-operative Publishing Co., 1951.

C. N. Callender and J. C. Charlesworth, "Ethical Standards in American Public Life," *The Annals, 280* (March 1952).

Zechariah Chafee, Jr., *Free Speech in the United States,* Cambridge: Harvard University Press, 1941.

Tris Coffin, *Missouri Compromise,* Boston: Little, Brown & Co., 1947.

K. G. Crawford, *The Pressure Boys,* New York: Messner, 1939.

Karl W. Deutsch, *Nationalism and Social Communication,* New York: John Wiley & Sons, 1953.

Donald Drew Egbert and Stow Persons, eds., *Socialism and American Life,* Princeton: Princeton University Press, 1952.

Arthur Hillman, *Community Organization and Planning,* New York: Macmillan Co., 1950.

Adolf Hitler, *Mein Kampf,* München: F. Eber, 1933. Variously translated.

A. N. Holcombe, *The Middle Classes in American Politics,* Cambridge: Harvard University Press, 1940.

Floyd Hunter, *Community Power Structure,* Chapel Hill: University of North Carolina, 1953.

V. O. Key, Jr., *Politics, Parties, and Pressure Groups,* 3d ed., New York: T. Y. Crowell Co., 1952.

Milton R. Konvitz, *Bill of Rights Reader: Leading Constitutional Cases,* Ithaca: Cornell University Press, 1954.

Petr A. Kropotkin, *Fields, Factories, and Workshops,* Boston: Houghton Mifflin Co., 1899.

Harry W. Laidler, *Social-Economic Movements,* New York: T. Y. Crowell Co., 1944.

Alfred McClung Lee, *How to Understand Propaganda,* New York: Rinehart & Co., 1952. Esp. Chaps. 1, 9–10.

Nicholai Lenin, *The State and Revolution,* New York: International Publishers, 1932.

Max Lerner, "Introduction," in N. Machiavelli, *The Prince and The Discourses,* New York: Modern Library, 1940, pp. xxv–xlvi.

Samuel Lubell, *The Future of American Politics,* New York: Harper & Bros., 1952.

Robert Morrison MacIver, *Democracy and the Economic Challenge,* New York: A. A. Knopf, 1952.

————, *The Web of Government,* New York: Macmillan Co., 1947.

Karl Marx and Frederick Engels, *The Communist Manifesto,* New York: Socialist Co-operative Publishers Association, 1901.

D. D. McKean, *The Boss: The Hague Machine in Action,* New York: Houghton Mifflin Co., 1940.

Charles E. Merriam, *What Is Democracy?,* Chicago: University of Chicago Press, 1941.

———— and Harold F. Gosnell, *The American Party System,* New York: Macmillan Co., 1940.

Robert K. Merton, Ailsa P. Gray, Barbara Hockey, and Hanan C. Selvin, eds., *Reader in Bureaucracy,* Glencoe, Illinois: Free Press, 1952.

Robert Michels, *Political Parties,* Glencoe, Illinois: Free Press, 1949.

Lucille Milner, *Education of an American Liberal,* New York: Horizon Press, 1954. From 1920 to 1945 Mrs. Milner was secretary of the American Civil Liberties Union.

Benito Mussolini, *My Autobiography,* New York: Charles Scribner's Sons, 1936.

Richard L. Neuberger, *Adventures in Politics,* New York: Oxford University Press, 1954.

James Hasting Nichols, *Democracy and the Churches,* Philadelphia: Westminster Press, 1951.

Ernest Minor Patterson, ed., "NATO and World Peace," *The Annals,* 288 (July 1953).

————, ed., "Progress and Prospects of the United Nations," *The Annals,* 252 (July 1947).

Leo Pfeffer, *Church, State, and Freedom,* Boston: Beacon Press, 1953.

David Riesman and Nathan Glazer, *Faces in the Crowd: Individual Studies in Character and Politics,* New Haven: Yale University Press, 1952.

J. T. Salter, ed., *Public Men in and out of Office,* Chapel Hill: University of North Carolina Press, 1946.

Karl Schriftsgiesser, *The Lobbyists,* Boston: Little, Brown & Co., 1951.

G. Sorel, *Reflections on Violence,* transl. by T. E. Hulme, New York: B. W. Huebsch, 1914.

U. S. Legislative Reference Service, Library of Congress, *Communism in Action,* Washington: Government Printing Office, 1946.

————, *Fascism in Action,* Washington: Government Printing Office, 1947.

H. Hubert Wilson, *Congress: Corruption and Promise,* New York: Rinehart & Co., 1951.

REVIEW QUESTIONS

1. Give four characteristics of the struggle for power between government and business?
2. What are four characteristics of the participants in the struggle for domination of public policy?
3. In the struggle for control of federal power, what are Prentis's especial concerns?
4. How would you analyze Prentis's piece in terms of Blaisdell and Greverus's theories?
5. What sort of a dictatorship does Clugston say that Pendergast had in Kansas City, Missouri? How did he operate?
6. When Pendergast was sent to the penitentiary, what happened to the political control of Kansas City?
7. For what purposes does Clugston say that the *Star* wields its power?
8. What do legal aid societies offer their clients?

9. Of what importance are legal aid societies to the community at large, including people who can afford to use regular legal advice and service?
10. What are some of the characteristics Schlesinger has found to be typical of those who fit into what might be termed "the fascist pattern"?
11. How threatening is this pattern to the American way of life?
12. What does Schlesinger have to say about granting the Communists full freedom of action?
13. What arguments are there for and against letting Communists teach in our schools?
14. What are the implications to Clevelands' quotation from Walt ("Pogo") Kelly: "Resolve then that on this very ground . . . we shall meet the enemy, and not only may he be ours, he may be us"?

Mass Communications

THE STRUGGLE to plant ideas in the minds of groups in order to control actions by those groups has increased in intensity and technical skill as the communications revolution has proceeded. The first selection in this chapter furnishes an approach through which "ultimate consumers" of propaganda may equip themselves to analyze and understand the efforts being made to control their minds and actions. The Mobilization for Understanding Private Enterprise shifts the emphasis and presents a program for a group of those who wish to plant ideas in our minds, in this case the members of the National Association of Manufacturers.

In the propaganda struggles of modern society, the great mass mediums of publicity—the press, radio, the motion pictures, and education—are the chief instruments of combat. Motion pictures and education are treated elsewhere, but press and radio are discussed here. The selection on "freedom of the press" analyzes ways in which the press, although free politically in the United States, has had its representativeness more and more limited by economic arrangements. The two tables following supply statistics on the trend toward local monopolies in the twenty-five largest cities and in the United States as a whole. Spingarn and Gruber offer data and make suggestions with regard to the current control and use of radio and television.

Can the Individual Protect Himself Against Propaganda Not in His Interest?
Alfred McClung Lee

Alfred McClung Lee (1906–   ), professor and chairman, department of sociology and anthropology, Brooklyn College of the City of New York. Principal works: *The Daily Newspaper in America* (1937, 1947); with Elizabeth Briant Lee, *The Fine Art of Propaganda* (1939); with N. D. Humphrey, *Race Riot* (1943); *How to Understand Propaganda* (1952). Editor and co-author: *Outline of the Principles of Sociology* (1946, 1951); *Readings in Sociology* (1951); with others, *Public Opinion and Propaganda* (1954).

A grasp of propaganda analysis is a central part of the promise of a liberal arts education. Those who have confidence in American liberal arts ideals thus answer the question faced in this paper quite simply and directly. They affirm that the individual can protect himself somewhat against propaganda not in his interest. The extent to which a person can so protect himself depends—within the limits of available knowledge and competence—upon the extent to which he has benefited from a liberal arts education. Variously stated and interpreted, the development of an ability to assess and accept or reject propaganda is one principal purpose of a liberal arts education. And the social sciences join powerfully with the humanities and the physical and biological sciences in contributing to the accomplishment of that purpose.

Large sections of social science methodologies

From "Can the Individual Protect Himself Against Propaganda Not in His Interest," *Social Forces*, 29 (1950–51): 56–61.

deal more or less popularly as well as technically with the nature of reports, statements, allegations, efforts to convince, efforts to describe, and efforts to confuse. These include the methodologies of documentary criticism, interviewing, statistics, and terminology as well as of psychology, political science, history, sociology, cultural anthropology, and related fields. Since any material can be used propagandistically, propaganda analysis represents in part an application of whatever of such methodologies are appropriate in any given case. The analysis of propaganda, adequately conceived, is thus an orientation of what an individual may know of science and art to the understanding of propaganda messages that reach him. This implies the acceptance of such a non-normative definition of propaganda as that it is the use of symbols with the intention of forwarding or attacking an interest, cause, project, institution, or person with a public. The symbols may be words, cartoons, paraphernalia, events, personalities, buildings, or whatever else might be appropriate and useful. Propaganda is aimed especially at achieving social action goals through changing attitudes, prejudices, opinions, loyalties, modes of living. [1]

If this idealistic answer were unchallenged, one could then go on to the more specific questions: *How* can an individual protect himself against propaganda not in his interest? And *to what extent?* But the traditional answer fails to reflect societal limitations, and it is being challenged quite insistently by noisy surrogates both of politico-economic and religious orthodoxy and of what is called by some, social science.

Let me touch briefly upon the problems, first from a professional and then from a popular pressure viewpoint. In a chapter on "The Orientation of Soldiers Toward the War" [2] in the much vaunted work, *The American Soldier,* it is contended that propaganda analysis grew out of "the re-evaluation which followed the First World War, . . . a debunking process which challenged the worthwhileness of the most recent major cause to which

they had given their allegiance," and it is then asserted as follows:

The moral drawn from this was that people became converted to supporting causes by a kind of trickery—"propaganda"—and that it was, therefore, wise to be on one's guard against being taken in by propaganda. As a result, the very discussion of abstract ideas, especially where they concerned themselves with values, was suspect. If a label has to be put to it, it might be said that the dominant philosophical tone of the period was a variety of positivistic materialism which belittled if it did not deny the validity of any concern with values.

Thus it would have been more convenient, in the view of certain managerial technicians working for the war effort,[3] had educators failed to stimulate a questioning attitude and had merely inculcated values drawn from the currently dominant politico-economic orthodoxy. Look at all the problems such teachers have raised for the military establishment, product advertisers, and other propagandists by telling their students it is "wise to be on one's guard against being taken in by propaganda"! Just think how much more difficult it would be for the managerial technicians if the teachers of propaganda analysis (under various labels) had made a really substantial contribution to the thought-habits of America's youngsters. After all, in spite of the sincere efforts by occasional teachers to maintain traditional American "oh, yeah?" and "so what?" attitudes in their students, Albert Einstein expresses the concerned observation of many when he says that "It is, in fact, nothing short of a miracle that the modern methods of instruction have not yet entirely strangled the holy curiosity of inquiry; for this delicate little plant, aside from stimulation, stands mainly in need of freedom; without this it goes to wrack and ruin without fail." [5]

The noisy popular advocates of an unquestionable orthodoxy are even more numerous than those within academic ranks, but space again permits only a suggestion of their volume and tactics.

---

[1] See the author's "Interest Criteria in Propaganda Analysis," *American Sociological Review, 10* (1945), pp. 282–288, and "The Analysis of Propaganda: A Clinical Summary," *American Journal of Sociology, 51* (1945–46), pp. 126–135.

[2] The chapter is by Shirley A. Star. See S. A. Stouffer, E. A. Suchman, L. C. DeVinney, S. A. Star, and R. M. Williams, Jr., *The American Soldier: Adjustment During Army Life* (Studies in Social Psychology in World War II, Volume I, Princeton: Princeton University Press, 1949), chap. 9, esp. p. 437.

[3] For the author's review of vols. 1 and 2 of *ibid.* see *The Annals of the American Academy of Political and Social Sciences, 265* (September 1949), pp. 173–175. For a complimentary review, see Paul F. Lazarsfeld, "*The American Soldier*—An Expository Review," *Public Opinion Quarterly, 13* (1949), pp. 377–404.

[4] See "We Say Au Revoir," *Propaganda Analysis, 4:* 13 (January 9, 1942), pp. 1–6.

[5] "Notes for an Autobiography," *Saturday Review of Literature, 32:* 48 (November 26, 1949), p. 11.

After analyzing their current efforts, Max Lerner [6] notes that those currently dominant in our public discussions have "come to hate and despise ideas as such, no longer examining them for validity, but attaching dirty names to them, and reducing them to a label and a personal attack." Henry Steele Commager elaborates this same theme further with these pointed comments:

The current program of suppression seriously endangers effective operation of our democracy. . . . It imperils freedom of teaching in elementary, secondary, and higher schools by requiring conformity in standards, by introducing the grave peril of censorship of textbooks and ideas, and by driving away from the teaching profession men and women of independent minds. It creates an atmosphere in which teachers find safety not in orthodox ideas—for they will never know surely just which ideas are orthodox —but in no ideas. . . .

The current program threatens the right and the necessity of criticism. No government can operate successfully without criticism, and no government that tries to distinguish between "safe" and "subversive" criticism will get the kind of criticism that it needs. . . .

The danger that confronts us . . . is graver by far than any danger that arises from the activities of Communists or subversives in America. [7]

Looked at from another viewpoint, we might approach current problems facing those promulgating such basic conceptions as propaganda analysis in this manner: Implicit or explicit in discussions of free popular education are two objectives which are usually presented as being compatible. These are what are usually considered to be the primary (1) personal and (2) social objectives. They call for (1) the provision of relatively equal opportunities for personal development along general and vocational educational lines, and (2) the nurturing of an "enlightened electorate." [8] The former objective appeals to the masses who see in such education a way to maintain or raise personal and family status. The social control potentialities of the latter appeal to those in positions of power. As George S. Counts [9] notes, "Undoubt-

edly the ability to read may merely make the individual citizen more subject to propaganda and a willing tool in the hands of some ruling caste." The popular orientation of education toward propaganda analysis becomes, of course, a threat to such an implementation of the second objective. From any given interested viewpoint, interpretations of both objectives may be worked out which make them appear compatible. In terms of the societal scene, however, they are more often incompatible. [10] For a vast complex of historical reasons, our schools have become institutions both of impoundment and of education, both of social control and manipulation and of personal development. Pressures are constantly exerted toward personally sterilizing impoundment and toward personally invigorating education.

In the foregoing we have faced briefly what might be called the first aspect of our question, whether or not the individual *should* be equipped to protect himself against propaganda not in his interest. It is fairly apparent that whether or not the individual *can* so protect himself depends at the present time to an alarming extent upon whether or not he will be permitted to have access to a knowledge of propaganda analysis facts and principles. In discussing this aspect of the question, we have run into the whole problem of freedom of inquiry and education and into the hysterical attacks now being made against those attempting to stimulate anything resembling objective propaganda analysis. One is reminded of the comment by E. A. Ross [11] twenty-five years ago that the *"puncturers of propaganda"* are the real butts of drives against "liberty of utterance." As Ross put it, dominant spokesmen are not greatly concerned "when a man in an important position—a pulpit, a sanctum or a university chair—leans toward socialism. What enrages them,—and I know from personal experience," he observed, recalling his many crusading years, "is the man who goes about effectively puncturing their vast propaganda *for* more battleships or the open shop or lower wages . . . etc., or *against* the excess profits tax or the child labor amendment or the shorter working day or labor unions or freedom of teach-

---

[6] "Broun, Pegler, and Reynolds," editorial column, New York *Post*, November 30, 1949.

[7] "The Real Danger—Fear of Ideas," *New York Times Magazine*, June 26, 1949, reprinted as a leaflet by the American Civil Liberties Union, October 1949, pp. 7–8.

[8] Adapted from George S. Counts, "Education: History," *Encyclopaedia of the Social Sciences*, 5 (1931), pp. 403–414, esp. p. 411.

[9] *Ibid.*, p. 411.

[10] See, as examples, "Propaganda in the Schools," *Propaganda Analysis*, 2: 8 (May 1, 1939), and "Propaganda Over the Schools," *Propaganda Analysis*, 4: 4 (February 25, 1941).

[11] In a private communication to Frederick Elmore Lumley quoted by the latter in his *Means of Social Control* (New York: Century Co., 1925), footnote p. 210.

ing for High School teachers . . . etc." Ross might have worded this in a different manner. He might better have said that reformist propositions couched in generalities are harmless enough. What draws fire is the comparison of powerfully sponsored ideas with contrary evidence. Especially in such tense times as those in which we are now living, it requires courage to instruct students in the implications of "oh, yeah?" and "so what?"— the popular and capsular abbreviations of the scientific attitude.

To the extent that we can and do teach propaganda analysis, how and to what extent can the individual protect himself against propaganda not in his interest? In facing these aspects of the general question, one needs to analyze the situation in terms of (1) value orientation, (2) configurational emphasis, and (3) objective data available in the bodies of knowledge to be used. These are not discrete considerations, nor are they all-inclusive, but they point to significant facets of the propaganda analysis problem.

By (1) value orientation, reference is made here to something more general than class, group, or personal interests even though the latter may be subsumed under the former. Reference is made to the deeply conflicting major orientations of thought, interest, and knowledge which may conveniently be labeled the (a) authoritarian, (b) pressure group, and (c) humanistic.

The (a) authoritarian orientation is one that it is respectable in academic circles to reject ritualistically and then, under a variety of guises, to exemplify. It is exemplified in the foregoing in the quotation from *The American Soldier* which attacks propaganda analysis as an unwarranted interference with official propaganda. But the orthodoxy may derive from any one of a number of other sources—political, economic, religious, or personal—or from several. Whatever the source of authority, institutional or personal, the typical approach in this orientation to so-called propaganda analysis is to contrast "error" with "truth," *their* "propaganda" with *our* "facts." Analytical principles thus become, for those with this orientation, techniques for discredit or glorification rather than for understanding. Even though the charisma of the authority may derive from something vaunted as "science," this orientation is regarded here as antithetical to any relativistic, functional, and hence possibly scientific approach to propaganda analysis.

The authoritarian orientation is commonly held by the cult-minded functionaries of movements and institutions in our society, those functionaries whose insecurities have made them over-protective of their status connection. Among academicians, it is a common viewpoint among the more conservative and also among the more radical devisors of managerial technology. In such anxiety ridden times as those at present, this and the pressure group orientations have crowded hard against the humanistic and have done much to silence its expression.

The (b) pressure group orientation is commonly exemplified by spokesmen for the more combative management, labor, and political organizations. It is a catch-as-catch-can attitude toward knowledge. It looks upon research as a way of manufacturing ammunition, not as a way to understanding. All facts and views thus become functions of intergroup and intragroup conflict. What validity facts and views might have is merely in terms of their relation to and utility in current and long-term struggles. Such theorists both of the left and of the right sneer at social scientists as available to stooge for whomever controls their status and income or offers them tips (consulting fees). The usual approach in this orientation to so-called propaganda analysis is to evaluate facts and views in terms of whose cause they help or handicap. Even though this orientation is a long stride away from the rigidities of authoritarianism, its cynical rejection of scientific procedures for those of combat makes its opposition to scientific propaganda analysis disastrously effective.

The pressure group orientation may be regarded as especially typical of such managerial technicians as public relations, advertising, administrative, personnel, and many commercial research specialists. When David Krech and Richard S. Crutchfield advise propagandists that *"Propaganda can be fought most effectively with counterpropaganda,"* [12] they are of course carrying coals to Newcastle. Their advice is directed to those less acquainted with the strategies of social combat. They would naturally be opposed to taking the next step with combative propagandists and regarding all knowledge as a function of social struggle.

The (c) humanistic orientation, the one espoused here as the one most truly representative

_____

[12] *Theory and Problems of Social Psychology* (New York: McGraw-Hill Book Co., 1948), p. 360. Italics theirs.

of the useful scientific and democratic traditions, centers about concern for the rights of mankind and about hope for the potentialities of human personality. It accepts not only (i) the position taken by Julius Lippert when he said, "Man is the focus for all our striving in the accumulation of knowledge." [13] It also assumes (ii) that scholarly and scientific work should serve primarily general interests rather than those of any specific class, (iii) that valuation in the arts and verification in science are processes in which all normal persons can participate, (iv) that what hope we have for alleviating mankind's pressing problems lies in contributions to mass processes making for societal adaptation, (v) that special efforts to preserve or magnify vested interests may hamper or even delay needed societal adaptations to changed life conditions, and (vi) that any person with courage can make a contribution to social welfare by accepting the challenge of social responsibility and speaking or acting in behalf of his inarticulate or cautious fellows. Such a person may be a Larry Gara [14] fighting for freedom to object to the war system, a Vashti McCollum [15] fighting for freedom of religious conviction, or a William G. Sumner, Thorstein B. Veblen, or Charles A. Beard, each in his way obnoxious to vested academic interests, fighting to expand our scientific knowledge of controversial and important aspects of human society. Morris R. Cohen spoke in this general tradition when he pointed out, "Those who are engaged in scientific work need not only leisure for reflection and material for their experiments but also a community which respects the pursuit of truth and allows freedom for the expression of intellectual doubt as to its most sacred or established institutions. Fear of offending established dogmas has been an obstacle to the growth of astronomy, geology and other physical sciences; and the fear of offending patriotic or respected sentiment is perhaps one of the strongest hindrances to scholarly history and social science." [16]

Propaganda analysis in the humanistic orientation aims primarily to help mass man directly and indirectly to understand more accurately the relation to his interests of propagandas directed at him. It recognizes the combat role of facts and views in propaganda, but it also points to the utility of disinterested and objective analysis in the provision of dependable perspectives upon propaganda and upon knowledge generally. It thus accepts the proposition that it is possible to have professional social scientists and scholars of integrity who, as Cohen has put it, "care more for the justice of their methods than for the value of any results obtained by using them." [17] This integrity can only be assured through scientific work in socially important fields which is then subject to popular review by tolerant but irreverent publics and through competition between ideas in a relatively free market place.

These value orientations should not be confused with the (2) configurational emphases mentioned as a second significant group of considerations to be analyzed in studying the problem, how and to what extent can the individual protect himself against propaganda not in his interest. In sociology and social psychology, theorists have tended to be (a) system-centered, (b) group-centered, or (c) person-centered in their emphases. Those who have erected methodology as a preoccupying screen between themselves and a study of human affairs—numerous and fashionable as such academicians are—are passed over here. These methodological futilitarians have the only configurational emphasis that necessarily functions to interfere with the development of a useful knowledge of propaganda analysis.

Some of the (a) system-centered theorists intrigue themselves with Pareto's systemic definition of equilibrium,[18] a conception which easily lends itself to the rationalization of administrative and managerial manipulations. To the extent that system-centered theory becomes distorted by concern for equilibrium maintenance, as it apparently has a strong tendency to become, it can become an authoritarian or pressure group instrument, opposed to the development of popular understanding of propaganda analysis materials and methods.

---

[13] *The Evolution of Culture* (1886–1887), transl. and ed. by G. P. Murdock (New York: Macmillan Co., 1931), p. 1.

[14] See "The Inner Voice," *Time, 54:* 7 (August 15, 1949), p. 55.

[15] See 8 to 1 U. S. Supreme Court decision in the case, People of the State of Illinois *ex rel.* Vashti McCollum, Appellant, *vs.* Board of Education of School District No. 71, Champaign County, Illinois *et al.*, 333 *U. S. Reports* 203 (1948).

[16] "Method, Scientific," *Encyclopaedia of the Social Sciences,* 10 (1933) p. 395.

---

[17] *Ibid.*

[18] See L. J. Henderson, *Pareto's General Sociology: A Physiologist's Interpretation* (Cambridge: Harvard University Press, 1937), pp. 85–86, and S. A. Stouffer and Others, *op. cit.,* vol. 1, pp. 33–34.

In this country, sociologists have been typically more (b) group-centered in their emphasis, and the psychological social psychologists have been typically more (c) person-centered. The influential cross-disciplinary work of many leading social scientists and of such bodies as the Social Science Research Council and the Society for the Psychological Study of Social Issues * is, however, gradually bringing about a synthesis of tested theories from these two viewpoints, supplemented by what is useful in the works of the systemic theorists. Actually, sound propaganda analysis cannot permit itself to be confined to any of these emphases. To be understood, propaganda must be seen in societal, group, and personal perspectives.

Granted access to a suitable (1) value orientation, the democratically and scientifically humanistic, and a multiple (2) configurational emphasis, just what (3) objective data are needed in order to understand a given propaganda effort? At this point, it needs to be insisted that content analysis, as usually understood,[19] falls far short of providing an understanding of a propaganda effort.[20] In addition to (a) an analysis of propaganda content, a propaganda effort must also be seen (b) in an over-all manner, to the extent possible. In other words, it needs to be seen in relation to the conflict or competition in which any given message is just one piece of ammunition. Then this effort and those of its friends, competitors, and antagonists need to be related to (c) the general societal situation, (d) the dynamics of pertinent publics, (e) the nature of available or significant communications instruments, and (f) the personalities of outstanding leaders and spokesmen, to the extent that these factors turn out to have significance in the over-all struggle.

In assimilating, assessing, and relating such data and generalities based upon them, an individual will have heavy difficulties, even though he

___

* And also, since 1951, the Society for the Study of Social Problems, now an affiliate of the American Sociological Society.

[19] "Content analysis is a research technique for the objective, systematic, and quantitative description of the manifest content of communication," according to Bernard Berelson and P. F. Lazarsfeld, *The Analysis of Communication Content* (mimeographed preliminary draft), March 1948, pp. 5–6. See also Irving L. Janis, "The Problem of Validating Content Analysis," chap. 4 in H. D. Lasswell, Nathan Leites, and others, *Language of Politics: Studies in Quantitative Semantics* (New York: George W. Stewart, 1949), esp. p. 55.

[20] See the author's "The Analysis of Propaganda," *loc. cit.*

may have benefited markedly from a broad liberal arts education. We are currently in a society in which, as Lerner and Commager were not needed to inform us, not only deviant ideas but all novel ideas and their purveyors are suspect. And this situation is reflected in academic circles, as one would anticipate, by a shift of emphasis from education for humanistic purposes to inculcation for managerial purposes, from a liberal arts orientation in education to human engineering and business administration.

Can the individual protect himself against propaganda not in his interest? What answers to this question can be suggested are sharply modified from the idealistically possible "Yes." Naturally, in facing such a question, available quantitative studies of opinion, attitude, and action do not go beyond helping to sketch background a little more accurately.

As William Allen White once concluded, "I think on the whole, sooner or later, in the long run, the American people do get the truth. But they often get it when it is cold potatoes, and does them no good."[21] To illustrate, how many Americans realize that in the fantastically "prosperous" year of 1948, marked by record corporate dividends, a total of 9.6 million American families earned $2,000 a year and less, according to the United States Bureau of the Census?[22] These were 25.1 per cent of American families, and 6.3 million of them were urban or nonfarm families. Of those whose newspapers reported these facts, how many readers had any way of assessing their significance? How many were reminded that this is not a new situation? It echoes 1929, and *Fortune* magazine carried an article in 1940 on "The Dispossessed" with the subtitle, "For nearly one-fourth of the population there is no economic system—and from the rest there is no answer." As *Fortune* then baldly put it, "There are simply too many people outside that system. They are wrenches, not cogs, in the machine."[23]

Down through the centuries in the more complicated societies, there have always been men with soil under their feet and an irreverent view of the pompous and the powerful. They were ones who could estimate the scrawniness of the trunk behind the stuffed shirt, the significance of a rus-

___

[21] Personal letter to the author, dated May 5, 1936.

[22] U. S. Joint Committee on the Economic Report, *Materials on the Problem of Low-Income Families* (Washington: Government Printing Office, 1949), pp. 3–5.

[23] 21: 2 (February 1940), 94.

tle which might warm of a coiled snake. More or less modestly, but similar in spirit to Mark Twain, Thorstein Veblen, Lincoln Steffens, and *The New Yorker* wits, these salty ones have imparted their clarifying and frequently deflationary perspectives to their fellows. Whether as "cold potatoes" as White asserted or no, the puncturers of special-interest propaganda have made constant and healthful contributions to the thought of millions.

Even though the effort falls far short of the need and our creeping anxiety is not to be brushed aside without peril, the history of the effort down through the years is one of the most inspiring in human annals. And it is an effort to which millions of insecure teachers, writers, clergymen, and other humanistically-minded spokesmen cannot help but continue to contribute.

How to Be a "Sentinel" for Private Enterprise
Mobilization for Understanding Private Enterprise

Mobilization for Understanding Private Enterprise is sponsored by the National Association of Manufacturers.

"I will be constantly on the alert for all attacks upon industry and I will stand ready at all times to clarify any misunderstandings which exist and to reply to unjustified criticism as forcefully and as effectively as I can."

This pledge, subscribed to by thousands of patriotic American business men, is the heart and soul of the MOBILIZATION FOR UNDERSTANDING OF PRIVATE ENTERPRISE, sponsored by the National Association of Manufacturers and local, state and national industrial associations. It enlists the business man as a *"sentinel"* for private enterprise.

Why a Sentinel? The radicals, the "pinks," the "economic planners," and other detractors of the private enterprise system gain headway by the personal evangelistic spirit that each of them gives to the movement which he is fostering. Personal time, personal effort, personal conviction, personal belief—these things often enable a handful of zealous people to make an impression far beyond their actual importance . . . or beyond what money will buy.

The MOBILIZATION FOR UNDERSTANDING OF PRIVATE ENTERPRISE has as its first objective the stimulation of each individual manufacturer to become equally as active in championing the economic system of which he is a part.

Imagine the impression that can be made by thousands of such manufacturers—willing to devote their time, their intelligence, their personal energy to the cause of private enterprise. Imagine the effect of thousands of manufacturers, each a *"sentinel"* on the alert to defend private enterprise when it is attacked.

More is at stake than the mere preservation of our businesses. A defense of private enterprise is a defense of the American way of life—for experience abroad has demonstrated that private enterprise usually is the first liberty to be attacked and that then other liberties vanish.

Why Are You Qualified to Be a Sentinel? By and large the business man gets around in the community. He has more contacts—business, social and cultural—than the average person. He is more active in civic affairs, in service and other clubs, than the rank and file. He keeps well posted on what is going on through these contacts and through his local radio stations and newspapers.

Thus he is in a better than average position to know about attacks on private enterprise and about activities of antagonistic or designedly subversive nature.

What you do as a *"sentinel"* is to make full use of these daily contacts and activities to promote understanding, and to correct misunderstanding, of the private enterprise system of which you are a part. . . .

What Do You Do? As a *"sentinel"* you remain ever on the alert, at home, at your club, in reading, in conversation to detect misunderstandings regarding our industrial system and to challenge

From "You Are a 'Sentinel' for Private Enterprise," pamphlet [1940]. Reprinted by permission.

such misunderstandings *with the facts.* . . .

Here are some of the things you can do as a *"sentinel."*

When You Read the Newspapers. . . . When you read the newspapers, keep a watchful eye for unjustified attacks on business and private enterprise in both news and editorial columns. Although the great majority of American newspapers recognize themselves as a part of private enterprise and are staunch defenders of it, their function is to report the news and many persons who are hostile to the private enterprise philosophy use them as a "sounding board."

If you see an attack of a local nature, but against industry in general, see that it is answered as quickly as possible by contacting the publisher or editor, writing a letter to the editor, or releasing a statement which sets forth the facts. If it has more than local scope, let the Mobilization staff at N.A.M. headquarters know immediately. . . .

When You Listen to the Radio. . . . Follow the radio programs and listen particularly to local speech programs which may develop untenable attacks on private enterprise.

When misstatements are made that are detrimental to industry, secure radio time for answering such attacks. . . .

When You Attend Group Meetings. . . . When you attend meetings of local groups, or hear or read about a local meeting at which there is spread misinformation about private enterprise, see to it that arrangements are made for another speaker to present industry's side of the story before the same audience. . . .

When You Go to the Movies. . . . The movies are the only great "see" and "hear" medium. They attract an audience of some 85,000,000 persons a week. If the films you see incorporate ideas and ideals that are hostile to the private enterprise philosophy, you have a perfect right to go to the theatre manager and ask him if he realizes how such films affect the business system of which he is a part.

Ask him for the name and address of the producer, so that you can write and register your complaint.

As a *"sentinel,"* ask your local theatre manager to show constructive films—and suggest to him the use of "Your Town" and other N.A.M. productions which are available to him free of charge.

When You Go to Church. . . . If you hear something preached from the pulpit by your clergyman which indicates either misunderstanding or misinformation, go talk with him at the earliest possible moment. Talk with him not about theology, which is his special field, but on the basis that if he is going to enter into the field of economics, he undoubtedly wants all sides of the story and would welcome information based on your own firsthand experience.

If, for example, you should hear manufacturing industry criticized for employing child labor, see that he knows that child labor is practically nonexistent in manufacturing industry and, furthermore, that industry has endorsed specific legislation to encourage the various states to eliminate what child labor may remain.

When You Talk with Your Children Who Are Home from School or College. . . . If you have children in school or college, talk with them about the material they are being taught regarding our economic system. Is it fair and unbiased, or are they hearing fallacious doctrines that are opposed to private enterprise?

In a spirit of cooperation and helpfulness, pay more attention to what the young people of your community are being taught. Talk with your local school principal or with the head of the board of education to see what textbooks are being used. See to it that the young people of your community are rightly informed of the fundamentals of industry and free enterprise in America and that they know the principles of the system under which they will live and in which they will be leaders tomorrow.

Tell your local education officials that factual information for use as study material is available on request from the N.A.M. and that it is already being used by thousands of schools that have requested it.

When You Talk with Your Wife About Her Club Meetings. . . . When you talk with your wife or daughter about her club meetings, take enough interest to find out what they are hearing and being told. Often women's groups are the first targets of antibusiness groups. They are told that advertising is a racket, that the manufacturers exploit the consumer, that profits are too high.

If your wife or daughter has heard a one-sided story that is antagonistic, she has the right to ask that the other side be presented. Help her to get facts—to put a business man before the same group to tell his—and your—side of the story.

Again, you can draw on N.A.M.—for suggestions as to local business men who may be asked to speak or, if it is preferred, for speech material and study courses on private enterprise designed especially for women's groups.

Other "sentinel" opportunities will, of course, suggest themselves to you in the course of your daily activities. . . .

Be sure to answer any and all attacks *immedi-*

ately when they occur or as soon thereafter as the facts of the matter can be obtained.

Don't fail to report immediately to N.A.M. Mobilization headquarters attacks of *national* character upon industry. The N.A.M. will endeavor to answer them.

NO UNJUST ATTACK UPON INDUSTRY, LOCAL OR NATIONAL, MUST GO UNANSWERED.

Freedom of the Press
Alfred McClung Lee*

What press freedom any civilized country has or has had may be regarded as a temporary by-product of the continuous struggle by economic, political, and religious interests for control of the press. Then, too, as Alexander Hamilton [1] asked in 1788, "What is the liberty of the press? Who can give it any definition which would not leave the utmost latitude for evasion?" He contended "that its security, whatever fine declarations may be inserted in any constitution respecting it, must altogether depend on public opinion, and on the general spirit of the people and of the government." Press freedom, in other words, to the extent that it corresponds to actual conditions, is defined by the mores of a time and place. Frequently students of Freedom of the Press [2] start with the assumption that some ideal version of the doctrine is the yardstick against which press freedom in practice can or should be graded. Sometimes they even go so far as to claim that Freedom of the Press, as described, is the ideal "towards which we *must* strive.". . .

Such legally sanctioned catch phrases as Freedom of the Press, then, inevitably produce a conflict in interpretation between those who would

cling to the "real meaning" of the fetish words of the constitutional heroes and those whose interests are better served by a "practical definition" in terms of present needs.[3] In periods of rapid change in life conditions, when popular acceptance of new rationalizations lags perceptibly, the gulf between these two viewpoints widens and tends to call forth efforts at sharper definition, at a reassessment of both the ideal and the practical in terms of realities. Popular doctrines, however, "are always vague; it would ruin a doctrine to define it, because then it could be analyzed, tested, criticized, and verified." [4] . . .

While legislators and judges, during the nineteenth and early twentieth centuries, were working out a definition of Freedom of the Press from a political standpoint, publishers were utilizing changing life conditions, mechanical and economic developments, and cultural tendencies to evolve, from an economic standpoint, a more "respectable" connotation for the Press. In a formal statement, Colonel Robert R. McCormick,[5] publisher of the Chicago *Tribune* and chairman

[1] "The Federalist, No. LXXXIV," *The Federalist,* ed. by E. G. Bourne, New York: M. W. Dunne, 1901, pp. 156–157.

[2] Throughout this paper, "Freedom of the Press" refers to the catch phrase of social discourse and struggle; "press freedom" refers to the actual social phenomenon as measured by the access of differing, competing, and even conflicting group spokesmen to press media of communication.

[3] For a further description of such differences, see the author's "Levels of Culture as Levels of Social Generalization," *American Sociological Review, 10* (1945): 485–495, and "Social Determinants of Public Opinions," *International Journal of Opinion and Attitude Research, 1:* 1 (March 1947): 12–29.

[4] W. G. Sumner, *War and Other Essays,* ed. by A. G. Keller, New Haven: Yale University Press, 1911, p. 36.

[5] "The Freedom of the Press Still Furnishes That Check upon Government Which No Constitution Has Ever Been Able to Provide," Chicago: The Tribune Co., 1934, pp. 33–34.

* See identifying note on page 239.

Revised from "Freedom of the Press: Services of a Catch Phrase," *Studies in the Science of Society,* ed. by G. P. Murdock, New Haven: Yale University Press, 1937, pp. 355–375, pp. 357, 364, 366–369, and 375 quoted. Used by permission.

of the Freedom of the Press Committee of the American Newspaper Publishers' Association, sums up the political rights of "decent" daily newspapers as he believes they are implied by the doctrine of Freedom of the Press: "The right of freedom of the press is 'a right which shall not be abridged by any law of congress.' The freedom of the press would be abridged by any law passed by congress which, by the exercise of a code or otherwise, would do any of the following things: First, unreasonably raise the cost of production . . . second, unreasonably decrease the return from

only with the greatest difficulty,[8] of advertising rates which yield no profit to new and even established small papers, of advertising contracts that effectively exclude or at least hamper "outsiders" and new papers,[9] and of buying arrangements available only to those able to purchase huge quantities of supplies.[10] Despite these and other changes, however, it should not be forgotten that it is still *possible* to start a daily in New York City with approximately the same capital as was employed a century or more ago—a daily of the same sort as those successful then. But it would

DIMINISHING COMPETITION AMONG DAILY NEWSPAPERS IN THE 25 LARGEST CITIES: 1900–1950 *

Year	Population	Morning newspapers		Evening newspapers		Average morning circulation	Average evening circulation	Total no.	No. of ownerships
		No.	Circulation	No.	Circulation				
1900	12,576,438	69	. . . . . .	84	. . . . . .	. . . . . .	. . . . . .	153	. .
1910	16,647,384	66	. . . . . .	86	. . . . . .	. . . . . .	. . . . . .	152	. .
1920	20,696,355	49	6,014,331	76	8,418,687	125,299	116,926	125	104
1930	25,477,606	43	9,116,889	69	11,358,463	217,069	164,617	112	96
1935	. . . . . .	39	9,004,188	62	9,981,351	236,952	160,990	101	86
1940	26,745,522	37	10,044,196	57	10,747,547	271,465	191,921	94	79
1945	. . . . . .	37	12,605,579	53	11,871,442	340,691	223,989	90	76 †
1950	29,292,742	35	11,995,590	51	13,146,912	342,731	257,783	86	72 †

* Adapted from Alfred McClung Lee, affidavit dated May 10, 1943, pp. 76–93, in U. S. Dept. of Justice, *Affidavits Filed in Support of Plaintiff's Motion for Summary Judgment* (U.S.A. v. A.P. et al., Civil Action No. 19–163, Dist. Court of the U. S. for the Southern Dist. of N. Y.), May 25, 1943, p. 85. The 1945 and 1950 figures have been added. Tabulated from lists in N. W. Ayer & Son, *American Newspaper Annual: 1901* and *American Newspaper Annual and Directory: 1911*, and the "International Year Book Numbers" of *Editor & Publisher* for 1920–21, 1931, 1936, 1941, 1946, and 1951. Only newspapers with a circulation of 1 per cent or more of the population of the city of publication were counted. This limitation was adopted to exclude trade and other special-interest papers and thus to confine the tabulation to newspapers of general circulation. All foreign-language papers were also excluded. Pp. 86–92 of the affidavit give details for each city for the 1900–1942 period.

† The further elimination of duplication due to newspaper "chains" extending to two and more cities reduces this total in 1945 to no more than 53 ownerships, in 1950 to no more than 46.

publishing . . . third, interfere with the transmission of news by telegraph or otherwise. . . . And, finally, anything that would unreasonably interfere with the freedom of the press in any way which may ever be invented.". . .

The story of the manner in which daily newspaper properties have been stabilized is long and complicated. It includes the development of monopolistic cooperative and other newsgathering memberships and franchises,[6] of monopolistic feature rights,[7] of efficient newspaper distributing organizations with which a newcomer can compete

not satisfy the current expectations of potential subscribers. Our folkways relating to newspaper reading, including the price we are willing to pay for a paper and our willingness to pay indirectly by purchasing advertised goods, contribute strongly to the stability of the relatively few dailies by which we are now served. We prefer newspapers which purchase costly features and run columns and columns of expensive cabled stories about the love affairs of royalty.

Such a brief summary of the factors restricting or prohibiting the entrance of new units into any field monopolized by established dailies inevitably

[6] See A. M. Lee, *Daily Newspaper in America*, New York: Macmillan Co., 1937, Chaps. 13 and 14.

[7] *Ibid.*, Chap. 15.

[8] *Ibid.*, Chap. 9.

[9] *Ibid.*, Chap. 10.

[10] *Ibid.*, Chaps. 7 and 8.

oversimplifies an extremely complicated situation. A more extensive survey of the facts than is here possible, however, merely modifies and refines the impression, and does not fundamentally alter the conclusions, which may be stated in a fashion paraphrasing the generalizations of McCormick.

established to an extent not accomplished politically in this country since long before the Revolution. And it has interfered with the transmission of news by telegraph and otherwise, through promoting the necessity of huge outlays for wire news as well as through monopolistic arrangements. . . .

DIMINISHING DAILY NEWSPAPER COMPETITION IN THE UNITED STATES: 1920–1950 *

Year	Cities with dailies	Cities with only one daily newspaper		Cities with only dailies under common control		Cities with competing dailies	
		Number	Per cent of total	Number	Per cent of total	Number	Per cent of total
1920	1292	724	56.0	743	57.5	549	42.5
1930	1402	1002	71.5	1114	79.5	288	20.5
1940	1426	1092	76.6	1245	87.3	181	12.7
1945	1388	1107	79.8	1273	91.7	115	8.3
1950	1410	1124	79.7	1314	93.2	96	6.8

* Adapted from Alfred McClung Lee, affidavit dated May 10, 1943, pp. 76–93, in U. S. Dept. of Justice, *Affidavits Filed in Support of Plaintiff's Motion for Summary Judgment* (U.S.A. *v.* A.P. *et al.*, Civil Action No. 19–163, Dist. Court of the U. S. for the Southern Dist. of N. Y.), May 25, 1943, p. 92. The 1945 and 1950 figures have been added. Tabulated from the lists of English-language daily newspapers in *Editor & Publisher* "International Year Book Numbers" for 1920–21, 1931, 1941, 1946, and 1951. The only papers eliminated were those outside of the geographical area of the 48 states and the District of Columbia and also certain special-interest trade and collegiate dailies which were included only in the 1946 and 1951 lists but which had been specifically excluded from previous lists by *Editor & Publisher*. Morning and evening papers were treated as competing units when under separate control.

The industry has raised the cost of production to a point prohibiting most newcomers.[11] It has decreased the return from publishing for the un-

[11] See Marshall Field, *Freedom Is More Than a Word*, Chicago: University of Chicago Press, 1945, part 3, and A. M. Lee, affidavits dated May 10, 20, and 22, 1943, in U. S. Dept. of Justice, *Affidavits Filed in Support of Plaintiff's Motion for Summary Judgment* (U.S.A. *v.* A.P. *et al.*, Civil Action No. 19–163, Dist. Court of the U. S. for the Southern Dist. of N. Y.), filed and served May 25, 1943, pp. 76–170, for statistical evidence.

Perhaps, despite the rapid technological, economic, and social adjustments in modern civilization, the kind of press freedom now covered in practice by Freedom of the Press as a doctrine will endure and prove "retrospectively rational." The facts cited and others referred to, however, suggest that the pathos surrounding this doctrine is cracking, and that its new adjustment, now formulating, will not meet with the full approval of the interests who have come to control most daily newspapers.

Radio Is No Gift Horse

Jerome H. Spingarn

Jerome H. Spingarn (1914–   ), lawyer (formerly with Federal Communications Commission) and writer.

Recently a public opinion survey was made to discover whether or not people were pleased with radio. To the dismay of the pollers, it was found

that most of the persons who were polled had no definite views. They had very clear-cut tastes in movies. But radio was free and it didn't seem

From "Radio Is Yours," Public Affairs Pamphlet No. 121, 1946, pp. 1–3. Reprinted by permission.

WHAT RADIO PUBLIC GETS FOR THEIR MONEY

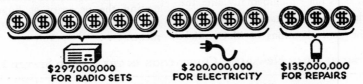

PUBLIC SPENDS $632,000,000 A YEAR ON RADIO

$297,000,000 FOR RADIO SETS $200,000,000 FOR ELECTRICITY $135,000,000 FOR REPAIRS

ADVERTISERS SPEND $397,000,000 ON BROADCASTING

$300,000,000 FOR BROAD-CASTING & PROGRAM $90,000,000 – PROFIT FOR BROADCASTERS

SO FOR EVERY DOLLAR PUBLIC SPENDS THEY GET 50¢ WORTH OF SERVICES.

(Graphic Associates for Public Affairs Committee, Inc.)

right to criticize it. If you don't like a radio program, you can always turn it off. And it's awfully nice of those people to go to all that trouble to broadcast.

Actually, of course, radio is no gift horse, and you have every right to look into the mouth of the loudspeaker. You definitely pay for your entertainment, and radio owes good broadcast service. You should not feel like a small boy sneaking a free peak at a ball game through a hole in the fence. You should feel more like a king in a royal box, witnessing a command performance.

To begin with, the public owns the airwaves. All of the channels for radio transmission belong to the public. It could hardly be otherwise because the number of channels are limited and without public control we should have utmost confusion. The government grants licenses without charge for three-year terms to applicants who pledge that they will operate "in the public interest, convenience, or necessity."

No charge is made to stations for the use of the airwaves. License fees and special taxes on the franchise have been suggested at times, most recently by members of the House Appropriations Committee.

Since it uses its channels without cost, the profits of the radio broadcasting industry are enormous. In 1944, the industry as a whole made an average profit of 223 per cent on the depreciated value of its physical property. In other words, in the course of one year, it made a profit of $2.23, before taxes, on every dollar's worth of tangible broadcast property at present book value. The networks and their key stations, taken alone, show a profit of 321 per cent on depreciated value.

But the listeners do more than give away the free use of the airwaves. Each one makes a financial investment, and in the aggregate it is a far greater investment than that made by the broadcasters. The original cost to the public of the 53,800,000 receivers manufactured from 1937 through 1944 was $2,078,000,000. The original cost to stations and networks of all tangible broadcast property as of December 31, 1944, was $82,997,650. In other words, the public spent $25 for receiving equipment to every $1 which the broadcasters spent for transmitting equipment.

The listener's upkeep bill, too, was larger than the advertiser's. He spent 3¢ a day per receiver to the advertiser's 2¢. And eventually, of course, the listener foots the broadcaster's part of the bill. Like other advertising costs, it is reflected in the price which consumers pay for advertised goods and services.

Radio channels have never been private property. The basic American philosophy of radio was stated by Herbert Hoover when he was Secretary of Commerce: "The ether is a public medium and its use must be for the public benefit. The dominant element for consideration in the radio field is, and always will be, the great body of the listening public, millions in number, country-wide in distribution."

Radio and Television and Ethical Standards
Frederick C. Gruber

Frederick C. Gruber (1903–   ), associate professor of education, University of Pennsylvania. Principal publication: with T. B. Beatty, *Secondary School Activities* (1954).

Responsible radio officials have recognized their duty to the general public and have developed codes of operational procedures. Each network and each station has developed its own code applicable to its specific situation, and practically all stations subscribe to the *Standards of Practice* as set forth by the National Association of Broadcasters (NAB) to which most network stations and many independent stations belong. The *Standards of Practice* is an eight-page pamphlet which sets standards covering almost every phase of radio broadcasting. . . .

There can be little doubt as to the high intent of the radio industry. But there seems to be considerable discrepancy between theory and practice. Many radio executives are devoted to the high ideals set forth in the Broadcasters' Creed, but their devotion does not appear to be great enough to overcome the pressures that they frequently meet from competition, Hooperatings, advertising agencies, mounting costs of operation, and the demands of stockholders for sizable profits. There is also no clear definition of what constitutes good taste. High aims seem to be implemented with wishful thinking—with inadequate and mild restrictions.

While much has been done by radio stations to promote civic projects, to uncover vice and corruption, and to keep the American public informed regarding current events with a fair degree of accuracy, the approach of many radio executives toward current issues is timid and fearful. They seem to be afraid to offend anybody, especially the potential customer and those with large accounts. "Radio is not in business for its health" is a familiar phrase among financial vice presidents. To take an extreme example, "in 1935 . . . Alexander Woollcott's 'Town Crier' broadcasts were discontinued when the sponsors complained Mr. Woollcott had criticized Hitler and Mussolini, and might thus offend some listeners."

American radio is sponsored for the most part by revenue from advertising, of which there are two types: network advertising and local advertising. About twenty-five agencies handle most of the 200 million dollars spent annually for big network advertisers. Of the 241 national advertisers on the four national networks in 1949, five major advertising groups accounted for almost three-quarters of the total network time sales. They were (1) Food and Food Products, (2) Toilet Goods, (3) Smoking Materials, (4) Drugs and Remedies, and (5) Soaps and Cleaners. Procter and Gamble spent over 17 million dollars, which represents almost twice as much as the next two advertisers combined.

When advertisers spend such sizable sums for advertising, it is not surprising that they tend to exercise considerable control over the content of the programs they sponsor. Advertisers are out

From "Radio and Television and Ethical Standards," *The Annals, 280* (March 1952): 116–124, pp. 117–118, 119–120, 121–122, 123–124 quoted.

for sales. They are interested that their message be carried to the largest number of potential buyers possible. The whole program is built around the commercial, the entertainment being calculated to induce the listener to stay with the program until the next commercial announcement. Advertisers by and large are not interested in the welfare or interests of minority groups or in the advancement of American culture or taste. One radio executive described "good taste" by saying: "We don't want anything that would be offensive. We don't want anything improper, that couldn't be heard in the home."

Such a point of view makes radio programming entirely subservient to the undiscriminating taste of the general public, with very little chance for improvement. Procter and Gamble probably has more to say about what the American public will hear than any other single organization in America.

Sponsors often use their commercial time to promote their own particular views with regard to social, economic, and even political questions rather than to use the time for a description of their product. . . .

In order to correct these abuses the radio industry has drawn up a great many restrictive rules. For example, the NAB *Standards of Practice* suggests how much advertising time should be allowed for each broadcast period, that no advertising copy should be approved without positive proof of the truth of its statements, that the word "cure" should never be used in drug advertisements, that advertising copy should never be so placed that it could be mistaken for a news item, and that wherever possible the newscaster should not read the commercials. These suggestions, however, are negative in their approach, and many of them are constantly violated.

Bad as radio commercials may be, it must be said for the industry that they are generally of higher quality and veracity than the type of advertising permitted in the tabloid newspaper and the pulp magazine. Any comparison of press and radio advertising would show that considerable more care is used in the investigation of the claims of the product by radio program departments than is exercised by some types of publications.

It is not so much the commercials as the cheap quality of the fill-ins that offends the listeners. One step in the right direction, it seems, is the building of a balanced program by the network programming departments and the development by the networks and their affiliated stations of package shows which are offered for sale to sponsors at such times as fit into the program pattern. Such a practice will return the responsibility for programming to the broadcasters, where it legally belongs. . . .

Any thoughtful person will realize how news is slanted by news analysts and even by newscasters and news commentators. The danger of such news slanting becomes especially acute when both press and radio in the same area are controlled by the same interests. Then, too, large corporations have been known to keep commentators on the air even when their Hooperatings have fallen far below those of other commentators whom they have dismissed, because the former express the political and economic point of view of the sponsor.

In a searching discussion of "Freedom of Speech on the Air," Siepmann cites a survey of radio news reporters in an issue of *Variety Magazine* dated July 25, 1945, to the effect that of 30 reporters studied, 12 were conservative (5 extreme reactionaries), 8 liberal (mildly so), 6 middle-of-the-roaders, 1 independently liberal, none extremely liberal, and the rest defying classification. Were the survey to be made today, it is likely that the proportion of conservatives would have increased.

In order to avoid criticism, the Columbia Network has declared that it has no editorial policy. Another suggestion is that each network should have a battery of news reporters representing different points of view. This latter suggestion is more positive, in theory at least. It would appear, however, that many radio stations are so afraid of being accused of being biased that they become ineffectual in the performance of their duty to the public. When the station has no editorial policy it leaves its air waves wide open to the sponsors, who usually have a very definite one. There is no harm in a station's having a point of view, openly acknowledged and openly expressed, provided that listeners in its service area have an opportunity to hear opposite points of view sincerely expressed at times convenient to them. Radio stations that have taken definite stands on public issues, especially on the local scene, have earned the gratitude of the communities they serve. . . .

Access to the air is by no means everywhere the same. Minority groups, racial, religious, and political, are frequently denied time on the ground that radio as a mass medium must appeal to the majority. But the success of democracy depends upon the encouragement and protection of the minority, for it is often within the minority groups that the seeds of progress are sown and nurtured. Even large groups are often denied free access to the air. Until recently, labor found it very difficult to secure air time. Fortunately this situation has been remedied. . . .

One of the weakest spots in radio-TV today is programming for children. Except for a few notable examples, the network entertainment for children consists of a schedule of horror on the one hand and saccharine condescension on the other. A survey of television offerings in the Los Angeles area during the first week of May 1951 revealed a total of almost 700 crimes, 82 per cent of which were committed before 9:00 P.M.—that is, before bedtime for most children. . . .

All the networks have extended codes for children's programs, that of N.B.C. being most worthy of comment for its implementation of these standards; but here again, many of the regulations are stated in the negative. The Mutual Broadcasting System, with its series of adventure programs for children, has been under greatest fire, and deservedly so. M.B.S. contends that right always triumphs; but it is to be doubted whether the thirty seconds wherein the criminal is brought to justice at the end of the program has much effect after the twelve, and in some cases twenty-five, minutes of exciting carnage and mayhem which precedes it. Such programs . . . are now supposed to be purified because the hero now devotes himself to solving modern social problems. But it is rather dangerous for youngsters to get the notion that one can set the world straight by liquidating all one's enemies. . . .

Radio and television need competent and vigilant critics. Fortunately such critics exist. John Crosby and Jack Gould delight thousands with their searching, though humorous, comments on radio and television. Leading magazines frequently carry critical articles on the subject. Various national organizations publish lists of things to view and to listen to. . . .

But the main responsibility for the improvement of broadcasting lies with the industry itself. Radio-TV stations virtually monopolize the nation's airwaves. These admittedly belong to the people; yet the American public can express itself on the air only in conformity with the interests and policies of the broadcasters, who are motivated all too often by a desire for large profits. Each of the major networks has its own characteristics and excellencies which should be developed to serve the various interests and needs of all the people. But the tendency is toward competitive simultaneous broadcasting of similar programs. What the public gets on the air is what the broadcasters want to give them. Ratings merely show the listeners' choice of what is offered.

To view programs as entertainment is not conducive to building a national culture. Many a good public service program has lost its character and effectiveness after it has become sponsored and has been gone over by the professionals.

Occasionally radio-TV stations promote the general welfare by coming out for pure water (who wouldn't approve of that?) or announcing stray dogs. Such programs are under the direction of the promotion or public relations department and are looked upon as publicity stunts to catch more listeners.

In many commercial stations the educational director is almost impotent. He often has little to say about what goes on the air under his direction. His programs can be swept aside at any time by the sales department. . . . Yet a properly qualified individual should be one of the most valuable members of the policy-making and program-making group.

There are some notable exceptions. A few stations devote their programs to good music and straight news reporting. One station reports a documentary about a reformatory that brought about needed changes. Another vigorously promotes a safety campaign. The Junior Town Meeting League annually chooses a topic of wide interest, such as juvenile delinquency, for discussion throughout the nation.

While highly commendable, these scattered programs are not enough. Radio-TV stations and networks must develop positive policies for the advancement of American life in all its desirable phases. . . .

The nation looks to the radio-television industry for leadership. Instead, it gets a singing commercial.

CROSS REFERENCES TO STANDARD TEXTS *

Bernard, *American Community Behavior*, pp. 88–89, 249–252, 599, 643–644.

Brown, *Social Pathology*, Chaps. 32–33.

Gillin, *Social Pathology*, p. 466.

—— and others, *Social Problems*, pp. 27–35, 281–282.

Herman, *Approach to Social Problems*, pp. 158–159.

Mihanovich, *Current Social Problems*, pp. 43–45.

Neumeyer, *Social Problems and the Changing Society*, Chap. 13.

Reinhardt and others, *Social Problems and Social Policy*, pp. 547–553.

* For complete bibliographical reference to each text, see page 13.

OTHER BIBLIOGRAPHY

Ray H. Abrams, *Preachers Present Arms*, New York: Round Table Press, 1933.

William Albig, *Public Opinion*, New York: McGraw-Hill Book Co., 1939.

Gordon W. Allport and Leo Postman, *The Psychology of Rumor*, New York: Henry Holt and Co., 1947.

Edward L. Bernays, *Public Relations*, Norman: University of Oklahoma Press, 1952.

Nathan B. Blumberg, *One-Party Press?*, Lincoln: University of Nebraska Press, 1954.

Emory S. Bogardus, *The Making of Public Opinion*, New York: Association Press, 1951.

Hadley Cantril and Mildred Strunk, eds., *Public Opinion, 1935–1946*, Princeton: Princeton University Press, 1951.

Wallace Carroll, *Persuade or Perish*, Boston: Houghton Mifflin Co., 1948.

Zechariah Chafee, Jr., *Free Speech in the United States*, Cambridge: Harvard University Press, 1941.

Mitchell V. Charnley, *News by Radio*, New York: Macmillan Co., 1948.

Harwood L. Childs and John B. Whitton, eds., *Propaganda by Short Wave*, Princeton: Princeton University Press, 1942.

Commission on Freedom of the Press, *A Free and Responsible Press*, Chicago: University of Chicago Press, 1947.

Leonard S. Cottrell, Jr., and Sylvia Eberhart, *American Opinion on World Affairs in the Atomic Age*, Princeton: Princeton University Press, 1948.

Leonard W. Doob, *Public Opinion and Propaganda*, New York: Henry Holt and Co., 1948.

Barrows Dunham, *Man Against Myth*, Boston: Little, Brown & Co., 1947.

Glenn and Denny Griswold, eds., *Your Public Relations: The Standard Public Relations Handbook*, New York: Funk & Wagnalls Co., 1948.

Ernest H. Gruening, *The Public Pays: A Study of Power Propaganda*, New York: Vanguard Press, 1931.

Helen MacGill Hughes, *News and the Human Interest Story*, Chicago: University of Chicago Press, 1940.

Institute for Propaganda Analysis, *Propaganda Analysis*, 4 vols., 1937–42.

Daniel Katz, Dorwin Cartwright, Samuel Eldersveld, and Alfred McClung Lee, eds., *Public Opinion and Propaganda*, New York: Dryden Press, 1954.

Judson T. Landis, "Social Action in American Protestant Churches," *American Journal of Sociology*, 52 (1946–47): 517–522.

Harold Dwight Lasswell, *Power and Personality*, New York: W. W. Norton & Co., 1948.

Paul F. Lazarsfeld and Harry Field, *The People Look at Radio*, Chapel Hill: University of North Carolina Press, 1946.

Alfred McClung Lee, "The Analysis of Propaganda," in Lee, ed., *Readings in Sociology*, New York: Barnes & Noble, 1951, pp. 297–312.

——, *The Daily Newspaper in America*, New York: Macmillan Co., 1937.

——, *How to Understand Propaganda*, New York: Rinehart & Co., 1952.

—— and Elizabeth Briant Lee, *The Fine Art of Propaganda*, New York: Harcourt, Brace and Co., 1939.

Daniel Lerner, *Sykewar: Psychological Warfare Against Germany, D-Day to VE-Day*, New York: G. W. Stewart, 1949.

—— and Harold D. Lasswell, eds., *The Policy Sciences*, Stanford: Stanford University Press, 1951. Esp. Chaps. 10–14.

Philip Lesly, ed., *Public Relations Handbook*, New York: Prentice-Hall, 1950.

Leo Lowenthal and Norbert Guterman, *Prophets of Deceit*, New York: Harper & Bros., 1949.

James L. and Julia B. McCamy, *Government Publications for the Citizen*, New York: Columbia University Press, 1949.

Carey McWilliams, *Witch Hunt*, Boston: Little, Brown & Co., 1951.

Robert K. Merton, Marjorie Fisk, and Alberta Curtis, *Mass Persuasion*, New York: Harper & Bros., 1946.

Merle Miller, *The Judges and the Judged*, New York: Doubleday & Co., 1952. The story of *Counterattack* and *Red Channels*.

William Miller, *The Book Industry: A Report of the Public Library Inquiry*, New York: Columbia University Press, 1949.

Gustavus Myers, *History of Bigotry in the United States*, New York: Random House, 1943.

Mildred Parten, *Surveys, Polls and Samples,* New York: Harper & Bros., 1950.

J. A. R. Pimlott, *Public Relations and American Democracy,* Princeton: Princeton University Press, 1951.

Oscar W. Riegel, *Mobilizing for Chaos: The Story of the New Propaganda,* New Haven: Yale University Press, 1934.

Lindsay Rogers, *The Pollsters,* New York: A. A. Knopf, 1949.

Jurgen Ruesch and Gregory Bateson, *Communication,* New York: W. W. Norton & Co., 1951.

George Seldes, *Facts and Fascism,* New York: In Fact, 1943.

———, *One Thousand Americans,* New York: In Fact, 1948.

———, *The People Don't Know,* New York: Gaer Associates, 1949.

———, *Witch Hunt: The Technique and Profits of Redbaiting,* New York: Modern Age Books, 1940.

Charles A. Siepmann, *Radio, Television, and Society,* New York: Oxford University Press, 1950.

Bruce L. Smith, Harold Dwight Lasswell, and Ralph D. Casey, *Propaganda, Communication, and Public Opinion: A Comprehensive Reference Guide,* Princeton: Princeton University Press, 1946.

Edmond Taylor, *Strategy of Terror,* rev. ed., Boston: Houghton Mifflin Co., 1942.

Television: A World Survey, New York: UNESCO (Columbia University Press, distributor), 1953.

U. S. Legislative Reference Service, Library of Congress, *Fascism in Action,* Washington: Government Printing Office, 1947. Esp. Chap. 2.

G. Henshaw Ward, *Builders of Delusion,* Indianapolis: Bobbs, Merrill Co., 1931.

William H. Whyte, Jr., *Is Anybody Listening?,* New York: Simon and Schuster, 1952.

Martha Wolfenstein and Nathan Leites, *Movies: A Psychological Study,* Glencoe, Illinois: Free Press, 1950.

J. Milton Yinger, *Religion in the Struggle for Power,* Durham, North Carolina: Duke University Press, 1946.

REVIEW QUESTIONS

1. What is the purpose of propaganda analysis?
2. What is the relationship between education and propaganda?
3. What does value orientation have to do with propaganda analysis?
4. What types of interest criteria must a propaganda analyst bear in mind? Why?
5. What are the purposes which the Mobilization for Understanding Private Enterprise believes will be served by its "Sentinels"?
6. What are they supposed to do?
7. In what ways are the families of "Sentinels" supposed to help them?
8. To what extent have we been able in this country to answer the question of Hamilton, "What is the liberty of the press?"
9. What are leading factors limiting freedom of the press in a functional sense in this country?
10. What has happened to daily newspaper competition during the past half-century in the twenty-five largest American cities?
11. What has happened to daily newspaper competition between 1920 and 1945 in the United States?
12. Of what significance are these trends toward local daily newspaper monopolies?
13. Who does Spingarn say pays for radio programs?
14. What sort of services does Spingarn think that the radio gives its publics?
15. What does Gruber regard to be the chief problems confronting us in the radio and TV fields?
16. What does Gruber say we can do about eliminating some of these problems?

CHAPTER 14

Recreation

IN THE RECREATIONAL FIELD, the needs and desires satisfied are different from those served in the other institutional areas we have been discussing, but the types of problem that arise have much in common. The problems stem, as usual, from the conscious and unconscious inhumanity of man to man—from the persecution of undefended minorities, inability or fear to face and adjust to life situations, insecurity of both real and imagined sorts, greed, exploitation, and deprivation. Theoretically, in a world so vast and with such adequate facilities for enjoyment as well as for sustenance—granted some degree of intelligent planning and cooperative direction—the world's several billion inhabitants should not want for the leisure as well as the facilities for recreation. Actually, of course, it is most trite to remark that mere sustenance is a pressing problem to uncounted millions and that recreation even in the United States of America is all too often a matter of snatched and neurotic flight from unpleasant reality.

In attempting to determine what a recreational problem might be, even though it be purely for the purpose of chapter arrangement, one is reminded of Clark Warburton's remark, "Drink, religion and such amusements as the moving pictures offer alternative modes of psychological compensation for the unsatisfactory character of actual life." *

The selections in this chapter focus attention on some of the pressing recreational problems of America today. DeBlois sketches some of the problems of alcohol in connection with recreation. Alcoholism is, naturally, taken up in connection with mental diseases in a later chapter. "Comic" books have been called the "marijuana of the nursery" and the "penicillin of a happy childhood." Wertham as a psychiatrist and Waugh as an artist with a social perspective analyze the problems the "comic" books present.

Motion pictures, sports, and bars probably consume the most time and money of Americans among the organized recreational programs. Rosten outlines part of the escapist pattern upon which a large share of the featured motion picture productions depends.

The chief problems in sports have traditionally been those associated with big-time gambling, with its concomitant wrecking of lives, bribing of legislators and police, and elimination of genuine sports interest from many events. Steigleman, upon the basis of a coast-to-coast investigation of the horse-racing racket, suggests the situation in terms of an especially flagrant example. Peterson describes some of the problems involved in efforts to enforce gambling laws.

---

* "Prohibition," *Encyclopaedia of the Social Sciences, 12* (1934): 499–510, p. 504 quoted.

The Drys Are on the March Again
Frank DeBlois

Frank DeBlois (1918–   ), associate editor, *Parade;* former staff member of *Yank.*

[We] Americans are maintaining our position as the world's heaviest drinkers. Paradoxically, we are also the only people in the world—with the possible exception of a few orthodox Mohammedans—who continue to pass laws forbidding each other to drink alcoholic beverages in freedom.

From *Parade* (August 24, 1947), pp. 5–7. Reprinted by permission.

One of the paradoxes of U. S. life is that we are the wettest people on earth—and also the driest.

It is a widely known but seldom appreciated fact that, despite our consistently prodigious drinking, one third of the U.S.A. is as dry—alcoholically speaking—as a church picnic. Three states—Kansas, Oklahoma and Mississippi—are completely dry [Kansas is no longer dry.—Eds.] and a half dozen others—including North Carolina, Kentucky and Texas—are arid in most of their counties. In addition, it is quite possible that we shall soon be even drier than we are today, for efforts to obtain legislation to submit the question of state prohibition to the voters of Alabama, Arkansas, North Carolina and Texas now are being made in these states and Dry leaders confidently expect to gain victories.

That this re-birth of Dry sentiment may eventually lead to the return of National Prohibition is frankly the hope of such forces of temperance as the Prohibition Education League, the World Prohibition Federation, the Anti-Saloon League, the Prohibition Party and the Women's Christian Temperance Union, but the gun sights of leading Drys today are trained on local prohibition which, once secured, may drive the entire nation to aridity again. Thus, Mrs. D. Leigh Colvin [past] president of the WCTU, believes that when enough congressmen from dry areas start voting dry, national prohibition will return.

"Then," she avers, "the two great evils, war and drink, will be replaced by peace and prohibition."

The establishment of local option laws, which enable the residents of a community to decide for themselves whether or not they want local prohibition, has proved a blessing to Dry leaders. In states where local option voting is permitted, the Drys have made consistent gains until today they are stronger by far than at any time since 1933.

"Three-fifths of the 15,000 local option elections since Repeal," says Mrs. Colvin, "have resulted in Dry victories.

"More than 20 million people," she adds, "are members of organizations committed to prohibition, a ban on alcoholic beverages by local option, or to total abstinence.". . .

On every debatable issue of Prohibition the Drys and the distillers have clashed. The Drys are continuously praising the administration of prohibition in bone-dry Oklahoma and Mississippi. . . . Distillers reply that in both Oklahoma and Mississippi bootleggers annually buy thousands of U. S. liquor stamps from the Federal government, then sell taxpaid liquor to anyone who has the price of a pint. . . .

On the effect of liquor upon the human brain and body the two forces are at issue once again. The Drys have produced from the writings of medical and psychological authorities testimony indicating that alcoholism is a disease. The Wets in rebuttal have introduced the testimony of Johns Hopkins psychiatrist Dr. Robert V. Seliger, who also has been frequently quoted by the Drys, that alcohol is a symptom of illness, not a disease in itself.

Both Wets and Drys have of late indicated deep interest in the work performed by such groups as Alcoholics Anonymous and the Yale Plan Clinic, where the alcoholic receives care designed to relieve him of his fears and misconceptions about drinking. The Drys, however, will ride only part of the way with the psychiatrists. They are primarily interested, they admit, in prevention rather than cure.

Biggest bone of moral contention between Wets and Drys today lies in their disagreement regarding the part played by the street-corner bar in contemporary society. The Drys, of course, view the bar as a cave of evil where husbands are led astray from their homes, youths are coaxed into careers of crime and maidens are enticed down the paths of evil. Wets, however, view the bar as a poor man's club where the American workman may enjoy a society that is frequently brighter than that of his home and where—in the words of H. L. Mencken—he may escape "the leathery delicatessen of his wife's cuisine."

The ills of drink, as chronicled by the Drys, include the promotion of sloth, ill-health, failure in business and marriage, boorishness, sterility, crime, madness and foulness of breath. In rebuttal, the Wets claim that drinking—in moderation—makes a man more generous and humane, more liberal, more tolerant, a better citizen, husband, father and friend.

Today the Drys, analyzing the gains they have made since Repeal, believe that the nation will continue to become drier each year because Americans, basically sober and religious, instinctively turn against evil. Wets, who attribute Dry gains in local option elections to hard work on the part of the campaigners and apathy on the part of most voters, believe that Dry territory soon will shrink, but predict that a soberer America will result once the nation's war nerves unwind. There need be no threat of Prohibition's return, the Wets believe, as long as the U. S. remembers that Prohibition in a number of ways is like a man's mother-in-law. It's easy to get her to visit you; it's much harder to get her to leave.

"Comic" Books: I
Fredric Wertham

Fredric Wertham (1895–   ), psychiatrist and neurologist; senior psychiatrist, New York City Department of Hospitals, and director of the general mental hygiene clinics, Bellevue and Queens Hospitals. Author: with Florence Wertham, *The Brain as an Organ* (1935); *Dark Legend: A Study of Murder* (1941, 1949); *The World Within* (1948); *The Show of Violence* (1949); *All Our Innocences* (1953).

A twenty-year-old youth in New York City has just killed a policeman. Is that so astonishing when he can see anywhere a typical comic-book cover showing a man and a woman shooting it out with the police to the accompaniment of these words: "We'll give those flatfeet a bellyful of lead"? A nineteen-year-old youth has just been sentenced to the electric chair for the murder of a girl of fifteen, despite the jury's recommendation of clemency, by a judge who had previously disregarded a recommendation of mercy in the case of a sixteen-year-old participant in a holdup with a fatal shooting. There are recent cases where young men branded girls' breasts with burning cigarettes and carved initials into their flesh with a knife. A thirteen-year-old boy in Chicago has just murdered a young playmate. He told his lawyer . . . that he reads all the crime comic books he can get hold of. He has evidently not kept up with the theories that comic-book readers never imitate what they read. He has just been sentenced to twenty-two years in jail; while the comic-book publishers who filled his mind with thoughts and methods of murder, and their experts who say his reading was good for him, continue as before.

All these manifestations of brutality, cruelty, and violence and the manner in which they are committed—that is the folklore of the comic books.

Comic books are the greatest book publishing success in history and the greatest mass influence on children. If I make the most conservative estimate from my own researches, one billion times a year a child sits down and reads a comic book.

Crime does not pay, but crime comics do.

Recently I walked in one of the crowded sections of New York City and saw a sign: "Saturday Morning [which is the Saturday matinee for children] Comic Books Will Be Given Out Free to the First 500 Attending." I looked to see what was playing in that movie that morning. There were two horror films: "The Son of Frankenstein" and "The Bride of Frankenstein." The posters calling attention to the movies showed girls in various stages of being overpowered. The movie was called the Ritz. As I stood there I was reminded of the story of the little boy who was asked what he wanted to be when he grew up and replied enthusiastically: "I want to be a sex maniac!"

There are two opinions about comic books. The one says they are very harmful to children; the other says they are good for the little kiddies. John Mason Brown [writing in *The Saturday Review of Literature* March 20, 1948] has called comic books the "marijuana of the nursery." The question can be put this way: Are comic books the marijuana of the nursery or the penicillin of a happy childhood? This difference of opinion is reflected also in the conflict in the child's mind. Briefly summarized, it is a conflict between superego and sub-machine gun. . . .

The worst sector of comic books is increasing and the best, if there is a best, is getting smaller. The comic-book publishers seduce the children and mislead the parents. Their mass production is a serious danger to the production of good inexpensive children's books. The publishers of these good children's books, instead of fighting

From "The Comics . . . Very Funny!" *Saturday Review of Literature*, 31: 22 (May 29, 1948): 6–7, 27–29, pp. 7, 27, 29 quoted. Reprinted by permission.

the experts of the comic-book industry and decoding their "codes," lie on psychoanalytic couches themselves, and delve into their own dreams instead of providing decent fare for the dreams of childhood.

"Comic" Books: II
Coulton Waugh

Coulton Waugh (1896–   ), comic strip cartoonist and painter. Conductor of "Dickie Dare" for Associated Press, 1935–44 and since 1949, and originator of "Hank" for *PM*, 1945.

One reaction to the tons of criticism which have been heaped on comic books was supplied by the publishers of the ones most under fire. It consisted of getting together boards of prominent educators and experts, who study the material before it is published, and pass on the suitability of such for childish minds. . . .

The use of these boards has been criticized in some quarters on the ground that they make a distinguished excuse for a very cheap product, and that since these people are connected with the magazines, their investigations are necessarily one-sided. Champions of the boards reply that the standing of the individuals involved, most of whom are connected with large colleges or study organizations, is a guarantee of good faith. The point is, they go on, these experts realize that comic books are a part of American life, and they intend to do their best to see the scientific approach applied to them. It is interesting that all of them agree to the need of a child for imaginative reading matter and for fantasy.

Dr. Lauretta Bender, for example, has pointed out that children read comics because of the need for experimenting with reality and its problems. In his own life, she says, a child cannot have the opportunity to meet any but a few of such problems; in his fantasy life, using such symbols as comics present, he may meet and adjust to a wide variety of the world's trials and difficulties. Children's fantasies she therefore regards, not as an escape from reality, but as a constructive approach to it. . . .

[In] spite of all the learned arguments of those college professors who endorse the lurid form of the comic books, the great mass of American people have been getting thoroughly annoyed at the alarming mass of cheap sensationalism their children have been buried under. These human torches and hornet men seem to have little connection with the sound values which the American people, generally speaking, strive for; and it seems that the people, in a number of ways, have been gradually making this clear to the publishers.

An example of the thing so many people object to, for instance, is the army of hooded and masked men, women, boys, and even girls, who were threatening to push the normal heroes off the stands. Why, in the name of a free republic, is all this hooding necessary? True, these people are always on the side of right, of democracy; but democracy's justice does not need to mask itself. From the picture point of view—and this means a great deal in comics—such hooded people suggest the Ku Klux Klan more than anything else, the very reverse of the process of democratic law. Protests of many kinds, from many sources, have poured in, to the point where at last a change is taking place; the furious sensationalism of the super-people is not as popular as it was. A new and healthier trend is on the way. The big news of the moment is not the emergence of a new supercreature; it is the growing popularity of the gay, animal comic book of the general Walt Disney Type, and the various titles devoted to teen-age interests.

These tendencies should silence most of the criticism. Teen-age comics are very normal and healthy as a rule. In addition, the animal group can develop fantasy, can supply that experimental adjustment to life through childish symbols, which the educators advise as good for the young mind.

Another happy point—these are funny books; the super-screamers were not.

From *The Comics*, New York: The Macmillan Company, 1947, pp. 348, 350–351. Reprinted by permission.

The Movies: Boy Gets Girl

Leo C. Rosten

Leo Calvin Rosten (Leonard Q. Ross, pseudonym; 1908–   ), author, political scientist. Best-known works: *The Education of H*y*m*a*n K*a*p*l*a*n (1937); *The Washington Correspondents* (1937); *Adventure in Washington* (1939); *Hollywood* (1941); *The Dark Corner* (1945).

In a world convulsed by catastrophe and change, Hollywood sells the oldest of allegories in its simplest and most consoling outlines: Boy Gets Girl. Those who berate the movies for their enslavement to Boy Meets Girl—Boy Loses Girl—Boy Gets Girl forget that this theme has been sovereign in the novel and the play for several thousand years, and in cultures ranging from the Greek to the Chinese. They forget that the unhappy ending was unpopular even in enlightened Athens. . . .

In the recondite naïveté of Hollywood's movies, life is a simple game between love and misunderstanding, between the pure in heart and the other kind. Optimism is basic, romance is of the essence, crises are rarely more than personal. In the movies, problems are solved by mere love, sheer will, or expiatory gestures; that is, by virtue, luck, or divine intercession. In the norms of the silver screen, virtue, luck, and divine intercession are incomparably more important than skill, intelligence, or reality. The Greek dramatists, it will be remembered, lowered an actor-Jove from the top of the stage so he could settle the destiny of the characters whenever the plot became too complicated for the author; Hollywood's *deus ex machina* is nowhere as crude: he resides in the very content of the movies, in the structure and values of the movies themselves.

In the movie story of mankind, the man who writes to Mother, steps aside for his friend, or places his sweetheart's happiness above his carnal desires is pretty sure to end as the ecstatic bridegroom, the president of the company, or the composer whose genius the audiences at Carnegie Hall acclaim by beating their palms into a pulp. The cad who kicks a dog, cheats at cards, betrays a friend, or attempts to seduce a maiden, is headed straight for the Big House, death, and eternal perdition beyond. To movie heroes, of course,

death is no more than the passport to eternal joy, its occurrence usually being accompanied by a majestic chorus of unseen angels hurling triumphant hosannahs at the audience while the screen swarms with moving clouds. It is surely consoling to discover that in the special logic of the movies, self-sacrifice always ends in successful (if unplanned) self-aggrandizement; and that selfishness is utter folly, doomed to a terrible fate.

All this means that in the moral lexicon of Hollywood, honesty is always rewarded, evil is always punished, and crime—in an exquisite reflection of the pragmatic emphases of our world —does not *pay*. The Lord Chief Justice of Great Britain, Lord Hewart, dismissed the contention that the movies help to "make" criminals, in this happy line: "If virtue triumphed in actual life as regularly as on the films, this world might be an easier place both to police and to understand." [1]

Hollywood's racial typologies are forever dismaying.* To the movie addict, Negroes are lazy, light-hearted mortals who tap dance on the slightest provocation and are prone to burst into spirituals during a thunderstorm. Italians seem to be a singularly specialized species, either childishly happy or dreadfully brutal; their talents, by some anthropological curse, are limited to restauranting or crime. Swedes, of course, are slow-witted behemoths dedicated to either the sea or the basement. In the realm of higher learning, teachers are depicted as frustrated, if female, or emasculated, if male. And the movie goer knows that a happy woman is one who enters a room with her arms full of packages. An entire social philosophy is reduced to that one classic image.

It is fitting to ask how a generation which has

[1] London *Times*, December 15, 1936.
*On this, see John T. McManus and Louis Kronenberger, "Motion Pictures, the Theater, and Race Relations," *The Annals*, 244 (March 1946): 152–158.—*Eds.*

From *Hollywood: The Movie Colony, The Movie Makers,* New York: Harcourt, Brace and Co., copyright 1941, pp. 357–360, 368. Reprinted by permission.

been innoculated with the inclusive romanticism of the movies—a romanticism which encompasses everything from individual armour to social issues —will cope with an increasingly hard and unpretty reality. To those intoxicated by the champagne of the film, everyday life and love may represent the deflation of periodically inflated expectations. One may be excused for wondering what are the consequences to psychological security when clerks are encouraged to believe in high destiny, when buck-toothed ingenues dream of Errol Flynn. True, there were Fairy Princes and Princesses long before celluloid was invented; but were they ever so real, and did they actually talk and kiss and sing?

The emphasis of the films upon action, violence, and brash conduct necessarily involves a devaluation of the thoughtful and the contemplative. This can hardly avoid influencing the manners of a society already predisposed to the physical solution of disputes, the mentality of a society most of whose inhabitants are more respectful of Hugh Johnson than John Dewey.† . . .

Whether the movies imitate life or whether life

† Rosten is speaking of General Hugh Johnson, a former Army officer who became an official in President F. D. Roosevelt's government and then a commentator for newspapers and radio stations and of John Dewey, Columbia University's world famous social philosopher.— *Eds.*

imitates the movies is for others to decide; this writer believes that like missionaries on a desert island, they begin to convert each other. Some critics say that audiences complain about the movies because the movies do not reflect reality; it is this writer's suspicion that more people lament the fact that reality does not reflect the movies. . . .

An advertisement in the *Saturday Evening Post* sang Hollywood's praises in these lyrical words:

Go to a motion picture . . . and let yourself go. Before you know it you are *living* the story—laughing, loving, hating, struggling, winning! All the adventure, all the romance, all the excitement you lack in your daily life are in—Pictures. They take you completely out of yourself into a wonderful new world. . . . Out of the cage of every-day existence! If only for an afternoon or an evening—escape! [2] . . .

It seems self-evident that Hollywood represents a challenge to the sovereignty of church, school, and family in the realm of values. The philosopher, the politician, the publicist, or the student may well agree with Mortimer J. Adler when he observes that the movies are "more than any other art the social and political problem of our day." [3]

[2] Quoted in Robert S. Lynd and Helen Merrell Lynd, *Middletown,* New York: Harcourt, Brace and Co., 1929, p. 265.

[3] Mortimer J. Adler, *Art and Prudence,* New York: Longmans, Green, 1937, p. 29.

Horse Racing: Seven-billion-dollar Racket!
Walter A. Steigleman

Walter A. Steigleman (1907–   ), associate professor of journalism, Indiana University; free-lance writer for magazines and former newspaperman. Author of *Horseracing* (1947); *Horse-play* (1948); *Newspaperman and the Law* (1950); and *Writing the Feature Article* (1950).

Every day except Sunday, about 1,000,000 people make one or more wagers on the races, even though fewer than 50,000 of them have ever seen a race horse. There is hardly a place so small, so remote, that one can't place a bet on a "sure thing" in the fifth at Belmont.

While the legalized pari-mutuel machines in some 65 U. S. race tracks were clicking off almost a cool two billion dollars last year, of which a fat slice went to the states as taxes, three times

that amount was being handled tax-free by the nation's thousands of illegal (except in Nevada) bookmakers. And while communities complacently shut their eyes, the 5½ illegal billions continued to pour in, corrupting public officials and stirring up turmoil among political and criminal groups competing for a share of the lush bonanza.

These are staggering facts, worth a moment's consideration. We bet a total in excess of seven billions yearly. How much is seven billion dollars

From *Coronet,* 22: 2 (June 1947): 14–18. Copyright, 1947, by Esquire, Inc., Coronet Building, Chicago 1, Ill. Reprinted by permission.

a year? Well, it's more than four times our national income from banking, more than twice what we allot each year for education, and nearly twice our combined medical care and death expenses. The sum is so great, in fact, that it means Americans are illegally betting more money *every week* on the horse races than is collected annually by the Red Cross and March of Dimes combined!

Some communities, like one in Illinois with a population of 40,000, actually share sub rosa in the illegal venture. Each month every bookmaker is raided and fined $500 to $1,500, depending upon the volume of business. Fines are estimated for a year in advance as a regular item in the municipal budget!

The postmaster in a western city of 120,000 was $15,000 in debt to the horses before he ended his life. A New York bookmaking ring, posing as jockeys, mulcted businessmen in the eastern United States of $300,000 by selling them fake tips. And none of their customers earned less than $15,000 a year. . . .

A few years ago, a woman widely celebrated as a shining example of American motherhood surprised interviewers by declaring that she preferred playing the horses to mending or washing dishes. Two thousand people at a matinee concert fidgeted while the guest artist waited backstage until the horses had crossed the finish line at a New York track. Local critics who called his performance "inspired" might have given credit to the artist's horse—which came home at odds of 3 to 1.

Bookie customers who feel their business or social prestige does not permit them to visit a betting parlor, maintain charge accounts and telephone their wagers. Some are like the Connecticut physician who employs an extra "nurse" to tabulate his betting system and call in wagers on race-to-race progression.

The large bookmakers maintain "runners" to make the rounds of office buildings on regular schedule. A horse player, no matter where he lives, can place a bet if he has a nickel to call his bookmaker or the energy to walk a block or two downtown. If his city is undergoing a periodical vice clean-up, or if he doesn't want his name on local bookmaking lists, he can simply wire his wagers to any metropolitan center.

Large bookmakers even in moderate-sized cities travel in the best circles, belong to exclusive clubs, contribute liberally to civic ventures. They send their sons and daughters to the best schools. The campus queen recently crowned at a Midwestern university believes her father's vocation is "broker"—but a few close associates know him as the biggest handbook operator in the state.

In addition to the big bookies and independent operators, there are all manner of marginal bookies not counted in the census of 15,000 horse-race parlors. Their rooms are little hideaways in the rear of poolrooms, cigar stores, barber shops and cheap restaurants. One bookie operated in the washroom of a New York public library. Still another received bets during a matinee intermission at the Metropolitan Opera. And a third bookie, serving a sentence in the District of Columbia jail, made $100,000 profit on an industrial magnate confined there with him. . . .

Although some reformers are still sniping at actual racing itself, it is the five-and-a-half-billion dollar-a-year-off-track betting that today is the target for heaviest attack. *But there is little likelihood that either attack will score much success.*

Attacks on racing itself are futile because of two vital changes. The invention of the pari-mutuel system of wagering permits the states to tap the racing dollar. Thus the state has become a partner of the track, and the principal racing states receive more than $85,000,000 a year as their share of the bettor's dollar. In fact, racing receipts are such important budget items that three states hurriedly summoned their legislatures to enact new taxes when tracks closed for five months during the war.

Municipalities, led by New York City, are finding that they can also share the racing wealth. Little Saratoga Springs, New York, following the example of its big sister downstate, also imposed a five per cent tax and in 1946 collected $1,062,000 —or $132,000 above its yearly total budget.

The second vital change that checks attacks on racing itself is the new complexion of the crowds. Even New York tracks receive the bulk of their $400,000,000-a-year wagers at the $2 windows. The little man has become the backbone of racing. He will never vote out of existence an institution that in little more than a minute-and-a-half may miraculously transform his $2 bill into $10 or $100.

The fight against the big-money side of racing —the four billion or more in off-track betting—is similarly doomed to failure. After all, a four-billion-dollar business is not easily outlawed—especially when again it is the little man with $2 who has the most important voice.

To date the only realistic method of control

suggested is the move to legalize bookie betting, license the bookmaking establishments and levy heavy taxes on all money bet. Curiously, the element which most strongly opposes such a move derives its chief support from the race tracks themselves, who argue that the idea of the sport—to "improve the breed of race horses"—would be destroyed.

But the track opposition loses force when one realizes that the race tracks should certainly have the power to eliminate the very backbone of the bookie business any time they desire—by merely stopping the wire services which supply the bookies (through 12,000 miles of wire) with play-by-play information.

A patron of the race track is virtually in a vacuum. No phones are available to him: the telegraph station under the grandstand "censors" outgoing messages if they contain the name of a horse. Yet despite this vacuum, the odds, results and other useful information are flashed instantaneously to bookie parlors from coast to coast. And believe it or not, the tracks say they have no idea how this information reaches the bookies!

Other efforts to stifle the bookies are completely ineffectual, because the public has clearly shown that it wants to bet on the horses—and if necessary will sneak down alleys and tap on doors to lay a wager.

Few large bookmakers are ever raided without their knowledge and tacit permission. In some cities, when the reform element becomes too vociferous, a token raid is staged as the "opening gun of an intensive war against vice." As zero hour approaches, the bookie tells his customers: "That's all today, boys. If you want anything in the late races, put it in now."

The customers are then shooed out, and bookie employees sit down nonchalantly to await the law. If the reform voice is not too strong, the raiding squad reports "no evidence." If the demands of justice are loud, one bookie employee takes the blame because he knows his fine will be reimbursed with a bonus. And the day's betting slips are carefully preserved to permit the bookie to settle accounts later.

And so it goes—a wealth of evidence on which to indict America's No. 1 industry—an industry which does good to no one and harm to millions of citizens. And when all the evidence is in, two indisputable facts remain: racing will continue exactly as long as the public wishes it to continue, and uncontrolled betting will continue just as long as racing does.

Obstacles to Enforcement of Gambling Laws
Virgil W. Peterson

Virgil W. Peterson (1904–   ), operating director of the Chicago Crime Commission; member of the Federal Bureau of Investigation, 1930–1942.

The laws prohibiting gambling are poorly enforced in most parts of the Nation. A report on the administration of justice in Cincinnati, Ohio flatly stated, "Several judges refuse to enforce the gambling laws." Many of the defendants found guilty were not required to pay either a fine or court costs, and jail sentences were virtually never imposed.[1] During one period studied in Chicago, of 5,585 persons arrested on charges of gambling, 5,023 were discharged without any penalty having been assessed against them. For the few defend-

ants found guilty, the average fine was $15.25. There were no jail or penitentiary sentences. An employee of one notorious gambling establishment was arrested four times within a short period. Once he was fined $10, and on his fourth court appearance the judge assessed a penalty of $15. There was a total absence of sincerity on the part of either the police or the judges in attempting to enforce the gambling laws.[2] Similar conditions prevail in numerous sections of the country.

Two factors are thought to contribute substan-

[1] Charles O. Porter, "Defects in the Administration of Justice in Hamilton County (Cincinnati) Ohio," *Journal of the American Judicature Society,* Vol. 32 (June 1948), pp. 14–22.

[2] "Racket Court Analysis—Dual Responsibility of Police and Judges in Law Enforcement," *Criminal Justice* (Journal of the Chicago Crime Commission), Number 72 (May 1945), pp. 7, 8, 16.

From "Obstacles to Enforcement of Gambling Laws," *The Annals,* 269 (May 1950): 9–20, pp. 9, 13–20 quoted.

tially to prevalent nonenforcement of the gambling laws. In the first place, it has been said that there has been developed in America a tradition of law-breaking. Any attempt to ascertain the basis for general laxity in the enforcement of the antigambling laws without considering public attitudes toward numerous other legislative enactments is unrealistic and will result in erroneous conclusions. In the second place, the tremendous importance of gambling as a source of political power has frequently made it possible for the gambling interests to dictate local law enforcement policies. . . .

Too frequently discussions of the enforcibility of gambling statutes have been confined to moral issues. Whether gambling in itself is morally permissible or immoral becomes the principal point of contention. Perhaps such considerations are inevitable, since wide-open professional gambling has usually flourished to the greatest extent in an atmosphere of easy morals. Underworld history reveals that there has always been a close working relationship between the vice lords and the gambling kings. Often the control of both prostitution and gambling in a municipality has been vested in the same individuals.

But any effort to determine the desirability or undesirability of the gambling laws on the basis of whether gambling in itself is moral or immoral serves no more useful purpose than to attempt an appraisal of the traffic laws by establishing the moral aspects of driving through a stop sign.

The emphasis frequently placed on the moral aspects of gambling has added to the problem of enforcement in two important respects. In the first place, the insistence of some religious groups that the act of gambling in itself is immoral is resented by those holding a contrary view. This resentment has given rise in part to the erroneous assumption that the antigambling laws resulted from a Puritanicle influence that attempted to impose its moral code on others. In the second place, the evasion of the law is justified by many on the ground that gambling is not immoral. Many character-building groups, including neighborhood and boys' clubs, patriotic organizations that specialize in developing good citizenship, and churches, resort to illegal gambling enterprises to raise money. They justify the law violation on the ground that gambling is not immoral—a type of rationalization which will permit an evasion of most laws.

The real motive, however, for disregarding the gambling statutes is "easy money." A well-known columnist, Herb Graffis, recently wrote: "Churches and charitable organizations run illegal gambling because that's the sure way of getting money for holy causes from people who otherwise wouldn't contribute if the Almighty pushed a .45 at them." But as to other law violators, Graffis observed, the attitude is usually expressed somewhat as follows: "Those commies—they ought to be run out of the country. They've got no respect for American laws." [18]

Ironically, many gambling ventures for worthy causes are actually operated on a concession granted to racketeering elements. And there have been many honest police executives who have had their law enforcement programs sabotaged by the insistence of character-building groups that illegal gambling operations be permitted for their worthy causes. Not infrequently these organizations have resorted to improper methods of pressure on law enforcement officers, identical with those employed by the criminal element. And these illegal activities, together with improper pressures, are all justified on the ground that gambling is not immoral per se, since the money raised through the law violation is for a worthy cause—in some instances to help others become good, law-abiding citizens.

Taking the cue from character-building organizations which evade the law, professional racketeers often engage in large-scale gambling enterprises which are identified with a real or fictitious charity. Recently in Chicago a large commercial bingo game was conducted by city employees, some of whom had long been associated with professional gambling. The alderman of the district admitted having given the venture his blessing. The promotors and the alderman explained that plans were being made to start a boys' club which would benefit from the proceeds of the bingo game. Commenting on the project editorially, a local newspaper realistically observed that "promoters and racketeers search for philanthropies which will lend the respectability of their name in return for a portion, often trifling, of the proceeds." [19]

A charity façade has long been utilized in connection with large-scale gambling enterprises, many times conducted by notorious racketeers. And when this subterfuge is not employed, the

---

[18] Herb Graffis, *Chicago Sun-Times,* Oct. 18, 1949.

[19] "Bingo Pays Off"—editorial, *Chicago Daily News,* Dec. 16, 1949.

gambler rationalizes that morally his business is no different from the enterprise operated by a charitable institution. The patron, in turn, rationalizes that morally there is little distinction between his patronage of a gambling venture operated in part for charity or one conducted for the welfare of an Al Capone. In either case, he is usually motivated principally by his desire to obtain "easy money."

The common assertion that America's antigambling laws stem from the early influence of Puritanism is without historical foundation. Mass gambling has always resulted in great social and economic ills; and almost every civilized nation in the world has from time to time found it necessary to resort to repressive legislation in an effort to protect its citizens. Egyptians, Greeks, Romans, and Hindus of ancient times invoked laws with severe penalties against gaming. The rabbis of the Second Temple classed gambling as a form of robbery and barred gamblers from the witness stand.[20]

Since ancient times, laws pertaining to gambling have followed a rather similar pattern in many nations. The evils of mass gambling have led to prohibitory legislation, which in turn has frequently been poorly enforced. The never ending quest for new sources of revenue, plus the difficulty of enforcing the antigambling laws, often prompted their repeal and the enactment of statutes which licensed games of chance with the state sharing in the profits. Legalization schemes have in turn increased mass gambling to the extent that the nation has found it necessary again to enact prohibitory laws. On some occasions efforts have been made to restrict legalized gambling to tourists, and the laws have prohibited local residents from entering the gaming resorts.[21]

By 1882, the laws of virtually every state in Europe prohibited gambling.[22] For many decades, legalized gambling has been a huge industry in South America. On April 30, 1946, the President of Brazil found it necessary to suppress most forms of gambling on the ground that it had become a "social cancer."[23]

It was during the early period in our national life, when the Puritan influence was the strongest, that the United States had its longest experience with legalized gambling. Lotteries had been commonplace during colonial times. After the Revolutionary War the various states were badly in need of revenue. But "taxes the people would not bear," wrote the historian John Bach McMaster. Hence, lotteries were authorized to raise money for bridges, school buildings, churches, colleges, and public works of all kinds.

The *Pennsylvania Mercury* reported on August 24, 1790, that "the lottery mania appears to rage with uncommon violence." Lotteries were flourishing in every part of the United States.[24] Unscrupulous promoters incited the "get rich mania" among the people through high-pressure tactics. Lottery frauds became scandalous. Legislatures were bribed. The poor people in particular suffered. Money needed for the bare necessities of life was poured into the state-authorized lotteries in the false hope of obtaining easy riches. Illegal private lotteries sprang up everywhere. The lotteries became a menace to the public welfare, and serious-minded citizens everywhere began agitating for their abolishment. As William Christie MacLeod has observed:

. . . the great mass of worthy citizens of New York and Massachusetts and Pennsylvania a century ago were opposed to public lotteries, not on abstract ethical grounds, but on the ground that they had become a serious social evil. . . . The campaigners against lotteries were primarily businessmen and professional men who saw around them everywhere the growing menace of the public lottery of the day.[25]

When most states outlawed lotteries in the early 1830's, the evils were fresh in the public mind. And in addition to enacting laws declaring lotteries illegal, many states inserted provisions in their constitutions which were designed to prevent future legislatures from ever again resorting to the folly of raising revenue through legalized gambling.

Following the Civil War, when the Southern States were poverty stricken, some turned to legalized lotteries as a means of raising revenue. Louisiana, in particular, engaged in large-scale lottery operations. The Louisiana lottery came

[20] Francis Emmett Williams, "A P-M Victory in Michigan," *The Lawyer and Law Notes,* Fall issue, 1946, p. 6.

[21] John Philip Quinn, *Fools of Fortune* (Chicago: G. L. Howe & Co., 1890), pp. 100, 101.

[22] Pierre Polovtsoff, *Monte Carlo Casino* (New York: Hillman-Curl Inc., 1937), p. 122.

[23] United Press dispatch dated at Rio de Janeiro, May 1, 1946.

[24] John Bach McMaster, *A History of the People of the United States* (New York: D. Appleton and Co., 1877), Vol. I, pp. 587, 588.

[25] William Christie MacLeod, "The Truth About Lotteries in American History," *The South Atlantic Quarterly,* April 1936, pp. 201–11.

into existence in 1868 under the regime of Governor Henry Clay Warmoth, a typical Reconstruction period official. Warmoth, a native of Illinois, had an unsavory earlier history which included a dismissal from the Army by General Ulysses S. Grant and an indictment in Texas for the embezzlement of government cotton. For over twenty years the lottery ruled the state of Louisiana. Governors, United States Senators, and judges were completely under the domination of this vast gambling enterprise.

During the first six years of its existence, the Louisiana lottery spent over $300,000 in bribes of legislators and state officers.[26] The poor squandered their money on tickets. The lottery company steadily grew in opulence, and the abuse of its tremendous political power became intolerable. In an election for the governorship of Louisiana in 1892, the sole issue of the campaign was the lottery. The people voted it out of existence.

To attribute America's laws prohibiting lotteries to the influence of Puritanism which considered gambling a "sin" is to ignore historical facts. State-authorized lotteries generated mass gambling resulting in social, economic, and political evils which caused the people to enact prohibitory legislation. England had a similar experience. In 1808, a committee of the House of Commons reported that

the foundation of the lottery system is so radically vicious, that your Committee feels convinced that under no system of regulations, which can be devised, will it be possible for Parliament to adopt it as an efficacious source of revenue, and at the same time, divest it of all the evils which it has, hitherto, proved so baneful a source.[27]

Various experiments with other forms of legalized gambling in the United States have usually resulted in mass gambling with attending social and economic evils to the extent that the licensing laws have soon been repealed. It is only in the state of Nevada that gambling in general is legalized in the United States today. And Nevada's liberal divorce and gambling laws "are condoned by many as a matter of economic expediency in lieu of more desirable ways of making a living."[28]

Various attempts at liberalizing the antigam-

bling statutes by permitting only certain types of games have usually resulted in many abuses, and the law enforcement problems have increased tremendously. In recent years the Montana legislature enacted laws permitting slot machines in private clubs. Punchboards were also legalized, with the state receiving 3 per cent of the value of each board. In the latter part of 1947, Governor Samuel C. Ford publicly deplored the gambling conditions in the state. He stated that his "two outstanding mistakes were when I signed the slot machine law and the punchboard law." Governor Ford said that he would recommend and insist "that both laws be repealed."[29] By 1949, there were over six hundred so-called private clubs in Montana, many of which were merely "fronts" for slot-machine interests.

In 1947, the Idaho legislature passed a law that enabled municipalities to license slot machines on a local option basis. Many communities took advantage of the law for the purpose of raising revenue. Because of the abuses which arose, several cities canceled all slot-machine licenses in 1949. Governor C. A. Robins of Idaho asked the 1949 legislature to repeal the law in its entirety.[30]

Experiments with the legislation of games of chance for the sole benefit of charitable organizations have at times resulted in serious abuses. Several years ago in Massachusetts, gambling czars established a mass of dummy charities to comply with the law, and engaged in large-scale commercial gambling activities. In several instances, the churches which were the alleged beneficiaries received only a few dollars or nothing at all, while the professional gamblers were fattening on the proceeds. Wholesale license revocations were necessary when the gambling craze got completely out of hand.[31]

The fact that a person may attend a race track in many states and be permitted legally to wager has added to the problems of enforcing the antigambling statutes in general. Poolrooms and handbooks have always been the source of many social and economic evils, particularly among the lower income groups. Proponents for legislation that would permit pari-mutuel wagering at the race tracks contended that their plan would elim

[26] Marquis James, *They Had Their Hour* (Cleveland: World Publishing Co., 1942), pp. 272, 273.

[27] John Ashton, *The History of Gambling in England* (London: Duckworth and Co., 1899), p. 238.

[28] Thomas C. Donnelly (Ed.), *Rocky Mountain Politics* (Albuquerque: University of New Mexico Press, 1940), p. 99.

[29] *Denver Post*, Nov. 23, 1947.

[30] State of California, *Second Progress Report of the Special Crime Study Commission on Organized Crime*, Sacramento, March 7, 1949, p. 66.

[31] "Beano and Bingo: Other 'O' Games Under Inquiry as Craze Becomes a Menace," *Literary Digest*, Aug. 29, 1936.

inate the handbook. A witness before a Senate committee in Washington in 1936 testified: "Whenever you find legalized racing you find few bookies . . . the bookies close up shop rather than compete with the organized forces of the law. It's history that legalized racing runs the bookies out of business." [32]

Such contentions were contrary to historical experience, which has established that the legalization of any form of gambling greatly increases its illegitimate offspring. Today it is well recognized that "bookmaking has increased enormously since the pari-mutuel machines were legalized in twenty-three states, although the conviction was that it would be uprooted." [33]

The pari-mutuel system of race-track betting theoretically affords the customer gambling that is honest. When wagering is confined to the race track, state control and supervision are possible to a greater extent than in any other form of gambling. Yet the history of race-track gambling contains many sordid chapters involving fraud on the part of horse owners, trainers, and jockeys. Many underworld characters have been identified directly or indirectly with racing. And the problem of enforcement of the gambling laws in general has been increased tremendously through the legal sanction of race-track wagering in several states.

Police officers, public officials, and many citizens chant a similar refrain in justification of a policy of tolerating illegal handbooks or in support of proposals to legalize them. They say that since those who can afford to do so are permitted to wager legally at a race track, the poor man should be provided with equal opportunities to gamble in a handbook. Unfortunately in the matter of indulgence in luxuries of a material nature, the poor man can never enjoy equal opportunities with the wealthy. And the sole objective of any intelligent legislation dealing with gambling and kindred matters should be social control in the interest of public welfare.

The distress caused by commercialized gambling has always fallen with greatest weight on families with low incomes. Gambling is merely a method whereby wealth is redistributed from the possession of the many into the hands of the few. The business of gambling is entirely parasitic, and exists for the sole purpose of exploiting a human weakness. The gambling-house patron as a class necessarily loses financially. The argument that handbook operators or other gambling-house proprietors should receive official sanction to exploit those who can least afford to lose runs counter to all concepts of enlightened social legislation. In fact, much of our modern legislation is designed to prevent exploitation on the part of legitimate businessmen who perform a genuine service to the community. Some of the stanchest supporters of these laws change their viewpoint with reference to the dubious business of gambling. Under the guise of liberalism they adopt the position that the state should legalize its exploitation.

In justification of such proposals, it is usually contended that the state would benefit in the form of increased revenue, and gambling would be placed under control. All legalized gambling schemes are primarily revenue measures; and legalized gambling as a means of obtaining revenue is incompatible with control. Since revenue is the principal end, it becomes expedient to issue more and more licenses in order to obtain more and more revenue.

Under our system of government the administration of the licensing laws inevitably falls into the hands of the dominant political party of a locality. Obviously, a political regime, including police, prosecutors, and courts, that has been impotent in the enforcement of the substantive laws prohibiting gambling, does not suddenly become efficient and honest with the mere enactment of laws which license gambling establishments. The issuance of licenses and the enforcement of the license laws would be based on political considerations with virtually unlimited opportunities for corruption. Given a legal status, gambling houses become located on main business streets and vie with competing places for patronage. Bright signs advertise their location. Over the radio, in the newspapers, and on huge billboards, people are urged to gamble. The "get something for nothing" appeal naturally is most alluring to the poor, to those who can least afford to contribute to the gambling fraternity. History has recorded that in America legalization has almost always resulted in mass gambling. [34]

The antigambling laws in the United States are not intended to regulate the private morals or habits of individuals. For example, "most

[32] John Richard O'Hare, *The Socio-Economic Aspects of Horse Racing* (Washington: Catholic University of America Press, 1945), pp. 80, 81.

[33] *Ibid.*, p. 22.

[34] Virgil W. Peterson, "Gambling—Should It Be Legalized?" *Journal of Criminal Law and Criminology*, Vol. 40, No. 3 (Sept.–Oct. 1949), pp. 259–329.

antigambling statutes do not make it unlawful to play or bet at cards at a private house or residence, from which the public is excluded. . . ." [35] In some jurisdictions, casual betting or gaming is not prohibited.[36] But most laws do prohibit the business of gambling which exists solely to exploit a human weakness and causes economic and social distress on entire families of many who patronize professional gambling houses.

Likewise, the laws that make gambling contracts unenforceable and gambling debts uncollectible are intended to afford social protection rather than to regulate private morals. It has frequently been contended that if a man wants to make a fool of himself by patronizing a gambling house, the law should not help him evade financial obligations arising from his folly.

The gambling-house proprietor relies on a mathematical percentage which assures him of financial success. The patron, on the other hand, defies the laws of mathematics and logic. Governed by his emotions, in which superstition frequently plays a strong part, he contributes to the gambling establishment. Often this emotional appeal becomes so overpowering that he gambles away his entire wealth as well as his earnings for some time to come. The principal sufferers in such cases are members of his family who are wholly dependent upon him for support.

To permit the inherently illegitimate gambling business to invoke the courts of justice or enforce hardships on children and other dependents, or to make the community support them while gambling debts are being paid, would be a reactionary move of the most vicious nature.

Likewise, the history of gaming clearly reflects that dishonesty and fraud have always been integral parts of the gambling business. A well-known mathematician, who has made a scientific study of gambling for many years, has properly concluded that "gambling has always been and always will be a crooked business." [37]

The desire to obtain "something for nothing" is present in most people. It constitutes a strong urge in many, and an all-consuming passion in others. Customers for various professional gambling schemes are always available in sufficiently large numbers to make the enforcement of the

antigambling statutes difficult. In addition, the tradition of lawbreaking which has become a part of the American character adds immensely to the problem. But gambling as a source of political power perhaps plays the most important role in the nonenforcement of the antigambling laws. In many well-governed municipalities, the antigambling laws are well enforced. The business of gambling can be largely forced out of existence everywhere if the police so desire "and if they are permitted by higher authorities to do so." [38] A commercial gambling establishment virtually never starts operating without the permission of responsible officials. Wide-open gambling never flourishes unless it has the sanction of the duly constituted authorities.

Alliances between those in control of commercialized gambling and professional politicians on a ward, city, or state level are almost expectable products of the American political system. Men of unusual ability and high integrity are not easily attracted to political life. They are able to utilize their talents to a greater personal financial advantage in private business or in their professions. The salaries offered to those holding most city, state, or Federal positions do not compare favorably with those in business or the professions. Men seeking honor, prestige, and distinction seldom look to politics to achieve those objectives.

But political life does afford excellent opportunities for exploitation by those who are not troubled by a high sense of integrity and public duty. Consequently, the ruling political classes in too many localities are comprised largely of opportunists. In order to remain in power they must maintain an efficient political organization, requiring continuous financial support and numerous workers. The highly lucrative gambling business is willing to make regular financial payments to political leaders who are in a position to give them needed protection. The alliance between political opportunists and the underworld leaders who control gambling is one of mutual advantage. As a result of such alliances, the law violators gain substantial control over the law enforcers and dictate many of the law enforcement policies of the community.

In many places large campaign contributions have been made by gamblers toward the election

[35] *American Jurisprudence* (Rochester: Lawyers Cooperative Publishing Co.), Vol. 24, p. 419.

[36] *Ibid.,* Vol. 24, p. 407.

[37] Ernest E. Blanche, *You Can't Win* (Washington: Public Affairs Press, 1949), p. 11.

[38] Edwin H. Sutherland, *Principles of Criminology* (Philadelphia: J. B. Lippincott Co., 1934), p. 205.

of a mayor, with the understanding that they would be permitted to name the head of the police department. The Wickersham Commission in 1931 reported that through alliances between politicians and the criminal element the professional gamblers had gained control of the police department, in Los Angeles, San Francisco, Detroit, and Kansas City.[39] These conditions are not unusual. They have been commonplace in American municipal history.

The political importance of the gambling business is not limited to its financial support to ward organizations. It is imperative to the gamblers that a friendly administration meets with success at the polls. Active election workers are furnished in substantial numbers. And these individuals have a selfish interest in the success of their candidates. For many years in Chicago, numerous precinct captains of the dominant political machines were gambling-house proprietors. Several were in partnership with members of the notorious Capone gang. Some political leaders who have won national attention for consistently amassing huge pluralities in elections owe much

of their political success to the financial aid of workers furnished by their underworld allies in control of gambling.

Whenever such conditions exist, it is only natural that considerable political power is vested in the gambling bosses. The political rulers must give consideration to their wishes when selecting slates of candidates for many offices, particularly those affecting the administration of justice or law enforcement.

The lenient attitude prevailing in many courts toward gambling offenders is easily explainable in certain localities. The tremendous political influence of professional gamblers would make it inexpedient for judges to arouse their ill will. In one important county, the gambling interests were so powerful politically that during a period of thirty years no candidate for sheriff was elected who pledged a policy of enforcing the gambling laws. The unlimited financial resources and election workers available to the gamblers made it political suicide to oppose them. At various times in many of our largest cities, gambling kings have also ruled over the political machinery and exerted tremendous influence over the police, the prosecutors, and the courts. Under such circumstances the nonenforcement of the gambling laws is no mystery.

---

[39] National Commission on Law Observance and Enforcement, *Report on Police,* No. 14 (Washington: Government Printing Office, 1931), p. 45.

CROSS REFERENCES TO STANDARD TEXTS *

Barnes, *Society in Transition,* pp. 445–446, 526–531, 534, 782.

Bloch, *Disorganization,* p. 424.

Brown, *Social Pathology,* p. 575.

Cuber and Harper, *Problems of American Society,* Chap. 16.

---

* For complete bibliographical reference to each text, see page 13.

Elliott and Merrill, *Social Disorganization,* Chap. 24.

Faris, *Social Disorganization,* pp. 175–180.

Gillin and others, *Social Problems,* pp. 33–34, 265–267.

Neumeyer, *Social Problems and the Changing Society,* Chap. 12.

Phelps and Henderson, *Contemporary Social Problems,* pp. 173, 183, 398.

Weaver, *Social Problems,* pp. 371–372, 718–719.

OTHER BIBLIOGRAPHY

David D. Allen, *The Nature of Gambling,* New York: Coward-McCann, 1952.

George D. Baker, ed., *Introduction to Community Recreation,* New York: McGraw-Hill Book Co., 1940.

Daniel Bertrand, W. Duane Evans, and E. L. Blanchard, "The Motion Picture Industry—A Pattern of Control," Temporary National Economic Committee Monograph No. 43, Washington: Government Printing Office, 1941.

Herbert Blumer, *Movies and Conduct,* New York: Macmillan Co., 1933.

——— and Philip M. Hauser, *Movies, Delinquency and Crime,* New York: Macmillan Co., 1933.

Gilbert Burck and Sanford S. Parker, "The Wonderful, Ordinary Luxury Market," *Fortune, 48:* 6 (December 1953): 117–119, 209–210, 212, 214, 218.

C. Delisle Burns, *Leisure in the Modern World,* New York: D. Appleton-Century Co., 1932.

Frederick W. Cozens and Florence S. Stumpf, *Sports in American Life,* Chicago: University of Chicago Press, 1953.

Paul G. Cressey, *The Taxi-Dance Hall,* Chicago: University of Chicago Press, 1932.

Winifred Johnston, *Memo on the Movies: War Propaganda, 1914–1939*, Norman, Oklahoma: Cooperative Books, 1939.

Juvenile Protective Association, *The Tavern: A Social Problem*, Chicago: Juvenile Protective Association, 1937.

Mirra Komarovsky, "The Voluntary Associations of Urban Dwellers," *American Sociological Review, 11* (1946): 686–698.

Siegfried Kracauer, *From Caligari to Hitler: A Psychological History of the German Film*, Princeton: Princeton University Press, 1947.

John T. McManus and Louis Kronenberger, "Motion Pictures, the Theater, and Race Relations," *The Annals, 244* (March 1946): 152–158.

J. P. Mayer, *Sociology of Film*, London: Faber and Faber, 1946.

Martin H. and Esther S. Neumeyer, *Leisure and Recreation: A Study of Leisure and Recreation in Their Sociological Aspects*, rev. ed., New York: A. S. Barnes and Co., 1949.

Morris Ploscowe and Edwin J. Lukas, eds., "Gambling," *The Annals, 269* (May 1950).

Leonard Reissman, "Class, Leisure, and Social Participation," *American Sociological Review, 19* (1954): 76–84.

Dero A. Saunders and Sanford S. Parker, "$30 Billion for Fun," *Fortune, 49:* 6 (June 1954): 115–119, 226, 228, 230, 232, 234.

Charles A. Siepmann, *Radio, Television, and Society*, New York: Oxford University Press, 1950.

Walter Steigleman, *Horseracing—The Greatest Money Sport*, New York: Prentice-Hall, 1947.

Jesse F. Steiner, *Americans at Play*, Recent Social Trends Monograph. New York: McGraw-Hill Book Co., 1933. See also his Chap. 18 in W. F. Ogburn, ed., *Recent Social Trends in the United States*, New York: McGraw-Hill Book Co., 1933.

Collis Stocking, "Gambling: General and Historical," *Encyclopaedia of the Social Sciences, 6* (1931): 555–558, 561.

Television: A World Survey, New York: UNESCO (Columbia University Press, distributor), 1953.

Thorstein Veblen, *The Theory of the Leisure Class*, New York: Modern Library, 1934.

Gordon S. Watkins, ed., "The Motion Picture Industry," *The Annals, 254* (November 1947).

Martha Wolfenstein and Nathan Leites, *Movies: A Psychological Study*, Glencoe, Illinois: Free Press, 1950.

REVIEW QUESTIONS

1. What is the disagreement between Wets and Drys, according to DeBlois, concerning the "street-corner bar"?
2. In what ways are the Drys now attempting to promote Prohibition again?
3. What are the chief charges Wertham and Waugh make against "comic" books?
4. What hopeful developments does Waugh point to? Why are they hopeful? Do current displays of "comic" books substantiate Waugh's predictions?
5. Do you think Rosten exaggerates in speaking of a "boy gets girl" pattern?
6. Hollywood propaganda is significant of what in this country?
7. How large is the horse-race "industry," according to Steigleman?
8. What problems does horse-racing present to the country?
9. What does Steigleman mean when he says that a patron at a race track is virtually in a "vacuum"?
10. In spite of his indictment of the race-track "industry," how long does Steigleman think it will continue to flourish in this country?
11. What is the connection between large-scale gambling and racketeers? And charitable organizations?
12. What abuses have followed attempts at liberalizing antigambling statutes?
13. Explain Peterson's statement that "alliances between those in control of commercialized gambling and professional politicians . . . are almost expectable products of the American political system."

PART V

The Atypical

The Physically Ill and Handicapped

MODERN MEDICINE has done much to minimize the ravages of disease and other physical impairments and to assist the handicapped and injured. As the material in this chapter indicates, however, there are still nearly 25,000,000 Americans who are physically or mentally impaired—men, women, and children, many of whose lives are marked by suffering and fear, and who are almost totally unproductive. From the selections comes an over-all view of the tubercular, cardiacs, blind, mentally afflicted, crippled, and others who make up this total. The selections in this and the next chapter help to round out this conception of society's needs and responsibilities among the physically ill and handicapped.

When one in four eighteen-year-old boys was rejected by Selective Service as unfit for general military duty in World War II, American leaders gave evidence of being shocked, of having ignored such potentialities too long. Mayo digests a survey of general child and youth health in the United States. Switzer and Rusk give recent statistics on the victims of handicapping conditions and indicate the growing tendency to consider all illness, of short or long duration, of mental or physical nature in cause or effect, as constituting a disablement that can be treated,

with rehabilitation to social usefulness as the potential outcome.

Few people realize that automobile accidents constitute the *largest* single source of maimed persons and accidental deaths in this country. Slaughtering and crippling automobile accidents have been called "worse than war." As the National Safety Council indicates, the all-accident death rate has declined since 1900 due to the work of safety specialists and organizations working in homes, factories, and public institutions, but a large share of such gains has been offset by the tremendous climb of traffic deaths to over 38,000 a year. The problem of adjusting human beings to our traffic machinery is a tremendous and a pressing one.

But what are we doing about our health problems? That we are making great headway through medical research is indicated by Cant, as well as that much remains to be done. Anderson, in the final selection, describes the volume and costs of personal health services experienced by families and shows that while many families have benefited through voluntary health insurance (one means of lowering the high cost of sickness), the burden of such costs is still tremendous.

Child and Youth Health in the United States
Leonard W. Mayo

Leonard W. Mayo (1899–   ), vice president, Western Reserve University; president, Child Welfare League of America, Inc. Author of *What About Our Town?* (1938).

In the years immediately preceding the second World War, seven countries had lower infant mortality rates than the United States, and from

seven to eleven countries had lower death rates among children.

One in every four eighteen-year-old boys was

From "The Findings of the National Commission on Children and Youth," *Proceedings of the National Conference of Social Work . . . May 19–23, 1946*, New York: Columbia University Press, 1947, pp. 371–378, pp. 372–374 quoted. Reprinted by permission. This summarizes findings of a commission headed by Henry Helmholz, Mayo Clinic.

rejected by the United States selective service system as unfit for general military service. Of these, hundreds of thousands were rejected for causes correctible in childhood. Physical defects found in children during school examinations are found again year after year at repeat examinations. No major steps have been taken in this country to correct this state of affairs. Health examinations are merely the first step in the process of building a healthy nation. Neither the provision of medical care nor the education of parents on how to use available facilities has kept pace with scientific knowledge.

In 1942, for the country as a whole, out of every 1,000 babies born, forty died before the end of their first year. In one state, the rate was ninety-eight; in another, only twenty-nine. The rate for Negro babies is almost twice as high as for white babies. Experience shows that infant mortality rates could be cut in half if we had the funds, the facilities, and the proper approach from the point of view of organization.

Each year some 200,000 babies are born without medical care; and yet the first day of a child's life is the most critical. More than 30,000 babies die each year because of premature birth. Deaths of infants on the first day of life have decreased little in the last decade. In the first year of life 9,000 infants die annually from gastrointestinal diseases; 17,000 from pneumonia and respiratory diseases; nearly 3,000 from measles, whooping cough, and other communicable diseases.

Maternal mortality decreased 56 per cent from 1935 to 1942, and yet in the latter year in the country as a whole twenty-six women died in childbirth for every 10,000 babies born. In one state the rate was fifty-three; in another, seven.

In July of 1944, agencies in the states dealing with crippled children had registered 373,000 such children. Out of every 1,000 children under sixteen years of age in the general population, there are eight, on the average, who are crippled. Recently a number of state agencies reported a total of 15,000 crippled children who could not be given care because of lack of funds.

Some 17,000 children are deaf, and approximatly 1,000,000 have impaired hearing. Some 15,-000 children are blind; 50,000 have only partial sight; nearly 4,000,000 have difficulties which require glasses.

Approximately 1,250,000 children are handicapped with asthma; 35,000 with diabetes; and 200,000 with epilepsy. Such children require prolonged and expert care. With one exception, no state has made provision in its crippled children's program for children suffering with diabetes, asthma, and epilepsy; and yet these are among the greatest and most powerful of the many enemies of childhood.

Lack of Facilities. In the light of these and other urgent needs our facilities are still woefully inadequate. The county is the fundamental local health unit of the country. Such a unit, according to the United States Public Health Service, should consist of at least one health officer, a sanitary engineer, and a public health nurse. Only three fifths of the nation's counties are thus equipped. Nearly 1,000 counties of the 3,000 in the nation still have no public health nurse.

Two out of every three rural counties has no child health conferences where mothers can bring their children for periodic checkups. These and other services are especially deficient in rural areas and in small towns.

One out of six small cities has no school nursing service.

Provision for corrective dental care of preschool and school children and of pregnant and nursing mothers is seriously inadequate. Many cities, towns, and counties do not have health or medical centers with adequate space, equipment, and personnel for prenatal clinics.

For maternal and child health the maximum Federal appropriation is still fixed at $5,820,000 a year. This must be distributed among forty-eight states, three territories, and the District of Columbia; some additional funds are spent locally, especially in the large cities. "Even the total of these two amounts obviously does not allow adequately for maternity and infant care, and for preventive and curative health service and dental care for preschool and school children and for children who have left school." [1]

---

[1] *Building the Future for Children and Youth*, Washington, D. C.: United States Children's Bureau for Commission on Children and Youth (1945), p. 9.

Disability and National Vigor
Mary E. Switzer and Howard A. Rusk

Mary E. Switzer (1900–   ), director, Office of Vocational Rehabilitation, U. S. Department of Health, Education, and Welfare. Howard A. Rusk (1901–   ), chairman of the Department of Rehabilitation and Physical Medicine, New York University College of Medicine and associate editor, *The New York Times*.

Every one of us, in childhood, youth, and maturity, has seen someone fall victim to a serious disease or disabling injury. Sometimes we remember them as shut-ins; others we hazily recall as being in the hospital for a long time. Some get around a bit, trying to work occasionally at odd jobs.

Many just seem to disappear from our personal lives. They join that army of disabled people who fill the chronic disease hospitals, the back bedrooms of thousands of homes, the mental institutions, the nursing and convalescent homes, the institutions for the aged and infirm, and homes for the poor. Doctors and nurses know about them, for these disabled people require a large part of the professional services which we have in this country. Social workers know about them, for the institutions are so crowded that applicants and their families must be carefully screened and checked to make sure that only the most urgent cases are accepted.

These and other victims of handicapping conditions make up the millions of disabled men and women in this country who could be rehabilitated and returned to places of usefulness in our society. No one knows the actual numbers or their heartaches or their suffering. But with proper services, thousands could leave their wheelchairs, their beds in hospitals and homes, able to care for themselves and with renewed interest in the world in which they live. Estimates by responsible organizations shed some light on the extent of disabling conditions among our citizens. They indicate some 260,000 blind persons, 2,000,000 with diabetes, 500,000 with tuberculosis. There are more than 200,000 amputees who require artificial limbs. The National Multiple Sclerosis Society reports that from 50,000 to 100,000 persons are victims of this disease. More than 750,000 have epilepsy, and about 10,500 new cases of

cerebral palsy appear each year. In poliomyelitis, 1952 was one of the worst years this country ever experienced, with 57,026 cases recorded for the 53-week period ended January 3, 1953.

These are only part of the picture. There are dozens of other disabling illnesses and accidents, and their victims number into the millions. Not all of them can be rehabilitated. Some have conditions beyond the reach of medical science today. But there are at least 2,000,000 disabled who *can* be rehabilitated and we, as individuals and as a nation, must bring them back into useful places in society.

The challenge they present is both a responsibility and an opportunity, for today we are in a position to do more to master the disabling effects of illness and accidents than ever before in history. The new medical knowledge which has been added to our scientific arsenal in recent years has made it possible to offer hope to thousands of disabled men and women who, even twenty-five years ago, would have been beyond help.

Yet the strong arm of science which has opened these opportunities for dealing with disabling conditions has, at the same time, been phenomenally successful in its life-saving mission and thereby has contributed to the number of disabled persons who survive today. Thanks to "wonder drugs," vastly improved surgery, better hospital facilities, and a host of other advances, thousands of our people are alive today who, with the same illness or injury fifty years ago, would have died. However, many of them who leave the hospital "cured" also leave with a serious disability. Each of them represents a precious human life saved—yet each raises the question of whether the same society which can save a life can also give meaning to it.

Our success so far in the constant struggle

From "Doing Something for the Disabled," Public Affairs Pamphlet No. 197, 1st ed., 1953, pp. 3–8, 9–11.

against disease and death has been the result of liver extract and insulin, good surgery and antibiotics, public health preventive measures and x-ray, vitamins and cortisone—these and the hundreds of other developments which have made medical care in America what it is today. Yet that very success has, in fact, created medicine's number one problem—the problem of chronic disease in a population in which the average age is rising.

We are becoming a nation of older people, with all the physical and other problems which go with advanced years. Two thousand years ago, man's average life expectancy was about 25 years. At the beginning of the twentieth century, it was forty-nine in this country. At present, the average for our entire population is nearly sixty-eight— and the figure promises to keep rising.

As our population becomes older, it can be expected that chronic disease and its resultant physical disability will increase correspondingly. Studies show that the higher the age group, the greater the percentage of chronic disease and disability. Lacking a cure for many of the chronic diseases that produce disability, we must depend on rehabilitation to teach the disabled to live within the limits of their disabilities and to the full extent of their capabilities.

Along with the human factors, there are economic considerations which touch every taxpayer in our country. Each year we spend large sums of state and federal money to maintain thousands of persons who have been forced onto public assistance rolls because they are disabled and unable to support themselves and their families. Most of us can readily understand the personal tragedies of these men and women, but few of us have realized that thousands of these people can be rehabilitated and returned to productive, satisfying lives, at a saving of millions in public funds.

We know this because it already has been done in hundreds of cases, covering all types of disabling diseases and injuries. The Office of Vocational Rehabilitation of the U. S. Department of Health, Education, and Welfare, working in cooperation with the eighty-eight State Divisions of Vocational Rehabilitation and Agencies for the Blind, recently completed a study of public assistance cases rehabilitated through the state-federal program of vocational rehabilitation during the year which ended June 30, 1951.

The study found that 66,000 persons had been rehabilitated during the year. Of these, more than 8,000—or one out of eight—had been receiving public assistance. They had been receiving assistance through the federally aided programs of Aid to the Blind, Aid to the Permanently and Totally Disabled, Aid to Dependent Children, and Old Age Assistance.

Assistance payments to these 8,000 men and women had been at the rate of about $5,700,000 annually. As rehabilitated, working members of their communities, their earnings are estimated at $14,000,000 in the first year after their rehabilitation. The expenditure of $4,000,000 to rehabilitate them was less than three-fourths of what it would have cost to maintain them *for one more year.* As contributing members of their communities, they will pay an estimated $1,000,000 annually in federal income taxes alone.

These national facts and figures were a reflection of similar patterns of experience in the individual states in 1952. One of the smaller states, for example, reported 69 disabled welfare recipients rehabilitated during the year. Involved in the fortunes of these 69 were 120 members of their families—wives, children, parents, and other relatives—all of whom had been dependent upon public welfare for the bare necessities of existence. Altogether, they had been drawing welfare payments at the rate of $45,760 a year.

It cost less than $14,000 for their rehabilitation. With this single investment in 69 human beings, the annual recurring public expense of more than $45,000 was at an end. They were earning their own way again—to the tune of over $133,000 a year in wages.

These are the brief facts on a few of those on public assistance who were rehabilitated. Behind them remain the thousands who could not be reached with the present resources of the vocational rehabilitation program—those who must wait and hope that some day they, too, will have their chance. Numerically, they are a large group one which could add greatly to the nation's strength. Financially, they represent a tremendous outlay of public funds.

Somehow, we must come to understand, as individuals, as communities, and as a nation, that neglect of disability is more costly than an aggressive program of rehabilitation which restores people to lives of productivity and satisfaction.

Pressing as the need is for a broader attack on disability among public assistance recipients, we need to balance our thinking and our planning by remembering the needs of those disabled persons *who have not yet been reduced to dependency on public aid*. To ignore them is to guarantee a continued flow of disabled people to welfare rolls.

In fact, all of the groups which constitute our disabled population today—the injured workman, the handicapped veteran, the crippled child, and the disabled person in advanced years—pose many questions of social and economic importance. Of all these groups, the aged present the most serious long-range problem.

There is no single answer to this problem. Part of the answer will come in our laboratories as we learn more and more about processes leading to deterioration in the human body. But there must develop, at the same time, an understanding of the possibilities of rehabilitation for these older persons and a comprehensive plan for bringing rehabilitation services to those who need them. . . .

These disabled people are, or used to be, your neighbors. They can't be identified as a group by age; they include the youngsters, the grown-ups, and the elderly, for disability strikes when it pleases. Some were clerks, some were captains of industry, others farmers, machinists, or housewives. Some, crippled in childhood, have never had a chance to work. There are the wealthy ones and the poor ones, though most are in the latter class, for severe disability is a costly business which soon wipes out life savings.

They are veterans and nonveterans, college alumni and public school graduates, blue collar and white collar, high IQ and mentally retarded. Some are the victims of accidents, others of serious infections and illness; still others were born with defects. They come from both sides of the track and vary in abilities and ambitions.

In short, the disabled are a fair cross-section of the American people. The only difference is that an unpredictable fate selected them to carry the burden of a disability.

The Office of Vocational Rehabilitation, analyzing the 66,000 persons rehabilitated during the year which ended June 30, 1951, found that:

The average age at time of acceptance for rehabilitation services was thirty-three. Of the group, 56 per cent were disabled by disease, 30 per cent by accidents, and 14 per cent by congenital conditions.

The greatest single group—30 per cent of the total—had lost the use of arms, legs, or back. Next came the amputees, accounting for 12 per cent; an equal number were blind or visually impaired.

Their financial situation, for the most part, varied between precarious and disastrous. One out of eight had never worked, and three-fourths were unemployed when rehabilitation was started. One in eight was on relief and one in twelve was living on insurance payments, most of which were temporary.

Accident Trends, 1913–1953
The National Safety Council

The National Safety Council is a cooperative, nonprofit organization formed in 1913 to serve as a clearinghouse for the industrial safety movement. It has since broadened its interests to accident prevention in every field. Its 7500 members include not only business firms but also schools, civic organizations, government departments, and individuals.

The total number of accidental deaths in 1953 was 15 per cent greater than in 1913—the year during which the National Safety Council was formally organized.* However, there were 63 per

* Comparisons are made with the single year 1913 because of the lack of certain detailed data for earlier years. However, all-accident death rates for 1900 to 1912 indicate that 1913 was an average year.

cent more people in 1953 than in 1913, and nearly 4,300 per cent more motor vehicles—the most important single agent of accidental deaths.

Comparisons between 1913 and 1953 should take into account changes in population. The rates below, which relate deaths to population, show that deaths from all causes were down 29 per cent in 1953 from 1913. Non-motor-vehicle

From *Accident Facts,* Chicago, 1954, p. 2. Reprinted by permission of the National Safety Council.

.deaths were down 56 per cent, but this great improvement was offset considerably by a 500 per cent increase in motor-vehicle deaths.

Deaths	1913	1953	Change
Total	82,500	95,000	+15%
Motor vehicle	4,200	38,300	+810%
Non-motor-vehicle	78,300	56,700	−28%

Rates (Deaths per 100,000 population)			
Total	85	60	−29%
Motor vehicle	4	24	+500%
Non-motor-vehicle	81	36	−56%

Class of accident

Deaths from motor-vehicle accidents, and from all other accidents (non-motor-vehicle) are shown above. The non-motor-vehicle classification includes work, home and public. Total deaths for these classifications can be estimated fairly accurately today, but this was not so in 1913. Comparisons, therefore, are not precise, but are about as follows:

	1913		1953		Rate
	Deaths	Rate	Deaths	Rate	Changes
Work	18,000 to 22,000	19 to 23	15,000	9½	−50% to −59%
Home	26,000 to 28,000	27 to 29	29,000	18	−33% to −38%
Public	29,000 to 32,000	30 to 33	16,000	10	−67% to −70%

Medical Research
Gilbert Cant

Gilbert Cant, medicine editor of *Time* magazine since 1949.

Because no drugs have yet been found which can kill any of the true viruses (the smallest of microbes) without risk to the patient, medical researchers have had to devise different weapons against such viral diseases as measles and German measles, chickenpox, mumps, and influenza itself. An excellent example is gamma globulin, a blood fraction given to ease the impact of measles, polio, and infectious hepatitis. While much has already been acccomplished with vaccines against various viruses, a great deal more remains to be done in the exciting future of medical research.

Totaling the saving of life which has been achieved since the discovery of the sulfa drugs and antibiotics, and largely because of their use, we find that from 1937 to 1952 the death rate for the United States as a whole declined by 15 per cent. In other words, if Americans had continued to die, through 1952, at the 1937 rate, there would have been 2,286,782 more deaths. In those fifteen years, about 8.4 years were added to the span of life that Americans could look forward to.

In half a century, twenty-one years have been added to the average American life expectancy. Thus, a baby born today has a far better chance of reaching the age of seventy than any of his forebears. However, a man who has already reached fifty can expect to live to 74, or about three and a half years longer than could his grandfather who reached fifty at the turn of the century. Medical research is challenged to extend its benefits with greater impartiality to both sexes and all age groups.

From "Medical Research May Save Your Life," Public Affairs Pamphlet No. 201, 1953, pp. 10–13.

Scientific man has fought his way to the crest of the ridge in his war on infectious diseases. From now on, though there may be many minor setbacks and even a few major ones, this campaign should be downhill most of the way if increasing research funds are available. That is why we are entering a new era. But it is not a time to relax our efforts against disease. Rather, it is a time to launch a new campaign against the disabling and crippling ailments. There is no single term to describe them aptly. Because they usually persist for a long time they are often dubbed "the chronic illnesses" or "degenerative diseases"— terms which are more misleading than informative. But individually the names of these maladies are household words: heart disease, cancer, mental illness, and rheumatism are the commonest. Then there is blindness, and also a group of diseases (with long names) which affect the nervous and muscular systems.

These illnesses blight the lives of millions and their families, destroying their emotional and economic well being and imposing an appalling burden on society as a whole. More effective weapons to be used against them must be forged in the laboratories of medical research. Before considering what needs to be done to bring these long-lasting illnesses under control, it will be worth while to review briefly how the enormous progress in the struggle against the infectious diseases was achieved.

Until very recently, most medical research was on a hit-or-miss basis and was starved for funds. Just before World War II, total medical research expenditures in the United States did not exceed $20,000,000 a year. Of this, the U. S. Public Health Service put up about $2,000,000. This was mainly for infectious diseases like Rocky Mountain spotted fever and syphilis which ranked as public health problems. Most of the remainder came from the meager funds of medical colleges and university hospitals. The carefully planned, all-out attack on a specific disease, from its ultimate origins to its final after-effects, was virtually unknown. Drug companies were doing a modest amount of research, but the major part of it was aimed at the quick perfection of products for profit. The idea that a business concern could properly spend stockholders' money on basic research that might never pay off in profits was slow in gaining general acceptance.

In these circumstances, it is remarkable that such rapid progress was made in finding ways to combat the infectuous diseases. The fact that penicillin was among the first of these drugs to be discovered was, in part, luck. Even then, but for the war, it might not have been rushed into mass testing and then mass production.

Today, the situation has improved considerably. Expenditures on medical research in the United States in 1952 are estimated to have topped $180,000,000 and may have approached $200,000,000. Nearly half of this sum represents developmental expenditures by pharmaceutical firms. The federal government has set up National Institutes to carry out basic research in several major classes of illness. These are the National Institutes of Cancer, Heart, Mental Health, Arthritis and Metabolic Diseases, Neurological Diseases and Blindness, and Microbiology. Fortunately, these are mainly the crippling and disabling diseases in which research is most urgently needed. The institutes also make grants to medical schools, hospitals, and research centers to enable thousands of researchers to carry on their work in their own institutions. Private organizations like the American Cancer Society and the American Heart Association are appealing to the public for funds and are striving in other fields for the successes which the National Foundation for Infantile Paralysis has achieved in connection with polio. Industry and industry-supported foundations have widened the scope of their research, so that while much is still aimed directly at finding new products (as was the case with isoniazid), more fundamental problems are being studied even though the effort cannot be expected to pay off for many years and may never pay off in dollars. The bulk of American medical research is being carried out in universities and hospitals, and many of these projects are financed by great private foundations such as the Rockefeller Foundation and the Commonwealth Fund. (The Rockefeller Foundation spent $3,599,698 on health and medical education and research throughout the world in 1952.)

Almost $200,000,000 a year for all types of medical research looks imposing; but this figure loses much of its impressiveness when compared with other expenditures. The total sum is only one-third of one per cent of the nation's defense budget, which is to prevent possible death from military attack. America spends less on research to prevent and cure disease among the living than on monuments and tombstones. And fifty times as much on alcohohlic drinks!

Family Medical Costs and Voluntary Health Insurance

Odin W. Anderson

Odin W. Anderson (1914–   ), research director, Health Information Foundation, New York City. Author of *Administration of Medical Care: Problems and Issues* (1947).

[The following material is from a preliminary report] on the extent of voluntary health insurance in the United States in July 1953, and the distribution of the volume and costs of personal health services experienced by families, permitting a comparison of families with some protection as against those with none. Disability insurance is not included although it is recognized that along with life insurance it may be used to defray the costs of personal health services, but neither type of insurance is designed specifically for that purpose, as is true of insurance covering hospital, surgical, and other medical costs.

The survey was conducted by the National Opinion Research Center, University of Chicago, and sponsored by Health Information Foundation. The general problem to be investigated was defined by Health Information Foundation in consultation with representatives of Blue Cross, Blue Shield, private insurance companies, medicine, public health, and the social sciences. . . . The field work was conducted during July 1953 covering the prior 12 months.

The survey is based on single interviews of 2,809 families in their homes. The families comprise 8,846 individuals representing a national sample of the population of the United States subdivided by age, sex, income, size of family, rural-urban, occupation and region.

A sample of "area probability" type was used in this study. It was drawn by the same methods as those used by the U. S. Bureau of the Census in the Current Population Survey. Estimates derived from it are, therefore, generally reliable within small margins. The representativeness of the sample was checked, wherever possible, by comparing estimates derived from it with data independently derived by the Bureau of the Census and other government agencies.

This study is a consumer survey, the first national survey of this kind since the series of studies conducted by the Committee on the Costs of Medical Care from 1928 to 1932. . . .

Part I. Extent of Voluntary Health Insurance as of July 1953.

Highlights:

1. Over 87 million people, or 57 per cent of the population, have some hospital insurance.
2. Over 74 million people, or 48 per cent, have some surgical and other medical insurance. Most of the 48 per cent have only surgery and in-hospital physicians' services but 4,900,000 have substantially complete physicians' services.
3. By occupation, there is a variation of 33 to 90 per cent with some type of health insurance.
4. By family income, 41 per cent of those under $3,000 have some type of health insurance, and 80 per cent of families over $5,000.
5. In urban areas 70 per cent of the families are enrolled in some type of health insurance and in rural-farm areas, 45 per cent.
6. 80 per cent of the families with health insurance obtained insurance through their place of work or through an employed group. . . .

Part II. Family Expenditures for Personal Health Services and Voluntary Health Insurance during the Survey Year.

Highlights:

1. The total annual charges for personal health services incurred by families in the United States is $10.2 billion.
2. Of these $10.2 billion, physicians charge $3.8 billion (37 per cent), hospitals $2.0 billion

From "National Family Survey of Medical Costs and Voluntary Health Insurance: Preliminary Report," Health Information Foundation, 1954, pp. 1–2, 11, 25, 53, 65.

(20 per cent), prescriptions and medicines $1.5 billion (15 per cent), other medical goods and services $1.3 billion (13 per cent), and dentists $1.6 billion (16 per cent).

3. Of all charges incurred by families 15 per cent is covered by insurance benefits. Broken down by type of service: hospital services, 50 per cent; all physicians' services, 13 per cent; surgery, 38 per cent; obstetrics, 25 per cent. The proportion paid by insurance for other benefits was non-existent or negligible because they are usually not covered.

4. The average charges for all personal health services is approximately $207 per family; one-half of the families have more than $110.

5. The families with insurance incurred a total median cost over twice as great as those without insurance, $145 compared with $63.

6. Seven per cent of the families, or approximately 3,500,000 families, incurred charges in excess of $495.

7. One-half of the families paid out 4.1 per cent or more of their incomes.

8. Approximately one million families paid out amounts equalling or exceeding one-half of their annual incomes, of which approximately 500,000 families paid out amounts equalling or exceeding 100 per cent of their incomes.

9. Among families receiving hospital insurance benefits, 50 per cent had 89 per cent or more of their gross hospital charges covered by hospital insurance.

10. Among families receiving surgical insurance benefits, 50 per cent had 75 per cent or more of their gross surgical charges covered by surgical insurance. . . .

Part III. Utilization of Personal Health Services and Voluntary Health Insurance during the Survey Year.

Highlights:

1. The general hospital admission rate for all families was 12 per 100 persons per year. Those with insurance had a rate of 13 and those without insurance a rate of 10.

2. The average length of hospital stay for all persons hospitalized was 9.7 days with virtually no differences between those with insurance and without insurance.

3. The number of hospital days for 100 persons per year was 100 days; for those with insurance the rate was 110 per 100 persons, and for those without insurance the rate was 80.

4. The insured rural-farm population had a hospital admission rate of 17 per 100 and the insured urban population had a rate of 12. There was no difference for those not insured.

5. The number of surgical procedures per 100 persons per year for all families was 6; among insured families the rate was 7 and among the uninsured the rate was 4.

6. Among all families, 34 per cent of the individuals sought dentists' services during a year, varying from 17 per cent for income groups under $2,000 to 56 per cent for income groups over $7,500. . . .

Part IV. Debt Among Families Due to Cost of Personal Health Services as of July 1953.

Highlights:

1. Among all families, 15 per cent are in debt to hospitals, physicians, dentists and other providers of medical goods and services, and their total debt is $900 million.

2. In absolute terms this means that approximately 7.5 million families have a medical debt and about one million of these families owe $195 or more.

3. The average debt among all families for bills owed to hospitals, physicians, dentists and other providers of medical goods and services is $121.

4. When debts to financial institutions and individuals are included, the national total is $1.1 billion.

5. A greater proportion, 21 per cent, of the families with children have a medical debt than those without children.

6. Four per cent of the families reported borrowing from financial institutions and individuals to pay charges for personal health services.

7. The greater the proportion of family income paid out for personal health services, the greater is the likelihood that the family seeks a loan.

CROSS REFERENCES TO STANDARD TEXTS *

Barnes, *Society in Transition*, Chap. 7.

Bernard, *American Community Behavior*, pp. 208–209.

Bloch, *Disorganization*, pp. 506–509.

Brown, *Social Pathology*, Chap. 16.

Cuber and Harper, *Problems of American Society*, Chap. 6.

Elliott and Merrill, *Social Disorganization*, pp. 205–208, 611–612.

Gillin, *Social Pathology*, Chaps. 2–4.

———————

* For complete bibliographical reference to each text, see page 13.

—––––– and others, *Social Problems*, Chap. 16.

Herman, *Approach to Social Problems*, pp. 240–252.

Landis, *Social Policies in the Making*, pp. 397, 453–455, 547–555.

Mihanovich, *Current Social Problems*, Chap. 11.

Neumeyer, *Social Problems and the Changing Society*, pp. 69–70, 150–155, 302, 307–310.

Odum, *American Social Problems*, Chap. 16.

Phelps and Henderson, *Contemporary Social Problems*, Chaps. 2–3.

Reinhardt and others, *Social Problems and Social Policy*, Chaps. 15, 16.

Weaver, *Social Problems*, Chaps. 6–7.

OTHER BIBLIOGRAPHY

American Dental Association, *A Dental Health Program for the Community, State and Nation*, Chicago, 1950.

Odin W. Anderson, *National Family Survey of Medical Costs and Voluntary Health Insurance*, New York: Health Information Foundation, 1954.

Roger G. Barker, Beatrice A. Wright, and Mollie R. Gonick, *Adjustment to Physical Handicap and Illness*, New York: Social Science Research Council, 1946.

Harry Best, *Blindness and the Blind in the United States*, New York: Macmillan Co., 1934.

———, *Deafness and the Deaf in the United States*, New York: Macmillan Co., 1943.

Alton L. Blakeslee, "Arthritis—And the Miracle Drugs," 3d ed., Public Affairs Pamphlet No. 166, 1952.

Gilbert Cant, "Medical Research May Save Your Life!" Public Affairs Pamphlet No. 201, 1953.

Hector Chevigny, *My Eyes Have a Cold Nose*, New Haven: Yale University Press, 1946.

——— and Sydell Braverman, *The Adjustment of the Blind*, New Haven: Yale University Press, 1950.

Loretta Chmiel, "Amputation—A Social Problem," *American Journal of Nursing*, 45 (1945): 1060–1061.

Michael M. Davis, *America Organizes Medicine*, New York: Harper & Bros., 1940.

Kathleen Cassidy Doyle, "Science vs. Chiropractic," 3d ed., Public Affairs Pamphlet No. 191, 1954.

Oscar R. Ewing, *The Nation's Health, A Ten Year Program: A Report to the President*, Washington: Federal Security Agency, 1948.

Miriam Forster Fiedler, *Deaf Children in a Hearing World*, New York: Ronald Press Co., 1953.

Lucy Freeman, "It's *Your* Hospital and *Your* Life," 2d ed., Public Affairs Pamphlet No. 187, 1953.

Oliver Garceau, *The Political Life of the American Medical Association*, Cambridge: Harvard University Press, 1941.

Franz Goldmann, *Public Medical Care*, New York: Columbia University Press, 1945.

——— and Hugh R. Leavell, eds., "Medical Care for Americans," *The Annals*, 273 (January 1951).

Samuel Perkins Hayes, *Contributions to a Psychology of Blindness*, New York: American Foundation for the Blind, 1941.

Helen Keller, *The Story of My Life*, New York: Doubleday, Page and Co., 1904.

———, *The World I Live In*, New York: D. Appleton-Century Co., 1914.

Baynard Kendrick, *Lights Out*, New York: William Morrow, 1946.

Alfred McClung Lee, "The Social Dynamics of the Physician's Status," *Psychiatry*, 7 (1944): 371–377.

William G. Lennox, *Science and Seizures: New Light on Epilepsy and Migraine*, New York: Harper & Bros., 1941.

Frances Cooke MacGregor, "Some Psycho-Social Problems Associated with Facial Deformities," *American Sociological Review*, 16 (1951): 629–638.

———, Theodora M. Abel, Albert Bryt, Edith Lauer, and Serena Weissman, *Facial Deformities and Plastic Surgery*, Springfield, Illinois: Charles C. Thomas, 1953.

Albert Q. Maisel, "Your Neighbor's Health Is *Your* Business," 2d ed., Public Affairs Pamphlet No. 180, 1953.

Harry S. Mustard, *Government in Public Health*, New York: Commonwealth Fund, 1945.

National Health Assembly, *America's Health*, New York: Harper & Bros., 1949.

Karsten Ohnstad, *The World at My Fingertips*, Indianapolis: Bobbs-Merrill Co., 1942.

Thomas Parran, *Shadow on the Land: Syphilis*, New York: Reynal and Hitchcock, 1937.

Louis H. Pink, "The Story of Blue Cross," 8th ed., Public Affairs Pamphlet No. 101, 1954.

Tracy J. Putnam, *Convulsive Seizures: A Manual for Patients, Their Families and Friends*, Philadelphia: J. B. Lippincott Co., 1943.

H. E. Sigrist, *Medicine and Human Welfare*, New Haven: Yale University Press, 1941.

Nathan Sinai, Odin W. Anderson, and Melvin L. Dollar, *Health Insurance in the United States*, New York: Commonwealth Fund, 1945.

Bernhard J. Stern, *Medicine in Industry*, New York: Commonwealth Fund, 1946.

——, *Society and Medical Progress*, Princeton: Princeton University Press, 1941.

Symposium, "The Health Status and Health Education of Negroes in the United States," *Journal of Negro Education*, Yearbook No. 18, 1949, Howard University, Washington, D. C.

T. Arthur Turner, *Organizing to Help the Handicapped*, Elyria, Ohio: National Society for Crippled Children, 1944.

U. S. Coal Mines Administration, *A Medical Survey of the Bituminous-Coal Industry*, Washington: Government Printing Office, 1947.

U. S. Social Security Board, *Medical Care and Costs in Relation to Family Income*, 2d ed., Washington: Government Printing Office, 1947.

H. G. Quaritch Wales, *Years of Blindness*, New York: T. Y. Crowell Co., 1948.

J. E. Wallace Wallin, *Children with Mental and Physical Handicaps*, New York: Prentice-Hall, 1949.

White House Conference on Child Health and Protection, *The Handicapped Child*, New York: D. Appleton-Century Co., 1933.

Charles-Edward Amory Winslow, *The Conquest of Epidemic Disease*, Princeton: Princeton University Press, 1943.

REVIEW QUESTIONS

1. To what does Mayo attribute the high percentage of rejectees among the eighteen-year-olds during World War II?
2. What are the chief lacks among health facilities for improving child and youth health?
3. Why are Switzer and Rusk convinced that the neglect of disability is more costly than an aggressive program of rehabilitation?
4. What is the general trend of the accidental death rate from all types of accidents?
5. What types of accidents are taking a more serious toll than formerly?
6. About how much a year is now spent on medical research? How does this compare with the amount spent on alcoholic drinks?
7. What percentage of the population has hospitalization insurance?
8. How many families have medical costs exceeding their annual income?

─CHAPTER 16─→

The Mentally Deficient and Diseased

MODERN PSYCHIATRY has helped to substitute scientific conclusions for the superstitious fears that once made the treatment of the mentally ill so difficult, and the mass mediums of communication are aiding by transmitting such findings to the public.

The toll of mental deficiency and illness is vast. Their varieties are many. And the job of interpretation to the public and of obtaining support for curative programs from the public is a complex one. Burgess discusses social factors in the causation and prevention of mental disorders and suggests areas for further research. Stevenson tells of the limitations of current treatment facilities and suggests steps that might be taken on a county or district level to help cope with the increasing problem.

Because alcoholics are so numerous in our society, their mental illnesses—roughly grouped under the term "alcoholism"—have received considerable attention, especially under the stimuli provided by Alcoholics Anonymous and by the Prohibition-worried brewers and distillers. Sociologists have been especially interested in alcoholism because of the striking manner in which societal conditions, especially cultural heritage, influence its incidence. Mowrer makes a psychocultural analysis of the alcoholic on the basis of clinical data. Bales describes the workings of Alcoholics Anonymous, one of the most effective means of rehabilitating the alcoholic.

In the final selection, Simpson deals with another of our more distressing problems—suicide. He suggests that "interrelating psychoanalytic discoveries on the motives for suicide with the social conditions under which suicide occurs" may aid our understanding and help us toward finding means of averting such tragedies.

The Causation and Prevention of Mental Disorders
Ernest W. Burgess *

This paper will propose a number of hypotheses concerning the causation and prevention of mental disorders, with special emphasis upon the social factors, and will then suggest certain problems in this field which call for interdisciplinary research.

As yet there is no general agreement on the causes of mental disorders. In the literature three groups of factors have been identified: the biological, the psychological, and the social.

Each of the three aspects of the mental disorder can and should be dealt with specifically but with recognition of the role of the other aspects. Franz Kallman has made an incisive statement of this point: "It is essential to understand the intricate etiological interaction of gene-specific biochemical dysfunctions, general constitutional (adaptational) modifiers, and precipitating outside factors arising from the effect of certain basic imperfections in the structure of modern human so-

* See identifying note on page 160.
From "Social Factors in the Etiology and Prevention of Mental Disorders," *Social Problems, 1* (1953–54): 53–56

cieties. Any approach which tends to be forgetful of one of these fundamental elements in the causation of a severe psychosis may be responsible for the crucial difference between therapeutic failure and success." [1] In the remainder of this section we shall confine our discussion to the social factors, it being understood that they operate in interaction with the biological and psychological.

Few or no authorities claim that social factors are the direct cause of mental breakdowns. Instead they may be regarded as precipitating rather than as predisposing factors.

People live in society which is a network of social relationships. Usually a person is in good mental health if he has free communication with his fellows and finds self expression and personal development in social groups such as the family, the peer group, the work group, and in recreational, educational, and religious activities.

If, however, he experiences rejection in the family, has no participation in a peer group, meets with frustration in occupational, recreational, and other activities, then he is unadjusted and may become maladjusted. One form of maladjustment is mental breakdown.

Some students of the problem assert that the most important factor affecting mental health is urbanization. The growth of cities has resulted in a number of changes in our institutions and social relations which would seem to exert an adverse influence on the mental health of the population. The effects of urbanization can be most readily perceived by contrasting life in the city with the old-time rural neighborhood. The change has been from low to high density of population, from simple to complex and complicated social relations, from face-to-face intimacy to impersonal contacts, from primary to secondary social control, from a family-centered economy to employment often in a gigantic industry, from a stable to an unstable home life, from the predominance of sacred to the growth of secular values. All these and other changes appear to have increased the stress and strain of adjustments in the city as compared with rural living. Specifically, certain aspects of urbanization seem to be related to problems of individual adjustment.

The greater complexity of living requires greater

adjustments in making choices of a mate, of associates, of an occupation, etc.

The increasing instability of the family leads to feelings of rejection on the part of the child, to behavior problems of children, and to juvenile delinquency.

The decline of the neighborhood results in a larger proportion of detached persons.

The growth of impersonal relations, loneliness, and isolation is particularly marked in rooming house areas and apartment house districts of our large cities.

The slums of the city are areas of high density of population, bad housing, overcrowding, neighborhood deterioration and the concentration of social problems, all of which may contribute to personal unadjustment and maladjustment.

The increasing tempo of city life, the growing intensity of the struggle for success and the maximization of stimulations, especially of the motion picture, radio, and television are other manifestations of urbanization making for complexity and confusion.

The total effect of this impact of urbanization on people may be sufficient to account for the increase of patients in mental hospitals. Why then has not the increase been much larger?

1. The lower proportion of persons with mental disorders who marry and the lower average number of their offspring as compared with the general population.

2. The improvement of the physical health of people in this country.

3. The betterment of working conditions in industry and the reduction of the hours of work resulting in less fatigue and strain among workers.

4. The introduction of labor-saving devices in industry, farming, business and the home.

5. The decline in commercialized prostitution and the increasing use of prophylactics against venereal diseases.

6. The lower per capita consumption of alcoholic beverages and the success of Alcoholics Anonymous and other methods of curing alcoholism.

7. The progress of medical science in the discovery of causes of specific mental disorders and advance in methods of treatment.

These counteracting factors may be regarded as approximately balancing or even outweighing the adverse effects of urbanization previously stated. If so, what is the explanation for the increasing proportion of patients in mental hospitals?

An urbanization factor not yet mentioned is probably sufficient to account for this fact. It is the growing willingness of families to send a mentally ill member to a mental hospital instead of caring for him at home. This change in be-

---

[1] Franz J. Kallman, "The Genetics of Psychoses: and Analysis of 1,232 Twin Index Families," *American Journal of Human Genetics,* 2 (1950), 390.

havior is the result of three chief causes. The first is the growing difficulty of keeping a mentally ill person in the family in the city because of the decreasing number of rooms in the dwelling, the absence of other family members at work or in school during the day, and the objections of other residents in apartment houses.

Second is the lessening of the sense of responsibility of the family, particularly for aged parents. The public is increasingly more disposed to regard the care of the mentally ill as the responsibility of the state rather than of the family.

Third is the decline in the stigma previously placed on admission to a mental hospital. This change of attitude is largely a result of public education in mental health. There is an increasing tendency to regard mental illness in much the same way as physical illness. The mental hospital is being thought of less and less as a place of custodial care of dangerous, incurable "crazy" individuals. It is now being considered more and more as a medical institution for the treatment and recovery of patients who will return to the community.

A program for the prevention of mental disorders to be successful must take account of the biological, psychological, and social factors in their causation.

The following discussion will include proposed as well as actual activities.

1. *Improvement of the physical constitution* of members of society by:

a) positive and negative eugenical measures, so far as they are feasible, to increase the reproduction of the biologically fit relative to those less fit;

b) raising the standards of health, housing, and nutrition;

c) extending the benefits of medical science to all groups in the population;

d) further reducing the strain and fatigue of work in industry, business, trades, and professions;

e) extension of social security to groups not yet covered and relating benefits to the cost of living;

f) specific preventive measures such as prophylaxis against infection in venereal disease, etc.

2. *Improvement in mental health* by dealing with *psychological factors* in its incidence:

a) parent education in the psychology of child rearing;

b) the expansion of preschool centers such as day nurseries and cooperative play groups;

c) early detection and treatment of behavior problems of children;

d) the extension of counseling in its various forms: vocational, premarital, industrial, personal, etc.

3. *Social measures* for the improvement of mental health:

a) stimulation of participation of persons of all ages in social groups to insure sense of belonging, of having friends, of security in social relations, and of status;

b) the development of competence in interpersonal relations in the various groups in our society: the family, the play group, at work, in voluntary associations, etc.

c) community organization to plan and operate a program for positive mental health;

d) a national program of social security planned and financed by co-operation of individuals, industry, and government, each assuming its legitimate area of responsibility;

e) a planning of recreational activities for wider participation, particularly of those groups and individuals which are not reached at present;

f) a campaign of public education not only to remove the stigma upon mental illness but to secure an understanding of the principles of mental health and social living.

The great body of research will and should continue to be within each of the several disciplines—biology, chemistry, cultural anthropology, psychiatry, psychology, and sociology—concerned with various aspects of mental health. But the opportunity and desirability of interdisciplinary research should not be overlooked where conditions are favorable.

Interdisciplinary research by its very nature is more complicated than a project carried on within one discipline. Yet a given problem may be one that cannot be adequately studied by each discipline separately. This is the situation which calls for cooperative effort. The problem needs to be stated in a larger framework than that offered by the separate disciplines. It requires the combined attack upon it by the research methods of two or more disciplines.

Certain problems in the field of mental health are now ready for interdisciplinary research. Three may be cited for purposes of illustration:

Detection of prepsychotic persons. The identification of adolescents and youths predisposed to mental breakdown is important for experiments in prevention. Various symptoms are important for study. These may be organic, psychiatric, psychological, and social.

An index of aging in relation to the senile psychoses. An index of aging should include physiological, psychological, and social data. A crucial question is the interrelation of physiological and psychological changes with increase or decrease of social activities, and success or failure in making adjustments to crises.

A community health program. A mental health project in a community might be directed to the education of the residents (and particularly of families with members under treatment in mental hospitals) in the nature of mental illness and in the way to accept recovered patients on their return home. An evaluation of the success of the project should be undertaken by an interdisciplinary group.

Other illustrations will occur to readers. The inclusion of staff members in mental hospitals to represent the different disciplines often creates a situation favorable for the prosecution of interdisciplinary research. The social scientist, functioning in such capacities as clinical sociologist or research associate, is receiving increasing recognition as a necessary member of such interdisciplinary teams.

Needed: A Plan for the Mentally Ill

George S. Stevenson

George Salvadore Stevenson (1892–   ), child psychiatrist, medical director of National Committee for Mental Hygiene. Author with Geddes Smith of *Child Guidance Clinics—A Quarter Century of Development* (1934).

Some miles outside almost any major American city, on a two-lane macadam road off the main highway, there is a group of large buildings, quite a few of them, probably of red brick. They sit on broad sweeps of beautiful greensward; a little network of small roads, all studded with signs that read "Speed Limit 15 M.P.H.," threads among them. This is the State mental hospital. Externally, the setting is attractive, the buildings of good architecture. Inside, the impression a visitor gets is something else again.

There is the pervading, indescribable institutional odor. There is the barrenness of the interior —little furniture, no pictures on the walls, nothing loose anywhere. Everything is colorless. Patients wear loose hospital clothing that has faded with years of laundering. They have no belts, no shoelaces, nothing with which they might harm themselves.

In one of the wards patients sit on benches or on the floor. They seem absorbed in their own private worlds. Some are weeping or groaning miserably; others are staring abstractedly through the barred windows at the grounds, which apparently are kept better than they are. In the small rooms where "disturbed" patients are confined individually there are no furnishings, no bed, just a soiled mattress. Perhaps in the next room there is a patient in a strait-jacket. In the large bathroom at the end of the hall a violent case reclines in a tub, his chin held above the water by a canvas harness; the swirling water soothes him. On a near-by table another patient lies swathed in a wet sheet; this is also a sedative device, one that tends to make him drowsy.

What goes on inside the hospital provides a vivid contrast with the orderly external appearance of the institution. And that contrast, to a great extent, symbolizes the status of public psychiatric treatment today. Throughout the United States we are confronted with a seriously ailing system of public psychiatry. The disturbing newspaper and magazine articles of the past few years which have described mental hospitals as "modern Bedlams" have been unpleasant because they couldn't be anything else and still tell the truth. And yet they have not told the worst, for they have criticized superficial conditions without getting at the core of this particular malady of American civilization. . . .

The dreadful mediocrity of our State institutions for psychotic and mentally deficient patients

From "Needed: A Plan for the Mentally Ill," *The New York Times Magazine* (July 27, 1947), pp. 11, 18–19. Reprinted by permission.

is merely a symptom of an outdated system that is crying for a complete remodeling. What we need today is an entirely new *concept* of public psychiatry. When the problem is viewed as a whole, the function of the mental hospital assumes its proper proportion. Then we can more accurately appraise our mental institutions and take up the more fundamental aspects of what is wrong with them.

The typical public mental hospital is indeed a sorry sight. Every State has one or more of these large—often monstrously large—facilities. Some are more handicapped than others. Very few can stand up under close examination, deficient as they are in doctors, nurses, attendants, social workers and other personnel, food, clothing, living space, sanitary facilities and recreation. . . .

First of all, our hospitals desperately need all types of personnel—especially doctors. Psychiatrists returning from the armed forces, where they have experienced the satisfaction of using their full scientific skill in the treatment of patients, are avoiding the many positions which are available in large public mental hospitals.

Young psychiatrists want good training, good supervision and an opportunity to live and work well. These conditions are not generally available under the present system of public psychiatry.

As psychiatrists are better trained—as they are now being trained—to treat patients scientifically and by tested methods they will be less and less attracted to our present system, which is focused primarily or even exclusively on large isolated hospitals separated from the past and future of the patient and from the community. Doctors who are interested in their patients do not accept without protest a system that ignores the earlier stages of illness, the conditions that produced it and the period of convalescence and adjustment which follows recovery. They want to control the conditions that keep people well or that produce a relapse.

With the extension of psychiatry into the community (such as in clinics and social agencies) and with private psychiatric practice growing enormously every year, the more competent psychiatrists are now looking toward the cities and private patients. Hence the future staff members in large hospitals are likely to be chosen from a less qualified group.

The mental hospitals also need psychiatric social workers. For a long time now hospitals have been unable to attract competent social workers as they formerly did.

The situation with these specialists is strikingly similar to that of the psychiatrists. . . .

In addition to doctors and social workers, the hospitals need nurses trained in psychiatric practice and the various kinds of therapists who can so effectively implement a good program of psychiatric care. They also need many more attendants—good ones. They need more inside space, facilities, appropriations—and public support.

But the solution does not lie entirely in the recruitment of good personnel any more than it lies in spending vast sums of money on hospital buildings. Having disposed of the needs of the hospitals themselves, we need now to go a step beyond the institutions. This entails a new concept of public psychiatry, viewed from a broader perspective.

What we need to realize is that the mental hospital constitutes *only one aspect* of the whole field of public psychiatry. We have to consider the needs of the millions who are not ill enough to require hospitalization but who still need help. (Private psychiatric practice, because of its expense, reaches only a minute proportion of our neuropsychiatric cases.)

The psychiatric function of society cannot work well while it is centered in a hospital building far out in the country. Every device should be used to bring it closer to the community and nearer to centers of research and learning. Perhaps the new system will be community-centered, with the hospital ward *as an adjunct service.*

Instead of having hospitals as the core of our psychiatric care, I suggest we look for administrative leadership to a district, municipal, county or regional Director of Psychiatry. He would have the responsibility for:

(1) The care and treatment of protracted, severe psychiatric cases needing hospitalization, the type now occupying most of the beds of our mental hospitals.

(2) The care and training of protracted cases of mental deficiency not returnable to the community who are now in an institution for mental deficiency or awaiting admission because the institution is too small or holds cases that should be in the community.

(3) The care and treatment of the legal offender whose offense is a symptom of psychiatric disorder. In this, public psychiatry would cooperate with public safety.

(4) The care of acute psychiatric cases needing hospitalization for a short period. This would be in the local general or special hospitals or in State hospitals if conveniently situated.

(5) The care and treatment of the psychoneurotic patient. This is to a limited degree a matter of hospitalization, and then usually in a general hospital. To a very extensive degree it is a matter of out-patient service.

(6) The care of behavior problems, especially those of children. In this, public psychiatry would cooperate with public health, public education and public welfare.

(7) Consultation to teachers, social workers, courts, public health nurses, ministers, general-practice doctors and others in the community who are dealing with people in trouble, so that they may more adequately deal with the lesser psychiatric problems involved in their work and know how and when to refer the more severe cases to a psychiatric clinic.

(8) The ferreting out and correction of defects in the community, such as inadequate recreational facilities and industrial hazards, which contribute to emotional disorders and mental breakdown.

The Director of Psychiatry would thus bring together not only the past and future of the hospital patient but the problems of those who will never need hospitalization, though they still need treatment. He would at the same time protect those who are well.

Such a change, moreover, includes a public-health principle: it deals with the conditions that contribute to mental illness and it builds up a greater public appreciation of the problem and the citizenry's responsibility. The Director of Psychiatry would have a challenging job—psychiatric service in his community would mean infinitely more than just hospitalization. A few such men backed up by community demand, which they would arouse, could change the whole complexion of a State hospital.

A Psychocultural Analysis of the Alcoholic

Harriet R. Mowrer

Harriet R. Mowrer (Mrs. Ernest R.) (1899–   ), consultant in domestic discord and personality adjustment. Chief works: with Ernest R. Mowrer, *Domestic Discord* (1928); *Personality Adjustment and Domestic Discord* (1935).

Drinking and the Cultural Milieu. In any analysis of the personality of the alcoholic, one must keep in mind the cultural milieu. Accordingly, the reasons men give for drinking and the circumstances surrounding it are in themselves of little scientific value. The alcoholic no more than the person experiencing domestic discord can give unaided the real causes of his difficulty. What he gives is the cultural definition of the situation, that is, those causes approved by the culture of his group. In our culture, such happy occasions as weddings, births, sudden good fortune, etc., call for and furnish excuses for drinking. Likewise, sorrows occasioned by death, financial reverses, disappointments in love and marriage, etc., are crisis situations which can be met and conquered by alcohol, the magic medicine. It keeps those happy who are already happy and makes the sad happy again. Wine is often the symbol of fruitfulness, and drinking to one's health is interpreted as expressing the wish that the life principle in wine may do him good. Alcohol, likewise, is supposed to make the shy become bold and the weak strong. It has long been associated with masculinity and sexual prowess. Quite consistent, then, are the reasons given by the alcoholics: "I drink to make me happy"; "I drink to forget my troubles"; "When I drink I feel like a man"; "Drinking helps me to make a sale"; "Drinking helps me forget that I have no wife"; and so on.

Here, of course, the alcoholic does not distinguish between normal drinking and chronic alcoholism. The average individual probably experiences a satisfying glow and a feeling of contentment and happiness as the result of an occasional drink. But does this average person experience the

From "A Psychocultural Analysis of the Alcoholic," *American Sociological Review*, 5 (1940): 546–557, pp. 554–557 quoted. Reprinted by permission.

same reaction in solitude as in the company of friends? This suggests a more general question: How much of the effect attributed to alcohol is due to the physiological response of the organism and how much to the social-psychological setting? This is not to deny that alcohol, particularly the chronic use of it, does not have any effect upon the physiological processes and psychological functions, but this paper is not concerned with this aspect.

It is doubtful, however, whether the chronic alcoholic experiences the oral satisfaction of the occasional drinker because he is inclined to drink hurriedly; in fact, his drinking often takes on the appearance of the performance of a ritual. While it is generally conceded that inhibitions are released through liquor, there is a wide variance as to how people behave under its influence. Not all shy persons become bold nor do all persons become happy. Many become sad and despondent; others, taciturn and unsociable; still others remain unchanged while under the influence of liquor. While the chronic alcoholic may say drinking enables him to meet his business associates and put across a deal, the clinical history may show this not to be the case. Alcohol, while it may increase sexual desire, decreases ability at performance, so in reality can hardly be said to increase sexual prowess. Thus it would seem that the chronic alcoholic is in a paradoxical situation. Rather than having been betrayed by his mother through the nursing experience, as some psychoanalysts have contended, he has instead been betrayed by his culture which has held out to him a false panacea for his problems.

The Alcoholic Personality Pattern. It seems apparent that the behavior of the individual under the influence of liquor is not as significant for an understanding of the alcoholic as has been believed in the past. What is more important are the attitudes of the members of his family toward him as a consequence of his alcoholism. The importance of these subsequent attitudes is suggested by the fact that, like the "neurotic" woman, he does not want to be cured of his social handicap.

Instead of slowly ruining his life, as the portrayals of the influence of alcohol would have one believe, the alcoholic, through his drinking, achieves satisfactions which he can realize in no other way. As an aftermath to his drinking, his role becomes equivalent to that played in earlier familial interaction. While some members of his family are disgusted with him, strict in their attitude, consider him an "inferior," a problem, etc., there are others who pamper him all the more, give him unlimited attention, always believe in and fasten hope upon his determination and pledge to "throw away the bottle." Even his wife, vacillating as is her attitude toward him, while inclined to criticize him, yet expresses sympathy and a maternal feeling for him.

How the alcoholic achieves the limelight as a consequence of drinking is illustrated in all the attention which he subsequently receives. Family conferences are held; plans are worked out to help him resist the temptation to drink; new inducements are offered him; and in general he occupies the center of the stage. Thus, for example, a program is worked out by the family requiring him to report each day to a sister, or a wife may meet him at the close of the day's work and thus protect him from the influence of drinking companions. The consequences are that the subsequent exemplary behavior under this regimen convinces those concerned that a cure has been effected. The moment the scheme is abandoned, however, the alcoholic relapses into drinking. Obviously, the cause of the relapse is not that new crises have arisen or that his former drinking companions have asserted their influence, but that he no longer receives the attention which he got under the regimen of supervision. Observing the collapse of his attention-consuming role, he again reinstates it through another drinking debauch.

How deceptive may be the immediate circumstances surrounding drinking may be illustrated by the following incidents. In one case, the alcoholic became drunk instead of appearing at the funeral of his brother. In another, he failed to go with his children to the hospital to see his wife, becoming drunk instead. At first sight, it would appear that drunkenness in each instance represented an avoidance of the sorrow and pain involved in these circumstances. More thorough analysis, however, revealed that the first person's relationship with his brother had not been such as to call out any deep sorrow and that the second quarreled recurrently with his wife, accusing her of infidelity, as a projection of his own sexual impotency. The more plausible interpretation of both instances is that each was a rebellion against the attention given another member of the family. The subsequent attention which each received as an aftermath of his drunkenness confirms this interpretation.

Thus it becomes clear that the behavior of the

alcoholic cannot be understood except with reference to the basic pattern of personality developed in early familial interaction. Alcoholism provides a way of recapturing at least temporarily the attention-receiving role of the early familial group. This recapturing of the childhood role, however, is much more the aftermath of drinking, than something which is obtained exclusively under the influence of liquor.

The consequence is, that in order to understand the alcoholic, it is necessary to keep in mind this basic pattern of personality. The moment segments of behavior are detached from the total configuration, the picture becomes distorted. In this distortion, single factors are considered causes of alcoholism with little realization upon the part of the researcher that these factors may have a wider application than the alcoholic, or if not, that they are but part of a larger causal complex.

Alcoholism and Group Therapy: Alcoholics Anonymous
Robert Freed Bales

Robert Freed Bales (1916–   ), lecturer and research associate, laboratory of social relations, Harvard University. Author of *Interaction Process Analysis* (1950) and, with Talcott Parsons and Edward A. Shils, *Working Papers in the Theory of Action* (1953).

There have been a number of popular movements in the history of therapy for alcohol addiction which have hit upon this basic principle [social reintegration through group therapy] and have utilized it with what was regarded in their time as spectacular success. Father Mathew's movement in Ireland, Mr. Bosshardt's group in Switzerland, the Washingtonian movement in the United States, the "Catch-My-Pal" movement in Ireland and England are a few examples from the last century and a half which would repay careful study. The most convincing present evidence that a group approach to the re-education of the compulsive drinker works on a large scale with an effectiveness and efficiency hardly approached by any other means of therapy is provided by Alcoholics Anonymous. This movement started with two compulsive drinkers searching for a way to keep sober, in Akron, Ohio, in 1935, and now has something over fourteen thousand members, all ex-alcoholics, with groups in practically all the large cities of the United States. This organization can certainly be said to have had spectacular success, even though various complications make any exact evaluation of their success in comparison with other methods quite difficult.

The new candidate for Alcoholics Anonymous finds that the group is made up exclusively of others who have been exactly in his own situation. He finds that they have schemed and planned and struggled and stolen to keep their supply of alcohol, just as he has. They have felt the same self-justification, inarticulate rage, and aggression. They have drunk their way into and out of every possible jam and, as a group, know every in and out of the life of the compulsive drinker.

That the members do know and understand the compulsive drinker comes out in the group meetings, which are given over chiefly to short narratives by the members of their drinking experiences, humorous and tragic, of their final realization that their attempt to adjust through drinking was hopeless, and of the way in which they were able to stop. It is customary for a new member to "qualify himself as a genuine alcoholic" by relating events from his drinking experience which undeniably identify him with the other members who know and recognize all the signs. The new candidate in such a group intuitively recognizes that he is among friends, and that when they speak of their experiences they speak of his own. They "talk the same language."

From "Social Therapy for a Social Disorder—Compulsive Drinking," *Journal of Social Issues*, 1: 3 (December 1945): 1–9, pp. 4–8 quoted. Reprinted by permission.

They feel as he feels. They do not condemn him. There is nothing to fight against.

The usual situation is here completely reversed; the alcoholic obtains recognition and response through the admission of thoughts and activities which, before, he had been desperately trying to hide, even from himself. In the course of time he opens out, and his experience becomes a part of the group experience. What he had thought were personal drinking secrets, monstrously invented and indulged in by himself alone, become trade secrets, and humorously or dramatically told, add to his effectiveness and sense of belonging. He becomes aware of habits of thought and feeling in himself which heretofore had been repressed and compulsively active. He undergoes a personal emotional catharsis, partly through the group meetings, partly through particular confidants he discovers in the group, and partly through his attempts to make amends to friends and associates for wrongs he feels he has done them in the course of his drinking career. The "Twelve Steps" which comprise a condensed statement of the therapeutic program and give it a religious rationale take care of these various aspects in a systematic way.[1] Although the program is admirably set forth in these twelve steps and individuals have been known to achieve sobriety through "The Book" alone without benefit of group contact, there is little reason to doubt that getting across the basic ideas in the personal and group setting is vastly more effective for the majority.

It seems reasonable to assume that ideas which come to the individual as convictions held by an organized group of which he feels irrevocably a part come to him with a greater clarity and intensity than information which comes to him in printed form, or as advice from a doctor or professional worker. A great many alcoholics, in fact, have a standing grudge against all professional workers, whom they tend to distrust and suspect of a lack of real sympathetic understanding at best, or of outright commercialism at the worst. It is a striking fact that an alcoholic will return to the doctor or social worker after a few meetings of Alcoholics Anonymous and will repeat to him with enthusiasm and conviction ideas of distinct therapeutic value which the profes-

sional worker had been unable to get over in a considerably longer time.

Many compulsive drinkers with long drinking careers and innumerable contacts with doctors come to recognize and emotionally accept for the first time as members of Alcoholics Anonymous that they are "alcoholics," that they cannot take even one drink without continuing on a spree, and that their only hope is absolute and complete abstinence. They learn that it is the *first* drink which they must avoid. They learn to detect and recognize their "screwey alcoholic thinking" for what it is, the first stirring fantasy which leads to the full-fledged craving and the fatal first drink. They learn that they must live in a world in which there is constant opportunity and encouragement to drink, and yet be sufficiently armed within themselves to say "no," without feeling resentment that others can drink and get away with it. These ideas and many others are constantly reiterated, infinitely varied in form and detail, in the context of impressive personal experience.

It is a fact which continues to provoke a sort of wonder and awe among the members and others who have seen the process actually at work that in the course of participation in Alcoholics Anonymous *the craving disappears.* "I did not leave alcohol—alcohol left me," is one phrase which the members use to express this phenomenal fact. The impressiveness of this fact is one of the concrete bases for the belief of the members in "a Power greater than the self." Belief in such a Power, stated in these very general terms, is gradually suggested to the candidate and gives the group a basically religious character.

The enthusiasm of the members is convincing evidence that the association gives them satisfactions and gratifications which they had previously been unable to attain. Membership and acceptance in the group alone provides a number of these satisfactions, but the action program gives still further opportunities for molding and confirming new, non-alcoholic modes of satisfaction to common human goals. The member is urged to work with other alcoholics and give them the opportunity to try the program for themselves. He has, in his own experience, the most effective possible "kit of tools" for this activity. No matter how ineffective he has been in other respects in the past, he has a good chance to succeed at this, since the number of alcoholics is very great, and some of those to whom he talks are bound to be

---

[1] For a complete statement and discussion of these twelve steps, *Alcoholics Anonymous,* New York: Works Publishing Co., 1942.

receptive to the proper approach, as he was. He knows his job, where to put in the entering wedge, what language to use, how far to go, what reaction to expect, and how to deal with it, for in their experience, and in their patterns of thought and feeling regarding drinking, alcoholics are very much alike.

In working to put over the new ideas which have enabled him to become sober, the member identifies himself still more strongly with the group. He confirms by repetition the effects it has had upon him. And in so doing, he feels a new sense of power, adequacy, and authority. His former position is reversed; whereas before he was the "child," the inferior and defensive "bad boy," or "the patient," he now is the wise and benevolent "father" or "mother," mature adult who has made good in the face of handicaps. He is "the doctor." He is consulted and depended upon by others in the group. His opinions and explanations are respected. Now he is the teacher instead of the pupil, and he can accept the idea of re-education with more equanimity, although actually the term is not much used in the group.

The leaders of the group become the principal links with the larger community, and are active in it both in a general way and in ways which draw upon community resources for the benefit of alcoholics. The bridge back to the parent social body, with the various aids it can offer, is completed. A series of intermediate roles is thus established, bridging the gap between the position of the isolated and rebellious compulsive drinker, and the position of a full-fledged responsible member of the larger community. The alcoholic, even when not an explicit leader of the group, can pass from one to the other of these intermediate roles with relative ease. Although the ex-alcoholic will probably always want and need to retain his membership and activity in the group, since the old thought and feeling patterns lie constantly in wait within him, he is no longer an outcast, but a full-fledged member of the larger community, participating in a way he would never have thought possible in his drinking days.

Perhaps it might be said that re-education in the larger sense always involves a reintegration of the individual with the parent social body and its common life, its institutions, its ways of thinking, its valued symbols, its particular and exclusive practices. Permanent belongingness in an organized, locally rooted, solidary social system is the only concrete matrix capable of grasping and involving the whole motivation of the man, his whole emotional and active life, as well as his intellectual processes. Consequently, this sort of matrix is ultimately the most effective setting for the re-educational process.[2] All other settings are partial and less effective. The most effective educative agencies—those in which the primary formative socialization takes place—(the family of orientation, friendship groups, the religious body)—all tend precisely toward this pattern, with a tendency to maximize solidarity, permanency, local and territorial segregation, common life and common rituals, and unlimited obligations of members to one another. Particular agencies are effective in the educative process pretty closely to the degree that they realize and embody this all-inclusive grasp on the individual.

Alcoholics Anonymous does not incorporate all of the elements mentioned, but it distinctly tends toward this pattern. It probably goes about as far in this direction as is easily compatible with our larger institutional system, certainly far enough to be remarkably effective in a task of re-education which has proved notably refractory to other, more superficial approaches. It is for this reason that it may provide concrete suggestions for other re-educative programs (e.g., racial prejudice, autocratic behavior) which are meant to modify individuals extensively, but must still fit into the context of the larger social system and complement its activities.

[2] Cf. Durkheim, Emile, L'Education Morale. Paris-Librarie: Felix Alcan, 1925, p. 95 ff.

On Suicide

George Simpson

George Simpson (1908–   ), assistant professor of sociology and anthropology, Brooklyn College of the City of New York. Principal works: *Conflict and Community* (1937); transl. and ed., Emile Durkheim, *Suicide* (1951); with Fritz Kafka, *Basic Statistics* (1952); *Science as Morality* (1953); *Man in Society* (1954).

Since Durkheim's work on suicide, the chief advances in our knowledge of the subject have come from actuarial and vital statistics, and psychoanalytic psychiatry.[1] The actuarialists have studied the over-all extent and trends of suicide, related it to race and color incidence, age and sex distribution, urban and rural areas, seasonality, economic conditions, religious affiliation, marital status. This type of approach is seen in Louis I. Dublin's and Bessie Bunzel's *To Be or Not To Be* (1933). An earlier work of Ruth S. Cavan, *Suicide* (1928), should also be mentioned at this point.

But the most important advances have been made in psychoanalytic psychiatry in literature which is certainly not well known among social scientists. To be sure, Dublin and Bunzel, and Cavan, append general discussions of this viewpoint in their works, but the psychiatric viewpoint and the sociological approach are nowhere integrated, as a whole, for aetiological ascription. On the other hand, the psychiatrists have done little to integrate their material with the sociological. . . .

It is the basic hypothesis here that interrelating psychoanalytic discoveries on the motives for suicide with the social conditions under which suicide occurs, offers the most fruitful method of advancing our knowledge of the phenomenon. Let us therefore follow the procedure of first stating summarily the present psychoanalytic viewpoint, and then seek to establish how it may be interrelated in research with sociological variables.

In 1918 at a psychoanalytic symposium on suicide in Vienna, Sigmund Freud summarized the discussion as follows: "Despite the valuable material obtained in this discussion, we have not succeeded in arriving at any definite conclusion. . . . Let us therefore refrain from forming an opinion until the time comes when experience will have solved the problem."[2] Since then, extensive work has been done on suicide by expert, highly trained psychoanalysts including Freud, Zilboorg, Abraham, Menninger, Brill, and others. For our purposes, Zilboorg's work is most pertinent.

On this subject of the aetiology of suicide, all investigators in psychiatry tread with great caution. Though psychoanalytic psychiatry holds that within the corpus of its interpretative principles of behavior there are tools for ferreting out the causes of suicide, no one yet seems ready to commit himself unreservedly to a set of aetiological postulates, based on either empirical data or inference from established principles. Zilboorg writes: "It is clear that the problem of suicide from the scientific point of view remains unsolved. Neither common sense nor clinical psychopathology has found a causal or even a strict empirical solution."[3]

An original and pervasive methodological obstacle must be clearly understood, an obstacle which is almost impossible wholly to overcome at the present time. Unless the individual who commits suicide has been under constant and long-time psychiatric examination (either through psychoanalysis or clinical study with full and detailed life-history records), an interpretation and classification of his suicide becomes an *ex post facto* reconstruction of his life-history. This is extremely difficult, and probably impossible in most cases. Not even the most ardent opinion-poller or attitude-tester can go around interview-

---

[1] In the tradition of Durkheim, there is, to be sure, the large-scale work of his friend and student, Maurice Halbwachs, *Les Causes du Suicide*, published in 1930.

[2] Quoted by Gregory Zilboorg, "Differential Diagnostic Types of Suicide," *Archives of Neurology and Psychiatry*, vol. 35, 1936, p. 272.

[3] *Op. cit.*, p. 271.

From "Methodological Problems in Determining the Aetiology of Suicide," *American Sociological Review*, 15 (October 1950): 658–663.

ing suicides, and representative samples of a population can scarcely be investigated solely on the anticipatory ground that some of the items in the sample will commit suicide.

To some small degree, this obstacle has been overcome by psychoanalytic psychiatrists who have re-examined the records of patients who were under treatment or examination and who committed suicide then or later, or of patients who attempted suicide unsuccessfully or toyed with the idea. Zilboorg particularly concerned himself with this problem, in a close study of institutionalized cases, and his conclusions must therefore be looked upon as a fairly definitive statement of where psychoanalytic psychiatry stands in this regard. He found that suicide appeared in those suffering from depressive psychoses, compulsive neuroses, and schizophrenia, and was led to the conclusion: "Evidently there is no single clinical entity recognized in psychiatry that is immune to the suicidal drive."[4] Suicide, according to Zilboorg, "is to be viewed rather as a reaction of a developmental nature which is universal and common to the mentally sick of all types and probably also to many so-called normal persons."[5] He feels that "further psychoanalytic studies . . . will probably permit one later to subject the data to statistical tabulation and thus facilitate and probably corroborate the work on the clinical typology of suicides."[6]

But perhaps the most important methodological obstacle of all, in the study of the aetiology of suicide, is the unreliability and inadequacy of the statistics. Zilboorg flatly states: "Statistical data on suicides as they are compiled today deserve little if any credence; it has been repeatedly pointed out by scientific students of the problem that suicide cannot be subject to statistical evaluation, since all too many suicides are not reported as such. Those who kill themselves through automobile accidents are almost never recorded as suicides; those who sustain serious injuries during an attempt to commit suicide and die weeks or months later of these injuries or of intercurrent infections are never registered as suicides; a great many genuine suicides are concealed by families; and suicidal attempts, no matter how serious, never find their way into the tables of vital statistics. It is obvious that under these circumstances the statistical data available cover

the smallest and probably the least representative number of suicides; one is justified, therefore, in discarding them as nearly useless in a scientific evaluation of the problem."[7]

Moreover, Fenichel, following Brill and Menninger, has pointed out the prevalence of "partial suicides," where death does not occur but which consist of "self-destructive actions, during melancholic states, carried out as self-punishment, as an expression of certain delusions or without any rationalization." The term, "partial suicides," Fenichel concludes "is absolutely correct in so far as the underlying unconscious mechanisms are identical with those of suicide."[8] It is clear that these "partial suicides" never find their way into the statistics of suicide. From the aetiological standpoint, they are identical with consummated suicides; but of them all, Fenichel writes: "The factors, doubtlessly quantitative in nature, that determine whether or when the result is to be a suicide, a manic attack, or a recovery are still unknown."[9]

Even were statistical regularity now ascertainable, a methodologist of science, Harold Larrabee, citing the statistics of female suicides in New York City, writes: "What makes the statistical regularity of long-run conduct so striking is the fact that it shows itself in acts which are not the simple outcomes of a few mechanical forces, like the movements of spun coins, but in masses of close decisions of a very complex sort."[10]

It appears inescapable to conclude that until we have better records and more literate classifications in terms of psychiatric nomenclature, we can draw few binding conclusions concerning regularity in terms of age, ethnic groups, social status, and other sociological variables. As an example, it may be pointed out that Durkheim, Dublin and Bunzel, and others show little if any suicide among children, whereas Zilboorg has deemed it significant enough to make a special study.[11]

A further result of the unreliability of the

[4] Op. cit., p. 282.
[5] Op. cit., p. 289.
[6] Op. cit., p. 285.

[7] Gregory Zilboorg, "Suicide among Civilized and Primitive Races," American Journal of Psychiatry, vol. 92, 1935–36.
[8] Otto Fenichel, The Psychoanalytic Theory of Neurosis, New York, 1945, p. 401.
[9] Ibid.
[10] Harold A. Larrabee, Reliable Knowledge, Boston, 1945, p. 436.
[11] Gregory Zilboorg, "Considerations on Suicide, with Particular Reference to That of the Young," American Journal of Orthopsychiatry, VIII, 1937.

statistics is that they have led many to the conclusion that suicide grows as civilization advances. This thesis has been seriously challenged by Zilboorg. He concludes that suicide is evidently "as old as the human race, it is probably as old as murder and almost as old as natural death. The lower the cultural niveau of the race, the more deep-seated the suicidal impulse appears. . . . The man of today, as far as suicide is concerned, is deficient, indeed, compared with his forefathers who possessed a suicidal ideology, mythology, and an unsurpassed technique." [12] Zilboorg speaks of a traditional, almost instinctive bias that results in "the misconception that the rate of suicide increases with the development of our civilization, that in some unknown way civilization fosters suicidal tendencies within us." [13]

Though this paper is restricted to a consideration of methodological problems, a few words are necessary concerning the psychoanalytic view of the *substantive* characteristics of suicide.

The most widely accepted view today in psychoanalysis is that suicide is most often a form of "displacement"; that is, the desire to kill someone who has thwarted the individual is turned back on the individual himself. Or technically stated: the suicide murders the introjected object and expiates guilt for wanting to murder the object. The ego is satisfied and the superego mollified through self-murder.

The emotional state of the suicide is not explicable in terms of an immediate situation; emotions relate back to the life-history of the individual. Feelings of melancholia, depression, or any of the other states which Durkheim describes when he comes to classifying what he calls morphological types of suicide in terms of their social causes, are not those of the moment of suicide; they have a long history in the individual, and although he may be stimulated to suicide by what looks like an immediate cause, no such stimulus would have resulted in the self-murder, unless the underlying patterns of behavior had already been set.

In the sense that all human beings have been subjected to the process of frustration and repression, of guilt and anxiety, to that extent suicide is a potential outlet under given kinds of emotional stress. The suicide-potential is thus universal and omnipresent. It is extremely susceptible to being aggravated even by what look like trivia, and the higher the potential the more susceptible is it. It may even erupt where the potential is slight if the aggravation is great enough. It may be nurtured and fed by offenses against the psyche in the school-room, the play-group, the high-school, the college, by economic disaster and success, by familial difficulties, real or imagined.

The basic problem for social research must be to interrelate the life-histories of individual suicides and attempted suicides with sociological variables, on the hypothesis that certain social environments may (a) induce or (b) perpetuate or (c) aggravate the suicide-potential. If we can correlate for masses of cases, suicide or attempted suicide with their having been induced, perpetuated, or aggravated by certain social environments, then we are in a position to establish laws of *generalized occurrence*. And now to the hazardous task of establishing pertinent hypotheses for today. . . .

The Family. The emotional patterns of those attempting or committing suicide are laid down in infancy and early childhood by familial relationships.

Socialization in the family is a process of frustration for all, and thus suicide is a potential outlet in everybody.

It is necessary to seek to interrelate the case-histories of suicides and attempted suicides with the type of family-rearing, including such variables as ethnic group, religious affiliation, income-group, size of family and place of the individual suicide in the family, educational level. . . .

Urban Life and Suicide. Present findings, that rates are high in urban areas, must be re-investigated in terms of the psychic aggravation of urban living. It is one thing to seek to discover whether urban rates are high because of aggravation and perpetuation of basic emotional patterns; it is quite another to hold that urban living *induces* suicide.

Suicide and Religious Affiliation. There is general agreement that the suicide rate for Catholics is lowest of all religious groups. This requires investigation into the emotional outlets offered to Catholics for repressed instinctual desires, as against other religious groups.

This leads to inquiry into the causes of suicide among those Catholics who do commit it. These should show up as confirmatory of causes among

[12] *American Journal of Psychiatry,* vol. 92, 1935–36, pp. 1361, 1362.
[13] *Op. cit.,* p. 1351.

non-Catholics. And what of the suicide rate among Catholic *converts;* is this lower or higher than among other Catholics, and among other religious groups?

This in turn raises the problem whether suicides of Catholics are being accurately reported, since the religious prohibition against suicide in the Catholic church may well lead to serious complications.

The suicide rate for Protestants everywhere shows itself as higher than that for Catholics, and often for the Jews. This has been ascribed by Morselli and Durkheim to the individualism emphasized by Protestantism and its emphasis upon reflective thinking and the individual conscience. If this holds true, then the most individualistic Protestant sects should show the highest suicide rates. For example, in the United States, Unitarians should show a very high rate, and high-church Episcopalians a very low rate. Do they? We do not know. Moreover, we have no data that relates psychiatric life-histories to religious affiliation.

Whereas in the nineteenth century, the suicide rate for the Jews appeared to be lowest of the three main currents of religion in Western civilization, more recent figures would probably show that it has increased beyond the other two.

The religious environment may be strictly linked with psychiatric interpretation of suicide. Durkheim's hypothesis of the comparative immunity of Catholics to suicide, which appears to be confirmed within the undoubtedly narrow limits of accuracy of contemporary actuarial and social statistics, may sink deep roots in psychiatric science. Durkheim ascribed Catholicism's immunity-giving power to the way in which it integrates the individual into the group, through a complete, thorough and all-encompassing body of common sentiments and beliefs. But to what do these common sentiments and beliefs refer? Catholic sentiments and beliefs seek to relieve the individual of guilt, make all sins expiable, establish an intricate, hierarchical system of father-substitutes, and an ingenious, poetic image of the mother.

And the less rigorous Protestant sects give no sublimatory outlet for infantile repression and frustration, through poetry, art, and ritual, and there is a rampaging of the sense of guilt which cannot be expiated through the confessional but which faces God and his elders' wrath in all its individual nakedness. Calvinism, and to no small degree, Lutheranism, deal with sin repressively and individualistically. In early Protestantism, the unconscious is thrown back upon itself, and later only exclusively non-religious social sanctions hold it fully in check.

Suicide and Sex. Consummated suicides are higher among men than among women, but it seems that attempted suicides are higher among women than among men. Laying aside the unreliability of the statistics, we may ask, is this because of the social position of women, or because of the emotional differences between men and women, or an interrelationship of both, and how and to what degree?

Suicide and Age. The suicide rate is believed to increase with age. But is this not possibly because early frustrations are aggravated by failures in middle life? And what relation is there between middle-age suicide rates and failure in intimate marital and familial relations?

The suicide rate increases, according to the statistics we have, with advance in age. It is particularly high among the aged. Several problems arise here. First, is it that there is less reluctance to admit that death resulted from suicide when the individual is aged? Second, old-age is the time when degenerative diseases reach their mortal climax, and the affect upon the psyche may be immense. Third, shall we also call suicide the self-murder which is perpetrated in the knowledge that death is not far off anyhow? Fourth, is the *social* oblivion to which the aged are subjected an invitation to what the psychoanalysts call the desire for *maternal* oblivion; that is, a return to the kindly sleep of the unborn? These questions, and others, must obviously be to the forefront in the new branch of medicine called geriatrics, particularly in the light of what has been termed our aging population.

Suicide and Income-Groups. Suicide rates are relatively high among the highest income-groups. Wealth, the touchstone of success in our type of society, is no assurance of immunity. Is this because of overprotection in infancy and youth? And what of suicides among self-made men? Dublin and Bunzel come to the conclusion that there is no simple causal relation between economic factors and suicide. Should, then, suicides among all economic groups show up confirmatory of the same emotional difficulties?

Suicide and War. In the midst of a shooting war, suicide rates tend to decline; so the statistics say. But a shooting war offers for those in battle optimum opportunity for suicide to be committed without anyone being aware of it. What looks like courage may be suicidal proclivity; and anyway one may not contemplate suicide if the chances are greater that life may soon be over.

As far as the civilian population is concerned, the whole question of the impact of war upon psychic desiderata remains to be investigated.

Suicide and Marital Status. Marital status and suicide are presumed to be strictly interrelated. Divorced men have a higher suicide rate than the undivorced, divorced women a higher rate than undivorced women but lower than divorced men. What of suicide rates among the divorced who have re-wed?

Among the widowed, childless marriages give high rates. But the interpretation of such phenomena seems to require generalization based on psychiatric case-histories, and some understanding of the relation of marital status to emotional life as patterned before marriage, divorce, or widowhood. And what of suicide rates of the widowed who re-wed? If marriage protects against suicide, particularly fertile marriage, why does it not protect all such marriages? Is it that the suicide-potential overcomes even the devotion to spouse and family in the case of suicides? And if so, how did the suicide-potential get so powerful?

Suicide and the Negro. The rate for Negroes is very low compared to whites in our society. There is obviously (if the statistics are correct) no correlation between Negro underprivilege and suicide, as might be expected. Is this because systematic oppression and underprivilege lead individuals to be adjusted to the misery and tragedy of human existence which is visited upon all? Expecting nothing of life, they may not be disappointed at how little it does offer them. But here a serious check must be made by studies of suicide among upperclass and well-educated Negroes, and among low-income and poorly-educated Negroes. Do Negroes who are on the margin of upper-class white standards of living, materially and intellectually, commit suicide more than do other Negroes?

But Negro women have a rate somewhat closer to white women than Negro men have to white men. Here intimate knowledge of the private lives of such Negro women would be of help. Also questions of high and low coloration may be necessarily involved throughout the problem of the relation of Negroes to suicide.

Suicide and Curative Therapy. Where, from analytic-room and clinic, the suicidal proclivity originally appeared high in given individuals, and curative therapy proved successful, what is the suicide rate in later life among these individuals? Has the proclivity been re-directed towards life? And what kind of life?

To raise questions such as these is certainly not to answer them. Since the respect for human personality in our society is so great, we hold as a fundamental value an abhorrence of suicide. This in turn raises the problem of what to do about combating suicide. From the psychiatric point of view, the answer would seem to be the vigorous training of parents and parents-to-be in the principles of mental hygiene, a rigorous training of nursery-school, grade-school, and high-school teachers in these principles, and an extensive system of psychiatric record-keeping in these "coming-of-age" organizations. Sociologically considered, it is necessary to assuage the suicidal proclivities of whatever social environments we find inducing and aggravating and perpetuating tendencies towards self-murder among individuals.

Some social scientists have for some time been chagrined by the increasing trend in our guilds to establish programs for research and not to give answers. Here, in the case of suicide, research has gone on for over fifty years, and some may feel that it is high time we had some answers. To this I can only say that it is only recently that we have found the key to this Pandora's box, but that this key itself can only open the box; it cannot quickly conquer the released wild and dark furies of irrationality to which humans are heir.

CROSS REFERENCES TO STANDARD TEXTS *

Barnes, *Society in Transition*, Chap. 14.
Bloch, *Disorganization*, Chaps. 20–22.
Brown, *Social Pathology*, Chaps. 5, 11–15, 17–19.

* For complete bibliographical reference to each text, see page 13.

Cuber and Harper, *Problems of American Society*, Chaps. 7–8.
Elliott and Merrill, *Social Disorganization*, Chaps. 7–9, 12–14.
Farris, *Social Disorganization*, Chaps. 5, 9.
Gillin, *Social Pathology*, Chaps. 5–8, 10.

——— and others, *Social Problems*, pp. 398–399, 417–419.

Herman, *Approach to Social Problems*, pp. 140, 316.

Landis, *Social Policies in the Making*, pp. 95, 110, 116, 120–128, 134.

Lemert, *Social Pathology*, Chaps. 8, 10, 11.

Merrill and others, *Social Problems*, Chaps. 5–7.

Mihanovich, *Current Social Problems*, Chap. 12.

Neumeyer, *Social Problems and the Changing Society*, Chap. 6.

Nordskog and others, *Analyzing Social Problems*, Chap. 5.

Odum, *American Social Problems*, Chap. 16.

Phelps and Henderson, *Contemporary Social Problems*, Chaps. 4–5.

Reinhardt and others, *Social Problems and Social Policy*, Chap. 16.

Weaver, *Social Problems*, Chaps. 8–10.

OTHER BIBLIOGRAPHY

Alcoholics Anonymous, New York: Alcoholics Anonymous, 1937.

Clifford W. Beers, *A Mind That Found Itself*, rev. ed., Garden City: Doubleday, Doran and Co., 1948.

Frank G. Boudreau and Jean Downes, eds., *Interrelations Between the Social Environment and Psychiatric Disorders*, New York: Milbank Memorial Fund, 1953.

Norman Cameron, "The Paranoid Pseudo-Community," *American Journal of Sociology*, 49 (1943–44): 32–38.

J. C. Coleman, *Abnormal Psychology and Modern Life*, New York: Scott-Foresman and Co., 1950.

Albert Deutsch, *The Mentally Ill in America*, 2d ed., New York: Columbia University Press, 1949.

John Dollard and Neal Miller, *Personality and Psychotherapy*, New York: McGraw-Hill Book Co., 1950.

Emile Durkheim, *Suicide: A Study in Sociology*, transl. by J. A. Spaulding and George Simpson, Glencoe, Illinois: Free Press, 1951.

Robert H. Dysinger, ed., "Mental Health in the United States," *The Annals*, 286 (March 1953).

Robert E. L. Faris and H. W. Dunham, *Mental Disorders in Urban Areas*, Chicago: University of Chicago Press, 1939.

R. H. Felix and Morton Kramer, "Extent of the Problem of Mental Disorders," *The Annals*, 286 (March 1953): 5–14.

Katherine Glover, "Mental Health—Everybody's Business," 3d ed., Public Affairs Pamphlet No. 196, 1954.

Herbert Goldhamer and Andrew Marshall, *Psychosis and Civilization*, Glencoe, Illinois: Free Press, 1953.

H. W. Haggard and E. M. Jellinek, *Alcohol Explored*, Garden City: Doubleday, Doran and Co., 1942.

Maurice Halbwachs, *Les Causes du Suicide*, Paris: Felix Alcan, 1930.

William Healy and Augusta F. Bronner, *Treatment and What Happened Afterward*, Boston: Judge Baker Guidance Center, 1939.

Andrew F. Henry and James F. Short, *Suicide and Homicide*, Glencoe, Illinois: Free Press, 1954.

E. Gartly Jaco, "The Social Isolation Hypothesis and Schizophrenia," *American Sociological Review*, 19 (1954): 567–577.

E. L. Johnstone, "What Shall We Do With the Mentally Deficient," *Mental Hygiene*, 30 (1946): 296–302.

Oscar J. Kaplan, ed., *Mental Disorders in Later Life*, Stanford: Stanford University Press, 1945.

Robert M. Lindner, *Rebel Without a Cause*, New York: Grune and Stratton, 1944.

Herta Loewy, *The Retarded Child*, New York: Philosopical Library, 1951.

A. H. Maslow, *Motivation and Personality*, New York: Harper & Bros., 1954.

——— and Bela Mittelmann, *Principles of Abnormal Psychology*, rev. ed., New York: Harper & Bros., 1951.

Karl A. Menninger, *Man Against Himself*, New York: Harcourt, Brace and Co., 1938.

John Rawlings Rees, *The Shaping of Psychiatry by War*, New York: W. W. Norton & Co., 1945.

Arnold M. Rose, ed., *Mental Health and Mental Disorder* (prepared for the Society for the Study of Social Problems), New York: W. W. Norton & Co., 1955.

William Seabrook, *Asylum*, New York: Harcourt, Brace and Co., 1935.

Leo W. Simmons and Harold G. Wolff, *Social Science in Medicine*, New York: Russell Sage Foundation, 1954.

Edith M. Stern, "Family Care for the Mentally Ill," *Survey Graphic*, 31 (1942): 31–32, 42–44.

Robert Straus and Selden D. Bacon, *Drinking in College*, New Haven: Yale University Press, 1953.

G. Aiken Taylor, *A Sober Faith: Religion and Alcoholics Anonymous*, New York: Macmillan Co., 1953.

W. I. Thomas, *The Unadjusted Girl*, Boston: Little, Brown & Co., 1923.

Helen M. Walker and Mary C. Schauffler, *The Social Adjustment of the Feeble-Minded*, Cleveland: Western Reserve University Press, 1930.

S. Kirson Weinberg, *Society and Personality Disorders*, New York: Prentice-Hall, 1952.

Orin Ross Yost, *What You Should Know About Mental Illness*, New York: Exposition Press, 1953.

REVIEW QUESTIONS

1. How does our society help to bring about mental breakdowns?

2. What proportion of the people in this country have nervous and mental disease?

3. How reliable are statistics on the incidence of mental illness?

4. How could case records be utilized in the study of mental disorders?

5. How does Stevenson criticize hospitals for the mentally ill?

6. How would Stevenson organize a district, municipal, county, or regional mental health program?

7. How does Mowrer relate drinking to the cultural milieu?

8. How does Mowrer describe the alcoholic personality pattern?

9. How adequate are the funds available for research in alcoholism? How would you account for this?

10. What is the underlying principle behind Alcoholics Anonymous? Can you suggest other areas where this might be applied?

11. Is there a relationship between suicide and urban life?

12. What can we do to combat suicide?

—CHAPTER 17→

The Delinquent and Criminal

SOCIETY traditionally defines a criminal as a person who has violated a criminal statute, has been caught, and has been adjudged guilty. This arbitrary social definition once coincided with that of the social scientists and is even yet regarded as adequate by some. But sociologists—even though they must accept that stereotyped social definition as a social datum to be studied—now believe that it leaves far too many significant questions unanswered to be accepted as close to a scientific concept. To what extent, to illustrate, do criminal statutes accurately specify what is socially damaging behavior? Of those who disobey legal injunctions, how many and who are likely to be arrested? Of those who are arrested, how many and who are likely to be convicted? Sutherland's essay on white-collar criminality forcefully raises such questions.

These questions sociologists are raising with regard to the definitions of delinquency and criminality are of far more than academic significance. Such questions, put forward also by many other spokesmen with increasing insistency during the past half-century, have helped to modify both judge-made law and legislature- and Congress-made statutes covering criminal offenses.

Even though delinquent children are admittedly off to an unfortunate start in many cases in their adjustment to community life, juvenile delinquency is far from being a uniform prerequisite to adult criminality. Barron sums up major aspects of what is known about juvenile delinquency and states his belief that "a theory that could be used most profitably by investigators is that juveniles in America are growing up in a 'delinquent society.'"

Five other problem areas in juvenile and adult delinquency and crime are regarded as important by sociologists and criminologists. These are: (1) the organization and operation of police work in such a way that it will serve broad social welfare; (2) the common patterns of relationship that exist between law enforcement agencies and the underworld; (3) drug addiction; (4) prostitution; and (5) punishment and/or rehabilitation and re-assimilation.

In connection with problem areas (1) and (2), Deutsch outlines and gives examples of the pressures under which honest police must frequently operate and ways in which dishonest police "cash in."

To the increasing problem of drug addiction and crimes by addicts (3), Stevens brings the suggestion, after discussion with medical and legal authorities, that "the fastest and surest way" to lessen these difficulties is to "make dope legal."

In discussing prostitution (4), Henderson and Shaw show its linkages in this country to venereal disease, organized gambling, and political corruption. Davis, in excerpts from a longer study, offers notes on a sociology of prostitution.

In that other highly complex area, (5) punishment and/or rehabilitation and re-assimilation, Hayner and Ash describe the processes through which prisoners are assimilated into the prison community and the obstacles prison organization raises against the re-assimilation of ex-prisoners into the outside community.

These selections, even with the indictment they make of criminological methods, still point to a "way out." The crux is probably in our philosophy of punishment as popularly held. Here, as in so many other departments of society, we traditionally adhere to a categorical impoundment device with which we presumably cope with our ills. Our mental hospitals and prisons entrust a defenseless and societally condemned population to underpaid persons, badly trained and motivated, who not infrequently abuse this tremendous power. Little wonder that such institutions, ignored in most cases by all but politicians and a few do-gooders, chiefly serve purposes other than rehabilitation. All credit, however, should certainly be given to servants of such institutions who do hold to their integrity in spite of the institutionalized system and who find ways to help their charges to find their way "back."

The selections in this chapter may be interpreted as suggesting such beginnings of solutions as these: We need to transfer the center of our criminological emphasis from impoundment, and this includes the rejection of a scapegoat attitude toward offenders and the eye-for-eye exactment of penalties. We need to place the emphasis upon (1) the development of a society that provides healthy patterns of maturation for the vast majority of our people, that distorts fewer minds and forces them into antisocial paths, and (2) the development of a criminological system that will function to rehabilitate unfortunate fellow human beings rather than to harden them in their antisocial tendencies. Beginnings are being made in certain police forces by the elimination of the traditional type of personnel from women's and children's divisions. The psychiatrically trained operatives in these areas are sufficiently successful to suggest their value elsewhere. Well-trained and suitably adapted social workers may well replace police of the traditional sort entirely. Certain courts and prisons, too, have programs that center upon re-assimilation into the larger community rather than upon the prisoner making "a good prison adjustment." Instrumental in this area are the indeterminate sentence and modernized parole techniques. Perhaps in these and other symptoms lie the beginnings of a saner approach to the whole problem.

White-collar Criminality
Edwin H. Sutherland

Edwin Hardin Sutherland (1883–1950) professor of sociology, Indiana University. Chief works: *Criminology* (1924); with H. J. Locke, *Twenty Thousand Homeless Men* (1936); *The Professional Thief* (1937); *Principles of Criminology*, 3rd ed. (1947); and *White Collar Crime* (1949).

The criminal statistics show unequivocally that crime, *as popularly conceived and officially measured*, has a high incidence in the lower class and a low incidence in the upper class; less than two per cent of the persons committed to prisons in a year belong to the upper class. These statistics refer to criminals handled by the police, the criminal and juvenile courts, and the prisons, and to such crimes as murder, assault, burglary, robbery, larceny, sex offenses, and drunkenness, but exclude traffic violations.

The criminologists have used the case histories and criminal statistics derived from these agencies of criminal justice as their principal data. From them, they have derived general theories of criminal behavior. These theories are that, since crime is concentrated in the lower class, it is caused by poverty or by personal and social characteristics believed to be associated statistically with poverty, including feeblemindedness, psychopathic deviations, slum neighborhoods, and "deteriorated" families. This statement, of course, does not do justice to the qualifications and variations in the conventional theories of criminal behavior, but it presents correctly their central tendency.

The thesis of this paper is that the conception and explanations of crime which have just been described are misleading and incorrect, that crime is in fact not closely correlated with poverty or with the psychopathic and sociopathic conditions associated with poverty, and that an adequate explanation of criminal behavior must proceed along quite different lines. The conventional explanations are invalid principally because they are derived from biased samples. The samples are biased in that they have not included vast areas of criminal behavior of persons not in the lower class. One of these neglected areas is the criminal behavior of business and professional men, which will be analyzed in this paper.

The "robber barons" of the last half of the nineteenth century were white-collar criminals, as practically everyone now agrees. Their attitudes are illustrated by these statements: Colonel Vanderbilt asked, "'You don't suppose you can run a railroad in accordance with the statutes, do you?'"

From "White-collar Criminality," *American Sociological Review*, 5 (1940): 1–12. Reprinted by permission. Thirty-fourth annual presidential address, American Sociological Society, delivered at Philadelphia, Dec. 27, 1939, in joint meeting with the American Economic Society.

A. B. Stickney, a railroad president, said to sixteen other railroad presidents in the home of J. P. Morgan in 1890, "I have the utmost respect for you gentlemen, individually, but as railroad presidents I wouldn't trust you with my watch out of my sight." Charles Francis Adams said: "The difficulty in railroad management . . . lies in the covetousness, want of good faith, and low moral tone of railway managers, in the complete absence of any high standard of commerical honesty."

The present-day white-collar criminals, who are more suave and deceptive than the "robber barons," are represented by Krueger, Stavisky, Whitney, Mitchell, Foshay, Insull, the Van Sweringens, Musica-Coster, Fall, Sinclair, and many other merchant princes and captains of finance and industry, and by a host of lesser followers. Their criminality has been demonstrated again and again in the investigations of land offices, railways, insurance, munitions, banking, public utilities, stock exchanges, the oil industry, real estate, reorganization committees, receiverships, bankruptcies, and politics. Individual cases of such criminality are reported frequently, and in many periods more important crime news may be found on the financial pages of newspapers than on the front pages. White-collar criminality is found in every occupation, as can be discovered readily in casual conversation with a representative of an occupation by asking him, "What crooked practices are found in your occupation?"

White-collar criminality in business is expressed most frequently in the form of misrepresentation in financial statements of corporations, manipulation in the stock exchange, commercial bribery, bribery of public officials directly or indirectly in order to secure favorable contracts and legislation, misrepresentation in advertising and salesmanship, embezzlement and misapplication of funds, short weights and measures and misgrading of commodities, tax frauds, misapplication of funds in receiverships and bankruptcies. These are what Al Capone called "the legitimate rackets." These and many others are found in abundance in the business world.

In the medical profession, which is here used as an example because it is probably less criminalistic than some other professions, are found illegal sale of alcohol and narcotics, abortion, illegal services to underworld criminals, fraudulent reports and testimony in accident cases, extreme cases of unnecessary treatment, fake specialists, restriction of competition, and fee-splitting. Fee-

splitting is a violation of a specific law in many states and a violation of the conditions of admission to the practice of medicine in all. The physician who participates in fee-splitting tends to send his patients to the surgeon who will give him the largest fee rather than to the surgeon who will do the best work. It has been reported that two thirds of the surgeons in New York City split fees, and that more than one half of the physicians in a central western city who answered a questionnaire on this point favored fee-splitting.

These varied types of white-collar crimes in business and the professions consist principally of violation of delegated or implied trust, and many of them can be reduced to two categories: misrepresentation of asset values and duplicity in the manipulation of power. The first is approximately the same as fraud or swindling; the second is similar to the double cross. The latter is illustrated by the corporation director who, acting on inside information, purchases land which the corporation will need and sells it at a fantastic profit to his corporation. The principle of this duplicity is that the offender holds two antagonistic positions, one of which is a position of trust, which is violated, generally by misapplication of funds, in the interest of the other position. A football coach, permitted to referee a game in which his own team was playing, would illustrate this antagonism of positions. Such situations cannot be completely avoided in a complicated business structure, but many concerns make a practice of assuming such antagonistic functions and regularly violating the trust thus delegated to them. When compelled by law to make a separation of their functions, they make a nominal separation and continue by subterfuge to maintain the two positions.

An accurate statistical comparison of the crimes of the two classes is not available. The most extensive evidence regarding the nature and prevalence of white-collar criminality is found in the reports of the larger investigations to which reference was made. Because of its scattered character, that evidence is assumed rather than summarized here. A few statements will be presented, as illustrations rather than as proof of the prevalence of this criminality.

The Federal Trade Commission in 1920 reported that commercial bribery was a prevalent and common practice in many industries. In certain chain stores, the net shortage in weights was sufficient to pay 3.4 per cent on the investment in those commodities. Of the cans of ether sold to the Army in 1923–1925, 70 per cent were rejected because of impurities. In Indiana, during the summer of 1934, 40 per cent of the ice cream samples tested in a routine manner by the Division of Public Health were in violation of law. The Comptroller of the Currency in 1908 reported that violations of law were found in 75 per cent of the banks examined in a three months' period. Lie detector tests of all employees in several Chicago banks, supported in almost all cases by confessions, showed that 20 per cent of them had stolen bank property. A public accountant estimated, in the period prior to the Securities and Exchange Commission, that 80 per cent of the financial statements of corporations were misleading. James M. Beck said, "Diogenes would have been hard put to it to find an honest man in the Wall Street which I knew as a corporation lawyer" (in 1916).

White-collar criminality in politics, which is generally recognized as fairly prevalent, has been used by some as a rough gauge by which to measure white-collar criminality in business. James A. Farley said, "The standards of conduct are as high among office-holders and politicians as they are in commercial life," and Cermak, while mayor of Chicago, said, "There is less graft in politics than in business." John Flynn wrote, "The average politician is the merest amateur in the gentle art of graft, compared with his brother in the field of business." And Walter Lippmann wrote, "Poor as they are, the standards of public life are so much more social than those of business that financiers who enter politics regard themselves as philanthropists."

These statements obviously do not give a precise measurement of the relative criminality of the white-collar class, but they are adequate evidence that crime is not so highly concentrated in the lower class as the usual statistics indicate. Also, these statements obviously do not mean that every business and professional man is a criminal, just as the usual theories do not mean that every man in the lower class is a criminal. On the other hand, the preceding statements refer in many cases to the leading corporations in America and are not restricted to the disreputable business and professional men who are called quacks, ambulance chasers, bucket-shop operators, dead-beats, and fly-by-night swindlers.[1]

The financial cost of white-collar crime is probably several times as great as the financial cost of all the crimes which are customarily regarded as the "crime problem." An officer of a chain grocery store in one year embezzled $600,000, which was six times as much as the annual losses from five hundred burglaries and robberies of the stores in that chain. Public enemies numbered one to six secured $130,000 by burglary and robbery in 1938, while the sum stolen by Krueger is estimated at $250,000,000, or nearly two thousand times as much. *The New York Times* in 1931 reported four cases of embezzlement in the United States with a loss of more than a million dollars each and a combined loss of nine million dollars. Although a million-dollar burglar or robber is practically unheard of, these million-dollar embezzlers are small-fry among white-collar criminals. The estimated loss to investors in one investment trust from 1929 to 1935 was $580,000,000, due primarily to the fact that 75 per cent of the values in the portfolio were in securities of affiliated companies, although it advertised the importance of diversification in investments and its expert services in selecting safe securities. In Chicago, the claim was made six years ago that householders had lost $54,000,000 in two years during the administration of a city sealer who granted immunity from inspection to stores which provided Christmas baskets for his constituents.

The financial loss from white-collar crime, great as it is, is less important than the damage to social relations. White-collar crimes violate trust and therefore create distrust, which lowers social morale and produces social disorganization on a large scale. Other crimes produce relatively little effect on social institutions or social organization.

White-collar crime is real crime. It is not ordinarily called crime, and calling it by this name does not make it worse, just as refraining from calling it crime does not make it better than it otherwise would be. It is called crime here in order to bring it within the scope of criminology,

---

[1] Perhaps it should be repeated that "white-collar" (upper) and "lower" classes merely designate persons of high and low socioeconomic status. Income and amount of money involved in the crime are not the sole criteria. Many persons of "low" socioeconomic status are "white-collar" criminals in the sense that they are well-dressed, well-educated, and have high incomes, but "white-collar" as used in this paper means "respected," "socially accepted and approved," "looked up to." Some people in this class may not be well-dressed or well-educated, nor have high incomes, although the "upper" usually exceed the "lower" classes in these respects as well as in social status.

which is justified because it is in violation of the criminal law. The crucial question in this analysis is the criterion of violation of the criminal law. Conviction in the criminal court, which is sometimes suggested as the criterion, is not adequate because a large proportion of those who commit crimes are not convicted in criminal courts. This criterion, therefore, needs to be supplemented. When it is supplemented, the criterion of the crimes of one class must be kept consistent in general terms with the criterion of the crimes of the other class. The definition should not be the spirit of the law for white-collar crimes and the letter of the law for other crimes, or in other respects be more liberal for one class than the other. Since this discussion is concerned with the conventional theories of the criminologists, the criterion of white-collar crime must be justified in terms of the procedures of those criminologists in dealing with other crimes. The criterion of white-collar crimes, as here proposed, supplements convictions in the criminal courts in four respects, in each of which the extension is justified because the criminologists who present the conventional theories of criminal behavior make the same extension in principle.

First, other agencies than the criminal court must be included, for the criminal court is not the only agency which makes official decisions regarding violations of the criminal law. The juvenile court, dealing largely with offenses of the children of the poor, in many states is not under the criminal jurisdiction. The criminologists have made much use of case histories and statistics of juvenile delinquents in constructing their theories of criminal behavior. This justifies the inclusion of agencies other than the criminal court which deal with white-collar offenses. The most important of these agencies are the administrative boards, bureaus, or commissions, and much of their work, although certainly not all, consists of cases which are in violation of the criminal law. The Federal Trade Commission recently ordered several automobile companies to stop advertising their interest rate on installment purchases as 6 per cent, since it was actually 11½ per cent. Also it filed complaint against *Good Housekeeping,* one of the Hearst publications, charging that its seals led the public to believe that all products bearing those seals had been tested in their laboratories, which was contrary to fact. Each of these involves a charge of dishonesty, which might have been tried in a criminal court as fraud. A large proportion of the cases before these boards should be included in the data of the criminologists. Failure to do so is a principal reason for the bias in their samples and the errors in their generalizations.

Second, for both classes, behavior which would have a reasonable expectancy of conviction if tried in a criminal court or substitute agency should be defined as criminal. In this respect, convictability rather than actual conviction should be the criterion of criminality. The criminologists would not hesitate to accept as data a verified case history of a person who was a criminal but had never been convicted. Similarly, it is justifiable to include white-collar criminals who have not been convicted, provided reliable evidence is available. Evidence regarding such cases appears in many civil suits, such as stockholders' suits and patent-infringement suits. These cases might have been referred to the criminal court but they were referred to the civil court because the injured party was more interested in securing damages than in seeing punishment inflicted. This also happens in embezzlement cases, regarding which surety companies have much evidence. In a short consecutive series of embezzlements known to a surety company, 90 per cent were not prosecuted because prosecution would interfere with restitution or salvage. The evidence in cases of embezzlement is generally conclusive, and would probably have been sufficient to justify conviction in all of the cases in this series.

Third, behavior should be defined as criminal if conviction is avoided merely because of pressure which is brought to bear on the court or substitute agency. Gangsters and racketeers have been relatively immune in many cities because of their pressure on prospective witnesses and public officials, and professional thieves, such as pickpockets and confidence men who do not use strong-arm methods, are even more frequently immune. The conventional criminologists do not hesitate to include the life histories of such criminals as data, because they understand the generic relation of the pressures to the failure to convict. Similarly, white-collar criminals are relatively immune because of the class bias of the courts and the power of their class to influence the implementation and administration of the law. This class bias affects not merely present-day courts but to a much greater degree affected the earlier courts which established the precedents and rules of procedure of the present-day courts. Consequently, it is justifiable to interpret the actual or potential failures of conviction in the light of known facts regarding the pressures brought to bear on the agencies which deal with offenders.

Fourth, persons who are accessory to a crime should be included among white-collar criminals as they are among other criminals. When the Federal Bureau of Investigation deals with a case of kidnapping, it is not content with catching the offenders who carried away the victim; they may catch and the court may convict twenty-five other persons who assisted by secreting the victim, negotiating the ransom, or putting the ransom money into circulation. On the other hand, the prosecution of white-collar criminals frequently stops with one offender. Political graft almost always involves collusion between politicians and business men but prosecutions are generally limited to the politicians. Judge Manton was found guilty of accepting $664,000 in bribes, but the six or eight important commercial concerns that paid the bribes have not been prosecuted. Pendergast, the late boss of Kansas City, was convicted for failure to report as a part of his income $315,000 received in bribes from insurance companies but the insurance companies which paid the bribes have not been prosecuted. In an investigation of an embezzlement by the president of a bank, at least a dozen other violations of law which were related to this embezzlement and involved most of the other officers of the bank and the officers of the clearing house, were discovered but none of the others was prosecuted.

This analysis of the criterion of white-collar criminality results in the conclusion that a description of white-collar criminality in general terms will be also a description of the criminality of the lower class. The respects in which the crimes of the two classes differ are the incidentals rather than the essentials of criminality. They differ principally in the implementation of the criminal laws which apply to them. The crimes of the lower class are handled by policemen, prosecutors, and judges, with penal sanctions in the form of fines, imprisonment, and death. The crimes of the upper class either result in no official action at all, or results in suits for damages in civil courts, or are handled by inspectors, and by administrative boards or commissions, with penal sanctions in the form of warnings, orders to cease and desist, occasionally the loss of a license, and only in extreme cases by fines or prison sentences. Thus, the white-collar criminals are segre-

gated administratively from other criminals, and largely as a consequence of this are not regarded as real criminals by themselves, the general public, or the criminologists.

This difference in the implementation of the criminal law is due principally to the difference in the social position of the two types of offenders. . . . The statement of Daniel Drew, a pious old fraud, describes the criminal law with some accuracy, "Law is like a cobweb; it's made for flies and the smaller kinds of insects, so to speak, but lets the big bumblebees break through. When technicalities of the law stood in my way, I have always been able to brush them aside easy as anything."

The preceding analysis should be regarded neither as an assertion that all efforts to influence legislation and its administration are reprehensible nor as a particularistic interpretation of the criminal law. It means only that the upper class has greater influence in moulding the criminal law and its administration to its own interests than does the lower class. The privileged position of white-collar criminals before the law results to a slight extent from bribery and political pressures, principally from the respect in which they are held and without special effort on their part. The most powerful group in medieval society secured relative immunity by "benefit of clergy," and now our most powerful groups secure relative immunity by "benefit of business or profession."

The hypothesis which is here suggested as a substitute for the conventional theories is that white-collar criminality, just as other systematic criminality, is learned; that it is learned in direct or indirect association with those who already practice the behavior; and that those who learn this criminal behavior are segregated from frequent and intimate contacts with law-abiding behavior. Whether a person becomes a criminal or not is determined largely by the comparative frequency and intimacy of his contacts with the two types of behavior. This may be called the process of differential association. It is a genetic explanation both of white-collar criminality and lower class criminality. Those who become white-collar criminals generally start their careers in good neighborhoods and good homes, graduate from colleges with some idealism, and with little selection on their part, get into particular business situations in which criminality is practically a folkway and are inducted into that system of behavior just as into any other folkway. The lower class criminals generally start their careers in deteriorated neighborhoods and families, find delinquents at hand from whom they acquire the attitudes toward, and techniques of, crime through association with delinquents and in partial segregation from law-abiding people. The essentials of the process are the same for the two classes of criminals. This is not entirely a process of assimilation, for inventions are frequently made, perhaps more frequently in white-collar crime than in lower class crime. The inventive geniuses for the lower class criminals are generally professional criminals, while the inventive geniuses for many kinds of white-collar crime are generally lawyers.

A second general process is social disorganization in the community. Differential association culminates in crime because the community is not organized solidly against that behavior. The law is pressing in one direction, and other forces are pressing in the opposite direction. In business, the "rules of the game" conflict with the legal rules. A business man who wants to obey the law is driven by his competitors to adopt their methods. This is well illustrated by the persistence of commercial bribery in spite of the strenuous efforts of business organizations to eliminate it. Groups and individuals are individuated; they are more concerned with their specialized group or individual interests than with the larger welfare. Consequently, it is not possible for the community to present a solid front in opposition to crime. The Better Business Bureaus and Crime Commissions,

composed of business and professional men, attack burglary, robbery, and cheap swindles, but overlook the crimes of their own members. The forces which impinge on the lower class are similarly in conflict. Social disorganization affects the two classes in similar ways.

I have presented a brief and general description of white-collar criminality on a framework of argument regarding theories of criminal behavior. That argument, stripped of the description, may be stated in the following propositions:

1. White-collar criminality is real criminality, being in all cases in violation of the criminal law.

2. White-collar criminality differs from lower class criminality principally in an implementation of the criminal law which segregates white-collar criminals administratively from other criminals.

3. The theories of the criminologists that crime is due to poverty or to psychopathic and sociopathic conditions statistically associated with poverty are invalid because, first, they are derived from samples which are grossly biased with respect to socioeconomic status; second, they do not apply to the white-collar criminals; and third, they do not even explain the criminality of the lower class, since the factors are not related to a general process characteristic of all criminality.

4. A theory of criminal behavior which will explain both white-collar criminality and lower class criminality is needed.

5. An hypothesis of this nature is suggested in terms of differential association and social disorganization.

The Delinquent: Society or the Juvenile?
Milton L. Barron

Milton L. Barron (1918–), associate professor of sociology, City College of New York. Author of *People Who Intermarry* (1946), *The Juvenile in a Delinquent Society* (1954).

A well-known American criminologist, Austin MacCormick, is credited with having once remarked: "There are few social problems about which the public has done more hysterical wringing of hands and less intelligent thinking, more talking and less doing, than juvenile delinquency." This has been continuously true since juve-

nile delinquency was set off from crime as a unique social problem by the Illinois legislature's enactment of the first juvenile-court law in 1899.

Many social problems show marked cycles or swings in their incidence. With respect to juvenile delinquency, when the New York State Youth Commission, using the year 1938 as a base line,

From "The Delinquent: Society or the Juvenile?" *The Nation, 178* (June 5, 1954): 482–484.

analyzed the trend of official court cases in New York State, it noted first that the number of cases reported annually increased between 1938, a time of peace, and 1941, a period of defense preparation. The war years, 1942 to 1945, showed a decided increase, the peak being reached in 1943. During the postwar years there was a steady and appreciable decline to a new twelve-year low in 1950. With our renewed defense preparation and involvement in the Korean war, delinquency again rose in 1951 and leveled off in 1952. Apparently it is now in another upswing.

We cannot yet fully explain these cycles, but at least we are aware of some of the important factors. Examination of all the cycles since 1929 shows that juvenile delinquency increases in periods of economic prosperity and declines in periods of depression, just as it increases in a time of defense preparation and war and drops in time of peace. In the past fifteen years defense preparation and war have coincided with prosperity, but it is likely that *either* war or prosperity would have increased the delinquency.

The incidence of adult crime follows exactly the opposite course. It generally declines in time of prosperity and war and rises during depressions and peace. The answer to the question why trends of delinquency and crime are diametrically opposed is believed to be that the patterns of economic boom-bust and war-peace have different psychological, social, and economic impacts on children than on adults.

In the new upswing of delinquency since 1953 another factor has been operating. The census of 1950 estimated that from 1953 to 1957 there would be an unprecedented increase of more than 400,000 children, about 25 per cent, in the age group from seven to fifteen. This increase obviously explains the greater size of the problem today, though the *rate* may not have changed.

Responsible analysts of juvenile delinquency today agree that it has many causes, not just one. Many self-appointed experts, however, persist in explaining delinquency as well as crime solely as a product of personality maladjustment; others look at the family and find it the source of all trouble; still others point to the influence of comic books. The proponents of these different views overlook the fact that probably the only recognizable common denominator in all cases of delinquency is that they are violations of law. No inherent personality trait or social background distinguishes delinquent children. The endless varia-

tions of circumstance, opportunity, and personal history must be taken into account.

Regardless of the reasons for the current increase, delinquency as a social problem now lends itself once again to self-righteous speech-making, newspaper exposés, and Congressional investigations. The hackneyed clichés concerning the "growing menace to law and order" presented by the second-generation children of "foreigners" and of Negro migrants in the North have been dusted off for re-use. Concern about the allegedly deteriorating behavior of youngsters is exploited by special-interest groups to further their own goals. What could be more effective, for instance, in attacking the public-school system than to charge it with being the "cause" of the mounting juvenile delinquency?

The recent series of twenty articles in the New York *Daily News* (February 28 to March 20) on "teen-age terrorism" in the public schools of New York City supports this point. The schools were accused of being a vast incubator of narcotic addiction, vandalism, gang warfare, and sexual promiscuity, largely because of their progressive methods of teaching. The *News* maintained that the facts were suppressed by the school authorities because of their desire to keep "the complete picture of disorder" from the taxpayers. In short, according to the *News,* "the left-wing, pseudo-intellectual, do-as-you-like progressive system prevalent in the local schools is breeding lawlessness in the classrooms—and outside schools, too."

Those who find the cause of delinquency in a social institution, such as the public-school system, need to be reminded of some of the conclusions of the Herlands Report of 1943. Many citizens of New York at the time expressed the same anxiety that we feel today about the growing problem. Accordingly, Mayor LaGuardia appointed a Committee on Juvenile Delinquency headed by William B. Herlands, the city's Commissioner of Investigation. In August, 1943, the committee released its report, an exhaustive analysis of Children's Court cases for the thirty months from January, 1941, to June, 1943. It was undoubtedly the most detailed and careful statistical analysis of juvenile delinquency in New York ever prepared. Although offenses centering around the home and the school—such as running away from home, disobeying parents, and truancy—together with burglary, were found to make up most of the increase since Pearl Harbor, the Herlands Report added an interesting and important observation.

The conclusion is unwarranted, it said, that because most delinquent acts during the period covered occurred at home or in the school, parents and teachers must have been mainly responsible. Statistics such as these merely indicate where the delinquency *occurred,* not where it was *caused.*

A more effective approach to the problem than that of the New York *Daily News* is being made by a bipartisan subcommittee of the United States Senate headed by Senator Robert C. Hendrickson of New Jersey, which opened public hearings in 1953. The subcommittee has a staff of three men who serve as legal counsel and investigators, and in addition has borrowed several experienced consultants from various public and private organizations throughout the country. In each of twenty cities where it planned to hold hearings the subcommittee first organized a task force of persons interested in delinquency—civic leaders, police, the juvenile-court judge, clergymen, and so on. Their responsibility has been to provide an estimate of the extent of the problem in the community, to indicate what is being done to solve it, and to point out the deficiencies in the local program. The subcommittee investigators have then moved in and directed the inquiry. The subcommittee has also sent thousands of letters to agencies and individuals all over the United States soliciting their help in determining the nature, extent, main causes, and contributing causes of juvenile delinquency.

The first interim report of the Hendrickson subcommittee appeared in March of this year and wisely emphasized at the outset that "an investigation of juvenile delinquency involves examination of many facets of our complex society." "The brief period in which the subcommittee has had to work," it continued, "has not enabled it to do more than make a beginning on its task. For this reason, no effort has yet been made to formulate definite conclusions or final recommendations." However, the subcommittee did offer some tentative conclusions which may be summarized as follows: (1) In recent years a steadily increasing number of American children have been involved in delinquency. (2) As a corollary to the growing incidence of delinquency, younger children are committing more serious offenses. (3) The problem is non-urban as well as urban. (4) Delinquent acts are committed by children in all economic groups. (5) Delinquency "is always the product of many and closely interrelated influences or forces," especially those of the family and the

community. (6) It follows that prevention of delinquency requires measures for improving family and community life for children.

The report is useful as a sober and realistic analysis of the problem, but it adds little to the store of knowledge already recorded in professional journals, monographs, and textbooks. What is most urgently needed, perhaps, is an inclusive theory which will (a) encompass and integrate the diverse threads of causation already uncovered, (b) suggest further lines of research, and (c) give direction to an effective program of treatment, control, and prevention. Such a theory is faintly suggested in one statement in the interim report to the effect that "through both acts of commission and omission, larger society may and does contribute to the development of delinquency."

This fits in with a school of thought in American social science which believes that the search for causation in social problems like juvenile delinquency has failed until now largely because it has not recognized the appropriate frame of reference for study and analysis—that is, American society as a whole. The forces impelling delinquency pervade our whole social structure. In other words, a theory that could be used most profitably by investigators is that juveniles in America are growing up in a "delinquent society."

According to this theory, the dynamic nature of American society is of primary importance. Continuing change has given a high degree of fluidity to our ideas of right and wrong. If American children were brought up in a culture where the pace of change was slow and the "right" ways had become firmly intrenched in tradition, they would be less prone to deviant behavior. Secondly, social relations in American society have become quite impersonal. The decline of face-to-face relations and responsibilities has meant the decline of an important form of social control, for adults as well as for children. Thirdly, the heterogeneous composition of American society has fostered a duality of loyalty and ethics. Children have consequently been inclined to follow one code of ethics in their relations with members of their own group and another code in their relations with the out-group.

But even more significant for delinquency, perhaps, are some of the values in American culture. For example, material success is generally believed to be emphasized more in our society than anywhere else in the world. This undoubtedly accounts for much of the energy and drive of Americans. But it also helps explain why other countries, even those with a standard of living considerably beneath ours, have lower delinquency rates. The majority of children elsewhere set up for themselves goals within reasonable reach, such as their parents have attained. Here we expect successive generations to achieve ever higher levels. Some children, when they realize they cannot reach their goals by thrift and hard work, turn to other means—those which spell delinquency.

Another pertinent American value, especially as it constitutes part of the personality make-up of the boy in our society, is toughness. American culture is permeated with violence in personal relations. Though social classes may differ in this respect, in general an inordinate pressure is placed on the male child to "fight back," not to be a "sissy." If the family does not cultivate this value in the boy, he will acquire it elsewhere.

The condoning of trickery as expressed in the sayings, "There's a sucker born every minute" and "Everything is a racket," is still another value related to juvenile delinquency. Ultimately juveniles acquire their values from the adults around them. And when adults take the attitude that laws dealing with intoxication, taxes, gambling, traffic, and many other things may be ignored if one can "get away with it," children follow their example.

Most programs and techniques now in effect for the control and prevention of delinquency penetrate no deeper than the superficial symptoms. New proposals are usually no better. Typical of many is the "solution" just advocated by the American Association of Health, Physical Education, and Recreation. The April, 1954, issue of the A.A.H.P.E.R. *Journal* maintains that juvenile delinquency can be combated swiftly and economically by providing a sound program of physical education and recreation for all children in the nation's schools. Prevention of juvenile delinquency calls for much more than this. It requires modification of the social and cultural pattern of American society.

Unfortunately, the Hendrickson subcommittee, if it ever reaches such a conclusion, will have difficulty in translating it into recommendations for action. We all know that bold revisions in the pattern of human relations have become taboo in mid-century America. We no longer pioneer freely in social affairs. Our way of life has come to mean, among other things, conservative correctness in social, political, and economic affairs. Proposals for planned change, so common a generation ago, are now frowned upon as the impractical speculations of "eggheads." Recommendations that social engineering be employed to alleviate our social problems are linked with political subversion or left-wing ideologies and dismissed —or investigated. The flexibility and social inventiveness that explained so much of the promise and hope of our earlier history have given way to fear and rigidity.

This, indeed, is one of the more important dilemmas of our time. Unless we solve it, our very existence, not merely the welfare of our children, will be threatened.

Police Corruption

The United States Special Senate Committee to Investigate Organized Crime in Interstate Commerce

In 1950–1951, the U. S. Senate Crime Investigating Committee, under the chairmanship of Senator Estes Kefauver, held hearings in 14 cities and took testimony from over 600 witnesses to determine the extent of the utilization of interstate commerce by organized crime and to determine whether such operations were developing corrupting influences in violation of federal and state laws. The material given here constitutes a small portion of the Committee's voluminous report.

Although the committee has seen and paid tribute to many fine, efficient, honest, and able law-enforcement officers and officials, law enforcement has broken down in many of the communities visited by the committee. Where criminal gangs and syndicates operate openly as they

From *The Kefauver Committee Report on Organized Crime*, New York: Didier, n. d., pp. 162–168.

have done in such places as Saratoga; Bergen County, N. J.; the Newport-Covington area of Kentucky; the Miami area of Florida; many of the parishes outside of New Orleans; many of the Illinois and California counties and the area of Jackson County outside of Kansas City, to cite only the most notorious examples, it is apparent that too many local police, sheriffs, prosecutors, and courts are failing to do their sworn duty.

The committee places no stock in the professed inability of many law-enforcement officials to detect violations of the law which are apparent to any informed citizen. The blindness which afflicts many law-enforcement officials in wide-open communities is for the record only.

There can be little question that these officials know perfectly well what is going on. Nor can there be little doubt in the mind of the committee that vigorous, honest law-enforcement can put an end to wide-open conditions in a very short time. The fact that Saratoga was run without open gambling in the racing season of 1950; that Sheriff "King" Clancy could give the order to shut down operations in Jefferson Parish; that Pat Perdue, the so-called "one-man vice squad" of Miami Beach, could boast that he could shut down operations in Miami Beach in 24 hours if he were given the order to do so, is an indication of what can be accomplished where law-enforcement officials really wish to act.

It can be assumed that this failure of law-enforcement officials to suppress gambling and vice conditions in their community affects their law-enforcement responsibilities in other fields. By refusing to act against the racketeers who run bookmaking operations, slot machines, gambling casinos, and houses of prostitution, law-enforcement officials give aid and encouragement to some of the worst hoodlums and criminal gangs in this country. These hoodlums and criminal gangs do not restrict their operations to exploiting the human desire to gamble.

They also engage in activities which are even more devastating to the community and to the welfare of the people; the sale and distribution of narcotics, various forms of extortion and shake-downs, various types of business and labor-union racketeering, as well as outright robbery, burglary, and larceny. Inevitably, their operations in gambling and other fields bring in their train aggravated forms of violence against persons and property. The ultimate weapon that these mobsters

have is murder and they have not hesitated to use it in communities all over the country.

Nor should it be assumed that law-enforcement agencies, which are ineffective in suppressing gambling operations, suddenly become efficient instruments of justice when confronted with other crimes. The record is clearly the other way. Police officials, sheriffs, and district attorneys who refuse to do their duty in enforcing the gambling laws because of corruption or the use of political influence do not prosecute vigorously when the racketeers and gangsters operating gambling enterprises become involved in other crimes.

If money or political influence will fix a gambling case, it will also fix a case involving a more heinous offense. The creeping paralysis of law enforcement which results from a failure to enforce the gambling laws, therefore, contributes to a breakdown in connection with other fields of crime.

It is axiomatic in the underworld that once a public official allows a case to be fixed, thereafter the underworld owns him.

One other aspect of this breakdown must be noted. Wherever organized criminal gangs are entrenched in a particular community and have been given the green light to operate, it is not unusual to see the forces of law enforcement being used against their competitors, while protected operations are left severely alone. This fact helps to explain the growth of such vast bookmaking conspiracies as the S and G Syndicate in Miami, the Guarantee Finance Co. in Los Angeles, and the Gross bookmaking empire in New York. Only too frequently, bookmakers, slot-machine operators, policy bankers and punchboard sellers have been given to understand that they must come to terms with the "syndicate" or the "combination" that has the "in" with law enforcement. The penalty for failing to come to terms is continual harassment by the police and other agencies of law-enforcement. In the Miami story, we saw this weapon of inequal enforcement of the law by a State official being used against the S and G as one of the weapons to compel it to capitulate to the demands of Accardo-Guzik-Fischetti crime syndicate.

The breakdown in law enforcement is not exactly due to corruption of law-enforcement officials or to the use of political influence to paralyze law-enforcement processes. Much of the responsibility must be placed upon the present organization of law-enforcement agencies. In metropolitan communities like Cook County, Ill., Los Angeles County, Calif., or Bergen County, N. J., there is a congerie of independent local police forces covering the county. In addition, a sheriff's office with wide law-enforcement responsibilities and the State police with a wide jurisdiction to enforce State laws, may also operate within the county.

There is no centralized direction or control and no centralized responsibility for seeing that a single uniform law-enforcement policy is applied over the entire geographic area of a county. The situation lends itself to buck-passing and evasion of responsibility which can only inure to the benefit of gangsters and racketeers. It makes it possible for hoodlums to find those cities and towns where law-enforcement is lax and to concentrate their operations there.

It is obvious that many factors contribute to the breakdown of law-enforcement agencies. No single panacea can make law-enforcement agencies more efficient and effective in dealing with organized crime. It is suggested, therefore, that each State make an over-all survey of its law-enforcement agencies to see whether or not they are adequately organized and equipped to cope with modern racketeering and gangsterism. It is obvious that a survey of this character must not only inquire into the organization and operation of law-enforcement agencies, it must also determine whether they are so beset by corruption and political influence that no matter how they were organized, they would continue to be ineffective.

Surveys in each State are necessary because of the difficulty of making suggestions which are applicable to the entire country.

The peculiar problems of each State vary and there are significant differences in the organization of their law-enforcement agencies. However, there is sufficient administrative know-how in the various States to make it possible to lay out a plan and a method for dealing with organized crime which will considerably curtail this threat to our insitutions.

The most shocking revelations of the testimony before the committee is the extent of official corruption and connivance in facilitating and promoting organized crime. Nevertheless, it should not be assumed that our revelations cast doubt as to the integrity of the great preponderance of law-enforcement and other public officials. On the contrary, our findings and conclusions relate only to a small but disturbing minority of such officials.

The committee found evidence of corruption and connivance at all levels of government—Federal, State, and local. The evidence of the corruption of Federal Government officials is primarily in connection with the enforcement of the income-tax laws. Certain officials of the Bureau of Internal Revenue in California conceived the scheme of selling stock which they owned in a company that they controlled to persons who were likely to have trouble with their income taxes. The stock was worthless, but its purchase assured immunity from a too-careful scrutiny of income-tax returns. This is not an indictment of the Bureau as a whole; most of these employees have been discharged and some have been indicted by a Federal grand jury.

The evidence of corruption and connivance with organized crime in State and local government is present in four different forms:

(1) Direct bribe or protection payments are made to law-enforcement officials, so that they will not interfere with specific criminal activities.

(2) Political influence and pressure of important officials or political leaders is used to protect criminal activities or further the interests of criminal gangs.

(3) Law-enforcement officials are found in the possession of unusual and unexplained wealth.

(4) Law-enforcement officials participate directly in the business of organized crime.

Just before his death, James Ragen, head of Continental Press, told the State's attorney that over a 3-year period, the wire service had in the past paid out $600,000 in political contributions.

At the local level, the committee received evidence of corruption of law-enforcement officers and connivance with criminal gangs in every city in which it held hearings. The testimony at the Tampa hearings indicates that Sheriff Culbreath, of Hillsborough County, was the center of the criminal conspiracy to violate the gambling laws. Evidence was received of direct and regular payments of protection money by gamblers to Culbreath and to other law-enforcement officials in Tampa.

The sordid story of direct payments to law-enforcement officials in return for the protection of criminals, is repeated in Philadelphia, where the "bag" man for a Captain Elwell, would come into the station house with his pockets bulging with money. Three thousand dollars to four thousand dollars a month was alleged to have been paid in each of 38 police districts or approximately $152,-000 a month, not counting payments to the higher ups. In New York City it has been estimated that the Gross bookmaking empire paid over $1,000,000 a year for police protection. In Dade County, Fla., a deputy sheriff is alleged to have turned over to the wife of the sheriff seven, eight, ten, and eleven thousand dollars at a time in cash and obtained signed receipts therefor. In Jackson County, Mo. (K. C.), some deputy sheriffs were on the payrolls of slot-machine distributors and taverns that violated the liquor laws. In Los Angeles, at least half a dozen police officers "borrowed" money from the Guarantee Finance Co., a big bookmaking operation. One suspended officer worked as a collector from bookmakers for the Guarantee Finance Co. during the period of his suspension. An entry of $108,000 on the books of the Guarantee Finance Co. for "juice" undoubtedly indicates payoffs to law-enforcement officials. The strong box which Sheriff Grosch of Orleans Parish, La., bought with such elaborate precautions at a time when he was a city detective, was intended to keep not his legitimate earnings but the fruits of his betrayal of the public trust—protection money from law violators. But his official behavior was similar to that of many other important law-enforcement officials in the New Orleans area. This is illustrated by the extraordinary story of Moity who discovered that he could not stay in the slot-machine business without paying "ice."

There is also the case of former Police Chief George Reyer, of New Orleans, who once was president of the International Association of Police Chiefs. Squeezed by a change in administrations, Reyer took his pension and switched to the wire service payroll at $100 a week without the loss of a payday.

Law-enforcement has been an easy road to affluence for many law-enforcement officials. The case of Dan "Tubbo" Gilbert, "the richest police officer in the world," who was chief investigator in the State attorney's office in Chicago, is well known. Such officials as "King" Clancy, sheriff of Jefferson Parish, La., and Walter Clark, sheriff of Broward County, Fla., have grown rich, powerful, and arrogant from their association with the underworld elements who ran the gambling and prostitution enterprises in their jurisdictions. There are many other illustrations in the testimony before the committee. Typical of this is the fortunate economic position of John English, the city commissioner in charge of the police department of East Louis, who was able to obtain a

$100,000 summer home, various interests in real estate in East St. Louis, interests in a restaurant and a gas station, on a salary of $4,500 to $6,000. The fact that the city was wide open for years and only two or three gambling arrests were made in 1950 may have some relation to the commissioner's wealth.

The attempt to paralyze law-enforcement by political means is encountered again and again in the testimony before the committee. The success of mobster Frank Costello in exercising control over the New York County Democratic organization is typical of what one can expect from the alliance between politics and crime. Mobster Joe Adonis' influence upon the Kings County (Brooklyn, N. Y.) Democratic organization may go far to explain why neither he nor a major subordinate like Anastasia was ever subjected to prosecution and punishment. The committee developed at great length the extraordinary attempt by Binaggio, a powerful political leader, to acquire control of the Police Board of Kansas City so that he could install his candidate Braun as chief of police. Binaggio finally offered a substantial bribe to one of the commissioners who had refused to go along with his program. Gene Burnett, police chief of Granite City, Ill., was apparently willing to close down the gambling places and the handbooks in his town, but the orders from the mayor were to let them operate as that is how the city council wanted it. There is more than a remote connection between the orders to Police Chief Short of Miami to "lay off" gambling, "although the city could be closed in a matter of hours," and the fact that one of Miami's councilmen had had many extremely profitable deals with Harold Salvey, a member of the S and G Syndicate. The story of Governor Fuller Warren of Florida is told elsewhere. After accepting a huge campaign contribution from William H. Johnston, who has close connections with present and past members of the Capone syndicate, Warren allowed the power of his office to be used by the Capone syndicate in its successful effort to muscle into Miami Beach gambling. Most recently Warren has reinstated Sheriff James Sullivan of Miami without any satisfactory explanation of the serious evidence and charges brought against Sullivan before this committee.

There was considerable evidence before the committee concerning contributions to political campaigns by gamblers and gangsters. For example, Molasky contributed $2,500 to the gubernatorial campaign in Missouri in the hope that he would be given the right to name a member of the St. Louis Police Board. When he was unable to do so he claimed to have been double-crossed. Pat Noonan, an associate of the mobsters in the Binaggio gang, did considerable political work in the campaign to elect Governor Smith. Much of his expenses were paid by persons involved in violations of the gambling laws. The fact that Emilio Georgetti, "the Gambling King of San Mateo County," worked "like hell" for the election of Sheriff McGrath and "accumulated a little money for the campaign," did not hurt him in his gambling operations.

Evidence has also been presented to the committee that certain law-enforcement officials or their relatives not only received protection money from gangsters but that they actually ran gambling operations themselves. The bookmaking operation which was run right in Sheriff Culbreath's office by his brother and an employee of the sheriff, may or may not have been as insignificant as the sheriff tried to show. But the same thing cannot be said for the partnership which Sheriff Clark of Broward County had in the Broward Novelty Co. This company operated bolita games (policy) and slot machines and provided the sheriff with his principal source of income. The participation of public officials in the New Orleans area in the operation of slot machines has almost come to have the status of an established institution.

It is obvious that law-enforcement officials who are themselves engaged in gambling operations will have no special desire to enforce gambling statutes.

The committee has been most gratified by the tremendous interest which the general public has demonstrated in the hearings conducted by the committee. . . . That interest has confirmed anew the committee's fundamental faith that the heart of America is basically sound.

The active participation of an informed public is essential to the correction of the conditions which the committee's investigation has shown to exist throughout the country. The committee has emphasized time and again that organized crime cannot exist without political protection. It is the responsibility of the voting public to insure that their representative governments at all levels are made up of men who are not open to corruption or persuasion by criminals and racketeers.

In the course of its investigations, the committee has seen numerous examples of public apathy toward the operations of organized crime and its alliance with officials at various levels of government.

In the State of Florida, it seemed clear to the committee that the highest officials in the State condoned, and in some cases, affirmatively aided the operations of organized gamblers. In the State of Illinois, where there can be no question as to the honesty and integrity of the Governor and his aides, the committee found evidence that numerous local law-enforcement officials made no effort to interfere with illegal gambling operations. More shocking than the defection of individual law-enforcement officials was the testimony before the committee that many of these men were elected and re-elected by a voting public which was well aware of their tolerance of illegal gambling.

Equally shocking is the fact that efforts to remove and punish such officials for their obvious acts of malfeasance are often nullified by juries that refuse to recognize the venality of such behavior.

There is a segment of public opinion in many cities that believes that gambling, in some cases "just a little gambling," is good for business, and that strict enforcement of the anti-gambling laws would be a mistake. This attitude on the part of normally law-abiding citizens can only come from a failure to comprehend the violence and racketeering which inevitably accompany gambling operations, and the extent of the resulting damage to the economic and social fabric.

The theory that gambling is good for business was expounded in Kansas City, in Las Vegas, and in Miami. The fact of the matter is that the huge sums which accrue as a result of gambling are pocketed by criminals, hoodlums, and corrupt politicians, and the general public receives little or no part of the income from the milking operations carried on by the big-time gamblers.

It is established practice for big-time gamblers and gambling syndicates to contribute generously to charities, fraternal organizations, and other worthy causes as part of their program to ingratiate themselves with the community and convince the public that while more or less illegal, their activities are thoroughly moral.

In the light of the tremendous profits which gamblers enjoy so long as the public will tolerate their operations, they can well afford to expend substantial sums of money to cloak themselves with an aura of public-spiritedness.

It is the hope of this committee that as a result of its investigations and report specific legislation aimed at dealing with organized criminal activity will be enacted; that certain changes recommended by the committee will be made in Federal, State, and local law-enforcement procedures.

However, the ultimate responsibility for the success of the suggested legislation and reforms rests squarely in the hands of the public. Unless the public expresses an affirmative desire for the elimination of organized criminal operations and official corruption through the continued exercise of the vote, through active participation in the work of such organizations as local and State crime commissions, and through the careful attention to the efficiency and honesty of the men whom they employ to govern them, there can be no real and lasting progress toward the elimination of organized criminal activity in this country.

Narcotic Addiction

Alden Stevens

Alden Stevens (1907–   ), free-lance writer. Major publications: *Arms and the People* (1942); with Roger Burlingame, *Victory Without Peace* (1944); *America: A Traveler's Guide* (1950).

Everyone wants the illegal drug racket broken and crime by addicts stopped. Everyone wants teen-age addiction conquered and adult addiction reduced to a minimum. The fastest and surest way to accomplish these ends is to make dope legal.

This doesn't mean that drug peddlers should be licensed by the state and made respectable nor that morphine should be sold freely in drugstores. It does not mean that international controls should be abandoned. It is not suggested that the federal narcotics hospitals should be closed. Illegal drug traffickers should still be prosecuted to the limit.

The plan proposed here is a modern development of an approach tried thirty years ago. This crude early effort showed great promise even though severely hampered by shortage of funds and shortage of time before it was cut down by ignorance and prejudice. Modern educators, welfare experts, physicians, and others have suggested safeguards and procedures which, added to the experience gained during this brief experiment, encourage the belief—shared by churchmen, citizens of the highest standing in the community, and incidentally addicts and ex-addicts—that this extensively revised plan offers an excellent prospect for public victory over narcotic addiction.

It is only fair to say that many experts disagree. Their reasons will be taken up later in this article.

Careful analysis of the objections leaves this writer more convinced than ever that the new approach is a sound one.

Few people know that narcotics clinics were conducted during 1919 and 1920 in no less than fifteen states. With a few possible exceptions all were closed by the federal government for reasons which seemed to many doctors and citizens at the time illogical and inadequate. Yet this action, exposed here for the first time in a magazine of general circulation, has made possible in large part the horrible business of dope pushing, teen-age addiction, and the crimes related to them.

The writer has talked with many addicts in recent weeks. He has talked with doctors about the problem, doctors both frightened and realistic. He has talked to enforcement officials of the Federal Bureau of Narcotics, social workers, churchmen, and citizens. And he is convinced that the problem is not being solved. It is, as New York State Attorney General Nathaniel Goldstein says, if anything, worsening.

Before outlining this suggested approach to the problem it should be emphasized that narcotic addicts are not "fiends." They are human beings, every pathetic, afflicted, unhappy one of them. Referring to them as "hoodlums" and "zoot-suit hellions" does not expel them from the human race. Furthermore, it has no effect upon their addiction and it only makes their problems worse. Actually, many addicts are housewives. Others

From "Make Dope Legal," *Harper's Magazine*, 205:1230 (November 1952): 40–47.

are business men, artists, musicians, doctors, nurses, politicians, lawyers, and clerks. Many others are hardly more than children, young people who should be cared for and treated with sympathy and understanding, who in all humanity should be rescued in a civilized manner instead of being driven into the underworld. These usually underprivileged adolescents, some through their own arrogant foolishness, far more through the ignorance, deception, and cowardice of others, are victims of something beyond human power to control, something certainly far beyond the power of a young person against whom the world conspires and whom the world is urged to despise.

Doctors agree that the full facts about addiction are not known, that there are many questions which remain unanswered, that there are many problems not yet solved. There are, however, some basic facts which *have* been established.

The habit-forming drugs which are most important and which give the most trouble at the present time are heroin and morphine. *Neither of these drugs incites anyone to crime.* Both are depressants, not excitants. They tend to make users sluggish and dopey, weak, and subject to dreams. In rare cases when a person under their influence gets hallucinations he may become irrational and violent. But such cases *are* rare. People become much more violent from drinking too much alcohol than from taking morphine or heroin.

It is not the drug itself which drives the addict to crime. It is the need for the drug. The criminal path is almost inevitable because an addict must spend from $15 to $75 every day for his drug. Usually less alert than non-addicts, less able to concentrate, less able to work (although many do hold down jobs), with less energy and less initiative, they can rarely earn what their addiction costs in addition to the regular costs of living. How many teen-agers living in city slums can honestly earn a hundred dollars a week? Answer: none.

Yet, robbed of will power by the drug itself, his personality usually ravaged far beyond his own dulled realization, the addict will do anything to get his dose. He is completely unable to stand the excruciating withdrawal symptoms which occasionally (though rarely) end in death. These begin with heavy sweating and running eyes and nose, progress through an intolerable restlessness, high blood pressure, and gooseflesh,

and culminate in fever, vomiting, diarrhea, and extremely severe cramps in the back, abdomen, and legs.

Is it any wonder that the problem of getting the next dose may occupy the addict's every thinking moment? The relentless urgency, coupled with fear of arrest, makes him tense and nervous. As tolerance to the drug builds up, an addict usually needs slightly increasing doses. Never being absolutely certain that he can get more drugs in time to avoid withdrawal symptoms, in constant fear of being picked up by police, never being quite sure whether his supply contains 10 per cent, 3 per cent, or 1 per cent, he finds his need building up with a terrifying rapidity brought about by these very fears and doubts. Overdoses, sometimes caused by the fear that he will not be able to get another shot and sometimes by the fact that he doesn't know how much his supply has been cut, are common—and sometimes fatal.

The actual cash value of a day's supply of morphine for an average addict is about thirty cents. Except in very rare circumstances it can't be obtained for that because it must be bought in the illegal market from ruthless brigands.

And just as long as two pounds of heroin can be bought for ten dollars and when cut can be sold for $80,000, it will be cut and sold. Half a million enforcement agents (the Federal Bureau of Narcotics now has about two hundred) could not prevent this so long as addicts must have it no matter what crimes must be committed to get the price.

Many states have, in the past few years, tightened laws against sellers, providing stiffer sentences and heavier fines. What effect has this policy had? It has driven the price of drugs sharply upward. It has thus made necessary more crime and more desperate crime by addicts who have no other way of getting money for the supply they need.

New York State has recently passed a law providing compulsory hospitalization of all minor addicts. The Federal Bureau of Narcotics wants to go further and forcibly hospitalize *all* addicts. What will be the effect of such a policy? Why, to drive the addict further underground and to make him cleverer than ever at hiding his drug and his addiction.

According to the New York City Mayor's Committee on Narcotics there were, in the summer of 1951, somewhere between 45,000 and 90,-

000 drug users in New York City alone. These figures are estimates, of course. The Federal Bureau of Narcotics says, and all experts agree, that there are no reliable figures on the total number of addicts. How can there be when every addict has, as one of his main problems, the need to conceal his addiction from the world? (Many gain incredible skill at this deception with years of practice.) How can there be figures when it is possible (as it *is* possible) for a person to become an addict in three weeks? How can a count be made on which to base any statement?

The Mayor's Committee does, however, give some figures which are reliable—and revealing. In 1946, 281 persons in New York City were sentenced for violation of narcotics laws. In 1950, 1,031 were so sentenced, and in the first nine months of 1951, 1,179 were so sentenced—more than five times as many per month during 1951 as during 1948. The Federal Narcotics Bureau confirms this trend nationwide by reporting 6,149 arrests in fiscal 1950—which was 1,048 more than in fiscal 1949.

Let's take a look at the success we've had in curing addiction, and at what it costs.

The chief treatment centers are the two federal hospitals, one at Fort Worth, Texas, with about 400 beds, and the older, better known one at Lexington, Kentucky. There is space at Lexington for about 1,500 patients. About 4,000 are admitted each year for a minimum treatment time of four and a half months. In 1946, 3 per cent of these patients were under twenty-one. In 1951, 18 per cent were under twenty-one; one was thirteen years old. It costs the Public Health Service $3,000,000 per year to run these two hospitals. Dr. John D. Reichard of Lexington says that of their patients, 13.5 per cent abstain after their "cure." He also says 39.9 per cent relapse in nine months to three years. The remainder are either dead or not known. This, a recent official report, indicates that at best not more than one-quarter of the people who go to Lexington are permanently cured. And many knowledgeable people scoff at these figures as being ridiculously high. One man who has been treated at Lexington and who has studied addiction for years says, "It's closer to 3 per cent cures."

Yet nearly everyone, doctors, social workers, enforcement officers, and addicts themselves, say cure without confinement is impossible. Or, at least, it's hardly ever been done.

Exact figures are not to be had, but each *cure* at Lexington (if we divide the cost of operation by the number of real cures) costs at least $4,000. A part of this expense is paid by some of the voluntary patients, and since no one actually knows how many cures are made, this figure is little more than a guess. To this cost of treatment should be added that of enforcement. The Narcotics Bureau will spend two and a quarter million dollars this year, its largest budget in history. Many states have their own narcotics squads; so do many cities. Clearly all these add up to astronomical even though unobtainable figures.

And still Americans, many of them normal people and far too many of them children who don't know what they are doing, are having their lives destroyed by drugs. The cost to these people in New York City alone is more than $100,000,000 per year.

It seems clear that our present efforts to eliminate or even control the drug traffic are not working. It's time to try something else. What should a rational narcotics program accomplish?

First, it should reduce the number of addicts sharply.

Second, it should prevent the making of new addicts, especially among our youth.

Third, it should eliminate crime caused by the need for drugs.

Fourth, it should take the fantastic profit out of the narcotics traffic.

Fifth, it should discover who the addicts are and how many there are.

Sixth, it should determine more facts about addiction, medically and psychologically. The ignorance of addicts about their affliction is abysmal and tragic, and doctors themselves admit they know far too little.

There is a way to win every one of these objectives. Useful citizens can at the same time be made out of addicts who happen to be incurable, as even the Federal Bureau of Narcotics, which hounds and reviles them, admits a great many probably are. There seems to be no doubt that many people must live as addicts until they die, and they rarely die of drugs. People have lived, twenty, thirty, even forty or more years as addicts.

What is this method and what reason is there to believe it will work?

For the answers to these questions we must go back to 1919 and the early nineteen-twenties, when many narcotics clinics were operating in the United States. Usually under control of state, city, or county health officials, these were run by physicians of excellent standing, with the blessing and active co-operation of medical societies, many of which were affiliated with the American Medical Association. In them addiction was recognized as a medical and public-health problem. Persons who came in and could establish the fact of addiction were given advice and information, and drugs were dispensed to them. Moral, social, and welfare aspects of the problem, however, surprising as it now seems, were generally ignored. In spite of this fact doctors in charge reported that their work reduced crime, made useful citizens, blasted the illegal drug traffic, and in some cases established cures.

These clinics existed, at one time or another, in fifteen or more states. New York City had such a clinic from July 17, 1919, until March 6, 1920, and sixteen other cities in New York State had them. Among the most successful were those at Los Angeles; Portland, Oregon; and Shreveport, Louisiana. Many states, such as Tennessee, had modified clinic systems providing for medical care of addicts and the dispensing of drugs to them.

What happened to these clinics? Why is there not a single such institution in the United States today? If they were so successful, why did they close?

The answer is simple—and shocking.

The basic federal narcotics law is the Harrison Act of December 17, 1914. This is a revenue act, not a prohibitory law. It neither forbade doctors licensed under it to prescribe drugs nor did it limit the amount they prescribed. It required only that they keep a record of how much they prescribed to which patients, with dates.

In 1921 a four-page advisory leaflet, inspired by a report of a committee of the American Medical Association, was issued by the Prohibition Bureau, then in charge of narcotics law enforcement. This leaflet stated that addicts should be confined during treatment for addiction. The four members of this committee were physicians of excellent reputation and there is no doubt they sincerely believed in their recommendations, but other members of the AMA of equal experience and reputation, who were actually running narcotics clinics, just as sincerely believed they had found the answer to the drug problem.

Yet on the basis of this leaflet, which had no legal status and for which none was claimed, the clinics were closed. Patients were driven to despair and crime. Many became dope peddlers to

protect their own supply, and in order to sell enough dope to earn the cost of their own they made addicts out of the easiest marks—young, ignorant, frustrated kids. This single bureaucratic step, unauthorized by Congress, destroyed all honest attempts, other than forced hospitalization, to treat addiction as a medical problem instead of a crime. Many observers have remarked that on this single, almost forgotten, leaflet the present narcotics trade, the narcotics crime picture which we see today, in fact much of the narcotics evil is based. In European countries today, where doctors can treat addicts as sick people, the appalling picture of crime and teen-age addiction does not exist. It did not exist in cities with clinics in this country as it does now, before the release of this leaflet.

This damaging misinterpretation of the Harrison Act has not gone unobserved. Doctors, welfare workers, and even the Supreme Court of the United States have noted it. The entire matter was succinctly and completely aired in Congress on June 15, 1938, by Congressman John M. Coffee of Washington. Mr. Coffee wanted to transfer the entire narcotics enforcement problem from the Bureau of Narcotics to the U. S. Public Health Service. He spoke of the $2,735,000,000 a year cost of addiction as a "needless burden imposed on the people, not by conditions inherent in the problem of drug addiction, and not by the operation of the law, but by the mistaken interpretation of law made by the Federal Narcotics Bureau." Continuing, he pointed out that "in examining the Harrison Special Tax Act we are confronted with the anomaly that a law designed (as its name implies) to place a tax on certain drugs, and raise revenue thereby, resulted in . . . developing a smuggling industry not before in existence. Through operation of the law *as interpreted* [italics ours] there has developed the racket of dope peddling; in a word, the whole gigantic structure of the illicit drug racket, with direct annual turnover of upward of a billion dollars."

Mr. Coffee went on to summarize the findings of the U. S. Supreme Court in the Linder Case of 1925 and the Nigro Case of 1928, both of which clearly established that the Harrison Act was a pure revenue act, and the AAA case of 1936 which established that federal law has no control over the practice of a profession. Said Coffee: "The Narcotics Bureau ignores these decisions and assumes authority to prevent physicians from even the attempt to cure narcotic addicts unless the patients are under forced confinement." Coffee went on to recommend putting addicts in the care of physicians who would prescribe what medicine they might need, presumably including narcotics. Confidently predicting the end of the narcotics traffic if this were done, Coffee asked why the Harrison Act should not function as originally intended and as the Supreme Court said it should. In reply to this question he said "the opposition comes from a small coterie of persons in authority who are in a position to benefit from the *status quo*." He particularly desired "to question the Commissioner of Narcotics and to observe how he may endeavor to justify the activities that cost the American people not far from $3,000,000,000 per year."

Actually Congress would have to pass no law to re-open these clinics, other than an appropriation measure. All that would be necessary would be a reversal in policy by the Federal Bureau of Narcotics. Unfortunately it is far too late to return to this simple clinic system. It is too late to legalize prescription by doctors which, although it works in Europe, never functioned well here. (In 1919 the Treasury Department estimated that thirty doctors in New York City wrote 1,500,000 legal prescriptions for drugs each year. Their "patients" were addicts, and no control was exercised over the drugs they bought freely on prescription. Abuses such as overdoses and resale of supplies were very common.)

The problem must now be handled in a different way in order to meet today's much more difficult conditions.

The federal government, probably through the U. S. Public Health Service, which runs the hospitals at Lexington and Fort Worth, should be enabled to open clinics in places where the problem is acute and to permit designated physicians to take over similar functions in smaller places. The purpose of these clinics would be to cure or alleviate addiction, to wipe out the illegal narcotic traffic, and to eliminate crime by addicts in need of drugs. There would also be secondary functions which will be discussed later.

Any person, regardless of age, should be able to come into one of these federal clinics and register as an addict by filling out a form. He would be required to state that it was his desire to be cured of addiction and would pledge co-operation with the physicians. Naturally, because of the nature of his affliction, this pledge would in no way relax the extreme care and close supervision which is always necessary. In other words, the physicians

in charge would not agree to believe everything they were told.

The addict would then get a thorough physical examination to determine whether he was truly an addict and to what degree. Great care would be necessary to prevent the deliberate picking up of the habit or reversion to it by former addicts, and this scrupulous medical attention would be an essential part of clinic operation. Each registrant would be photographed and his fingerprints sent to the FBI to check the legitimacy of his identification and to prevent registry at another clinic under another name. Each registrant would receive a tamper-proof laminated card with his signature, address, photograph, and fingerprints on it. Corresponding records, with space for recording each medication given, would be kept at the clinic office.

The addict's identification cleared, the physician in charge would proceed to determine how much of what drug he had been taking and what quantity of morphine might lead to a balanced dosage. (Heroin, not in the United States Pharmacopoeia, would probably not be dispensed; morphine is less harmful and can be substituted.) A balanced dosage is the smallest amount which will keep an addict reasonably free from the nightmarish withdrawal symptoms. Its establishment is far from easy and may take weeks, even months, of careful watching, recording, and analysis. But it is an important step on the long, hard road to recovery.

At this point three important things will have been accomplished for the addict himself. First, he will have gone onto the least harmful drug which will satisfy his need; second, he will know how much he really needs; third, he will be released from the tension of worry over where the next dose is coming from. A gradual relaxation may be expected to follow which will make a balanced dosage and a reasonable attitude easier to establish. An actual cure would not be attempted until much later, in a few cases perhaps never. There would be no urgency to get an addict off drugs in a hurry, since this would defeat the whole purpose of the clinic by driving him back to the illegal market.

Dosages would be carefully measured and recorded, not cut, as is universally done in the illegal traffic. Instruments would be sterile, not contaminated. Advice would be freely given, questions honestly answered.

The dosage established would always be dispensed at the clinic. Neither prescriptions nor a supply—not even enough to last one day—would be put in the hands of the addict to carry away. Whether by needle or mouth, all doses would be taken at the clinic. The price of each dose, regardless of size, would be nominal—probably ten cents. This would cover the actual cost of the drug. Pauper addicts would be treated free.

Each registered addict would be given a booklet on the first visit explaining the medical facts of his affliction. He would watch educational films and listen to lectures. He would have what psychiatric help could be made available. His personal, home, employment, and other problems would be discussed with social workers and job specialists. Efforts would be made to find him a job. He would be referred to religious counsel of his choice. Whether contrite or not, he would be treated as a person with serious problems, as a medical and social case, not as a criminal.

No registrant would ever formally be told he was incurable, even though the doctors thought so. Whether or not ambulatory cures are actually possible no one has ever conclusively proved or disproved under properly controlled conditions. There are doctors who believe they are possible. Here again, we are dependent on information which would be scientifically gathered through the experience of the clinics. The hospitals would remain open in any case and would be more effective because the clinics would provide follow-up treatment, advice, and aid not now available to the discharged addict. Patients of both hospitals and clinics would, in fact, be required to report to the clinics for check-ups at intervals for some time after their cure had been accomplished, if indeed it had been accomplished.

What would be the effect of this modern, comprehensive clinic program? First, it would provide every addict who registered with complete information about addiction and what could be done for it.

Second, it would place his photograph and fingerprints on file. The primary purpose would be to prevent duplicate registration in another clinic. But it would also be easier to catch up with addicts who, in spite of the removal of their needs for big money, got into trouble.

Third, while criminal addicts could be caught more easily, this program would itself make crime quite unnecessary for most addicts, as indicated above. In addition, it would make addicts very wary of criminal activities because not only would they be almost certainly caught, but once caught they would subject to the ordeal addicts most fear—immediate, total withdrawal of their drug supply. It might even, in some cases, lead to speedy reform of minor criminal tendencies.

Fourth, many experts believe that the program would virtually wipe out the illegal drug traffic by removing the profit from it. (Only addicts afraid to register would have to pay the high illegal prices.) If no stigma and no publicity were attached to registry few would avoid it. And the capture of unregistered criminal addicts would become far easier.

Fifth, the program would give youths the true facts of addiction and make them more amenable to cures, which are much easier for young people than for old and much easier for new addicts than for those of long standing. Thus it would reduce both the number of addicts and the degree of their addiction.

Sixth, and this is most important, it would tend to save teen-agers from addiction. At present teen-agers get their first few doses free. Once "hooked" they must pay, and through the nose. However, from the peddler's point of view, what would be the use of giving away expensive drugs to get another customer if, the minute addiction was established, he was lost to the federal clinic? And the peddler who sold drugs only to get his own supply, as many do, would immediately remove himself from the market. It would no longer be necessary to make sales by infecting young people who knew no better. He could get his own supply at the clinic, and help and advice with it.

Seventh, it would provide medical information which we now sadly lack.

Certainly the proposed federal clinics would not solve all drug problems. Hospitals would still be needed, and narcotics police to prosecute the illegal traffic, and international agreements and co-operation. But without such clinics all our present efforts are useless; with them as an integral part of the plan, there is promise of a solution.

What are the objections to such a plan? Many people feel that nothing should be done for addicts, that they are worthless, vicious, and dangerous, and that the only real answer is to wipe them off the face of the earth. In 1936 the Chinese government of Chiang Kai-shek was calmly shooting as many as a hundred of them at a time for no crime other than smoking opium—which actually kept them out of trouble by putting them into a sound sleep. Our Occidental culture would recoil from such inhuman methods even if they were effective. In China they were not effective.

The reason is quite simple. You cannot kill all addicts because you cannot find all addicts, and the ones you don't find will infect others to protect their own supply. You can kill people of whom you are blindly afraid for no good reason, but when you have finished you will be no better off. You will simply have a fresh crop.

Other people raise their hands in horror at the suggestion that the federal government dispense drugs to addicts. Well, addicts will get their drug anyway. Why not give it to them under controlled, safe conditions instead of driving them into the criminal jungle? Why shouldn't the government dispense drugs if by so doing it can better the condition of the addicts, sharply reduce crime, blast the illegal narcotics racket, and, most important of all, save its youth from a living death?

"Addicts won't register," say other critics. Maybe a few of them won't. But on the first day the New York City clinic opened in 1919, no less than 1,500 did register, and others trooped in on following days. And fifteen states didn't support health programs that had no patients. Obviously they *had* patients—addicts *did* register and there is no reason to think they won't again.

Several addicts objected to the idea of getting dope only at the clinic. "Some people need a shot every three or four hours," they said.

But unfortunately the experience of the twenties indicates that this is the only way doses can be given without cheating by addicts. It's more trouble and more costly but it's the only way to prevent fraud and safeguard the program. However, there are various ways of increasing the intervals between doses when physicians are in charge and it is quite unlikely that this would be a serious problem except in a few cases which ought to be hospitalized anyway. These clinics would be run less for the comfort and convenience of addicts than for the good of the nation.

"It would cost too much!" Yes, it would be expensive. But if you add the cost of enforcement, cures, and crime to the amount of money thrown to the jackals who sell the drug today, even the cost of running clinics as they should be run does not look so large. Nothing more than a guess is possible, but probably the clinics would cost less than one-third as much as the nation spends on addiction today.

"Some addicts will cheat." Yes, some will. What of it? Under present conditions they *all* cheat. And cheating can be cut to a minimum by watchfulness on the part of clinic personnel.

"Ex-addicts will revert if they know they can get the stuff free." The answer to this objection is slightly more complicated but very important. The determination of actual addiction is medically far from simple. It is, however, possible, and would become increasingly certain as clinical experience built up. It is quite unlikely that more than a very small percentage of ex-addicts would be able to deceive the clinic physicians. And suppose a few *do* revert? It's still a vast improvement. As things are now, nearly all revert!

The recognition of addiction as a complex socio-medical problem offers the only hope of getting rid of it. Clinics would reduce sharply the making of new addicts, would cut the illegal drug traffic and crime caused by it, and would save our youth. By the grace of God addicts, like other people, eventually die. If no new addicts are made, addiction would disappear with them. And in the meantime federal clinics would make them useful citizens until that, for them, happy time.

V.D. for Sale
Harry Henderson and Sam Shaw

Harry Henderson (1914–   ) and Sam Shaw (1912–   ) are a free-lance writer-photographer team who have contributed to many national magazines, principally *Collier's*. Authors of *War in Our Time* (1942) and *World War II in Pictures* (1942).

Wheeling is the core of a loosely organized prostitution circuit which fans out from West Virginia into the four states of Ohio, Pennsylvania, Michigan and New York.

Besides Wheeling, the key cities of the circuit are Detroit, Buffalo, Cleveland, Canton, and Steubenville in Ohio, and Pittsburgh and some of its large suburbs—Homestead, Braddock and Du-

From "V.D. for Sale," *Collier's, 118*: 21 (November 23, 1946): 22–23, 112–113, pp. 23, 112 quoted. Reprinted by permission.

State Laws Against Prostitution

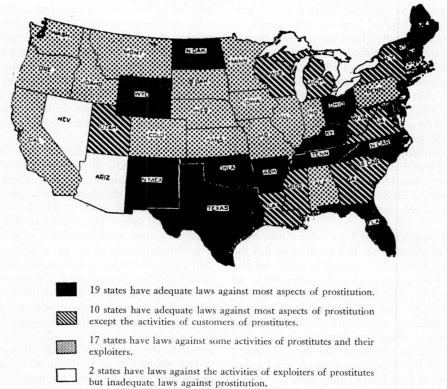

19 states have adequate laws against most aspects of prostitution.

10 states have adequate laws against most aspects of prostitution except the activities of customers of prostitutes.

17 states have laws against some activities of prostitutes and their exploiters.

2 states have laws against the activities of exploiters of prostitutes but inadequate laws against prostitution.

Many states have adequate legislation for the repression of prostitution. Such laws can and should be used not only against prostitutes but also against third persons, such as keepers, "madams," procurers, go-betweens, or other facilitators who exploit prostitutes and their customers for profit. (Reprinted by permission from "State Laws to Guard Family Life," American Social Hygiene Association leaflet, January 1947.)

quesne. As far as could be learned, the circuit is not operated by a syndicate; in all of these cities the brothels appear to be individually owned. But there are several syndicates, headed by racketeers with political pull, which control from two to twenty girls each and transfer them from one city to another exacting a fee from the prostitute.

For example, if a girl gets into trouble or otherwise wears out her welcome in Cleveland, she is sent down to Canton, or to Pittsburgh, Detroit or Buffalo. There's always room for her, and the madams are glad to see new faces. And when a girl can't go anywhere else, there's always Wheeling. But some of the Wheeling madams, especially those who take pride in running a "nice house," resent the fact that their town is used as a sort of sanctuary.

"Most of the girls we get here," one said, "are tramps who come to us because they can't get along anywhere else. It's hard to keep them, too, because this is a dirty town and prices are cheap. We don't get what I'd call a nice class of trade."

As rapidly as protection can be arranged and the madams can find the necessary housing, the syndicates are moving girls into other localities; operations have already begun, on a comparatively small scale, in such widely separated cities as Erie, Pa., Wilmington, Del., and Akron, Ohio. And there seems to be plenty of room not only for the expansion of this particular circuit, but for the formation of others.

According to a report of the American Social Hygiene Association, which recently completed a survey of 1,100 cities, the number of communities in which organized vice has obtained a foothold has quadrupled since the war. A member of the syndicate which handles girls in the Pittsburgh area said that the time was ripe for a real big shot to muscle into the business and organize prostitution from the Mississippi to the Atlantic.

"Somebody like Al Capone or Johnny Torrio," he said. "Then you'll really see something! What we're doing now is peanuts."

And such a thing is not unlikely, for the rewards are certainly there. In all of the cities where vice has become more or less firmly entrenched within the past year or so, the take from prostitution and its principal ally, gambling, runs into big figures. The madam of a three-girl house in Youngstown, which was one of the "good towns" until an energetic sheriff cleaned it up a few months ago, rang up a gross business of more than $6,000 in one month, although her dive was on a side street and she didn't sell liquor.

Similarly staffed brothels, in better locations and operated by more enterprising madams, are known to have averaged from $8,000 to $10,000 a month over a considerable period. Not long ago a Duquesne minister, appearing before the city council to demand action against the dives which infest that city, declared that the proceeds from gambling and prostitution in Duquesne amounted to almost $1,000,000 a year. Mayor Frank J. Kopriver indignantly said:

"There's nothing going on in Duquesne that isn't going on in every mill town in the valley."

And the chief of police said:

"There's nothing to check, but we'll check anyway."

Aside from the corruption which they create and foster, the red-light districts of Wheeling and other cities of the prostitution circuit are important because they help spread venereal disease. As the girls travel back and forth, they carry with them syphilis and gonorrhea. Many are unaware for months that they have these diseases, and few go to the trouble of taking treatments because they fear it might interfere with business. It is true that in some cities the health authorities require weekly examinations, but in the opinion of most medical authorities this does little or no good.

To be really effective, inspections should be made at least once a day, and preferably after each exposure. And since many professional prostitutes entertain as many as 50 or 60 men a night, this would require a great many doctors and cost a great deal of money.

During the war, by tracing infections reported by soldiers, the Army established that the major source of venereal disease was prostitution, and found that more than 90 per cent of the professional prostitutes apprehended by military and local police were infected. By working in co-operation with local agencies and closing the brothels in 715 cities, the Army reduced venereal disease rates to the lowest point in American military history, while there was a similar decline in civilian rates. For the first time, venereal disease was virtually under control.

But in a little more than a year this situation has been reversed to such an extent that the country faces an epidemic of venereal disease as widespread and as virulent as that which followed World War I. Even in New York, where there is proportionately less organized vice than in any other large American city, the venereal disease rates during the first six months of 1946 increased 29 per cent, as compared to a similar period in 1945. A statement issued recently by the American Social Hygiene Association said:

"In the rest of New York State a 100 per cent increase is indicated for 1946 over last year, and New York has always been one of the better states. Lesser but still shocking rates are reported from the Pacific Coast. The curve is definitely up throughout the country."

In addition to Wheeling, the really "good towns" of the circuit are Pittsburgh and Canton, the latter an industrial city in Stark County, Ohio, about sixty miles southeast of Cleveland. Unlike the grimy manufacturing cities of the Ohio Valley, Canton is clean and pleasant. The people of Canton are proud of their many churches, and on Sundays they are well filled. One local minister said, "People are pretty religious here."

But in the underworld, Canton is known as a "racket town." Gambling houses have sprung up all over the city within the past year, and many of them operate under the guise of veterans' clubs. At Bingoville, on the edge of the city, the play is tremendous.

During the war Canton's brothels, most of which are within five minutes' walk of the city hall, were supposed to be closed. Many were, but others simply shut their front doors and otherwise carried on as usual. Since the end of the war Canton has opened up with a bang—there were 27 houses of prostitution in June of 1946, ten more in July, and forty by the end of August. Most of them are two- and three-girl places. Some have Negro girls and cater to white men only;

one has both Negroes and whites and admits all comers.

As in Wheeling, all the rackets in Canton are under the protection of one man, who is a political power throughout northeastern Ohio. He operates the numbers game, gets a percentage of the take from the gambling houses and horse parlors, and collects from the madams and the inmates of the brothels. Most of the prostitutes work for him as numbers writers; that is, they take bets on the numbers from their customers. The girls used to get their books free; now the big shot charges them two cents each.

He cheats the deluded numbers players, too. In Pittsburgh the payoff on winning numbers is 800 to one, and in other cities it runs from 500 to 700. But in Canton it's only 400. One of the city's religious leaders defended the racketeer and, by implication, the things the racketeer does:

"He's not as bad as he's painted. He does many things for the poor. He gives a great deal to charity."

It was pointed out that this paragon of virtue had once shot a man in front of a Canton hotel, in full view of a policeman, and had never been arrested, nor had the incident been reported in the local newspapers.

"But," said the religious leader, "did you know he paid the man's hospital bills?"

A year or so ago a group of businessmen and ministers organized to break up the rackets and rid Canton of prostitution. They accumulated a great deal of information about bribery of police and corruption in the city government and courts, and engaged a nationally known detective agency to send detectives into Canton to get conclusive evidence. The operatives worked for a week, then left in a hurry; they said they'd be killed if they stayed in Canton any longer. Before leaving, they made several affidavits which were turned over to the police, but the latter refused to act unless the detectives returned to Canton. This the detectives flatly refused to do.

Notes on the Sociology of Prostitution
Kingsley Davis*

To the theoretical even more than to the applied sociologist, prostitution sets a profound problem: Why is it that a practice so thoroughly disapproved, so widely outlawed in Western civilization, can yet flourish so universally? Social theorists, in depicting the power of collective representations and the mores as determinants of human conduct, have at times implied that institutions are maintained only by *favorable* attitudes and sentiments. But prostitution is a veritable institution, thriving even when its name is so low in public opinion as to be synonymous with "the social evil." How, then, can we explain its vitality? . . .

Prostitution embraces an economic relation, and is naturally connected with the entire system of economic forces. But to jump from this truism to the conclusion that prostitution can be abolished by eliminating its economic causes is erroneous. Economic causes seldom act alone, and hence their removal is seldom a panacea.

The causal ramifications of commercial coitus extend beyond the economic sphere. At least three separable but related problems must be recognized: (1) the causes of the existence of prostitution; (2) the causes of the *rate* or *amount* of prostitution; and (3) the causes of *any particular individual's entrance into, or patronage of,* prostitution. The existence of prostitution seems related both to the physiological nature of man and to the inherent character of society, both of which include more than the sheer economic element. These basic factors, constantly operative, account for the ubiquity of prostitution, but not for the variations in its rate. This second problem must be dealt with in terms of the specific institutional configuration existing at the time, in which economic factors are highly but not exclusively im-

* See identifying note on page 120.

From Kingsley Davis, "The Sociology of Prostitution," *American Sociological Review*, 2 (1937): 744–755. Reprinted by permission.

portant. Finally, any particular person's connection with prostitution is a result of his or her own unique life-history, into which an infinite variety of strands, some economic and some not economic, are woven. The factors in (1) and (2) are operative in the individual's life, but are never sufficient in themselves to explain his or her behavior. . . .

Why should a girl enter prostitution *only* through economic necessity? Is the occupation so arduous? On the contrary, we often speak as if harlots "would rather prostitute themselves than work."[1] It is even true that some women enjoy the intercourse they sell. . . . The harlot's return is not primarily a reward for abstinence, labor, or rent. It is primarily a reward for loss of social standing. She loses social esteem because our moral system condemns the commercialization of intercourse. If, then, she refuses to enter the profession until forced by sheer want, the basic cause of her hesitation is not economic but moral. Only when the moral condition is assumed, do wages or economic want take on any importance. Prostitution, therefore, is not purely a matter of economic factors alone.

We have taken for granted that in the face of moral condemnation, only starvation wages can drive girls into prostitution. Actually this is only partly true. But even if it were, the proposal to eliminate prostitution by raising wages would not work. In a competitive system as soon as the salaries of working girls are increased, the supply of prostitutes diminishes. The resulting scarcity increases the effective demand, in the form of price, which rises as the supply diminishes. (The demand rests upon a constant imperative need, not always conveniently satisfiable by substitutes.) With the rise in price, working girls even with good salaries will be tempted into the profession. Moreover, it will be possible for more women to live on the proceeds of prostitution alone—without performing arduous labor in store or restaurant. The net result will be as much prostitution as before, and in terms of actual money invested and changing hands, there may be more.[2] The

facts seem to bear out these theoretical propositions, for apparently prostitution does not increase greatly with low wages for women nor decrease with high, although other factors, such as the correlation between men's wages and women's wages, must be considered in working out the relationship.[3] . . .

When outlawed, prostitution falls into one peculiar category of crime—a type exceedingly hard to deal with—in which one of the willful parties is the ordinary law-abiding citizen. This kind of crime, of which bootlegging is the archetype, is supported by the money and behavior of a sizeable portion of the citizenry, because in it the citizen receives a service. Though the service is illegitimate, the citizen cannot be held guilty, for it is both impossible and inadvisable to punish half the populace for a crime. Each citizen participates in vital institutional relationships—family, business, church, and state. To disrupt all of these by throwing him in jail for a mere vice would be, on a large scale, to disrupt society. . . . But the eagerness of otherwise decent citizens to receive illicit service attests powerful forces behind the demand element.

On the one hand, the demand is the result of a simple biological appetite. When all other sources of gratification fail, due to defects of person or circumstance, prostitution can be relied upon to furnish relief. None of the exacting requirements of sex attraction and courtship are necessary. All that is needed is the cash, and this can be obtained in a thousand ways. . . .

But in addition to the sheer desire for sexual satisfaction, there is the desire for satisfaction in a particular (often an unsanctioned) way.

The common and ignorant assumption that prostitution exists to satisfy the gross sensuality of the young unmarried man, and that if he is taught to bridle gross sexual impulse or induced to marry early the prostitute must be idle, is altogether incorrect. . . . The prostitute is something more than a channel to drain

---

[1] W. L. George's novel, *Bed of Roses*, vividly contrasts the hard life of the working girl with the easy life of the prostitute.

[2] Another difficulty is that the wages of prostitution are already far above the wages of ordinary women's work. "No practicable rise in the rate of wages paid to women in ordinary industries can possibly compete with the wages which fairly attractive women of quite ordinary ability can earn by prostitution" (Ellis, [*Studies in the Psychology of*

Sex, vol. 6] p. 263). The discrepancy between the wages of ordinary work and the wages of prostitution results from the fact, as indicated above, that the latter is morally tabooed. This increases the wage differential until there is *every economic* incentive for entering.

[3] The wages of one class cannot be arbitrarily raised without affecting those of all other earners. Under competition women's wages could scarcely be raised without also raising men's. Men would then have more to spend on prostitution. A. Deprés, *La prostitution en France* (1883), concluded that as wealth and prosperity increased, so did prostitution.

off superfluous sexual energy, and her attraction by
no means ceases when men are married, for a large
number of men who visit prostitutes, if not the majority, are married. And alike whether they are married or unmarried the motive is not one of uncompli-
cated lust.[4]

The craving for variety, for perverse gratification,
for mysterious and provocative surroundings, for
intercourse free from entangling cares and civilized pretense, all play their part. . . .

There is no reason to believe that a change in
the economic system will eliminate either side of
demand. In any system the effective demand as
expressed by price will vary with current economic and moral forces, but the underlying desire
both for sheer gratification and for gratification
in particular ways will remain impregnable.

We can imagine a social system in which the
motive for prostitution would be completely absent, but we cannot imagine that the system could
ever come to pass. It would be a regime of absolute sexual freedom, wherein intercourse were
practiced solely for the pleasure of it, by both
parties. . . .

The conclusion that free intercourse for pleasure and friendship rather than for profit is the
greatest enemy of prostitution emerges logically
from our statement that a basic trait of prostitution is the use of sex for an ulterior purpose.
Should one wish to abolish commercial coitus,
one would have to eliminate this trait. This proposition, however, is unacceptable to moralists, because, as we saw, the underlying trait of prostitution is also a fundamental feature of reputable
sexual institutions, and intercourse for sheer pleas-

ure is as inimical to our sacred institutions as it
is to the profane one of mercenary love. Though
Lecky's suggestion that harlotry sustains the family is perhaps indefensible, it seems true that prostitution is not so great a danger to the family as
complete liberty. . . .

Not only in Soviet Russia has pleasurable sex
freedom invaded and reduced prostitution, but
also in America and England, where "amateur
competition" is reputedly ruining the business of
street-walkers and call girls.[5] This indicates that
independently of communism or capitalism, due
to factors more profound than mere economic organization, sex freedom can arise and, having
arisen, can contribute to the decline of prostitution. Its rise seems correlated with the growth of
individualization in an increasingly complex society where specialization, urbanism, and anonymity prevail—factors which are also inimical to
reproductive institutions of the familial type.

But even if present trends continue, there is no
likelihood that sex freedom will ever displace
prostitution. Not only will there always be a set
of reproductive institutions which place a check
upon sexual liberty, a system of social dominance
which gives a motive for selling sexual favors,
and a scale of attractiveness which creates the
need for buying these favors, but prostitution is,
in the last analysis, economical. Enabling a small
number of women to take care of the needs of a
large number of men, it is the most convenient
sexual outlet for an army, and for the legions of
strangers, perverts, and physically repulsive in
our midst. It performs a function, apparently,
which no other institution fully performs.

---

[4] Ellis, *op cit.,* pp. 295–296. The author describes in
detail the various motives involved.

[5] . . . "Prostitution," *Encyclopaedia Sexualis,* p. 665.
J. K. Folsom, *The Family,* New York: Wiley, 1934,
Chap. 13.

The Prison as a Community
Norman S. Hayner and Ellis Ash

Norman S. Hayner (1896–   ), professor of sociology, University of Washington. Ellis Ash (1914–
), director of management, Housing Authority of Baltimore City, Maryland.

The prisoner comes from a community and,
after an average stay of two and one-third years,
will return to a community. If he is to be ac-

cepted as a law-abiding person on his return, he
must learn in prison to play the role of a citizen.
He cannot learn those things that will enable him

From "The Prison as a Community," *American Sociological Review,* 5 (1940): 577–583, pp. 577–580 quoted. Reprinted by permission.

to participate as an acceptable member of the outside community, if he is engaged in activities that are foreign to people on the outside. If the prisoner learns on the inside, that to fit in with institutional routine, he must walk close to the wall, this will not help him on the outside. In fact, it may mark him as peculiar.

We are aware of the real difficulties in the way of fundamental reforms. Unless there is a dramatic escape, a bloody riot, or a "mass whipping," as reported recently at San Quentin, the press and the public are apathetic. J. Edgar Hoover's vigorous defense of the "machine-gun school of criminology" with its hatred of "slimy criminals" and its belief in long prison terms as the only means of punishment and his pungent attacks on "the cream-puff school" with its "moo-cow sentimentalities" and its faith in rehabilitation have swung the pendulum of public opinion in this country in the direction of a hostile attitude toward the offender and away from an attitude of inquiry. It is our conviction, however, that the punitive attitude has been adequately tried and found wanting. The most promising method of progress is through experimentation. Why not, for example, make a sincere attempt to save money for a higher salary level and a better quality of personnel by housing a larger proportion of carefully selected prisoners in the less expensive minimum security institutions? Furthermore, why not make "the prison as a community" the guiding concept for administration?

As it is, the present-day American treatment of men in prison reminds us of the relations between lions and their trainer. The function of a trainer is to make his beasts respond to the crack of a whip. Although the lion goes through his set of tricks every day, the trainer has found that he must always be on the defensive. He is never so certain of the complete friendliness of the beast that he does not have a chair in his hand or a pistol in his pocket. Likewise, when imprisoned men are treated as beasts, they either sink into apathy or stir up rebellion.

In penal institutions as they are today, the constant hostility between guards and inmates is one of the major obstacles in the reformation of prisoners.[1] The division into "cons" and "screws"

(guards) in prison society is even more basic than the Middletown dichotomy into workers and business men. This conflict situation helps to explain the widespread lack of sympathetic and understanding relationships between guards and convicts. Low pay and long hours do not attract a high type of custodial officer. Hence, the most important link that prisoners have with the outside world, their contact with guards, yields little social profit.

Just as the Southern cotton plantation during slavery times exhibited a sharp division into two major groups, the white masters and overseers on the one hand and the black and brown slaves on the other, so also does the American prison. The process of socialization, for example, is twofold. This dual process will be discussed in the following paragraphs as a concrete illustration of the two social worlds in prison society. Achieving a status role in the world of guards is one thing; in the prison group, another. Tannenbaum describes a guard showing every sign of fear and lack of ease in the beginning, who, nevertheless, within two months, had become the most uncompromising officer in the institution. Nelson reports that it is a social error for a prisoner to be seen talking to a guard. For both staff members and convicts, the roles they are expected to play have been defined by their respective groups and wide deviations are not easily tolerated.

The politically appointed warden may give the new officer a book of rules and a speech about proper behavior. Then the deputy warden, who, like the foreman of a plant, has the responsibility for running the institution, will probably emphasize the maintenance of discipline and the avoidance of disorder. To achieve this end, he urges the new man to "put them in their proper place at all times." When the guard comes back to the dormitory after his first day on the job, his fellow officers give him additional advice—often phrased in lurid folk language. As in the outside community, these definitions are frequently conflicting. In the absence of a special training school, the new guard must work out his own policy by trial and error.

The "fish," or new prisoner, undergoes an experience analogous to that of the new guard. He, too, meets the deputy warden and is advised: "Keep your nose clean and you won't have trouble." In his conversation with other officers of the classification committee, lip service may be given to the ideal of reformation. The prisoner does not

[1] The method used in our study of the Washington State Reformatory, with data on the attitudes and connivings of convicts, has already been set forth in "The Prisoner Community as a Social Group," *American Sociological Review*, 4 (1939): 362–369.

live with the officers, however, but with his fellow convicts. They tell him very definitely what he is supposed to do as a con. Since they are the people with whom he eats, works, sleeps, and talks, he will naturally try to adjust by "getting along." As Riemer has pointed out: "If an inmate desires favorable status in the opinions of his fellows, he must adopt patterns of behavior in line with their culture."[2] Riemer, a voluntary prisoner, by swearing at an officer and being ordered into solitary confinement as a punishment, won wholehearted inmate approval. In perhaps no other social world do men "watch each other and study every gesture and action" as they do in prison. The first-timer is tested and rated in a variety of ways. If he happens to draw a "rat," or informer, as a cell-mate, this will not help his reputation. He probably knows nothing about conniving when he first comes, but he soon learns. As Halfpint told Stanley in the *Jack-Roller:* "Don't antagonize the guards; hate them all you want to, but work them for your own good."

Inmate "politicians" play a role in prison similar to that of their prototypes in a corrupt city government. As in the outside community, they must grant favors in order to hold their position and yet they are frequently hated for their self-seeking attitude. The "right guys," on the contrary, can always be trusted to remain loyal to their fellow cons. Clemmer found that "being right" was the essential and most admired trait of prison leaders. A prison mythology, Riemer reports, plays a role in defining the mores for the newcomer. Remarkable escapes, great strikes and riots, and tales of outstanding men are included in these stories.

In the normal community, conflict tends to be adjusted by "accommodation." Eventually the fusion of opposing cultures results in "assimilation." In the prison community, the chronic hostility between cons and screws—to some extent and extension of the progressive conflict between criminals and police on the outside—may lead to superficial and temporary forms of accommodation, but rarely to assimilation. Deciding to "make the best of it," the new prisoner usually undertakes some form of self-culture. As he adjusts to the dull monotony of prison life, however, there is likely to be a "decline of profitable reflection" and a weakening of the attempts at self-improvement. Daydreaming becomes more frequent. "Prison stupor" or becoming "stir simple" are common end results. As the prisoner grows "con-wise," however, he learns that things denied him by the prison administration may be available through conniving. These *sub rosa* activities provide variety, help break the deteriorating monotony, and constitute another type of accommodation.

How important are these characteristics of the prison community for later careers? Is the common conception of prisons as schools for crime justified? In general, it is our conclusion that the conventional prison situation is the antithesis of the normal community and does not prepare for it. Monotonous routine, sex starvation, lack of self-direction, and isolation from law-abiding culture patterns do not rehabilitate. They demoralize. . . .

Institutional services sponsored by the staff are in general too formal, rigid and superordinated to provide training for community life. The real objective for the administration is maintenance. Providing housing, food, clothing, and work for the inmates tend to become ends in themselves rather than means for preparing the men to return to outside communities. The work program may be called "trade training," but such skills as are acquired can seldom be used on the outside. Present educational programs in prisons are largely stereotyped replicas of the conventional educational organization. They are neither adapted to the prison situation nor are they designed to prepare the convict adequately for the role of law-abiding citizen in a somewhat disorganized outside community.

---

[2] Hans Riemer, "Socialization in the Prison Community," *Proceedings, Sixty-Seventh Annual Congress, American Prison Association,* 1937, pp. 151–155. See also Donald Clemmer, "Leadership Phenomena in a Prison Community," *Journal of Criminal Law and Criminology,* 28 (1937–38): 869–872; and Victor F. Nelson, *Prison Days and Nights,* Boston: Little, Brown & Company, 1933.

CROSS REFERENCES TO STANDARD TEXTS *

Barnes, *Society in Transition,* Chaps. 15–17.
Bernard, *American Community Behavior,* pp. 490–500, 528–550.

---

* For complete bibliographical reference to each text, see page 13.

Bloch, *Social Disorganization,* Chaps. 7–16, 18.
Brown, *Social Pathology,* Chaps. 21, 31.
Cuber and Harper, *Problems of American Society,* Chap. 9.
Elliott and Merrill, *Social Disorganization,* Chaps. 5–8.

Faris, *Social Disorganization*, Chaps. 5–7.
Gillin, *Social Pathology*, Chaps. 15, 17, 18, 30, 31.
——— and others, *Social Problems*, Chap. 18.
Herman, *Approach to Social Problems*, pp. 115–132.
Landis, *Social Policies in the Making*, Chaps. 9–10.
Lemert, *Social Pathology*, Chaps. 8–9.
Merrill and others, *Social Problems*, Chaps. 8–10.
Mihanovich, *Current Social Problems*, Chaps. 4–5.
Neumeyer, *Social Problems and the Changing Society*, Chap. 14.

Nordskog and others, *Analyzing Social Problems*, Chaps. 7–8.
Odum, *American Social Problems*, pp. 108, 259.
Phelps and Henderson, *Contemporary Social Problems*, Chaps. 7, 18–19.
Reinhardt and others, *Social Problems and Social Policy*, pp. 288–291, Chap. 14.
Weaver, *Social Problems*, Chaps. 11–12, 14–17.

OTHER BIBLIOGRAPHY

David Abrahamsen, *Crime and the Human Mind*, New York: Columbia University Press, 1944.
Harry Elmer Barnes and Negley K. Teeters, *New Horizons in Criminology*, 2d ed., New York: Prentice-Hall, 1951.
Milton L. Barron, *The Juvenile in a Delinquent Society*, New York: A. A. Knopf, 1954.
David Bogen, "Juvenile Delinquency and Economic Trends," *American Sociological Review*, 9 (1944): 178–184.
Croswell Bowen, *They Went Wrong*, New York: McGraw-Hill Book Co., 1954.
Ernest W. Burgess, "The Study of a Delinquent as a Person," *American Journal of Sociology*, 28 (1922–23): 657–680.
Nathaniel Cantor, *Crime and Society*, New York: Henry Holt and Co., 1939.
L. J. Carr, *Delinquency Control*, rev. ed., New York: Harper & Bros., 1950.
Ruth Shonle Cavan, *Criminology*, New York: T. Y. Crowell Co., 1950.
Caryl Chessman, *Cell 2455 Death Row*, New York: Prentice-Hall, 1954.
Courtney Ryley Cooper, *Here's to Crime*, Boston: Little, Brown & Co., 1937.
Albert Deutsch, "What We Can Do About the Drug Menace," Public Affairs Pamphlet No. 186, 1952.
Mabel A. Elliott, *Crime in Modern Society*, New York: Harper & Bros., 1952.
"Federal Program of Venereal Disease Education: A Symposium," *Journal of Social Hygiene*, 30 (1944): 1–42.
John R. Ellingston, *Protecting Our Children From Criminal Careers*, New York: Prentice-Hall, 1948.
John L. Gillin, *Criminology and Penology*, 3d ed., New York: D. Appleton-Century Co., 1945.
Sheldon Glueck, *Crime and Correction: Selected Papers*, Cambridge: Addison-Wesley Press, 1952.
Gladys Mary Hall, *Prostitution in the Modern World*, New York: Emerson Books, 1936.
Leonard Harrison and Pryor Grant, *Youth in the Toils*, New York: Macmillan Co., 1938.
Alfred Hassler, *Diary of a Self-Made Convict*, Chicago: Henry Regnery Co., 1954.
William Healy and Augusta F. Bronner, *New Light on Delinquency and Its Treatment*, New Haven: Yale University Press, 1936.

Samuel Koenig, Clyde B. Vedder, and Robert E. Clark, *Criminology: A Book of Readings*, New York: Dryden Press, 1953.
Wilbur LaRoe, Jr., *Parole With Honor*, Princeton: Princeton University Press, 1939.
Alfred R. Lindesmith, *Opiate Addiction*, Bloomington, Indiana: Principia Press, 1947.
———, "The Drug Addict as a Psychopath," *American Sociological Review*, 5 (December 1940): 914–920.
Robert M. Lindner, *Stone Walls and Men*, New York: Odyssey Press, 1946.
Geoffrey May, "Prostitution," *Encyclopaedia of the Social Sciences*, 12 (1934): 553–559.
Maud A. Merrill, *Problems of Child Delinquency*, Boston: Houghton Mifflin Co., 1947.
Alan S. Meyer, ed., *Social and Psychological Factors in Opiate Addiction*, New York: Bureau of Applied Social Research, 1952.
Florence Monahan, *Women in Crime*, New York: Ives Washburn, 1941.
Martin H. Neumeyer, *Juvenile Delinquency in Modern Society*, New York: D. Van Nostrand Co., 1949.
Thomas Parran, *Shadow on the Land—Syphilis*, New York: Reynal and Hitchcock, 1937.
Bertram Pollens, *The Sex Criminal*, New York: Macaulay Co., 1938.
Walter C. Reckless, *The Crime Problem*, New York: Appleton-Century-Crofts, 1950.
Louis S. Reed, "Fee Splitting," *Encyclopaedia of the Social Sciences*, 6 (1931): 178–179.
Ben L. Reitman, *The Second Oldest Profession*, New York: Vanguard Press, 1931.
Louis N. Robinson, *Jails*, Philadelphia: John C. Winston Co., 1944.
Kenyon J. Scudder, *Prisoners Are People*, New York: Doubleday and Co., 1952.
Clifford R. Shaw, ed., *Brothers in Crime*, Chicago: University of Chicago Press, 1938.
———, *The Jack-Roller*, Chicago: University of Chicago Press, 1930.
———, *The Natural History of a Delinquent Career*, Chicago: University of Chicago Press, 1931.
——— and Henry D. McKay, *Juvenile Delinquency in Urban Areas*, Chicago: University of Chicago Press, 1942.

Bruce Smith, *Police Systems in the United States*, rev. ed., New York: Harper & Bros., 1949.

"Social Protection in Action in the Community: Symposium," *Journal of Social Hygiene, 31* (1945): 261–307.

Edwin H. Sutherland, *Principles of Criminology*, 4th ed., Philadelphia: J. B. Lippincott Co., 1947.

——, *The Professional Thief*, Chicago: University of Chicago Press, 1937.

——, *White Collar Crime*, New York: Dryden Press, 1949.

Donald R. Taft, *Criminology*, rev. ed., New York: Macmillan Co., 1950.

Paul W. Tappan, *Contemporary Correction*, New York: McGraw-Hill Book Co., 1951.

——, *Delinquent Girls in Court*, New York: Columbia University Press, 1947.

——, *Juvenile Delinquency*, New York: McGraw-Hill Book Co., 1949.

Negley K. Teeters and John Otto Reinemann, *The Challenge of Delinquency*, New York: Prentice-Hall, 1950.

Frederick M. Thrasher, *The Gang*, Chicago: University of Chicago Press, 1927.

Simon H. Tulchin, *Intelligence and Crime*, Chicago: University of Chicago Press, 1939.

Hans von Hentig, *Crime: Causes and Conditions*, New York: McGraw-Hill Book Co., 1947.

Clyde B. Vedder, *The Juvenile Offender: Perspective and Readings*, Garden City: Doubleday and Co., 1954.

Willoughby Cyrus Waterman, *Prostitution and Its Repression in New York City, 1900–1931*, New York: Columbia University Press, 1932.

William A. Westley, "Violence and the Police," *American Journal of Sociology, 41* (July 1953): 34–41.

Donald P. Wilson, *My Six Convicts*, New York: Rinehart & Co., 1951.

Arthur E. Wood and J. B. Waite, *Crime and Its Treatment*, New York: American Book Co., 1941.

Howard B. Woolston, *Prostitution in the United States*, New York: D. Appleton-Century Co., 1921.

Pauline V. Young, *Social Treatment in Probation and Delinquency*, New York: McGraw-Hill Book Co., 1937.

REVIEW QUESTIONS

1. How does Sutherland think that criminal statistics have given a biased view of criminal behavior?
2. What question did Sutherland find to be useful in revealing white-collar criminal practices in a given occupation?
3. What are chief types of white-collar crime that Sutherland found in business? In the professions? In politics?
4. Sutherland says that his conception of white-collar crime supplements convictions in the criminal courts in four respects. What are these respects?
5. In what ways does Sutherland conclude that white-collar and lower-class criminality differ?
6. What are Barron's objections to newspaper exposés of "teen-age terrorism"?
7. What are his suggestions for a more effective approach to the problem of juvenile delinquency?
8. What are some of the typical difficulties of the honest policeman?
9. How does the corrupt police executive operate?
10. Describe Stevens plan for the control of narcotic addiction.
11. What is the role of prostitution, according to Henderson and Shaw, in organized vice generally? In political corruption?
12. What are the three separate problems which Davis believes must be recognized in studying prostitution?
13. What obstacles, according to Hayner and Ash, stand in the way of fundamental prison reforms?
14. How is the prison community organized?
15. What happens to the attitudes of prisoners in prison?
16. How would Hayner and Ash improve prison organization?

—CHAPTER 18—→

Leaders

MAN's QUEST for certainty and security in an ever-changing world has frequently led him to pay huge prices for what looked like a degree of what he sought. These prices have often been paid to leaders and especially to charismatic leaders, men who are endowed by their followers with qualities beyond those possessed by human beings. As Albig notes, in the selection from his writings, there is "more belief in authority than in fact and experimentation, because the members of large publics have more confidence in their ability to discern personal qualities than in their capacity to winnow out the pertinent facts."

Leadership and genius present democracy with the horns of a dilemma, and sound democratic thinking must somehow find a path between them. On the one hand, democracy needs to encourage its gifted sons and daughters to make their maximum contributions to society, and on the other hand, it cannot afford to permit them to seize thereby extraordinary power and to tyran-

nize their fellow human beings. That our society does erect barriers which keep many gifted children from making their maximum contributions is demonstrated by Sibley as the result of an extensive statistical study. The caste barriers associated with race erect ever higher barriers, but these are treated in other chapters. Dimock and Hyde discuss the bureaucratic devices by which innovators are kept from high positions in government and business.

Where do the gifted come from? What factors make for their appearance and success? Several selections deal with these questions. Terman tells of the part played by the spirit of the times in the development of unusual talent. Blumer outlines the ways in which leaders get opportunities to break through repressing barriers and distinguish themselves in social movements. Drake and Cayton describe the types of leaders who appear in an urban Negro community.

The Quest for Leadership
William Albig

John William Albig (1899–   ), professor of sociology and chairman of the department, University of Illinois. Author of *Public Opinion* (1939).

The quest for personal leadership is based in part upon fear and uncertainty. In projecting the father image onto the leaders of the great society, millions of followers seek for the security and personal response of an intimate primary group. There is more belief in authority than in fact and experimentation, because the members of large publics have more confidence in their ability to discern personal qualities than in their capacity to

winnow out the pertinent facts. And uncertainty is terrifying to the average man. Publics seek for charismatic leaders. . . .

Today, the quest for certainty, the quest for simple, understandable, comprehensible plans in a world of complex social relationships, has intensified the quest for trustworthy personal authority. Authoritarian political leaders are not merely officials, directors, organizers and guides. They are

By permission from *Public Opinion* by William Albig, copyrighted by McGraw-Hill Book Co., Inc., New York, 1939, pp. 94, 98, 106.

spiritual chiefs. Reliance upon them may be misplaced confidence, but it is psychologically understandable. . . .

The characteristics of successful leaders and the processes of leadership in influencing opinion differ with the size and type of groups and with the situation or "field structure." There do not appear to be general characteristics of leadership that are everywhere effective in influencing the opinions of followers. The psychologist's quest for general leadership "traits" has been futile. The characteristics of leaders of small discussion groups—committees, gangs, families, clans, neighborhoods and other small groups—differ from leadership qualities in large publics consisting of thousands and hundreds of thousands of members. There is some experimental literature on leadership in small groups.[1] Certainly, opinions are influenced in all such groups, but we shall not discuss the studies of face-to-face relations. In the large groups and publics, there are diverse preferences for leader-

ship qualities, depending upon the group's size, organization, purposes, relation to other groups, the prevailing attitudes and values and, in general, upon its field structure. The situation must always ultimately determine the preferred qualities. Leadership qualities vary under democracy, fascism, communism; in different ages, periods, cultures; under national ascendency or degradation; in an expanding or contracting economy. . . .

In the creation of contemporary symbols, modern publicity plays a dominant role. The process is speeded up. In the great society, ideas about leaders are acquired primarily from press, radio and motion picture. The leader symbol of the past could not emerge so suddenly for large publics. Moreover, although gossip, legend and rumor could distort the popular image of the great man, there could not be so much conscious propaganda of his legend. In Nazi propaganda, the build-up of Hitler, Goering, Goebbels, von Hindenberg, Horst Wessel and Schlageter has been blatant. The way in which personalities are presented to the public will depend in large part upon the interests controlling particular sectors of the means of communication.

[1] Examine the publications of *The Inquiry*, especially: A. D. Sheffield, *Creative Discussion, A Statement of Method for Leaders and Members of Discussion Groups*, 1926; H. S. Elliott, *The Process of Group Thinking*, 1932.

Social Barriers to Gifted Children
Elbridge Sibley

Elbridge Sibley (1903–   ), sociologist; executive associate, Social Science Research Council. Author of *The Recruitment, Selection, and Training of Social Scientists* (1948); *Support for Independent Scholarship and Research* (1951).

Differential birth rates, while less spectacular than either technological changes or mass immigration, have made about as great a contribution as either of the former to the upward tide in American society. Relatively low fertility in the white-collar workers has produced what Sorokin[1] calls "a social vacuum within the upper strata." Recruits from the more prolific families of farmers and laborers have been constantly flowing into the vacuum. In 1928, by rough calculation, approximately 80 per cent of the babies born in the United States were children of manual workers[2]; but manual workers represented only about 70

per cent of the total population. Assuming that three out of five infants survive and become workers, it appears that when the 1928 cohort of babies reaches maturity, there will be an annual shift of about 160,000 persons from blue-collar to white-collar work.[3] American vital statistics do not yet afford a sound basis for asserting that fertility differentials are generally diminishing; but if the experience of more "mature" European countries is any guide, such a trend may be expected.

Most American demographers have described

[1] Pitirim Sorokin, *Social Mobility*, New York: Harper and Bros., 1927, p. 346.

[2] U. S. Bureau of the Census, *Birth, Stillbirth, and Infant Mortality Statistics, 1928*, Table 10.

[3] On the assumption, of course, that the occupational patterns that existed around 1928 continue to prevail. . . .

From "Some Demographic Clues to Stratification," *American Sociological Review*, 7 (1942): 322–330, pp. 325–327, 329–330 quoted. Reprinted by permission.

the negative correlation of fertility and social status as an unmixed evil, and many of them used to take a similar view of immigration—especially of the "New Immigration." Little attention has been given to the role played by these processes in keeping the United States free from rigid social strata. Will the net upward movement of from 300,000 to 400,000 or more American workers per year be more or less permanently reduced? The last three decades have seen one of the three sources of the movement, namely immigration, choked off, once for the duration of a war and later seemingly permanently. Another source, differential fertility, may conceivably be drying up. The future of the third source, technological progress, depends upon the not-yet-demonstrated ability of the nation's leaders to readjust political-economic institutions so as to produce a genuine "economy of plenty."

Even if the favorable balance of vertical mobility should disappear, it would be theoretically possible to prevent the development of rigity in the social structure by developing an increase volume of downward movement of the less "fit" and correspondingly increasing the opportunities for ascent. If this does not occur (and it cannot be expected to happen automatically), general realization of the fact that an individual's chances of rising are no better than his chances of falling may lead to the erection of arbitrary barriers to social circulation. If well-to-do citizens come to believe that their own (and their families') privileges are menaced by the ascent of numerous Horatio Algers, their reaction will likely take the form of efforts to restrict by law admission to the more lucrative vocations and the dissipation of established fortunes. Moves in the former direction have already been made by organizations representing various "overcrowded" professions. In such a situation, the less successful may also develop group consciousness in an attempt to exchange their traditional birthright of unlimited individual opportunity for a mess of the pottage of collective security. The defensive attitudes of the *rentier* may tend to supplant the optimistic liberalism of the *speculateur*.[4] . . .

Can the Educational System Produce More Vertical Circulation? If we must look forward to a slackening of the upward tide that has sustained our liberal democratic optimism, it is appropriate to examine the educational system by which, sup-

posedly, the ablest members of each generation are selected for advancement to higher social-economic positions. Heretofore, the mechanism has seemed to work sufficiently well if it has caught in its meshes enough promising youngsters to fill the actual vacancies in high places; henceforth it must perform the more strenuous function of pulling up a large number of the best-qualified boys and girls even at the expense of pushing down others who are initially more fortunate but inherently less able.

It is well known that from the lowest to the highest level of the educational system, pupils of inferior intelligence are continually being eliminated; it is also well known that school "mortality" is higher among those whose parents' social-economic status is relatively low. But so far, these two selective factors have usually been studied separately and their respective relationships with school progress stated in the form of raw correlations. It has remained the privilege of the apologist for the *status quo* to attribute the failure of poor children to their low intelligence, while the revolutionary has had at his disposal statistics which can be interpreted as showing that the children of the poor fail because their fathers are not rich.

Strangely enough, data adaptable to an appraisal of the relative roles of intelligence and social-economic status as factors influencing children's school progress appear to have been collected on a large scale in only one American study. Late in 1934, as an emergency work project, the Pennsylvania Department of Public Instruction collected records of some 23,000 boys and girls who were in the sixth grade in selected public schools of that State in 1926 or 1928. The items recorded include highest grade attained at the time of the survey, intelligence quotient, and father's occupational rating.[5] . . .

[After describing a retabulation of these data, Sibley summarizes his conclusions as follows:] With the influence of parental status eliminated, a boy with an intelligence quotient of 112 or over enjoys a 50 per cent better chance of completing nine grades than one rated 87 or less; his chances of finishing high school are somewhat more than twice as great as those of the dull boy; and his

[4] Vilfredo Pareto, *Traité de Sociologie Générale*, Paris, 1919, sec. 2231–2235.

[5] A monograph by Harlan Updegraff, *Inventory of Youth in Pennsylvania*, was issued in "preliminary draft" by the American Youth Commission, Washington, D. C., in 1936. This report stopped short of exploring adequately the interrelationships of parental status, intelligence, and educational attainment.

chances of spending at least a year in college or other higher institution are about four times those of members of the dullest group. Stated in general terms, this shows that the higher levels of the educational system are more selective of intelligence than the lower levels.

But the net influence of the father's status on his son's chances is a different matter. At the ninth grade and at the twelfth grade level, father's status has less influence than intelligence on educational opportunity; but at the college level, the situation is sharply reversed. While the most intelligent boys have only a 4 to 1 advantage over the least intelligent, the sons of men in the highest occupational category enjoy an advantage of more than 10 to 1 over those from the lowest occupational level. A particularly striking feature . . . is the sudden rise of a boy's chances of going beyond high school which takes place near point 10 on the Barr scale—the point which roughly divides white-collar from blue-collar workers.

These statistics indicate that as a boy passes through the educational sifting process, his parents' status assumes increasing importance, both absolutely and in comparison with his own intelligence, as a factor influencing his chances of continuing his preparation for one of the more advantageous vocations. Although there has been (in Pennsylvania) an approach to the "social-economic democratization" of high-school education, college education and higher vocational training remain to a large extent the special privilege of children of superior social-economic backgrounds.

Even on the lower levels, perfect apportionment of educational opportunity to ability as indicated by the I.Q. is not achieved.

As recruitment for the higher paid and otherwise more desirable occupations tends increasingly to be limited to those who have had higher education, it is evident that the American educational system is far from being as effective as it might be in counteracting tendencies toward social stratification. Increased enrollment on any particular level of the system does not automatically mean progress toward the goal of assorting individuals into positions commensurate with their own abilities. A system of higher education might admit only a small minority of applicants and yet stimulate rather than retard vertical circulation in society, provided that the minority were selected for admission solely on the basis of their abilities; and *vice versa.*

If we propose to preserve the American faith in freedom from social-class barriers to individual achievement, some institutional changes must be planned and effectuated in order to offset the previously discussed diminution of the favorable balance of vertical circulation. Educational institutions appear to offer the most promising field for such changes. If the changes are made well enough and quickly enough, they may forestall the onset of an acute case of class conflict and indefinitely postpone the death of a leading American ideal. If not, our social arteries are likely to become sclerotic.

The Relation of Executive Leadership to Bureaucracy

Marshall E. Dimock and Howard K. Hyde

Marshall Edward Dimock (1903–   ), professor of political science, Northwestern University. Recent works: *The Executive in Action* (1945); with G. O. Dimock, *American Government in Action* (1946). Howard K. Hyde (1911–   ), director, Division of Recruitment and Manning, U. S. Maritime Commission. Also author of *Social Control of Business* (1936).

Among the personnel causes of bureaucracy of which business executives and students of administration most often complain is the lack of competent, effective leadership. As the head of one enterprise has remarked, "there aren't enough first-class executives to go around. They are almost

From "Bureaucracy and Trusteeship in Large Corporations," U. S. Temporary National Economic Committee Monograph No. 11, Washington: U. S. Government Printing Office, 1940, pp. 44–45, 49–54.

as rare as inventors and first-class research men, so unusual a combination of qualities—plus an ounce of 'devine spark'—must they possess." Herbert Emmerich has criticized the popular idea that "a good executive is a 'no man' entirely surrounded by 'yes men.' " "Executive management," he has said, "is a constant process of evoking from the human beings who comprise an organization their best contributions toward its work. This cannot be accomplished in a negative atmosphere. The top executive of the future will bend most of his efforts toward discovery and release of the creative forces of his organization, not to their suppression."[1] . . .

For our present purposes the discussion of the relation of executive leadership to bureaucracy may be confined to five general requirements. These are that the executive not be too old upon appointment; that he possess a broad outlook; that he reached office primarily on the basis of merit; that he remain in office long enough to be effective but not so long as to become senile; and that positions of leadership be attractive to potential leaders. It is recognized that these are capable of broad interpretation; we may, however, note tendencies in each of them.

A leading figure in the field of industrial management maintains: "It is hardly to be gainsaid that with the steadily increasing age at which executives reach the top rank of president or chairman of the board, they find themselves physically, as well as intellectually less able than under former conditions of corporative simplicity to cope with the question of future progress and growth."[2] It cannot be flatly said, of course, that advanced chronological age means a corresponding loss in mental resiliency. Daniel Willard, president of the Baltimore & Ohio Railroad, and the late Justice [Oliver Wendell] Holmes serve amply as refuting examples. There can be no doubt, however, that there is a general tendency in this direction—that, in general, resiliency is lost with age. Because of this, summary figures on age have meaning in relation to corporate leadership. [The authors then present such data for groups of corporation presidents, Presidents of the United States, and federal department and agency heads.] . . .

Insofar as direct comparisons are possible, the following may be said in summary: the appointment age of top officials of the Nation's largest corporations is about the same or slightly above that of the top layers of Government officials. The average current age, however, is considerably higher than that of Government officials. To the extent that the undesirable aspects of bureaucracy are due to the advanced years of some of the top executives, it is apparent that this cause exists in the large corporation to at least the same degree if not more than it does in Government.

The second aspect of executive leadership is broadness of outlook. In even a moderately large corporation the administrative problems are many and diverse. The executive must be capable of harmonizing a multitude of conflicting forces. In the giant corporation, therefore, the ability to see things broadly and in relation is correspondingly more essential. Since most of the heads of the largest companies are promoted from within the question should be raised as to whether broad-gage executives can readily be developed in such enterprises.

A number of executives believe that the large corporation develops outstanding executives with considerable difficulty. The head of one company went so far as to say that "large corporations do not produce great executives. The men tend to become too specialized. The man in a smaller organization gets to know the business as a whole at an earlier age." Another phrases the problem in this way: "Specialization results in a dearth of top executives. You can't find men to integrate because they themselves aren't integrated. I know more good all-around business men in small concerns than I do in big corporations." Or again, "As activities become more specialized and routinized it becomes more difficult to develop ability in the ranks. . . . It may not be safe for us to rely upon securing a sufficient number from the ranks who will qualify for executive leadership."[3]

The benefits of specialization, of course, constitute one of the principal advantages of the large corporation and can ill be sacrificed. Although some top executives demonstrate that specialization is not an insuperable barrier in the development of leaders, nevertheless it remains an

---

[1] Herbert Emmerich, "Some Folklore of Executive Management," *Public Management, 20* (1938): 264–267.

[2] Harry A. Hopf, in the *Georgetown Law Journal, 24* (1938): 1067.

[3] James O. McKinsey, *Organization Problems Under Present Conditions,* New York: American Management Association, 1936, General Management Series No. 127, p. 13. The late Mr. McKinsey was chairman of the boards of Marshall Field and Co. and of the American Management Association.

impediment in the process of such development and is, therefore, a contributing cause of bureaucracy in big business.

In the Federal Government the bureau chiefs are probably specialized to about the same degree as the corporation executives. Among the higher political heads, however, there is a characteristically broader experience and outlook. It is the business of the politician to compose differences and to recognize the implications of particular policies over a broad realm. To the extent, then, that specialization is a cause of bureaucracy, the large corporation suffers as much as and perhaps more than Government.

The third general requirement for good leadership is that the executive shall have reached his position on the basis of merit. The degree to which merit now plays a part in appointments is difficult to determine. With the diffusion of ownership, which is characteristic of the large corporation, there is a corresponding decline in the practice of placing the chief owner or his son or some other relative in the higher executive positions. Although the propensity to "play ball" with the existing control is doubtless a factor in the selection of executives, this relative disappearance of inheritance as a selector opens the way for an emphasis on merit per se and it is possible that this will be the future trend. Inheritance is too unreliable a determinant for us to weep over its eclipse.

Although merit has doubtless played an increasingly important part in the selection of the top executives of large corporations, one nevertheless hears the complaint, from other than those who may be expected to be prejudiced, that seniority has been too much emphasized. This is particularly true, for example, among the railroads and doubtless contributes to the relatively high age at which men in this field are appointed to top positions. The idea of promotion by seniority permeates the railroads all the way down the hierarchy, where men are apt to think more in terms of the time in their records than in how effectively that time has been spent.

But promotion by seniority is not confined to the railroads. Some executives feel that the practice is generally characteristic of the large corporation. Moreover, even if it were no more common there than in the small enterprise, the process of reaching the top would take longer because of the greater number of steps in the hierarchy. In any case, it is at least certain that the big companies as a rule do not have an adequate system of executive recruitment. . . .

On the whole, then, we cannot say that merit for the particular jobs to be done is given any less consideration in government than in business. Politics, of course, plays a part in both. As one executive expressed it: "Politics exists in all large corporations. Whenever there is a change at the top in our company there is a shake-up all along the line." There is much room for improvement in both business and government, and, in each, some of the policies of executive recruitment result in defective leadership and contribute to bureaucracy.

The fourth qualification for leadership is that the executive remain in office long enough to be effective. Just what this term may be is difficult to say. Some executives claim that "a creative man delivers all he has in 3 to 5 years on one job." While this may be true at some of the lower levels of the hierarchy we doubt that it accurately describes the situation at the top. A well-conceived program of action would require 3 to 5 years to be properly developed and put into operation. An even longer period would be required for it to become an integrated part of the enterprise as a whole. Continuity of office is essential to smooth continuity of policy. Our general conclusion, therefore, is that although the exact length of appointment cannot accurately be determined, 10 years is not too long for a capable man to direct an enterprise while even 3 years is too long for a poor one. The problem is to select well and then to allow a sufficient length of time for the executive leader fully to put his ideas into effect. . . .

[On] the basis of turn-over of leadership, big business compares favorably with Government. Both business executives and bureau chiefs have quite satisfactory terms of office. Above the bureau level, however, turn-over is generally more rapid—too rapid, in fact, for effective administration.

Finally we should mention briefly the ability of the two groups to attract executive talent. Three elements may be mentioned: Salary, security, and prestige. Annual salaries of over a hundred thousand dollars for the top men are common among the largest corporations, though of course there are variations. Since most top executives have risen within their companies, however, and there is little cross-over among companies, the variations do not result in a flow of executive talent to those paying the highest salaries. Remuneration schedules appear to be at least sufficient to make the top positions attractive from that angle to subordinate executives within particular concerns—which is about all that matters in practice, except perhaps in the case of the railroads where there is some transfer among them.

Judging from the length of service of top executives of the largest corporations, security of tenure at that level at least would also seem to be adequate. Likewise the position of head of one of the large corporations carries with it a good deal of prestige in the corporate family and is therefore an inviting goal.

In comparison with business, government is generally less attractive from the standpoints of salary and security for men at the top levels. In all of government there is no salary of a hundred thousand dollars. The term of office of those above the bureau level is also considerably shorter than that which obtains in the largest corporations. In regard to the element of prestige, however, the situation is different, for identification with the public service has always appealed to men and in recent years this attraction has considerably increased due in large part to the expanding role of government in modern life.

In summary, therefore, it may be said that business leadership often contributes to bureaucracy because of defects in regard to age, narrowness of outlook, and the too frequent resort to seniority in making promotions. The rate of turnover among the top business executives of the largest corporations is small—in fact, so small that complaints are sometimes made of stoppage at the top. In comparison with business, Government executives are no older, they probably have a broader outlook, and seniority has been less important in appointments above the bureau level, while tenure, at this point, on the other hand, has been relatively short. The prestige attached to the top governmental positions has been as great as that of the top business positions for the past decade and will probably continue to be high, though the attractiveness of salary and tenure are somewhat below the level of the major positions in big business. In short, the defects of leadership contributing to bureaucracy bulk about as large in business as they do in Government.

Exceptional Talent

Lewis M. Terman

Lewis M. Terman (1877–   ), professor emeritus of psychology, Stanford University; widely known for his development of the Stanford-Binet test and his studies of gifted children.

But however efficient our tests may be in discovering exceptional talents, and whatever the schools may do to foster those discovered, it is the prevailing *Zeitgeist* that will decide, by the rewards it gives or withholds, what talents will come to flower. In Western Europe of the Middle Ages, the favored talents were those that served the Church by providing its priests, the architects of its cathedrals, and the painters of religious themes. A few centuries later the same countries had a renaissance that included science and literature as well as the arts. Although presumably there are as many potential composers of great music as there ever were, and as many potentially great artists as in the days of Leonardo da Vinci and Michaelangelo, I am reliably informed that in this country today it is almost impossible for a composer of *serious* music to earn his living except by teaching, and that the situation is much the same, though somewhat less critical, with respect to artists.

The talents most favored by the current *Zeitgeist* are those that can contribute to science and technology. If intelligence and achievement tests don't discover the potential scientist, there is a good chance that the annual Science Talent Search will, though not until the high school years. Since Westinghouse inaugurated in 1942 this annual search for the high school seniors most likely to become creative scientists, nearly

From "The Discovery and Encouragement of Exceptional Talent," the first Walter Van Dyke Bingham lecture, delivered at the University of California at Berkeley, March 25, 1954, *American Psychologist*, 9 (1954): 221–230, pp. 227–228 quoted.

4,000 boys and girls have been picked for honors by Science Service out of the many thousands who have competed. As a result, "Science Clubs of America" now number 15,000 with a third of a million members—a twenty-fold increase in a dozen years. As our need for more and better scientists is real and urgent, one can rejoice at what the talent search and the science clubs are accomplishing. One may regret, however, that the spirit of the times is not equally favorable to the discovery and encouragement of potential poets, prose writers, artists, statesmen, and social leaders.

But in addition to the over-all climates that reflect the *Zeitgeist,* there are localized climates that favor or hinder the encouragement of given talents in particular colleges and universities. . . .

Scores on aptitude tests show that the intelligence of students in a given institution is by no means the sole factor, though it is an important one. Other important factors are the quality of the school's intellectual climate, the proportion of able and inspiring teachers on its faculty, and the amount of conscious effort that is made not only to discover but also to motivate the most highly gifted. The influence of motivation can hardly be exaggerated.

Leadership in Social Movements
Herbert Blumer

Herbert Blumer (1900–   ), professor and chairman of the department of sociology, University of California, Berkeley. Author: *Movies and Conduct* (1933); *Movies, Delinquency and Crime* (1933); *Appraisals of Social Research I* (1939). Editor: *Human Side of Social Planning* (1935). Co-author: *Man and Society* (1937); *Outline of the Principles of Sociology* (1939, 1946).

[The] "leaders" of a general social movement play an important part—not in the sense of exercising directive control over the movement, but in the sense of being pace-makers. Such leaders are likely to be "voices in the wilderness," pioneers without any solid following, and frequently not very clear about their own goals. However, their example helps to develop sensitivities, arouse hopes, and break down resistances. . . .

Agitation operates in two kinds of situations. One is a situation marked by abuse, unfair discrimination, and injustice, but a situation wherein people take this mode of life for granted and do not raise questions about it. Thus, while the situation is potentially fraught with suffering and protest, the people are marked by inertia. Their views of their situation incline them to accept it; hence the function of the agitation is to lead them to challenge and question their own modes of living. It is in such a situation that agitation may create social unrest where none existed previously. The other situation is one wherein people are already aroused, restless, and discontented, but where they either are too timid to act or else do not know what to do. In this situation the function of agitation is not so much to implant the seeds of unrest, as to intensify, release, and direct the tensions which people already have.

Agitators seem to fall into two types corresponding roughly to these two situations. One type of agitator is an excitable, restless, and aggressive individual. His dynamic and energetic behavior attracts the attention of people to him; and the excitement and restlessness of his behavior tends to infect them. He is likely to act with dramatic gesture and to talk in terms of spectacular imagery. His appearance and behavior foster the contagion of unrest and excitement. This type of agitator is likely to be most successful in the situation where people are already disturbed and unsettled; in such a situation his own excited and energetic activity can easily arouse other people who are sensitized to such behavior and already disposed to excitability.

The second type of agitator is more calm, quiet, and dignified. He stirs people not by what he does, but what he says. He is likely to be a man sparing in his words, but capable of saying very caustic, incisive, and biting things—things which get "under the skin" of people and force them to view things in a new light. This type of agitator is more suited to the first of the social situations

From "Collective Behavior," Part 4 of A. M. Lee, ed., *New Outline of the Principles of Sociology*, New York: Barnes & Noble, 1946, pp. 165–222, pp. 201, 204–205, 209 quoted. Reprinted by permission.

discussed—the situation where people endure hardships or discrimination without developing attitudes of resentment. In this situation, his function is to make people aware of their own position and of the inequalities, deficiencies, and injustices that seem to mark their lot. He leads them to raise questions about what they have previously taken for granted and to form new wishes, inclinations, and hopes.

The function of agitation . . . is in part to dislodge and stir up people and so liberate them for movement in new directions. More specifically, it operates to change the conceptions which people have of themselves, and the notions which they have of their rights and dues. Such new conceptions involving beliefs that one is justly entitled to privileges from which he is excluded, provide the dominant motive force for the social movement. Agitation, as the means of implanting these new conceptions among people, becomes, in this way, of basic importance to the success of a social movement. . . .

[The] emergence of a saint cult . . . is to be discerned in every enduring and persisting social movement. There is usually a major saint and a series of minor saints, chosen from the popular leaders of the movement. Hitler, Lenin, Marx, Mary Baker Eddy, and Sun Yat-sen will serve as convenient examples of major saints. Such leaders become essentially deified and endowed with miraculous power. They are regarded as grossly superior, intelligent, and infallible. People develop toward them attitudes of reverence and awe, and resent efforts to depict them as ordinary human beings. The pictures or other mementos of such individuals come to have the character of religious idols. Allied with the saints of a movement are its heroes and its martyrs. They also come to be regarded as sacred figures. The development of this whole saint cult is an important means of imparting essentially a religious faith to the movement and of helping to build up the kind of convictions [necessary to give the adherents of the movement morale].

Negro Leadership

St. Clair Drake and Horace R. Cayton

St. Clair Drake (1911–   ), associate professor of sociology and anthropology, Roosevelt University, Chicago. Horace Roscoe Cayton (1903–   ), sociologist; United Nations correspondent for the *Pittsburgh Courier*. Author, with George S. Mitchell, of *Black Workers and the New Unions* (1939).

Any objective estimate of the success of Race Leaders in organizing discontent would probably reveal that there has been a lot more unity displayed than the people give themselves credit for. . . . In winning these victories the decisive factor has been the Negro's *political* power implemented by the threat of mass action, and even of violence. Paradoxically enough, they have come not from a monolithic unity but from a diversity of competing leaders stimulating each other to win gains for the Negro people. There has been a kind of informal and even unplanned division of labor, with the "accepted leaders" negotiating and pleading for the Negroes, while the "radicals" turned on the heat. A shrewd leader can always remind the white folks that he's trying to control the unruly Negro masses, but that he doesn't

know whether he can continue to do so if some concessions aren't made right away. This—coupled with the power of the Negro vote, desired by both major parties—is an effective minority technique. It hasn't broken the Job Ceiling nor abolished restrictive covenants, but it has won numerous isolated victories here and there.

Negroes are a minority in the midst of a white majority. They can win concessions only because certain sections of the white society need their votes or their labor, and because white America "respects the rights of minorities." An ethnic minority has to learn how to maneuver, to play balance-of-power politics, and to appeal to the conscience of the majority. Negroes have to learn how much the traffic will bear, and not to exceed this maximum. Race Leaders grow astute in

From *Black Metropolis: A Study of Negro Life in a Northern City*, New York: Harcourt, Brace and Co., 1945, pp. 730–737. Reprinted by permission.

measuring the factional alignments of the white community and in throwing, in just the right manner, the weight of the economic and political power they control.

Leaders must present a program of racial advancement and win enough support to put it through. Race Leaders of all class levels are agreed upon the necessity for cultivating a set of attitudes built on the basic fact of widespread "race consciousness." As they see it, "race consciousness" should be transformed into "race pride," replacing shame and lack of confidence. "Race pride," they feel, should then be made the basis of "race loyalty"—and all these should produce "race solidarity": a solid front facing the white world. From this point on, however, there is wide divergence on a program of action. . . .

"Accepted" Leadership. It has been evident in the story of Black Metropolis as we have traced it from the time of the Flight to Freedom up to the First World War, that there were certain Negroes who were looked upon by the white people of power and influence as the "accepted leaders" of the Negro community. These were usually the more successful businessmen, the more prominent preachers, the outstanding Negro politicians, and here and there a professional man. These Negro leaders could always count upon a small group of whites—"the friends of the Negro"—to lend financial and moral support to colored churches and community institutions. Among "the friends of the Negro" were prominent white political leaders, socially conscious and not-so-socially conscious businessmen, and white liberals and radicals of varied hue. Negroes were not a "problem" to Chicago in those days and leaders seldom found it necessary to lead any dramatic protests against flagrant injustices. They concentrated upon trying to widen economic opportunity so that Negroes as individuals and families could "advance themselves," and they constantly urged Negroes to "take advantage of every opportunity."

The Great Migration created the "Negro problem." Numerous Negroes smarting from the rebuffs of a white community that did not seem to want them, took refuge in a kind of defensive racialism. Individuals arose on the lower and lower-middle-class level who fervently preached "race pride" and "race solidarity.". . . [The] Commission on Race Relations in 1922 appealed to the "accepted leaders" to curb "agitators." A distinction emerged in the minds of white people between "safe leaders" and "radicals." The for-

mer were those who counseled thrift, patience, education and "wise" political action as the key to racial advancement. They were expected to throw their weight against violence and the blandishments of radicals—both economic and racial—and the enticements of labor unions. Many of the older Race Leaders accepted this role of "safe leaders," but numerous Negroes in the growing professional and business class were far less docile than a "safe leader" was supposed to be. They did not hesitate to voice their disapproval of any attempts to infringe upon the rights of Negroes or to deny them equal opportunity. Most of the community leaders had their hands full however, maintaining Bronzeville's institutional life. They were the people who knew how to organize fund-raising drives and to make a budget and stay within it. They were people who were "uplifting the masses"—not leading them. Discontent was well dispersed in the prosperous Twenties.

The Challenge of the Racial Radicals. With the outbreak of the Depression, a small group of militant Race Men began to organize discontent into a "Spend Your Money Where You Can Work" Campaign, and this involved a new weapon, the boycott. The "intellectuals" of the movement were upper-middle-class businessmen and newspapermen; but the "leg work" was done by young high-school-trained Negroes who needed white-collar jobs, and by a few aspiring Negro labor leaders and "jack-leg" preachers. They expressed the sentiments, however, of the Negro masses, who loyally rallied around them. The idea of the boycott as a weapon persisted throughout the Depression and was supported by some Negro businessmen, a few politicians, and a group of militant young men and women organized into a Negro Labor Relations League. Inevitably, these activities involved sporadic violence, for the less disciplined hangers-on about such a movement often think in terms of a "squeeze play." A convenient brick tossed through a recalcitrant merchant's window may make him decide to negotiate with the leaders of the boycott.

The "accepted leaders" had to adjust to the threat of the Racial Radicals. The Chicago Urban League, for instance, had always been considered the citadel of "safe leadership" but when the Bronzeville masses began to picket for jobs, the Urban League ". . . not only gave its sanction to the movement, but also placed the facilities of its offices at the disposal of the leaders. . . . Beyond this whole-hearted support and encouragement, however, the League took no active part in the campaign. Its organization was such that it could not co-operate directly in the use of coercive methods." Yet, on October 9, 1930, a prominent official of the Chicago League wrote the national office in the following vein:[1]

"The time has come for a more aggressive attitude on the part of the Negroes. We, of the Chicago Urban League, realize that fact, and our future programs will be far more aggressive than they have been in the past."

Throughout the Depression, the Urban League gave its moral support to the younger radicals who were channelizing the discontent of Black Metropolis into non-violent patterns of aggressive action.

Thunder on the Left. The accepted leaders not only had to maintain their ties with the sources of white economic and political power in Midwest Metropolis. They also had to adjust to the moods of racial radicalism, and were forced to take cognizance of pressure from the Left. . . .

There has been much loose talk about Negroes going Red. A few hundred Negroes in Midwest Metropolis did "join the Party," some of them becoming prominent officials in the American Communist movement. They studied Marxism and became ideologically committed to the extension of World Socialism. But the Negro masses who "could not hate Reds" were not Marxian Socialists dreaming of a Socialist society—they were hungry, frustrated, angry people looking for a program of action. And the Reds had a plan. So Negroes joined the parades, attended the picnics, and fought bailiffs and policemen. As they did so they found white men marching and fighting beside them. Together they carried the signs, BLACK AND WHITE UNITE, and demonstrated for more relief and better houses; but most of them were attracted to the Communists

[1] O. C. Cox, "The Negroes' Use of Their Buying Power in Chicago as a Means of Securing Employment," unpublished manuscript, 1932, quoted from an article in *The Crisis*, July, 1931, p. 126.

primarily because the "Reds" fought for Negroes *as* Negroes. Thousands of Negro preachers and doctors and lawyers, as well as quiet housewives, gave their money and verbal support to the struggle for freeing the Scottsboro Boys and for releasing Angelo Herndon. Hundreds, too, voted for Foster *and* Ford. Browder *and* Ford, for what other party since Reconstruction days had ever run a Negro for vice president of the United States? And who had ever put Negroes in a position where they led white men as well as black? Every time a black Communist appeared on the platform, or his picture appeared in a newspaper, Negroes were proud; and no stories of "atheistic Reds" or "alien Communists" could nullify the fact that here were people who accepted Negroes as complete equals and asked other white men to do so. Some of the preachers opposed the Reds publicly, but remarked privately, "If the Reds can feed the people, let 'em." Politicians dutifully denounced them, but privately admired their spunk. A few Negroes sincerely hated them.

"The Reds" won the admiration of the Negro masses by default. They were the only white people who seemed to really care what happened to the Negro. Yet few Negro sympathizers were without reservations. Some thought Communists were "using Negroes." Others felt that "if they ever gain power they'll be just like the other crackers." Many regarded the interracial picnics and dances as "bait." But Negroes are realists. They take "friends" and allies where they can find them. . . .

The Passing of the "Safe Leader." The old style "safe leader" has virtually disappeared from Bronzeville. Challenged on one hand by the Communists and on the other by the racial radicals, the "accepted leaders" have had either to accommodate themselves to new techniques or give way to men who could do so. The major community institutions (exclusive of the churches) are now in the hands of people who know how to steal a little of the radical's thunder, and "when they can't lick 'em, to jine 'em."

CROSS REFERENCES TO STANDARD TEXTS *

Bernard, *American Community Behavior*, Chap. 27.
Brown, *Social Pathology*, pp. 551–554.
Gillin, *Social Pathology*, p. 413.
——— and others, *Social Problems*, p. 119.

Landis, *Social Policies in the Making*, Chap. 24.
Neumeyer, *Social Problems and the Changing Society*, pp. 437–440.
Nordskog and others, *Analyzing Social Problems*, p. 644.
Odum, *American Social Problems*, Chap. 17.
Phelps and Henderson, *Contemporary Social Problems*, pp. 193, 207.

* For complete bibliographical reference to each text, see page 13.

OTHER BIBLIOGRAPHY

T. W. Adorno, Else Frenkel-Brunswik, Daniel J. Levinson, and R. Nevitt Sanford, *The Authoritarian Personality*, New York: Harper & Bros., 1950.

Herbert Agar, *The People's Choice*, Boston: Houghton Mifflin Co., 1938.

Jack Anderson and Ronald W. May, *McCarthy: The Man, the Senator, the "Ism,"* Boston: Beacon Press, 1952.

H. G. Barnett, *Innovation*, New York: McGraw-Hill Book Co., 1953.

Emory S. Bogardus, *Leaders and Leadership*, New York: D. Appleton-Century Co., 1934.

Walter G. Bowerman, *Studies in Genius*, New York: Philosophical Library, 1947.

Crane Brinton, *The Anatomy of Revolution*, New York: W. W. Norton & Co., 1938.

Joseph W. Eaton, "Experiments in Testing for Leadership," *American Journal of Sociology*, 52 (1946–47): 523–535.

Robert E. L. Faris, "Sociological Causes of Genius," *American Sociological Review*, 5 (1940): 689–697.

René Fülöp-Miller, *Leaders, Dreamers, and Rebels*, New York: Viking Press, 1935.

S. C. Gilfillan, *The Sociology of Invention*, Chicago: University of Chicago Press, 1935.

Noel P. Gist, C. T. Pihlblad, and Cecil L. Gregory, *Selective Factors in Migration and Occupation: A Study of Social Selection in Rural Missouri*, Columbia: University of Missouri, 1943.

——— and Carroll D. Clark, "Intelligence as a Selective Factor in Rural-Urban Migrations," *American Journal of Sociology*, 44 (1938–39): 36–58.

Robert Aaron Gordon, *Business Leadership in the Large Corporation*, Washington: Brookings Institution, 1945.

Alvin W. Gouldner, ed., *Studies in Leadership*, New York: Harper & Bros., 1950.

Leta S. Hollingworth, *Gifted Children: Their Nature and Nurture*, New York: Macmillan Co., 1927.

Sidney Hook, *The Hero in History*, New York: John Day Co., 1943.

Orrin E. Klapp, "Heroes, Villains and Fools, as Agents of Social Control," *American Sociological Review*, 19 (1954): 56–62.

Otto Klineberg, "Genius," *Encyclopaedia of the Social Sciences*, 6 (1931): 612–615.

R. H. Knapp and H. B. Goodrich, *Origins of American Scientists*, Chicago: University of Chicago Press, 1952.

R. H. Knapp and J. J. Greenbaum, *The Younger American Scholar: His Collegiate Origins*, Chicago: University of Chicago Press, 1953.

Hans Kohn, "Messianism," *Encyclopaedia of the Social Sciences*, 10 (1933): 356–364.

Wilhelm Lange-Eichbaum, *The Problem of Genius*, transl. by E. and C. Paul, New York: Macmillan Co., 1932.

Harold D. Lasswell, *Power and Personality*, New York: W. W. Norton & Co., 1948.

Alfred McClung Lee, *How to Understand Propaganda*, New York: Rinehart & Co., 1952, esp. Chaps. 4, 6, 7.

Elizabeth Briant Lee, *Eminent Women: A Cultural Study*, MS. Ph.D. Dissertation, New Haven: Graduate School of Yale University, 1937.

Harvey C. Lehman, *Age and Achievement*, Princeton: Princeton University Press, 1953.

Ferdinand Lundberg, *America's Sixty Families*, New York: Vanguard Press, 1937.

Charles Allan Madison, *Critics and Crusaders*, New York: Henry Holt and Co., 1947.

John M. Mecklin, *The Passing of the Saint: A Study of a Cultural Type*, Chicago: University of Chicago Press, 1941.

M. C. Otto, "Fanaticism," *Encyclopaedia of the Social Sciences*, 6 (1931): 90–92.

Fritz Redl, "Group Emotion and Leadership," *Psychiatry*, 5 (1942): 573–596.

Ralph Lord Roy, *Apostles of Discord*, Boston: Beacon Press, 1953.

Richard Schmidt, "Leadership," *Encyclopaedia of the Social Sciences*, 9 (1933): 282–287.

Joseph Schneider, "The Cultural Situation as a Condition for the Achievement of Fame," *American Sociological Review*, 2 (1937): 480–491.

———, "Social Origin and Fame," *American Sociological Review*, 10 (1945): 52–60.

Melvin Seeman, "Role Conflict and Ambivalence in Leadership," *American Sociological Review*, 18 (1953): 373–380.

George Seldes, *One Thousand Americans*, New York: Boni and Gaer, 1947.

Pitirim A. Sorokin, *Social and Cultural Dynamics*, New York: American Book Co., 4 vols., 1937–41, esp. Vol. 3.

Donald S. Strong, *Organized Anti-Semitism in America*, Washington: American Council on Public Affairs, 1941.

L. M. Terman and others, *Genetic Studies of Genius*, Palo Alto: Stanford University Press, 4 vols., 1925–32.

U. S. Legislative Reference Service, Library of Congress, *Fascism in Action*, Washington: Government Printing Office, 1947.

Stephen S. Visher, "Environmental Backgrounds of Leading American Scientists," *American Sociological Review*, 13 (1948): 65–72.

Wilson D. Wallis, *Messiahs: Their Role in Civilization*, Washington: American Council on Public Affairs, 1943.

Lester Frank Ward, *Applied Sociology,* Boston: Ginn and Co., 1906.

Sanford Winston, "The Mobility of Eminent Ameri-cans," *American Journal of Sociology, 41* (1935–36): 624–634.

P. Witty, ed., *The Gifted Child,* Boston: D. C. Heath and Co., 1951.

REVIEW QUESTIONS

1. Why does Albig think there is such a dangerous search for charismatic leadership?
2. What does Albig say about the characteristics of leadership?
3. What evidence does Sibley present to indicate that there are social barriers against the advancement of many gifted American children?
4. What does Sibley mean by the "vertical circulation in society"?
5. What influence does our school system have upon vertical circulation in society?
6. In what ways does the lack of effective leadership lead to bureaucracy in business and in government?
7. In what ways does bureaucracy keep effective leadership from working into positions of trust and authority?
8. What do Dimock and Hyde give as the five general requirements for the relation of leadership to bureaucracy?
9. What are favorable environmental conditions to the production of persons likely to achieve eminence in American society?
10. What does Blumer regard to be the chief importance of leaders for general social movements?
11. In what kinds of situations does Blumer say that agitation operates? What kind of agitators function in each kind of situation?
12. What does Blumer mean by a "saint cult"?
13. What do Drake and Cayton believe that Negro leadership has accomplished?
14. Who are the "accepted" Negro leaders? How do they function?
15. Who are "racial radicals"? How do they function?
16. What do Drake and Cayton say is happening to the "safe leader"?

PART VI

Social Division

—CHAPTER 19—→

Class and Status

Parents are frequently ambitious for their children, but they etch ideals and customs on the minds of their offspring which tend to confine them to limited groups of vocations and to bind them for better or for worse to the social class of their birth. As other chapters indicate, the opportunities available to the children of the various classes are far from similar in the United States. Educational opportunities are a noteworthy example of this. Jobs, crime and punishment, recreation, sex life, church membership, and many other social areas all have class involvements.

These evidences of a class society are with us even though traditional American political orators persistently assure us that the United States is a "classless society." Since sociologists are concerned with the job of describing and attempting to understand what exists, they have ignored such orations and have proceeded to examine the extent, workings, and problems of the class system in America and its relations to our racial caste barriers and to the major social institutions. Every chapter of this work touches upon some aspect of class stratification, but the present chapter attempts to bring together some central characteristics and problems of social classes. Warner and his associates define the class system, as they observed it, in Yankee City. The Useems and Tangent tell of the kind of stratification that is becoming common in an American prairie town.

In our society, the chief problems of class are those associated with interclass friction, extreme social mobility (both from group to group within a class and vertically from class to class), class-making and class-rigidifying tendencies, class-caste relationships, and disproportionate control of social power by the leaders of a class.

Angell deals with the first of these problems and shows how interclass misunderstandings confront one with "a vicious circle: differentials in the distribution of income and property make the classes unable to appreciate one another's positions, and this inability makes it impossible for them to agree on any measures that would reduce the differentials." He advocates an approach to the whole problem by indirection rather than by a head-on attack.

Whyte, in his articles, points out some of the characteristics of the next managerial class, both men and their wives, and raises questions as to the possible rise here of a new and eventually inbred caste. Johnson, in part of an essay on caste and class in an American industry, indicates how the realistic problems of mutual class needs tend to break down caste distinctions. This has been otherwise illustrated in many instances by large industrial unions such as the United Automobile Workers. In the final selection, the report of the U. S. Senate Committee on Education and Labor on an investigation of the National Association of Manufacturers comes to conclusions concerning that body that are indicative of its powerful roles in American political, economic, and social life.

Class-making and class-rigidifying tendencies are, of course, touched upon in several other chapters.

Some Characteristics of Yankee City's Social Classes

W. Lloyd Warner, Leo Srole, and Paul S. Lunt

W. Lloyd Warner (1898–   ), professor of anthropology and sociology, University of Chicago. Co-author of: *A Black Civilization* (1937); *Color and Human Nature* (1941); with P. S. Lunt, *Status System of a Modern Community* (1942); *Who Shall Be Educated?* (1945); *Social System of a Modern Factory* (1947); *Measurement of Social Status* (1948); with M. Meeker, and K. Eells, *Social Class in America* (1949); *American Life, Dream and Reality* (1953). Paul Sanborn Lunt (1902–   ), director, Lunt Research Associates. Leo Srole (1908–   ), visiting professor of sociology and psychiatry, Cornell University Medical College.

The . . . six social strata of the community . . . are of importance in determining the behavior of everyone in the community. The top level, or upper-upper class, consists of members of "old families" who are born to their position; their family genealogies show them to be products of several generations of upper-class living. This old aristocracy is the keystone in the Yankee City status system. Below this level are the "new families" or newly rich (lower-upper) who are busy transforming their money into acceptable behavior through participation with those who preceded them to the top level. On the step below them are the "pillars of society," the successful men and women, who are the powerful upper-middle class who do things and see that things are done in Yankee City. These three classes, comprising no more than 15 per cent of the total, are "the big people" who are above the common run of men.

Below them, but at the top of "the little people," are the members of the lower-middle class, the small tradesmen, the skilled workers, and the white-collar workers who cling to the virtues of the "protestant ethic," despite the fact that many are members of other religions. Beneath them are the poor and respectable workers, who hope and strive to do better than they are doing, but who worry for fear of falling into the class below them, the lowest in society, where the "shiftless Yankees" and the "ignorant immigrants" are found. . . .

An upper-upper person in Yankee City belongs to a class having a much larger number of women than men and a larger percentage of females (over 60 per cent) than any other class in the community. In this respect it differs markedly from the lower-lower class, which has the smallest percentage of women, and is most like the upper-middle class, which also has an excess of females. . . .

The upper-upper class has the smallest percentage of children and the largest proportion of people over sixty years of age. In both respects it stands in strongest contrast to the lower-lower class, containing about 11 per cent of persons under twenty-one, as against 28 per cent, and over 39 per cent of persons sixty years of age or older, as against fewer than 11 per cent. The upper-upper most closely resembles the lower-upper and upper-middle classes in numbers of old people, the upper-middle in percentage of children. The excess of older people in the upper-upper population is accounted for in part by the large number of unmarried females who are the sisters and maiden aunts of other members of the group, in part by the number of "ladies" who have lived on in the old family houses after their parents' death and after their brothers and sons have gone elsewhere to marry and rear their families.

All members of the upper-upper class are Yankees, none belonging to any ethnic group in the community. The lower-upper class, which con-

From W. Lloyd Warner and Leo Srole, *The Social Systems of American Ethnic Groups*, New Haven: Yale University Press, 1945, pp. 1–2, 295–296, and W. Lloyd Warner and Paul S. Lunt, *The Social Life of a Modern Community*, New Haven: Yale University Press, 1941, pp. 422–423, 426–428, 435, 438, 447, 449. Reprinted by permission.

tains less than 5 per cent with an ethnic background,* all of them Irish whose families have been in America for several generations, approximates the upper-upper class most closely in this. By contrast, 57 per cent of the lower-lower and 61 per cent of the upper-lower classes belong to ethnic minorities, with large concentrations of Irish, Poles, Russians, Greeks, French Canadians, Italians, Jews, Armenians, and Negroes. Upper-upper individuals rarely associate with persons of other ethnic stocks. Lower-class Yankees try hard not to do so and sometimes join associations having "racial" prejudices; physically, however, they are continually in the company of people with traditions which differ from their own.

Upper-upper individuals marry later than those of any other class.[1] Their median age at marriage is almost twenty-eight years (27.90), which is closest to that of the lower-upper class (26.60 years) and furthest from that of the lower-lower class (23.20 years). . . .

Members of the upper-upper and lower-upper classes give their children a different formal and informal education. No children of the former attended the local high school at the time of our census, and, as far as we could determine, but few had attended this institution previously. Moreover, only four lower-upper-class children were enrolled in the high school. Most of the children of the two upper classes are sent to private preparatory schools, where they not only prepare for college but also acquire the etiquette and attributes of their group. . . .

The frequency with which members of a class are arrested and get their names on the police blotter is a fair index both of the kind of authority exercised by political organization over each class and of the kind of behavior in each class which is sufficiently disapproved by the whole community to warrant the more drastic sanctions of police action. Of the total arrests in the city, the upper-upper class accounts for but one half of 1 per cent, while the lower-lower accounts for 65 per cent. As regards the figures within the class itself, only a little over 1 per cent have been arrested, a slightly larger percentage than the classes

just below it, while 11 per cent of the lower-lower class have had their names placed on the police records. Moreover, none of the upper-upper and lower-upper-class arrests is below twenty-one years of age, while 30 per cent of the lower-lower-class arrests are juveniles. This great disparity is not to be accounted for by the fact that "criminal behavior" is proportionately higher among lower-class juveniles or that there are more ethnic members whose children have been imperfectly adapted to Yankee City life. It must be understood as a product of the amount of protection from outside interference the parents can give the members of their families. Our interviews together with police records demonstrate that the lower-lower adolescent boys are guilty of crimes against property, and that some girls are caught in sexual delinquencies. But these same interviews likewise demonstrate that boys and girls in the higher classes as frequently commit the same acts but do not get on the police records. They are not arrested because social pressure prevents the police from taking action when they make threats to do so or forces them to overlook the behavior at their own volition, or, more important, because the social controls of the class system operate in such a way as to hide successfully all such activities from the authorities.

The security of younger members of upper-upper-class families from outside interference is further demonstrated by the fact that all charitable associations, in which the upper classes are represented in large numbers, serve to subordinate the lower classes and interfere with their ordinary family life. An organization such as the Society for the Prevention of Cruelty to Children, for example, is ostensibly free from class bias; yet all of the cases with which it dealt came from below the two upper classes, and most of them, from below the three uppermost classes. In brief, the social power of the upper classes highly protects their families, while the subordinate position of the lower classes leaves their families more vulnerable to the sanctions of the rest of the community. . . .

Eighty-three per cent of the upper-middle are Yankee by birth and tradition, being most like the lower-upper and least like the upper-lower class. This class is also most like the lower-upper class (next like the lower-middle) in the composition of its ethnic population, most of which is Irish, less than 1 per cent of the class membership being from any other ethnic group. About 6 per

---

* This term refers to any ethnic background other than a native white American ethnic background such as is found in Yankee City.—Eds.

[1] Cf. pp. 94 ff. [in Warner and Lunt, *The Social Life of a Modern Community*] for a full description of marriage in Yankee City. Each characteristic which is summarized in this general description of the six classes is fully described in earlier chapters of this book.

cent of the Irish, 3 per cent of the Jews, 2 per cent of the Greeks, 1 per cent of the Armenians, and less than 1 per cent of all other ethnic groups in Yankee City belong to the upper-middle class. It contains no Russians, Poles, or Negroes. The total membership of the upper-middle class comprises 10 per cent of the total population of the city. . . .

This class accounts for but 2 per cent of all the arrests in Yankee City. Its members are socially powerful enough to prevent their arrests for many crimes such as drunkenness which would ordinarily cause arrest in the lower classes. Less than 1 per cent of the members of the class have been arrested. In this respect they are exactly the same as the lower-upper class. . . .

All the Negroes, about nine tenths of the Poles, seven tenths of the Russians, more than half of the Greeks, slightly less than one half of the French Canadians, and Italians are in the lower-lower class. But only one third of the Armenians, one tenth of the Irish, and one fourteenth of the Jews are in this class. . . .

The police arrest the members of the lower-lower class more frequently than any others in the community. . . . By way of comparison, about one out of every three people in the lower-lower class, three out of a hundred in the upper-lower class, one out of a hundred in the upper-upper and lower-middle classes, and still less in the lower-upper and upper-middle classes have been arrested. About one fourth of those arrested in the lower-lower class are below eighteen years of age, and about 33 per cent are below twenty-one. The lower-lower class has not sufficient power to protect its young from the police. . . .

The future of American ethnic groups seems to be limited; it is likely that they will be quickly absorbed. When this happens one of the great epochs of American history will have ended and another, that of race, will begin.

Paradoxically, the force of American equalitarianism, which attempts to make all men American and alike, and the force of our class order, which creates differences among ethnic peoples, have combined to dissolve our ethnic groups. Until now these same forces have not been successful in solving the problem of race. The Negro and other dark-skinned groups are still ranked as color castes.

How we will solve the problem of race in the future is problematical. The major areas of the earth, including the United States, are now closely interconnected into an interdependent totality. The effects of important racial and social movements in Europe, Asia, and South America are felt in the United States; our color-caste structure is an ever-present reality in the thoughts of the leaders of China, India, and Latin America. The dark-skinned races' struggle with the dominant whites for social equality is rapidly being organized on an international basis. To calculate the future we must interpret what happens in the United States in this larger setting. Whether we try forcibly to subordinate dark-skinned people, and thereby face certain failure, or use democratic methods, and thereby increase our chances of success, may depend more upon how this decision is made in the rest of the world than upon what happens in this country.

Stratification in a Prairie Town
John Useem, Pierre Tangent, and Ruth Useem

John Useem (1911–   ), professor of sociology and anthropology, Michigan State College. Ruth Hill Useem (1915–   ), sociologist. Pierre Tangent (1913–   ), associate minister, Calvary Baptist Church, Washington, D. C.

While social stratification is characteristic of all societies, its form and meaning in any particular society vary with prevailing values and operative social forces.[1] Evidence accumulates that a type of

stratification new to the towns and rural areas of

[1] See Max Weber, *Wirtschaft und Gesellschaft*, 631–640, 1922; P. A. Sorokin, *Social Mobility*, 12–17, New York, 1927; Talcott Parsons, "An Analytical Approach to the Theory of Social Stratification," *American Journal of Sociology*, 45 (1940): 841–862; and Ralph Linton, *The Study of Man*, New York: D. Appleton-Century Co., 1936, pp. 113–131.

From "Stratification in a Prairie Town," *American Sociological Review*, 7 (1942): 331–342, pp. 331–332 quoted. Reprinted by permission.

the country is rapidly taking place.[2] Heretofore social positions were contingent upon individual achievements and opportunities for climbing the social ladder were thought to be open to everyone; recent years have witnessed a curtailment of social circulation and a division of society into fixed social classes in many of the communities of the prairie states.

The earlier traditions of the Great Plains were those common to the recent frontier culture: much neighborliness, informality in social interaction, indifference to ancestors, evaluation of persons in terms of their immediate roles in the social order. Although there were differences with regard to the means of attaining desired ends, the ends themselves were never questioned: the family was patriarchal; the church, fundamentalistic; the school, an unlimited good; and belief in Jeffersonian democracy, axiomatic. The only requisites for social acceptability were adherence to established institutions and conformance to the mores. Advancement in status was achieved by work, "good horse sense," and ownership of land. Public assistance for an able-bodied person was regarded as an absurdity because little wealth was required to become an entrepreneur and any man could secure a freehold. Social life was leisurely,

being a combination of frontier and old-world rural patterns.[3]

The past two decades have witnessed profound upheavals in the Great Plains: drought, heavy mortgages, tax delinquencies, farm foreclosures, business failures, and exodus of populations.[4] There is an increasing tendency for towns to be composed of a smaller entrepreneur class and a larger submerged group composed of ex-farmers, unemployed farm and town workers and stranded itinerants. While doctors, school teachers, craftsmen, and retired farmers still live in towns, they are proportionately fewer in number and less significant in community life. The impact of these changes has led to the development of communities sharply divided into distinct strata.[5] The present generation has experienced a shift in the system of assigning status from evaluating an individual according to personal achievements to ranking by family affiliation. Climbing the ladder has practically ceased. Today it requires capital beyond the means of the lower class to secure a commercial farm or to open a business enterprise with any promise of success. Nearly every major area of interaction has been affected because social relations in prairie towns continue to be face-to-face and social institutions are shared by the total population.

[2] See Roy H. Holmes, *Rural Sociology*, 73–75, New York, 1932; T. Lynn Smith, "Trends in Community Organization and Life," *American Sociological Review, 1* (1940): 325–344; Paul H. Landis, *Rural Life in Process*, McGraw-Hill Book Co., 1940, p. 285; Grace Browning, *Rural Public Welfare*, 333, Chicago, 1941; Edgar Schmiedeler, "Will History Repeat in Rural America?" *Rural Sociology, 6* (1941): 291–299; Carl C. Taylor, "Rural Life," *American Journal of Sociology, 47* (1942): 841–853.

[3] See, for example, Everett N. Dick, *The Sod-house Frontier*, New York: D. Appleton-Century Co., 1937.

[4] *The Northern Great Plains*, National Resources Planning Board, Washington, D. C., 1940; R. S. Kifer and H. L. Stewart, "Farming Hazards in the Drought Area," W.P.A. Research Monograph VI, Washington, D. C., 1938; and Allen D. Edwards, "The Sociology of Drought," *Rural Sociology, 4* (1939): 190–202.

[5] See J. M. Gillette, "Socio-economic Submergence in a Plains State," *Rural Sociology, 5* (1940): 57–68.

Misunderstandings between Classes
Robert Cooley Angell

Robert Cooley Angell (1899–   ), professor of sociology, University of Michigan. Principal works: *The Campus* (1928), *A Study in Undergraduate Adjustment* (1930); with C. H. Cooley and L. J. Carr, *Introductory Sociology* (1933); *The Family Encounters the Depression* (1936); *The Integration of American Society* (1941); *The Moral Integration of American Cities* (1951).

The lessening of the misunderstandings between classes is an extraordinarily difficult task. One is confronted with the operation of a vicious circle: differentials in the distribution of income and property make the classes unable to appreciate one another's positions, and this inability makes it impossible for them to agree on any measures that would reduce the differentials. It is easy to say, "Drastically reduce the income differences by legislation, and understanding will increase." The point is that you cannot do this without destroying our democracy. The attempt would either bring about a capitalist fascism or a working-class dictatorship. In this situation it appears that the only hope lies in approaching the problem by indirection.

Whatever increases the intimacy of association of different social classes encourages the understanding that is requisite as a basis for realizing our common values. The decentralization of our great industries so as to throw population back into smaller, more "natural" communities would certainly have this effect. There has been a hope among garden city enthusiasts and regional planners that increasing use of electrical power in factories would make such decentralization possible.[1] Perhaps the establishment of a compulsory labor service for young men and women of eighteen or nineteen, a service performed in camps where members of the different social classes would live together for a few months, would produce, even among city dwellers, the intimacy requisite for full understanding. Sometimes college life gives a similar opportunity, though usually not, because the students from different social strata tend to keep to themselves on the campus. Those who have worked within the consumers' cooperative movement can testify that it also frequently affords the occasion for close acquaintance across class lines. All such developments, however, run counter to the main current of our life, that of diversification and stratification, and no one should expect them to have any marked effect in the near future.

A more immediate possibility is the reduction of friction and conflict without increased intimacy among classes, by securing more likeness of judgment with respect to the degree to which our common values are being realized under modern conditions. Children might perhaps receive instruction in school concerning contemporary social conditions and their compatibility with American values, although the effectiveness of this is likely to be weakened by after-school contacts which introduce divergent biases. Any thorough interchange of experience and views across

class lines would tend toward similarity of perception and interpretation. One of the great benefits of collective bargaining is that, through it, employers and employees have the opportunity to become well acquainted over the conference table. And many charitable organizations are finding that a gratifying insight develops when well-to-do contributors and volunteer workers are brought into close contact with the underprivileged.

But in a society in which most needs can be satisfied with money, one cannot ignore the importance of lessening disparities of property and income as a means to similarity of interpretive position. We have indicated that such lessening cannot be achieved abruptly without running the danger of killing our democracy. Perhaps we can accomplish it gradually and alongside the cultivation of class understanding through other channels. Indeed something must be done in this direction if the cooperation of the working classes is to be secured. They will interpret the interest exhibited by the well-to-do classes in their problems as a pseudo interest and a sham unless positive meliorative efforts come out of it. But once a start is made the gains should be cumulative. A reduction in property and income differentials should breed more understanding and more understanding should bring into the area of discussion programs aiming at further reduction. Then members of different classes could argue intelligently and constructively over policies. No one expects that they would easily agree upon particular solutions, but they could at least canvass alternatives with mutual respect.

One must have no illusions that this will be easy to bring about. The line of least resistance would be to ignore the whole problem. In a country where the standards are as materialistic as in the United States, many will continue to regard improvement in technology as the main line of progress. They will not realize that such improvement does nothing to strengthen the foundations of our society. But we cannot leave them in ignorance. They must be brought to see that only increased common orientation can lead us to more societal integration. Though it is foolish to make predictions of imminent decline and fall, it is significant that more and more social scientists realize the danger. We are faced with the necessity of taking positive and vigorous action. The supreme test of democracy will be the promptness and the intelligence with which we meet this challenge.

[1] For a careful examination of this whole question, see Lewis Mumford, *The Culture of Cities,* New York: Harcourt, Brace & Co., 1938.

Management Man: Permanent Transient
William H. Whyte, Jr.

William H. Whyte, Jr., assistant managing editor, *Fortune* magazine. Author of *Is Anybody Listening?* (1952).

For a quick twinge of superiority there is nothing quite like driving past one of the new Levittown-like suburbs. To visitors from older communities, the sight of rank after rank of little boxes stretching off to infinity, one hardly distinguishable from the other, is weird, and if they drive along the streets at dusk, when the little blue lights of the television sets begin to shine out of the picture windows, they can speculate that if they were to blink their eyes in proper rhythm the scene flashing by would freeze into one motionless picture. Appalling! If this is progress, God help us . . . 1984. But, onlookers are also likely to conclude, one must be sympathetic too; after all, it is a step up in life for the people who live there, and one should not begrudge them the opiate of TV; here, obviously, is a group of anonymous beings submerged in a system they do not understand.

The onlooker had better wipe the sympathy off his face. Underneath the television aerials lies a revolution. What he has seen is not the home of little cogs and drones. What he has seen is the dormitory of the next managerial class.

The most important single group in these communities is what has been variously called business bureaucrats, industrial civil servants, technicians of society—the junior executives, research workers, young corporation lawyers, engineers, salesmen. The bond they share is that they are (1) between twenty-five and thirty-five, (2) organization men, (3) and all on the move. It is significant enough that there are now so many of them that whole towns have to be built to hold them; more significant, it is these unostentatious, salaried nomads who will be running our business society twenty years from now.

Many future managers, of course, do not live in such places; and many work for companies that don't require them to move. Nevertheless, it may be the new suburban communities that pro-

vide the sharpest picture of tomorrow's management. Not only are managerial transients concentrated here, they are concentrated almost totally free of the pressures of older traditions and older people that would affect them elsewhere. In such propinquity, they bring out in each other—perhaps at times caricature—tendencies latent elsewhere, and one sees in bold relief what might be almost invisible in more conventional environments. To an older eye, perhaps the picture is abnormal, but what may be abnormal today is very likely to be normal tomorrow.

For some months *Fortune* has been making an intensive study of four of the new suburbs. As we will report . . . there is a remarkable similarity, in attitudes toward politics, education, economics, sex, religion, from suburb to suburb. Almost a new way of life is in the making in these communities, and it is not a synthetic way of life "sold" by mass producers of suburbs; it is the expression of the younger people's needs and wants.

Before looking under the TV aerials, however, there are some immediate questions to take up: How has this new mobility been brought to pass? Is it likely to decline or increase? Does it signal the rise of a new and eventually inbred caste? To attempt a definitive answer to any of these would be presumptuous. But on one thing at least the evidence is clear: America's social structure is going through a shake-up the full effects of which are yet to be felt.

Thirty years ago the notion that the U. S. had a fairly fluid society would not have been particularly controversial—"classless" America, indeed, was almost a universal cliché. Today, however, the dominant school of thought on American society maintains that the country's pride in "classlessness" and in the idea that a good man can always rise is illusion. After two centuries, some social students hold, the American system is finally shaking down into a fixed, stable hierarchy.

From "The Transients," *Fortune* (May 1953), 112–117, 221–222, 224, 226, pp. 113–115, 116–117, 226 quoted. Reprinted from the May 1953 issue of FORTUNE Magazine by Special Permission of the Editors; Copyright Time Inc.

As interpreted in terms of the six ranks of anthropologist Lloyd Warner,[1] American society is a traditional community in which the Hill, local business ties, and interlocking family relationships firmly fix the individual's position, from which he can move upward (from the Elks, say, to the Rotary) only by sanction of the next-upper group. Furthermore, other studies indicate, what with the unionization of labor and the professionalization of management, the way up the ladder is growing tougher. The solution, it has been argued, lies not in the individual's cherishing illusions that he's going to go up but in adjusting to the realities of his home environment.

We do not agree. Such studies have done a service in sensitizing Americans to class and status factors they like to pretend don't exist. Their very emphasis on what is static, however, has obscured what is dynamic. What about the people who *leave* home?

It is the thesis of this article that the man who leaves home is not the exception in American society, but the key to it. Almost by definition, the management man is a man who left home, and like the man who went from the Midwest to Harvard, kept on going. There have always been, of course, people who left home, but the number of them has increased—and so vastly that those who stay put are as affected by the emigration as those who leave.

The growing importance of the transients has been obscured by a sort of economic time lag; organization people don't make the big money, and they are making less real income than they did ten years ago. But though it may be the automobile dealer and the owner of the local bottling franchise who drive the Cadillacs, it is the organization man who now makes the decisions that most affect the lives of others. "Those fat cats around here are falling all over themselves entertaining Charlie," says the wife of a plant engineer. "They could buy and sell us twice over, but he's going to decide the location of the new chemical plant." The story has endless variations; from the man in the investment division of an insurance company whose brief may decide a whole industry's future to the new-product engineer, Organization Man is becoming dominant.

Even if part of the American Dream is still

---

[1] Whose "upper upper," "lower upper," etc., classification of Newburyport, Massachusetts, was handled so roughly by ex-Newburyporter John P. Marquand in *Point of No Return*.

true, one big chunk of it is dead, finished, kaput. For the future will be determined not by the independent entrepreneur or the "rugged individualist" whom our folklore so venerates; the future will be determined by Organization Man. It is not occasion for cheer; but neither is it occasion for pessimism. It is, however, occasion for reflection. Wherever it is we are going, we are going there very, very fast.

After the war, one thing looked sure. Americans had had their bellyful of moving; now, everybody agreed, they were going to settle down and stop this damned traipsing around. Here is the way things worked out:

Americans are moving more than ever before: Never have long-distance movers had it so good; according to figures provided by the five leading firms, moving is now at a rate even higher than in wartime. And compared with prewar, the five firms are all moving at least three times as many families, and one is moving ten times as many. Furthermore, not only are more families moving, those who move move more frequently; one out of every seven of its customers, Allied Van Lines reports, will *within a year* pick up stakes and move again to a new state, and seven out of ten will be "repeaters" within the next five years.

This is not just a matter of moving from one part of town to another; in 1951, 7 per cent of all male adults moved away from their county, and of these roughly half moved out of the state entirely. Concentrate on the twenty-five to thirty-five-year-old group and the figure goes up sharply; in 1951 roughly 12 per cent of men twenty-five to thirty-five years old moved outside of their county, and 6 per cent moved to a new state.

The more education, the more mobility: If a man goes to college now, the chances are almost even that he won't work in his home state. Recent census figures and *Time*'s study, *They Went to College,* indicate that the educational level is higher among migrants than among non-migrants, and the higher the educational level, the more intensive the migration. In the twenty-five to thirty-five-year-old group, to extrapolate from census figures, about sixteen out of every hundred men who have only a high-school education have been interstate migrants, vs. 29 per cent of those who have had at least one year of college. Of men who complete college, 46 per cent move. Of those who worked their way through in a college outside their home state, about 70 per cent don't go back. And for all college men, incidentally, the higher the grades, the more likely they are to go to work elsewhere than in their home states.

Organization people move the most: To judge from studies by direct-mail experts of *Time, Life, Fortune,* and McGraw-Hill, the greatest amount of address changing occurs among managerial people. Similarly, records of long-distance movers show that the greatest single group among their customers, upwards of 40 per cent, consists of corporation people being transferred from one post to another (with the employer usually footing the bill). If to this group are added government, Army, and Navy people, and men joining new companies, over 70 per cent of all moves are accounted for by members of large institutions.

The impact of this transiency on U. S. society is incalculable. The small town, for example, has long exported some of its youth; but what was once a stream has become a flood. It is no longer a case of the special boy who had to get out of town to cross the tracks or find an outlet for his energies; now as many as three-quarters of the town's young college men may be in the same position. Where are they to go after college? Back home? Lawyers and doctors can, and the majority do; they are in the happy position of being able to go home, to keep professionally alert, and to make a good bit of money at the same time. But for the others, opportunity seems to be elsewhere —not just for the delivery boy who became an Air Force lieutenant, but for the young man on the Hill who's gone off to join du Pont.

In terms of status it is difficult to say whether the migrants have gone up or down. But they have moved more than geographically; what is taking place is a horizontal movement in which the transients have come together in a new kind of group that fits none of the old social categories. . . . As sociologist Max Weber long ago noted, before the turn of the century the trend to a "bureaucratic" organization of society was already in high motion. Since then the trend has been steadily accentuated, until today most college men almost automatically see their future in terms of the salaried life of an organization.

The reasons are obvious enough. While there is an undue assumption by many young men that entrepreneurship equals insecurity, if the young man has no independent income or capital what is he to do? The big organization wants him; wants more of him, in fact, than are available. Its recruiters go to him before he graduates from college, and they promise good starting salaries (cur-

rently: $275 to $335 a month), good extra training, and a secure future. To join up seems not only the line of least resistance but the logical course as well.

Clearly, the big organization is now the prime vehicle for a career, and in more institutions than the corporations. At their present size, the armed forces, a great institutional career in themselves, are in effect a great training ground for indoctrinating each new age group in the organization way. So are the government bureaus. Even in the professions the emphasis has switched to the organization; of the professional men who graduated in the last decade, only about one in five is working for himself; the bulk are to be found in group clinics, law factories, AEC labs, corporation staff departments, and the like. Academic life has been similarly affected; what with the growth of foundations and huge government research grants, academics now find it's easier to obtain $200,000 for a group project than a few thousand for somebody doing something all by himself— if the businessman were to eavesdrop on some of the grant-raising shoptalk of the academics he wouldn't throw the term "ivory tower" around so loosely.

In the wake of this shift to the big organization is the moving van. Certainly the recruit does not join up because he *wants* to move a lot, and it is often in spite of it. But moving, he knows, has become part of the bargain, and unsettling as transfer might be, even more unsettling are the implications of not being asked to transfer. "We never plan to transfer," as one company president explains, a bit dryly, "and we never make a man move. Of course, he kills his career if he doesn't. But we never *make* him do it." The fact is well understood; it is with a smile that the recruit moves—and keeps on moving, year after year; until, perhaps, that distant day when he is summoned back to Rome.

It is not just more moves per man. Even companies reporting no increase in the number of times each individual moves report an increase in the sheer number of men being moved. G.E. has compared a cross section of its forty-five-year-old executives with one of its thirty-five-year-olds; in the ten years after they were twenty-five, 42 per cent of the older group had moved at least once; during the same age period, 58 per cent of the younger had moved.

Corporations never planned it quite that way. Decentralization and expansion, rather than deliberate personnel policy, have determined the pattern. Companies have systematized it, to be sure; moves are settling into more of a rhythm, almost invariably they are sweetened with a raise, and in some companies, sweetened by special departments that handle all the housekeeping fuss of the trip. By and large, however, the question of the man's personal development—however emphasized when the boss breaks the news to him—has been secondary to the day-to-day necessity of filling vacancies out in the empire.

That is, up until now. Periodic transfer, some companies are coming to believe, is a positive good in itself; and even where no immediate functional reason exists, it might often be important to move the man anyway. What better way, they ask, to produce the well-rounded executive?

Instead of leaving transfer to be determined haphazardly by different departments, some companies, like G.E., have made such decisions part of a systematic managerial program. By thus making a man's "permanent" assignment (i.e., one lasting at least three years) part of a deliberate rotation policy, the man is given "more choices in life to make," and the company, as a result, is given a pool of seasoned talent. Other companies agree; by deliberately exposing a man to a succession of environments, they best obtain that necessity of the large organization—the man who can fit in anywhere. "The training," as an I.B.M. executive succinctly puts it, "makes our men interchangeable. . . ."

What has already happened to the salaried transient suggests that if mobility continues to increase it may produce a rootlessness that can have far-reaching consequences. What, in the years to come, will be the effect on the younger members of management, on their children—and on the organizations some will one day head—of a way of life so much more nomadic than that of their elders? The development of new values in the transients' suburban villages indicates that the effect will be profound. . . . The young organization people in many ways have made a surprisingly good adjustment to their transiency, yet, under the congenial surface, there boil some tensions which hint that more changes are yet to come.

How much to the good, or bad, this change will be is a question we must defer. There is no virtue, certainly, in change per se; whether or not it is to be for the good depends on what the change is to. But for the moment at least, there is one hopeful conclusion we can draw. If the sheer fact of change is true, the picture of a society gradually stratifying is wrong. Those are mistaken who hold that the routes of mobility are being closed; that we are finally shaking down into a stable system; that we are, at last, on a plateau. Quite the opposite; the evidence indicates that our society has never been more dynamic—and the best thing about our system, perhaps, is that there isn't too much of it. Not just yet, anyway.

Management Man's Wife
William H. Whyte, Jr.*

There is a person, it would appear, to whom the modern corporation is beginning to pay a good bit of attention. Over the last few decades, as is now so frequently observed, the corporation has been evolving a social community able to provide its members with more and more of their basic social wants. Yet, the corporation now concedes, one of the principal members of its community remains officially almost unnoticed; to wit, the Wife. For

the good of the corporation, many executives believe, it is time the matter was remedied. "We control a man's environment in business and we lose it entirely when he crosses the threshold of his home," one executive says mournfully. "Management, therefore, has a challenge and an obligation to deliberately plan and create a favorable, constructive attitude on the part of the wife that will liberate her husband's total energies for the job."

* See identifying note on page 353.
From "The Wives of Management," *Fortune* (October 1951), 86–88, 204, 206–208, 210, 213, pp. 86–88, 213 quoted. Reprinted from the October 1951 issue of FORTUNE Magazine by Special Permission of the Editors; Copyright Time Inc.

Others, though they might not put it quite so baldly, agree that the step is logical.

Just how to do this . . . is a problem that has many a management understandably baffled. On one very basic matter, however, management is not in the slightest baffled. It knows exactly what kind of wife it wants. With a remarkable uniformity of phrasing, corporation officials all over the country sketch the ideal. In her simplest terms, she is a wife who is: (1) highly adaptable, (2) highly gregarious, (3) realizes her husband belongs to the corporation.

Are the corporation specifications presumptuous? It would appear not. For the significant fact is not that corporations are trying to get this kind of wife. The significant fact is that her kind is precisely what our schools and colleges—and U. S. society in general—seem to be giving the corporation.

Let us define terms: we are discussing the wives of the coming generation of management, whose husbands are between twenty-five and forty, and in junior or middle management or with logical aspirations of getting there. There is, of course, no sharp dividing line between age groups, but among older executives there is a strong feeling that this younger generation of wives is the most cooperative the corporation has ever enlisted. "Somehow," says one executive, "they seem to give us so much less trouble than the older ones." "Either the girls are better or the men are marrying better," says another. "But whatever it is with these people, *they get along.*"

Perhaps it is merely that this generation of wives has not yet grown older and more cantankerous. Perhaps. But there is evidence that this group-mindedness is the result of a shift in values more profound than one might suppose. The change is by no means peculiar to the corporation wife, but by the nature of her job she may be the outstanding manifestation of it. And a preview, perhaps, of what is to come.

First, how do the wives conceive their own role? Critical literature has been answering the question rather forcefully, with the result that many Americans (and practically all Europeans) assume that the wife of the American businessman is not only the power behind the scenes but wants to become more so. The picture needs considerable revision. For the striking thing that emerges from wives' comments is the negativeness of the role they sketch. As they explain it, the good wife is good by *not* doing things—by *not* complaining

when her husband works late; by *not* fussing when a transfer is coming up; by *not* engaging in any controversial activity. Moreover, they agree heartily that a good wife can't help a husband as much as a bad wife can hurt one. And the bad wife, clearly, is one who obtrudes too much—whether as a "meddler," a "climber," a "fixer," or, simply, someone who "pushes" her man around.

This conservatism is fairly recent. Slick-magazine fiction, that excellent index of accepted values, documents the shift. As late as the mid-thirties, a plot analysis indicates, stories were full of "dumb" smart girls, manipulating their amiable but often oafish husbands to business success. No longer. In affairs of commerce today's heroines are lovable nitwits, while the husbands, with tousled hair and lopsided grin, definitely run the show. It is still, in short, a man's world.

So, at least, it is to the executive wife. Resolutely anti-feminist, she conceives her role to be that of a "stabilizer"—the keeper of the retreat, the one who rests and rejuvenates the man for the next day's battle. "A man gets so frustrated at the office—it's such a rat race—he should be able to come home to calmness". . ."You make it so he can relax". . ."I try to see that there aren't any problems left around the house."

This stabilizing calls for more than good homemaking and training the kids not to bother Daddy before dinner. Above all, wives emphasize, they have to be good listeners. They describe the job somewhat wryly—they must be "sounding boards," "refueling stations," "wailing walls"—but they speak without resentment. Nurturing the male ego, they seem to feel, is not only a pretty good fulfillment of their own ego but a form of therapy made increasingly necessary by the corporation way of life. Management psychologists couldn't agree more. "Most top executives are very lonely people," as one puts it. "The greatest thing a man's wife can do is to let him unburden the worries he can't confess to in the office."

In addition to listening, she can do some judicious talking. If she is careful about it, she can be a valuable publicity agent for the husband. "In a subtle way," says one executive, "they put in a plug for the husband, they tell things he wouldn't dare tell for fear of seeming immodest." In similar fashion they can humanize him if he's a boss. "About the time I get fed up with the bastard," says a junior executive, "here I am going over to dinner at his house. And she's so nice—she jokes about him, kids him to his face—I figure he can't be so bad after all."

Good, low-key "stabilizing," then, the wife sees as her main task. There is another aspect to her role, however, and it is a good bit less passive. For the good corporation wife must also be a social operator—and when husbands and wives sketch out the personal characteristics of the ideal wife it is the equipment for this role that comes first to their minds. What they ask for, more than any other quality, is gregariousness—or a reasonable facsimile. Here are some of the ways in which they spell it out.

Executive: She should do enough reading to be a good conversationalist . . . Even if she doesn't like opera she should know something about it, so if the conversation goes that way she can hold her own. She has to be able to go with you if you're going to make a speech or get an award, and not be ill at ease.

Executive: The hallmark of the good wife is the ability to put people at their ease.

Wife: The most important thing for an executive's wife is to know everybody's name and something about their family so you can talk to them—also, you've got to be able to put people at their ease.

Executive: Keeping herself so she is comfortable with people on the boss's level is important. I don't think reading and music and that kind of stuff are vital.

Executive: The kind you want is the kind that can have people drop in any time and make a good show of it even if the baby's diapers are lying around.

Wife: It's a very worth-while bunch we have here. Edith Sampson down on Follansbee Road is sort of the intellectual type, but most of the gang are real people.

For the corporation wife, in short, being "sociable" is as important as stabilizing. Like the Army wife (an analogy she detests), she must be a highly adaptable "mixer." In fact, she needs to be even more adaptable than the Army wife, for the social conditions she meets are more varied. One year she may be a member of a company community, another year a branch manager's wife, expected to integrate with the local community—or, in some cases, to become a civic leader; and frequently, as the wife of the company representative, to provide a way station on the route of touring company brass.

As a rule, she is inextricably bound up in the corporation "family," often so much so that her entire behavior—including what and where she drinks—is subtly conditioned by the corporation. "It makes me laugh," says one wife in an eastern city dominated by one corporation. "If we were the kind to follow the Pattern, I'll tell you just what we would do. First, in a couple of years, we'd move out of Ferncrest Village (it's really pretty tacky there, you know). We wouldn't go straight to Eastmere Hills—that would look pushy at this stage of the game; we'd go to the hilly section off Scrubbs Mill Pike. About that time, we'd change from Christ Church to St. Edwards, and we'd start going to the Fortnightlies—it would be a different group entirely. Then, about ten years later, we'd finally build in Eastmere Hills." It just makes her laugh, she says, because that would be the signal to everybody that she had become a wife of the top-brass bracket. Which she probably will.

Few wives are as articulate as that on the social role, but intuitively they are generally superb at it; their antennae are sensitive, and the rules of the game they know by heart. Second nature to the seasoned wife, for example, are the following:

Don't talk shop gossip with the Girls, particularly those who have husbands in the same department.

Don't invite superiors in rank; let them make the first bid.

Don't turn up at the office unless you absolutely have to.

Don't get too chummy with the wives of associates your husband might soon pass on the way up.

Don't be disagreeable to any company people you meet. You never know. . . .

Be attractive. There is a strong correlation between executive success and the wife's appearance. . . .

Be a phone pal of your husband's secretary. Never—repeat, never—get tight at a company party (it may go down in a dossier).

One rule transcends all others: *Don't be too good.* Keeping up with the Joneses is still important; but where in pushier and more primitive times it implied going substantially ahead of the Joneses, today keeping up means just that: keeping up. One can move ahead, yes—but slightly, and the timing must be exquisite. "We will have a grand piano" says one wife, "when we are ready for it"—which is quite different from "when we can afford it." Whatever the move, it must never be openly invidious. Perhaps it is for this reason that the Buick is such a preferred car; it envelops the whole executive spectrum and the jump from a Special to a Super, and from a Super to a Road-master, can be handled with tact.[1]

Neither must one be too outstanding in more personal ways. The good corporation wife does not make her friends uncomfortable by clothes too blatantly chic, references to illustrious forbears, or excessive good breeding. And intellectual pretensions she avoids like the plague. It is interesting to watch one wife rearrange her magazine basket as she primps for callers; almost automatically, she shuffles her *Harper's* and *Atlantic Monthly* beneath the pile. The Girls might not understand.

Are these rules of the game merely the old fact of conformity? In part, yes. But something new has been added. What was once a fact has now become a philosophy. Where people used to like to talk, at least, of "individualism," today's young couple are without hypocrisy on the matter; not only do they concede their group-mindedness, they are outspokenly in favor of it. They blend with the group not because they fear to do otherwise, but because they approve of it.

And in this, they can correctly point out, they are no more than in tune with currents in American thought and pedagogy; from the "group integration" of the progressive schools to the growing emphasis in the universities on group dynamics, human relations, and industrial psychology, the young couple have impressive material at hand with which to rationalize group living as the key to the pursuit of happiness.

Even the fiction they read has picked up the moral. To return to magazine plots a moment: Today, good people simply don't buck the system. In 1935–36 the heroine was quite likely to tell the boss off or do something equally contentious. Rarely now; if she has troubles, she solves them

by patience, understanding, and compromise. She practices human relations.

The net effect is more than the mere Babbittry young couples' frankness so often makes it sound. A "real" person the wife explains, is one "whose satisfactions are not sought selfishly" within oneself, but "with others." Her search, to be sure, includes popularity but it also includes civic activities, P.T.A., and all the intangible satisfactions of *esprit de corps*. Even her tensions are in character; for it is almost an article of faith with her that her deepest personal desires and the values of the group contain no conflict that a little "adjusting" can't fix up. It does not, unfortunately, always work out that way . . . .

College? Here is the *summum bonum*. There are some obvious reasons; because virtually all executives now go to college, the couple in such cases start off with shared values. But corporation people mention a reverse factor almost as much. It is not so important for the wife, they say, to have gone to college: but it is very important not to have *not* gone to college. If she hasn't, corporation people warn, she is prey to an inferiority complex that makes it difficult for her to achieve real poise. Some corporations, accordingly, make it their business to find out whether or not the wife has a degree.

The corporation would seem to have reason for optimism. Since more girls are going to college, the proportion of executives' wives who are college graduates has been steadily increasing. In part, as a result of this, the problem of the out-grown wife appears to be less acute among the younger wives.

And the omens in some other respects would seem as good. The younger wives are afflicted with all of the old problems of adjustment—and some new ones of the corporation's own making—but rarely has there emerged a generation of wives so dedicated to the job of grappling with them. On almost every point of contact—from entertaining to moving across the continent, their background is making them the most tractable material the corporation has ever had.

---

[1] In one eastern steel town, where cars have always been the accepted symbol of rank, this convenient arrangement has been thoroughly disrupted. The Chairman of the Board has a Cadillac—certainly a high enough ceiling. The President, however, has taken to buying Buick Supers, with the result that people in the upper brackets are chafing because it would be unseemly to go higher. Except for the Chairman, accordingly, only the local tradespeople drive Cadillacs and Roadmasters.

Caste and Class in an Industry

Charles S. Johnson

Charles Spurgeon Johnson (1893–   ), sociologist; president, Fisk University. Principal works: with others, *The Negro in Chicago* (1922); *The Negro in American Civilization* (1930), *Shadow of the Plantation* (1934), *The Negro College Graduate* (1936), *Growing Up in the Black Belt* (1941), *Patterns of Negro Segregation* (1943), *Into the Main Stream* (1946), *Education and the Cultural Crisis* (1951).

Considering its unique history, the tobacco industry offers a peculiarly interesting illustration of the character assumed by the class struggle when complicated by racial antagonisms and caste tradition. A class struggle is implicit in the free competition on which capitalism and the capitalistic organization of industry is based. But in the early period of the tobacco industry the classes had all the features and limitations of a caste. New conditions inherent in the industry itself, and changes in the formal status of the Negro workers, have created conditions under which typical economic classes have developed and are now seeking to function. In the tobacco manufacturing industry, with its white and Negro workers, the class alignment, because of the persistence of the caste tradition, has been imperfectly achieved. Social habits and customs change less rapidly than artifacts and the division of labor incidental to the expansion of industry.

A modern industry is too complex and changes too rapidly to sustain a caste system. The progressive substitution of machinery for hand processes has created new tasks and destroyed old and honorable skills. With each advance in machinery there has been an increase in white male and female labor. Lacking the protection of that caste sentiment which preserved to the Negro jobs in which he once seemed to have some sort of vested interest, these workers have found themselves holding only those jobs which were "secured" to them by low wages, disagreeable dust, and by tasks regarded as too heavy for native-born white Americans.

Curiously enough, the existing racial division in work is rationalized by both white and Negro workers in essentially the same terms. A white worker who had come into one of the factory towns some years before from farm labor explained the racial division of labor as something having a biological basis. . . . In like manner, a Negro prizer, doing heavy work, assumed that these jobs fell to Negroes because they alone could sustain them. . . .

If the exigencies of the economic system have given Negroes and whites the common interests of members of the same economic class, traditions supported by the familiar racial fictions and enforced by racial etiquette have continued to maintain the moral isolation of the races. It is the undercurrent of hostility which this isolation of the two groups inevitably fosters and the festering suspicions, which are more or less justified by the use which can be made of this internal conflict by the industry itself, that keep these two groups actively and impotently in conflict.

From "The Conflict of Caste and Class in an American Industry," *American Journal of Sociology*, 42 (1936–37): 55–65, pp. 57–59 quoted. Reprinted by permission.

Organized Industrialists

United States Senate Committee on Education and Labor

This report was prepared under the direction of the subcommittee on Senate Resolution 266 of which Senator Robert M. La Follette, Jr., was chairman and Robert Wohlforth, secretary. Senator Elbert D. Thomas was chairman of the Committee on Education and Labor.

The National Association of Manufacturers is largely financed by a small group of powerful corporations. . . . A much smaller clique of large corporations, not more than 60 in number, have supplied it with active leadership. . . .

With the funds of this group of powerful corporations, the National Association of Manufacturers has flooded the country with biased propaganda directed against organizations of American workingmen and against social legislation adopted by Congress. This propaganda, for the most part unidentified to the public as coming from the National Association of Manufacturers, is reiterated day after day through the means of every channel of public expression, in the press, over the radio, in schools, on billboards, by public speakers, by direct mail, and in pay envelopes. In some cases the National Association of Manufacturers has contrived to arrange for the sponsorship of its propaganda by others, for the purpose of misleading the public into believing that it came from an independent source. Much of this propaganda is intended to influence the public with reference to elections, and, officials of the association have boasted that its propaganda has influenced the political opinions of millions of citizens, and affected their choice of candidates for Federal offices. . . .

The National Association of Manufacturers' campaign of propaganda stems from the almost limitless resources of corporate treasuries. Not individuals but corporations constitute the membership of the association and supply its funds. It is this fact that makes the political aspects of the association's campaign of propaganda a matter of serious concern. In effect the National Association of Manufacturers is a vehicle for spending corporate funds to influence the opinion of the public in its selection of candidates for office. It may be questioned whether such use of the resources of corporate enterprise does not contravene the well established public policy forbidding corporations to make contributions in connection with political elections. The National Association of Manufacturers is to be condemned for cloaking its propaganda in anonymity and for failing clearly to disclose to the public whom it is trying to influence that this lavish propaganda campaign has as its source the National Association of Manufacturers. . . .

Finally, the committee deplores the failure of the National Association of Manufacturers and the powerful corporations which guide its policies to adapt themselves to changing times and to laws which the majority of the people deem wise and necessary.

CROSS REFERENCES TO STANDARD TEXTS *

Barnes, *Society in Transition*, pp. 51, 408–409.
Bernard, *American Community Behavior*, pp. 5, 85, 377, 388–389, Chap. 10.
Bloch, *Disorganization*, Chap. 19.
Cuber and Harper, *Problems of American Society*, Chaps. 12, 23.
Elliott and Merrill, *Social Disorganization*, pp. 6–9, 22–25, 45–47, 55–57, 61–62, 72–75, 105–107, 127–128,

133–135, 139–143, 145–147, 158, 181–183, 198, 404–405, 411–412, 444–445, 460–461, 499–500, 546–547, 639–642.
Gillin, *Social Pathology*, Chap. 21.
——— and others, *Social Problems*, Chap. 3, pp. 59, 118–119.
Landis, *Social Policies in the Making*, pp. 39, 42, 55–56, 95, 210–212, 281–282, 309, 564, Chap. 19.
Merrill and others, *Social Problems*, pp. 34–38.
Mihanovich, *Current Social Problems*, Chaps. 6–7, pp. 441–442.

* For complete bibliographical reference to each text, see page 13.

From *Violations of Free Speech and Rights of Labor* . . . *The National Association of Manufacturers*. 76th Congress, 1st session, Senate Report No. 6, Part 6, Washington: Government Printing Office, 1939, pp. 220–222.

Neumeyer, *Social Problems and the Changing Society*, pp. 139–142, 237.

Nordskog and others, *Analyzing Social Problems*, Chap. 4, pp. 231, 607.

Odum, *American Social Problems*, pp. 154–166, 504.

Phelps and Henderson, *Contemporary Social Problems*, Chap. 13.

Reinhardt and others, *Social Problems and Social Policy*, Chap. 5.

Weaver, *Social Problems*, pp. 53, 465, 543–544.

OTHER BIBLIOGRAPHY

E. L. Anderson, *We Americans: A Study of Cleavage in an American City*, Cambridge: Harvard University Press, 1937.

H. P. Beck, *Men Who Control Our Universities*, New York: King's Crown Press, 1947.

Reinhard Bendix and Seymour Martin Lipset, *Class, Status and Power: A Reader in Social Stratification*, Glencoe, Illinois: Free Press, 1953.

Robert Bierstedt, "An Analysis of Social Power," *American Sociological Review*, 15 (1950): 730–738.

Donald C. Blaisdell and Jane Greverus, "Economic Power and Political Pressures," Temporary National Economic Committee Monograph No. 26, Washington: Government Printing Office, 1941.

Robert A. Brady, *Business as a System of Power*, New York: Columbia University Press, 1943.

A. M. Carr-Saunders and P. A. Wilson, "Professions," *Encyclopaedia of the Social Sciences*, 12 (1934): 476–480.

Richard Centers, *The Psychology of Social Classes*, Princeton: Princeton University Press, 1949.

W. H. Crook, *The General Strike*, Chapel Hill: University of North Carolina Press, 1931.

Allison Davis and R. J. Havighurst, "Social Class and Color Differences in Child-Rearing," *American Sociological Review*, 11 (1946): 698–710.

Kingsley Davis and Wilbert E. Moore, "Some Principles of Stratification," *American Sociological Review*, 10 (1945): 242–249.

Leonard W. Doob, "Poor Whites: A Frustrated Class," Appendix I in John Dollard, *Caste and Class in a Southern Town*, New Haven: Yale University Press, 1937.

G. Franklin Edwards, *The Negro Professional Class*, Glencoe, Illinois: Free Press, 1954.

Evelyn Ellis, "Upward Social Mobility Among Unmarried Career Women," *American Sociological Review*, 17 (1952): 558–563.

Nelson Foote, "Destratification and Restratification: An Editorial Foreword," *American Journal of Sociology*, 58 (1952–53): 325–326.

W. H. Form, "Status Stratification in a Planned Community," *American Sociological Review*, 10 (1945): 605–613.

Carl Joachim Friedrich, "Plutocracy," *Encyclopaedia of the Social Sciences*, 12 (1934): 175–177.

Eli Ginzberg and others, *The Unemployed*, New York: Harper & Bros., 1953.

Walter R. Goldschmidt, "America's Social Classes: Is Equality a Myth?" *Commentary*, 10 (1950): 175–181.

Milton M. Gordon, "Social Class in American Sociology," *American Journal of Sociology*, 55 (1949–50): 262–268.

Llewellyn Gross, "The Use of Class Concepts in Sociological Research," *American Journal of Sociology*, 54 (1948–49): 409–421.

Paul K. Hatt, "Occupation and Social Stratification," *American Journal of Sociology*, 55 (1949–50): 533–543.

J. O. Hertzler, "Some Tendencies Toward a Closed Class System in the United States," *Social Forces*, 30 (1951–52): 313–323.

Stanley Hetzler, "An Investigation of the Distinctiveness of Social Classes," *American Sociological Review*, 18 (1953): 493–497.

E. T. Hiller, *The Strike*, Chicago: University of Chicago Press, 1928.

A. B. Hollingshead, *Elmtown's Youth*, New York: John Wiley & Sons, 1950.

Leo Huberman, *The Labor Spy Racket*, New York: Modern Age, 1937.

A. W. Jones, *Life, Liberty and Property*, Philadelphia: J. B. Lippincott Co., 1941.

Harold Kaufman, "Prestige Classes in a New York Rural Community," Ithaca: Cornell University Agricultural Experiment Station, Memoir No. 260, March 1944.

Arthur Kornhauser, Robert Dubin, and Arthur M. Ross, eds., *Industrial Conflict*, New York: McGraw-Hill Book Co., 1954.

Gerhard Lenski, "American Social Classes: Statistical Strata or Social Groups," *American Journal of Sociology*, 58 (1952–53): 139–144.

Max Lerner, "Vested Interests," *Encyclopaedia of the Social Sciences*, 15 (1935): 240–243.

A. Lindsey, *The Pullman Strike*, Chicago: University of Chicago Press, 1943.

Arthur Livingston, "Gentleman, Theory of the," *Encyclopaedia of the Social Sciences*, 6 (1931): 616–620.

Lewis L. Lorwin, "Class Struggle," *Encyclopaedia of the Social Sciences*, 3 (1930): 538–542.

Ferdinand Lundberg, *America's Sixty Families*, New York: Vanguard Press, 1937.

T. H. Marshall, ed., *Class Conflict and Social Stratification*, Ledbury: Institute of Sociology, Le Play House, 1938.

Kurt Mayer, "The Theory of Social Classes," *Harvard Educational Review* (Summer 1953), pp. 149–167.

C. Wright Mills, "American Business Elite: A Collective Portrait Based on the Dictionary of American

Biography," *Journal of Economic History*, supplement 5 (December 1945): 20–44.

———, *The New Men of Power*, New York: Harcourt, Brace and Co., 1948.

———, *White Collar*, New York: Oxford University Press, 1951.

Paul Mombert, "Class," *Encyclopaedia of the Social Sciences*, 3 (1930): 531–536.

Barrington Moore, Jr., "A Comparative Analysis of the Class Struggle," *American Sociological Review*, 10 (1945): 31–37.

———, "The Relation Between Social Stratification and Social Control," *Sociometry*, 5 (1942): 230–250.

Gaetano Mosca, *The Ruling Class*, transl. by H. D. Kahn, New York: McGraw-Hill Book Co., 1939.

National Resources Committee, *The Structure of the American Economy*, Washington: Government Printing Office, 1939.

Charles Hunt Page, *Class and American Sociology*, New York: Dial Press, 1940.

Omar Pancoast, Jr., *Occupational Mobility*, New York: Columbia University Press, 1941.

S. H. Patterson, *Social Aspects of Industry*, New York: McGraw-Hill Book Co., 1943.

Harold W. Pfautz, "The Current Literature on Social Stratification: Critique and Bibliography," *American Journal of Sociology*, 58 (1952–53): 391–419.

Max Radin, "Status," *Encyclopaedia of the Social Sciences*, 14 (1934): 373–378.

Arthur F. Raper, *Tenants of the Almighty*, New York: Macmillan Co., 1943.

——— and Ira DeA. Reid, *Sharecroppers All*, Chapel Hill: University of North Carolina Press, 1940.

J. A. Ryan, *Distributive Justice*, New York: Macmillan Co., 1942.

George Seldes, *One Thousand Americans*, New York: Boni and Gaer, 1947.

Gideon Sjoberg, "Are American Social Classes Becoming More Rigid?" *American Sociological Review*, 16 (1951): 775–783.

Celia Burns Stendler, *Children of Brasstown*, Urbana: University of Illinois, 1949.

Edwin H. Sutherland, *White Collar Crime*, New York: Dryden Press, 1949.

W. Lloyd Warner, R. J. Havighurst, and M. B. Loeb, *Who Shall Be Educated?* New York: Harper & Bros., 1944.

——— and Paul S. Lunt, *The Social Life of a Modern Community*, New Haven: Yale University Press, 1941.

———, Marchia Meeker, and Kenneth Eells, *Social Class in America*, Chicago: Science Research Associates, 1949.

James West (pseudo.), *Plainville, U.S.A.*, New York: Columbia University Press, 1945.

Clair Wilcox, "Competition and Monopoly in American Industry," Temporary National Economic Committee Monograph No. 21, Washington: Government Printing Office, 1940.

REVIEW QUESTIONS

1. What six social strata have Warner and his associates found in Yankee City?
2. What are the special characteristics of each of these six social strata?
3. How do the Yankee City ethnic minorities fit into the sixfold class system?
4. What do Warner and associates say is happening to American ethnic groups? What do they contend will follow the ethnic "epoch" in American history?
5. What sort of class system is developing in "a prairie town"?
6. What factors have brought about this class system?
7. What influences, according to Angell, make for misunderstandings between classes?
8. What influences help to counteract inter-class misunderstandings?
9. What does Angell propose as ways to diminish inter-class friction?
10. What qualities of Whyte's managerial transients incline him to speculate on the possible "rise of a new and eventually inbred caste"?
11. If, as Whyte indicates, the wives of management are more and more compliant in their group-mindedness, what influence could this have on our class system?
12. Why does Johnson claim that modern industry cannot sustain a caste system?
13. How have advances in machinery changed the Negro-white relationships and the white class structure in factories?
14. What bearing on social problems of class and status has the report of the U. S. Senate Committee on the N.A.M.?

━CHAPTER 20━➔

Race

RACE is a term which refers to physiological differences. It labels the futile efforts once made by anthropologists to divide mankind up into categories, and it now can refer scientifically only to the fact that wide ranges of racial types do occur in the one human race.

Man's racial differentiation is a by-product of his agelong diffusion and wanderings over the face of the earth. Over many centuries pools of human beings, confined by such natural barriers as mountains and seas, developed distinct and somewhat unified characteristics—skin color, hair texture, and the rest. Even in primitive times, however, such barriers did not keep trickles of people from being absorbed back and forth among the differentiating types, and the vast majority of mankind remained racially "in between."

As the transportation revolutions of recent centuries rapidly shrank the world, men of differing racial characteristics ceased to be occasional curiosities. Masses of men of white, yellow, black, and intermediate shades came into contact with each other. While ethnic differences can be erased by assimilation in a relatively brief period of time, racial differences are more persistent. And especially in the United States where the mistreatment of the Negro is a longtime national disgrace, racial distinctions have become the basis for caste discriminations. A caste is especially featured by a taboo on marriage across caste barriers, but it involves various forms of deprivation and exploitation of the submerged caste, as this and other chapters in this book indicate.

Minorities distinguished both by racial and ethnic differences have been persecuted, and the mental mechanism that serves to justify many such persecutions is the scapegoat device. Allport describes how human beings all too often blame their problems on a defenseless minority which they feel they can abuse with impunity. Stonequist's restatement of Park's theory of the marginal man points to problems of racial difference that afflict the racially different themselves. As another writer,* a Negro himself, has put it, "I can conceive of no Negro native to this country who has not, by the age of puberty, been irreparably scarred by the conditions of his life. All over Harlem, Negro boys and girls are growing into stunted maturity, trying desperately to find a place to stand; and the wonder is not that so many are ruined but that so many survive."

As the decades of the twentieth century have gone on, sociologists have given more and more attention to problems of interracial relations. Gordon and Roche sum up vividly and incisively the price we all pay for prejudice in our society with special reference to the Negro. The expert testimony of the thirty social scientists to the U. S. Supreme Court points out the effects of segregation on both minority and majority groups. That their testimony should have borne so much weight in the Court's judicial consideration is an indication of the advances the social sciences have made in recent decades. Fine gives a summary of the findings of the extensive survey of Negro education carried on under the auspices of the Ford Foundation's Fund for the Advancement of Education.

The racially different minorities in this country naturally include more than the Negro even though the Negroes are the largest. Collier reminds us of our long abuse of the Amerind aboriginals—familiarly and inaccurately called the Indians—by telling of recent legislative moves to dissolve federal trusteeship of Indian properties. One of our recent rejections of tenets of decency and democracy in interracial relations was our condemnation of thousands of Americans of Japanese descent to concentration camps—after seizing their property—because of their ancestry. The President's Committee on Civil Rights recounts this shameful story of "guilt by heredity."

---

* James Baldwin, "The Harlem Ghetto: Winter 1948," *Commentary*, 5 (1948): 165–170, p. 170 quoted.

As a careful student * of sociology notes, " 'Racial' differences fail to explain the obvious and profound differences in human societies. Ways of living differ as widely as do those current in China and in Sweden, in the Congo and in Hollywood. The scientific explanation of these differences in social behavior lies in the study of cultural behavior, not in the details of bodily differences." This perspective on race is gradually penetrating the thinking of Americans, and it may eventually help to place the emphasis in human relations more commonly where it belongs: on the worth and capabilities of the individual regardless of race, creed, or ethnic background.

* Douglas G. Haring, *Racial Differences and Human Resemblances*, Syracuse: Syracuse University Book Store, 1946, p. 22.

Scapegoating
Gordon W. Allport*

> *And the goat shall bear upon
> him all their iniquities.*
> —Leviticus 16:22

From the earliest times, among all peoples, there is to be found the notion that guilt and suffering can be transferred to some other being or person. To the primitive mind this transferring of blame and sorrow seems reasonable enough, for the primitive mind commonly confuses the physical with the mental. For example, if a load of wood can be lifted from one man's back to another's, why not a load of guilt or sorrow? The primitive thinker concludes that the shift is not only possible but entirely natural.

Today the transfer is usually from person to person, but in ancient times, a living animal was often chosen. The most famous of these ceremonies is the ritual of the Hebrews, described in the Book of Leviticus. On the Day of Atonement, a live goat was chosen by lot, and the high priest, robed in linen garments, laid both his hands on the goat's head, and confessed over it the iniquities of the children of Israel. The sins of the people having thus been symbolically transferred to the beast, it was taken out into the wilderness and let go. The people felt purged and, for the time being, guiltless.

Everywhere we see our human tendency to revert to this primitive level of thinking and to seek a scapegoat—some object or animal, or more often some luckless human being—who may be saddled with blame for our own misfortunes and misdeeds. "Civilized" people are still primitive in their thinking.

Though an ever present and universal phenomenon, it is especially during times of stress—of war, famine, revolution, depression—that the motivations to scapegoating are strengthened and scapegoating increases. If in ordinary times we have an impulse to "take it out on the dog," in times of severe social tension, this impulse is so greatly magnified that deeds of incredible savagery may result.

I need not tell again the story of the bestial torture and massacre of a large fraction of the Jewish population in Poland and Germany. Such sadistic deeds are almost too revolting for belief, but the unfortunate facts are known; and the facts must be faced.

We say that these violent persecutions are simply an expression of the sadistic Nazi mentality, but if we look closely we see that the Nazis are, in reality, trying to shift a burden of intolerable shame, guilt and frustration from the German people to a convenient goat, in this case selected not by lot but by the unhappy course of history. Illogical though it is, Hitler and his henchmen have ceaselessly placed the blame for the humiliating defeat of 1918 upon the Jews, likewise the blame for the famine that followed the war, for the inflation and subsequent bankruptcy, for the harshness of the Versailles Treaty, for the political turmoil and moral degeneracy of the 1920's, and for all other German misfortunes.

* See identifying note on page 90.
From "Foreword," to *ABC's of Scapegoating* (written by his students in a seminar at Harvard University), Chicago: Central YMCA College, undated, pp. 4–8. Reprinted by permission.

Irritation, shame, and a sense of failure had been smouldering in German bosoms since the first world war. Then, under direction from Hitler, Rosenberg, Streicher, and Goebbels, these fierce emotions became focused upon the Jew, and pent-up savagery overflowed with unspeakable violence.

Such events, we know, have occurred all through the course of history. The victims have always been relatively small minority groups who because of conspicuousness and tradition became the goats saddled with the burden of blame.

It is not necessary to assume that in every case of persecution the victim himself is lily-white in his innocence. History often records provocative acts (or at least defensive and retaliatory conduct) on the part of the victim. But there is in scapegoating always an element of projected, excessive and unwarranted blame. . . .

Prejudice, we know, exists. This prejudice actively manifests itself in discrimination against certain "races" and groups. Proceeding to still lower levels of human nature, we know that scapegoating through aggressive and hostile words and deeds is also prevalent. And occasionally, as in the . . . race riots in Los Angeles and Detroit [in 1943], extreme violence breaks out.

Our mixed population provides fertile soil for prejudice and scapegoating and the strains and irritations of wartime, combined with the confusion of thought that occurs in times like these, augment the difficulty. A public opinion poll revealed that eighty-five per cent of our population accuses one or more of the following groups of profiting selfishly from the war: farmers, Negroes, Jews, foreign-born, Protestants, Catholics, business men, labor-leaders, wealthy people. The seeds of suspicion are already sown. In most of our minds one special group of our fellow Americans is singled out for blame. In place of a sense of national unity, most of us have a feeling of distrust, if not actual hostility.

In the list, the groups most frequently accused are labor-leaders and Jews—precisely the Nazi pattern of slander and attack. We know from other studies that half our population harbors the suspicion that the Jews in this country have undue influence. Many of those who are suspicious are undoubtedly victims of the vague Coughlinite propaganda concerning "international bankers." It is never said that Episcopalians or Quakers or white men have more influence in this country than their numbers warrant, although if the contribution of groups must be proportionate to their size, then these groups surely have "undue influence."

In ordinary times the resiliency of democracy is so great that mixed populations manage to live side by side peacefully enough, even though minor frictions and prejudices exist. Our peril today lies in the fact that our pet prejudices combined with our tendency to fix the blame for our woes upon others, may break over into irrational, degenerative scapegoating, destructive of our chances to win a victory for democracy and a lasting peace of equality and opportunity for all men.

The Problem of the Marginal Man
Everett V. Stonequist

Everett V. Stonequist (1901–   ), professor of sociology and chairman of the department, Skidmore College; chief, Research Division, Office of War Information, 1944–1945. Author of *The Marginal Man* (1937).

Probably the great majority of individuals in the world live and have their being within a single cultural system. Each individual is likely to be born, mature, and die within the boundaries of one tribal or national tradition, learning to communicate in one tongue, developing loyalties to one sovereign government, conforming to the expectations of one moral code, believing in the way of life approved by one religion. The deepest part of his personality—his sentiments, conception of self, style of life, and aspirations, whether articulate or inarticulate, conscious or unconscious

From "The Problem of the Marginal Man," *American Journal of Sociology*, 41 (1935–36): 1–12, pp. 1–3 quoted. Reprinted by permission.

—are formed out of and identified with these more or less harmonious patterns of the social heritage. From the standpoint of material culture it is true that his well-being today is at the mercy of a world-wide economic system; but the elements which make up his personality are formed in a much more restricted system. He is English, French, Japanese, American. This relatively restricted system of non-material culture—of nations and nationality—cannot, of course, escape some inner cultural conflicts in proportion to the degree that it is dynamic. Nevertheless, it has a powerful tendency toward unity, consistency, and harmony, for each national system, resting upon common historical memories, faces a world of other striving national systems, each bound within a framework of governmental institutions, economic interests, and ethnocentric sentiments.

However, largely because the economic system has expanded so much more rapidly than have the other aspects of culture, we find today many individuals growing up in a more complex and less harmonious cultural situation. They are unwittingly initiated into two or more historic traditions, languages, political loyalties, moral codes, and religions. Migration has transplanted individuals and cultures to such an extent that nearly every land and every city is something of a melting-pot of races and nationalities. The individual who grows up in such a situation is likely to find himself faced, perhaps unexpectedly, with problems, conflicts, and decisions peculiar to the melting-pot. This is true particularly of those who are expected to do most of the melting, that is, those who belong to a minority group, or to a group which has an inferior status in the land. The

more powerful or dominant group does not expect to adjust itself to the others; it is the subordinate group which is expected to do the adjusting, conforming, and assimilating—or remain apart.

Some of the members of the subordinate or minority group are able to live their lives within their own cultures, or at least to live in them sufficiently not to be greatly disturbed by the culture of the dominant group. They have a symbiotic rather than a social relationship. Others, however (and the proportion will be small or large depending upon the conditions), find themselves more strongly influenced and attracted by the dominant group. The personality development of such individuals is of interest and significance both to theoretical and practical students of human behavior. Living as they do, in between the two cultures, their personalities and careers are interwoven and linked with both systems. They thus mirror in their own personalities aspects of the two cultures, and especially the *relations* of the two cultures.

We are indebted to Professor Robert E. Park [1] for identifying this personality type, which he has called the "marginal man" and defined as one who is "living and sharing intimately in the cultural life and traditions of two distinct peoples, never quite willing to break, even if he were permitted to do so, with his past and his traditions, and not quite accepted, because of racial prejudice, in the new society in which he now seeks to find a place." [2]

[1] "Human Migration and the Marginal Man," *American Journal of Sociology, 33* (1927–28): 881–893.
[2] *Ibid.,* p. 892.

The Price of Prejudice
Milton M. Gordon and John P. Roche

Milton M. Gordon (1918–   ), assistant professor of sociology, and John P. Roche (1923–   ), associate professor of political science, are both faculty members at Haverford College.

"I'll not take my wife and children South. I grew up in Mobile and I know how the system works—we're just not having any." This sentiment has been echoed many times by Negroes, but the unusual aspect of this reiteration, and the

one which reveals segregation's other face, was that the author of it was white, a Government lawyer who, until released by the new Administration, had spent ten years in New York. Although offered a good job in a Southern city, he

From "Segregation—Two-Edged Sword," *The New York Times Magazine,* (April 25, 1954).

accepted a less remunerative one in New England.

It is, indeed, odd that so little has been said about this consequence of racial segregation. Justifiably, most of the emphasis has been on the unfortunate impact of discrimination and segregation on the Negro community. But it should be remembered that segregation is a two-edged sword that cuts both ways. A white person in a Southern state or municipality that enforces segregation does not have the option of deciding whether or not he wishes to sit in the rear of a bus, attend an educational meeting with Negroes, send his child to a school which enrolls Negro children, or dine in a restaurant with a Negro colleague or friend. He is forced to observe the segregation pattern. Are not his civil rights, too, being violated?

Furthermore, there is persuasive recent evidence from the social sciences to the effect that discrimination and segregation, both the Northern and Southern varieties, produce harmful practical effects for the white majority. The fact of the matter is that, seen in its larger context, racial segregation in the United States constitutes a deprivation of the rights and the welfare of both whites and Negroes, not Negroes alone.

While the Supreme Court, employing a restricted interpretation of the Fourteenth Amendment, has not yet held this interference with the personal liberty of whites and Negroes to be "unconstitutional," * segregation clearly runs against the dictates of the democratic conscience. And the problem is not exclusively a Southern one. The Northern white person, for instance, who wishes to live in a neighborhood composed of individuals of all racial backgrounds finds it exceedingly difficult to do so, especially if he resides in a desirable residential location.

If it should be claimed that the rights of those whites who favor segregation would be violated were segregation to be abolished, it must be pointed out that the fundamental right of any person to choose his own intimate social companions is in no way threatened. The point at issue is the essentially impersonal access of all persons to the general rewards of society in terms of individual merit and general ethical norms, and precisely the right of individuals to effect such intimate social relationships as they personally prefer.

* In Chapter 10, see excerpts from the recent Supreme Court ruling against segregation in the schools.—*Eds.*

Indeed, the fact that those whites who favor segregation insist so vigorously on legal sanctions indicates their perhaps inarticulate recognition that without governmental guarantees, the system would fall of its own weight. As Ralph Bunche has so well pointed out, "An underlying assumption behind the segregation laws has to be that in the absence of such laws many Southern whites would voluntarily associate with Negroes."

Not only does segregation constitute an unmistakable deprivation of the rights and privileges of whites (as well as Negroes) in America, but it also works to the practical disadvantage of the white community. A growing number of whites are aware of the two-edged nature of the sword of segregation and view with dismay the violations of the rights and welfare of all people. A larger proportion, particularly in the South, support or acquiesce in segregation because its harmful consequences for them tend to be concealed and are only gradually becoming apparent, and because historic prejudices becloud and overwhelm the kind of rational thinking which would reveal them most clearly and unmistakably. Furthermore, some whites believe that they are the beneficiaries of "short-run" gains as a result of keeping the Negro "in his place." The larger and "long-run" picture is the more important one, however, and it is this picture which makes apparent the substantial losses to whites arising out of the discriminatory pattern.

For the purpose of this article, four major areas of substantial loss to the white citizens of the United States may be distinguished: the economic, the psychological, the moral, and the international.

(1) **Economic.** *Discrimination and segregation severely restrict the best possible training and use of human skills, lower the potential productive and purchasing power of the nation, make necessary the uneconomic provision of duplicate facilities and add to the taxpayer's social service burden.*

The total cost doubtless runs into the billions annually. In an analysis concerned solely with purchasing power, John E. O'Gara, then vice president and general manager of Macy's, stated several years ago that the net loss for the nation's buying power of not utilizing Negroes at their highest skills amounted to $6 billion. Employment discrimination, he declared, takes away from American business a "no-cost big market right here at home."

When to this deprivation of potential purchasing power is added racial discrimination in housing, the result is the piling up of many Negroes in depressed and blighted areas. The slum conditions thus produced add considerably to the social service burden borne by the entire taxpaying public. In one study of the cost of slums in Cleveland, it was found that the income from taxes on real estate in one such area totaled $225,-000, whereas the costs of public and private social services, including relief, the handling of juvenile offenders, fire-fighting and tax delinquencies came to $1,360,000, a ratio and loss of six to one. . . .

In addition to purely quantitative considerations, there is the qualitative one of waste of leadership and special ability potentials. The research scientist who is potentially equipped to take the final step in the conquest of cancer may have a black or brown or yellow skin. If this potential is shriveled and stunted in a sharecropper's cabin, the peoples of the world, including the whites, are the losers.

(2) Psychological. *In the realm of psychology and personality factors, there is increasing evidence that prejudice and discrimination exact a toll of undesirable consequences from those who discriminate as well as those who are discriminated against.*

Not long ago, a large group of psychologists, sociologists and cultural anthropologists were polled for their opinions on the psychological effect of enforced segregation, even when equal facilities were provided, on both the segregated and the segregating groups. As might perhaps be expected, out of the approximately 500 respondents, 90 per cent expressed the opinion that enforced segregation, even with equal facilities, was detrimental to those at whom the segregation was directed. What may come as more of a surprise to many is that nearly as large a group, 83 per cent, recorded their belief that enforced segregation had detrimental effects on the group which enforced the segregation.

These detrimental effects on the majority group may manifest themselves, as George E. Simpson and J. Milton Yinger, Oberlin College sociologists, have pointed out, in at least two ways. For some persons in our society, who pick up their prejudice from the cultural environment in rather predictable fashion and are not greatly involved emotionally with it, there is posed an internal dilemma between discrimination and the democratic and Hebraic-Christian values of what Gunnar Myrdal has called the American Creed.

On the one hand, such a person is taught that equal treatment for all persons and the brotherhood of man under the Fatherhood of God are the values by which to guide one's conduct. On the other hand, he is exposed to forces which dictate behavior patterns of hostility, superiority and avoidance toward certain minority groups. This provides a setting for internal conflict, tension and feelings of guilt. While it cannot, in the present state of our knowledge, be safely asserted that all prejudiced majority persons in the United States experience this inner conflict, it is entirely likely that at various levels of awareness and consciousness, many do.

Many psychologists have come to the conclusion that the more deeply felt and rabid types of group prejudice found in some people are the product of rather complex processes of personality functioning which operate somewhat as follows: These people have met with severe frustrating experiences in life; these frustrations have generated a reservoir of "free-floating aggression." In many cases, it seems dangerous or impossible to them to release this aggression in action against the source of the frustration, since this source may be too powerful, may be defined as a loved one or a member of the "in-group," or may be unknown. The hostility may then be "displaced" onto a group which is socially defined as weak and undesirable.

The great harm this kind of prejudice does to the person who carries it is that it prevents him from sizing up his problems realistically and meeting them constructively. If racial and religious prejudice functions for some people as a substitute for a rational view of self and surroundings, then it is causing immense harm, not only to the minority group, but to those of the majority who tilt at shadows while the true sources of their unhappiness or insecurity go unchallenged.

(3) Moral. *The gap between creed and deed in American life with regard to racial and other forms of group discrimination constitutes a weakening of the moral tone of America and doubtless contributes to the flabbiness of moral codes in other important areas.*

We have mentioned above the clash of the Hebraic-Christian and democratic values of brotherhood and equality with the values and patterns of prejudice which make up the daily round of existence in the United States. This is the clash which Myrdal, in his monumental study of the American Negro, has called "An American Dilemma." The consequences of this dilemma are that American life functions in the constant shadow of a patent evasion of a major moral imperative. The child growing up in such a culture is faced with the perpetual reminder that creeds are one thing, deeds another; and that the adult world, to a large degree, countenances this hypocrisy.

But the results of such a learning process may easily be applied to other areas of life. The "five-percenter," the grafter, the political opportunist who uses truth and falsehood as equal weapons of aggression—and, what is even worse, the atmosphere of half-approving cynicism in many areas of American life which allows these types to fatten and prosper—all these have a logical relationship to the point of view which affirms that "ideals of racial equality are all right in their place, but——."

The conscience of America is, of course, not entirely dormant on the issue of prejudice and discrimination. Many men and women of goodwill are working to bring ideals and behavior into harmony. The larger picture, however, still represents a tragic hiatus. If it did not, even in the North racial segregation in housing—to take one instance—would end tomorrow. From one point of view, the Negro may be said to have won a bitter moral victory over the whites—he has forced them, in their attempted justification of racial discrimination, to sell their ideals short.

(4) International. *At a time when the free nations are engaged in a world-wide struggle with the pseudo-egalitarian Soviet Union, it seems hardly necessary to make the point that, in international affairs, the Negro situation is America's Achilles' heel.*

One of the writers recently returned from western Europe, where he found, to his surprise, that the first question on the lips of young democrats was not "What about McCarthyism?" but "What about the future of the Negro in America?" In this connection, one might quote the statement of former Assistant Secretary of State A. A. Berle that "It is no exaggeration, I think, to say that the habit of race discrimination practiced in considerable parts of the United States is the greatest single danger to the foreign relations of the United States . . ."; or the even more recent assertion of Chester Bowles, arising out of his experience as Ambassador to India: "No American returning from Asia can doubt that the status of the American Negro is a key to our country's relationship with the awakening nations of Asia and Africa."

In short, the actions of those American whites who have so far supported segregation as a public policy are working to the harm of the nation in the international arena. The advocacy of democracy requires that those who press it practice it.

Racial segregation, we have said, violates the rights and injures the welfare of whites as well as Negroes. Nothing in the preceding remarks is to be interpreted as suggesting that the rights and welfare of whites, even those opposed to segregation, should be considered as of greater moment than the rights and welfare of Negroes at whom the segregation is fundamentally directed.

The final victory over discrimination and segregation, when it comes, will be a victory for man entire. Nevertheless, it may be of value to have taken a somewhat unfamiliar stance and examined the imposition and effect of segregation on the white majority in American society. For then one catches a revealing and sobering glance at segregation's other face.

The Effects of Segregation: A Social Science Statement to the United States Supreme Court

On May 17, 1954, in two historic decisions, the United States Supreme Court ruled against racial segregation in the nation's public schools.* In those decisions, the Court for the first time based findings upon sociological and social psychological research. It gave especial attention to the testimony of a group of thirty-two social scientists on the effects of segregation upon personality development. Authorities in sociology, anthropology, psychology, and psychiatry, who had worked in the area of American race relations, drafted and signed a statement which represented a summary of the best available scientific evidence and their consensus with respect to the issues involved. A considerable portion of that statement appears here.

In dealing with the question of the effects of segregation, it must be recognized that these effects do not take place in a vacuum, but in a social context. The segregation of Negroes and of other groups in the United States takes place in a social milieu in which "race" prejudice and discrimination exist. It is questionable in the view of some students of the problem whether it is possible to have segregation without substantial discrimination. Myrdal [1] states: "Segregation . . . is financially possible and, indeed, a device of economy only as it is combined with substantial discrimination" (p. 629). The imbeddedness of segregation in such a context makes it difficult to disentangle the effects of segregation per se from the effects of the context. Similarly, it is difficult to disentangle the effects of segregation from the effects of a pattern of social disorganization commonly associated with it and reflected in high disease and mortality rates, crime and delinquency, poor housing, disrupted family life and general substandard living conditions. We shall, however, return to this problem after consideration of the observable effects of the total social complex in which segregation is a major component.

At the recent Mid-century White House Conference on Children and Youth, a fact-finding report on the effects of prejudice, discrimination and segregation on the personality development of children was prepared as a basis for some of the deliberations.[2] This report brought together the available social science and psychological studies which were related to the problem of how racial and religious prejudices influenced the development of a healthy personality. It highlighted the fact that segregation, prejudices and discriminations, and their social concomitants potentially damage the personality of all children—the children of the majority group in a somewhat different way than the more obviously damaged children of the minority group.

The report indicates that as minority group children learn the inferior status to which they are assigned—as they observe the fact that they are almost always segregated and kept apart from others who are treated with more respect by the society as a whole—they often react with feelings of inferiority and a sense of personal humiliation. Many of them become confused about their own personal worth. On the one hand, like all other human beings they require a sense of personal dignity; on the other hand, almost nowhere in the larger society do they find their own dignity as human beings respected by others. Under these conditions, the minority group child is thrown into a conflict with regard to his feelings

[1] Myrdal, G., *An American Dilemma*, 1944.

[2] Clark, K. B., *Effect of Prejudice and Discrimination on Personality Development*, Fact Finding Report, Mid-century White House Conference on Children and Youth, Children's Bureau, Federal Security Agency, 1950 (mimeographed).

* See Chapter 10 for excerpts from the Court's decisions.

From "Appendix to Appellants' Briefs, The Effects of Segregation and the Consequences of Desegregation: A Social Science Statement," in the cases of Oliver Brown, *et al., vs.* Board of Education of Topeka, Kansas, *et al.;* Harry Briggs, Jr., *et al., vs.* Members of Board of Trustees of School District No. 22, Clarendon County, S. C., *et al.;* and Dorothy E. Davis, *et al., vs.* County School Board of Prince Edward County, Virginia, *et al.,* cases numbered respectively 8, 101, and 191, October Term, 1952, pp. 3–11, 18–19.

about himself and his group. He wonders whether his group and he himself are worthy of no more respect than they receive. This conflict and confusion leads to self-hatred and rejection of his own group.

The report goes on to point out that these children must find ways with which to cope with this conflict. Not every child, of course, reacts with the same patterns of behavior. The particular pattern depends upon many interrelated factors, among which are: the stability and quality of his family relations; the social and economic class to which he belongs; the cultural and educational background of his parents; the particular minority group to which he belongs; his personal characteristics, intelligence, special talents, and personality pattern.

Some children, usually of the lower socio-economic classes, may react by overt aggressions and hostility directed toward their own group or members of the dominant group.[3] Anti-social and delinquent behavior may often be interpreted as reactions to these racial frustrations. These reactions are self-destructive in that the larger society not only punishes those who commit them, but often interprets such aggressive and anti-social behavior as justification for continuing prejudice and segregation.

Middle class and upper class minority group children are likely to react to their racial frustrations and conflicts by withdrawal and submissive behavior. Or, they may react with compensatory and rigid conformity to the prevailing middle class values and standards and an aggressive determination to succeed in these terms in spite of the handicap of their minority status.

The report indicates that minority group children of all social and economic classes often react with a generally defeatist attitude and a lowering of personal ambitions. This, for example, is reflected in a lowering of pupil morale and a depression of the educational aspiration level among minority group children in segregated schools. In producing such effects, segregated schools impair

the ability of the child to profit from the educational opportunities provided him.

Many minority group children of all classes also tend to be hypersensitive and anxious about their relations with the larger society. They tend to see hostility and rejection even in those areas where these might not actually exist.

The report concludes that while the range of individual differences among members of a rejected minority group is as wide as among other peoples, the evidence suggests that all of these children are unnecessarily encumbered in some ways by segregation and its concomitants.

With reference to the impact of segregation and its concomitants on children of the majority group, the report indicates that the effects are somewhat more obscure. Those children who learn the prejudices of our society are also being taught to gain personal status in an unrealistic and non-adaptive way. When comparing themselves to members of the minority group, they are not required to evaluate themselves in terms of the more basic standards of actual personal ability and achievement. The culture permits and, at times, encourages them to direct their feelings of hostility and aggression against whole groups of people the members of which are perceived as weaker than themselves. They often develop patterns of guilt feelings, rationalizations and other mechanisms which they must use in an attempt to protect themselves from recognizing the essential injustice of their unrealistic fears and hatreds of minority groups.[4]

The report indicates further that confusion, conflict, moral cynicism, and disrespect for authority may arise in majority group children as a consequence of being taught the moral, religious and democratic principles of the brotherhood of man and the importance of justice and fair play by the same persons and institutions who, in their support of racial segregation and related practices, seem to be acting in a prejudiced and discriminatory manner. Some individuals may attempt to resolve this conflict by intensifying their hostility toward the minority group. Others may react by guilt feelings which are not necessarily reflected in more humane attitudes toward the minority group. Still others react by developing an unwholesome, rigid, and uncritical idealization of all authority figures—their parents, strong political and economic leaders. As described in *The*

[3] Brenman, M., The Relationship Between Minority Group Identification in A Group of Urban Middle Class Negro Girls, *J. Soc. Psychol.*, 1940, *11*, 171–197; Brenman, M., Minority Group Membership and Religious, Psychosexual and Social Patterns in A Group of Middle-Class Negro Girls, *J. Soc. Psychol,* 1940, *12*, 179–196; Brenman, M., Urban Lower-Class Negro Girls, *Psychiatry*, 1943, *6*, 307–324; Davis, A., The Socialization of the American Negro Child and Adolescent, *J. Negro Educ.*, 1939, *8*, 264–275.

[4] Adorno, T. W.; Frenkel-Brunswik, E.; Levinson, D. J.; Sanford, R. N., *The Authoritarian Personality*, 1951.

Authoritarian Personality,[5] they despise the weak, while they obsequiously and unquestioningly conform to the demands of the strong whom they also, paradoxically, subconsciously hate.

With respect to the setting in which these difficulties develop, the report emphasized the role of the home, the school, and other social institutions. Studies [6] have shown that from the earliest school years children are not only aware of the status differences among different groups in the society but begin to react with the patterns described above.

Conclusions similar to those reached by the Mid-century White House Conference Report have been stated by other social scientists who have concerned themselves with this problem. The following are some examples of these conclusions:

Segregation imposes upon individuals a distorted sense of social reality.[7]

Segregation leads to a blockage in the communications and interaction between the two groups. Such blockages tend to increase mutual suspicion, distrust and hostility.[8]

Segregation not only perpetuates rigid stereotypes and reinforces negative attitudes toward members of the other group, but also leads to the development of a social climate within which violent outbreaks of racial tensions are likely to occur.[9]

We return now to the question, deferred earlier, of what it is about the total society complex of which segregation is one feature that produces the effects described above—or, more precisely, to the question of whether we can justifiably conclude that, as only one feature of a complex social setting, segregation is in fact a significantly contributing factor to these effects.

To answer this question, it is necessary to bring to bear the general fund of psychological and sociological knowledge concerning the role of various environmental influences in producing feelings of inferiority, confusions in personal roles, various types of basic personality structures and the various forms of personal and social disorganization.

On the basis of this general fund of knowledge, it seems likely that feelings of inferiority and doubts about personal worth are attributable to living in an underprivileged environment only insofar as the latter is itself perceived as an indicator of low social status and as a symbol of inferiority. In other words, one of the important determinants in producing such feelings is the awareness of social status difference. While there are many other factors that serve as reminders of the differences in social status, there can be little doubt that the fact of enforced segregation is a major factor.[10]

This seem to be true for the following reasons among others: (1) because enforced segregation results from the decision of the majority group without the consent of the segregated and is commonly so perceived; and (2) because historically segregation patterns in the United States were developed on the assumption of the inferiority of the segregated.

In addition, enforced segregation gives official recognition and sanction to these other factors of the social complex, and thereby enhances the effects of the latter in creating the awareness of social status differences and feelings of inferiority.[11] The child who, for example, is compelled to attend a segregated school may be able to cope with ordinary expressions of prejudice by regarding the prejudiced person as evil or misguided; but he cannot readily cope with symbols of authority, the full force of the authority of the State—the school or the school board, in this instance—in the same manner. Given both the ordinary expression of prejudice and the school's policy of segregation, the former takes on greater force and seemingly becomes an official expression of the latter.

Not all of the psychological traits which are

[5] Adorno, T. W.; Frenkel-Brunswik, E.; Levinson, D. J.; Sanford, R. N., *The Authoritarian Personality,* 1951.

[6] Clark, K. B. & Clark, M. P., Emotional Factors in Racial Identification and Preference in Negro Children, *J. Negro Educ.,* 1950, *19,* 341–350; Clark, K. B. & Clark, M. P., Racial Identification and Preference in Negro Children, *Readings in Social Psychology,* Ed. by Newcomb & Hartley, 1947; Radke, M.; Trager, H; Davis, H., Social Perceptions and Attitudes of Children, *Genetic Psychol. Monog.,* 1949, *40,* 327–447; Radke, M.; Trager, H.; Children's Perceptions of the Social Role of Negroes and Whites, *J. Psychol.,* 1950, *29,* 3–33.

[7] Reid, Ira, What Segregated Areas Mean; Brameld, T., Educational Cost, *Discrimination and National Welfare,* Ed. by MacIver, R. M., 1949.

[8] Frazier, E., *The Negro in the United States,* 1949; Krech, D. & Crutchfield, R. S., *Theory and Problems of Social Psychology,* 1948; Newcomb, T., *Social Psychology,* 1950.

[9] Lee, A. McClung and Humphrey, N. D., *Race Riot,* 1943.

[10] Frazier, E., *The Negro in the United States,* 1949; Myrdal, G., *An American Dilemma,* 1944.

[11] Reid, Ira, What Segregated Areas Mean, *Discrimination and National Welfare,* Ed. by MacIver, R. M., 1949.

commonly observed in the social complex under discussion can be related so directly to the awareness of status differences—which in turn is, as we have already noted, materially contributed to by the practices of segregation. Thus, the low level of aspiration and defeatism so commonly observed in segregated groups is undoubtedly related to the level of self-evaluation; but it is also, in some measure, related among other things to one's expectations with regard to opportunities for achievement and, having achieved, to the opportunities for making use of these achievements. Similarly, the hypersensitivity and anxiety displayed by many minority group children about their relations with the larger society probably reflects their awareness of status differences; but it may also be influenced by the relative absence of opportunities for equal status contact which would provide correctives for prevailing unrealistic stereotypes.

The preceding view is consistent with the opinion stated by a large majority (90%) of social scientists who replied to a questionnaire concerning the probable effects of enforced segregation under conditions of equal facilities. This opinion was that, regardless of the facilities which are provided, enforced segregation is psychologically detrimental to the members of the segregated group.[12]

Similar considerations apply to the question of what features of the social complex of which segregation is a part contribute to the development of the traits which have been observed in majority group members. Some of these are probably quite closely related to the awareness of status differences, to which, as has already been pointed out, segregation makes a material contribution. Others have a more complicated relationship to the total social setting. Thus, the acquisition of an unrealistic basis for self-evaluation as a consequence of majority group membership probably reflects fairly closely the awareness of status differences. On the other hand, unrealistic fears and hatreds of minority groups, as in the case of the converse phenomenon among minority group members, are probably significantly influenced as well by the lack of opportunities for equal status contact.

With reference to the probable effects of segregation under conditions of equal facilities on majority group members, many of the social scientists who responded to the poll in the survey cited above felt that the evidence is less convincing than with regard to the probable effects of such segregation on minority group members, and the effects are possibly less widespread. Nonetheless, more than 80% stated it as their opinion that the effects of such segregation are psychologically detrimental to the majority group members.[13]

It may be noted that many of these social scientists supported their opinions on the effects of segregation on both majority and minority groups by reference to one or another or to several of the following four lines of published and unpublished evidence.[14] First, studies of children throw light on the relative priority of the awareness of status differentials and related factors as compared to the awareness of differences in facilities. On this basis, it is possible to infer some of the consequences of segregation as distinct from the influence of inequalities of facilities. Second, clinical studies and depth interviews throw light on the genetic sources and causal sequences of various patterns of psychological reaction; and, again, certain inferences are possible with respect to the effects of segregation *per se*. Third, there actually are some relevant but relatively rare instances of segregation with equal or even superior facilities, as in the cases of certain Indian reservations. Fourth, since there are inequalities of facilities in racially and ethnically homogeneous groups, it is possible to infer the kinds of effects attributable to such inequalities in the absence of effects of segregation and, by a kind of subtraction to estimate the effects of segregation *per se* in situations where one finds both segregation and unequal facilities. . . .

The problem with which we have here attempted to deal is admittedly on the frontiers of scientific knowledge. Inevitably, there must be some differences of opinion among us concerning the conclusiveness of certain items of evidence, and concerning the particular choice of words and placement of emphasis in the preceding statement. We are nonetheless in agreement that this statement is substantially correct and justified by the evidence, and the differences among us, if any, are of a relatively minor order and would not materially influence the preceding conclusions.

[12] Deutscher, M. and Chein, I., The Psychological Effects of Enforced Segregation: A Survey of Social Science Opinion, *J. Psychol.*, 1948, 26, 259–287.

[13] Deutscher, M. and Chein, I., The Psychological Effects of Enforced Segregation: A Survey of Social Science Opinion, *J. Psychol.*, 1948, 26, 259–287.

[14] Chein, I., What Are the Psychological Effects of Segregation Under Conditions of Equal Facilities?, *International J. Opinion and Attitude Res.*, 1949, 2, 229–234.

Floyd H. Allport
Gordon W. Allport
Charlotte Babcock,
    M.D.
Viola W. Bernard,
    M.D.
Jerome S. Bruner
Hadley Cantril
Isidor Chein

Kenneth B. Clark
Mamie P. Clark
Stuart W. Cook
Bingham Dai
Allison Davis
Else Frenkel-Brunswik
Noel P. Gist
Daniel Katz
Otto Klineberg

David Krech
Alfred McClung Lee
R. M. MacIver
Robert K. Merton
Gardner Murphy
Theodore M. New-
    comb
Robert Redfield
Ira DeA. Reid

Arnold M. Rose
Gerhart Saenger
R. Nevitt Sanford
S. Stansfeld Sargent
M. Brewster Smith
Samuel A. Stouffer
Wellman Warner
Robin M. Williams

Book Digest: Harry S. Ashmore's "The Negro and the Schools"

Benjamin Fine

Benjamin Fine (1905–   ), education editor of *The New York Times*. Chief works: *A Giant of the Press* (1933), *Educational Publicity* (1943), *Democratic Education* (1945), *Our Children Are Cheated* (1947), *Opportunities in Teaching* (1952).

Despite the efforts made in recent years by the South to improve Negro education, a substantial gap still exists between the schooling received by Negro and white children.

Measured in terms of physical facilities, curricula, school libraries, teacher supervision and financial support, the white pupils have superior educational opportunities.

However, education in the South is inferior to that in the rest of the country. This is true even though the South spends a greater proportion of its income for schools than does any other section.

These conclusions are reached by the Ford Foundation's Fund for the Advancement of Education in a report on school segregation. Fifty educators, economists and sociologists took part in the survey, believed to be the most intensive study of Negro education ever undertaken in this country.

The 228-page report, "The Negro and the Schools," was published yesterday. It was prepared by Harry S. Ashmore, executive editor of The Arkansas Gazette.

The Supreme Court has before it * five cases seeking to eliminate pupil segregation, but even

if it outlaws separate schools for Negro and white children the immediate gains will not be promising, the report declares.

Underlying Problems Cited

A reshuffling of the South's school children, permitting Negro pupils to go to white schools, would not solve the pressing problems of inadequate educational facilities, it adds, saying that "the same general deficiencies in physical facilities, teacher training, curricula and the like would exist."

Although abstract justice might be achieved by ending segregation, in that the deficit would fall evenly upon members of both races, "the over-all standard of public education would not be materially improved," the report suggests. The South is only now reaching the point where there are enough classrooms and enough teachers to meet the minimum demand of its children for education, it is added.

"There has been discrimination against Negroes, it is true," the report says, "but it could have been corrected only by pouring additional money into the total system or by lowering the standards of white schools. If at any point in the past discrimination had been wiped out by total integration the effect would have been that some

---

* See Chapter 10 for the Supreme Court's decisions against segregation in the schools.—*Eds.*

From *The New York Times* (Sunday, May 16, 1954), p. 78.

Negroes would have gone to better schools and some whites to worse."

Among the findings in the report are these:

Although the South ranks far below the other regions of the United States in terms of per capita income, it ranks well above most of the rest of the country in terms of the proportion of its income it has been spending for the education of its children in public schools.

From 1940 to 1952 expenditures per pupil in Southern schools increased more than three-fold. Every state in the South showed a substantial increase.

The disparity between white and Negro education in the South is much greater in rural areas than in metropolitan areas.

By 1952 the gap between the average number of years of college training received by white and Negro teachers in the South had been virtually closed. The gap between the salaries of white and Negro teachers in the South is rapidly closing.

One of the gaps between white and Negro education in the South that has remained wide is that between the number of books in the libraries of white and Negro schools. The number of books per pupil in the libraries in Negro schools in five Southern states was considerably less than half the number for the white schools.

The report asserts that the period since 1940 has seen the South exert its greatest efforts in behalf of public education and it is giving to Negro children the largest share of the total outlay they have ever known.

Expenditure Comparisons

In 1951–52, thirteen Southern states spent $1,-200,000,000 for school operations, nearly four times the expenditures for 1939–40, according to the report, and $220,000,000 went for Negro schools. When these figures are adjusted to offset the effects of inflation, it is noted, the operational expenditures for both races in 1951–52 was nearly twice as great as in the pre-war years.

The statistics cover Alabama, Arkansas, Florida, Georgia, Kentucky, Louisiana, Mississippi, North Carolina, Oklahoma, South Carolina, Tennessee, Texas and Virginia. The report says that, over and above operating expenditures, these states spent $315,000,000 for school construction and maintenance in 1951–52—eight times the amount spent in 1939–40. Between 1940 and 1952 the total value of school buildings in these states rose from $1.2 billion to more than $3 billion, the report adds,

and $65,000,000 to $70,000,000 of the capital expenditures in 1951–52 went into Negro schools and equipment, for the first time approximating the 25 per cent portion of Negro attendance.

Despite these accelerated efforts, the report declares, the differential between white and Negro education in the South has remained large.

The gap between school expenditures for whites and Negroes has been narrowed, the report says, but in 1951–52 it was still wide, $115 per Negro pupil against $165 per white pupil. In federally-aided school lunchrooms almost twice as much was spent in serving each white child, it is added, the difference being $8 a year.

The general disparity between white and Negro schools in the South has variation in the inequalities between urban and rural schools, according to the report. In every state, it asserts, there are counties in which the best white schools by any standard of comparison are inferior to the worst Negro schools in the larger cities. The educational problems of the rural South have been increased, it is added, by recent population trends, it being noted that the decade after 1940 there was a population loss of 4,200,000 in the farm areas of thirteen states.

Rural School Needs Acute

The South's rural schools have only begun to scratch the surface of the accumulated deficiencies, the report asserts, even though the proportion of state funds channeled to them through equalization programs has risen sharply. The recent statistics, according to the report, show that in instruction expenditures per pupil in metropolitan and rural counties a gap had widened from $20 to $44 and that in capital outlay a gap had gone from $2 to $37.

The legal drive for equalization of Negro facilities has already had a sharp impact upon the whole of the Southern educational structure, the report declares, and along with this has come the less dramatic but equally persistent pressure to close the gap between rural and urban schools for the children of both races. However, the report points out, there are districts where local school taxes would have to be doubled if the racial discrepancy in per pupil expenditures was to be wiped out at a stroke.

Besides the task of replacing sub-standard schools for both races, the South is faced with the urgent need of providing additional classrooms to accommodate net additions to its school population. The report estimates that by 1962 the South's average daily school attendance will reach 9,100,000, an increase of 16 per cent over that of the current school year. The region's building program is already subject to the special pressures created by the shift in population from rural to urban areas, the report says, commenting:

"This brings about a greater demand for new facilities than even the rapid increase in attendance would indicate, with new consolidated structures required in rural areas of declining population while new buildings must also be built in the growing metropolitan suburbs. It is estimated that the cost of new facilities—quite apart from the cost of eliminating the present capital deficit for both races—would be about $1.3 billion."

Southern educators have recognized, the report declares, that the gap between white and Negro schools is only one aspect of the region's school problem, that there is no way by which it can be considered apart from the overall deficiencies of the school system.

To meet its growing school needs, for white as well as Negro schools, the South might need some form of Federal aid to education, the report suggests. In his 1954 State of the Union Message, the report notes, President Eisenhower endorsed the principle of Federal aid for school construction.

Referring to the migration of Negroes from the South, the report says that problems arise even where segregation is not legally enforced. Educational segregation in the non-South has been more the product of residential patterns than of law, the report observes, but there is abundant evidence that many school administrators have adopted segregation as a conscious policy without formal sanction and in defiance of the statutes.

Such practices as gerrymandering of school districts, encouraging "voluntary" choice of separate schools by Negro pupils, careful regulating of transfer permits and other comparable administrative arrangements have been common, the report asserts.

In recent years, however, there has been a strong counter trend, according to the report. In some of the border states, laws prescribing or permitting some degree of educational segregation have been repealed or liberalized, it adds, and in other states, where the law has never condoned segregation, legal and administrative action has been directed toward elimination of the separate pattern.

A review of twenty-five communities that had recently made, or were in the process of making, transition from segregation to integration in their public schools, indicates that little difficulty is experienced from the public, the report declares. The only incidents of disorder found, it notes, were in Cairo, the southernmost city of Illinois, and "this is hardly surprising, since the history of the old river town often has been marked by violence, corruption and, in recent years, economic blight."

The matter of integrating school faculties is asserted to be generally regarded as more of a problem than that of mixing classes. In many communities school authorities who have experienced no serious difficulty in admitting Negroes to formerly all-white schools expressed the fear, the report says, that white parents would not tolerate Negro teachers for their children. However, the report found that whenever there had been a well-planned program to "sell" integration to the community it had succeeded.

New Jersey is cited in the report as a notable example of a situation in which a well-staffed state agency made it its business to work closely with communities that had long practiced segregation and appeared resistant to compulsory change. The change was required by the new state Constitution. Although New Jersey's Division Against Discrimination was armed with the power to withhold state funds, and even to bring misdemeanor charges against school officials who refused to comply, the report records, it accomplished the integration of forty formerly-segregated school districts without invoking these powers in any instance.

"Massive Change" Begun

The report, observing that the South is moving into a new era, suggests that there is abundant evidence that a "massive change" is taking place. The economic time lag which kept the region behind the great American industrial march is being wiped out, the report declares. The South is still sending its sons out to seek opportunity in other regions, it is remarked, but it is receiving a substantial number of managerial migrants to operate its new factories and these are bringing with them national social and political concepts.

"All in all, the cultural, political and economic isolation which is necessary to the preservation of the region's special identity is breaking down," the report declares. "Southerners themselves are speeding the process in many ways, whether or not they are always pleased with the results.

"In the long sweep of history the public school cases before the Supreme Court may be written down as the point at which the South cleared the last turning in the road to reunion—the point at which finally, and under protest, the region gave up its peculiar institutions and accepted the prevailing standards of the nation at large as the legal basis for its relationship with its minority race.

"This would not in itself bring about any great shift in Southern attitudes, nor even any far-reaching immediate changes in the pattern of biracial education. But it would redefine the goal the Southern people, white and Negro, are committed to seek in the way of democracy."

Indian Takeaway
John Collier

John Collier (1884–   ), professor emeritus of sociology and anthropology, City College of New York; United States Commissioner of Indian Affairs, 1933–1945; president of the Institute of Ethnic Affairs. Principal works: *The Indians of the Americas* (1947), *American Colonial Record* (1947), *Patterns and Ceremonials of the Indians of the Southwest* (1949).

The United States is trustee for Indian properties worth tens of billions of dollars. Further, through treaties and other bilateral compacts it is trustee over the political, social, and cultural institutions and group enterprises of the several hundred Indian groups. The Administration and Congress are driving toward the destruction of the trusteeship obligation, after a preliminary costly perversion of it, and thereby toward turning over the Indian properties to whites. In justice it must be stated that this jettisoning of the national obligation toward Indians was begun under Dillon S. Myer, Commissioner of Indian Affairs under Truman. Since the Eisenhower Administration took over, the process has been expedited almost frantically. Comprehensively, the facts are these:

The 460,000 Indians in the United States are citizens, having all the rights and duties of citizens, with one perilous exception. Congress, in Indian matters, exercises a plenary authority. For a century and three-quarters Indian life has been organized within a framework of treaties, agreements, and legislation. No constitutional inhibition can say "Thou shalt not" if Congress acts unilaterally to destroy the Indian political, economic, and cultural organizations formed and developed within the bilateral federal-Indian relationship. And this is what Congress, under the Administration's leadership, is now doing. The demolition goes on behind a smoke screen of fabrications.

Of these fabrications the central one is the denial, through word and action, of the historical basis of the Indian-government relationship. The second is the assumption that the Indians need to be forced to become full and equal citizens—which they already are—and therefore that the structures they have built for mutual aid, self-protection, self-regulation, and economic advancement must be destroyed through administrative or legislative action. The third is that the Indians have been consulted and that they want this havoc wrought on themselves. Now to some of the details.

Just before Congress recessed at the end of July, 1953, a bill was rushed to passage without hearings on its essential provision. That bill became Public Law 280. Signing it, President Eisenhower lamented it as "most un-Christian" and voiced the hope that a future Congress would amend its —and his—errors. There has been no amendment. This Public Law 280 authorizes any state government, in its own discretion, to substitute its own law for federal Indian law and its own codes for the Indian tribal codes.

In the session of Congress recently adjourned the Interior Department pressed its onset, this time not through an "omnibus" bill but through numerous separate bills purportedly dealing with local situations. An example is Senate bill 2745, now signed by President Eisenhower, directed at the Indians of the Klamath reservation in Oregon. This law forcibly fee-patents—that is, re-

From "Indian Takeaway: Betrayal of a Trust," *The Nation*, 179: 14 (October 2, 1954): 290–291.

moves from trusteeship status—all individually owned Klamath lands and authorizes any enrolled Klamath member to force the tribe to sell its corporate holdings in order to buy him out; it also brings to an early end federal supervision of the immense timber operation in the Klamath forest. Here, for once, the truth came out from the Interior Department—that the termination might result "in abandonment of sustained-yield management presently enforced by the federal government" and that "accelerated cutting would result eventually in serious injury to the entire economy of the Klamath basin."

The Klamath action is a massive one, as is the comparable Menominee, Wisconsin, action now also made law by President Eisenhower. A law directed toward four small bands of Utah Indians will have a statistically infinitesimal effect but is massive as to precedent and policy and representative as to method. These 177 full-blood Paiutes are owners, as groups, of 45,000 acres of poor land believed rich in subsurface oil and minerals. Entitled by law to federal aid and protection, these Paiutes have not been receiving it; hence the Watkins bill (Senate 2670) provided that hereafter they should not receive federal aid and protection. Congress and the public were told that these groups had been fully consulted and by implication had indorsed the bill. In fact, all but one of the groups have officially objected to the measure. Search of the hearings and reports reveal nothing regarding the adequacy of consultation. The only indorsement of the bill was wrung from a minority of one of the groups, admittedly counseled by the representative of an oil company which "desired to negotiate a lease without going through the procedure" of competitive bidding. Trivial as well as heartless when locally viewed, this bill, now law, was announced as a model for all termination bills. The federal legal obligation to scores of thousands of Indians has not been fulfilled; past devastating wrongs—such as those done to the five civilized tribes of Oklahoma—have not been righted: therefore, the federal government shall be prohibited by statute from meeting the unmet obligations or righting the unrighted wrongs.

This article must omit other details and conclude with the really massive, all-embracing betrayal. The Indian Reorganization Act of 1934, together with subsequent amendatory acts, reaffirmed the bilateral Indian–federal-government relation. It empowered the several hundred Indian groups to organize for domestic self-rule and to incorporate for economic self-help and self-defense. The ensuing years saw the creation, by the Indians, of 182 tribal constitutions and 154 tribal corporate charters. The act created a revolving credit fund, resting on the communal aspirations and responsibilities of the tribes but fully attending to individual requirements; the account of this fund until about two years ago stood as a "record-breaker." There was developed a multiform, far-flung, and almost uniformly successful organization of Indian life, in which the individual through his group entered into the wider commonwealth.

Beginning with Dillon S. Myer as Indian Commissioner in 1950, the ruling purpose, harshly intensified by the present Administration, has been to atomize and suffocate the group life of the tribes—that group life which is their vitality, motivation, and hope—and to prevent the continuance and adaptation of those Indian civilizations which have produced great human beings through hundreds of generations. The present Administration's central method is to destroy the Indian Reorganization Act and the life structures which the Indians have built within its authority. The technique is not to use an omnibus bill but a host of special bills—effective in scattering the opposition—designed to destroy the Reorganization Act and its results tribe by tribe and region by region. A looted Indian estate will be the most apparent result, as it was in the case of the allotment acts of sixty and fifty years ago. A less apparent result will be a looted Indian soul and looted national honor, a United States shamed before the forty million Indians of the hemisphere. These results, except in local cases, have not yet been realized. The American public, if it would, could still forbid their irremediable accomplishment.

Stop.

Guilt by Heredity

The President's Committee on Civil Rights

The President's Committee on Civil Rights was created by Executive Order of President Truman on December 5, 1946; composed of Charles E. Wilson (chairman), Sadie T. Alexander, James B. Carey, John S. Dickey, Morris L. Ernst, Rabbi Roland B. Gittelson, Frank P. Graham, Bishop Francis J. Haas, Charles Luckman, Francis P. Matthews, Franklin D. Roosevelt, Jr., Bishop Henry Knox Sherrill, Boris Shishkin, Dorothy Tilly, and Channing Tobias. Report submitted October 29, 1947.

The most striking mass interference since slavery with the right to physical freedom was the evacuation and exclusion of persons of Japanese descent from the West Coast during the past war. The evacuation of 110,000 men, women and children, two-thirds of whom were United States citizens, was made without a trial or any sort of hearing, at a time when the courts were functioning. These people were ordered out of a large section of the country and detained in "relocation centers." This evacuation program was carried out at the direction of the Commanding General of the West Coast Command, who acted under an Executive Order authorizing the Secretary of War and the military commanders to prescribe military areas from which any person or group could be excluded.

The ground given for the evacuation was that the military security of the nation demanded the exclusion of potentially disloyal people from the West Coast. We have not felt that it would be proper or feasible for this Committee to try to review all of the facts to the evacuation program. We remember well the doubts and fears of the early months of the war and we recognize that the evacuation policy seemed a necessary precaution to many at the time. But we are disturbed by the implications of this episode so far as the future of American civil rights is concerned. Fundamental to our whole system of law is the belief that guilt is personal and not a matter of heredity or association. Yet in this instance no specific evacuees were charged with disloyalty, espionage or sedition. The evacuation, in short, was not a criminal proceeding involving individuals, but a sort of mass quarantine measure. This Committee believes that further study should be given to this problem. Admittedly in time of modern total warfare much discretion must be given to the military to act in situations where civilian rights are concerned. Yet the Committee believes that ways and means can be found of safeguarding people against mass accusations and discriminatory treatment.

Finally it should be noted that hundreds of evacuees suffered serious property and business losses because of governmental action and through no fault of their own. The War Relocation Authority, charged with the administration of the evacuation program, recommended in its final report that some provision be made in federal law that claims for evacuation-caused property losses be "considered promptly and settled with a minimum of delay and inconvenience." Over a year has passed since then.

Also disturbing, though less spectacular, was the issuance by military authority during the recent war of individual orders of exclusion against citizens scattered widely throughout the "defense zones" established by the Army. These orders rested on the same Executive Order as did the mass evacuation of Japanese Americans. In the case of these individual orders a citizen living perhaps in Philadelphia, Boston, or San Francisco was ordered by the Army to move. He was not imprisoned, for he could go to any inland area. He was not accused of criminal or subversive conduct. He was merely held to be an "unsafe" person to have around. Fortunately these violations of civil rights were not numerous. Moreover, the Army lost confidence in the exclusion orders as effective security measures and abandoned them —but not until more than 200 citizens had moved under military compulsion.

From *To Secure These Rights,* Washington: U. S. Government Printing Office, 1947, pp. 30–32.

CROSS REFERENCES TO STANDARD TEXTS *

Barnes, *Society in Transition*, Chaps. 5–6.

Bernard, *American Community Behavior*, Chaps. 16–17.

Brown, *Social Pathology*, pp. 382–384.

Cuber and Harper, *Problems of American Society*, pp. 223–224, 229, Chap. 13.

Elliott and Merrill, *Social Disorganization*, Chap. 31.

Faris, *Social Disorganization*, pp. 393–404.

Gillin, *Social Pathology*, Chap. 21.

—— and others, *Social Problems*, Chaps. 4–5.

Herman, *Approach to Social Problems*, pp. 211–222, 360–371, 461–463.

——————

* For complete bibliographical reference to each text, see page 13.

Landis, *Social Policies in the Making*, Chap. 11.

Lemert, *Social Pathology*, pp. 28–30.

Merrill and others, *Social Problems*, Chaps. 14–16.

Mihanovich, *Current Social Problems*, Chap. 14.

Neumeyer, *Social Problems and the Changing Society*, pp. 93–94, 131–136.

Nordskog and others, *Analyzing Social Problems*, Chap. 3.

Odum, *American Social Problems*, Chap. 15.

Phelps and Henderson, *Contemporary Social Problems*, Chap. 11.

Reinhardt and others, *Social Problems and Social Policy*, Chap. 13.

Weaver, *Social Problems*, Chap. 23.

OTHER BIBLIOGRAPHY

Gordon W. Allport, ed., "Controlling Group Prejudice," *The Annals*, 244 (March 1946).

——, *The Nature of Prejudice*, Boston: Beacon Press, 1954.

Harry S. Ashmore, *The Negro and the Schools*, Chapel Hill: University of North Carolina Press, 1954.

Ruth Benedict, *Race: Science and Politics*, rev. ed., New York: Viking Press, 1943.

—— and Gene Weltfish, "Races of Mankind," 15th ed., Public Affairs Pamphlet No. 85, 1953.

Brewton Berry, *Race Relations*, Boston: Houghton Mifflin Co., 1951.

Franz Boas, "Race," *Encyclopaedia of the Social Sciences*, 13 (1934): 25–36.

Ina Corinne Brown, *Race Relations in a Democracy*, New York: Harper & Bros., 1949.

F. J. Brown, J. S. Roucek, and others, *One America*, rev. ed., New York: Prentice-Hall, 1945.

Kenneth Bancroft Clark, "Desegregation: An Appraisal of the Evidence," *Journal of Social Issues*, 9 (1953): 4:1–77.

J. M. Corrigan and G. Barry O'Toole, eds., *Race: Nation: Person: Social Aspects of the Race Problem*, New York: Barnes & Noble, 1944.

O. C. Cox, *Caste, Class, and Race*, New York: Doubleday and Co., 1948.

Dwight W. Culver, *Negro Segregation in the Methodist Church*, New Haven: Yale University Press, 1953.

Maurice Rea Davie, *Negroes in American Society*, New York: McGraw-Hill Book Co., 1949.

Allison Davis and John Dollard, *Children of Bondage*, Washington: American Council on Education, 1941.

——, Burleigh B. Gardner, and Mary R. Gardner, *Deep South*, Chicago: University of Chicago Press, 1941.

John Dollard, *Caste and Class in a Southern Town*, New Haven: Yale University Press, 1937.

St. Clair Drake and Horace R. Cayton, *Black Metropolis*, New York: Harcourt, Brace and Co., 1945.

W. E. B. DuBois, *Black Folk, Then and Now*, New York: Henry Holt and Co., 1939.

——, *Color and Democracy*, New York: Harcourt, Brace and Co., 1945.

Grant Foreman, *Indian Removal: The Emigration of the Five Civilized Tribes of Indians*, Norman: University of Oklahoma Press, 1953.

E. Franklin Frazier, *The Negro in the United States*, New York: Macmillan Co., 1949.

Mary E. Goodman, *Race Awareness in Young Children*, Cambridge: Addison-Wesley Press, 1952.

E. L. Hartley, *Problems in Prejudice*, New York: King's Crown Press, 1946.

Charles S. Johnson, *Growing Up in the Black Belt*, Washington: American Council on Education, 1941.

——, *Patterns of Negro Segregation*, New York: Harper & Bros., 1943.

—— and associates, *Into the Main Stream*, Chapel Hill: University of North Carolina Press, 1947.

Otto Klineberg, ed., *Characteristics of the American Negro*, New York: Harper & Bros., 1944.

John LaFarge, *Race Question and the Negro*, New York: Longmans, Green and Co., 1943.

Bruno Lasker, *Race Attitudes in Children*, New York: Henry Holt and Co., 1929.

Alfred McClung Lee, "Race Riots Aren't Necessary," 3d ed., Public Affairs Pamphlet No. 107, 1947.

—— and N. D. Humphrey, *Race Riot*, New York: Dryden Press, 1943.

—— and others, "How 'Open' Is the Unitarian Door?" *Christian Register*, 133: 4 (April 1954): 10–18.

Everett S. and Anne S. Lee, "The Differential Fertility of the American Negro," *American Sociological Review*, 17 (1952): 437–447.

Alexander H. Leighton, *The Governing of Men: The*

Lessons of Japanese Relocation, Princeton: Princeton University Press, 1945.

Kurt Lewin, *Resolving Social Conflicts*, New York: Harper & Bros., 1948.

Sinclair Lewis, *Kingsblood Royal*, New York: Random House, 1947. A novel based upon an interracial problem theme.

Andrew W. Lind, *Hawaii's Japanese: An Experiment in Democracy*, Princeton: Princeton University Press, 1946.

F. S. Loescher, *The Protestant Church and the Negro*, New York: Association Press, 1948.

Herman H. Long and Charles S. Johnson, *People vs. Property*, Nashville: Fisk University Press, 1947.

Katharine Du Pre Lumpkin, *The Making of a Southerner*, New York: Alfred A. Knopf, 1947.

Robert Morrison MacIver, *The More Perfect Union: A Program for the Control of Inter-Group Discrimination in the United States*, New York: Macmillan Co., 1948.

Carey McWilliams, *Brothers Under the Skin*, Boston: Little, Brown & Co., 1943.

———, *Prejudice: Japanese Americans*, Boston: Little, Brown & Co., 1944.

Robert K. Merton, "The Self-Fulfilling Prophecy," *Antioch Review*, 8 (1948): 193–210.

M. F. Ashley Montagu, *Man's Most Dangerous Myth: The Fallacy of Race*, 3d ed., New York: Harper & Bros., 1952.

Gunnar Myrdal, R. Sterner, and Arnold M. Rose, *An American Dilemma: The Negro Problem and Modern Democracy*, New York: Harper & Bros., 1944, 2 vols.

Herbert Northrup, *Organized Labor and the Negro*, New York: Harper & Bros., 1944.

Mary White Ovington, *The Walls Came Tumbling Down*, New York: National Association for the Advancement of Colored People, 1947.

Robert Ezra Park, *Race and Culture*, Glencoe, Illinois: Free Press, 1950.

President's Committee on Civil Rights, *To Secure These Rights*, Washington: Government Printing Office, 1947.

Arnold M. Rose, *The Negro in America*, New York: Harper & Bros., 1948.

Gerhart Saenger, *The Social Psychology of Prejudice*, New York: Harper & Bros., 1953.

Richard Schermerhorn, *These Our People: Minorities in American Culture*, Boston: D. C. Heath and Co., 1952.

Muzafer and Carolyn W. Sherif, *Groups in Harmony and Tension*, New York: Harper & Bros., 1953.

Lillian Smith, *Killers of the Dream*, New York: W. W. Norton & Co., 1949.

Everett Y. Stonequist, *The Marginal Man*, New York: Charles Scribner's Sons, 1937.

Dorothy S. Thomas, Charles Kikuchi, and James Sakoda, *The Salvage: Japanese American Evacuation and Resettlement*, Berkeley: University of California Press, 1952.

———, Richard C. Nishimoto, and others, *The Spoilage*, Berkeley: University of California Press, 1946.

Helen G. Trager and Marian R. Yarrow, *They Learn What They Live*, New York: Harper & Bros., 1952.

Ruth D. Tuck, *Not With the Fist: Mexican Americans in a Southwestern City*, New York: Harcourt, Brace and Co., 1946.

Evon Z. Vogt, *Navaho Veterans: A Study of Changing Values*, Cambridge: Peabody Museum of American Archaeology and Ethnology, Harvard University, 1951, Vol. 41, No. 1.

Robert C. Weaver, *Negro Labor: A National Problem*, New York: Harcourt, Brace and Co., 1945.

Joseph E. Weckler, *Negro Platform Workers*, Chicago: American Council on Race Relations, 1945.

Robin M. Williams, Jr., *The Reduction of Intergroup Tensions*, New York: Social Science Research Council, 1947.

Richard Wright, *Black Boy*, New York: Harper & Bros., 1940.

REVIEW QUESTIONS

1. From what does the term "scapegoating" derive?
2. What does "scapegoating" mean?
3. How is prejudice related to scapegoating?
4. How is insecurity related to scapegoating?
5. What is a marginal man?
6. To whom is the marginal man a problem? Why?
7. How are tensions resulting from interracial frictions passed on to the Negro child?
8. How do social scientists analyze the frequency of hypertension among Negroes?
9. How does educational segregation work in the southern states?
10. What are the accumulating consequences of the southern states producing a disproportionate share of the country's children?

11. What reasons other than humanitarian ones do Gordon and Roche find for ending segregation?
12. What actions on the part of the white Americans have brought Indians to their present intense problems?
13. What is meant by "guilt by heredity"? Is it tenable under the American traditions of law and justice?
14. What is the case against the United States government in connection with its mistreatment of persons of Japanese descent, as summed up and analyzed by the President's Committee on Civil Rights?
15. To what extent did the Army "relocate" persons for security reasons on the East coast?

—CHAPTER 21—→

Ethnic Difference

In a land to which so many different peoples have migrated as the United States, ethnic difference might be thought to provide the basis for fascinating varieties of custom and ceremony, tradition and folklore. But unfortunately ethnic difference has implicit in it both romantic and colorful possibilities and also what sociologists call ethnocentrism, a term for the "view of things in which one's own group is the center of everything, and all others are scaled and rated with reference to it. . . . Each group nourishes its own pride and vanity, boasts itself superior, exalts its own divinities, and looks with contempt on outsiders. Each group thinks its own folkways the only right ones, and if it observes that other groups have other folkways, these excite its scorn." * American society is called by some a melting pot, but it is more realistically a social structure in which ethnic minority members face great compulsion to exchange their ethnic identities for those of American groups and classes.

Many of the problems of race and caste sketched in the previous chapter are problems of ethnic difference which are aggravated, justified, and maintained by racial characteristics. Many similar rationalizations serve to justify keeping the Negro in "his place" in the United States and the Irish and the Cockney submerged in Great Britain. An American Negro who assumes the identity of a visiting Latin American or Hindu personage speedily learns the degree to which caste stigmata are social rather than physiological.

Once early European immigrant groups had established beginnings of social structure in the American colonies, each successive wave of immigration found itself torn between old-world

ethnic-group loyalties, the punishments for deviation from American patterns, and the rewards for assimilation or Americanization. Or the immigrant group found itself pushed back upon its ethnic ties and traditions by the rejection of it by dominant groups. Thomas and Znaniecki tell of the impact of the new world upon the immigrant as a person. Wirth discusses similarities and differences in the segregation and assimilation of Negroes and Jews. Bloomgarden reports on the "quota system" in medical schools. Barrabee and Von Mering describe their investigations of variations in mental stress as related to differing ethnic backgrounds, whether Irish, Jewish, Italian, or Yankee-American.

What forms do segregation, discrimination, and rejection take? Other chapters touch upon instances in real estate, employment, politics and government, education, entertainment, the armed forces, and elsewhere. Here it suffices to point to common problems of ethnic difference in this country which are not mentioned in the preceding chapter. One selection tells of the form of activity taken recently by "hate groups." The complacency of the majority to the persecution of minority members frequently raises the question: Does social discrimination really matter? McWilliams mentions some of the ways in which social discrimination does matter and the fact that it is frequently stimulated in the case of Jews by members of our most powerful social circles. One particular form of social discrimination, that apparent in college fraternities and sororities, is described in the next reading. Galarza deals with problems of the Mexican-American minority in the United States. The Mexican-Americans are a huge minority and one with pressing problems, but they are so localized geographically that they have been ignored by most Americans.

---

* William Graham Sumner, *Folkways*, Boston: Ginn and Co., 1907, p. 13.

Demoralization among Immigrants

William I. Thomas and Florian Znaniecki*

The peasant immigrant is able to maintain his moral status in spite of the weakened social response and control only because of the power of mental habits. When a strong set of active associations has once been formed, even a weak social stimulus is sufficient to provoke the usual kind of behavior; a letter from home, the response or recognition of a friend, even the mere remembrance of past social influences may be for a time almost as efficient in keeping the individual within the limits of normality as the consciousness of a direct social control by his old primary-group. But when the habit is broken, because the individual's social education was insufficient in the old country or because his temperament is more than usually refractory to the given social influences or because the stress of new conditions proves too strong, the average immigrant lacks the necessary preparation to construct for himself a new life-organization with such elements as abstract individualistic morality, religious mysticism and the legal and economic systems which he finds in America. In order to reorganize his life on a new basis he needs a primary-group as strong and coherent as the one he left in the old country. The Polish-American society gives him a few new schemes of life, but not enough to cover all of his activities. A certain lowering of his moral level is thus inevitable. Though it does not always lead to active demoralization, to anti-social behavior, it manifests itself at least in what we may call passive demoralization, a partial or a general weakening of social interests, a growing narrowness or shallowness of the individual's social life.

Of course the second generation, unless brought in direct and continuous contact with better aspects of American life than those with which the immigrant community is usually acquainted, degenerates further still, both because the parents have less to give than they had received themselves in the line of social principles and emotions and because the children brought up in American cities have more freedom and less respect for their parents. The second generation is better adapted intellectually to the practical conditions of American life, but their moral horizon grows still narrower on the average and their social interests still shallower. One might expect to find fewer cases of active demoralization, of anti-social behavior, than in the first generation which has to pass through the crisis of adaptation to new conditions. And yet it is a well-known fact that even the number of crimes is proportionately much larger among the children of immigrants than among the immigrants themselves.

* See identifying note on page 17.

From *The Polish Peasant in Europe and America,* New York: copyright by Alfred A. Knopf, Inc., in 1927, pp. 1649–1651. Reprinted by permission.

The Jews and the Negroes: Contrasting Educational Problems

Louis Wirth

Louis Wirth (1897–1952), late professor of sociology, University of Chicago; president, American Council on Race Relations. Chief works: *The Ghetto* (1928); with others, *Our Cities: Their Role in the National Economy* (1937) and *Urban Government* (1938). Editor: *Contemporary Social Problems* (1939), *1126: A Decade of Social Science Research* (1940).

The survival of the Jews has probably depended more upon the segregation and internal solidification of the Jewish community as a response to exclusion and persecution than upon toleration by the outside world. In the light of the history of the Jewish people up to the rise of

From "Education for Survival: The Jews," *American Journal of Sociology, 48* (1942–1943): 682–691, pp. 690–691 quoted. Reprinted by permission.

naziism, the adaptability of Jewish life to changing situations is scarcely subject to doubt as a powerful factor in survival. But the will to live is perhaps more convincingly manifested in the adjustment of Jewish education to changing needs and circumstances than in any other phase of Jewish social life. While it has been concerned with the transmission of knowledge and skills of a sort, it has been primarily designed to nurture a consciousness of a common past and a common destiny. The most important part of the education which the Jewish family and community has provided its members, especially the youth, has served to inculcate in the individual a sense of belonging to a historic people with deep roots in the past and of sharing the future of that people despite the seeming discrepancy between the fortune of the one and the fate of the many.

It should be noted, of course, that in all the countries of the Western world except those under the dominance of Nazi doctrines the education of the Jews, except for the religious education, is part and parcel of the general educational system of the country. The disproportionate crowding of the Jews into the professions in the past few generations has to some extent repeated what their concentration in business and finance had done in an earlier period: It gave rise to a reaction expressing itself in Jewish quotas in many higher educational institutions, if not complete exclusion in the case of some. Incidentally, it may also be noted that the quota system in higher educational and professional institutions has mainly resulted in intensifying the individual struggle for admission and advancement.

The fascination which higher education and professional careers have had for the Jews may be traced to at least three factors: (1) the traditionalist scheme of learning cultivated as a social value for centuries and now translated into secular terms; (2) the relatively high degree of urbanization of the Jews; and (3) the lack of interest in or opportunity for entering other occupations. It is a striking fact that agricultural vocational education (except in the retraining of refugees in an emergency like the present or as stimulated by nationalistic enthusiasm, as in Zionism, or as a deliberate policy by philanthropic and resettlement agencies) has failed to attract more than a trivial segment of the Jews.[1] In the

higher brackets of education anti-Semitism has frequently generated a personal sense of frustration and embitterment. Among the Jews, as among other minority peoples, discontent is not confined to the lower strata but extends on up into the top reaches of the social hierarchy and is perhaps most acute among those who, despite their abilities, have found their path to advancement or acceptance barred. . . .

The experience of the Jews may well stand as the classic example of the survival of a people and the perpetuation of a culture from which others similarly situated may draw appropriate inferences for their policies, both positive and negative. There probably is no people more unlike the Negroes than the Jews. The latter have long been sophisticated, urbanized, and literate. While immersed in the stream of Western civilization, the Jews have retained a profound consciousness of their separate identity and past. The Negroes in these respects are virtually exactly opposite. The Jews, for instance, have no need for an urban league as do the Negroes, for the Jews, having grown up with the city, find urban life their natural milieu. Whereas the Jews on many occasions faced their supreme problem in resisting assimilation, the Negroes only rarely have been permitted to assimilate. Whereas the Jews have inherited their communal organization, the Negroes have had to build up their community structure painfully and laboriously. The Negroes have no minority language, ritual, religion, and culture to speak of, for which they must seek toleration as do the Jews. It is interesting to speculate how much of the anomalous status of the Jews today is due to the progress of the industrial revolution and how different the contemporary position of the Negroes would be if they had been permitted to share in the industrial, commercial, and professional roles which the Jews have played. Despite the obvious differences between the Jews and the Negroes, however, none can perhaps profit more by the historic experiences of the Jews than the Negroes themselves.

We already see in the crystallization of schools of thought among Negro leaders striking likenesses between the issues and the strategy of adjustment. Assimilationism and nationalist separatism are the extreme poles in both instances. Intermediate between these lie a series of variant policies which have close resemblances in the two

---

[1] See Arthur Ruppin, *The Jews in the Modern World*, London, 1934, Chap. x. For an account of the chief experiment in agricultural education and settlement see Gabriel Davidson, *Our Jewish Farmers and the Story of the Jewish Agricultural Society*, New York, 1943.

peoples. Accommodation, submission, and sublimation are three distinctly recognizable intermediate forms of proposed adjustment. The Jews have perhaps more of a recognizable will to live as a people and as a culture than have the Negroes. Moreover, the Jews, as a historic people, have a core of cultural traditions to knit them together and enable them to face a hostile world with an inner sense of equality and with equanimity despite their dispersion. The greater visibility of the Negroes, on the other hand, furnishes a not always welcome basis of racial identity from which the individual cannot, even if he would, escape.

The fact that the Jews have, through the centuries of their dispersion and their struggle for recognition and survival, acquired certain unmistakable successes within the framework of Western civilization no doubt gives them an advantage over the Negroes, who have had to traverse the road from African folk culture to Western civilization more recently and in a much shorter time, which did not permit them to share even those opportunities which the Jews until recently thought they could take for granted as permanent gains. On the other hand, it is the very success of the Jews in surmounting the obstacles put into the path of their progress which has made them the object of envy, hate, and persecution and which makes them vulnerable to the propaganda of organized anti-Semitism.

Despite the momentary and, we hope, temporary vicissitudes of history which have allotted to the Jews a more precarious prospect than there was reason to hope would face them in the age of liberalism, it is not unlikely that they will continue to enjoy in the long run certain advantages over the Negroes which even the aftermath of naziism cannot completely cancel. There is no doubt, however, about the fact that large masses of Jews who thought they were well on the road of assimilation have, through their setbacks incident to the advent of racism and anti-Semitism as political weapons, come to a point of seeing themselves and their fate with a greater feeling of kinship and sympathy for the Negroes. For both peoples the goal of a happier adjustment to the world in which they must live is seen to be further distant than either had expected. They have the consolation that they can travel at least part of that road in companionship.

Medical School Quotas
Lawrence Bloomgarden

Lawrence Bloomgarden (1907–   ), attorney, formerly case consultant to the Physicians' Committee of the National Refugee Service, and presently staff member of the Civil Rights Department, American Jewish Committee.

Numerous, subjective, and shifting criteria for admission to medical schools make the picture a scrambled one and considerable patience and ingenuity are required before the claims, counterclaims, and highly inaccessible statistics can be fitted together into a coherent whole.

The overriding element in the whole medical school picture is the simple fact that not everyone who wants to can become a doctor. Of course not everyone who wants to can become a millionaire, or, for that matter, a chorus girl, either. But there is no conscious, well-organized effort on the part of others to limit the number of chorus girls or millionaires.

For the prospective doctor the case is far different. For even if he has the brains, the ability, and the money, he may not be able to become a doctor. Of the more than 20,000 qualified applicants who yearly apply to medical schools, only about 7,000 can be accepted. The medical schools can and will take no more. This anomalous situation, where about one out of three qualified candidates for a profession are accepted for training, is in itself a novelty in America, where it is customary to think of careers being open to all who wish to pursue them. . . .

The whole quota policy was once known under the less delicate term of the *numerus clausus*, instituted in Poland and other East European countries on openly anti-Semitic grounds. From al-

From "Medical School Quotas and National Health," *Commentary*, 9:1 (January 1953): 29–37.

most any point of view, the argument in favor of quotas has been found lacking in logic, fairness, or good sense. It is manifestly subversive of the democratic ethic that citizens be treated and judged as members of racial, religious, or national blocs, and not as individuals. It is clearly an argument of convenience, never used to justify expansion of opportunity for minority groups, but only for limitation. It is never said, for example, that Negro medical students should constitute 10 per cent of the total to correspond to the Negro percentage of our population; nor is it ever argued that Jewish executives in banks and insurance companies, two fields in which Jews are poorly represented on the administrative level, should equal 4 per cent of the total to correspond to the Jewish percentage of the American population.

A great deal has happened . . . [of recent years.] For one thing, it is no longer good form to justify or even admit discrimination. For another, several states, including New York, have laws specifically prohibiting such practices.

Another factor in the modern medical picture is the acute national shortage of physicians which became obvious at the end of World War II. Medical educators themselves estimated in 1945 that 20,000 more physicians were badly needed, and the report of the President's Committee on Health Needs of the Nation indicates a prospective shortage of 30,000 physicians by 1960.

In the face of these clear needs, the AMA seems to have revised its earlier views on the overproduction of doctors. In June 1951 it announced that "it has no desire to limit the production of properly trained physicians to serve the American people." And it emphasized its willingness to encourage the expansion of medical training facilities. The AMA has also reversed its attitude toward foreign medical schools. State licensing boards have been urged that graduates of foreign schools "be accorded the same opportunities for licensure as graduates of approved medical schools in the United States." It should be noted, however, that the Council on Medical Education, in its 1952 report, observes that "opportunities for American students to obtain a medical education in the better foreign medical schools are diminishing." The medical schools in Great Britain, for example, are now accepting very few Americans because of their own need for more doctors.

This combination of changed public attitudes, new state laws, and an acute shortage of doctors has brought some important changes in the techniques of admission by medical schools. "Techniques" is the correct word here, for the aims, and the results, would appear to be about the same. The Jewish applicant still too often finds himself on the outside, a victim this time of one or another of current admissions criteria.

The problem of criteria is worth some investigation because the medical schools rest their whole case upon it. The dialogue generally begins when a rejected Jewish applicant notices that other applicants, with grades lower than his own, have been admitted. He wants to know why. He is told that personality factors have also been considered. . . .

Admittedly, such personality factors as "diction, voice, physical appearance, grooming" may contribute to the well-known bedside manner and therefore to the average doctor's success. But a pathologist or research worker may go through his entire career without ever seeing a live patient, while a surgeon who leaves a sponge or a clamp inside his victim would need an unusual bedside manner indeed to mollify his outraged patient, or placate the bereaved family. And when one considers the personalities of some outstanding pioneers in medical history, and finds that a frequent common characteristic is a kind of pig-headed obstinacy, a quality seldom associated with a sunny disposition but very useful in overcoming the opposition of eminent fools, it is cause for thanksgiving that men like Ehrlich, Koch, and Freud did not need the assent of . . . [an] Admissions Committee in order to study medicine.

Even when personality criteria are not used as a conscious—or unconscious—cover for prejudice, objective evidence seems to cast great doubt on the worth of such criteria for admissions. The Menninger Clinic in Topeka, Kansas, has recently been studying methods of improving the selection of physicians for psychiatric training. Teaching psychiatrists gave intensive interviews to the candidates and then rated them as to probable aptitudes. No applicants were excluded by this process, the sole purpose being to determine the value of personality interviews in selecting physicians for the training program. Comparison between the performance of the candidates and their interview ratings with *trained psychiatrists* revealed a correlation of only +.2. This is only slightly better than the interviewers could have done by flipping a coin. Seven out of the ten top trainees, rated on performance at the conclusion of the training, would have failed to qualify if results of the personality interviews had been used to bar candidates.

Obviously, physicians on admissions committees do not have the competency of trained psychiatrists in judging personality qualifications. Yet they have not hesitated to use these subjective criteria in deciding who shall and who shall not enter medical school. . . .

Geographical criteria may constitute a legitimate admissions requirement where some private medical schools wish to establish a national character. As for state medical schools maintained with tax funds, they are under obligation to prefer residents. Yet geographical criteria are only legitimate where they are fairly and scrupulously administered. In New York, private medical schools use highly elastic geographical criteria for reasons which are at least dubious.

In 1950, the New York State Department of Education studied the admissions practices of nine medical schools in the state. The study threw grave doubt on the real purpose of geographical criteria in some of these schools. It was discovered, for example, that non-Jewish residents of New York found it just as easy as non-residents to get into private medical schools. Only Jewish residents found it more difficult to get into such schools—ostensibly because they were New Yorkers. It appears that geographical criteria are indeed used—but only if the applicant is Jewish.

The study also showed that more than 30 per cent of the Jewish applications whose grades on a comparative basis should have entitled them to admittance to some school failed to get into any medical school in the state. This figure of rejections would have been much higher had it not been for the liberal and eminently fair admissions policy of two of the nine schools, New York University and the State University at Long Island Medical College. These two accounted for more than two-thirds of all the Jewish medical students in the state. The other seven showed a sharp distortion in the proportion of Jews to non-Jews accepted on a comparative scholarship basis. . . .

Unfortunately, the restrictive admissions practices of New York medical schools are by no means unique. Although the greatest problem exists in that state, discrimination in American medical schools elsewhere can be equally documented. Studies of admissions at Pennsylvania medical schools, for example, show similar practices. . . .

Nor is there any evidence that present interview techniques and personality criteria are even successful in eliminating the emotionally unstable among prospective doctors. Indeed, what evidence there is would indicate the contrary. A study in 1942 of medical students at Cornell, Illinois, and Chicago revealed that about 25 per cent were in serious need of help for various emotional problems or psychiatric disabilities. And in a recent study by Edward A. Strecker and colleagues, of a senior medical class, 46.5 per cent were found to have neurotic handicaps of major character. Facts such as these impelled the American Psychiatric Association at its recent Conference on Psychiatric Education to urge the rapid development of objective indices for measuring the emotional stability and psychological fitness of medical candidates, to replace the hit-or-miss methods of present admission boards. And it is worthy of note that the conference concluded that "for the present, grades are probably the best single criteria for admission since . . . we do not know as yet what special qualities make a good medical student or a proficient physician, and thus do not have other criteria."

The moral or practical case against discrimination in medical schools need not be labored here. It has been found to lack any justification whatsoever apart from that of protecting vested interests at the expense of the health and welfare of the nation. Yet even those who admit the fallacies of quotas will sometimes refer to the "disproportionate" Jewish interest in medicine. This point needs no refutation, only comprehension.

The interest of Jewish students in medical education is, of course, a fact. The interest of Italians in the opera is also a fact. The particular talents and interests of ethnic or cultural groups have always served to enrich mankind and, particularly in the United States, have traditionally been seen as forces to be encouraged and nurtured. . . .

Undoubtedly, the interest of able young Jews in medicine is accentuated by lack of opportunity for them in many other attractive pursuits. So long as the junk business rather than steel, and the loan business rather than banking, are the choices available, enthusiasm for rewarding professions like medicine will be great. This simply illustrates the unbalancing effect on the whole economy of discrimination in any particular field. The tragedy is that the medical profession, which serves the nation so directly, should work to strengthen discriminating tendencies in American life instead of combating them.

The larger tragedy is that the medical educators responsible for recruiting new members to the profession should be selecting them on grounds of prejudice, not competence. As a result, our doctors are not as good as they should and could be. So while prejudice in medicine hurts Jews directly, it also hurts everybody else indirectly.

Ethnic Variations in Mental Stress
Paul Barrabee and Otto Von Mering

Paul Barrabee (1912–   ), research fellow, department of psychiatry, Harvard Medical School. Otto Von Mering (1922–   ), assistant professor of social anthropology, University of Pittsburgh School of Medicine.

In this paper [1] we shall report the results of research concerned with ethnic variations in mental stress observed in families with psychotic children. In view of the paramount importance of the socialization process within the family in shaping the individual into a functioning member of society, we designed a research project focusing on the dimensions of authority and solidarity within the family. Our goal was to understand the relationship between family social structure and the production of individual stress. Families belonging to various ethnic subcultures were expected to differ from one another in a way reflective of their subcultures. Therefore, we decided to see how they were different and what it was that made them different.

The ethnic [2] groups we finally chose for study are the Irish, Jewish, and Italian. As a kind of baseline for comparison, we also selected a group of families which we consider to be typically Yankee-American. The material for our research was obtained from the analysis of 69 families, 18 each in the Italian, Irish, and Jewish groups and 15 in the Yankee. In selecting our cases we chose patients between the ages of eighteen and thirty-five because we felt that that period of life during which the individual made his first major adjustments as an adult would be most pertinent to our interest in the relationship between stress and the social structure of the family. In general, our choice of cases was not restricted by marital status or type of diagnosis, but we tried to obtain an equal number of male and female cases in each group.

The cases admitted to the Boston Psychopathic Hospital came from many different sources. Since it is a state-supported diagnostic and treatment hospital it receives both unselected patients directly from the community and many transfers from other state hospitals. Most patients come from the Metropolitan Boston Area. We fully appreciate the geographic limitations of our sample. We assume that any one member of an ethnic group living either alone or in contact with other members of his group in other geographical areas of the United States might well experience some different stresses, or that they might at least be phrased somewhat differently.

Families of the Jewish, Irish, and Italian groups all belonged to the lower socio-economic level as determined by standard procedures. In contrast, the Yankee group belonged to the middle level.

---

[1] This is a preliminary report of a two-year study financed by the Russell Sage Foundation, conducted at the Boston Psychopathic Hospital, and now in preparation for publication in book form.

[2] For our purpose we define a member of an ethnic group as a person who regards himself or is regarded by others as distinguished by religion or national origin from the native-born white Protestant majority. The ethnicity of a member of an ethnic group refers to the degree to which his behavior reflects the values, language, and customs characteristic of his ethnic group. We restrict our choice to persons of lower socio-economic status whose parents were both born in rural Ireland, Southern Italy, or the semi-urban areas of Jewish settlement in Eastern Europe. A Yankee is defined as a person of Anglo-Saxon white Protestant ancestry, with native-born grandparents, who is regarded by himself and others as Yankee.

From "Ethnic Variations in Mental Stress in Families with Psychotic Children," *Social Problems, 1:* 2 (October 1953): 48–53.

Total family membership of all groups included 439 persons.

Our basic methodological tool was a semi-structured interview which allowed the interviewee complete freedom to formulate his answers within the framework of the outline used by the interviewer. Interviews were conducted by the authors. They averaged approximately twenty hours per case. In addition to the patient, every available relative was interviewed, and full use was made of other sources of information such as doctors and social workers who, in turn, often had interviewed family members other than those contacted by the authors. Finally, case records and other pertinent documents were examined. Notes were taken at all interviews and tape recordings were made at approximately two-fifths of them. Certain categorized material was placed on a master chart that eventually contained about five thousand entries.

We wish to make it clear that our findings primarily apply to the families we studied. Nevertheless, the fact that these families include at least one psychotic member does not necessarily preclude cautious generalizations to other families in the same ethnic group comparable in social background. We do not know what causes psychosis and in the families studied there are other siblings who did not become psychotic. Perhaps the families in our study are different in some respect from corresponding ethnic families without mentally ill members. Nevertheless, as a study in the relationship between family social structure and mental stress, we suggest that our findings will be useful as a basis for a better understanding of those fundamental values that characterize the family social structure of the ethnic groups selected and as a stimulus to a greater awareness of the sociodynamics of mental stress.

Our basic premises are that: 1) family social structure is a product of the values originally held by the parents and subsequently internalized by the children; 2) the stability of the cultural pattern of a family through time is encouraged by the transmission of values from one generation to the next primarily in the medium of the family setting through the performance of roles; 3) the nature of these values is of utmost importance in the determination of what the individual family member perceives to be stressful. Since the totality of values in a given family is, in large measure, what has been transmitted from preceding generations, it is reasonable to assume that they

will contain many values that we call ethnic. Accordingly, we would expect that particular modes of stress experienced by children of ethnic families would tend to vary with their ethnic values.

For our purposes, stress is a state of unpleasant emotional tension engendered in an individual when he feels that he is unable to satisfy his needs within his situation of action. If the individual is unable to resolve this problem, his state of tension tends to manifest itself in behavior that reflects anxiety and/or hostility laden with guilt about an immediate or anticipated loss of gratification. To satisfy the demands of both clarity and brevity we will confine ourselves here to a consideration of the experience of stress in the male child.

In the area of intra-familial emotional relations there is an alliance or mutual preference between the mother and son in our Irish families. The mother exhibits a sex-linked preferential solicitude. However, she shows a lack of overt affection, which is coupled with strict discipline and a failure to reward in general for parentally approved behavior. The son experiences stress over this constellation of factors and tends to react to them with excessive dependency feelings on his mother which are punctuated by frequent verbal aggressions. The Irish father remains somewhat detached from his son but maintains a supervisory right that is all-inclusive. Like the mother, the father frequently belittles his son about his "looks" and behavior to make him feel subordinate, which is very stressful to and resented by the son. However, the Irish son does not develop strong emotional reactions toward his father and is apt to accept his subordination to him with little conflict because the number of situations in which he could experience subordination to him is much less in comparison to those he experiences with his mother.

The mother-son relationship in our Jewish families tends to be highly emotional. The mother is apt to be overprotective and overtly affectionate. She employs the withdrawal of love technique as her primary means of control. This emotional situation engenders in the son a distressful concern over the inconstancy of maternal love. He responds to it with highly ambivalent feelings to his mother, combining an exaggerated dependency and deep-rooted repressed hostility. The Jewish father is not very punishing, but he also yields much of the control over his home life to his wife. The Jewish son is not likely to have strong negative feelings toward his father, but neither is he likely to accept him as a role model.

The Italian son is the recipient of sex-linked preferential treatment from both his parents. There is little concern with affection and practically no overt display of it, but the Italian mother is apt to be oversolicitous, partly due to the superior status of males, and partly due to her concern over her son's physical welfare. The father's rigidity and propensity for physical punishment induces the mother to act as a buffer between father and son. The son reacts to this situation by feeling obligated to carry out maternal commands without hesitation, which tends to increase his emotional dependence on her. While the son enjoys the protection provided by his mother against his father, neither parent shows interest in his personal problems. Moreover, the father's extreme strictness tends to create a fear-ridden respect for him in the son, so that the latter feels he cannot dare reject the father as a role-model though he rejects him as a symbol of warmth. It is these aspects of the son's emotional position in the Italian home which prove very stressful to him in the long run because role expectations are not supported by emotional security.

The element of positive affect is important in the Yankee family, but there is a pronounced tendency not to display it overtly. The mother is quite overprotective and restrictive in the care of her son, who often must compete with his sisters for the affections of his father. The competition for parental affection between siblings of both sexes is both intense and highly stressful for the Yankee boy, especially since he has to reach constantly for indirect signs of love in things that his mother does for him rather than to look for and find evidence of love in a more direct fashion. The Yankee father is not very dominant, nor inclined to make much use of physical punishment. He is likely to be rejected as a role model, but also is not apt to be the object of the intense affect that the son feels toward his mother. The great difficulty in identifying with his father in a specific area of conduct and in having to rely almost exclusively on his mother's emotional guidance appears to be very stressful to the Yankee boy. The Yankee mother uses the withdrawal of love technique of control more importantly than any other, but she differs from the Jewish mother by emphasizing the moral implications of transgression rather than its impact upon her personal attitudes. The vague pervasiveness of the moral implications of all his conduct appears to be highly stressful to the Yankee boy, who responds with a deep emotionality to his mother that contains a high degree of guilt and a strong sense of inadequacy.

In the area of role performance Irish and Italian boys are expected to make financial contributions to the family which enhance their prestige in the family. Although this expectation is very mild for Jewish and Yankee boys, what contributions they do make are viewed as love gifts. When such financial contributions are unsatisfactory, the Irish and Italian boys find the situation very stressful in that their family status is jeopardized. In contrast, the Jewish and Yankee boys are inclined to find their inability to contribute to the family exchequer of relatively minor importance. Being a good Jewish or Yankee son in the sense of earning some money is not a function of family service but rather a function of to what "good" or useful personal ends the money earned is put, such as savings or personal future advancement. If a Yankee or Jewish boy does not live up to these expectations, he is apt to experience as much stress in the area of making money as is the Italian or Irish boy who does not contribute sufficiently to the family exchequer.

Both Jewish and Yankee boys are continuously urged to achieve good school marks, to obtain higher education, and to be upwardly socially mobile. The underlying reason is that the Jewish boy is essentially oriented by his parents to satisfy the personal ambition needs of his parents, particularly his mother. The Yankee boy is pushed by his parents to live up to similar expectations, which are primarily based on moral justifications and upon standards of family reputation. Both Jewish and Yankee boys experience stress when they are unable to fulfill parental expectations regarding education and mobility. They see themselves as having failed in respect to values which they do not question because such values seem to be in complete accord with the highly esteemed American values of education and success.

The Italian and Irish do not encourage their sons to risk the benefits of a regular income from a steady job for the hazards of a promising but uncertain position. This includes not sacrificing immediate earning capacity by going to school in the interests of future occupational advantages. Far from urging their sons to excel in school, Irish and Italian parents in the families we investigated tended to be satisfied if the boys "got by." These boys perceived the situation as stressful, of course, when they were unable to meet even these moderate requirements. However, in contrast with the Jewish and Yankee boys, they experienced stress when they preferred to get a better education and to seek a career conducive to upward social mobility. For them, to do so meant to reject the values of their parents, whom they saw as obstacles to their desires.

The performance of chores is a source of stress most often with Yankee boys. While Irish and especially Italian boys are expected to do chores, they are usually *ad hoc* and for visibly pragmatic reasons. Moreover, their chore load is very small if compared with that of their sisters. In comparison, Yankee boys are assigned routine chores which apparently are not practically necessary, but rather are justified on a moral basis, that it is "right" to have regular obligations, or it is good character training. Further, the Yankee boy is unable to shift any part of his chore load to his sisters, who are expected to do about as much as he. What chores are expected of the Jewish boy is predicated upon practical or moral reasons, or both, but the whole matter is greatly subordinated to other expectations such as doing homework or practicing music lessons. Thus, the Jewish boy seldom experiences as much stress over this as the Yankee boy.

The ability to maintain adequate social relationships outside the family is of great concern to our Yankee families. Thus Yankee families emphasize neatness, pleasant appearance, social amenity, and "good" social contacts. In part, this is linked with social mobility, and in part, with family status. Although social competence receives less emphasis in our Jewish families, it is important, and it is primarily functional insofar as it enhances the opportunity for upward social mobility. Considerable stress for both Yankee and Jewish boys arises from the incessant concern of

their parents that they behave "properly." By comparison, our Italian and Irish parents pay little attention to their sons' social competence other than that they don't get into "trouble." Their sons experience stress only indirectly when they feel that they are inadequately prepared for the social intercourse they deem essential to their own plans. This usually occurs when the level of their personal aspirations is higher than that their parents have for them.

Membership in the ethnic group can be a source of stress. This is most frequent with Jewish boys who see their Jewishness as impeding the fulfilment of social or occupational ambitions. Much depends upon the environmental conditions. Indeed, a Jewish boy can select avenues to success that bypass his Jewishness. However, since this implies a restriction in his freedom of choice, he often cannot quite shake off a diffuse sense of deprivation about his ethnic membership. In Boston, due to the large Irish population, being Irish is generally not a serious obstacle to an ambitious Irish boy. According to our sample, being an Italian rarely seemed to be stressful by itself as an obstacle to upward social mobility. Rather it appears to be parental values discouraging upward social mobility that produce stress in those of our Italian boys who are ambitious.

The above represents selected abbreviated findings which we use to support our basic contention that there are variations between ethnic groups in the modes of stress experienced by their members and that these differences are related to differences in family social structure as influenced by ethnic values. We believe that the application of these findings can be of service to all persons such as physicians, marriage counselors, nurses, social workers, and social scientists who have professional dealings with individuals from the relevant ethnic groups whose adjustment to their social environment is stressful.

"Hate" Groups
Civil Rights Department of the American Jewish Committee

Many anti-Semites have abandoned their former brash and obvious tactics. The more skillful hate-mongers and cunning publicists have now

developed a sense of public relations. They exploit current legitimate issues, toning down, if not eliminating, open anti-Semitism. They aim to win

From "Anti-Semitic Activity in the United States: A Report and Appraisal," pamphlet report of a study conducted by the Civil Rights Department, American Jewish Committee, 1954, pp. 3–7, 17.

the support of respectable elements, rather than the lunatic fringe following which they so highly prized in Christian Front days.

Thus, in the Presidential elections of 1952, when several thousand citizens in the states of California, Texas, Missouri, Arkansas, North Dakota, and Washington voted for General Douglas MacArthur on the Christian Nationalist Party ticket, these voters were expressing their confidence in an American hero. They were unaware that the General had not accepted the nomination, and that the party was actually a front for one of the most vicious and implacable anti-Semites in the country.

Similarly, when many people in Los Angeles protested against the schools teaching about UNESCO (United Nations Educational, Scientific and Cultural Organization), they had at heart what they sincerely, albeit mistakenly, believed to be the best interest of our country. They did not know that many of the alarming rumors they had heard about UNESCO came from the propaganda of a man who makes his living stirring up hatred, and who once headed an organization which the Attorney General of the United States listed as "fascist."

Such are the maneuvers whereby anti-Semites currently seek to influence public opinion. Thus far, their success has not been impressive; but the support and alliances they have gained by their deceptive tactics nevertheless constitute a potential danger.

Overt anti-Semitism reached its high-water mark in the United States in 1939, when several hundred anti-Jewish groups, launched with Nazi money, tried to convince Americans that Hitler was right. Mainly composed of crackpots and presided over by petty fuehrers, these organizations held storm-troop meetings; they picketed; they published reams of abusive literature. But such blatant demagoguery was offensive to the overwhelming majority of Americans; mostly the so-called lunatic fringe rallied to their banners.

On Pearl Harbor Day most of the rabble-rousers scurried for cover, remaining there for the duration of the war. By 1947, organized anti-Semitism had reached its lowest ebb.

The advent of the cold war brought many of these agitators back into the open. Some resumed their rabid fulminations against the Jews. Others, having learned from experience that racist appeals violated a basic American ethic, now courted public approval by exploiting the controversial issues of the day. The glibness of their arguments and the vigor of their attacks appeal especially to "ultra-nationalist" groups.

Ultra-nationalist groups have been a factor in American life since the first World War. They have opposed all progressive moves to meet the needs of government and society in these complex, industralized, modern times. After almost a generation of collective bargaining, social security measures, and government welfare programs, ultra-nationalists still seek a return to the nineteenth century. Their view of "states rights" would even preclude SEC regulation of security markets.

Although three wars have proven their thesis fallacious, the ultra-nationalists are still vehemently isolationist. They oppose foreign aid, bitterly resent United States participation in the United Nations, and favor amending the Constitution to curtail the treaty-making power of the Federal Government. Suspicious of foreigners, they have consistently resisted immigration into this country, except by persons of certain "approved" racial and national origins, and have fought all efforts to improve our immigration laws.

Most of the ultra-nationalists assert there is no difference between Republican and Democratic policies and call for "a new political party" or, at least, "a realignment of political forces."

Though often led and financed by reputable individuals, and spending millions of dollars to advertise their views via press, platform, radio, and other media, ultra-nationalists made little headway with the average American until the cold war brought about the present tense atmosphere of our national life.

While some of the ultra-nationalist groups espouse retrogressive economic reforms, and others have political aims, all favor extremist techniques in combating communism—free-swinging, wild-accusation tactics which indiscriminately charge liberals with being communistic. Ultra-nationalists are now appealing to the American people on this basis, equating everything they oppose with communism, subversion, and a newly-invented phenomenon—"creeping socialism."

During the past decade, ultra-nationalists organizations have increased measurably and they now offer tempting opportunities for infiltration by anti-Semitic elements. In setting out to cultivate these groups, the professional bigot plays his hand adroitly, exploiting the particular political issues which are currently the focus of concern in ultra-nationalist circles.

Anti-Semites, using justifiable public exposés of

Communist activity as springboards, have stepped up their smear of Jews as being Communists or Communist-influenced. Projection of this theme ranges from featuring Jewish names in unfavorable context, to outright charges of a Jewish conspiracy for world domination through the Communist movement.

It is expected that ultra-nationalist groups will soon launch their strongest attack upon such long-accepted features of our national way of life as unionism, social security, government welfare assistance, and similar social reforms of the past generation. Tied in will be appeals to "save America from creeping socialism" and return to "constitutionalism," "economic freedom," and "freedom of choice." Anti-Semites add the "Jewish angle" to these lines, alleging prominent Americans of Jewish background to be Machiavellian agents of a super-government.

The "third party" is not a new feature in American politics. Theodore Roosevelt's Bull Moose Party, LaFollette's Progressives and the more recent political venture of Henry Wallace, bearing the same title, come readily to mind. Adapting this idea to their own objectives, ultra-nationalists contend that the present Republican Administration is little more than a carbon copy of the Democratic Administrations which preceded it. Many anti-Semites have sedulously taken up the "third party" cry; in so doing, their propaganda generally charges that both major political parties are controlled by Jews.

A notorious instance of this dovetailing occurred during the 1952 Republican primary fights when both the ultra-nationalists and the anti-Semites opposed the nomination of General Eisenhower. The former proclaimed what they considered his failings, and the latter blamed these shortcomings on Jewish influence. In some localities, leaflets penned by as many as ten agitators in different parts of the country were assembled into kits and distributed on main thoroughfares. A typical piece showed a Streicher-like caricature of a Jew pointing to Eisenhower and saying, "Ikie vill keep us boys in power." This broadside was produced by Independent Republicans for MacArthur, a front organization established by Gerald L. K. Smith—without MacArthur's approval.

Exploiting legitimate public discussion of United States foreign policy, anti-Semites denounce and "expose" the United Nations and UNESCO with varying degrees of calumny, ranging from brashness to subtle innuendo. UN is depicted as designed to subvert American sovereignty to communism, Zionism, and Jewish control. Findings of official investigative bodies concerning individual UN employees are distorted into mass-indictments. The colors of the UN and Israeli flags are compared for hidden significance. UNESCO is invariably portrayed as the communistic, atheistic propaganda arm of UN, aimed at corrupting American schools and their children. Ultra-nationalist groups exploit a similar line, though without patent anti-Semitic content.

The McCarran-Walter Act has been severely criticized by Christian organizations—Protestant and Catholic—as well as by Jewish and many other reputable groups. Much ultra-nationalist and anti-Semitic propaganda, aimed at stirring anti-alien sentiment, has attacked critics of the Act, while minimizing or ignoring the opposition of Christian church groups. Played up instead is a portrayal of the Jews as seeking the law's repeal because they wish to get millions of their coreligionists into this country. Hints of Jewish power are frequently woven into this argument.

The onslaught of ultra-nationalists against modern education has gravely harassed the school systems of many towns during the past several years. In some instances, so-called "education" groups, dominated or influenced by anti-Semites, have smeared modern educational methods as communistic and atheistic. Such features as intercultural education, especially, have come under vicious attack; leading educators have been vilified as Communists and their textbooks investigated. UNESCO teaching materials and the display of the UN flag have been frequently used as starting points for these attacks. The momentum produced by the earlier organizational and propaganda efforts of ultra-nationalists promises to keep the issue of modern educational methods alive for some time to come.

In a grotesque effort to exploit the fears and phobias of the public, the anti-Semites have seized upon proposals in some sections of the country to fluoridate drinking water as a community health measure. Demagogic interpretations range from outright scares of "mass-poisoning" and "mass suicide" to innuendoes that fluorine saps the individual's will-power—an end, it is charged, desired by the Government. Also suggested, if not openly asserted, is that a "Super-Secret World Government" backs the project. Fantastic? Yet, huge quantities of such propaganda were distributed in

Cincinnati. They may well have influenced the negative vote which this proposition received in November 1953. . . .

Organized anti-Semitic activity today bears little resemblance to the noisy, unruly assemblages of pre-Pearl Harbor days with their spewing of unvarnished racial hatred easily recognizable as Nazi-inspired. Using as a point of reference the year 1947, when the anti-Semitic movement reached its lowest ebb, several changing trends in dynamics and tactics are discernible:

First, more emphasis is laid on disseminating literature, rather than staging meetings, picket-lines, rallies, and other demonstrations.

Second, more subtle approaches are made to public opinion by exploiting such issues as com-munism, United Nations, and national economic policies.

Third, there is a pronounced tendency among prominent ultra-nationalist organizations and leaders to accept—or at least tolerate—hatemon-gers and their propaganda products. In many cases this amenability is the result of unwariness; many would be more discerning, were it not for their own extremist viewpoints.

And finally, professional fomenters of discord are in positions where they can cause much trouble, for they have learned how to salt public debate with hate propaganda, and have discovered the usefulness of general mailing lists, instead of relying on the private rosters of crackpot followings in years gone by.

Does Social Discrimination Really Matter?
Carey McWilliams

Carey McWilliams (1905–   ), writer; editorial director, *The Nation*. Publications: *Factories in the Field* (1939); *Ill Fares the Land* (1942); *Brothers Under the Skin* (1943); *Prejudice* (1944); *Southern California Country* (1946); *A Mask for Privilege* (1948); *North From Mexico* (1949); *California* (1949); *Witchhunt: The Revival of Heresy* (1950).

In a society verbally devoted to democratic ideals, invidious distinctions are often masked, for even the rich acknowledge allegiance to these same ideals. Still and all, in our kind of social order, what passes for society will be seen to be based on wealth in its own right. The very absence of a landed gentry and titles of nobility, coupled with the pervasiveness of democratic shibboleths, compels the moneyed classes in this country to emphasize a rigid social exclusiveness as a means of protecting economic and political power. Indeed, social exclusiveness takes on a peculiar significance in a nominally democratic society, for it is entirely arbitrary and therefore impenetrable. . . .

In a democracy, social discrimination requires the exclusion of *groups,* since the comparative fluidity of the social structure makes the exclusion of *individuals* both difficult and awkward. From the point of view of wealth, social grace, and culture, individual Jews clearly meet the canons of social acceptability; nor can they be distinguished racially. Hence they must be excluded as a group, by name, as a matter of policy. . . .

Of the various "white" groups, Jews are about the only element that can be readily excluded from the category of the socially acceptable. They are not Christians; they are mostly late-comers; and they often occupy a special niche in the economy. Other ethnic groups would unquestionably have been excluded were it not for the curiously mixed character of the American population and the peculiar geographical concentration of minority elements. Where Scandinavian immigrants, for example, have been settled and concentrated since an early date, it has been difficult to exclude them as individuals have prospered and acquired status. Admitted to upper class symbols in one community, the bar against Scandinavians would lose its snobbish effectiveness elsewhere.

It should be noted, too, that while the Negro cannot be accepted because he is regarded as a member of an inferior race, this charge is practi-

From "Does Social Discrimination Really Matter?" *Commentary*, 4 (1947): 408–415, pp. 409–411, 415. Reprinted by permission.

cally never raised against the Jew. This tacit admission of racial and cultural equality outlines the purpose of exclusion more sharply. Social discrimination, involving the unequal treatment of equals, directly implies "an alteration in competitive power of those presumed to possess a freely competitive status" (*Encyclopaedia of the Social Sciences*), and lays bare the meaning of exclusion. Other ethnic groups have also been denied access to social power in relation to their numbers and wealth; but, over the years, it has been impossible to exclude these groups, *as groups,* with anything like the effectiveness with which Jews have been excluded. . . .

The failure of both Jews and Gentiles to admit the importance of social discrimination—to see that it has a function—is to be explained by the tendency in American culture to deny the existence of realities which conflict with our equalitarian ideals. "Democracy of feeling is expected of us," as Charles Horton Cooley once said, "and if we do not have it we usually simulate it." Thus we rationalize social discrimination as "freedom of association" or the right to select associates. The folk-belief that any American can become a millionaire and therefore eventually entitled to practice some form of social discrimination has, in effect, robbed this type of exclusion of its edge. As long as Jews are given a theoretical right to enter any trade, business, or profession, and their civil rights are safeguarded, they are almost powerless to object to a form of discrimination which they, in turn, are also privileged to practice in a limited way should they so desire. . . .

The effect of this "closed shop" attitude on the part of the industrial and financial giants is to intensify the pressure of Jewish applicants for jobs in those businesses which have pursued a less systematic policy of exclusion, and to re-double the pressure to enter the free professions. These pressures, in turn, perpetuate the marginal economic position of the Jews. Issues of this kind take on, furthermore, an ever-increasing gravity as more of the national economic life falls within the orbit of exclusive trusts and monopolies.

That social discrimination *is* important is fully realized by those who practice it, despite their pious disclaimers and innocent assurances. A year or so ago, Judge Harry Hollzer, long a distinguished and highly respected federal district court judge, died in Los Angeles. Judge Hollzer was one of the leaders of the Jewish community. A meeting to plan a memorial in his honor was called at the California Club. "There we were," as one of the members present told me, "planning a memorial for Judge Hollzer in a club which would have refused his application for membership. It occurred to me, as we sat there at luncheon, talking about Harry Hollzer, that the best way we could have honored him, if we had really wanted to honor him, would have been to eliminate a certain section from the by-laws. For a moment, I thought of suggesting this as a memorial, and then I glanced around at those present and a good impulse was inhibited."

Discrimination in College Fraternities and Sororities

Alfred McClung Lee*

When its Amherst chapter pledged a Negro in November, 1948, Phi Kappa Psi chose to disown the chapter rather than to depart from its tradition of racist membership restrictions. But the decision was not painless. Several prominent alumni resigned, and many individuals and chapters served notice that they would not rest until the fraternity constitution was changed.

This incident again focussed national attention on the racial and religious membership restrictions of college social organizations and threw the fraternity world into turmoil. Other groups were also torn with dissension on the same issue. In 1953, when Phi Delta Theta suspended its chapters at Amherst and Williams for violating the constitutional clause limiting membership to

* See identifying note on page 239.

From "Discrimination in College Fraternities and Sororities," *School and Society, 79* (June 26, 1954): 198–199.

persons of "full Aryan blood," other chapters rushed to the support of the ones ousted. Again alumni resigned in protest. The Williams chapter received hundreds of letters of support from alumni, including one from the late Chief Justice Fred N. Vinson. A constitutional amendment to change the offending clause had been supported by a clear majority at the 1952 national Phi Delta Theta convention, but it failed to gain the three-fourth vote necessary to effect a change. Now the suspended chapters are awaiting hopefully the 1954 convention.

At the University of Connecticut, four fraternities—Lambda Chi Alpha, Sigma Nu, Kappa Sigma, and Sigma Chi—were forced to sever their national ties in order to comply with a university ban on discriminatory membership policies.

Amherst, Dartmouth, and Columbia are preparing to withhold recognition from any group which limits its membership for reasons of race or religion. Hoping to reform rather than punish, Columbia and Dartmouth have set a 1960 deadline in order to give the fraternities several national conventions at which to accept what is for them a new conception. The Dartmouth action has the support of a student referendum.

But only a few colleges have taken so firm a stand. A more popular position, held by perhaps two dozen schools, bans new discriminatory societies, but it permits those already on the campus to remain on condition that they make "sincere efforts" either to reform their parent organizations or to gain freedom of action.

By and large, the struggle is being led neither by the colleges nor by national fraternity leaders but by undergraduates. These student leaders find that college action is necessary to consolidate their gains, but most schools have yet to take a stand on the issue.

In 1949, moved by undergraduate pressure, the National Interfraternity Conference recommended that those of its constituent organizations which had discriminatory membership policies should review such provisions with a view to their removal. Since then, however, more conservative elements in the Conference have prevailed. Its most recent resolution on the subject calls for "fraternity autonomy." This means: "National fraternities will determine membership standards. Colleges please keep hands off."

To date, a few of the discriminatory groups have yielded to undergraduate and college pressures and have eliminated bias-laden constitution-al provisions. A few others may be about to do so. The great majority still appears to be unmoved. In fact, about half of the national societies still have restrictive membership policies. The public, then, may well be alarmed when it sees a large segment of the nation's future leadership being prepared for citizenship in a setting which endorses racial and religious discrimination as a pattern of daily life.

Princeton's eating clubs and Amherst's fraternities have gone even further toward the elimination of exclusiveness or snobbishness in their membership policies than the social organizations in other colleges and universities. They may well then point the way toward the adaptation of fraternities to more enlightened standards of democratic living.

In both Princeton and Amherst, all interested men may join the social societies, and all social organizations are required among them to find places for all interested men. Members of minority groups are not segregated in special clubs but find themselves assimilated into a range of eating clubs and fraternities. The highly successful Princeton and Amherst systems are perhaps the best answer to those who contend that fraternities must be snobbish.

What are the prospects for change in this situation? Henry M. Wriston, president, Brown University, has observed that racial and religious restrictions in fraternities would disappear if left to the students themselves. This view is corroborated by such evidence as a nationwide survey of college students which revealed that 60% of them opposed *any* discrimination while only 20% favored exclusion. An additional 20% believed partial restrictions to be a solution.

Unfortunately the students themselves are a part of a system which prevents them from exercising the right of free association. Most national fraternities are governed by alumni, many of whom caricature the worst aspects of fraternity life and are completely wedded to the *status quo.* Nonconformist chapters occasionally rally large groups of former graduates to their support, but these forces rarely have been able to sustain the effort necessary to effect a change.

Each year a few more schools undertake, with varying degrees of stringency, to reform fraternity policies. And every so often a Greek-letter social organization reforms its membership practices from within. But it seems apparent that no significant change will occur unless the efforts of college administrations, alumni, and students are greatly stimulated and encouraged.

In order to provide the facts and research which make for such stimulation, a group of college educators and community leaders have formed an organization known as the National Committee on Fraternities in Education. This group believes that discrimination in fraternity membership can be overcome so that campus groups may perform useful roles as adjuncts to college education.

The committee plans to achieve its goal by providing information on developments in fraternity and sorority policies and programs; undertaking appropriate research and study, including further examination of the damage to educational objectives and to personality development already indicated by preliminary evidence; making information and consultation services available to fraternities and sororities, colleges, other student organizations, and the general public; stimulating conferences among alumni, undergraduate fraternity leaders, and college administrators and trustees to promote understanding of the problem and corrective action, campus by campus; and encouraging colleges, national organizations, and alumni to recognize the importance of permitting young people to select their own companions on the basis of personal criteria.

The National Committee on Fraternities in Education is just getting its program under way. It is dealing with a social problem in which there is now sufficient interest and agitation for results of a beneficial nature to be achieved. With the support which the committee has already achieved, it can look forward to furnishing undergraduates and others interested in eliminating discriminating practices with the services of a stable source of experiences and other information for their efforts. From the faculty standpoint, an important contribution will be to help decrease the social distance between professors and the future social actionists of business, politics, and union affairs who frequently find more stimulation in social fraternities than in college classrooms.

The Mexican American
Ernesto Galarza

Ernesto Galarza (1905–   ), university professor and director, research and education, National Farm Labor Union, American Federation of Labor.

The conditions of life and work of the Spanish-speaking minority in the United States are no longer a problem only of the borderlands. A historical process has been at work lifting this problem above local and sectional concern. It now involves communities as distant from the United States–Mexican border as Chicago, New York, and Detroit. It shows up in the rural slums that lie on an arc stretching from Arkansas to northern California. It is documented in federal reports on employment and in community conferences on human relations in the urban industrial East as well as in the rural agricultural Southwest. It has become a skeleton in the closet of our Latin American policy. The Mexican agricultural migrant and itinerant railway maintenance worker have been the primary agents in this process.

Over the past fifty years they have moved into practically every state of the Union. Today, while the bulk of over 2,500,000 of this minority is still anchored in California, Texas, Arizona, and New Mexico, thousands can be found in Illinois, Michigan, Ohio, Pennsylvania, and Kansas.

Within the group, the inferiority complex has been disappearing. From the uncomplaining ranks of Mexican "stoop labor" have emerged trained men and women to spoil the myth of the innate servility and incompetence attached to this group, with some romantic concessions, by the finance farmers and railway corporations that long have exploited them. Two world wars proved the courage, tested the loyalty, broadened the experience, and tempered the will of young men born and bred in a no-man's-land of social

From "The Mexican American: A National Concern. Program for Action," *Common Ground*, 9 (Summer, 1949): 27–38, pp. 27–29.

rejection and lack of civic opportunity for adult citizenship.

In the cotton fields, the truck farm, and the corporation ranches, as well as in the armed services, the Mexican has mingled with other minority groups more experienced in the defense of human rights and dignity, especially the Negro. He has rubbed shoulders with the militant Nisei GI's who did not come back from Monte Cassino to take it lying down. Through these contacts, methods of action have been learned and technics of organization have been discovered and communicated. The language of protest, pure and simple and almost always unheeded, has been supplemented by self-education and the discovery of the methods of redress available in the larger society by which he is surrounded. In this process, not a few Mexicans have discovered the weaknesses of civic and political organization, locally and nationally, as well as the mirages of international relations which have affected their welfare. For half a century they have experienced, intuitively rather than rationally, the red tape, obscure diplomatic deals, misrepresentations, and legal taffy in which the civil liberties and economic opportunities of Mexicans in the United States have been entangled. But as the American school system has inevitably rescued a few of the more fortunate ones from the *colonias* of the rural countryside or the gashouse districts of the large cities, understanding has become more rational, supported by knowledge and experience.

As the individual capacity of certain Mexicans has been developed and as their collective insight has become sharper and more meaningful, the attempt to stop the clock on them by some social groups has also taken on different forms. In Washington an Associated Farmers' lobby prevents the extension of social security, minimum wages, and other forms of protection to the Mexican rural workers. The same lobby inspires highly confidential agreements with the Mexican government for the recruitment of Nationals or *braceros*, whose major strategic function is to depress wages in California and Texas. Men who are highly sympathetic to the policies of the Associated Farmers sit securely in control of the machinery of the Inter-American System, thereby heading off constructive multilateral action to tackle the problems of inter-American labor migration at its roots.

On this and other aspects of the changing context of the problem of the Mexican minority in the United States, an abundant literature has developed. This literature runs all the way from the serious, compact, and sustained scholarship of Dr. Paul Taylor's studies to the articles, newspaper accounts, and books of the "protest" type. In between are the shelves of catalogued masters' and doctoral theses, government reports, case studies, and monographs numbering thousands of items. Bibliographically, at least, the Mexican minority has come of age.

CROSS REFERENCES TO STANDARD TEXTS *

Barnes, *Society in Transition*, Chaps. 4–6.
Bernard, *American Community Behavior*, Chaps. 16–20.
Brown, *Social Pathology*, pp. 29, 51–52, 384–386, 460–462, 499–500.
Cuber and Harper, *Problems of American Society*, pp. 281–284, Chap. 21.
Elliott and Merrill, *Social Disorganization*, Chaps. 30–31.
Faris, *Social Disorganization*, pp. 455–457.
Gillin, *Social Pathology*, pp. 187, 416, 423.
—— and others, *Social Problems*, Chaps. 3–5.
Herman, *Approach to Social Problems*, pp. 64, 81, 83,

86–87, 133–134, 208–213, 224, 255–256, 383–384, 464–466.
Landis, *Social Policies in the Making*, Chaps. 8, 11.
Lemert, *Social Pathology*, pp. 39–41, 43–44.
Merrill and others, *Social Problems*, Chaps. 14–16.
Mihanovich, *Current Social Problems*, Chaps. 1, 14.
Neumeyer, *Social Problems and the Changing Society*, Chap. 5.
Nordskog and others, *Analyzing Social Problems*, pp. 84–90, Chap. 3.
Odum, *American Social Problems*, Chap. 15.
Phelps and Henderson, *Contemporary Social Problems*, Chaps. 10–11.
Reinhardt and others, *Social Problems and Social Policy*, Chaps. 9, 13.
Weaver, *Social Problems*, Chaps. 22–23.

* For complete bibliographical reference to each text, see page 13.

OTHER BIBLIOGRAPHY

N. W. Ackerman and Marie Jahoda, *Anti-Semitism and Emotional Disorder*, New York: Harper & Bros., 1950.

Gordon W. Allport, ed., "Controlling Group Prejudice," *The Annals*, 244 (March 1946).

————, *The Nature of Prejudice*, Boston: Beacon Press, 1954.

Steuart Henderson Britt and Isacque Graeber, eds., *Jews in a Gentile World*, New York: Macmillan Co., 1942.

F. J. Brown, J. S. Roucek, and others, *One America*, rev. ed., New York: Prentice-Hall, 1945.

John H. Burma, *Spanish-Speaking Groups in the United States*, Durham: Duke University Press, 1954.

Irvin L. Child, *Italian or American?* New Haven: Yale University Press, 1943.

Israel Cohen, *The Zionist Movement*, rev. ed., New York: Zionist Organization of America, 1946.

Maurice Rea Davie, *Refugees in America*, New York: Harper & Bros., 1947.

S. A. Fineberg, *Overcoming Anti-Semitism*, New York: Harper & Bros., 1943.

Else Frenkel-Brunswik and others, "The Antidemocratic Personality," in T. M. Newcomb and E. L. Hartley, eds., *Readings in Social Psychology*, New York: Henry Holt and Co., 1947, pp. 531–541.

Manuel Gamio, *The Mexican Immigrant*, Chicago: University of Chicago Press, 1930.

M. Gottschalk and A. G. Duker, *Jews in the Post-War World*, New York: Dryden Press, 1945.

Arnold W. Green, "Why Americans Feel Insecure," *Commentary*, 6 (1948): 18–28.

Eugene L. Hartley, *Problems in Prejudice*, New York: King's Crown Press, 1946.

Oscar I. Janowsky, *Nationalities and National Minorities*, New York: Macmillan Co., 1945.

Ruby Jo Reeves Kennedy, "Single or Triple Melting-Pot? Intermarriage Trends in New Haven, 1870–1940," *American Journal of Sociology*, 49 (1943–44): 331–339.

Samuel Koenig, "The Problem of Anti-Semitism," in Koenig, Rex D. Hopper, and Feliks Gross, eds., *Sociology: A Book of Readings*, New York: Prentice-Hall, 1953.

Alfred McClung Lee, "Fraternities: Schools for Prejudice?" *American Jewish Committee Reporter*, 2: 5 (September–October 1954): 2–3.

———— and Elizabeth Briant Lee, *The Fine Art of Propaganda: A Study of Father Coughlin's Speeches*, New York: Harcourt, Brace and Co. and the Institute for Propaganda Analysis, 1939.

Kurt Lewin, *Resolving Social Conflicts*, New York: Harper & Bros., 1948.

James G. Leyburn, "World Minority Problems," Public Affairs Pamphlet No. 132, 1947.

Leo Lowenthal and Norbert Guterman, *Prophets of Deceit: A Study of the Techniques of the American Agitator*, New York: Harper & Bros., 1949.

Robert Morrison MacIver, ed., *Group Relations and Group Antagonisms*, New York: Harper & Bros., 1944.

————, *The More Perfect Union: A Program for the Control of Inter-Group Discrimination in the United States*, New York: Macmillan Co., 1948.

Carey McWilliams, *A Mask for Privilege: Anti-Semitism in America*, Boston: Little, Brown & Co., 1948.

J. M. Mecklin, *The Ku Klux Klan: A Study of the American Mind*, New York: Harcourt, Brace and Co., 1924.

Robert K. Merton, "The Self-Fulfilling Prophecy," *Antioch Review*, 8 (1948): 193–210.

C. Wright Mills, Clarence Senior, and Rose Kohn Goldsen, *The Puerto Rican Journey: New York's Newest Migrants*, New York: Harper & Bros., 1950.

M. F. Ashley Montagu, *Man's Most Dangerous Myth: The Fallacy of Race*, 3d ed., New York: Harper & Bros., 1952.

J. L. Moreno, *Sociodrama: A Method for the Analysis of Social Conflicts*, New York: Beacon House, 1944.

Hortense Powdermaker, *Probing Our Prejudices*, New York: Harper & Bros., 1944.

Arnold M. Rose, ed., *Race Prejudice and Discrimination*, New York: Alfred A. Knopf, 1951.

Fred W. Ross, "Get Out If You Can: The Saga of Sal Si Puedes," a pamphlet, California Federation for Civic Unity, 101 Post St., San Francisco, Calif., 1953. An account of an American Friends Service Committee project among Mexican-Americans in a Northern California community.

Gerhart Saenger, *The Social Psychology of Prejudice*, New York: Harper & Bros., 1953.

Richard Schermerhorn, *These Our People: Minorities in American Culture*, Boston: D. C. Heath and Co., 1952.

Thorsten Sellin, *Culture Conflict and Crime*, New York: Social Science Research Council, 1938.

J. P. Shalloo and Donald Young, eds., "Minority Peoples in a World at War," *The Annals*, 223 (September 1942).

Muzafer and Carolyn W. Sherif, *Groups in Harmony and Tension*, New York: Harper & Bros., 1953.

George Eaton Simpson and J. Milton Yinger, *Racial and Cultural Minorities: An Analysis of Prejudice and Discrimination*, New York: Harper & Bros., 1953.

Donald S. Strong, *Organized Anti-Semitism in America*, Washington: American Council on Public Affairs, 1941.

Raymond Gram Swing, *Forerunners of American Fascism*, New York: Julian Messner, 1935.

Leon E. Truesdell, *The Canadian Born in the United States*, New Haven: Yale University Press, 1943.

Robin M. Williams, Jr., *The Reduction of Intergroup Tensions*, New York: Social Science Research Council, 1947.

Wendell L. Willkie, *One World*, New York: Simon and Schuster, 1943.

Louis Wirth, *The Ghetto*, Chicago: University of Chicago Press, 1928.

——, "The Problem of Minority Groups," pp. 347–372 in Ralph Linton, ed., *The Science of Man in the World Crisis*, New York: Columbia University Press, 1945.

Donald R. Young, *American Minority Peoples*, New York: Harper & Bros., 1932.

Florian Znaniecki, *Modern Nationalities: A Sociological Study*, Urbana: University of Illinois Press, 1952.

REVIEW QUESTIONS

1. What reasons do Thomas and Znaniecki give for the inability of the immigrant to construct for himself a new life-organization?

2. What reasons do they give for saying that the "second generation . . . degenerates further still" unless certain conditions are met?

3. How does the segregation of the Jews differ from that of the Negroes?

4. Upon what chief factors does Wirth say that the survival of the Jews depends?

5. Why does Wirth believe that the Negroes can benefit from the historic experiences of the Jews?

6. How does Bloomgarden account for medical school quotas?

7. What relationships did Barrabee and Von Mering find between stress and Irish family social structure? How do these differ from those found in Yankee-American, Jewish, and Italian families?

8. Since 1947, what changes in the activities of "hate" groups are observable?

9. What does McWilliams indicate are interests served by anti-Jewish discrimination?

10. What does the incident of the Judge Hollzer meeting illustrate?

11. Is discrimination in college fraternities and sororities of much social consequence?

12. How does Galarza characterize the Mexican-Americans?

13. What does Galarza see as the chief problems confronting Mexican-Americans in the United States?

PART VII

Social Crises

CHAPTER 22

Depressions and Catastrophes

UNEMPLOYMENT, dust storms, floods, droughts, and inflations have stalked the land and its people, and, with wars, they represent our principal social crises of a general sort. Between depressions, droughts, and wars, some thought is given to preventive and ameliorative measures, but it has always been difficult for us to concern ourselves with a possible catastrophe when there are always current problems and opportunities of an absorbing and demanding nature.

The selections on the depression of the 1930's are to remind students in the vivid language of sensitive contemporary investigators just how drastic such experiences were and again may be. Palmer and Wood furnish detail concerning those who, in May 1934, were on relief in urban areas. The staff of the Living Newspaper, in a scene based on newspaper dispatches, catches the drama, tenseness, and pathos of farmers about to lose their land. *Fortune* recounts the extent and nature of the remaining unemployment at the time of the outbreak of World War II in Europe and mentions war as one of a number of possible ways to bring the "dispossessed" within our economic system.

During World War II, the manpower situation was reversed. But even though the people worried about the depression around the corner, they were perforce more concerned by the wage-price spiral that confronted them during and after the war. Men are so busy struggling against one another for advantages in the markets of the country that they give little attention and effort to effective measures for planning in the public interest.

To typify the problems of dust, flood, earthquake, and other natural catastrophes, two selections are reproduced, one on drought and dust storms and another on disaster relief. The chapters on physical resources, urban and rural problems, and economic problems touch upon other aspects of man's fight with natural disasters of a sudden or creeping sort.

Urban Workers on Relief
Gladys L. Palmer and Katherine D. Wood

The principal findings with regard to the occupational and social characteristics of the urban relief population in the 79 cities as a whole may be summarized briefly. Of the 165,000 relief households studied,[1] 10 per cent reported no employable person in the household, 18 per cent reported some person engaged in private employment on a part- or full-time basis, and slightly less than three-fourths of the total reported all persons of working age unemployed. Since some of the persons seeking work were handicapped by physical or mental disabilities, it is estimated that approximately 20 per cent of the households surveyed could be classified as without an employable member. Eighty per cent of the cases studied were therefore dependent upon public aid because of complete or partial unemployment, or, in a small proportion of cases, inadequate earnings from full-time employment. Three-fourths of the

---

[1] Changes later made in the sampling ratios, to better represent cities of all sizes, resulted in a weighted summary of about 202,000 cases.

From "Urban Workers on Relief, Part I: The Occupational Characteristics of Workers on Relief in Urban Areas May 1934," Works Progress Administration Research Monograph 4, Washington: Government Printing Office, 1936, pp. xxiii–xxv, xxvii.

families were white and one-fourth were of Negro or other racial extraction. The average size of white families was 3.8 persons and of Negro families 3.4; and more than one-half of all families studied had only one employable person per family.

About 400,000 persons 16 to 64 years of age were included in the study. Of this number, over half were unemployed persons seeking work, a third were for specific reasons not seeking work, and approximately one-tenth were engaged in private employment at the time of the study. Among those not seeking work, there were five times as many women as men. In general, those not seeking work were older and had a higher physical disability rate than the other groups. The majority of the persons not seeking work were women engaged in household activities (64 per cent of the total). Most of the persons in the younger age groups were attending school, and the majority of older men not seeking work were physically unable to work.

Interest naturally centers around the characteristics of the 235,000 workers reported unemployed and seeking work. There were almost three times as many men as women in this group. The vast majority of unemployed workers were a part of the experienced labor supply of their communities. The typical unemployed person on urban relief rolls in May 1934 was a white man 38 years of age who was the head of a household. He had not completed an elementary school education, but had had, on the average, 10 years experience at the occupation he considered his customary or "usual" one. This occupation varied considerably with the type of community in which he lived but was most frequently a semiskilled or unskilled occupation in the manufacturing or mechanical industries. Perhaps the most significant fact about the average urban worker on relief in 1934 was that he had lost the last job at his usual occupation in the winter of 1931–32.

The largest single group (34 per cent) of unemployed men on urban relief rolls had formerly been employed in unskilled occupations. One-fourth of the total had worked in skilled and another fourth in semiskilled occupations. The remainder had been engaged in professional, proprietary, and clerical pursuits. Proprietary workers were the oldest group of unemployed men on urban relief rolls and clerical workers the youngest. In general, skilled and unskilled workers had been unemployed longer than semiskilled and

white collar workers. White collar workers had a better educational background than other workers. Skilled workers had been to school longer than semiskilled and unskilled workers, and had had greater experience at their usual occupation than any group except proprietors.

The average unemployed woman on urban relief rolls in 1934 was 5 years younger than the average man. She had had a slightly better education but had worked for a shorter period at her customary occupation. She had lost the last job at her usual occupation in the fall of 1932 and had had no non-relief job of 1 month or more for approximately 1½ years.

The majority of all women in urban relief rolls had formerly been employed in semiskilled and unskilled occupations and had been out of work for shorter periods of time than men. Women who had been clerical workers were the youngest of all and were in general better educated, but had worked shorter periods at their usual occupations. Of the occupations in which women were numerous, clerical workers had been unemployed for the longest periods of time. Women from domestic and personal service, on the other hand, who constituted over half of all women on urban relief rolls, tended to be older than the average, and had been unemployed for shorter periods of time.

Every type of occupation and industry was represented on urban relief rolls in May 1934, but a significant proportion of all men (36 per cent) and over half of all women were found to be concentrated in the 10 largest occupations reported. These 10 occupations (in order of decreasing size) were the following: (1) servants, (2) chauffeurs, truck and tractor drivers, (3) laborers (building and general), (4) salesmen, (5) carpenters, (6) painters, (7) clerks, (8) operatives in the iron and steel industries, (9) operatives in the clothing industries, and (10) coal mine operatives. Five of these occupations are among the 10 largest occupations reported by gainful workers in cities with a population of 25,000 or over in 1930. . . .

The highest average length of time out of a job was reported by white men from occupations in the extraction of minerals, by white women in transportation and communication, by Negro men in manufacturing and mechanical industries and mining, and by Negro women in transportation and communication. The five types of industrial establishments from which workers on relief reported the highest average length of time out of any job lasting 1 month or more (in order of decreasing averages) were: blast furnaces and steel mills, metal factories other than iron and steel, oil and gas wells, coal mines, and other iron and steel industries.

The pre-depression unemployed were represented on urban relief rolls in May 1934, although the proportion they formed of the total was small. In the group which had held no job since 1929 or before there were three times as many women as men. This may have been the result of the depression which forced many women to re-enter the labor market after several years of not seeking work. It is significant, however, that 5 per cent of the men on urban relief rolls had held no job lasting over 1 month for more than 5 years and that 14 per cent had lost the last job at their usual occupation prior to the spring of 1929. . . .

Perhaps the most significant facts [in this study] are those which demonstrate the cumulative effects of prolonged unemployment. The longer persons are out of work the worse their chances are for re-employment at their customary occupation or, in fact, at any type of job. Although the majority of unemployed workers on relief stay on relief for relatively short periods of time, there appears to be a residual group of long-time unemployed who are the core of a permanent unemployment problem. This group will not be able to qualify for unemployment benefits under the provisions of the Social Security Act. Their number is relatively small when compared with the total number of persons in the urban relief population. Their proportion of the total rises, however, in certain communities and in certain occupations and age groups. Some of them are out of work in isolated and specialized industrial centers which have been characterized by steadily declining employment opportunity in recent years. Others were formerly employed in occupations which are now obsolescent. Still others are too old to secure employment readily in the occupations in which they were formerly employed, or for which they have been trained, and are too young to secure old age pensions. Together they constitute a group of workers who are "stranded" in every sense of the word.

A Depression Farm Auction
The Staff of the Living Newspaper

VOICE OF LIVING NEWSPAPER (*over loudspeaker*): Farmers lose their land—their homes—unpaid mortgages are foreclosed; land is sold at public auction. The farmers take matters in their own hands.[1]

(*The scene is a farmyard, but there is no attempt at realism; blue cyclorama, gray platform for auctioneer, barrel on platform. . . . FARMERS are in overalls, a few WOMEN in crowd. One MAN conspicuous in business clothes stands apart. All this is discovered at rise. The time is clearly afternoon, the day bright.*)

FIRST NEIGHBOR (*beckoning*): Hey, Sam! Albert's going to do the talkin'. John'll speak up first.

WILSON:[2] There's a fellow here I don't know.

FRED: He was asking me questions about the place.

FIRST NEIGHBOR: Point him out, Sam, and I'll watch.

(WILSON *nods his head backward toward a well-dressed man, who is walking about. The* MAN *finally stops in front of a group of farmers, and engages them in casual conversation.*)

STRANGER: Nice day for an auction. (*The group of* FARMERS *look at him in disgust, turn away.* STRANGER *shrugs shoulder, and turns to* FIRST *and* SECOND NEIGHBOR *standing near.*)

AUCTIONEER: We're all ready, folks, soon's the sheriff reads his notice. (SHERIFF *reads in an unintelligible fast monotone, 'State of Wisconsin . . .'* WILSON *goes through* GROUP OF FARMERS, *from person to person, speaking so that the audience can hear.*)

WILSON: Albert's going to do the rest of the

---

[1] *Literary Digest*, January 21, 1933.
[2] Fictional character.

From "Triple-A Plowed Under," in *Federal Theatre Plays*, ed. by Pierre de Rohan, New York: Random House, 1938, pp. 1–57, pp. 21–23 quoted. Reprinted by permission.

talkin'. (*Each* FARMER *nods in understanding manner.* WILSON *continues as he reaches* JOHN) You speak up first. Albert'll do the talkin'. (*As* SHERIFF *completes his reading of the notice, the* AUCTIONEER *comes down with his hammer.*)

AUCTIONEER: Folks, today you're going to be able to buy a lot of up-to-date modern machinery, and the best piece of farm land this side of the Mississippi River, and I want to see some spirited bidding. (FARMERS *watch him grimly and silently*) The valuation of the farm alone is twenty thousand dollars, three hundred acres under cultivation. Lock, stock and barrel, I should say it's worth, conservatively speakin', thirty thousand dollars. I leave it to you, gents, as to how we bid. All to oncet, or piece by piece? What'dya say we keep the pikers out. . . . (*Meaningly, to* STRANGER) All to oncet. (STRANGER *nods slightly.* FARMERS *all turn their heads in unison toward* STRANGER *who is still occupied by two farmers talking to him*) . . . Any objection? (*There is no answer*) . . . All right, thirty thousand dollars on the block. What am I bid? (*Slight pause.*)

JOHN (*quietly, unemotionally*): Twelve cents.[3]

(*Pause.* FARMERS *remain grimly silent.*)

AUCTIONEER (*forcing a laugh*): That's a good one. Twelve cents. . . . Ha! Ha! Well, now, let's have a bid!

JOHN: That's my bid. (AUCTIONEER *looks around and is sobered by the dead earnestness of the* FARMERS. *His next speech, in dead earnestness*

---

[3] *New York Times*, February 2, 1933.

likewise, is spoken meaningfully, directly to the stranger.*)

AUCTIONEER: All right, I've got a bid. I'm bid twelve cents on thirty thousand dollars' worth of property, twelve cents. (*Right at* STRANGER) Who'll bid a thousand? Do I hear a thousand? (STRANGER *opens his mouth to speak. He starts to raise his arm. The* FIRST NEIGHBOR *grabs his hand.* THIRD NEIGHBOR *spins him around, tips his hat over his eyes and the two lead him off,* THIRD NEIGHBOR *speaking.*)

THIRD NEIGHBOR: . . . and when it rains around these parts, Mister, it pours. And you ought to see the pigs down to my place. It's the likeliest litter of little devils anybody ever seen. (*His voice trails off as they disappear off stage. The auctioneer's jaw sags. He looks at the* SHERIFF *and tries to catch his glance.* SHERIFF *deliberately turns his back and starts whittling.*)

JOHN: Whattya waitin' for? You got a bid.

AUCTIONEER: All right. Twelve cents, twelve cents, what do I hear? I've got to have another bid. 'Tain't legal less I have another bid.

ALBERT: Thirteen cents. (*Dead pause. The* AUCTIONEER *looks beaten, as if he hadn't heard the bid*) You got your bid. (*There is another, shorter pause, during which the* AUCTIONEER *looks more helpless than ever*) Well, whattaya waitin' for? Call it!

AUCTIONEER (*thoroughly licked, smacks his hammer down hard*): All right, thirteen cents once . . . thirteen cents twice . . . thirteen cents. . . . Are you all done? Sold for thirteen cents.

Challenge of Unemployment: 1939
From "Fortune"

October, 1939, tenth anniversary of the Wall Street crash, marked the end of a ten-year industrial depression in the U. S. In that month the Federal Reserve Board index of industrial production rose to 121, which was two points higher than the average for 1929. But factory employment in October, 1939, stood at 104, which is two points below the 1929 figure. There were some nine million American citizens who were,

as the term is, "unemployed." And there may be more today.

There are two reasons why employment has failed to keep pace with production. One is the technological reason,* which cannot be measured; but it is known that the U. S. worker, with the help of machines, produces much more per hour

---

* See selections on the social impacts of technological change in Chapters 4 and 6.

From "The Dispossessed: For nearly one-fourth of the population there is no economic system—and from the rest there is no answer," *Fortune*, 21: 2 (February 1940): 94–96, 118, 120–121, 123–124, 126, p. 94 quoted. Reprinted by permission.

than he did ten years ago. . . . The other reason is anything but technological, and is much more important. At least six million of the nine million "unemployed" were neither tractored off the farm nor rationalized out of the roundhouse nor spray-gunned off the scaffold nor mechanized out of the mine nor even eroded onto the highways. Six million, as a strictly statistical matter, have never had jobs at all. They are the net increase in the working population. By simply growing up during the last ten years, the members of this idle horde silently inform their nation that to achieve in 1939 the production levels of 1929 is no achievement at all.

Such, in simplified form, is the problem that like the ghost of his guilt freezes the tongue of any honest American who is otherwise proud of his economic system. There are simply too many people outside that system. They are wrenches, not cogs, in the machine. A meager and infrequent market, they would be no market at all were it not for public largess, which, since the beginning of the New Deal, has totaled no less than $19,000,000,000 in federal, state, and local expenditures to keep them alive. When they produce, it is to hear themselves called shovel-learners; and even a skilled hand fumbles work that he knows is an excuse for, not a cause of, the pay. As animals they are sick twice as often as their neighbors. As souls they seem considerably more hopeful of the future than they have any reason to be. . . . As citizens they begin to lose interest. They are, in fact, dispossessed.

There are several simple ways in which the economic system could get this incubus off its conscience. War might do it.* "I'd just as soon go to war," said Silas, a forty-year-old ex-miner of Birmingham shortly after he was dismissed from WPA last summer. In the December [1939]

* Observe that this was written shortly after the formal outbreak of World War II in Europe.—Eds.

FORTUNE Survey on war feeling, wherein only 2.5 per cent of the people voted to go to war at once, 8.4 per cent of the unemployed so voted, a higher percentage than in any other group. "This war is overdue," said a New York subway bum a couple of months ago, not too drunk to figure that "every so often there get to be too many people in the world. Take me. I can't get a job. Well, let's *have* a war."

Another easy solution would be to ignore the problem entirely. If all public help were eliminated, the dispossessed would probably not revolt. In Governor Bricker's recent social experiment in Ohio, when sixteen thousand hungry people were refused relief for two weeks or more, there was no rioting and little disorder. "A man without enough calcium in his bones, or food under his belt," points out Harry Hopkins, the authority on the subject, "has more inertia in him than rebellion." If the Ohio experiment had been carried to its logical extreme, the ex-reliefers might not have voted Republican next year, but they probably would not have mobbed the capitol either. Ultimately, by the rules of the Darwinian game, they and their children would die off.

Other solutions are communism and fascism. The problem does not compel such solutions, but it invites them. The plan of production for use, now being tried on a small scale in southern California, is also a possible solution. So, for that matter, is the New Deal: most of the dispossessed are now receiving public help, and U. S. business has demonstrated that it can make excellent profits without employing them. The fact remains that they are dispossessed. The fact remains that from the standpoint of the economy, they have no reason to be alive. The fact remains that none of these "solutions" can be entertained if the functioning part of our system desires to keep its own health and self-respect.

Drought and Dust
Seth S. King

Seth S. King (1920–   ), Midwest correspondent, *The New York Times*.

To most residents of the Great Plains the summers of 1934 and 1936 have a special and very un-

happy significance. For these were the years of the great droughts. These were the years when

From "Drought in the Great Plains States—A Repetition of the 1930's?" *The New York Times* (July 25, 1954).

thousands of acres of crop and range lands were ruined, when hordes of grasshoppers ate every shred of vegetation, when cattle and sheep were driven from the ranges and sold at calamity prices.

This week, from Texas northward to South Dakota and from the Rockies almost to the Mississippi, there was a sickening feeling that all this might be starting again.

For days the temperatures in most of this area have ranged above the hundred mark. On the ground itself thermometers have recorded readings of 135 and 140 degrees. Skies have been cloudless, and high winds, which seemed to come straight from some gigantic blast furnace, have pulled up what little moisture was left in the ground. The scattered rains that did fall ran off the baked earth and did no good.

In addition, the grasshoppers were back. In southern Iowa they were leaving the fence rows, where the weeds had dried up, and were starting to eat the corn. In Missouri it was so hot they were reported leaping out of the fields and into barnyards and onto porches in search of shade.

The extent of the drought and the effect it has had on agriculture and business has varied throughout the stricken region. But in general the pattern is the same as in 1934 and in 1936, and the final results can be as bad or even worse if the rains do not come soon.

In Texas the central sections of the state were the hardest hit. The Fort Worth and Dallas areas had temperatures around the 100-degree mark most of the week. For more than thirty days the rainfall throughout central and northwestern Texas was from 25 to 50 per cent of normal.

In most of Oklahoma the temperatures were running from 6 to 9 degrees above normal. In Tulsa and Oklahoma City the thermometer hovered between 100 and 112 degrees for nearly two weeks. Rainfall, which had been excellent in early June, was far below normal and long range forecasts did not call for any more in the near future.

Kansas and Nebraska were consistently producing some of the highest temperatures in the nation. Fort Scott was without rain for forty-seven consecutive days, and temperatures there and in several other Kansas localities throughout the state reached 116 degrees.

Rainfall in the Kansas City area has averaged 4.49 inches below normal since the beginning of 1954. In other sections of Missouri, it has been below normal for the past three years, and this year was described by Gov. Phil M. Donnelly as the worst of them all.

In Iowa, which was recently hit by floods and cloudbursts in its northern section, the southern third of the state was suffering for the second straight year. At the moment rainfall there was 2.4 inches below what should have fallen in the past month. In many other sections in this area it was only 10 per cent of normal.

Colorado and Wyoming, although less seriously affected by high temperatures, were suffering seriously from lack of rain. In addition, the past winter produced much less snow than normal, and streams in southwestern Colorado were at the lowest level since 1934.

The amount of damage already caused by these extreme conditions varies with the type of crops raised in the various sections.

In Oklahoma, Kansas and Nebraska a great number of farmers had already harvested one of the best wheat crops in their memories before the worst of the drought struck. Since their land will lie fallow until this fall or next year, they are free from worry for the moment.

In other sections oat, barley and other small-grain crops were generally good and were either harvested or "made" and not in danger.

However, in southern Iowa, northeastern Kansas and Nebraska and much of Missouri one of the best-looking corn crops in many years was on the brink of serious damage. Some agriculture officials estimated that nearly one-third of the Missouri corn was already lost and in sections of eastern Kansas the corn had been burned so badly by the hot winds that even a three-inch rain would fail to help it.

In Iowa, the nation's leading corn producer, the dryness and the hot days were speeding up the tasseling of the plants. If this trend continued, it would mean small and poorer quality ears and a much lower yield per acre than normal. Crop forecasters said that rains over the southern half of the state within the next ten days were the only thing that would prevent a serious corn loss.

But the ones who were feeling the sharpest pains from the heat and dryness were the cattle ranchers and sheep raisers. Many of these men had already suffered through three and four years of below-normal moisture and were on the verge of going under. To them drought might mean the final downward shove.

Pasture conditions in parts of Oklahoma and

Nebraska, and most of eastern Colorado and Wyoming were at a critical stage. The hot winds had dried out much of the subsoil moisture left by the spring rains, and the sun was burning up any grass that grew. In southeastern Wyoming, range conditions had deteriorated 18 per cent in June. This was the largest drop since records were first taken thirty-two years ago. The state's Co-operative Crop-Reporting Service said feed and water on the ranges were only 70 per cent of normal, the lowest since 1936. The service also rated the condition of range cattle at 82 per cent of normal and that of range sheep at 83 per cent, again the lowest since 1936.

These same conditions existed in central and west Texas, except that in these areas the drought was in its fourth year and the strain on foundation herds was being felt even more severely.

This drying up of pastures and ranges meant that the cattle and sheep producers would have to begin emergency feeding if they wanted to keep their livestock from starving. If they had sufficient reserve funds they could weather the crisis. But if they didn't they would have to start moving their cattle and sheep to market before they were ready and sell them under conditions that would keep getting worse before they got better again.

Already there were signs that many ranchers were being forced to sell their poorer grades of range stock.

In Colorado the slaughter of range cattle jumped 16 per cent in one week. In Oklahoma the market price received for the poorer grades of cattle dropped five cents a pound. In Kansas City the slaughter rates on some cattle and sheep was 34 per cent higher for the past five months than for a year ago.

In contrast to this, in Oklahoma the cost of alfalfa hay for range feed had jumped as much as $15 per ton, and cottonseed cake, a popular supplement feed, was getting scarce.

Faced with these conditions, the ranchers and farmers have appealed to Washington for Federal aid. In Colorado and Texas twenty-three counties in each state have been declared drought emergency areas and sections of Wyoming have been similarly designated. Officials in Oklahoma and Missouri were asking for this type of aid and were expected to receive it.

The designation of states as disaster drought areas entitled farmers and ranchers within them to receive Government loans and to get money to defray the transportation costs of hay bought as supplemental feed. In addition to this help, cattlemen's associations and Congressmen from these states have asked the Department of Agriculture to resume its buying of low-grade beef as a means of bolstering the sinking cattle market. These spokesmen were also asking that the Commodity Credit Corporation be allowed to sell surplus corn and feed grains to livestock owners at reduced prices.

These emergency measures were about the only recourse left to farmers and ranchers, except the rainmakers, and even some of these were being hired. There was little in the way of emergency tillage or other soil conservation measures that could be taken.

The only thing that would restore the land was rain. In some of the range and pasture areas the grass could make a respectable comeback if it got moisture within the next few days. In others, the land was over-grazed and would not recover effectively until cattle numbers were reduced and the rains came.

Catastrophe
Lewis M. Killian

Lewis M. Killian (1919–   ), associate professor of sociology, Florida State University, Tallahassee.

In a study of the reactions of people in four Southwestern communities to physical disasters—explosions and tornadoes—made by the University of Olahoma Research Institute, it was found that conflicting group loyalties and contradictory roles resulting from multiple-group membership were significant factors affecting individual behavior in critical situations. The dilemmas created

From "The Significance of Multiple-Group Membership in Disaster," *American Journal of Sociology,* 67: 4 (January 1952): 309–314, pp. 310–314 quoted. Footnotes deleted.

by the disasters also brought to light latent contradictions in roles not ordinarily regarded as conflicting.

In spite of the fact that multiple-group memberships do create dilemmas and inconsistencies, the majority of people in modern urban society manage to function efficiently as members of many groups, often being only vaguely aware of contradictions in their various roles. . . .

When catastrophe strikes a community, many individuals find that the latent conflict between ordinarily nonconflicting group loyalties suddenly becomes apparent and that they are faced with the dilemma of making an immediate choice between various roles. In his classic study of the Halifax disaster, S. H. Prince noted this conflict when he wrote:

But the earliest leadership that could be called social, arising from the public itself, was that on the part of those who had no family ties, much of the earliest work being done by visitors in the city. The others as a rule ran first to their homes to discover if their own families were in danger.

People who had been present in the explosion port of Texas City and in three Oklahoma tornado towns during disasters were asked, among other questions, "What was the first thing you thought of after the disaster struck?" and "What was the first thing you did?" Their answers revealed not only the conflict between loyalties to the family and to the community, described by Prince, but also dilemmas arising from conflicting roles derived from membership in other groups. The individuals concerned were not always conscious of the dilemmas or of the existence of "cross-pressures," but even in such cases the choice of roles which the person made was significant in affecting the total pattern of group reaction to the disaster. In some cases subjects indicated that they recognized *after* the emergency that their reaction had been of critical social importance. On the basis of the experiences of people involved in these four community disasters it is possible to suggest the types of groups between which dilemmas of loyalty may arise in modern communities. Tentative generalization as to how these dilemmas will be resolved and as to their significance for *group* reactions to disaster may also be formulated.

The choice required of the greatest number of individuals was the one between the family and other groups, principally the employment group or the community. Especially in Texas City, many

men were at work away from their families when disaster struck and presented a threat to both "the plant" and "the home." In all the communities there were individuals, such as policemen, firemen, and public utilities workers, whose loved ones were threatened by the same disaster that demanded their services as "trouble-shooters." Even persons who had no such definite roles to play in time of catastrophe were confronted with the alternatives of seeing after only their own primary groups or of assisting in the rescue and relief of any of the large number of injured persons, regardless of identity. Indeed, only the unattached person in the community was likely to be free of such a conflict.

How these conflicts between loyalty to the family group and loyalty to other membership groups, including the community and "society-at-large," were resolved was of great significance for the reorganization of communities for rescue, relief, and prevention of further disaster. In Texas City, at the time of the first ship explosion, many men were working in oil refineries, where failure to remain on the job until units were shut down could result in additional fires and explosions. In all the communities studied, failure of community functionaries, such as firemen and policemen, to perform the duties appropriate to their positions could result in the absence of expected and badly needed leadership in a disorganized group. This, in turn, could cause costly delay in the reorganization of the community for emergency rescue, traffic control, and fire-fighting activity. Preoccupation of large numbers of able survivors with their own small primary groups could result in the atomization of the community into small, unco-ordinated groups, again delaying reorganization into a relatively well-integrated, unified, large group. As Prince indicated in his statement, quoted above, this would increase the dependence of the community on outside sources of leadership.

The great majority of persons interviewed who were involved in such dilemmas resolved them in favor of loyalty to the family or, in some cases, to friendship groups. Much of the initial confusion, disorder, and seemingly complete disorganization reported in the disaster communities was the result of the rush of individuals to find and rejoin their families. Yet in none of the four communities studied did the disastrous consequences contemplated above seem to have materialized. In the first place, there were important exceptions to the tendency to react first in terms of the family. Most of the refinery workers in Texas City did stay on the job until their units were safely shut down, as they had been trained to do. The significance of conflicting group loyalties in a disaster situation is underlined, however, by the importance of the actions taken by a few exceptional individuals in each town who were not confronted with such conflicts. In Texas City the chief of police remained at his post from the moment of the first explosion until seventy-two hours later, never returning to his home during the entire period and playing a vital part in the reorganization of the community. He ascribed his ability to give undivided attention to his official duties to the fact that he knew that his family was safely out of town, visiting relatives, at the time of the explosion. One member of the volunteer fire department of a tornado town told of the thin margin by which his community escaped a disastrous fire following the "twister":

I was at my home, right on the edge of where the storm passed, when it hit. Neither me nor my wife was hurt. The first thing I thought of was fires. I knew there'd be some, so I went to the fire station right away. On the way I could see that there was a fire right in the middle of the wreckage—a butane tank had caught fire. I got out the truck, drove over there, and fought the fire by myself until the army got there to help me.

All the rest of the firemen had relatives that were hurt, and they stayed with them. Naturally they looked after them. If it hadn't been that my wife was all right, this town probably would have burned up. It's hard to say, but I kind of believe I would have been looking after my family, too.

Devotion to the family as the primary object of loyalty did not always redound to the detriment of aid to other groups, however. Many people who served as rescue workers, assisting injured people whom they did not even know, were drawn to the areas of heavy casualties because of concern for members of their own families whom they believed to be there. Apparently they found their identification with society-at-large, and the emphasis of American culture upon the importance of human life, too great to permit them to pass an injured stranger without assisting him. Hence, many stayed to assist in the common community task of rescuing the injured, in both Texas City and in the tornado towns. In one of the latter a man sensed the approach of the tornado only minutes before it struck. In spite of

great personal danger he rushed through the storm to a theater where his children were attending a movie. There he prevented the frightened audience from pouring forth into the storm by holding the doors closed. Later he was acclaimed as a hero whose quick action had saved the lives of many of his fellow-citizens. He himself denied that he had any thought of taking the great risk that he took for the sake of the anonymous audience itself; he was thinking only of his own children.

A second, but less common, type of conflict was found in the case of people who were confronted with the alternatives of playing the "heroic" role of rescue worker and of carrying out what were essentially "occupational roles." In terms of group loyalty, they were impelled, on the one hand, to act as sympathetic, loyal members of society-at-large and to give personal aid to injured human beings. On the other hand, they were called to do their duty as it was indicated by their membership in certain occupational groups.

One such person was a minister in Texas City who, upon hearing the explosion, started for the docks with the intention of helping in the rescue work. On the way he became conscious of the choice of roles which confronted him. He said:

After I heard the first explosion my first impulse was to go down to the docks and try to help there. But on the way down I saw two or three folks I knew who had husbands down there. I saw then that my job was with the families—not doing rescue work. I had a job that I was peculiarly suited for, prepared for, and I felt that I should do that.

More important for the reorganization of a tornado-stricken town was the choice made of a state patrolman between his role as a police officer and his role as friend and neighbor to the people of the community in which he was stationed. His story was:

As I drove around town after the tornado had passed I realized that the best thing I could do was to try to make contact with the outside and get help from there. I started out to drive to the next town and try to call from there. As I drove out of town people I knew well would call me by name and ask me to help them find their relatives. Driving by and not stopping to help those people who were looking to me as a friend was one of the hardest things I ever had to do.

As a result of this difficult decision, this man became the key figure in the development of organized rescue work, after he recruited and organized a large force of rescue workers in a nearby community.

A similar dilemma faced many public utilities workers who were forced to disregard the plight of the injured if they were to perform their task of restoring normal community services. Unlike the minister and the patrolman, these workers reported no awareness of a conflict of roles, regarding it as a matter of course that they concentrated on their often quite dangerous jobs. Some indicated that preoccupation with the job was so intense that they were scarcely aware of what went on around them. Yet the instances of devotion to prosaic duty cited above were exceptional. Many policemen, firemen, and other functionaries acted heroically but quite outside the framework and discipline of their organizations.

For people whose usual occupational roles bore little or no relationship to the needs created by a disaster, identification with the community as a whole and disregard of their occupational roles came still more easily. Many merchants and clerks rushed from their stores to aid in rescue work, leaving both goods and cash on the counters. The postmaster in one tornado town left the post office completely unguarded, even though the windows were shattered and mail was strewn about the floor. This was, it is true, an extreme case of abandonment of the occupational role.

A third type of conflict of loyalties was that between the loyalty of employees to "the company" as an organization and to fellow-employees as friends and human beings. It might seem that the choice, essentially one between life and property, should have been an easy one; but the fact that different choices were made by men with different degrees of identification with other workers reveals that a basic conflict was present. In Texas City many plant officials were also residents of the community and friends of the workers. After the explosions, in which several top executives were killed, some men found themselves suddenly "promoted" to the position of being in charge of their company's damaged property. At the same time men with whom they had worked daily for several years were injured or missing. The most common, almost universal, reaction was to think of the men first and of the plant later. One plant official, active in rescue work in spite of a broken arm and numerous lacerations, described his reaction to the sudden, dramatic conflict between loyalty to the company and loyalty to the workers as follows:

Property! Nobody gave a damn for property! All that was important was life. I've often wondered just how it would be to walk off and let a plant burn up. That was the way it was. We didn't even consider fighting the fire.

In sharp contrast to this reaction, however, was that of a man in charge of a neighboring plant. While he was in Texas City at the time of the first blast, he had never lived in the community and scarcely knew his workers. He described his first reaction in the following words:

I got in my car and drove over to another refinery to find out what had happened. The assistant superintendent told me that their top men had been killed and asked me what I thought he should do, I told him, "You should take charge of the company's property. That's what the president of your company would tell you if he were here. You look after the property. I'm going over to Galveston to call our president, and I'll call yours at the same time."

While this reaction was exceptional, it is significant as suggesting an alternate way of resolving the conflict between loyalty to "the company" and "the men."

Finally, some individuals suddenly discovered, in the face of disaster, that there was a conflict between loyalty to the community and loyalty to certain extra-community groups. At the time of two of the disasters telephone workers in the Southwest were on strike. In both communities the striking workers were allowed to return to duty by union leaders but were ordered to walk out again a few days later. In both cases the union officials considered the emergency to be over sooner than did the townspeople of the stricken communities. In one town the workers obeyed the union's orders only to find themselves subjected to harsh criticism by their fellow-townsmen. In the other community the workers resigned from the union rather than forsake their loyalty to their other membership group. It was almost a year before union officials were able to reorganize the local in this town, and some workers never rejoined. . . .

Further research is needed to make possible the prediction of the choices that will be made by individuals in these conflicts. The frequency with which individuals thought and acted first in terms of family and close friends suggests that loyalty to primary groups stands first in the hierarchy of group loyalties, as might be expected. On the other hand, important exceptions in which persons played relatively impersonal roles as leaders or working with matériel, rather than people, indicate that some factors, such as training or feelings of responsibility, may predispose the individual to adhere to secondary-group demands even in a disaster. Knowledge of what these factors are and how they may be induced would contribute to greater understanding of group reactions to disorganization and of methods of facilitating group reorganization.

CROSS REFERENCES TO STANDARD TEXTS *

Barnes, *Society in Transition,* pp. 55, 61, 135–137, 358–363, 587.
Bernard, *American Community Behavior,* pp. 458–459, 483–485.
Brown, *Social Pathology,* pp. 500–503.
Elliott and Merrill, *Social Disorganization,* pp. 314–316, 438–439, 565–571, 596–597, 600–602, 606–609, 616.
Gillin, *Social Pathology,* Chaps. 25–26, 28.
——— and others, *Social Problems,* pp. 200–206.

* For complete bibliographical reference to each text, see page 13.

Herman, *Approach to Social Problems,* pp. 60–61, 104–105, 257–258, 279–280, 340–341.
Landis, *Social Policies in the Making,* pp. 391–392, 428, 437–439, 447, 571.
Neumeyer, *Social Problems and the Changing Society,* pp. 68, 196, 242–243, 247, 259–266, 297–300, 314–316.
Odum, *American Social Problems,* pp. 247, 518–519.
Phelps and Henderson, *Contemporary Social Problems,* Chap. 12.
Reinhardt and others, *Social Problems and Social Policy,* Chap. 5.
Weaver, *Social Problems,* Chaps. 3, 26.

OTHER BIBLIOGRAPHY

Nels Anderson, *The Right to Work,* New York: Modern Age Books, 1938.
Robert Cooley Angell, *The Family Encounters the Depression,* New York: Charles Scribner's Sons, 1936.
Louise V. Armstrong, *We Too Are the People,* Boston: Little, Brown & Co., 1938.
Aleta Brownlee, "Disasters and Disaster Relief," *Encyclopaedia of the Social Sciences,* 5 (1931): 161–166.
Erskine Caldwell and Margaret Bourke-White, *You Have Seen Their Faces,* New York: Modern Age Books, 1937.
L. J. Carr, "Disaster and the Sequence-Pattern Concept of Social Change," *American Journal of Sociology,* 38 (1932–33): 207–218.
Ruth Shonle Cavan and Katherine H. Ranck, *The Family and the Depression,* Chicago: University of Chicago Press, 1938.
F. Stuart Chapin and Stuart A. Queen, "Research Memorandum on Social Work in the Depression," Bulletin No. 39, New York: Committee on Studies on the Social Aspects of the Depression, Social Science Research Council, 1937.
Dwight W. Chapman, ed., "Human Behavior in Disaster: A New Field of Social Research," *Journal of Social Issues,* 10 (1954): 3: 1–73.
Stuart P. Chase, *The Tragedy of Waste,* New York: Macmillan Co., 1935.
Ewan Clague, Walter J. Couper, and E. Wight Bakke, *After the Shutdown,* New Haven: Yale University Press, 1934.
W. T. and D. E. Cross, *Newcomers and Nomads in California,* Stanford: Stanford University Press, 1937.

Paul H. Douglas, *Controlling Depressions,* New York: W. W. Norton & Co., 1935.
Fairfax Downey, *Disaster Fighters,* New York: G. P. Putnam's Sons, 1938.
J. A. Estey, *Business Cycles: Their Nature, Cause, and Control,* New York: Prentice-Hall, 1950.
Paul B. Foreman, "Panic Theory," *Sociology and Social Research,* 37 (1952–53): 295–304.
Corrington Gill, *Wasted Man Power,* New York: W. W. Norton & Co., 1939.
R. R. Grinker and J. P. Spiegel, *Men Under Stress,* Philadelphia: Blakiston Co., 1945.
J. Blaine Gwin, "Do Disasters Help?" *Social Forces,* 8 (1929–30): 386–389.
Marie Dresden Lane and Francis Steegmuller, *America on Relief,* New York: Harcourt, Brace and Co., 1938.
A. Leighton, "Psychological Factors in Major Disasters," *Medical Projects Reports,* Rochester: University of Rochester, 1951.
National Research Council (Division of Medical Science) and Walter Reed Army Medical Center, *Symposium on Stress,* Washington: Army Medical Service Graduate School, 1953.
Maurice Parmelee, *Farewell to Poverty,* New York: John Wiley & Sons, 1935.
J. J. Robinson, "Men on the Bargain Counter," *American Mercury,* 25 (1932): 136–151.
James Harvey Rogers and Lester V. Chandler, "Inflation and Deflation," *Encyclopaedia of the Social Sciences,* 8 (1932): 28–33.

Paul B. Sears, *Deserts on the March,* Stillwater: University of Oklahoma Press, 1935.

Ivan R. Tannehill, *Hurricanes,* Princeton: Princeton University Press, 1937.

J. S. Tyhurst, "Individual Reactions to Community Disaster: The Natural History of Psychiatric Phenomena," *American Journal of Psychiatry, 107* (1950–51): 764–769.

U. N. Department of Economic Affairs, *Inflationary and Deflationary Tendencies,* Lake Success, N. Y.: United Nations, 1949.

U. S. Strategic Bombing Surveys, *Reports,* Washington: Government Printing Office, 1946–47.

Thorstein Veblen, *The Engineers and the Price System,* New York: B. W. Huebsch, 1921; Viking Press, 1933.

———, *Essays in Our Changing Order,* ed. by Leon Ardzrooni, New York: Viking Press, 1934.

T. O. Waage, *Inflation: Causes and Cures,* New York: H. W. Wilson Co., 1949.

A. F. C. Wallace, *Human Behavior in Extreme Situations: A Survey of Literature and Suggestions for Further Research,* report for Committee on Disaster Studies, National Research Council (mimeo.), 25 pp.

Henry A. Wallace, *Sixty Million Jobs,* New York: Reynal and Hitchcock, 1945.

Dixon Wechter, *The Age of the Great Depressions: 1929–1941,* New York: Macmillan Co., 1948.

Norbert Wiener, *The Human Use of Human Beings,* Boston: Houghton Mifflin Co., 1950.

James Mickel Williams, *Human Aspects of Unemployment and Relief,* Chapel Hill: University of North Carolina Press, 1933.

REVIEW QUESTIONS

1. What proportion of the urban unemployed did Palmer and Wood find to be part of the experienced labor supply of their communities?
2. What was the background of the women whom Palmer and Wood found on urban relief rolls?
3. Do the findings of Palmer and Wood support the tragic generalization that the Negroes are the last hired and the first fired?
4. How would you try to cope with the problems Palmer and Wood describe?
5. What impressions did you get from the dramatic incident reported by the staff of the Living Newspaper?
6. After the trials of the depression during the 1930's, does the *Fortune* account concerning the "dispossessed" suggest that any great gains had been made in coping with economic deprivation?
7. How many people were apparently still unemployed in 1939? How did this compare to the number unemployed in 1929?
8. What "moral" does *Fortune* apparently attempt to point to with its reference to Governor Bricker's "recent social experiment in Ohio"?
9. What do farmers have to gain and lose from an inflationary spiral?
10. What were the consequences of the midwestern droughts described by King?
11. What efforts are being made to cope with the dust and drought problem?
12. What can science and engineering contribute to the mitigation of such calamities as dust storms, floods, disasters, and earthquakes?
13. What can organization contribute to the mitigation of such calamities?
14. What dilemma faces disaster relief workers, according to Killian?

CHAPTER 23

Riots and Wars

POPULAR SPOKESMEN in civilized countries persist in talking as though wars are catastrophes into which their "peaceful" countries are willy-nilly precipitated every now and then by "aggressors." That wars are catastrophes can certainly be accepted, but that any civilized country is peaceful is open to serious doubt. The fact is that in "the history of states and nations a war occurs on an average in every two or three years." Almost two-fifths of the years the United States has existed have been marked by war. "If the Indian wars are included, the figures for the United States exceed 60 per cent." * With the magnitude of wars, the proportion of casualties, and the cost in lives ever mounting through recent centuries and years, the wonder is that wars have not long ago been recognized for what they are: They are a constant threat to human welfare. They are an integral part of societal structure and function as we have known it and know it now. The wonder is also that so little really serious attention is given to planning and working for peace.

Taken out of context war can be regarded as an unmixed evil. But in context war can quickly absorb tremendous support because war appears to solve personal problems for vast numbers of people. It furnishes a socially sanctioned scapegoat upon which to vent aggression. It breaks monotony. It provides a temporary divorce from marriage. It is thought to be a road to glory. And those who chant its ritual point to victims past and remote, not to the victims of the future. In prospect, war does not promise capture, torture, disease, twisted minds, mutilation, death, weakened and crippled civil rights, unemployment, heedlessly wasted natural resources, the transfer of power into fewer and more ruthless hands, and an endless burden of pensions and taxation. In retrospect, men and women have perennially wondered what happened to those ideals for which they deprived themselves, fought, and sacrificed their children.

* Pitirim A. Sorokin, *Society, Culture, and Personality,* New York: Harper & Bros., 1947, Chap. 32, p. 497 quoted.

The forces that make for war can perhaps better be understood by starting with units smaller than a state fighting a state. Freud, upon the basis of his clinical experiences, frequently insists on the extent to which we neglect the presence in man of "a powerful measure of desire for aggression." He emphasizes especially the failure of the law and of other human controls to cope with "the more discreet and subtle forms in which human aggressions are expressed." War becomes a common channel into which the aggressive desires of millions may flow without the frustrating restraints of peacetime.

The most shocking peacetime examples of violence in the United States have been lynchings, strikes, and riots. The selection dealing with race riots is presented to serve as illustration of such small-scale conflicts. The description of the 1951 Cicero race riots, from the report written by Abrams, sets forth some of the background and the chief occurrences in that running series of conflicts.

Just how wars occur is a never-ending subject for both loose theorists and careful students of human affairs. Sumner points to the role of doctrines and of the catch phrases which label them. Even in 1903, when wars were comparatively inexpensive, he concluded that there "is no state of readiness for war; the notion calls for never-ending sacrifices." Sorokin chooses to ignore power drives by individuals, corporations, cartels, and politico-economic cliques and to place the chances of war largely on changes in social relationships and cultural values, a basis sufficiently abstract to avoid offense to the powerful.

The impact of war upon persons and social institutions is highly complex, but some of its problem aspects are suggested by the next five selections. Case and Oxnam tell about the various types of conscientious objectors and how they have been treated in the United States in World Wars I and II. Oxnam then suggests a program for the treatment of conscientious objectors in World War III. The Institute for Propaganda

Analysis describes the confusion with which the clergy of the Prince of Peace reacted to demands to sanction World War II. Haber summarizes the economic and social impacts of World War II with special reference to problems of finance, employment, production, standards of living, and readjustment to a so-called peacetime economy.

Even though World War II occasioned the launching of many new lethal weapons and the development of others for future use, the atomic bomb overshadowed all others. Arthur reports his first-hand observations of what he saw when he got to Nagasaki as a member of the first mission dispatched to evacuate prisoners of war. The development of the hydrogen bomb and even more deadly ones has followed in recent years. Their impact is reported to be many times more powerful than that of the atomic bomb and the possible consequences of their use in warfare that much more horrendously destructive.

The next two selections debate universal military training. Spokesmen for the armed forces make a case for such compulsory training. The Church of the Brethern attempts to bring together into a short series of statements the arguments pro and con. The last selection presents a cross section of public opinion on peace and means of bringing it about as ascertained by Roper and Quayle in a 1954 poll.

Aggressive Cruelty Awaits Provocation
Sigmund Freud

Sigmund Freud (1856–1939), Austrian neurologist and psychiatrist, founder of psychoanalysis, professor of neuropathology, University of Vienna, 1902–1938. Principal works in English translation: *Group Psychology and the Analysis of the Ego* (1922) and *The Basic Writings of Sigmund Freud* (1938).

[Men] are not gentle, friendly creatures wishing for love, who simply defend themselves if they are attacked, but . . . a powerful measure of desire for aggression has to be reckoned as part of their instinctual endowment. The result is that their neighbor is to them not only a possible helper or sexual object, but also a temptation to them to gratify their aggressiveness on him, to exploit his capacity for work without recompense, to use him sexually without his consent, to seize his possessions, to humiliate him, to cause him pain, to torture and to kill him. *Homo homini lupus;* who has the courage to dispute it in the face of all the evidence in his own life and in history? This aggressive cruelty usually lies in wait for some provocation, or else it steps into the service of some other purpose, the aim of which might as well have been achieved by milder measures. In circumstances that favor it, when those forces in the mind which ordinarily inhibit it cease to operate, it also manifests itself spontaneously and reveals men as savage beasts to whom the thought of sparing their own kind is alien. Anyone who calls to mind the atrocities of the early migrations, of the invasion by the Huns or by the so-called Mongols under Jenghiz Khan and Tamurlane, of the sack of Jerusalem by the pious Crusaders, even indeed the horrors of the last world-war, will have to bow his head humbly before the truth of this view of man.

The existence of this tendency to aggression which we can detect in ourselves and rightly presume to be present in others is the factor that disturbs our relations with our neighbors and makes it necessary for culture to institute its high demands. Civilized society is perpetually menaced with disintegration through this primary hostility of men towards one another. Their interests in their common work would not hold them together; the passions of instinct are stronger than reasoned interests. Culture has to call up every possible reinforcement in order to erect barriers against the aggressive instincts of men and hold their manifestations in check by reaction-formations in men's minds. Hence its system of methods by which mankind is to be driven to identifications and aim-inhibited love-relationships; hence the restrictions on sexual life; and hence, too, its ideal command to love one's neighbor as oneself, which is really justified by the fact that nothing is so completely at variance with original human nature as this. With all its striving, this endeavor of culture's has so far not achieved very much. Civilization expects to prevent the worst atrocities of brutal violence by taking upon itself the right to employ violence against criminals, but the law is not able to lay hands on the more discreet and subtle forms in which human aggressions are expressed. The time comes when every one of us

has to abandon the illusory anticipations with which in our youth we regarded our fellow-men, and when we realize how much hardship and suffering we have been caused in life through their ill-will. It would be unfair, however, to reproach culture with trying to eliminate all disputes and competition from human concerns. These things are undoubtedly indispensable; but opposition is not necessarily enmity, only it may be misused to make an opening for it.

Riot: The Time Bomb That Exploded in Cicero
Charles Abrams

Charles Abrams (1901–   ), attorney; professor, graduate faculty, New School for Social Research; New York State Rent Administrator. Author: *Revolution in Land* (1939); *The Future of Housing* (1946); *Race Bias in Housing* (1947); *A Housing Program for America* (1947); *Current Land Policies* (1952); *Forbidden Neighbors* (1955).

On the 18th of September, 1951, a Cook County grand jury, investigating the recent housing riot in Cicero, Illinois, handed down a curious indictment. Instead of indicting the hoodlums responsible for the vandalism which denied a Negro the right to live where he chose, it indicted the attorney for the National Association for the Advancement of Colored People who was defending him in that right. Along with him, the owner of the house, her lawyer, and her rental agent were all charged with conspiracy to injure property by causing "depreciation in the market selling price." The right of a Negro to buy or rent a home, which is guaranteed by the federal Civil Rights Law of 1866, was thus declared to be null and void in Illinois.

For many, the implications of the riot and of the indictment were too ugly to be faced. The riot was variously held to be a nasty incident that doesn't happen too often, a wicked occurrence in a wicked city that is the haunt of Al Capone's former mob, an eruption provoked by "alien" Czechs and Poles who have not yet learned the American way of life, a teen-agers' lark that got out of control, a rumpus started by Communists —and it is not surprising that the grand jury added the interpretation it was all a "Negro plot."

Yet behind the Cicero affair lies one of the most

disturbing, and what may yet prove to be one of the most widespread, violations of civil rights in American history. Its most ominous aspect is the growing use of legal processes to flout civil rights. The Cicero riot and the Cook County indictment are only the most recent phases of the development.

The Cicero rioting started when a Mrs. DeRose, who owned a $100,000 apartment house, got into a controversy with her tenants and was ordered to refund a portion of the rent. Shortly after, it became known that she had rented an apartment to Harvey E. Clark, a Negro war veteran and a graduate of Fisk University. Movement of Negroes into white areas is nothing new in Chicago. But it was new in Cicero, which, like Dearborn (Michigan) and many similar communities, has successfully resisted Negro settlement.

When it was learned that a Negro was moving into the apartment house, a high Cicero official arrived to warn Mrs. DeRose there would be "trouble" if Clark moved in. The city, he said, could not be responsible for keeping order. Two policemen then came to tell Mrs. DeRose she could not "get away with it." At 2:30 P.M., on June 8, a moving van containing $2,000 worth of Clark's furniture drove up to the house and was

From "The Time Bomb That Exploded in Cicero," *Commentary* (November 1951), 407–414, pp. 407–409, 410, 411, 412, 413–414 quoted.

halted by the police. The rental agent was ushered out with a drawn revolver at his back. "At about 6 P.M.," reads his affidavit, "the Chief of Police of Cicero rushed out of the alley nearby followed by about twenty men and grabbed my arm." The Chief told him to " 'get out of here fast. There will be no moving into this building.' . . . He hit me about eight times while he was pushing me ahead of him toward my car which was parked across the street. I was trying to walk but he was trying to make me move faster. When we reached my car, I opened the door and the Chief shoved me inside and said 'Get out of Cicero and don't come back in town or you'll get a bullet through you.' "

When suit was brought against the Cicero police through the NAACP, United States District Judge John P. Barnes, on June 26, enjoined the city from "shooting, beating or otherwise harassing Clark"—one of the most unusual injunctions in legal annals. "You are going to exercise the same diligence in seeing that these people move in as you did in trying to keep them out," said the judge.

Word was then passed along that there would be "fun" at the apartment house. Crowds gathered, tensions rose, and a rock smashed the window of Clark's apartment.

On Wednesday, July 11, some of the white families in the apartment house, warned of impending trouble, stored their furniture and moved out. By dusk, a crowd of 4,000 cut the ropes put up by the police. Only 60 policemen were assigned to the scene. The uniformed policemen in front of the building stepped out of the way when the crowd moved forward; the plain-clothes men simply mixed with the crowd. Women supplied rocks from a nearby rockpile which were hurled at the windows while policemen cracked jokes with the mob and made anti-Negro remarks. Flares, bricks, and burning torches were thrown into the house, radiators and walls were ripped out, furniture thrown from the windows, and trees torn up by the roots to be burned as the mob cheered. While this was happening, the Mayor and Chief of Police were "out of town."

A few state police and twenty deputy sheriffs under County Sheriff John E. Babb, who arrived Wednesday evening, were at the scene, but little was done to disperse the mob. When the sheriff's deputies asked Cicero firemen to turn hoses on the crowd, the firemen refused to do so without orders from their lieutenant, and he too was un-available. After $20,000 in damage had been done to the building, Babb requested the Governor to send in the state militia. The militia finally pushed back the mob at bayonet point, while four militiamen were felled, and only their superb discipline kept the riot from turning into a massacre.

In the end, 19 persons were injured and 117 persons from Chicago and Cicero were arrested. After it was all over, the town council president made a simple explanation—"outsiders invaded our town."

The Cicero riot received more notice in Chicago than usual. For two days the news had been played down and in fact most Chicagoans saw the riot on television before they read it in their newspapers. But when the Governor called out the National Guard, the news broke all over the country, forcing the grand jury to investigate. The jury's bizarre indictment then again made the headlines and protests by the press moved the district attorney to drop the indictment against the NAACP lawyer. (The other indictments were dropped October 22.) All this adds up to more "action" than is usually given these matters in Cook County.

What has been forgotten is that the Cicero riot is only the most recent of a series in Cook County. The other riots have either not been publicized or have been reported like local fires. From July 1949 to August 1951, there were three such riots in Chicago, and there have been six altogether since 1945. In addition, since 1949 there have been more than a hundred lesser "incidents" in the Chicago area: bombings, fires, or organized assaults against Negro families, one of these by a hit-and-run incendiary who started a fire that cost ten lives. Another "incident" was the bombing of the home of Dr. Percy Julian, co-discoverer of cortisone, a few days after the Cicero riot.

A major outburst, in fact, occurred only a few days before the Cicero riot and it never broke into the headlines. It began toward evening on Sunday, July 1, when Leon Yonik, publisher of a local Lithuanian newspaper, gave shelter to three Negro delegates to the "American Peace Crusade," a Communist front organization then meeting in Chicago. A crowd gathered, the Negroes were spirited out the back door by policemen, a co-editor of the newspaper was slugged, and rock-throwing began. The windows in Yonik's house and the plateglass in his newspaper shop were shattered. The cops stood around the house three or four feet apart, ducking the missiles as the crowd cheered. Only a sergeant was in command. Next morning a false fire alarm was sounded and the mob rushed in with the hook and ladder. One of the men leaving the house, which was being "protected" by the police, was assaulted in their full view. When he visited the police station to sign a complaint, he was jailed. When arrested rioters came up for trial, policemen didn't show up as witnesses.

The Chicago Council Against Racial and Religious Discrimination called the police action "a poor job of mob diagnosis, mob dispersal, force deployment.". . .

It would only be repetitive to recite the details of the other riots since 1945. One required 1,500 policemen to quell it.

The immediate cause of the flare-ups differs in each case, but the underlying cause is always the same: Negroes try to move out of their overcrowded slum areas and are met with violence, or the presence of an occasional Negro is interpreted as signalizing an influx. Groups are permitted to gather around the target; they draw larger groups, including the subnormal, the prejudiced, the emotionally immature, and youth seeking "fun." Rumors begin to fly, emotion rises, order breaks down, and normally law-abiding citizens become part of the mob action. Frustrated by not being able to get at the target, the mob looks for a scapegoat upon which to vent its aggressions— Negroes, Jews, Communists, strangers, intellectuals. In all the outbreaks but one, police showed no willingness to protect the Negroes in their rights, and in some their forces were even deployed to let the victims take their beatings. The pattern is now a commonplace in Chicago, but the potential for miniature race wars exists in other parts of urban America. . . .

There was of course no conscious "plot." But the real-estate and home-building group played an important role in supplying the intellectual justification for housing prejudice; they are a powerful lobby locally and in Washington, and, since the expansion of federal housing programs, were able to get at least one important housing agency to incorporate their ideas in its policy.

The influential texts on real estate and housing written since the 1920's, one can find such items as:

(1) A listing of the order of racial "desirability," with the English, Germans, Scotch, Irish, and Scandinavians at the top, Jews, South Italians, Negroes, and Mexicans at the bottom.

(2) A statement by a former chief economist for the Federal Housing Administration to the effect that: "A family should never live in a neighborhood with those in a higher or lower income scale than its own."

(3) A warning to home owners, written by the "dean" of American appraisers, against "any deviation from the typical" in selecting tenants by race, color, nationality, income level, or social position.

(4) A declaration that: "The colored people certainly have a right to life, liberty, and the pursuit of happiness, but they must recognize the economic disturbance which their presence in a white neighborhood causes and forego their desire to split off from the established districts where the rest of their race lives. . . . Segregation of the Negro population seems to be the reasonable solution of the problem, no matter how unpleasant or objectionable the thought may be to colored residents."

(5) An assertion that all foreigners should be segregated and that only citizens who are "100 per cent American" are good for residential neighborhoods, which will become "anemic and even diseased if polluted with a large percentage of unassimilated aliens, who neither understand nor are in sympathy with American ideals and standards."

In a recent article in the *Appraisal Journal,* the chief appraiser for the liquidation operations of the General Services Administration asserts that real estate values are threatened, not only by Negroes, but by "people of foreign birth" and their children as well.

These and similar biases were written into the "Code of Ethics" of the National Association of Real Estate Boards and into the codes of local boards throughout the country. Thus, discrimination against minorities became a tenet of real estate "morality." It is true that the national code was modified somewhat last year, but the local codes still carry the old rule. As a result, American neighborhoods are at present being erected almost without exception as homogeneous units. The more races excluded, the more exclusive the area is considered. . . .

The most fruitful approach to a solution of this problem today would be through new building that would serve as an escape valve for the population pressure of the segregated minorities. But neither Cook County, Illinois, which has enough lots to accommodate 4,000,000 families, nor Chicago, with enough lots to house 500,000 families, find themselves capable of building new homes for a fraction of the 100,000 Negro families that need them. The only hope for creating new unsegregated housing is a large-scale public housing program or a different FHA policy—but public housing has been held down to a trickle by claims that it means "Negro infiltration," and today almost all FHA developers build "for whites only." As for city officials, most won't talk about the problem—it's too loaded with political dynamite.

Actually, in both Chicago and Detroit the very public housing program that would seem to offer some hope to minorities has been perverted into an instrument for ousting them from their present overcrowded homes. Under the pretext of "slum clearance," 50,000 Chicago Negroes face wholesale eviction. The city officials have obstinately refused to build on empty lots—this would let Negroes into white areas. So the net effect of "slum clearance" in the Chicago area is to reduce the number of housing units available to Negroes.

In the last few years, some progress has been made in breaking down segregation in a few cities. But neither the Supreme Court's ruling against the enforceability of restrictive covenants, nor FHA's decision two years ago to modify its manual, has been able to undo the damage already done throughout the country. A whole generation has been reared on the propaganda of "homogeneity," and "all-white, non-alien" neighborhoods exist from coast to coast. Many of them are still covered by restrictive covenants or substitute devices.

As things now stand, the effect of Negroes moving into new areas is that home-owners—educated by the real estate profession to believe that their houses will collapse in value if a single Negro moves nearby—offer their houses in panic and actually do bring down selling prices. Homeowners in other areas, seeing the decline of values through panic sales, form "neighborhood improvement" associations to keep the "intruders" out. More than a hundred such associations exist in Chicago and are a powerful force in the City Council. In Detroit these organizations have federated and become one of the most potent political organizations in the area. The ethical standards of business conduct in these cities have been neatly inverted and the inalienable right to buy and sell is now viewed as a conspiracy against the general welfare. . . .

In sum, Cicero is no isolated incident, chargeable to local conditions or to some single criminal segment of the population; it is only the most prominent symptom of a major disease in the American scene. The jury that indicted the landlady, her lawyer, her agent, and the NAACP lawyer was not corrupt. Nor were the rioters all vandals or gangsters. They had the sanction of their elders, of the community, of the police, and of parts of the press. The police who tried to prevent the Negro family from moving in undoubtedly believed they were acting in the interests of their community. When the mayor and chief of police "couldn't be found," it was because they knew that if they stopped the riot they would lose any chances of re-election. The sheriff of Cook County was politically embarrassed when he tried to enforce the law. Even the Governor who courageously called out the militia may have to pay a price in votes for his action. Is it not the plain fact that for the local community, segregation—and breaking the law to protect it—represents the prevailing morality, the "higher law"?

The recent decision by United States Attorney General McGrath to hold a federal grand jury investigation into the Cicero riot may be a beginning in the major effort required to tackle this problem. However, it is likely that the standards of any jury trying the culprits of Cook County will be no higher than that of the citizenry from which it is drawn.

What is called for is a full-scale drive to change both the conditions of segregation and the attitudes of prejudice that breed under these conditions and help sustain them.

The first thing is to keep the Cicero pattern from spreading to other areas, and this requires review and action at the highest Washington level. If we are to meet our housing needs in the next twenty years, we shall have to build housing equal to half our existing supply. Most of this will be built with the help of FHA, the Housing and Home Finance Agency, or the Federal Home Loan Bank System. On the government itself therefore devolves the chief responsibility for deciding whether the future neighborhoods of America will be democratic communities hospitable to all classes and groups—or be like Cicero and Dearborn.

Furthermore, there must be a direct moral and educational attack at various levels on the social attitudes which support the "all-white" Ciceros throughout the country. For it is not only the residents of these communities themselves and their leaders who are at fault. The members of Chicago's Union League club, who refused to admit Dr. Percy Julian to a luncheon of scientists, must share the blame for the moral climate of Cicero and Chicago. So must Mayor Kennelly for failing to assert leadership in Chicago. So must the industrialists who recruit workers from minority groups but take no responsibility for seeing that they are housed. So too must the private builders who attach the free and pernicious label of "exclusive" as a means of selling their houses. And so too must FHA, until it bars federal mortgage insurance to builders who discriminate in favor of one race as against another.

Further, "slum clearance" must be stopped until there is an adequate supply of houses available for the displaced families. (It is obvious that the solution of America's housing needs will not be satisfied by tearing down more houses occupied by minorities than are being built.) Simultaneously, a comprehensive program must be launched in which housing will be supplied on the basis of need, not race or color. The defense housing program can make a start in that direction, but a long-range program is needed as well.

Lastly, the creation of new non-segregated communities is itself an essential step in changing the attitudes which supply the fuel for race riots. In New York City, Pittsburgh, Philadelphia, Seattle, and Portland (Oregon) housing projects involving more than a billion dollars in investments have integrated Negroes and whites successfully. Negroes and whites live side by side in four hundred million dollars of public and private projects for middle-income families in New York City. Numerous studies have demonstrated that real estate values do not decline simply because Negroes or other minority groups move into an area.

In short, the race problem in housing will not be resolved by pious preaching of civil rights by government or community leaders while the very environments that frustrate these rights are being created under their noses. Unless the issue is met by a full-scale program of building, by public education, and by the support of top-level officials, prejudice and political power will continue to move hand in hand to reinforce the pattern of racial lawlessness that is now a spreading blight upon the American scene.

Notes on War
William Graham Sumner[*]

If you want war, nourish a doctrine. Doctrines are the most frightful tyrants to which men ever are subject, because doctrines get inside of a man's own reason and betray him against himself. Civilized men have done their fiercest fighting for doctrines. The reconquest of Holy Sepulcher, "the balance of power," "no universal dominion," "trade follows the flag," "he who holds the land will hold the sea," "the throne and the altar," the revolution, the faith—these are the things for which men have given their lives. What are they all? Nothing but rhetoric and phantasms. Doctrines are always vague; it would ruin a doctrine to define it, because then it could be analyzed, tested, criticised, and verified; but nothing ought to be tolerated which cannot be so tested. . . .

If you allow a political catchword to go on and grow, you will awaken some day to find it standing over you, the arbiter of your destiny, against which you are powerless, as men are powerless against delusions. . . .

There is no such thing nowadays as a state of readiness for war. It is a chimera, and the nations which pursue it are falling into an abyss of wasted energy and wealth. When the army is supplied with the latest and best rifles, someone invents a new field gun; then the artillery must be provided with that before we are ready. By the time we get the new gun, somebody has invented a new rifle and our rival nation is getting that; therefore

[*] See identifying note on page 46.

From "War" (1903), pp. 3–40 in his *War and Other Essays,* ed. by A. G. Keller, New Haven: Yale University Press, 1911, pp. 36, 38–40 quoted. Reprinted by permission from A. G. Keller and M. R. Davie, eds., *Essays of William Graham Sumner,* New Haven: Yale University Press, 1934, Vol. 1, pp. 169–171.

we must have it, or one a little better. It takes two or three years and several millions to do that. In the meantime somebody proposes a more effective organization which must be introduced; signals, balloons, dogs, bicycles, and every other device and invention must be added, and men must be trained to use them all. There is no state of readiness for war; the notion calls for never-ending

sacrifices. It is a fallacy. It is evident that to pursue such a notion with any idea of realizing it would absorb all the resources and activity of the state; this the great European states are now proving by experiment. A wiser rule would be to make up your mind soberly what you want, peace or war, and then to get ready for what you want; for what we prepare for is what we shall get.

The Necessary Cause of War
Pitirim A. Sorokin

Pitirim Alexandrovitch Sorokin (1889–), professor of sociology and director, Research Center in Creative Altruism, Harvard University. Principal English works: *Social Mobility* (1927); *Contemporary Sociological Theories* (1928); *Principles of Rural-Urban Sociology* (1929); *Social and Cultural Dynamics,* 4 vols. (1937–1941); *Russia and the United States* (1944); *Society, Culture and Personality* (1947); *Reconstruction of Humanity* (1948); *Altruistic Love* (1950); *Social Philosophies of an Age of Crisis* (1950); *S.O.S.: The Meaning of Our Crisis* (1951).

Other conditions being equal, *each time when in the relationship of two or more states, or of any social groups, the system of social relationships and cultural values involved tends to become shattered, or muddled, or indefinite, such a change favors the chances of war. And vice versa, when the network of the relationships and cultural values moves toward greater crystallization, stability, and clear integration, such a change favors peace in their interrelationship.* Such is the hypothesis in a nutshell. . . . Unfolded, the hypothesis implies the following particular cases.

A. If and when, for whatever reason, the intragroup system, either of relationships or of cultural values, or both, undergoes a rapid and deep change within each party (state), such an inner "revolution" within one party tends, for obvious reasons, to unsettle the existing *status quo* in its relationship to the other party(ies); it therefore increases the chances of antagonism, conflict, and war between them.

B. Still greater is the facilitation of the chances of war if *both* parties experienced a profound, but opposite, modification of their intragroup web of relationships and system of cultural values. In that case, the interrelationships that existed between them will be doubly shattered and perturbed, and consequently lead to more conflicts and finally to war.

C. When in the interacting parties the *tempo and the profoundness or magnitude of change* of their organization and culture are so fast and so great that there is hardly any possibility for them to settle and crystallize, because before they have a chance to do so in regard to the latest change, it is gone and is replaced by a new one, *such a tempo and magnitude of social and cultural change unsettles more and more the system of the intergroup social and cultural relationships, and greatly facilitate antagonisms, conflicts, and war.* There is, of course, a theoretical possibility of a rapid change which is harmonious and orderly and which does not disrupt the crystallization of the relationships, but systematically, like a healthy growing organism, changes it from one crystallized form into another. In empirical social reality, however, such a case is exceedingly rare, practically nonexistent. Empirically, to use an analogy, the rapid tempo and magnitude of change are similar to driving a car at increasing speed on a road with increasingly sharper turns. Such driving, as we know, increases the chances of accidents. Likewise, increase of magnitude and tempo of change in one interacting party, and especially in both, increases the chances of conflict.

The hypothesis, then, is sociological *par excellence.* It sees the necessary and immediate factor of war, not in the sunspots or other cosmic and

From "A Neglected Factor of War," *American Sociological Review, 3* (1938): 475–486, pp. 483–486 quoted. Reprinted by permission. See also Sorokin, *Society, Culture, and Personality,* New York: Harper & Brothers, 1947, Chaps. 32 and 33.

biological factors, nor in any specific social and cultural conditions, economic, demographic, religious, psychological, or any other, but in the *stable or shattered status of the whole web of social relationships and of the system of cultural values of the parties involved*. It says that if the status is definite, crystallized, and stable, the chances for war are small, no matter whether or not the economic or other conditions of the parties involved are satisfactory from our standpoint. If the status of relationships and cultural system is amorphous and unsettled, the slightest pretext is sufficient to call forth a war-explosion. . . .

Such is the hypothesis. I regard the factor named as the necessary and real, though not always sufficient cause of war, in the same sense as an infection with the germs of diphtheria is the necessary and real, though not always sufficient (as when one is inoculated and is immune) cause of diphtheria. The concrete circumstances under which the infection takes place vary infinitely in regard to place, time, ways of infection, and the

persons or things from which the infection is obtained. Likewise, the concrete circumstances under which a shattering of the stability of the social and cultural relationships occurs, may be very different in various conditions and societies; but the shattering remains, like infection in diphtheria, the necessary cause of war. . . .

In the light of the hypothesis, the real medicine against war consists in all actions and measures that work for restabilization and reintegration of the contemporary shattered system of social relationships and cultural values. The real forces for war consist in all actions and measures that increase shattering and hinder reintegration of the social and cultural system, no matter for what noble or ignoble purposes. Such is the general formula of the cure against war. Being sufficiently clear in its general nature, it points out the concrete ways and forms of organized social action for decreasing or eliminating war. Enumeration of these concrete forms and measures is outside the task of this paper.

Conscientious Objectors
Clarence Marsh Case*

A conscientious objector is one who passively resists the effort of some social group, usually the state, to compel him to do something against which he holds conscientious scruples. The behavior of the conscientious objector is purely defensive and non-aggressive and is often, although not necessarily, a result of pacifistic views. . . .

The [First] World War brought into prominence various types of objectors. In addition to the religious objector opposed to war in general there was the socialist objector who was opposed to the war on international and humanitarian grounds, and especially because it was held to be the work of capitalistic interests arraying the masses against one another. Some socialist objectors, however, expressed their willingness to participate in a war of the proletariat against capital. A third type, the individualist objectors, often called "absolutists," denied the right of government to force the citizen to fight or do any-

thing else contrary to his own conscience. Their objection was directed at conscription in and of itself, regardless of the righteousness of the particular war or of war in general. It is this third group of objectors on whom considerable attention was centered during the war. Many objectors accepted non-combatant service without compromising their conscience, but not so the individualist objector. In Germany those refusing non-combatant service were commonly declared insane. In France, where there was no legal recognition of objectors, they were put to death as deserters. In both Great Britain and the United States, where conscription systems were put into effect, certain exemptions were allowed but did not include the individualist objector. . . .

Testimony is not wanting to show that the absolutist conscientious objectors found their bitterest opponents in religious leaders of almost every kind. The Federal Council of Churches of Christ

* See identifying note on page 7.
From "Conscientious Objectors," *Encyclopaedia of the Social Sciences*, 4 (1931): 210–212. Copyright, 1931, by The Macmillan Company and used with their permission.

in America, the separate denominational establishments and the Y.M.C.A. all neglected to bespeak mercy for the conscientious objectors, much less to defend them, while they suffered under excessive prison sentences. This attitude of organized religion reflects the almost universal hostility of the public toward conscientious objectors. Even the policy of the administration and the army was far less bitter than that of the popular newspapers and their readers, whose severe criticism of the government's alleged leniency hampered its efforts and condemned its results. This popular hostility was followed after the war by widespread admiration for the reconstruction work done by religious objectors and by an extraordinary revulsion against war on the part of the great Christian denominations.

The conscientious objector has always stood as a most difficult challenger of the political state's claim to absolute authority over its citizens. Conscientious objection is itself simply a special case under nonconformity, and heresy is another aspect of the same thing. The list of conscientious objectors therefore includes most of the intellectual and moral innovators in human history. The future role of conscientious objection is momentous and problematical. As a solution to the conflict between the state and the allegiance of the individual Laski suggests a future state in which the rights of the minority and the judgments of conscience will be respected and wherein the state will receive the individual's allegiance "only where it commands his conscience."

Freedom of Conscience in World War II
G. Bromley Oxnam*

No one knows how many conscientious objectors faced draft boards during World War II. Aside from those who accepted noncombatant service in the army, approximately 11,000 were classified for civilian service as persons whose conscientious objection was based upon religious training or belief. They were assigned to alternative civilian service in special work camps.

An additional 6,000 who claimed conscientious objection were sentenced to prison. These men fell into many different categories: those who refused to register because they opposed conscription as well as war; those who rejected civilian public service for one reason or another; those who failed to gain recognition of their position, but who nevertheless refused to accept induction into the army.

In the group of 11,000 were men from 150 religious bodies, one third of whom were Mennonites. In the second group of 6,000, two thirds were Jehovah's Witnesses, who were not pacifists but who insisted they were ministers and entitled to the exemption granted to clergymen. Their claim to be ministers was denied and, upon their refusal to serve, they were tried and sent to prison.

The largest group, those who accepted noncombatant service, was estimated by some to be more than 100,000. They were to be found almost exclusively in the Army Medical Corps. Colorful articles have been written about the "medics" and also about the men from Civilian Public Service who were assigned to special projects, in which they became "guinea pigs" in experiments in medical and scientific research. These articles have praised the bravery and sacrificial spirit of such men. . . .

A Ten-point Program

From the experience of this war, what propositions should guide us in present and future handling of the conscientious objector?

1. Democracies must respect the conscience of the individual citizen.

A citizen who breaks the law must be tried and suffer the penalty of disobedience. However, when a citizen is convinced that law is morally wrong, the community should do all in its power to make it possible for him to follow the dictates of his conscience. For instance, a man who has conscien-

---

* See identifying note on page 118.
From "Freedom of Conscience in the USA," *Survey Graphic, 35* (1946): 309–313, pp. 309, 313 quoted. Reprinted by permission.

tious objection to taking an oath in court is nevertheless allowed to testify. It is impossible in law to reach perfection in this matter, and individuals who in conscience must disobey certain laws must be prepared to take the consequences. In the matter of conscientious objection to war, because the number of such objectors is relatively insignificant and because of the validity of the objection, I believe provision should be made for the absolute exemption of the individual whose sincerity is unquestioned.

2. Conscientious objection to war should not be based upon religious training and belief alone.

If a man in conscience is opposed to participation in war upon intellectual grounds, or humanitarian ideals, or even on grounds of philosophical anarchism, I believe we should respect his conscience. To single out religious belief as the sole basis is to penalize a sincere unbeliever whose conscience is nonetheless his guide. The American Friends Service Committee is right in advocating "sincerity of conviction rather than religious training and belief as the test of conscience."

3. Full responsibility for the classification and assignment of all men claiming to be CO's should be vested in civilian boards.

The boards should be composed of men competent to deal with this issue. Uniform principles should govern these boards, procedures should be established, full records kept, and proper rights of appeal provided; the proceedings throughout to be in civilian control including final appeal.

4. Noncombatant service should be made more attractive to the CO.

This could be done by regulations forbidding a commanding officer to assign any duty to such a person other than strictly noncombatant service.

5. For those who cannot undertake noncombatant service, alternative service of national importance should be provided.

This should be under civilian administration throughout, and should not be administered by the churches. It would appear that there are enough services for private and governmental agencies to keep all CO's busy at socially valuable work and eliminate the necessity for camps.

6. CO's would seem to be entitled to support similar to the soldier's, with family allowances.

All men who serve as noncombatants or in alternative service have been drafted by the people. Noncombatants who were in the army did receive such support; we deal here with but a small group of men in alternative service. We should not penalize conscience by starving the objector.

7. Conscience must be no protection for cowards.

All attempts to avoid military service by claims of conscientious objection to war that are not sincere should be dealt with severely.

8. CO's who strike to effect reforms should face the same discipline a soldier would face if he struck.

CO's should not ask for nor receive special privileges in terms of 40-hour weeks and the like. They should be willing to face some of the hardships borne by the soldier.

9. CO's should try to avoid the holier-than-thou attitude.

This is all too often present, perhaps unconsciously but nonetheless offensively. Belligerent pacifism is really a contradiction in terms, but belligerency in advocating views and in fighting to realize them creates an unfortunate community reaction. Parading as martyrs is not a pleasing performance when thousands of soldiers and sailors are risking and giving their lives.

10. There is only one final answer to the question of conscientious objection to war.

That is the creation of a warless world in which law and order have supplanted international anarchy, in which power has been brought under democratic control, and justice established by democratic process. It is in this struggle that Conscientious Participator and Conscientious Objector can unite.

Soldiers of the Lord
The Institute for Propaganda Analysis

The Institute for Propaganda Analysis was a nonprofit organization established by the late Edward A. Filene to help citizens analyze and understand propaganda; active in 1937–41.

There is nothing at all strange in this support given by organized religion to the state in time of war. This dual alliance between war and religion is as old as civilization itself.

As far as Christianity is concerned, there is a lengthy and notable war record. Professor Ray H. Abrams, in his *Preachers Present Arms,*[1] suggests that "Of all the great world religions, with the possible exception of Mohammedanism, none has been more devoted to Mars than has Christianity. Founded by one who was adored as the 'lowly Nazarene,' 'The Prince of Peace,' and 'The Lamb of God,' his followers have, nevertheless, when occasion demanded, pictured him as a mighty warrior in the forefront of the battle. They have participated under his Banner in the bloodiest wars know to man.". . .

In the United States, the Government has always been able to rely upon the churches for support in time of any major war. Before the shooting started in the Revolutionary period, the pulpits of New England were preparing the minds of the members of the congregation for an open break with the mother country. When it did come, preachers everywhere joined the colors and used their pulpits as recruiting stations.

In the Civil War, the churches—North and South—were for the most part loyal to their repective sides.

In the Spanish-American War the Government again relied upon the forces of organized religion.

In the World War, as the Interchurch World Movement phrased it: "Every office of the Government with a war message to deliver appealed to the ministers first of all.". . .

In the period of disillusionment following the World War, churches joined the peace movement. Practically every denomination went on record as being opposed to war. . . . The *World Tomorrow,* in May 1931, gave the results of a questionnaire distributed to 53,000 clergymen over the United States. There were 19,372 replies and of these 10,427 or fifty-four per cent stated it was their "present purpose not to sanction any future war or participate as an armed combatant.". . .

Outside the Quaker and Mennonite folds, following their pacifist line, and, by propaganda, seeking to persuade others to follow it, are hundreds of American clergymen. . . . Numerically, they comprise but a small minority of American clergymen. Although their effectiveness as propagandists is limited by the disinclination of many newspapers and radio stations to disseminate pacifist views, they reach large and influential groups by sermons, conferences, and peace meetings.

Pacifism, however, represents but *one* of the Christian attitudes toward war. Most Christians accept the tradition that stems from St. Augustine, who believed the State to be morally obligated to protect its citizens against attack from other nations. He also sanctioned punitive wars fought for the restoration of justice. In other words, to most Christians, there is such a thing as a thoroughly *just* war. To such a war, or to preparation for it, clergymen holding this view are giving their sanction and that of God. . . .

During the World War only a few religious organizations such as the Society of Friends, the Mennonites, and the Church of the Brethren were deeply interested in conscientious objectors. These church groups, together with the Fellowship of Reconciliation and what is now the American Civil Liberties Union, bore the brunt of the fight for the C.O. in 1917. But in 1941, virtually every church body in the country is on record as favoring non-combatant duty for the C.O. The Methodist, Baptist, Presbyterian churches want all objectors to war on grounds of conscience to be exempt from military service—not merely the members of the Society of Friends.[2] . . .

[1] New York: Round Table Press, 1933, p. 3.

[2] "Official Statements of Religious Bodies Regarding the Conscientious Objector," The Department of International Justice and Goodwill of the Federal Council of the Churches of Christ in America, no date.

From "Soldiers of the Lord," *Propaganda Analysis,* 3 (1939–40): 61–70, pp. 61, 67–68 quoted, and "Religious Propaganda Against the War," *ibid.,* 4: 3 (January 25, 1941): 1–10, pp. 2–3, 7–9 quoted. Reprinted by permission.

When conscription came before Congress, the Federal Council of the Churches of Christ in America, representing over twenty communions, appointed a committee through which a document setting forth the policy of the churches on the conscientious objector was presented to the chairmen of the Senate and House Committees on Naval Affairs.[3] . . .

The Fellowship of Reconciliation propagandizes on a nation-wide scale, its members motivated by missionary zeal. . . . At its meeting in September, 1940, at Chautauqua, N. Y., the Fellowship[4] declared that in the event of actual invasion "the American people would have the organizing genius, if they will, to organize nonviolent non-cooperation with the invaders." It held that the development in America of a "democracy that worked" would "constitute a far more sure defense than bombers and battleships."[5] . . .

In 1941 pacifist ministers and groups are better organized and more active than they were in 1917. Moreover, in addition to the Quakers and the F.O.R., . . . there are many other peace groups. The strongest and most influential which are for the most part supported by the church people are: The National Peace Conference (representing about 40 national organizations, many

of which are church groups), the National Council for the Prevention of War, and the Women's International League for Peace and Freedom. The strongest peace organization within the larger Protestant bodies is the Peace Commission of the Methodist Church.

While the Jews have no historic traditional teaching against war such as has existed in some of the Christian bodies, rabbis in many parts of the country have been active anti-war propagandists. Many organizations, such as the Women's International League for Peace and Freedom, receive support from Jews.

The Catholics have a Catholic Association for Peace and another organization called Pax. The journals, *Catholic Social Action* and the *Catholic Worker,* are pronouncedly against the war. In November 1940, *Catholic Social Action,* discussing pro-British propaganda in America, declared: "We have here in America a group of super-propagandists who mask their true intentions with high words. But their deeds speak more loudly than their words. Hiding behind their official positions, positions of respect and even the clerical cloth, they are revealed now as hyphenated Americans who are being duped the same way in which the intellectuals were duped and misled during the first World War."

War opinion among Catholics is divided as it is among most of the Protestant and Jewish groups. Most Catholics and the Church itself take the position that there are "just" wars. Various Popes at various times have found some wars just and some unjust.

---

[3] *Federal Council Bulletin,* October 1940.

[4] "As War Comes Nearer," a statement by the Twenty-fifth Annual Conference of the Fellowship of Reconciliation, Chautauqua, New York, Setpember 6–8, 1940; issued by the F.O.R., New York.

[5] *Christian Century,* October 16, 1940.

Economic and Social Impacts of War
William Haber

William Haber (1899–   ), professor of economics, University of Michigan. Chief works: *Unemployment, A Problem of Insecurity* (1931) and *Unemployment Relief and Economic Security* (1936); co-author of *How Collective Bargaining Works* (1942) and *Post War Economic Reconstruction* (1945).

[Note] the changes which have taken place as a result of wartime pressures: The war has affected the size and composition of our labor force; production levels have reached unprecedented heights; there have been radical changes in the level of consumption and the standard of living; the status of many groups in our national life— the prewar unemployed, youth, women, and minority groups—have been radically influenced by the expansion of job opportunities. . . .

From "Economic and Social Readjustments in the Reconversion Period," *Proceedings of the National Conference of Social Work . . . 1945,* New York: Columbia University Press, 1945, pp. 26–44, pp. 25–31 quoted. Reprinted by permission.

Under the spur of war, our total production of goods and services has reached levels never approached in peacetime; the 1944 total of $198,000,000,000 compares with $97,000,000,000 in 1940 and $99,000,000,000 during the boom times of 1929. In 1944 the value of war production alone was equal to 160 per cent of the total production in 1939, the last year unaffected by rearmament and war production; yet nonwar production is also above the 1939 level.

The increase in total output was accompanied by a sharp increase in our physical plant and in our consumption of raw materials. About $20,000,000,000 has been invested in new or expanded industrial plants since 1940. Of this total, about $16,000,000,000 represents facilities owned by the Government. About $10,000,000,000 worth of these new facilities will be usable for civilian production—aircraft and synthetic rubber capacity, most of the aluminum and magnesium, and a good share of the steel and machine tools.

In contrast with every other major warring nation, our outpouring of weapons and munitions has been achieved without cutting the total supply of goods and services available to consumers. Many durable goods, such as automobiles, have of course not been produced during the war. The shortages of some foods and consumers' goods have been annoying rather than serious. In fact, the total expenditure for consumers' goods and services rose from about $66,000,000,000 in 1940 to nearly $98,000,000,000 in 1944. Even if price changes are taken into account, this means that the average American family has been able to purchase more food, clothing, and other goods and services than before the war. Thus we shall enter the transition period, unlike most other countries, with a population which is physically sound and potentially capable of a high level of productivity.

America's war production record was achieved as a result of many factors in addition to a prodigal use of materials and facilities. Production processes were improved and new ones were invented. Mass production methods were applied so that most workers engaged in making highly complex products performed simple repetitive tasks. Partly as a result, it was possible to employ and train millions of workers who had no previous industrial experience. The general adoption of a longer work week gave us the equivalent of several million additional workers.

These developments have important implications for the postwar period. Productivity per worker will increase as wartime technological improvements are adapted for civilian work, and hourly wage rates may be increased in a number of industries, with no increase over prewar production costs. New civilian products will be placed on the market, thus increasing potential job opportunities but, at the same time, causing a decline in some established industries.

Just as wartime production has implications for the postwar economy, the wartime mobilization of manpower will also affect the transition period. The chronic unemployment of the 1930's has been replaced by full employment. In fact, the war has brought into the labor force millions of workers whose employment interferes with education or family responsibilities which should normally be paramount.

Between October, 1940, and October, 1944, our total labor force rose from 55,000,000 to 65,000,000. Of this total, 12,000,000 were in the armed forces—an increase of more than 11,000,000 during the four-year period. This drain of manpower was not quite balanced by other increases in the labor force; the civilian labor force declined during the same period. This net decline, however, conceals tremendous shifts within the civilian labor market.

Employment in manufacturing rose from a monthly average of less than 11,000,000 in 1940 to nearly 17,000,000 in 1943, declining to about 16,000,000 in 1944. In the so-called "munitions industries," employment rose from about 4,000,000 in 1940 to more than 9,000,000 in 1944. This vast industrial army was recruited from the ranks of the unemployed, by transfer from other industries, and by use of persons not previously in the labor market.

About 7,000,000 persons who would not normally be in the labor market took jobs, or were added to the armed forces. About 3,000,000 of this group were boys and girls who left school earlier than they would have in peacetime. Some 2,000,000 married women took jobs instead of remaining as housewives; and about 2,000,000 aged persons returned to work, or postponed their retirement to stay in war jobs. The number of women in nonfarm jobs today is about 6,000,000 greater than it was in 1940. Many of these women, after the war, will undoubtedly prefer to be wage earners rather than housewives.

Millions of Negro workers have been able, for the first time, to obtain steady jobs at high wages.

Government-sponsored fair employment policies have helped them to come closer to obtaining an equal opportunity to share job opportunities.

The vast tide of movement into munitions production required mass migration of workers and their families. About 3,000,000 persons have moved across state lines to take war jobs. In many war production centers postwar employment is unlikely to require as many workers as are needed now.

Agriculture, with an average of 8,100,000 workers in 1944 (compared with 9,200,000 in 1940), has been able to produce more food than ever before to feed, not only this country, but also our Allies.

The movement to war industries has meant long hours of work and greater pay for most workers. The scheduled work week in manufacturing increased from about forty hours to forty-eight hours, and average weekly earnings rose from $26 to $47. For millions of families, the war has brought a higher standard of living, more food and clothing, and steadier work than ever before.

Despite these economic benefits, the war has created social dislocations which must receive attention in the transition period. Families in which both parents are working have been unable to give children the supervision and guidance they normally require. The absence of men in the service leaves many children who have never seen or do not recall their fathers, and many wives who have had little chance to work out normal homes for themselves and their husbands.

Migration has interrupted the schooling of children, and overcrowding in war centers has caused hazards to health. Many young workers have earned high wages without ever being exposed to the need for competing for jobs on a basis of efficiency. Millions of young men have gone directly from school to the armed forces and have not yet had a chance to make a real adjustment to normal employment.

A wartime economy differs from the normal operation of a competitive economic system in that a large segment of all business activity is devoted to serving a single customer—the Government. In order to assure an adequate supply of materials and manpower for war production and war-supporting activities, it is necessary to interfere with the normal freedom of action of employers and wage earners. Materials must be allocated to essential users, and some products and services must be curtailed or even eliminated. The freedom of workers to accept any job they choose and the freedom of employers to hire workers as they choose have been sharply modified by manpower regulations, such as those which provide for employment ceilings, statements of availability, and the hiring of certain workers only through the United States Employment Service.

To prevent inflation, it has been necessary to maintain rigid controls of prices and wages. For some commodities, the lack of balance between supply and consumer demand has made it necessary to institute rationing, which limits the amount of consumption by any individual in order to make sure that all consumers receive at least their minimum needs. . . .

Millions of our families have known for the first time what it is to have steady work and a high standard of living. They have had the truest kind of economic security—the knowledge that there are enough jobs to go 'round. In the postwar period, we will have the same resources, productive plant, and managerial skills that we have now; we will have even greater human resources. Properly used, they can give us a higher standard of living and personal dignity than we or any other nation have ever known.

The Atomic Bomb at Nagasaki
From the "Saturday Review of Literature"

EDITOR'S NOTE: The Saturday Review *makes no apology for sponsoring so grim and unpalatable a picture as emerges from the following letters.*

What happened at Hiroshima and Nagasaki is the responsibility of the American people. It was officially denied at the time that the bomb had

From editor's note and John Arthur's letters to his brother Bob, "The Atomic Age: Anniversary of a Letter," *Saturday Review of Literature*, 29: 38 (September 21, 1946): 12–14. Reprinted by permission.

any lingering deadly effects, or that the Japanese were suffering from an "atomic bomb disease." Yet the fact remains that the radioactivity produced by the bomb was literally a death ray, belonging in many respects to the poison gas classification outlawed by the Geneva convention, which the United States warned other nations to respect many times during the war. The significance and implications of this fact cannot be ignored by the American people. These implications take on added meaning in the letters that follow.

Major John Arthur was a member of the first mission dispatched to Nagasaki to evacuate prisoners of war. His party was flown to Japan, reaching Nagasaki some ten days before the official occupation. For a while, they were the only Allied troops in an area occupied by thousands of armed Japanese soldiers.

* * * *

By John Arthur

The Japs . . . apparently started to clean up immediately after the fire, which followed the bomb, burned itself out. In many places they arranged the dead—20,000 or more killed outright —in rows like cordwood. Then many survivors began dying from delayed-action radiation burn effect. This scared them and the city was abandoned for days. The dead remained where they had been placed.

We found one long row in which bodies had been stacked to shoulder height. The top layers were tattered skeletons—the buzzards and vultures had been at work. The lower layers were flyblown and maggoty. The bottom layers had been worked on by the rats—the rats apparently survived the atom bomb better than the humans! (Wonder whether this offers any clues as to the identity of the survivors of a general atomic war of the future?) . . .

In the immediate center, for a diameter of perhaps half a mile, there is nothing left at all. Even the rubble has been spread evenly so that nothing is more than a foot high from the normal ground level. . . .

The hospitals and school buildings that remain are jammed with the dying, who can only wait for death to take them—people who were in the vicinity when the bomb went off. Some were burned, some seemed quite unharmed at the time. Apparently a delayed radiation effect on the blood and tissues is killing them now, and the few remaining doctors hold no hope for them. The situation of the doctors here is symbolic of the tragedy. They don't know what to do, nor do they have facilities with which to do anything. All they can do is make a patient comfortable— and when he dies, admit another to take his place. . . .

The Japanese, being less technically organized, and therefore less dependent on the services and cooperation of other individuals have probably fared better, on the whole, than the residents of highly integrated American cities would. What would happen, for instance, if a salvo of bombs killed 500,000 people in New York? Doubtless all food distribution systems would be destroyed. You might have more deaths from starvation than from blast or radiation effect. I can easily imagine a breakdown that would result in wholesale murder for a few scraps of food, and—but draw your own pictures.

Having seen an atomized city, I can tell you that those who have seen it with me know that nothing that has ever happened to soldiers on the battlefield can be so horrible as what will happen to civilians.

Official Purposes of Universal Military Training
Public Relations Division, United States War Department

It is a sound and democratic principle that each physically and mentally fit male and alien residing in the United States owes an obligation to this country to undergo training which will fit him to protect it in an emergency; that adequate preparedness will prevent aggressive wars against this country and the needless sacrifice of human life; that a well-trained citizenry is the keystone

From *A Plan for Universal Military Training*, Washington: Government Printing Office, 1946, pp. 1–2 quoted.

of preparedness; and that such preparedness can best be assured through a system of military training for the youth of the Nation. . . .

The purpose of the Universal Military Training Program is to promote the national defense of the country by providing a large reservoir of men trained as individual specialists and as members of teams in order that:

a. Mobilization and training of the Nation's wartime Army can be completed rapidly in an emergency.

b. The readiness of the Regular Army, the National Guard, and the Organized Reserve Corps can be maintained at the highest level during peace due to prior intensive training of enlistees.

Men will be trained as specialists and as members of teams for voluntary enlistment in the National Guard and Organized Reserve Corps.

c. Qualities of leadership can be developed and outstanding leaders can be selected for further training, on a voluntary basis, as commissioned and non-commissioned officers in the Regular Army, the National Guard, and the Organized Reserve Corps. A substantial basis of military knowledge and experience on which to build officer training will be provided.

d. Aptitudes can be established and classified and special skills required in modern war can be developed to the highest degree.

e. Each civilian community throughout the country can be composed in part of men who have received intensive training in the latest methods of scientific warfare and who would be able to defend and assist the community in the event of local disasters resulting from initial enemy action, which may be expected in the early stages of a war of the future.

f. Although not a primary purpose of Universal Military Training, an important result will be that the welfare of the Nation can be improved because:

(1) Opportunity will be provided for the raising of the standard of education for the Nation's young manhood.

(2) The physical well-being of all trainees will be improved to the maximum extent by means of athletics, adequate medical care, and physical conditioning.

Both Sides of Peacetime Military Conscription
The Church of the Brethren

Proponents Urge—

Military conscription is insurance against attack.

It prepares us to win if we are attacked.

It encourages justice and order through world organization.

It fosters community responsibility and good citizenship.

It is a small premium for securing our high standard of living.

It will bring great benefits to the United States in health, vocational training and democratization of the youth.

But Opponents Respond—

It cannot save our cities from the atom bomb and guided rocket bombs.

It increases the danger of attack.

It weakens our capacity to resist attack.

It defeats the possibility of world community free of imperialism.

It undermines democracy through habits of authoritarian control and obedience.

It reduces the standard of living by removing many men and large resources from productive activity.

It will divert us from attacking the causes of ill-health, inadequate vocational training and undemocratic attitudes and practices.

From "Look at Both Sides of Peacetime Military Conscription" (leaflet), Elgin, Illinois, 1947, a section entitled, "In Short . . ." Reprinted by permission.

American Attitudes on World Organization
Elmo Roper and Oliver A. Quayle III

Elmo Burns Roper (1900–   ), marketing consultant; research director, *Fortune* Survey of Public Opinion; assistant professor of journalism, Columbia University; director, International Public Opinion Research, Inc. Oliver A. Quayle III is his associate in the last.

American Attitudes on World Organization

9% We shouldn't get tied up in any more alliances or joint commitments with other countries and we should aim at getting out of as many as we can as soon as we can. (This is the isolationist view.)

21% We should continue to work along with United Nations just about as we have been, gradually trying to make it better as time goes on. (This is the United Nations "as is" view.)

35% We should immediately get behind strengthening the United Nations and do everything necessary to give it more power and authority than it has—enough to actually keep even a strong nation from starting a war. (This is the stronger United Nations view.)

6% In addition to continuing with the United Nations, we should also unite with the friendly democratic countries into one government in which each member nation would in effect become a state, somewhat like the different states in this country. (This is the democratic union view.)

11% We should start now working toward transforming the United Nations into a real world government of all nations of the world, in which every nation would in effect become a state, somewhat like the different states in this country. (This is the world government view.)

7% Some of these ideas are good, but we won't get any of them working in time to prevent war, so we'd better not rely on them. (This is the hopeless view.)

11% No opinion.

Most Americans believe that mankind's best hope for peace and survival lies in some form of world organization.

This conclusion dominated a national public-opinion survey conducted by our organization some months ago. Over-all, we found that 73 per cent of the population are oriented toward internationalism. Only 9 per cent—to us a surprisingly low figure—indicated that they were isolationist in viewpoint.

The largest of the six basic groups into which our results broke down favors a strengthened United Nations.

We set out to discover how many people—and what kinds of people—believe in world cooperation, and why. We also wanted to measure attitudes toward isolationism, and toward several kinds of world organization that this country might support in order to achieve peace.

We decided to interview a cross section of Americans 21 years of age and over. The 3,502 interviews were distributed proportionately for geographic section and size of place according to the 1950 census figures. In places of 25,000 or more, a method of "modified area sampling" was used: Interviewing locations were selected at random and interviewers were required to make their interviews in a prescribed area. Within these areas, controls for both sex and age were used. In places of less than 25,000 a highly controlled quota method of sampling was used: Interviewers were given assignments in specific places and each assignment was controlled for age, sex, race and socio-economic and employment status.

For purposes of this study, we gave people six alternate choices, and asked them:

"While everyone seems to agree that peace is an important thing, there are a good many different views as to how to bring it about. Here are some different ideas—there's one on

From "Internationalism—73, Isolationism—9," *The 1954 Federalist Annual*, produced and published by the Writers Board for World Government, 1954, 15–17, p. 15 quoted.

each of these cards. Will you look through them and tell me which you come closest to agreeing with?"

The choices and answers to each are shown in the accompanying chart.

CROSS REFERENCES TO STANDARD TEXTS *

Barnes, *Society in Transition*, pp. 3–7, 17, 47–48, 62, 138, 342–343, 385, 485–486, 489–491, 689–690.

Bernard, *American Community Behavior*, pp. 20, 337–349, 474–475, 506–509, 654–655, 658–660.

Brown, *Social Pathology*, Chap. 34.

Cuber and Harper, *Problems of American Society*, pp. 84–85, 109, 114–115, 121, 242, 259, 426.

Elliott and Merrill, *Social Disorganization*, Chaps. 32–34, pp. 657–658.

Faris, *Social Disorganization*, Chap. 4, pp. 372–376.

Gillin, *Social Pathology*, Chap. 24.

—— and others, *Social Problems*, pp. 91–92, Chap. 6.

Herman, *Approach to Social Problems*, pp. 157–163, 194–197, 217–218, 455–456.

Landis, *Social Policies in the Making*, pp. 95, 223, 244, 260, 383, 386–401, 406–407, 480–483.

Mihanovich, *Current Social Problems*, Chap. 3.

Nordskog and others, *Analyzing Social Problems*, pp. 162–168, Chaps. 13–14.

Odum, *American Social Problems*, Chap. 25.

Phelps and Henderson, *Contemporary Social Problems*, pp. 22, 57–58, 64, 68, 149, 178, 182, 415.

Reinhardt and others, *Social Problems and Social Policy*, pp. 559–569.

Weaver, *Social Problems*, Chap. 28.

* For complete bibliographical reference to each text, see page 13.

OTHER BIBLIOGRAPHY

Theodore Abel, "The Element of Decision in the Pattern of War," *American Sociological Review*, 6 (1941): 853–859.

Ray H. Abrams, *Preachers Present Arms*, New York: Round Table Press, 1933.

Devere Allen, *The Fight for Peace*, New York: Macmillan Co., 1930.

C. Arnold Anderson and Bryce Bryan, *War Came to the Iowa Community*, Ames: Iowa Agricultural Experiment Station, Iowa Agricultural Extension Service, Iowa State College, 1942.

Paul Russell Anderson, ed., "Universal Military Training and National Security," *The Annals, 241* (September 1945).

Thurman Arnold, Leo M. Cherne, and Neil H. Jacoby, *War Profits*, University of Chicago Round Table No. 214, April 19, 1942.

"The Atomic Age Begins," *Time, 46:* 8 (August 20, 1945).

Luther Lee Bernard, *War and Its Causes*, New York: Henry Holt and Co., 1944.

Crane Brinton, *The Anatomy of Revolution*, rev. ed., New York: Prentice-Hall, 1952.

Bernard Brodie, ed., *The Absolute Weapon*, New York: Harcourt, Brace and Co., 1946.

Vannevar Bush, *Modern Arms and Free Men*, New York: Simon and Schuster, 1949.

Clarence Marsh Case, *Non-Violent Coercion: A Study in Methods of Social Pressure*, New York: Century Co., 1923.

Dwight W. Chapman, ed., "Human Behavior in Disaster: A New Field of Social Research," *Journal of Social Issues, 10* (1954): 3: 1–73.

Maurice Rea Davie, *Evolution of War*, New Haven: Yale University Press, 1925.

John Dewey, "Outlawry of War," *Encyclopaedia of the Social Sciences, 11* (1933): 508–510.

Leonidas Dodson, ed., "The Shadow of War," *The Annals, 175* (September 1934).

John Dollard, *Fear in Battle*, Washington: Infantry Journal, 1944.

Wilma T. Donahue and Clark Tibbitts, eds., "The Disabled Veteran," *The Annals, 239* (May 1945).

E. F. M. Durbin and John Bowlby, *Personal Aggressiveness and War*, New York: Columbia University Press, 1939.

Sylvanus M. Duvall, "War and Human Nature," Public Affairs Pamphlet No. 125, 1947.

Howard M. Ehrmann, ed., "Foreign Policies and Relations of the United States," *The Annals, 255* (January 1948).

Paul Einzig, *Economic Warfare*, New York: Macmillan Co., 1941.

Paul French, *We Won't Murder: The History of Non-Violence*, New York: Hastings House, 1940.

Anna Freud, *War and Children*, New York: Ernst Willard, 1943.

William Gellerman, *The American Legion as Educator*, New York: Teachers College, Columbia University, 1938.

Justin Gray with Victor H. Bernstein, *The Inside Story of the Legion*, New York: Boni and Gaer, 1948.

R. R. Grinker and J. P. Spiegel, *Men Under Stress*, Philadelphia: Blakiston Co., 1945.

C. Grove Haines and Ross J. S. Hoffman, *The Origins and Background of the Second World War*, New York: Oxford University Press, 1943.

John Hersey, *Hiroshima*, New York: Alfred A. Knopf, 1946.

Guy Franklin Hershberger, *War, Peace, and Non-resistance,* Scottdale, Pennsylvania: Herald Press, 1944.

E. T. Hiller, *The Strike: A Study in Collective Action,* Chicago: University of Chicago Press, 1928.

Institute for Propaganda Analysis, "War Aims in War Propaganda," and "Strikes, Profits, and Defense," *Propaganda Analysis,* 4: 5 and 6 (March 27 and April 29, 1941).

I. L. Janis, *Air War and Emotional Stress,* New York: McGraw-Hill Book Co., 1951.

Alvin Johnson, "War," *Encyclopaedia of the Social Sciences,* 15 (1935): 342–347.

Abram Kardiner, *The Traumatic Neuroses of War,* Washington: National Research Council, 1941.

——, *War Stress and Neurotic Illness,* New York: Paul Hoeber, 1947.

Harold D. Lasswell, *World Politics Faces Economics,* New York: McGraw-Hill Book Co., 1945.

Alfred McClung Lee and Norman D. Humphrey, *Race Riot,* New York: Dryden Press, 1943.

William Draper Lewis, ed., "Essential Human Rights," *The Annals,* 243 (January 1946).

Mulford Q. Sibley and Philip E. Jacob, *Conscription of Conscience: The American State and the Conscientious Objector: 1940–1947,* Ithaca, N. Y.: Cornell University Press, 1952.

Hans Speier, *Social Order and the Risks of War: Papers in Political Sociology,* New York: George W. Stewart, 1952.

John M. Swomley, Jr., *Militarism in Education,* Washington: National Council Against Conscription, 1013 18th St., N. W., 1950.

Edmund Taylor, *The Strategy of Terror,* Boston: Houghton Mifflin Co., 1940.

Arnold J. Toynbee, *Armenian Atrocities,* London: Hodder & Stoughton, 1915.

——, *The German Terror in Belgium: An Historical Record,* New York: George H. Doran Co., 1917.

——, *The German Terror in France,* London: Hodder & Stoughton, 1917.

——, *Turkey: A Past and a Future,* New York: George H. Doran Co., 1917.

——, *War and Civilization,* New York: Oxford University Press, 1950.

F. J. Veale, *Advance to Barbarism,* Appleton, Wisconsin: C. C. Nelson Co., 1953.

Willard Waller, *The Veteran Comes Back,* New York: Dryden Press, 1944.

——, *War and the Family,* New York: Dryden Press, 1940.

——, ed., *War in the Twentieth Century,* New York: Dryden Press, 1940.

Quincy Wright, *A Study of War,* Chicago: University of Chicago Press, 1942, 2 vols.

REVIEW QUESTIONS

1. How frequently do wars occur in civilized countries? In the United States?
2. What does Freud mean by aggression?
3. How dangerous is aggressive cruelty to the maintenance of civilized society?
4. What might be said to have caused the 1951 Chicago race riot?
5. What roles did rumor play in the race riot?
6. Interpret the account of the 1951 Chicago race riot in terms of Freud's discussion of aggression.
7. What is the role of scapegoatism in a race riot?
8. How can race riots be prevented?
9. What influence does Sumner attribute to doctrines and catch phrases?
10. Does Sumner believe we can be prepared for war? Why?
11. Do Sumner's points apply with equal force to our situation today?
12. What does Sorokin regard to be the necessary cause of war?
13. Why does Sorokin say he regards this factor to be "the necessary and real, though not always sufficient cause of war"?
14. How would you criticize Sorokin's analysis?
15. What is a conscientious objector? How many types of them are there?
16. How extensive was conscientious objection in World War II?
17. What are the chief points in Oxnam's program for the treatment of conscientious objectors in World War III?
18. What attitude did many clergymen take toward the belligerents in World War II?
19. What change was there in the attitude of churches toward conscientious objectors between World War I and World War II?
20. How well organized were the religious pacifist forces in 1941?
21. Compare the Haber selection to "Challenge of Unemployment: 1939," in the previous chapter. Are the "dispossessed" of 1939 likely to be dispossessed again after World War II's demands are passed?
22. How would the American citizens of New York, Detroit, Chicago, or Los Angeles react to such an experience as the citizens of Nagasaki had?
23. What are the major justifications offered by the federal government for the installation of universal military training?
24. How would you sum up the UMT debate?
25. What is your interpretation of Roper's poll findings on means of attaining peace?

PART VIII

Toward Adjustment

CHAPTER 24

Social Work and Social Action

THE major approaches to the mitigation or solution of social problems are roughly three. These are: (1) social work, which emphasizes the adjustment or readjustment of the person or family to environmental factors; (2) social reform, which stresses the modification of parts of the social structure; and (3) social revolution, which insists that only drastic and far-reaching changes can cope with societal maladjustments. The second and third approaches are frequently spoken of as forms of social action.

The first four selections in this chapter present four different general viewpoints on social work and efforts at social reform. Marx and Engels take the position that "redressing social grievances" is a bourgeois procedure for blocking proletarian revolutionary moves. Keller attacks social ameliorism from a quite different angle; it is his contention that humanitarianism may be counter-selective, that it may help to swamp the "fit" with the "unfit." Sumner is thankful that men cannot do much to change societal tendencies.

Following World War I and especially during the 1930's, social work in the United States expanded tremendously, developed a large corps of professionally trained workers, came to cost a great deal of money, and grew into a complex network. Those who are associated with the work of social agencies very shortly find, if they are at all observant, that case and group techniques must be supplemented by community organization or social action techniques. Pray discusses this relationship between social work and social workers and social action. Watson gives a keen example of the utility of social action techniques in one highly significant problem area, intergroup relations. Cohen tells of the application of social science findings to the work of the practitioner in the intergroup relations field and of some of the problems remaining, both for research and for its practical utilization.

When social action is mentioned, those who take an overprotective attitude toward existing social structures frequently become disturbed and classify all ameliorists as "left-wingers" or "reds" or "radicals." Madison sketches in summary form the history of radicalism in this country and poses some of the basic issues with which radicals have attempted and are still seeking to deal. Bernard describes the dilemma in which vested interests find themselves in relation to a revolution in their own country or another.

On Redressing Social Grievances
Karl Marx and Friedrich Engels*

A part of the bourgeoisie is desirous of redressing social grievances, in order to secure the continued existence of bourgeois society.

To this section belong economists, philanthropists, humanitarians, improvers of the condition of the working class, organizers of charity, members of societies for the prevention of cruelty to animals, temperance fanatics, hole and corner reformers of every imaginable kind. This form of Socialism has, moreover, been worked out into complete systems. . . .

The socialistic bourgeois want all the advan-

* See identifying note on page 34.

From "Manifesto of the Communist Party" (1848), transl. by S. Moore and F. Engels, in K. Marx, *Capital . . . and Other Writings,* ed. by Max Eastman, New York: Modern Library, 1932, pp. 320–355, pp. 349–350 quoted.

tages of modern social conditions without the struggles and dangers necessarily resulting therefrom. They desire the existing state of society minus its revolutionary and disintegrating elements. They wish for a bourgeoisie without a proletariat. . . .

Bourgeois Socialism attains adequate expression when, and only when, it becomes a mere figure of speech.

Humanitarianism May Be Counterselective
Albert Galloway Keller*

[The] "individualistic tendency of humanitarianism" * . . . means the tendency to regard a case of relief, let us say, as a relation merely of individuals, in which the society is conceded no interest. Humanitarianism in general is, of course, counterselective, in that it always eases the struggle for existence and so operates—as perhaps its chief aim—against the elimination of those who are losing in the conflict.[1] Carried to senseless excess, as in Spain of the late Middle Ages, it foists upon the really wholesome and vital body of society a parasitic burden; beggar-migrations at one time literally invaded Spain, where undiscriminating charity was one of the surest titles to heavenly bliss—undiscriminating, not because it was assumed that none of the beneficiaries was unworthy, but because of the religious peril from turning away a single worthy soul.

Nobody denies the social value of willingness to aid the unfortunate with discrimination; what is lost biologically is doubtless made up for so-cially. No one denies the social virtue, to say nothing of the personal obligation to society, of succoring a fellow-man in distress, whatever form the affliction may take.[2] That, however, benevolence should extend to the assurance of the "right" to procreate, is another matter. "The individualistic tendency" of Schallmayer is one that is blind to all those larger group-interests which at times dictate refusal of aid where the personal inclination would be to afford it. No one is fit to give charity whose sentiment overweighs his intelligence, and whose perspective is bounded by the individual relation of giver and recipient. . . .

It is easy enough to vote funds for more comfortable prisons; but somebody pays for them. Who? Not the philanthropists alone, or at all. Taxes take the pennies of the self-supporting, law-abiding, common people, who can ill spare the loss. The "white man's burden"—keeping hordes of Orientals alive, that they may propagate an increasing burden for the self-supporting—is largely the "Forgotten Man's."[3]

---

* Keller is quoting W. Schallmayer, *Vererbung und Auslese im Lebenslauf der Völker,* Jena, 1903, pp. 111 ff. —*Eds.*

[1] "The Conflict between Benevolence and Biology," reporting an attack by Karl Pearson, rebutted by others, in *Science and Discovery.*

* See identifying note on page 30.

From *Societal Evolution: A Study of the Evolutionary Basis of the Science of Society,* rev. (1931) ed., New Haven: Yale University Press, 1947, pp. 258–260. Reprinted by permission.

[2] W. G. Sumner, *What Social Classes Owe to Each Other* (1883), New Haven: Yale University Press, 1925, Chaps. 4, 11.

[3] "French Doctors Save African Native Race," in *The New York Times,* Dec. 26, 1929.

A Tough Old World
William Graham Sumner*

If this poor old world is as bad as they say, one more reflection may check the zeal of the headlong reformer. It is at any rate a tough old world. It has taken its trend and curvature and all its twists and tangles from a long course of formation. All its wry and crooked gnarls and knobs

---

* See identifying note on page 46.

From "The Absurd Effort to Make the World Over," *Forum,* 17 (1894): 92–102, pp. 101–102 quoted. Reprinted by permission from A. G. Keller and M. R. Davie, eds., *Essays of William Graham Sumner,* New Haven: Yale University Press, 1934, vol. 1, pp. 104–106.

are therefore stiff and stubborn. If we puny men by our arts can do anything at all to straighten them, it will only be by modifying the tendencies of some of the forces at work, so that, after a sufficient time, their action may be changed a little, and slowly the lines of movement may be modified. This effort, however, can at most be only slight, and it will take a long time. In the meantime spontaneous forces will be at work, compared with which our efforts are like those of a man trying to deflect a river; and these forces will have changed the whole problem before our interferences have time to make themselves felt. The great stream of time and earthly things will sweep on just the same in spite of us. It bears with it now all the errors and follies of the past, the wreckage of all the philosophies, the fragments of all the civilizations, the wisdom of all the abandoned ethical systems, the debris of all the institutions, and the penalties of all the mistakes. It is only in imagination that we stand by and look at it, and criticise it, and plan to change it. Everyone of us is a child of his age and cannot get out of it. He is in the stream and is swept along with it. All his sciences and philosophy come to him out of it. Therefore the tide will not be changed by us. It will swallow up both us and our experiments. It will absorb the efforts at change and take them into itself as new but trivial components, and the great movement of tradition and work will go on unchanged by our fads and schemes. The things which will change it are the great discoveries and inventions, the new reactions inside the social organism, and the changes in the earth itself on account of changes in the cosmical forces. These causes will make of it just what, in fidelity to them, it ought to be. The men will be carried along with it and be made by it. The utmost they can do by their cleverness will be to note and record their course as they are carried along, which is what we do now, and is that which leads us to the vain fancy that we can make or guide the movement. That is why it is the greatest folly of which a man can be capable, to sit down with a slate and pencil to plan out a new social world.

The Social Worker in Social Action
Kenneth L. M. Pray

Kenneth L. M. Pray (1882–1948), late dean of the University of Pennsylvania School of Social Work.

Social action, once more commonly called social reform, has always been an integral and often a decisive element in social work practice as a whole. From the early days of the charity organization and settlement movements in England, down to the mental hygiene and public welfare movement of our own time, there has never been a moment when professionally conscious social workers have been content wholly to separate their day-to-day service of particular individuals and groups from some measure of responsibility for controlling or preventing some of the broad social factors that caused, complicated, or intensified the problems with which they dealt. And the reason, I believe, is that there is no possibility of such separation in fact. In accepting responsibility for administering particular services, social workers accept, also, the inherent obligation to see that those services find their mark, so far as possible, in the lives of those that seek and use them. The special knowledge and skill and discipline upon which the professional character of our whole function rests are directed precisely to that end. Otherwise it would be empty pretense. But suppose, in that effort, we discover circumstances beyond the immediate control of ourselves or our clients which frustrate or obstruct the full and fruitful use of our service? That cannot absolve us from our inherent responsibility to make our service available and useful in fact, as well as in theoretical purpose. And how can we discharge that full responsibility without undertaking somehow to help in removing the obstructions that confront us and our clients? And what is this but social action? . . .

There is . . . one focal point . . . whose spe-

From "Social Work and Social Action," *Proceedings of the National Conference of Social Work . . . 1945,* New York: Columbia University Press, 1945, pp. 348–359, pp. 350–353 quoted. Reprinted by permission.

cific significance sets off our tasks from every other part of social welfare enterprise. That is our concern with the actual impact of any or all of these problems upon the individual life, and the way in which human beings face and meet these problems, and thus attain, through social relationships, their mastery over them. We do not know, for instance—we have no way to find out through our own professional service or training —what constitutes a good and complete health program in any community, in terms of the technical components of such a program. We do know and we must know, because we are responsibly helping people to face their health problems as factors in their social adjustment, what stands in the way of the maintenance of health and the full use of health resources. We know the effect upon individual people of inadequate or inaccessible health resources, inadequate provision for meeting the economic hazards of illness, inadequate appreciation and, therefore, inadequate provision of integrated treatment, of the interacting physical, social, and emotional factors of illness. We know some of the conditions, mechanisms, and processes that are prerequisite for the attainment of recognized standards of health. With respect to these aspects of the community's health problem we have a clear professional responsibility to make our help available, not only in the realization, but also in the formulation of its own health standards and health program.

Take another example: We do not know, nor can we conceivably learn—as a part of our own professional study and practice—all that must go into the organization and operation of an adequate and satisfying economic system. But we do know the impact of economic factors of life upon individual human beings and groups, and we know the problems that people face in the actual process of adjusting to these fundamental realities of social living, because we have been responsibly and studiously engaged in helping people through that actual process. We do know, therefore, not only the fact, but the meaning to real people of inadequate income, of intermittent employment and unemployment; we know the meaning to the individual of real work, of creative, free, self-respecting participation in the economic process and in the determination of his own working conditions. This does not entitle us to prepare or to endorse a detailed blueprint of a total reform of the economic system. It does obligate us to contribute of our special knowledge and our professional judgment to the formulation of acceptable criteria of the validity of economic arrangements, and to exert our influence toward the introduction into our economic structure of those mechanisms and processes that make it possible for people continuously to find positive satisfactions, through sound relationships, in all their working life.

The province of professional social work, then, either in its direct service or in its social action, does not encompass the total life problem of anybody, not the whole of any problem. We are concerned with social process—the impact of social structure and policy upon individuals, and the process by which people are enabled to meet and master the problems this impact presents.

Social Action to Improve Intergroup Relations
Goodwin Watson

Goodwin Barbour Watson (1899–   ), professor of education, Teachers College, Columbia University. Principal works: *Creating a Culture Adapted to Modern Life* (1932); *Human Resources* (1936); *How Good Are Our Colleges?* (1938); *Psychology of Civilian Morale* (1942); *Bureaucracy* (1946); and *Youth after Conflict* (1947).

Fresh efforts to improve inter-faith and inter-racial relations in any community should build on what has gone before. There is no way to begin at the beginning. New agencies inherit, along with the community's problems and conflicts, various patterns of habitual action. Organizations within and among racial and religious groups have long been at work. Programs, some militant

From *Action for Unity*, New York: Harper & Bros., 1947, pp. 1, 5–6, 17, 23, 25, 27–30, 64–65, 78, 91–94. Reprinted by permission.

and others limited to the area of ready agreement, have been accumulating experience. Mistakes that may have been made are quite as important for guiding future programs as are the previous successes. . . .

The visitor going to a strange city to learn how problems of inter-racial and inter-religious tension are met, is likely to be struck at first with the large number of organizations that claim to be working in some way in this field. They seem to overlap in title and in programs. (It is hard, at first, to remember whether the committee that meets next Tuesday is the one for inter-racial collaboration or the one against inter-racial conflict.)

The next discovery is that at each meeting, whatever its title or auspices, many of the same faces reappear. Despite the impressive paper structure, only a handful of citizens are really active. They meet one week to help get better housing for Negroes, a few days later as part of a different conference assembled to consider how to fight a proposed G. L. K. Smith rally, and the next week on a committee to help displaced Nisei find jobs. This overlapping directorate of good will reduces the number of persons who have to be interviewed in order to cover all the activities. Further, and more important, it gives experienced citizens a good basis for comparing the many different types of program. Finally it suggests one criterion for a good new project. Any agency which comes into a community to improve what is being done about inter-racial and inter-religious understanding should plan to develop a broader base of action than now exists. Seldom are all the interested citizens engaged in the existing programs. The few are overworked until they come to think of themselves as almost indispensable and to fear that there are no others upon whom to call. A movement which deliberately went beyond the men and women who have for years carried the burden of promoting community co-operation might tap undiscovered resources of leadership and ingenuity.

But, even though the same persons appear in many different programs, this does not make the programs alike in effectiveness. Organizations develop characteristic ways of acting. The same man may find himself part of one strategy committee which works quietly behind the scenes and of another which blares forth with every available organ of publicity. . . .

One of the most striking facts about inter-faith, inter-racial, and intercultural programs is that they are seldom undertaken on a basis which deserves the name "research." There is often a little "survey" or fact finding, but the methods used to meet the situation have rarely been given any objective appraisal.

Usually any research on community interrelations is done by university staff members or by research departments in social agencies. In the latter case, the research must be limited. The research committee of a welfare agency, for example, seldom has funds or personnel adequate for its own most urgent problems. One lesson which has not yet been carried over from successful corporations to social agencies is the importance of large investments in laboratories and scientific workers. . . .

The first impression of the inquirer is that there are too many overlapping organizations. A second thought is likely to suggest that since the problem is so widespread and so serious there can't be too many agencies attacking it. The numerous committees may be desirable if they enlist more participants and stimulate experiment with new methods. The most regrettable aspect of the present situation is the energy that goes into inter-agency disparagement and dispute. . . .

The activities which make up the programs of agencies now working to improve community relations can be analyzed in seven patterns, termed for convenience: (*a*) exhortation, (*b*) education, (*c*) participation, (*d*) revelation, (*e*) negotiation, (*f*) contention, and (*g*) prevention. . . .

Exhortation to good will abounds. On Race Relations Sunday, exhortations come from the pulpit. During Brotherhood Week or Unity Week or Good Will Week, the Mayor, the school superintendent, and representatives of various racial or cultural minorities speak on the importance of co-operation. The citizen rides beneath car cards and past billboards which frame the good will theme in slogans. . . .

Thoughtful observers tend to question whether those ceremonial re-enforcements of the cultural ideal have much positive effect on real community relations. The doubts seem to lie along four lines: . . .

First, research in character development has shown that preachments have little effect on conduct. . . .

Second, this pattern of action is notoriously apt to reach only those already converted. The audience at meetings assembled to promote good will is made up almost entirely of persons anxious to promote the cause. A meeting of this kind may be helpful in keeping up the morale of the people who are fighting prejudice and intolerance, but it seldom reaches the serious offenders. The same observation must be made of the literature distributed in such quantities. . . .

The third limitation of this good-will pattern is that it usually evades the points of conflict. . . . The propaganda "accentuates the positive," but it leaves everyone with his objections and reservations unexamined. . . .

The fourth reservation is serious because it indicates that activities of this pattern may be, not merely innocuous and wasteful, but harmful. Expressions of good will often serve to salve the American conscience. They become substitutes for constructive action or a compensatory offering to make up for violations in practice. People pay their verbal tribute to the ideal and use those symbolic acts to excuse the actual inequities. Sometimes the preaching is an actual cloak, as when notorious anti-Semites and reactionaries participate on good-will programs to gain a reputation for Americanism. . . .

One of our most fundamental hypotheses, growing out of this survey,* is that *it is more constructive to attack segregation than it is to attack prejudices.* One reason for this is that segregation is a public matter; prejudices are private affairs and therefore not so subject to social control. A more important argument is that, if we try to change people's feelings while the caste barriers remain tacitly accepted, the habits built around those barriers will silently undo anything we accomplish. On the other hand, persons with strong prejudices who have to live and work together soon experience human qualities and relationships which tend to break down the prejudice. Our survey presented many illustrations of this important truth. White workers in factories forced by the war, the FEPC, and the CIO unions to accept Negro co-workers came to tolerate and eventually to like their new companions. Families which planned to move out of housing projects when Negroes came in but were delayed in this moving discovered that they liked their new neighbors and that they no longer cared to move. . . .

Organizations which are uncompromising in

exposing racial and religious bias become storm centers in community life. They generate apprehension. Their activities offend the fence-sitters who are more afraid of "bad publicity" than of injustice. . . .

The persistent danger with individuals and organizations who seek to be useful only as "fixers" is that they seldom take a stand as a matter of principle. They tend to become merely an expression of the balance of forces. They themselves are not a force. They are like the pointer on a scale moved back and forth as the weights are shifted. Their prestige and apparent influence is out of all proportion to the effect that they actually exert. The driving pressure groups, pro and con, determine the dynamics of the situation, and the negotiators and diplomats become only the mouthpiece which makes the score official. Their influence on the course of events may be reduced to that of the score keeper on the course of a hockey match. . . .

Mediation is not always so limited in usefulness, however, because sometimes the invention of an ingenious compromise releases efforts for new social advance. Often the neutral observer, the third party, the negotiator, can play a therapeutic role. Since he understands each contender, the contenders themselves are relieved. Tension is reduced. Positions are clarified and even modified in the light of the third party's objectivity. Because of the presence of the mediator, conflicts are harmoniously resolved.

Negotiation can make a significant contribution in the case of tense community interrelations. The fact that in our observation most individuals and agencies which specialized in this function were regarded by the radicals as rather "unprincipled" constitutes a serious warning. Pressures are apt to be strong. Compromise tends to be regarded as good in itself, regardless of the principles and interests at stake. . . .

Experience has shown that, though inflexible people are unpleasant, they do often get their own way. It is especially true that, when a community places a high premium on good will and harmony, groups which threaten disturbances get a lot of attention and a great many concessions. "Better give them what they want and avoid a row," concludes the uneasy administrator.

One of our most instructive interviews was with a man who had just retired after several years of work as the head of an active Mayor's Committee in a large city.

---

* Watson's book, *Action for Unity,* from which only brief excerpts are given, sets forth in detail the results of an extensive field survey.—*Eds.*

"What would you say has made the biggest contribution to improving inter-race and inter-faith relations in this community?" we asked. He considered his reply and then said, "Well, it caused us a lot of headaches and it is probably full of potential dynamite for the Negroes them-selves, but I would have to admit that it was the aggressive, militant, uncompromising demands of some of the Negro organizations that made us move further than anything else. They cause us a lot of trouble, but they get attention."

Social Research and Intergroup Relations
Oscar Cohen

Oscar Cohen (1908–   ), national program director, Anti-Defamation League of B'nai B'rith.

It was not too many years ago that those of us working in the field of intergroup relations enter-tained great expectations for the social sciences. It was generally thought that in a comparatively few years there would be created a positive body of doctrine which could give definitive answers to the problems facing those who were trying to affect social change at the community level. We found, however, that instead of reaching the pot of gold just beyond the horizon, the horizon kept getting further away. Among practitioners, there has been some disillusionment about the useful-ness of social science knowledge. I believe this stems from four factors: the lack of relevance of research; difficulties of communication; loss of confidence in social science and the fact that social science had been originally oversold to commu-nity workers.

The practitioner who becomes aware of some of the conclusions of research in his field is fre-quently bewildered. He finds it difficult to dis-cover any practical application in what appear to be substantial and worthwhile research projects. There is not much research that seems to have any relevance to his day-to-day activities. He looks at a treatise on the authoritarian personality and wonders how he can use it. He reads of evidence concerning the relation between frustrated indi-viduals and prejudice. Does this mean that the practitioner should set about trying to eliminate the frustrations of individuals? Moreover, the practitioner soon notes that a good deal of re-search takes place with small and controlled groups in which personality factors are not con-sidered. For example, Rosenthal found that it was not possible to apply results obtained from stu-dent groups at Harvard to student groups at the University of Chicago.[1] If this is the case, how can one generalize from group studies? The prac-titioner wonders how to apply such research re-sults to the political and organizational atmos-phere in which he lives. Again and again, I have heard comments about research to this effect, "Interesting—but what do I do about it?"

This is not to gainsay the necessity for and the importance of basic research. Such pure research must continue even where there is no likelihood of applying the results. The results of social sci-ence research, of course, cannot be evaluated merely in terms of their usefulness to practition-ers. The practitioner, in any case, cannot read the great volume of material produced by social sci-entists, and the well known jargon language of social science raises a communication barrier which is difficult to penetrate.

I have indicated that undue optimism on the part of social scientists may have resulted in the practitioner's loss of confidence. There is also the professional's disappointment in the practical benefits he feels should derive from the many volumes and treatises now appearing. The results of research are frequently inconclusive or con-flicting. The practitioner is tempted, under the pressure of daily exigencies, to look upon social science findings with varying degrees of interest and intellectual curiosity. But he will, very likely, go about his business without giving the social sciences much thought.

At this point, it might be well to take a look at the practitioner. What kind of a person is he?

[1] B. Rosenthal, at 1953 Cleveland meeting of American Psychological Association.

From "The Application of Social Research to Intergroup Relations," *Social Problems,* 2: 1 (July 1954): 20–25.

And why does the nature of his work sometimes throw roadblocks between himself and the social scientist?

The practitioner in our field is not usually graduated from a course in intergroup relations. He doesn't, as a rule, enter this field by virtue of a diploma. Intergroup relations in this respect is vastly different from the social work field. Practitioners in our field have widely divergent backgrounds, and my own acquaintances in this field include men and women who have come from such occupations and professions as law, journalism, teaching, salesmanship, music, dentistry, parole work, public relations, radio, the clergy, social work and organized labor. However, despite this difference in background, a common core of understanding develops.

Most practitioners are oppressed by the overwhelming pressure of their jobs. They are constantly involved in practical situations which require decisions, situations in which organizational ability is more important than intellectual depth. So when there may arrive on his desk a three or four-hundred page volume which contains considerable discussion of displaced aggression, it is not difficult to see why the practitioner may become a little dismayed.

Having said this, I would now like to point out as emphatically as I can that social science findings have had a considerable effect upon action in the field of intergroup relations.

There has been a marked evolution in thinking on the part of the practitioner in this field, and, in fact, over the past twenty years, there has been a dramatic change. In the 1930's, when work in the field of intergroup relations was tremendously accelerated, techniques were fairly simple and few in number. They were confined largely to the areas of mass communication and the protest meeting. Since then, there has been a marked change in the basic assumptions which underlyy activities on the community level and, in addition, in the techniques which have stemmed from these assumptions. There is no doubt that the social sciences have contributed greatly to the changes which have resulted in increased effectiveness.

In the first place, practitioners have drawn heavily upon the work of many social scientists in establishing public recognition of the fact that Negroes are not an inferior race.[2] The practitioners' efforts to destroy widely accepted but falla-

cious notions about racial inferiorities have been immeasurably assisted by their ability to refer to authoritative and scientific sources.

There has been a very marked trend away from speeches exhorting audiences toward brotherhood. The trend now is toward the use of the discussion group as a device for affecting the attitudes of individuals.

The motion picture became a very widely used device in the presentation of intergroup themes to wide varieties of audiences. The emphasis upon group discussion rather than exhortation led to the practice of encouraging discussion after the presentation of motion pictures. This is an important change, and the technique is now widely accepted in the intergroup relations field.

At one time the belief was current among practitioners that understanding would be promoted if "only people knew each other." For this reason, efforts were made to achieve situations in which people of different races and religions would meet together as in Tredwell Smith's classic study.[3] The situations were frequently artificial and sometimes highly contrived. Social scientists found that the artificial juxtaposition of individuals of different faiths and races does not necessarily bring about understanding. Social scientists have indicated that personal contact is not the only consideration, but that equality of status is an all important factor in bringing together diverse groups whose understanding of each other was to be promoted.

Another important contribution to the practitioner has been the finding of the social scientist that recognition of racial and religious differences, and inculcation of prejudices, begin at a much earlier age than was previously thought possible. This resulted in the encouragement of intercultural educational practices in the schools, at lower grade levels than had previously been thought desirable.

Still another contribution of the social scientist has been the finding that integration of white and colored individuals in specific situations can be achieved amicably and with benefit to all concerned. The work of Deutsch and Collins in the field of inter-racial housing,[4] and Stouffer on the American soldier,[5] have helped in lending support

---

[2] Cf. the material summarized in G. Myrdal, *An American Dilemma*, New York: Harper, 1943, pp. 137–153.

[3] F. T. Smith, *An Experiment in Modifying Attitudes Toward the Negro*, New York: Teachers College, 1943.

[4] M. Deutsch and M. E. Collins, *Interracial Housing*, Minneapolis: University of Minnesota Press, 1951.

[5] S. A. Stouffer *et al.*, *The American Soldier*, Princeton: Princeton University Press, 1949.

to efforts to fight segregation in housing and in the armed forces.

The study of such techniques as group dynamics and socio-drama have had considerable effect upon practical work at the local level. There is evidence that the techniques based on studies of group dynamics are being generally utilized. In particular, socia-drama has become a highly regarded and much used technique in study groups, workshops and as a prelude to group discussion.

Perhaps one of the most widely used educational devices in the intergroup relations field is the Rumor Clinic, described in Allport and Postman's *Psychology of Rumor*.[6] Slides have been made from the drawings utilized by Allport, and the Rumor Clinic has been presented many thousands of times before audiences in all parts of the United States.

The Rumor Clinic is based on the device of selecting people from the audience, the first of whom sees the slide projected, after which his impressions are transmitted to the others, one at a time. During this presentation, the audience sees the projected slide, but those describing the message they have received do not see it. The most frequently used slide depicts a subway car in which a poorly dressed white man with a razor in his hand stands talking to a well dressed Negro. It is remarkable how the third participant in the Rumor Clinic generally passes the razor from the hand of the white man to the hand of the Negro. The visible effect upon audiences of such distortions is usually very impressive.

I should also mention very briefly the work done in applying human relations to police training which has proved extremely helpful to practitioners throughout the country.[7]

Finally, there is an increasing awareness on the part of practitioners of the importance of the reference group in affecting the attitudes and actions of the individual. The change in thinking and emphasis which previously was centered upon "reaching" the individual is now being increasingly directed toward the group. The pioneering work of Kurt Lewin in this connection is bearing fruit, and I believe that the work of social scientist in this area will be accorded increasing attention and response.

In order to help the community level practitioner achieve quality as well as quantity, it might be useful to suggest some of the areas in which further research is needed.

The question of the use of mass media continues to be a troublesome one for the practitioner. The use of mass communication can have a boomerang effect. The problem is not whether mass media will be used. Mass media are here to stay. They are imbedded in the American way of life, and the newspaper, car card, radio and television are as American as Coca-Cola. We may not like the singing commercial, but it works.

The problems of mass media are not "if" but "how." Some of the ill effects of the use of mass communication can be readily predicted but others are more subtle and obscure. Leo Srole has made some helpful initial explorations in this regard in a study sponsored by the Anti-Defamation League.[8]

An assumption generally held by practitioners is that knowledge promotes tolerance. This is the basis for a tremendous amount of activity, particularly of the interfaith variety. Whereas knowledge may promote tolerance under certain conditions, what are the limits of the validity of this generalization?

Much has been written about the effectiveness of legislation in the field of intergroup relations. I think legislation and litigation as techniques for combatting discrimination are now solidly accepted. However, there is a long way to go in the field of legislation both on the federal, state and local levels. Investigation could be helpful in ascertaining the preparatory steps of an educational and social action nature necessary to insure the passage of legislation. In addition, we need to know more about those steps which are necessary after the passage of legislation in order to assure public acceptance.

A sensitive area in which research could be tremendously helpful is the study of the reactions of minority groups. If, as a number of researches indicate, the attitude of a minority group toward itself will affect the attitude of a majority group, we have here an important area of concern. The phenomenon of self-hate on the part of a minority group is not uncommon. Moreover, it might be very helpful if we know more about how members of a minority group should handle incidents

[6] G. Allport and C. Postman, *Psychology of Rumor*, New York: Henry Holt, 1947.

[7] For instance, J. D. Lohman, *The Police and Minority Groups*, Chicago: Chicago Park District, 1947.

[8] L. Srole and C. Y. Glock, *A Controlled Study of the Impact of Anti-Discrimination Car Cards*, New York: Anti-Defamation League and Bureau of Applied Social Research, 1953.

of prejudice and discrimination. The Incident Control technique of Chein and his associates is a helpful beginning.[9] There is more work required here, particularly in the assistance that parents require in counselling children who meet with racial and religious prejudice. The work of Lewin and Bettelheim constitutes at least an initial step.

An enormous amount of activity is taking place in the field of intercultural education and increasingly, schools and school systems are adopting intercultural education techniques. Lynd[10] and others have pointed up the dichotomy between what youngsters are taught in school and what actually faces them in the world outside. This involves a study of the interrelationship of the school and community with particular focus upon intergroup relationships.

A study might be made of community self-surveys. Varying claims have been made for the efficacy of the community survey. Some have maintained that these surveys are full of sound and publicity with no significant change following in their wake. It might be found, for example, that techniques of community surveys are faulty; that the involvement in a survey covering a multitude of problems so exhausts the participants that no energies are available for remedial action. It might be found that a community survey is largely useless unless there is understanding and determination at the outset that remedial action will be taken. There are many aspects of this problem which, if explored, would be very helpful to practitioners who are lured into the monumental task of a community survey with sometimes disappointing results.

Finally, I would urge that a great deal more attention be given to the study of power and power structure as a basic consideration in the efforts toward social change.

The works of Lasswell,[11] and Floyd Hunter[12] are important contributions to this somewhat neglected field. It may well be that social change can be greatly accelerated by concentration upon certain community elements. Sometimes we have the disconcerting suspicion that social changes can be (and are being) achieved very rapidly on a local level by a relatively small number of people, none of whom have had a course in group dynamics.

An important problem, related to power, which has occurred to many persons in the intergroup and human relations field, is the reconciliation of persuasive techniques with true democratic processes. Even where we might all agree that our objective is the improvement of the human condition, we must be aware of the ethical issues involved in our trying to persuade other people to our point of view. The engineer of consent is always susceptible to criticism, no matter how worthy his goal.

There should be an improvement in the methods available for making research resorts available to the practitioner, and it is encouraging to note the extent to which social scientists are gaining first hand experience of action at the community level. Robin Williams has summed up the present situation with respect to the relation between research and practice ". . . . systematic research in race relations has had conspicuously little *direct* application to meaningful practice."[13] This is a pretty harsh indictment and I am not sure it is entirely earned. But I would suggest that the problem does exist, that it is a serious one, and that something should be done about it.

---

[9] A. F. Citron and J. Harding, *Answering the Bigot,* New York: Commission on Community Interrelations, no date.

[10] R. S. Lynd, *Knowledge for What,* Princeton: Princeton University Press, 1937.

[11] H. D. Lasswell, *Power and Personality,* London: Chapman and Hall, 1949.

[12] F. Hunter, *Community Power Structure,* Chapel Hill: University of North Carolina Press, 1953.

[13] R. Williams, "Application of Research to Practice in Intergroup Relations, *American Sociological Review,* 18 (1953), p. 79.

Radicals in America

Charles Allan Madison

Charles Allan Madison (1895–   ), college editor, Henry Holt and Company. Author of *Critics and Crusaders* (1947), *American Labor Leaders* (1950).

A radical may be many things and he may be moved by complex motives, but in the last analysis he is an idealist who feels impelled to right existing wrongs. His rebelliousness may be a form of compensation for suffering from authority or poverty, from thwarted ambition or personal maladjustment. But while others who are similarly conditioned, yet lack the noble impulse, become gangsters or millionaires, clowns or cranks, the radical is driven by a messianic urge to remake the world.

There have always been radicals because society has never been free of inequality and oppression. The majority of men, like Cain, are averse to becoming their brothers' keepers; the small band of critics and crusaders, however, emulate Moses in their zeal to deliver their brethren from bondage. They are quick to become indignant at the shortcomings of society and they try to rectify them in ways congenial to their time and culture. From the very beginning of communal life these radicals have held the mirror up to mankind and pointed to the obvious blemishes.

In the very real sense the United States was conceived and firmly established by the radicals of 1776. It was Samuel Adams and Thomas Jefferson and many others like them who risked their liberty, if not their lives, in their efforts to overthrow British rule and unite the colonies into a nation dedicated to the ideals of the Declaration of Independence. Because Jefferson most eloquently expressed the principles of freedom and equality—ideals consonant with the demands of the prevailing handicraft civilization—he became the patron saint of the radicals who came after him. From his time to ours many Americans have found inspiration in the doctrines of Jeffersonian democracy and have fought for them on the platform, in the polling booth, and on the battlefield. It was a continuous struggle because new wrongs always rose, phoenixlike, out of the ashes of old iniquities; yet these idealists, now few and ineffectual

and now numerous and strong, were ever ready to battle for the rights of the poor and the oppressed.

Probably no other wrong in the life of the American republic generated so much altruism and exaltation as Negro slavery. Although the Abolitionists were in a sense the apostles of an emerging industrialism, they were even more—at least individually and consciously—the exponents of a democratic ethics. They believed literally that God made all men free and equal and they could not abide the thought that millions of human beings were living in bondage. They insisted on proclaiming their ideal of freedom with a forcefulness that in the end made it irresistible.

The Abolitionists, like other groups of radicals, were not of one mind. Among them were a number of wealthy men who opposed slavery on moral grounds but who were staid conservatives in everything else. The majority might be classed with their leader Garrison: they were genuine democrats who loved liberty and suspected authority; who revered God and challenged orthodoxy; who abominated chattel slavery in the South and failed to recognize the economic oppression of their neighbors who worked in mills and factories. Their radicalism ended with the adoption of the Thirteenth Amendment. Only a few followed Wendell Phillips in the new crusade against industrial exploitation.

After the Civil War the struggle for economic justice brought about a new realignment of forces: it was no longer Southerners against Northerners but the mass of people against the powerful corporations. The latter were taking full advantage of the prevailing laissez-faire doctrine and were greedily exploiting an almost virgin continent. In their efforts to get rich quick the financiers and managers of the large companies oppressed their workers in the factory and their customers on the farm; in their eagerness to obtain special privileges they corrupted the agencies of government by means of lobbying and bribery.

Radicals and humanitarians readily took up the cause of economic justice. The fight was long and yielded meager reforms. The reason is twofold. The nature of economic democracy directly affects the very life of modern capitalism, since it implies limitations upon the freedom of enterprise that must ultimately dry up the source of the profit motive. Up to the depression of the 1930's businessmen, riding the crest of industrial development, had little difficulty in brushing aside the attempts to impede their progress. The reformers, moreover, either unaware of the logic of their economic doctrine or yielding to wishful thinking on the effectiveness of palliatives, pursued an obsolescent social philosophy and attacked the symptoms rather than the causes of industrial exploitation. Thus they fought for monetary reforms, for honesty in government, for free land, for free trade, for this law and that. Their agitation, however, failed to check the evils of an aggressive capitalism. Corporations continued to grow larger, stronger, and more monopolistic.

The complexity of human nature made it inevitable for the critics of the economic status quo to take divergent paths in their eagerness to reach the goal of social democracy. Although the utopians spent most of their idealism on experiments with Fourieristic phalanxes and perfect communities, not a few continued to dream of a paradise on earth. Edward Bellamy conceived his idealized society within the framework of a socialistic economy. When *Looking Backward* won a large number of eager followers, Bellamy devoted himself to the movement he had initiated with an enthusiasm that quickly exhausted his meager strength. The Nationalist party disintegrated after a few years, but the book which had brought it into being continues to contribute to the agitation for economic equality.

Equally utopian but emphatically individualistic were the early anarchists. They believed that all social wrongs were rooted in governmental authority and that the remedy lay in the curbing of this authority. Let each man live as he wished and permit no man to rule over his fellows—and society will function freely, harmoniously, and advantageously. Thoreau had the vision and the courage to demonstrate the feasibility of anarchistic way of life. For more than a quarter of a century Benjamine Tucker's *Liberty* advocated the philosophy of individualist anarchism with a gusto that made it stand out among the periodicals of the day. In the 1880's other libertarians, recognizing the cogency of industrial interdependence, advanced a theory of communism which eschewed all centralized authority. Their strong attacks upon capitalistic exploitation and their ominous "propaganda of the deed" subjected them to severe persecution and made the term "anarchism" synonymous with violence and criminality. Nevertheless they persisted in holding high the ideal of freedom from restraint and in fighting for the rights of the oppressed.

Although American economists have not especially distinguished themselves either for originality of thought or for radical ideas, several of them have contributed notably to a realistic understanding of modern economic society. Confronted by conditions which did not square with established theory, these few dissidents evolved principles more consonant with the facts as they found them. Their ideas influenced the thinking of many liberals in and out of government service and thereby contributed considerably to social progress. Thus Henry George's economic agitation, which sought to abolish poverty by stopping the private exploitation of land, for a time assumed the character of a crusade. Brooks Adams, having studied the nature and history of Western civilization, pointed out that the greed and blind selfishness of big business were driving the United States to the abyss of revolution. Thorstein Veblen's writings tore the underpinnings from classical economics and demonstrated the obsolescence of the principles supporting the system of capitalism. Although his books had few readers, there were among them those who gave force and direction to our current economic thinking.

The post-Civil War liberals were Jeffersonian idealists. Suspecting bigness and great wealth and provoked by the get-and-grab methods of the aggressive corporations, they saw the country despoiled of its wealth, the nation robbed of its birthright, and the farmers and laborers deprived of their just share. They worked hard to right these wrongs, but their proposed reforms went against the tide of capitalistic development. For a time their spirited agitation could put only an occasional brake upon the aggrandizement of the powerful monopolies or expose the misfeasance of men in office. Nevertheless, the attacks upon special privileges and corrupt government made by Henry D. Lloyd and John Peter Altgeld in the 1890's and by Robert M. La Follette, the muckrakers and the Progressives after the turn of the century prepared the way for the triumphant New Dealers in the 1930's. In the course of this long struggle for social justice, however, radically altered economic conditions forced the liberals to reject the Jeffersonian tenet of a weak government and embrace the contrary principle advocated by Alexander Hamilton. They found that only a strong central government was in a position to cope with the capitalist leviathan and safeguard the rights of the mass of the people.

The Marxian socialists have been the most persistent and the most radical critics of the status quo. Their agitation proved ineffective because their basic principles of the class struggle and the cooperative commonwealth seemed both pernicious and preposterous to a people imbued with the rightness of the laissez-faire doctrine. Few were ready to scrap a system that enabled a poor man to become a millionaire through his own efforts. For many years, therefore, the socialists received the same treatment as the early Abolitionists: they were either scorned or ignored. After 1900 the widespread social consciousness generated by the muckrakers served to give all radicals a favorable hearing. But the success of the Russian Revolution and the after-effects of World War I gave Marxism a frightening immediacy. The resulting hysteria drove most of the socialists into the underground camp of the communists—the faction that had joined the Third International. Relatively few in number and frequently treated like traitors and outcasts, these radicals nevertheless took a leading part in the struggle for social justice.

Notwithstanding their theoretical confusion and wide practical divergence, the various groups opposing the status quo have achieved notable success in their work to strengthen the democratic base of the American people. One need only recall the grievous conditions existing long after the Civil War—when men labored twelve hours a day for subsistence wages, working conditions were brutal and unsafe, trade unions were few and ineffective, social protection was unknown, farmers were at the mercy of the bankers and the railroads, and corporations practised fraud and chicane at will—to realize that the sum of social legislation enacted in recent years is of a truly revolutionary character. It is at least partly due to the agitation of these critics and crusaders that the American people are at present enjoying a combination of political freedom and economic well-being which is the envy of the world.

What of the future? To consider this question is to deal with conditions that differ fundamentally from those that confronted the radicals of the previous century. Before the 1930's men of wealth were firmly in the saddle. They enjoyed the privileges and powers bestowed upon them by a government functioning under a laissez-faire interpretation of the Constitution. For many decades judges upheld the farce of equality under the law, which presumed a day laborer to be as free and independent as his multi-millionaire employer. When state legislatures and the Congress, besieged by burdened workers and farmers, agreed to rectify the egregiously bad practices of the corporations, the courts refused to budge from the letter of the law. They declared unconstitutional acts to shorten the hours of labor or to protect workmen against obvious hazards—insisting that these laws deprived individuals of their inalienable right to work where and when they pleased. By the same reasoning they granted injunctions to employers in labor disputes and sanctioned the use of thugs to break up strikes.

Big business enjoyed these privileges until the early 1930's, when the severe economic depression gave rise to the New Deal. The election of Franklin D. Roosevelt on a liberal platform transferred the government of the country to a body of key men—many of whom had grown up under Thorstein Veblen—who knew that the laissez-faire policy had become completely anachronistic in an age of vast technological and electronic development. It was painfully obvious to them that the individual urban workman, entirely dependent upon his job for his livelihood, was not the equal of the wealthy corporation and must be shielded from exploitation and unemployment; that the small investor and the poor farmer were alike in need of protection from Wall Street and from Main Street respectively. To bring our basic law up to date—that is, to rectify existing inequalities—the Roosevelt administration had Congress enact a number of statutes that, taken together, amount to a social Magna Carta. Workmen and farmers were the chief beneficiaries. The National Labor Relations Act not only permitted employees to organize as they wished but also protected them against unfair practices on the part of their employers. What this meant in effect was that the government ceased favoring capital and looked benevolently upon labor. Shrewd union officials, finding the

American Federation of Labor unwilling and unwieldy, quickly formed the Committee on Industrial Organization (later changed to Congress of Industrial Organizations) for the purpose of unionizing the workers in the mass-production industries. Employing such spectacular methods as the "sit-down" strike and mass picketing, labor organizers soon enrolled millions of members into the new CIO unions. Before long there was considerable general improvement in both wage rates and working conditions. By the end of World War II more than fourteen million union members, conscious of their important part in the amazing rise in production, were determined to get their full share of the nation's augmented income. . . .

[The reaction against labor unions which followed World War II placed labor in a position which was] defensive and by no means so strong as its opponents insist. But in its favor are the positive trends in social and industrial development. There is no going back: science and invention impel us ever forward; and the problems they originate require fresh methods of treatment. The complexity of modern industrialism, requiring large concentration of workers and a completely urban mode of existence, has given organized labor a tremendous potential power; the operation of any major industry has become so essential to the life of the nation that no government can permit its interruption. As a consequence the doctrines of "free enterprise" and

"rugged individualism" have gone the way of human slavery and the horse and buggy. It was well enough, for instance, for the government to serve as a silent partner of the railroads in the strike of 1878, when trains were not yet the basic arteries of the nation's lifeblood; the same attitude on the part of the Cleveland administration in 1894 brought forth the Altgeld-Bryan rebellion; to act similarly in 1946 would invite chaos or revolution. In a highly technological society, social planning and control are both necessary and unavoidable. President Truman's proposal to draft strikers and force them to work was a desperate measure and was as regressive as it would be unworkable. And even that formula is based on government operation of the affected industries—which is not at all what the corporations want.

An examination of the problem of capital-labor relations leads, willy-nilly, to the following alternatives: either big business will be intelligent enough to concede the loss of its special privileges and seek a satisfactory working arrangement with labor—and this seems at present highly unlikely—or, on the failure of industrial peace, the government will be forced to take over and operate the basic industries—as Great Britain, France, and other countries are compelled to do by the logic of unavoidable events. Whether the latter solution will lead to state socialism, a modified fascism, or a liberalized communism is for the future to determine.

The Dilemma in Revolution

L. L. Bernard

Luther Lee Bernard (1881–1951), late professorial lecturer in sociology, Pennsylvania State University. Principal publications: *Instinct* (1924); *Introduction to Social Psychology* (1926); *The Development of Methods in Sociology* (1928); *Introduction to Sociology* (1942); with Jessie Bernard, *Origins of American Sociology* (1943); and *War and Its Causes* (1944).

The people who are responsible for the fixing of social relations and institutions, and thus for the blocking of normal social change, are often as helpless as are the people who revolt, when the question of loosening up on the social system is raised. All of their interests and obligations are tied up with the social system as it stands. To promote or to resist change often would be

equally destructive to them. The question thus frequently comes to be, "Shall we perish with the system or shall we be swept away by the flood that is loosed by breaking down the system?" In the French Revolution, for example, that was exactly the problem. A generation before the final debacle came it was clearly understood by the king and the nobles that they were destined to

From *Social Control in Its Sociological Aspects*, New York: Macmillan Co., 1939, pp. 340–343. Copyright, 1939, by The Macmillan Company and used with their permission.

lose, whatever might be the final solution—reform or revolution. Since it is at least as difficult for a class as for an individual to commit suicide of its own free will, they chose revolution in preference to a reform program which would also have destroyed them, and that is the meaning of Louis XV's famous aphorism, "After us, the deluge." Even in England, where not infrequently, perhaps usually, reform has been permitted to take the place of revolution, the ruling classes have not willingly surrendered their powers and privileges. Perhaps it is psychically impossible that they should be able to do so. It was a member of the English nobility, Lord Lansdowne, who at the end of the great war of 1914–1918 advised his government to end the war short of complete destruction of German political organization, lest a proletarian revolution should follow and spread to other countries and sweep away all of the privileges of the upper classes. It is interesting also that some of the commentators upon the puzzling surrender of England and France to the dominance of Germany in Europe in 1938 have contended that the decision was dictated not so much by fear of a German victory in case of war as by fear of a proletarian victory in case of the second defeat of Germany. In other words, the hypothesis advanced by these commentators was that the ruling (tory) classes of England found themselves confronted by the dilemma of choosing between a victory for the allies and a loss of their class privileges to the proletarian forces at home or the sacrifice of British prestige in Europe and possibly the ultimate sacrifice of the British empire to German aggression, with an implied Nazi guarantee to their class dominance at home. Consequently, if this is the correct interpretation, they sacrificed the empire to their class interests. Thus, even when the nation as a whole stands clearly to gain by a reform or a course of action it nevertheless must be fought for by much strenuous effort over equally strenuous opposition by the privileged classes or groups. That the existence of this barrier of the class struggle to reform in England has long been recognized, although it has often yielded to force of circumstances, is evidenced by the following analysis of British politics made more than half a century ago.

In the earlier part of the last century, when men began to awake to their natural rights, philosophical minds of the Continent of Europe were struck with the composition of English society. They gave credit to the government; but it was a society, formed to independent thought and existence, on which they paused in admiration. Now, English authority, of all in Europe, has been the most liberal; but what administration of it can be named to which England is indebted for liberty, or for any portion or atom of it? . . . England owes her prosperity to her liberty, and her liberty to the efforts of society. . . .

Liberty is the shame of authority in all countries. . . . Even political movements of mere humanity, improvements of the poor, of the prisons, of the law, have been forced on the English authority by society, and uniformly regarded by authority as loosening its reins.[1] . . .

Even today those who have made the capitalistic system and who are part and parcel of it in their sympathies and interests face the same sort of difficulty. Many leaders of the capitalistic system have contributed, intentionally or otherwise, to piecemeal and partial reforms by giving great sums for scientific endowments and for welfare work, but to abandon the system itself is possible neither mentally nor socially without a revolutionary disruption of the social order as the directors of the capitalistic system understand it. Because of their identification with the system they are unable to see such an abandonment as anything but irreparable social catastrophe which would destroy civilization itself. In such a manner was the French Revolution regarded by even as otherwise liberal a man as Edmund Burke, and so do the defenders of the capitalistic system now regard the Bolshevik revolution in Russia. Since *their* social system would be destroyed by such a revolution, and since almost everyone by psychological necessity regards *his* social system as the *one and only* feasable social system, it is impossible for a social class to give its cordial consent to a major social change. Hence the frequent inevitability of revolution as a cataclysmic form of social change which readjusts human relationships on a more equitable basis. The gradual growth of the technique of social reform during the nineteenth and twentieth centuries offers some hope that violent revolutions may not always be inevitable, but that a more rational form of social change may in time be made to work universally. This should be possible when men learn to think scientifically and objectively instead of emotionally about the social problems that most intimately concern them.

[1] From Charles Ingersoll, *Fears for Democracy*, Philadelphia: J. B. Lippincott and Co., 1875, pp. 251–252.

CROSS REFERENCES TO STANDARD TEXTS *

Barnes, *Society in Transition,* pp. 440–441, 515, 518, 583–585, 603.

Bernard, *American Community Behavior,* pp. 206–210, 589, Chap. 29.

Brown, *Social Pathology,* Chaps. 28, 33.

Cuber and Harper, *Problems of American Society,* Chap. 4, pp. 181–182.

Faris, *Social Disorganization,* Chap. 14.

Gillin, *Social Pathology,* Chaps. 32–33.

——— and others, *Social Problems,* Chap. 19.

Herman, *Approach to Social Problems,* pp. 316–319.

Landis, *Social Policies in the Making,* pp. 317, 397, Chap. 20.

Lemert, *Social Pathology,* pp. 56, 63, 260–263, 307, Chap. 7.

Merrill and others, *Social Problems,* Chaps. 4, 7, 10.

Mihanovich, *Current Social Problems,* Chaps. 1, 15.

Neumeyer, *Social Problems and the Changing Society,* pp. 24–25, Chap. 11.

Nordskog and others, *Analyzing Social Problems,* pp. 16–18, 318, Chaps. 11–12.

Odum, *American Social Problems,* Chaps. 17, 26–27.

Phelps and Henderson, *Contemporary Social Problems,* Chap. 20.

Reinhardt and others, *Social Problems and Social Policy,* Chap. 2.

Weaver, *Social Problems,* Chap. 29.

* For complete bibliographical reference to each text, see page 13.

OTHER BIBLIOGRAPHY

Edith Abbott, *Public Assistance: 1, American Principles and Policies,* Chicago: University of Chicago Press, 1940.

Charles A. Beard, "Individualism and Capitalism," *Encyclopaedia of the Social Sciences, 1* (1930): 145–163.

Herbert Bisno, *The Philosophy of Social Work,* Washington: Public Affairs Press, 1952.

Herbert Blumer, "Social Movements," Chap. 22 in A. M. Lee, ed., *Principles of Sociology,* 2d ed. rev., New York: Barnes & Noble, 1951, pp. 199–220.

Esther Lucile Brown, *Social Work as a Profession,* New York: Russell Sage Foundation, 1942.

Baker Brownell, *The Human Community: Its Philosophy and Practice for a Time of Crisis,* New York: Harper & Bros., 1950.

Grace Browning, *Rural Public Welfare,* Chicago: University of Chicago Press, 1941.

Frank J. Bruno, *Trends in Social Work,* New York: Columbia University Press, 1948.

Hadley Cantril, *The Psychology of Social Movements,* New York: John Wiley & Sons, 1941.

Zechariah Chafee, Jr., *Free Speech in the United States,* Cambridge: Harvard University Press, 1941.

Community Service Society, *Social Work as Human Relations,* New York: Columbia University Press, 1949.

Dan W. Dodson, "Social Action and Education," *Journal of Educational Sociology, 22* (1949–50): 345–351.

Leonard W. Doob, *Plans of Men,* New Haven: Yale University Press, 1940.

Seba Eldridge, *Dynamics of Social Action,* Washington: Public Affairs Press, 1952.

Bertram Fowler, *The Cooperative Challenge,* Boston: Little, Brown & Co., 1947.

David G. French, *An Approach to Measuring Results in Social Work,* New York: Columbia University Press, 1952.

L. M. French, *Psychiatric Social Work,* New York: Commonwealth Fund, 1940.

Gordon Hamilton, *Theory and Practice of Social Case Work,* rev. ed., New York: Columbia University Press, 1951.

Shelby M. Harrison and F. Emerson Andrews, *American Foundations for Social Welfare,* New York: Russell Sage Foundation, 1946.

Charles E. Hendry, ed., *Decade of Group Work,* New York: Association Press, 1947.

Arthur Hillman, *Community Organization and Planning,* New York: Macmillan Co., 1950.

Earle Hitch, *Rebuilding Rural Communities,* New York: Harper & Bros., 1950.

Rex D. Hopper, "The Revolutionary Process," *Social Forces, 28* (1949–50): 270–279.

Donald S. Howard, ed., *Community Organization: Its Nature and Setting,* New York: American Association of Social Workers, 1947.

Robert Hunter, *Revolutions: Why, How and When?* New York: Harper & Bros., 1940.

Ray Johns and David De Marche, *Community Organization and Agency Responsibility,* New York: Association Press, 1951.

Horace M. Kallen, "Radicalism" and "Reformism," *Encyclopaedia of the Social Sciences, 13* (1934): 51–54 and 194–195.

Clarence King, *Organizing for Community Action,* New York: Harper & Bros., 1948.

John A. Kinneman, *The Community in American Society,* New York: Crofts, 1947.

Harry W. Laidler, *Social-Economic Movements,* New York: T. Y. Crowell Co., 1944.

Benson Y. Landis, *Rural Welfare Services,* New York: Columbia University Press, 1949.

Judson T. Landis, "Social Action in American Protestant Churches," *American Journal of Sociology*, 52 (1946–47): 517–522.

Ruth Lerrigo and Bradley Buell, "Social Work and the Joneses," 2d ed., Public Affairs Pamphlet No. 97, 1945.

Emma O. Lundberg, *Unto the Least of These: Social Services for Children*, New York: Appleton-Century-Crofts, 1947.

John Eric Nordskog, *Contemporary Social Reform Movements*, New York: Charles Scribner's Sons, 1954.

Cleveland Rodgers, *American Planning: Past, Present, Future*, New York: Harper & Bros., 1947.

Guido de Ruggiero, "Liberalism," *Encyclopaedia of the Social Sciences*, 9 (1933): 435–442.

S. R. Slavson, *An Introduction to Group Therapy*, New York: Commonwealth Fund, 1943.

Lee R. Steiner, *Where Do People Take Their Troubles?* Boston: Houghton Mifflin Co., 1945.

Elwood Street, *A Handbook for Social Agency Administration*, New York: Harper & Bros., 1948.

Herbert Hewitt Stroup, *Community Welfare Organization*, New York: Harper & Bros., 1952.

Goodwin Watson, *Action for Unity*, New York: Harper & Bros., 1947.

R. C. White, *Administration for Public Welfare*, New York: American Book Co., 1940.

Gertrude Wilson and Gladys Ryland, *Social Group Work Practice: The Creative Use of the Social Process*, Boston: Houghton Mifflin Co., 1949.

REVIEW QUESTIONS

1. What are three major approaches to the mitigation or solution of social problems?
2. How do Marx and Engels dismiss ameliorative efforts?
3. In what ways does Keller maintain that humanitarianism may be counterselective?
4. In what ways does Keller believe we should discriminate in aiding the unfortunate?
5. What does Sumner believe that a reformer can accomplish?
6. What qualifications does Pray think qualify the social worker for participation in social action?
7. In what kinds of social action should the social worker participate?
8. How important does Watson believe the duplication of effort to be in social action to improve intercultural relations?
9. What are the roles of the fence sitters in social action?
10. What kind of organizations does Watson believe achieve results in social action? Why?
11. What social science findings have influenced intergroup workers, according to Cohen?
12. What social science research would be helpful to such workers?
13. What is a radical?
14. What brings about the appearance of radicals?
15. In what sense does Madison regard Adams and Jefferson as radicals?
16. What were the major outlines of the struggle for economic justice after the Civil War?
17. What stimulated radicalism in the United States after 1900?
18. What contributions does Madison believe critics and crusaders have made to American political and economic well-being?
19. What does Madison regard to be the future of radicalism in this country?
20. Who faces a dilemma in a revolution, according to Bernard?
21. How does Bernard believe that the danger of revolutions could be eliminated?

Social Science and Social Policy

THE social scientist perennially faces the conflict between "theory" and "practice," between the conclusions of the scientists based upon evidence and the decisions of the man of action based upon evidence *and* special interest. As the sciences have matured and have made contributions to phase after phase of our social life, the impatience of the actionist with the theorist has perforce been tempered. The invasion of the scientist has proceeded, and the actionist has developed a lurking respect and a suspicion that the freethinking investigator might not be so much of a fool as other nonscientific deviant thinkers.

When a person is bound by the traditional technological, economic, or other mores of a group, he cannot function as a scientist within the specialty of that group and make contributions to that specialty. The scientist—as a scientist —is concerned with criticizing, with the merits of modifying, even with the possibility of sweeping aside existing mores of a given group of specialists, technologists, or other workers. The battle of the scientist for freedom to work and to report has achieved great gains in many of the physical and even biological sciences, but the battle is still joined in the social sciences. Vested interests use their power and the services of their rationalists to discourage all but the hardy and the "unreasonable" from functioning as social scientists.

The selections in this chapter deal with aspects of the theorist-actionist relationship, otherwise stated as the relationship between social science and social policy. They also indicate kinds of areas in which social scientists are now and may be helpful in the solution of social problems.

In the first selection, Sumner warns against having a placid faith in "clear strides towards the millenium" and especially in laws as panaceas. "Man wins by the fight," he says, "not by the victory, and therefore the possibilities of growth are unlimited, for the fight has no end." He also makes a distinction between purposes and con-sequences in social science and especially in studying social problems. The sociologist, when functioning as a sociologist, Sumner observes, must regard both pessimism and optimism as "alike impertinent." Facts and probable consequences are the things to be watched.

As actionists in business, trade unions, politics, and civic affairs have discovered sociology to be an increasingly useful tool, more funds have come to social investigators, but the gadgets of the physical scientists continue to attract the lion's share of the support. Fosdick discusses this problem and pleads for a "foundation of hard, painstaking work" upon which social issues may be more "clearly defined and understood." This will require far greater investments in social science by a great range of types of organizations and individuals. For the future welfare of society, investments in telescopes are not going to be enough.

The 1950's gave new emphases to interdisciplinary cross-fertilization. Menninger expresses the belief that through cross-fertilization social scientists can narrow the discrepancy between the extent and the usability of their knowledge. In this, psychiatrists can contribute, he states, if they "do nothing more than throw light on the power of man's unconscious—its primitive and illogical and irrational nature."

The problems of how and for whom the social scientist should work in studying social problems have been variously handled but seldom solved to the satisfaction of many scientists. Concerned with such problems, Bierstedt differentiates between the sociologist as social scientist and as citizen and points out the compatibility of these two roles, as he sees them. The Society for the Study of Social Problems Committee goes further and suggests specific areas in which research contributions might be made to the national welfare, without loss to the scientific integrity of the individual researchers involved.

In closing, Clinard and Clark sketch important

new areas of applied sociology. Clinard tells how group techniques are now applied to prevent and to treat social and personal disorganization. He urges the further development and use of sociologically based group therapy. In connection with the acceptance of social science findings in policy-making litigations—a recent development of historic significance—Clark indicates that in this new role social scientists are placed under burdens of maximum accuracy and objectivity and that they must have courage.

The Solution of One Problem Leads to Another
William Graham Sumner*

It is a matter of course that a reactionary party should arise to declare that universal suffrage, popular education, machinery, free trade, and all the other innovations of the last hundred years are all a mistake. If any one ever believed that these innovations were so many clear strides towards the millennium, that they involve no evils or abuses of their own, that they tend to emancipate mankind from the need for prudence, caution, forethought, vigilance—in short, from the eternal struggle against evil—it is not strange that he should be disappointed. If any one ever believed that some "form of government" could be found which would run itself and turn out the pure results of abstract peace, justice, and righteousness without any trouble to anybody, he may well be dissatisfied. To talk of turning back, however, is only to enhance still further the confusion and danger of our position. The world cannot go back. Its destiny is to go forward and to meet the new problems which are continually arising. Under our so-called progress evil only alters its forms, and we must esteem it a grand advance if we can believe that, on the whole, and over a wide view of human affairs, good has gained a hair's breadth over evil in a century. Popular institutions have their own abuses and dangers just as much as monarchical or aristocratic institutions. We are only just finding out what they are. . . . The conquest of one difficulty will only open the way to another; the solution of one problem will only bring man face to face with another. Man wins by the fight, not by the victory, and therefore the possibilities of growth are unlimited, for the fight has no end.

* * * *

The observation ** that motives and purposes have nothing to do with consequences is a criterion for distinguishing between the science of society and the views, whims, ideals, and fads which are current in regard to social matters. . . . Motives and purposes are in the brain and heart of man. Consequences are in the world of fact. The former are infected by human ignorance, folly, self-deception, and passion; the latter are sequences of cause and the effect dependent upon the nature of the forces at work. When, therefore, a man acts, he sets forces in motion, and the consequences are such as those forces produce under the conditions existing. They are entirely independent of any notion, will, wish, or intention in the mind of any man or men. Consequences are facts in the world of experience. . . .

Serious study of human society shows us that we can never do anything but use and develop the opportunities which are offered to us by the conditions and conjunctures of the moment.

Other motives of action are derived from the authoritative or dogmatic precepts of some sect of

** From William Graham Sumner, "Purposes and Consequences" (written between 1900 and 1906), pp. 67–75 in his *Earth-Hunger and Other Essays*, ed. by A. G. Keller, New Haven: Yale University Press, 1913, pp. 67, 74–75 quoted. Reprinted by permission from A. G. Keller and M. R. Davie, eds., *Essays of William Graham Sumner*, New Haven: Yale University Press, 1934, vol. 1, pp. 11, 18–19.

* See identifying note on page 46.

From "The Challenge of Facts" (written during 1880's), pp. 17–52 in his *The Challenge of Facts and Other Essays*, ed. by A. G. Keller, New Haven: Yale University Press, 1914, pp. 49–50 quoted. Reprinted by permission from A. G. Keller and M. R. Davie, eds., *Essays of William Graham Sumner*, New Haven: Yale University Press, 1934, vol. 2, pp. 119–120.

philosophy or religion. These are what is commonly called ethics. In the ordinary course of life it is best and is necessary that for most of us, and for all of us most of the time, these current rules of action which are traditional and accepted in our society should be adopted and obeyed. This is true, however, only because it is impossible for nearly all of us to investigate for ourselves and win personal convictions, and it is impossible for any of us to do so except in a few special matters. Nevertheless, all this sets out only in so much clearer light the pre-eminent value of science, because science extends, over the whole domain of human experience, a gradually wider and wider perception of those relations of man to earth and man to man on which human welfare depends. Science is investigation of facts by sound methods, and deduction of inferences by sound processes. The further it goes the more it enlightens us as to consequences which must ensue if acts are executed by which things and men are brought into the relations which science has elucidated. At the present moment civilized society stands at a point in the development of the applications of science to human interests, at which the thing of the highest importance is the subjection of societal phenomena to scientific investigation, together with the elimination of metaphysics from this entire domain.

* * * *

From * the stand-point of the sociologist pessimism and optimism are alike impertinent. To be an optimist one must forget the frightful sanctions which are attached to the laws of right living. To be a pessimist one must overlook the education and growth which are the product of effort and self-denial. In either case one is passing judgment on what is inevitably fixed, and on which the approval or condemnation of man can produce no effect. The facts and laws are, once and for all, so, and for us men that is the end of the matter. The only persons for whom there would be any sense in the question whether life is worth living are primarily the yet unborn children, and secondarily the persons who are proposing to found families. . . . The sociologist is often asked if he wants to kill off certain classes of troublesome and burdensome persons. No such inference follows from any sound sociological doctrine, but it is allowed to infer, as to a great many persons and classes, that it would have been better for society, and would have involved no pain to them, if they had never been born.

---

* From "Sociology," *Princeton Review*, 57 (1881): 303–323, pp. 318–319 quoted.

Telescopes Are Not Enough
Raymond B. Fosdick

Raymond Blaine Fosdick (1883–   ), lawyer; former president, Rockefeller Foundation and General Education Board. Author: *European Police Systems* (1915); with E. F. Allen, *Keeping Our Fighters Fit* (1918); *American Police Systems* (1920); *The Old Salvage in the New Civilization* (1928); with A. L. Scott, *Toward Liquor Control* (1933); *The Story of the Rockefeller Foundation* (1952); and *Within Our Power* (1952).

While we cannot put brakes on intellectual adventure, it must be admitted that there is a lack of balance about our studies and our research that emperils the future. The disproportion between the physical power at our disposal and our capacity to make good use of it is growing with every day that passes. We are in the midst of a revolution in our physical environment so vast and so rapid that our minds can scarcely keep up with it. But there are other things that cannot keep up with it, either—notably our social ideas, our habits of life and our political and economic institutions. Our political institutions, for example, are mainly rooted in the eighteenth century, but our swiftly evolving technology is largely a twentieth century phenomenon. We have one foot in a civilization that is dying and another foot in a civilization that is struggling to be born. Consequently we live a kind of bifurcated existence, and the gap between what we

---

From *The Rockefeller Foundation: A Review for 1946*, New York, 1947, pp. 29–32. Reprinted by permission.

know and what we need to know becomes wider and deeper.

As a result there is developing a dangerously tilted situation in our society, an intellectual imbalance, which can no longer be ignored. Our knowledge of human behavior and social relations is not adequate to give us the guidance we need; and the fundamental issue of our time is whether we can develop understanding and wisdom reliable enough to serve as a chart in working out the problems of human relations; or whether we shall allow our present lopsided progress to develop to a point that capsizes our civilization in a catastrophe of immeasurable proportions.

What is needed is a broader basis of research, a more vigorous backing of objective and competent efforts to define and analyze the intricacies of human relationship. We need to know what our social organization is, how it operates, how it will react to alterations and changes. We have created a society so interdependent that issues are no longer simple, individual and local; they are complex, social and world-wide. And they are beyond the experience of most of us. . . .

A prominent figure in Washington recently remarked that we must have "a sufficient mastery of nature so that permanent world peace will be a reality and not a mere hopeful expression of faith." With all due respect, it is this mastery of nature which threatens to blow our civilization into drifting dust. What we really need is a mastery of man's social nature—knowledge and more knowledge of the on-rushing social consequences of our machines, consequences which, because they are too intricate to be easily understood, are shaping our lives to ends we do not want but cannot escape.

The encouraging factor in this whole situation is the universal ground swell of interest in the direction of greater emphasis on the social sciences—an interest that is developing in colleges and universities everywhere, as well as in public bodies and foundations. This interest is heightened by the proof, which recent years have afforded, that the objective investigation of problems of human relations can produce results of incalculable practical value, when properly trained research workers, imbued with scientific detachment and integrity, are given an opportunity to carry on their activities with adequate resources.

This is the encouraging part of the picture. The discouraging part is that the public generally —and this is true of our legislatures and some of our universities as well—does not appreciate the fact that the problems included in this kind of research are for a variety of reasons far more involved and complex than the problems which the natural scientists are facing. These new problems in social relations cannot be solved by literary pontification, by speeches, by partisan appeals, by emotional surges or amateur efforts. There seems to be a widespread belief that we are all social scientists, all of us are economists; and in this egalitarian democracy of ours any man's ideas on any problem in sociology are as good as any other man's. We need to realize that what is true of physics and biology is true in this area also. The same degree of special knowledge is required. Social issues cannot be clearly defined and understood except on the foundation of hard, painstaking work. We must have disciplined minds and the high integrity of objective scholarship; and the flow of first-class talent into these fields must be continuous and uninterrupted.

Psychiatry and Social Problems
William C. Menninger

William C. Menninger (1899–   ), psychiatrist, general secretary, The Menninger Foundation, Topeka, Kansas.

In every field of science, each of us tends to pursue his own goal with no or only minimal consideration or knowledge of the side effects of his efforts on other areas. This may be a partial explanation of the slow progress that has been made in finding solutions of social problems.

From "Social Change and Scientific Progress," Fifth Little Memorial Lecture, Massachusetts Institute of Technology, May 1, 1951, pp. 7–10, 34–35, 37.

Cross-fertilization between disciplines has begun to take place, and, if one stretches a point, he might regard my remarks tonight as a step in that direction. Collective pooling of knowledge has become essential since, even though we may make progress in one particular area, we may unknowingly create interference with scientific advance in another area of human activity and behavior.

Elementary Questions

In considering how science and the industrial revolution have affected the mental health of society, one is faced with the need to look for answers to some all-important basic questions.

Are people today any more or any less happy than they were in more rigorous and primitive cultures or in other civilizations?

Has our progress in the field of pragmatic materialism blighted or minimized our aesthetic and spiritual values?

Have scientific, technical, and industrial developments which have so greatly increased our material comforts robbed many people of deep-seated satisfactions without offering suitable substitutions?

Have those great technological advances that make it possible for us to defend ourselves against an enemy stimulated man's instinctive, hostile aggressiveness beyond his capacity to handle it?

Is the resistance to change in human nature so great that anxiety has been aroused by the speed of our technological advance?

Many other similar questions could be asked. In the absence of "scientifically validated" evidence, any answers could be fairly classified as merely an impression or an opinion. Such questions as these are raised because they are in the minds of all of us but as yet no group of scientists has come up with an adequate answer.

It is presumed that the answers will most likely come from the group of social sciences—cultural anthropology, sociology, economics, social psychology, and political science. They may be expected to rely heavily on contributions from philosophy, ethics, religion, and statistics. As yet, however, because of the youth of these sciences, they have had little time to develop and apply scientific methods of study comparable to the progress made in the natural sciences. Furthermore, we have no right to expect the social sciences to have made much greater gain than they have with the meager financial support that they have received. Their past achievements and future possibilities are well presented by Stuart Chase.[1] But as yet no millions of dollars of either private or governmental money have been made available for their research. Apparently we have not yet accepted the responsibility to advance our knowledge and skill in these fields that we have accepted in the physical and natural sciences. In fact, only two years ago a presumably intelligent Congressman, discussing the formation of the National Science Foundation, seriously questioned whether the social sciences could be called sciences. The bill was passed without mention of them.

A further reason for our inability to answer these basic questions at the present time is that they are so emotionally surcharged. Expressions of opinion about them, even by scientifically trained persons, may tend to place one group of scientists on the offensive, and, automatically, another group of scientists on the defensive. . . .

Among students of physics and chemistry, the early feuds have died out and no such emotional division exists. Probably both our lack of knowledge in the fields of social science, and this emotional resistance to the understanding of human behavior contribute to the so-called "cultural lag." I am aware that there is some argument as to whether this alleged lag exists, but no one can dispute the fact that the increase in the efficiency and use of our destructive power has very far eclipsed the growth of our ability to exert social control over it.[2] Furthermore, there is an admitted discrepancy between the extent of knowledge and the usable contributions that have been produced by the social sciences as compared to those of the physical and natural sciences.

We have reached a point in our scientific progress where we can almost annihilate time and space, and in a split second demolish a metropolitan city. Not enough of us have focused on the reason for our inability to understand and get along with each other. Great hope lies in the upward surge of those sciences that can help us understand and effect social change. I want to express the opinion that psychiatry might make a contribution, both as a medical and a social science, to these problems. While it focuses primarily on the health of the individual, it must of

[1] *The Proper Study of Mankind*, New York: Harper & Bros., 1948.
[2] Hornell Hart, "Social Science and the Atomic Crisis," *Journal of Social Issues*, Supplement No. 2 (April 1949).

necessity be concerned with the environment and the society in which that individual tries to make a life. . . .

My own conviction is that value systems are necessary even in pure science, although I understand this is disputed by some scientists. In psychiatry (and all medicine) they are basic; they serve not only as the goal for the physician but the types of values accepted by the patient determine the status of his mental health. They serve as criteria for judging a man as a social being. Thus one individual may be a conceited, selfish, bigoted exhibitionist; another a gracious, generous, considerate person.

But note that these typically descriptive terms refer to their relationships to people. Mental health is dependent not on our ability to relate ourselves to things but upon the degree to which we relate ourselves in a mutually satisfying fashion to those about us.

A value system in terms of goals, ethical standards, ideals, and convictions is the guiding light by which all men live. If these are really important to us they provide needed psychological support in times of pressure. If we believe strongly enough, we will die for that belief.

Some of our technological achievements have added to our comfort and our pleasure in life; others have seemed to deprive us, at least momentarily, of some previously established satisfactions; still others threaten us. But our deepest satisfactions do not come from these technological advances; they come because of our capacity to love, and to be loved—by our parents, our family, our friends, and the world. Our ability to participate in these relationships determines our mental health. . . .

My own belief is that psychiatry can and will make an important contribution towards the solution of some of our social problems, even if we psychiatrists do nothing more than throw light on the power of man's unconscious—its primitive and illogical and irrational nature. We can and must keep a sharp focus on the unlimited power of man's instinctive aggressive drive, and on the absolute necessity to neutralize it by fostering the potentially equally strong instinctive drive of Eros in its manifestations of creativeness, constructiveness, and love.

Social Scientist and Citizen
Robert Bierstedt

Robert Bierstedt (1913–   ), professor and chairman, department of sociology and anthropology, City College of New York.

Physicists, financiers, and philosophers, publicists, politicians, and poets have all had something to say about the atomic bomb, about the international control of atomic energy, and about the possibilities and potentialities of a durable world peace. The physicists in particular have conferred in private and argued in public, have issued sober reports and impassioned pleas, and have properly harangued the populace at large. Some of them have formed federations to advise on these problems, some have assumed the unfamiliar rôle of lobbyists, and still others serve on official committees and commissions of the Government. Where, in all of these councils, are the persons who presumably know most about the processes of society? Where are the scientists who study social organization and social change? Where, in short, are the social scientists? And what is their relation to social policy?

It cannot be denied that in all of these colloquies sociologists have been conspicuously silent. Neither as individuals, with some exceptions, nor as members of professional groups, have they had anything to say about the most distressing issues of our time.* The American Sociological Society

* As of 1948. Note that the following selection, dated 1952, came from the Society for the Study of Social Problems, an organization of sociologists founded in 1951 and affiliated in 1954 with the American Sociological Society. —Eds.

From "Social Science and Social Policy," *Bulletin of the American Association of University Professors, 34* (Summer 1948): 310–319, pp. 310, 311–312, 317–319 quoted.

has drafted no resolutions on questions of public policy. Nothing has been said by that organization about the impact of atomic technologies upon society, nothing about the social implications of atomic energy, and nothing about growing tensions in any part of the world. If the physicists are terrified, the military apprehensive, and the politicians nonplused, why are the sociologists indifferent? Why do they hesitate to contribute their recommendations to a world which stands in sore need of all the knowledge it can have in the field of human relations? . . . .

In order to suggest an answer to these questions it is necessary to recognize at the outset that some of them proceed from an inadequate knowledge of the nature of the sociological enterprise. The relationship between sociology and social policy is a complicated one and requires for its analysis some understanding of the rules and methods of science. For sociology is, or at least tries to be, a science. And science as such can have nothing immediately to do with policy. Sociologists as scientists, therefore, are not the saviors of society. In spite of a history which was linked in part with problems of social welfare—poverty, unemployment, crime, delinquency, and other kinds of social pathology—sociology is neither a substitute nor a synonym for social reform. Nor, in addition, are sociologists publicists, and they have far fewer recommendations about the direction which our American society ought to take and about the way human relations, including international relations, ought to be directed than have the columnists who speak with such authority and omniscience in the daily newspapers. If sociologists hesitate to give advice on problems of domestic and foreign policy, if they are chary of anything that even vaguely resembles a recommendation on matters of social and political action, it is for reasons which have seemed clear and cogent to them. These reasons it is profitable to explore, in an endeavor first to re-examine their cogency and second to inquire into possible limitations upon their relevance.

All of these reasons concern the fact, suggested above, that sociology, as distinguished from all other approaches to the human scene from the literary to the philosophic, is a science. It is a science or it is nothing. And in order to be a science it must diligently avoid all pronouncements of an ethical character. As a science it cannot answer questions of value. It can have no traffic with normative statements because there is

no logic of the normative. It can deal, as can the other sciences, only with questions of fact, with propositions, with statements capable of being true or false. It cannot deal with questions of good or bad, better or worse, right or wrong, or any question at all containing the word "ought." The sociologist, in company with his brother scientists, has taken seriously the famous remark of Jeremy Bentham, that the word "ought" ought never to be used, except in saying it ought never to be used. . . .

But these are urgent and vexatious times. Admitting the cogency of these considerations, it remains true that we should all like to be fugitives from urgency and that for all of us it is later than we think. If the obligations of science are international, so also are the obligations of citizenship. And citizenship has claims upon all of the sciences. The atomic bomb has no respect for ivory towers. Is there not some way in which the rigorous requirements of the scientific method can be squared with the responsibilities of citizenship? Can the sociologist continue to dwell in a scientific stratosphere of his own in which no problems of public policy ever intrude?

An answer to these questions appears with the recognition that the virtues of ethical neutrality, of normative silence, and of objectivity, while wholly relevant to scientific inquiry itself, have nevertheless a reduced relevance to the total activity of the scientist. For there are four ways at least in which questions of value enter inevitably into the scientific situation. The first of these appears in the rôle of hypotheses. If the scientist cannot properly handle normative propositions, he can and does handle hypothetical ones. That is, *if* certain ends are desired, the scientist may, without compromising his scientific integrity, decide which of several alternative means can best be utilized for realizing these ends. Once the values of a society are determined and once the goals are set, the sociologist should be able, when he does not know the answers, to initiate researches which will supply them. He need have nothing to do with setting the goals themselves; he need, as a scientist, neither praise them as good nor condemn them as bad. It is required of him only to phrase his problem in such a way that he may determine, with the theoretical knowledge and experimental techniques at his command, what it is necessary to do in order to achieve the goal.

Thus, *if* a stable financial system is the desired social goal . . . the economist should be able to answer whether raising the gold content of the dollar at a particular time is a more effective means of achieving it than not raising it. And *if* a world at peace is one of the common sentiments and devout desires of all mankind, the sociologist should be able so to direct his researches and reflections as to illumine the ways in which it can be won. Hypotheses and hypothetical propositions are no strangers to science; they are an essential part of the scientific method. They can be utilized as a bridge between science and social policy, between sociology and social action.

The second and third ways in which questions of value legitimately attach themselves to the scientific enterprise concern the kinds of problems to which to apply the scientific method and the order in which to try to solve them. Prior to the solution of any specific social problems it is a matter of nonscientific determination that some are susceptible to scientific exploration and that others are not. Similarly, of those that are susceptible to scientific exploration, it is a matter of nonscientific decision that some ought to be investigated first and others at a later and more propitious time. As a matter of fact, the choice of problems for scientific scrutiny is grounded in social and cultural conditions, and it is incumbent upon the sociologist, in some sense at least, to attend to the problems which his society sets for him. He has, in a deeper sense, no alternative. If he has no alternative it is in no way gratuitous to encourage him to concentrate his attention and his energy upon the earlier solution of the more pressing of these problems.

Finally, it is time for the scientist to acknowl-

edge that the ultimate test of his activity lies in the social use and consequence of his conclusions. Whatever freedom the sociologist may achieve from the exigencies of time and circumstance, it is still important, and now more than ever before, to narrow the gap between the discovery of new principles and their application to the sphere of human relations. Society should not be the victim of a cultural lag between sociological knowledge and social use. No scientific scruples, therefore, as important as those scruples are, should delay a constantly increasing sensitivity to the social rôle of social science.

The conclusion seems inescapable that the sociologist can be a scientist and still accept some civic responsibility for the society in which he lives. If the world is full of tensions, he can indicate some of the ways in which they can be reduced. If the prospect of a new world war looms over the horizon, he ought to help to lay the specter. If the dissipation of national sovereignties and the establishment of a world government are the only ultimate insurance against renewed conflicts between the nations, then he has the duty to show how such insurance can be purchased in the shortest possible time and at the lowest possible premium. The sociologist, in short, can help to build that one world whose only political boundaries are the outer atmosphere. In these days of the planet's malaise he can have no higher office and no more important function than this, to dedicate his science and his citizenship alike to a world community in which he, along with his fellow members of the human race, can live in peace.

Sociological Research Projects in a Preparedness Culture
Society for the Study of Social Problems

The American sociologist is heir to traditions of objectivity, of courageous observation and theorizing, and of service to humanity without reference to national boundaries. He is also subject to

responsibilities in the transient affairs of the nation that may be at variance to his services and his findings as a social scientist. How should the sociologist deal with these conflicting demands

From "Sociological Research Projects in a Preparedness Culture," report of the Committee on Standards and Freedom of Research, Teaching, and Publication of the Society for the Study of Social Problems at its second annual meeting, September 3, 1952, Ritz-Carlton Hotel, Atlantic City, mimeographed.

upon him? What projects and areas of investigation should absorb his research interests at this time?

In days of domestic and international tension, should the sociologist throw aside the role of scientist for that of the technician? In a period in which national leaders believe our country to be facing a life and death struggle with a drastically different system of authority, should the sociologist decide that these are times in which our society cannot afford the luxury of truly scientific investigations and contributions?

The way in which a sociologist or a society of social scientists chooses to resolve this issue depends upon the value attached to science. The most dependable source of useful new ideas mankind has developed is science. Sociology and social psychology, if untrammeled, promise great new gains for human knowledge in the near future. Such gains a society in transition can ill afford not to have available to it.

Sociologists see their academic fellows in the physical and biological sciences don uniforms, actually or figuratively, and continue their research under federal auspices. Many sociologists have looked longingly at the facilities thus made available. A substantial number of sociologists have donned uniforms during the 1940's and 1950's and continued to carry on what they have told themselves is scientific work.

But there is a striking difference between the sociologist in uniform and the physical or biological scientist in uniform. The sociologist in uniform, by the very nature of his work, must immediately renounce one of the basic necessities of truly scientific sociological research. He may no longer question many basic assumptions with which his research project starts. He cannot ask whether or not it is possible to convert the young male products of a peace culture into warriors with any assurance that the warriors can later become useful members of a peace economy. He cannot question whether or not a basic propaganda line is sound.

When the sociologist enters the employment of government or industry, therefore, he may cease to be a scientist and become a hired technician. The frank recognition of this transition would clear up a lot of cynical pretentions that have done much to discredit sociology.

Under auspices as independent as possible, there are a number of areas in which important research contributions might be made to the national welfare and to humanity, in our preparedness culture today. Some of these areas are as follows:

1. Attitudes of selected groups in the American population—especially young people—towards preparedness and the international emergency. Especially important here are age-groups—particularly the young men and women of draft age—ethnic groups, socio-economic classes, regional groups, political groups.

2. Minority groups in a preparedness culture. What assurances do Negroes, Jews, Mexicans in the Southwest, Puerto Ricans, and others have that the defense of democracy will serve to enhance their democratic rights in American culture?

3. Totalitarian tendencies in democratic preparedness.

4. Popular stereotypes of the Communist. How do these popular stereotypes compare with actual cases of known Communist party members?

5. Pacifist tendencies in American groups today. How deep-set and significant are they? With what other tendencies are these tendencies linked?

6. Youth expression and preparedness. To what extent are youth organizations available to our young people in which they actually find challenging opportunities for self-expression?

7. Reactions of children to air-raid drills and precautions.

8. Changes in mating patterns under preparedness conditions.

9. Status and role in the officers' corps of a standing army. How do status and role in the American officers' corps compare with those in other armies? Comparisons with anthropological findings would be helpful.

10. The doctrine of personal dependability under preparedness, the role of the social scientist, and the concept of national security.

11. The life-history technique applied to conscientious objectors.

12. Preparedness as a social movement, including analysis of changing power-relations under preparedness.

These topics are merely suggestions. Some are specific, and some rather general. We hope that they will help to stimulate discussion and to point to the great opportunities that sociologists as scientists have for constructive contributions to national and human welfare.

What has been said is not meant to suggest that technicians cannot also make contributions, but their contributions must necessarily be of a different and less fundamental order. They can only solve problems within a tightly preconceived value framework. The sociologist as a social scientist can attack a problem in as fundamental a manner as his abilities, courage, and facilities will permit.

The Group Approach to Social Reintegration
Marshall B. Clinard

Marshall B. Clinard (1911–   ), professor of sociology, University of Wisconsin. Principal work: *Black Market: A Study of White Collar Crime* (1952).

One suggestion for a unique point of view for the sociologist interested in social disorganization is that he should study and analyze value conflicts in a society.[1] The possibilities for such an integrated sociological approach appear encouraging. Queen has suggested that the definition of the field as well as research should be carried on within the framework of social participation.[2] Fundamentally, the role of the sociologist working in social and personal disorganization should be not only analysis of formal and informal group structures but of the relation of the person to social groups.

Despite their previous training and the need for a unique point of view, sociologists working in the field of social disorganization have largely neglected to place research emphasis on social groups.[3] Some research actually represents historical investigations, legal surveys or journalistic accounts of human experience without utilization of a unique point of view. Much of the research work is still concentrated on the individual, on multiple factor studies such as the tabulation of statistically convenient items in connection with prisoners, probation or parole prediction studies, ecological studies, and the like, studies which may represent excellent demonstration of techniques but whose factors are seldom meaningful in terms of human behavior, group behavior, or to a theory of social disorganization. Rather than getting at the subjective meaning of the world to the deviant and at the nature of group attitudes and integration, the typical so-called prediction study, for example, consists chiefly of an analysis of a long list of easily devised taxonomic factors.[4]

There is, moreover, an increasing tendency to accept claims, without adequate supporting evidence, that forms of deviant behavior such as functional mental disease and chronic alcoholism, are primarily an outgrowth of personality traits developed largely in a single group experience, namely early family association, and that interaction in this one group virtually supersedes all subsequent interaction in the person's life. This is not to say that there is not already considerable

[1] While this concept is implicit in Thomas and Znaniecki's *The Polish Peasant in Europe and America,* see particularly the writings of Frank, Waller, Fuller, and lately John F. Cuber and Robert A. Harper, *Problems of American Society: Values in Conflict,* New York: Henry Holt and Co., 1948.

[2] Stuart A. Queen, "The Concepts of Social Disorganization and Social Participation," *American Sociological Review,* VI (June, 1941), 307–316. Also see Stuart A. Queen and Jennette R. Gruener, *Social Pathology,* New York: Thomas Y. Crowell Co., 1940. Queen, by extending this concept beyond personal group participation, uses this concept much more broadly than implied in this paper.

[3] The current emphasis on industrial sociology represents in part the discovery by many sociologists that interaction in social groups is important for the understanding of human behavior.

[4] Although most prediction studies seldom take into account such factors, in a study of recently released inmates of a reformatory, men who had never been in such an institution before, we have found considerable evidence, as one might expect, of variations in group integration. Many of the old ties had been broken or forbidden, and there was fear of the neighbors' knowing of their incarceration, stories having been invented about their absences. In some cases families had moved or they had no home; in other cases the family even ostracized them, and generally they had lost many of their previous friends and had difficulty in securing new ones. Many were alone in the world, faced by stigma and filled with bitterness. "Family and Community: The Ex-Inmate's View," unpublished manuscript.

From "The Group Approach to Social Reintegration," *American Sociological Review,* 15 (April 1949): 257–261.

evidence to indicate the importance of childhood family experience, and the role of psychogenic traits in human behavior, but that the development of an adequate theory of social and personal disorganization as well as the solution of pressing treatment problems needs further research into the nature of social interaction within all groups, both in childhood and adult life.

There have been numerous developments, primarily during the past ten years, involving the application of group methods in the prevention and treatment of social and personal disorganization. Such efforts are not only suggestive as applied situations in developing sociological theory, but also represent the possibility of a vocational opportunity for sociologists. In most instances sociologists have not been involved in these group experiments, either in therapy or research; in others their relationship has been numerically insignificant. This work has included efforts of experts working with groups of persons to overcome difficulties which have been known in various forms as group therapy, clinical group work, therapeutic group work, group psychotherapy, sociometrics, and psychodrama. Other work has consisted of neighborhood councils, or of activities like Alcoholics Anonymous, Recovery for mental patients, and lately Addicts Anonymous in which expert guidance has been kept at a minimum. Still other work, such as that of Lewin and his Research Center for Group Dynamics, has been a combination of theory and application in the study of group dynamics in problem areas,[5] and certain group experiences of members of the armed services have contributed valuable information to the understanding of the role of group integration in the behavior of the individual. These efforts to apply the orientation of the group have ranged over areas such as neuroses and psychoses, delinquency and criminality, alcoholism, adolescent problems, family problems, old age adjustments, as well as racial and religious prejudice.

In the field of mental disease it is conceivable that the explanation may be found not only in certain trait structures but in the nature of social integration and interaction within social groups. The research of Faris has indicated that certain neuroses and schizophrenia may represent social isolation from group association.[6] Isolation of old persons from group participation may be significant in producing the senile psychoses. It has even been suggested that manic-depressive psychoses are produced by extremely intimate and intense social contacts.[7] Some validation of these views was revealed by the relation of group integration to neuroses in the armed services during the recent war. There it was learned that integrating or non-integrating forces immediate in the social environment around the individual were far more important than either the personality make-up of the individual, his personal maladjustment, or an examination of his family structure. The presence or absence of group supportive elements, particularly identification with a group under conditions of stress, was found to be one of the most important keys to the development of mental disorder even in those with little supposed tendency in that direction.[8] One commission of civilian psychiatrists who studied combat neuroses found that "When an individual member of such a combat group has his emotional bonds of group integration seriously disrupted, then he, *as a person,* is truly disorganized. The disruption of the group unit is, in the main, a primary causal factor, not a secondary effect of personal disorganization." [9] As the psychiatrist, William Menninger, puts it, "We seemed to learn anew the importance of the group ties in the maintenance of mental health. We were impressed by the fact that an individual who had a strong conviction about his job, even though his was a definite, unstable personality, might make remarkable achievement against the greatest of stress." [10] Such information, while limited, suggests that it might be well to analyze similar situations in civilian life which cause mental breakdowns.

---

[5] Kurt Lewin, *Resolving Social Conflicts,* New York: Harper & Brothers, 1948.

[6] Robert E. L. Faris, "Cultural Isolation and the Schizophrenic Personality," *American Journal of Sociology,* 40, September, 1934. Also his *Social Disorganization,* New York: The Ronald Press Co., 1948, Chapter 8.

[7] Robert E. L. Faris and H. Warren Dunham, *Mental Disorders in Urban Areas,* Chicago: University of Chicago Press, 1939, p. 173.

[8] William C. Menninger, "Psychiatric Experience in the War, 1941–1946," *American Journal of Psychiatry,* 103: 577–586, March, 1947. See also his *Psychiatry in a Troubled World,* New York: The Macmillan Co., 1948, Chapters V and VI, and S. Kirson Weinberg, "The Combat Neuroses," *American Journal of Sociology,* 51: 465–78, March, 1946.

[9] L. H. Bartemeir, L. S. Kubie, K. S. Menninger, J. Romano, and J. C. Whitehorn, "Combat Exhaustion," *Journal of Nervous and Mental Diseases,* 104: 370, October, 1946.

[10] William C. Menninger, "Psychiatric Experience in the War, 1941–1946," *op. cit.,* p. 581.

Group psychotherapy, the current emphasis having chiefly grown out of the physical impossibility of treating cases individually during the war, is suggestive for sociological research on mental disease. The usual method is for a psychiatrist and from six to twenty patients to conduct frequent discussions as a group in which there is group sharing of experience. Sometimes additional tools such as the psychodrama are employed where conflict situations are acted out in a group. These efforts have a history of development in many directions, including the work of Pratti with tubercular patients, of Marsh, Wender and Lazell in mental hospitals, of Moreno and his associates in the psychodrama, and of Schilder, Redl, Slavson and Klapman on theory.[11]

Without subscribing to the often weird symbolism and extreme theoretical views held by some, or the overly psychiatric emphasis in general in these experiments, the approach appears to be not only sociologically sound but to furnish significant research possibilities. While no carefully controlled experiment has as yet been made of the results of group therapy, there is an almost unanimous opinion, among those who have been engaged in this work, that group therapy is effective.[12] Although little fundamental research has been done on what takes place in such group sessions, it seems possible that the encouraging results obtained are due not to the theoretical scheme of the group analysis but to informal group adjustment. Certainly the work of Alcoholics Anonymous, without the presence of a psychiatrist, would indicate this. In group psychotherapy the members appear to develop an identification with one another and a degree of group integration, sometimes the opinion of the group appears to change the personality pattern and attitudes of one of its members, and each member secures an opportunity for new roles and a new conception of himself. In the light of the problems of others it is possible for the patient to see his own difficulties and relieve his feelings of social isolation.[13] The principal contribution to mental patients appears to be in the modification or elimination of egocentricity and social isolation.[14] The sociologist willing to do research in this field and approach it with his background of training and insights, may conceivably expect to contribute not only to a theory of disorganization but to therapy as well. As one psychiatrist states the problem, "It is the group itself that becomes the therapeutic agent as a result of the interaction between the individuals who form the group. It is the lack of knowledge of the dynamics of the group that at present limits the extent of the new therapeutic procedure." [15]

Some procedures also suggestive for sociological research have gone beyond the restricted approach of group therapy to methods of reintegrating the mental patient under more normal group situations. The treatment of the mentally ill at Gheel, Belgium, for example, consists chiefly of a procedure whereby some 3,000 patients are incorporated into a small city, living as part of the community rather than under the general method of institutionalization. The method of placing patients in individual homes has also been established in several other European countries, and while the number is relatively small, it is estimated that some 7,000 patients are receiving family care in some ten states in this country. The results, while not conclusive, appear to be quite successful.[16]

What we have suggested here in these various group treatments of mental disorders is that the etiology may not lie primarily in the conventional individualistic, early childhood explanation of psychiatry and psychoanalysis, but may develop out of a much more extensive process of group interaction. One psychiatrist, in discounting the individual or personal problems of the patient, has stated that "since he worked up his psychoses in the group, he can never be cured until he has worked out his recovery in a group." [17] As a re-

[11] The literature in this field is growing rapidly. See particularly S. R. Slavson, *An Introduction to Group Therapy*, New York: The Commonwealth Fund, 1943, and J. W. Klapman, *Group Psychotherapy*, New York: Grune and Stratton, 1946.

[12] Norman Q. Brill, "Group Psychotherapy," *Proceedings of the National Conference of Social Work*, 1946, New York: Columbia University Press, 1947, p. 240. Also see Klapman, *op. cit.*, pp. 330–332.

[13] William Menninger, *Psychiatry in a Troubled World*,

pp. 316–317. Also see Thomas P. Malone, "Socio-Psychological Factors in the Treatment of the Psychoneuroses in Group Psychotherapy," Ph.D. Dissertation, Duke University, 1947.

[14] S. R. Slavson, *op. cit.*, p. 1.

[15] Bruno Solby, "Group Psychotherapy and the Psychodramatic Method," in *Group Psychotherapy, A Symposium*, New York: Beacon House, 1948, pp. 50–51.

[16] See Hester B. Cruthers, *Foster Home Care for Mental Patients*, New York: The Commonwealth Fund, 1944. Also George Kent, "Family Care for the Mentally Ill," *Survey Graphic*, June, 1948.

[17] Cody Marsh, "Group Treatment of the Psychoses by

cent research statement on the relation of mental hygiene and socio-environmental factors indicated, "the possible existence of group character structures, the stresses put on man by changing conditions or by the excessive demands of the culture, the sources of and the effect of loneliness and social isolation, and the techniques and effects of social esteem and social punishment on personality, these and many other problems need careful and continued investigation." [18]

While sociologists have used the group approach in their research in criminology more than in any other field, the verification of the findings through experimental manipulation of the social world of offenders, using group methods, has not been extensively investigated. Here the problem is not so much group integration in the narrower sense, for that is usually present, but of group reintegration into the norms of the larger society. Individual clinical methods of treating potential or actual delinquency where, incidentally, a sociologist is rarely on the staff, have not demonstrated any marked success. [19] Some have suggested that rehabilitative efforts in correctional institutions should be on a group basis, with constant observation of the inmates' informal group structure and with efforts made to redirect these natural groups, rather than individuals, into a rehabilitative program. [20] Similar group programs might be employed in probation and parole work. Unfortunately, there are few skilled persons available for this type of approach. Efforts have been made in some directions to work on problems of deviant attitudes on a group basis, incorporating, for example, an entire delinquent group within a conventional framework. In one example of this type the California Youth Authority, in co-operation with the War Department, in 1944 placed two groups of about 150 seriously delinquent boys in army arsenals to work side by side with several thousand civilian men and women. The army furnished barracks and met the boys' needs. Efforts were made to restore the delinquents' confidence in themselves and to change their roles by incorporating them into the norms and objectives of conventional society. It was a group process enabling individuals to get rid of unacceptable behavior by participation. On the surface the program seems to have made marked changes in work habits, in the conceptions of themselves, and in changing anti-social group objectives which are reinforced in conventional institutional groups. [21] Some of the recent changes in the Swedish correctional system which involve rather extensive social participation also present experimental leads. [22] In several correctional institutions chapters of Alcoholics Anonymous have been established which may affect other attitudes of offenders through group interaction.

During the recent war the armed services, and lately various state correctional institutions, have introduced group psychotherapy into the treatment of offenders. In New Jersey where they have recognized that all prison inmates are by no means mentally abnormal this work is called "guided group interaction." Again, the success that has been encountered in efforts of this type may not be the result of psychiatric theory or of the therapist but of the group situation. It sets in operation group forces directed toward socially accepted goals partially to counteract the anti-social group conniving that goes on so extensively in correctional institutions. The limited literature indicates that these groups objectively examine their experiences and the reasons for their confinement rather than relying upon prison rationalizations, that there is growth in the capacity of the individual and the group to adjust, and that frequently an *esprit de corps* develops, particularly in the realization that they are helping others. Even personality characteristics appear to be modified for "the belligerent, over-assertive, anti-social rehabilitee is brought into line by his fellows and the asocial, shy, withdrawn person is drawn into the conversation." [23]

One of the most promising research leads in social disorganization has undoubtedly been the efforts to bring about local community reintegration through the group approach and citizen participation. Known as neighborhood councils or other

---

the Psychological Equivalent of the Revival," *Mental Hygiene*, 15: 341, April, 1931.

[18] R. H. Felix and R. V. Bowers, "Mental Hygiene and socio-Environmental Factors," *The Milbank Memorial Fund Quarterly*, 26: 134, April, 1948.

[19] See Sheldon and Eleanor Glueck, *Juvenile Delinquents Grown Up*, New York: Commonwealth Fund, 1940.

[20] *Bulletin Correctional Service Associates*, Volume I, No. 1, 1947.

[21] Described in John R. Ellington, *Protecting Our Children from Criminal Careers*, New York: Prentice-Hall, Inc., 1948, pp. 95–111.

[22] Thorsten Sellin, "The Treatment of Offenders in Sweden," *Federal Probation*, 12: 14–18, June, 1948.

[23] Joseph Abrahams and Lloyd W. McCorkle, "Group Psychotherapy of Military Offenders," *American Journal of Sociology*, 51: 458, March, 1946.

names, they are becoming increasingly widespread and appear to have a sound theoretical basis, both in accomplishing group redefinitions of situations and in giving the individual a place of belonging in the local structure. Studies of the success and failures of such efforts at group organization, as well as their relation to rates of delinquency, crime, mental disease, suicide, race and ethnic conflict, and alcoholism should be of primary interest to the sociologist. Here he can make his contribution by studying the social processes involved and the group variables which must be taken into account in successfully controlling the situation from a scientific point of view. Studies of informal groups and of agencies of moral risk such as the tavern, the dance hall, the political club, might well go along with investigations of the local community program.[24] Since sociologists assume that the disintegration of the community and the lack of consensus result in the increase of various forms of disorganization, the reintegration of the groups in the community should reduce such disorganization. If the answer is negative, then the factors should be isolated and studied. It appears, for example, that in dealing with ethnic, racial and religious group tensions the small intimate groups are the source of the individual's definition and that such problems must be dealt with on a group basis. As Williams has pointed out, however, there is a need in this field for the "further development of methods and materials for direct study of group behavior."[25]

Probably the most intriguing of all group approaches to social reintegration have been those where groups have informally assumed a major responsibility for dealing with a common problem, as those formed to aid in the rehabilitation of the tubercular, of youth councils to deal with delinquency and other adolescent difficulties, of those formed to overcome the loneliness of old age, and of groups for alcoholics and former mental patients. In each instance the group helps to integrate the individual, to overcome stigma, to change his conception of himself, and to make him feel again the solidarity of the group behind the individual. Without going into the question of whether the high claims of success for Alcoholics Anonymous are entirely justified, we are still in the dark as to exactly what effect takes place. After contrasting European and American group methods of working with alcoholics, Bales has indicated that A. A. involves a "network of personal relations that are made up of obligations, friendships, and other personal influences. The network insures that each person is a focal point of strong inter-personal relations."[26] There are indications that in these group processes there is established "we" feelings for the "I," the individual is given a feeling of group incorporation, and group oriented rather than individualistic and materialistic goals are furnished. Probably most important is the redefinition, through group experience, that is made in social values including those related to alcoholic drinking. Possibly we have an indication of the essential etiology of such behavior as alcoholism in this group treatment in that we also see other factors involved besides mere childhood emotional insecurity, for the alcoholic appears to have increasingly pulled himself away from meaningful or conventional group situations. In fact, the so-called religious emphasis in A. A. may be explained in terms of Durkheim's thesis that religion represents essentially the group and the feeling of getting outside of one's self by identification with others.[27] Such organizations represent, in part, the restoration of many of the characteristics of a folk society in the modern urban world.

Experiments with group integration have been developed generally without the aid of sociologists. At the risk of possibly destroying some of the mysteries which contribute therapeutically to their activities it is suggested that scientific analysis of these and similar activities may make possible more unique contributions by sociologists. Certainly it seems likely that psychiatrists and clinical psychologists are in no position to make as adequate studies of these or of the other types of group therapy approaches. Their background of theoretical training and point of emphasis have not been oriented in either the direction of social groups, with the possible exception of the family,

[24] See William F. Whyte, *Street Corner Society*, Chicago: University of Chicago Press, 1943, for a model of this type of research.

[25] Robin M. Williams, Jr., *The Reduction of Intergroup Tension: A Survey of Research on the Problems of Ethnic, Racial and Religious Group Relations*, New York: Social Science Research Council, 1947. No. 57, p. 134.

[26] Freed Bales, "Types of Social Structure as Factors in 'Cures' for Alcohol Addiction," *Applied Anthropology*, April–June, 1942, p. 8. Also see his "The Therapeutic Role of A. A. as Seen by the Sociologist," *Quarterly Journal of Studies in Alcohol*, 5: 267, 1944.

[27] Emile Durkheim, *The Elementary Forms of Religious Life* (Swaine Trans.), 1912.

or of the general society and its cultural value systems. Out of such study by sociologists could come not only additions to a body of theory but more adequate control of social and personal disorganization as well. Such knowledge as we could achieve about the group in relation to social dis-

organization could, in turn, be applied to social organization. Such emphasis on group situations would furnish not only a point of view for sociologists but also the necessary requirements of all science, the testing of knowledge in an attempt to control a problem situation.

The Social Scientist as an Expert Witness in Civil Rights Litigation*

Kenneth B. Clark

Kenneth B. Clark (1914–   ), associate professor of psychology, City College of New York and associate director, Northside Center for Child Development.

During the past three years, the Legal Division of the National Association for the Advancement of Colored People has been making a frontal attack on state laws which require racially segregated elementary and high schools. For the first time these lawyers have extensively used expert social science testimony [in the lower courts]. . . .

This new legal approach formed the basis for four of the five cases argued before the United States Supreme Court in January 1953: Clarendon, South Carolina; Topeka, Kansas; Wilmington, Delaware; and Richmond, Virginia. In addition to the testimony of professional educators, there was an extensive use of expert social science witnesses in these cases. . . .

In evaluating the testimony of the witnesses who were called by both sides in these school cases, it is clear that there were no essential differences among these social scientists on the crucial issue of the detrimental effects of segregation. Now that the precedent of admitting social science testimony has been established, it is certain that social scientists will be used in similar cases in the future.

The future use of expert social science witnesses in civil rights litigation, however, raises some fundamental questions concerning the objectivity of testimony, the basis of testimony—(research data, theoretical considerations, or personal opinion), and complex ethical considerations. As the

gap between social science and legal considerations narrows, it becomes increasingly necessary for the social scientist to deal effectively with the responsibilities which accompany his activities in this area. This is particularly true since the present school cases may be viewed as merely the beginning of this type of social science—legal collaboration.

This additional role of the social scientist places upon him at least the following burdens: The social scientist who participates in civil rights or civil liberties litigation as an expert witness must exercise the maximum degree of care and objectivity in the collection and interpretation of the relevant data. Further, he must be clear and courageous in his social values and he must be willing to assume social responsibilities even under conditions that would place him in a position contrary to the social beliefs which are popular at a particular time and place.

As the collaboration between social science and the legal profession increases, it will be necessary for the professional societies among the social and psychological sciences to develop safeguards against possible ethical abuses; e.g., flagrant manifestations of prejudice, distortion of data and deliberately misleading interpretations. While it would be impossible to prevent honest disagreement among social scientists reflecting differences in interpretations and emphasis, it is nonetheless

* See Chap. 20, "The Effects of Segregation: A Social Science Statement to the United States Supreme Court," pp. 371–375.

From "The Social Scientist as an Expert Witness in Civil Rights Litigation," *Social Problems, 1* (1953–1954): 5–10, pp. 5, 7, 9–10 quoted.

important to minimize the possibility of the presentation of conflicting testimony by equally competent scientists concerning the available facts. Professional organizations among social scientists now have the obligation to set up some kind of machinery which will prevent social scientists from being haunted by the same spectacle which has long bedeviled the field of psychiatry—two or more psychiatrists offering with equal certainty contradictory testimony concerning the sanity of a given defendant.

If social scientists assume the responsibility of developing their own safeguards, the social and psychological sciences are at present on the threshold of making direct and significant contributions to the progress of a rapidly changing society. The social science testimony in the public school segregation cases has opened the door of the courts to the social sciences. This now makes possible the direct use of social science findings in the process of social change.

CROSS REFERENCES TO STANDARD TEXTS *

Bernard, *American Community Behavior*, Chap. 29.
Bloch, *Social Disorganization*, pp. 3–7, 598–602.
Brown, *Social Pathology*, Chap. 28.
Cuber and Harper, *Problems of American Society*, Chaps. 1, 24.
Faris, *Social Disorganization*, Chap. 15.
Gillin, *Social Pathology*, Chap. 33.
——— and others, *Social Problems*, Chap. 20.
Herman, *Approach to Social Problems*, Chap. 11.

* For complete bibliographical reference to each text, see page 13.

Landis, *Social Policies in the Making*, Chaps. 21–26.
Merrill and others, *Social Problems*, Chap. 1.
Mihanovich, *Current Social Problems*, Chap. 1.
Neumeyer, *Social Problems and the Changing Society*, Chap. 16.
Nordskog and others, *Analyzing Social Problems*, Chap. 12.
Odum, *American Social Problems*, Chap. 28.
Phelps and Henderson, *Contemporary Social Problems*, Chap. 20.
Reinhardt and others, *Social Problems and Social Policy*, Chaps. 1–2.
Weaver, *Social Problems*, Chap. 29.

OTHER BIBLIOGRAPHY

Bernard Barber, *Science and the Social Order*, Glencoe, Illinois: Free Press, 1952.
L. L. Bernard, "The Social Sciences as Disciplines: United States," *Encyclopaedia of the Social Sciences, 1* (1930): 324–349.
Crane Brinton, "Humanitarianism," *Encyclopaedia of the Social Sciences, 7* (1932): 544–549.
Lyman Bryson, "Writers: Enemies of Social Science," *Saturday Review of Literature, 28; 41* (October 13, 1945): 9–11.
Cyril Burt, *Contributions of Psychology to Social Problems*, New York: Oxford University Press, 1953.
Lowell Juilliard Carr, *Situational Analysis*, New York: Harper & Bros., 1948.
Isidor Chein, Stuart W. Cook, and John Harding, "The Field of Action Research," *American Psychologist, 3: 2* (February 1948): 43–50.
———, "The Use of Research in Social Therapy," *Human Relations, 1* (1948): 497–511.
Morris R. Cohen, *The Faith of a Liberal*, New York: Henry Holt and Co., 1946.
James B. Conant, *Science and Common Sense*, New Haven: Yale University Press, 1951.
Lawrence K. Frank, *Nature and Human Nature: Man's New Image of Himself*, New Brunswick: Rutgers University Press, 1951.
Sigmund Freud, *Civilization and Its Discontents*,

transl. by Joan Riviere, New York: J. Cape and H. Smith, 1930.
William Ernest Hocking, "The Atom as Moral Dictator," *Saturday Review of Literature, 29: 5* (February 2, 1946): 7–9.
Karen Horney, *The Neurotic Personality of Our Time*, New York: W. W. Norton & Co., 1937.
Elliott Jacques, ed., "Social Therapy," *Journal of Social Issues, 3: 2* (Spring 1947).
David Krech, ed., "Action and Research—A Challenge," *Journal of Social Issues, 2: 4* (November 1946).
Alfred McClung Lee, "Individual and Organizational Research in Sociology," *American Sociological Review, 16* (1951): 701–707.
———, "The Person and Social Policy," Chap. 35 in Lee, ed., *Principles of Sociology*, 2d ed. rev., New York: Barnes & Noble, 1951, pp. 337–341.
———, "Responsibilities and Privileges in Sociological Research," *Sociology and Social Research, 37* (1952–53): 367–374.
———, "Sociologists in an Integrating Society," *Social Problems, 2* (1954–55): 57–66.
Alexander H. Leighton, *Human Relations in a Changing World: Observations on the Use of the Social Sciences*, New York: E. P. Dutton and Co., 1949.
Robert S. Lynd, *Knowledge for What? The Place of*

Social Science in American Culture, Princeton: Princeton University Press, 1939.

Karl Mannheim, *Diagnosis of Our Time,* New York: Oxford University Press, 1944.

———, *Freedom, Power, and Democratic Planning,* New York: Oxford University Press, 1950.

Roberto Michels, "Conservatism," *Encyclopaedia of the Social Sciences,* 4 (1931): 230–233.

Svend Riemer, "Social Planning and Social Organization," *American Journal of Sociology,* 52 (1946–47): 508–516.

George Simpson, *Science as Morality,* Yellow Springs, Ohio: Humanist Press, 1953.

Willard Waller, "Insight and Scientific Method," *American Journal of Sociology,* 40 (1934–35): 285–297.

REVIEW QUESTIONS

1. Of what does Sumner think "progress" consists?
2. What reasons does Sumner give for distrusting what he calls "clear strides towards the millenium"?
3. What are purposes and consequences in the senses used by Sumner?
4. What does one gain from studying consequences?
5. Why does Sumner believe that pessimism and optimism are "impertinent" to the work of the social scientist?
6. What problems does Fosdick say result from the fact that our political institutions "are mainly rooted in the eighteenth century"?
7. What proposals does Fosdick make for the solution of social problems?
8. Menninger raises what he terms "basic" questions. What does he give as an explanation for our inability to answer them?
9. What contribution can psychiatry make to the solution of social problems?
10. What does Bierstedt give as the relation of social scientists to social policy?
11. In what four ways do values enter into the scientific situation, as outlined by Bierstedt?
12. The S. S. S. P. committee suggests that independent research could profitably, for the nation and humanity, be carried on in a number of areas. Name several of these.
13. Clinard stresses the need for sociological research on the relationship of the person to the group. How is this different from other approaches to group therapy as he describes them?
14. What are Clark's concerns over the new role of social scientists in policy-making litigation? What professional problems does he see ahead for the social scientists?

Index